DATE DUE

For Reference

Not to be taken

from this library

THE GREAT SPY PICTURES

by
James Robert Parish
and
Michael R. Pitts

editor:
T. ALLAN TAYLOR

research associates:
JOHN ROBERT COCCHI
FLORENCE SOLOMON

The Scarecrow Press, Inc.
Metuchen, N.J.   1974

Library of Congress Cataloging in Publication Data

Parish, James Robert.
  The great spy pictures.

  Bibliography: p.
  1. Spy films--Catalogs. I. Pitts, Michael R.,
joint author. II. Title.
PN1998.P26   016.79143   73-19509
ISBN 0-8108-0655-X

Dedicated to

LOIS COLE

who inspired the concept for this volume

"While nations have armies and navies, while there is greed, hatred and selfish ambition among men, there will be work for and great need of the spy. While others receive the plaudits of those they have saved, the spy risks his or her all and lives or dies without glory."

Foreword to <u>After Tonight</u> (1933)

TABLE OF CONTENTS

AUTHORS' NOTE and ACKNOWLEDGMENTS

The aim of this cinema history volume is to trace the development of the spy film as the genre progressed through the decades of 20th-century motion picture production. The entries detailed in this study are intended to be representative, rather than all encompassing.

The authors would be grateful for any suggestions, amplifications and corrections regarding the text that readers care to supply.

Grateful acknowledgment of their helpfulness is given to Elliott Adams, Gene Andrewski, Richard Bojarski, the Cinemabilia Book Shop (Ernest Burns), Olivier Eyquem, Filmfacts (Ernest Parmentier), Film Fan Monthly (Leonard Maltin), Films in Review, Pierre Guinle, David McGillivray, Norman Miller, Movie Poster Service (Bob Smith), Jack E. Nolan, Joel Rageot, Screen Facts (Alan G. Barbour), Mrs. Peter Smith, Vinnie Terrace, and Dr. William Tomlinson.

And especial thanks to Paul Myers, curator of the Theatre Collection at the Lincoln Center Library for the Performing Arts, and his staff: Monty Arnold, Rod Bladel, Donald Fowle, Steve Ross, Maxwell Silverman, Dorothy Swerdlove, Betty Wharton, and page Juan Hodelin.

James Robert Parish
2039 Broadway #17F
New York, N.Y.   10023

Michael R. Pitts
1823 East 8th Street
Anderson, Indiana   46012

ABBREVIATIONS OF FILM STUDIOS

AA	Allied Artists Picture Corporation
AIP	American International Pictures
COL	Columbia Pictures Industries, Inc.
FOX	Fox Film Corporation
MGM	Metro-Goldwyn-Mayer, Inc.
MON	Monogram Pictures Corporation
PAR	Paramount Pictures Corporation
RKO	RKO Radio Pictures Corporation
20th-Fox	Twentieth Century-Fox Film Corporation
UA	United Artists Corporation
UNIV	Universal Pictures, Inc.
WB	Warner Brothers, Inc.

Note: A capital letter "C" following a title and preceding the running time denotes the picture is in color.

HISTORY OF THE SPY FILM

As long as there have been conflicts between peoples and nations there has been spying. The Bible describes how Joshua dispatched spies into Egypt, how Moses sent agents into Canaan to spy out the land, and of course, how Queen Esther's secret operatives advised her of the upcoming pogrom to be visited on her Jewish people. The Macedonian conqueror, Alexander the Great, utilized a spy force to gain knowledge of Persia and its inhabitants before he attacked the land; Julius Caesar employed a task squadron of "exploratores" to ferret out the weak points of his opponents both on the battlefields of Gaul, England, Spain, and Germany and at home in the senate of Rome. The Venetian Republic in medieval Italy retained its notorious spies known as the "sbirri" to gain the upper hand on its rival neighboring city-states. Queen Elizabeth I of England had her secret service organized under Sir Francis Walsingham, while a century later, under Queen Anne, the progenitor of the modern British Intelligence service was shaped by Daniel Defoe. And so it went, with wealthy individuals, church and state maintaining their various espionage organizations, each bent on obtaining supremacy over, or at the very least, retaining the status quo with their enemies or friends. The 20th century with its remarkable technological advances has made it possible for armies to be shipped around the globe. Likewise, the new-style spy, equipped with a wide variety of futuristic eavesdropping devices and defensive-offensive equipment, is called upon to become a world traveler, hopping from place to place as the job demands. In this war-fraught century, there seems to be an increasing "need" for, and use of, this professional insinuator, traitor, patriot, or what have you.

9

In a similar manner, as long as there have been motion pictures, the phenomenon of espionage has been used to entertain as well as to propagandize for national or governmental causes. Thus the spy film has been an intricate part of the motion picture industry, justly ranking in popularity with the western, detective film, musical, horror movie, and comedy as a popular cinema form.

In order to have a genuine spy content, a motion picture must concern itself in some way with national interest and with the interest being in some way threatened by a foreign power. In most cases an actual war is concerned, either a national one such as the revolutions in the United States, Spain, or France or Russia, or a World War, including the two World Wars, Korea, Vietnam, and the Cold War. These films tend to depict the agents of one power infiltrating another power's domain in order to aid the homeland in its determined cause to overpower the latter. (Motion pictures focusing on the battles of individual governments against the Mafia, counterfeiters, and dope and liquor smugglers within the confines of their own countries are not really spy movies and, as such, are not discussed in the text.)

Obviously, spy movies are prevalent usually during a time of national involvement in war. Although the Spanish-American War did not produce any such films, due mainly to the infancy of the motion picture industry, newsreels, both real and staged, tended to heavily propagandize for the American cause, and this practice continued with the U.S. entry into the First World War in 1917. Motion pictures, however, had developed sufficiently by this time, that when war fever broke out in the country as early as 1914, several films were already mongering for the Allied cause.

One of the first films to use the spy motif seriously was a 1914 Universal serial, Lucille Love, Girl of Mystery. This Francis Ford-Grace Cunard chapterplay dealt with a man who becomes an international spy in order to revenge the loss of the girl he loved, by stealing defense plans from the man who had won her. A film imported from England called England's Menace (London Films, 1914) was a two-reeler about two boys foiling a German invasion

by picking up their radio coded messages.   The next year Our
Secret Wires (Kay-Bee, 1915) was openly hostile to the Axis powers by depicting a U. S. secret service operator discovering German
spies sending messages to an enemy submarine stationed off the
coast of Oregon.   By 1916, more films urged American war involvement by making Germans the villains of their plots.   The Hero
of Submarine D-2 (Vitagraph, 1916) dealt with an attempt by German
operatives to destroy a U. S. naval base while As in a Looking Glass
(World, 1916) starred Kitty Gordon as a double agent who halted
the Prussian attempts to copy the fortification plans for New York
harbor.   Two serials of the year also stressed spying in their chapters.   The Secret of the Submarine (American/Mutual, 1916), a
Juanita Hansen vehicle, had agents of Japan and Russia and some
wicked Americans attempting to steal an invention which would allow a submarine to remain underwater indefinitely.   Liberty, A
Daughter of the U. S. A. (Universal, 1916) found Marie Walcamp involved with spies and a revolution down Mexico way.

      With America's belated entry into the war in 1917 a
goodly number of spy films were released.   Grant, Police Reporter
was a series film which traced a newspaperman's discovery of a
secret German submarine base located in New England.   America's
sweetheart, Mary Pickford, starred in The Little American (Art-
craft, 1917), which had her doing war relief work in Belgium and
being taken prisoner by the Germans and held as a spy.   War and
the Woman (Pathé, 1917) told of a foreign-born girl (Florence La
Badie) who turned in her stepfather as a spy, while the Fox film,
The Spy, openly called for a distrust of foreign-born residents with
its hysterical ads exclaiming, "Do you know your neighbor?"   Less
lurid was Triangle's Daughter Angele, about a young couple (Pauline
Starke and Philo McCullough) who encounter a German spy sig-
nalling U-boats off the New England coast and concentrate their
efforts on rounding up the enemy.   In A Soul in Pawn (American
Mutual, 1917) a woman (Gail Kene) became a spy in order to revenge the death of her husband, while in The Greatest Power
(Metro, 1917), Ethel Barrymore turned her lover over to the

the authorities upon discovering that he was a Prussian agent.   Another spy feature of 1917 was Vitagraph's The Stolen Treaty with
Corinne Griffith and Earle Williams.   In the serial field, dancer
Irene Castle starred in Patria (International Film Service-Pathé,
1917), a film William Randolph Hearst produced in which she
played a girl involved in an attack on the U.S. by Japan and Mexico
while also becoming involved with a U.S. secret service agent.

In the final year of World War I there was an avalanche
of spy dramas, all feeding the American filmgoer's preconceived
notion of patriotism, romanticism, and dastardly villainy.   In Raoul
Walsh's The Prussian Cur (Fox, 1918), a lynch mob, modeled after
the Ku Klux Klan, hanged several men of German parentage suspected of being saboteurs.   That year Walsh also directed his
brother, George Walsh, in I'll Say So (Fox, 1918), a story about
a man who rounds up a foreign spy ring.   The next year George
Walsh starred in Luck and Pluck (Fox, 1919), playing a reformed
crook who saves the daughter of a U.S. agent from marrying a
German spy.

Other 1918 spy films included The Hun Within (Paramount, 1918), about a second generation German-American becoming a spy for Germany, while Me und Gott (When America
Awoke) (Romayne-Super, 1918) dealt with a second generation
German-American boy who turns in his disloyal father when the
latter demands he blow up a U.S. munitions factory.   An Alien
Enemy (Hodkinson, 1918) had vamp Louise Glaum doing her exotic
best to woo unsuspecting German-American males into working for
the home country.   The complicated movie, The Kaiser's Shadow
(Paramount, 1918), told of two double agents (Dorothy Dalton,
Thurston Hall) who were working for Germany but were loyal to
the U.S.   Their plan was to steal the blueprints for a "ray rifle"
from its U.S. inventor (Edward Cecil) in order to locate the top
man of a Prussian espionage gang.   More simplistic in storyline
was Suspicion (Hoffman, 1918), a drama of a neglected wife who
finds out her new lover is actually a German spy out to destroy an
aircraft factory of which her husband is the superintendent.

In The Highest Tramp (Vitagraph, 1918) Earle Williams
played a dual role as U.S. and German agents, brothers in real
life, with the former taking the latter's place when he is killed and
thereafter capturing an undercover organization. In Pursuit of Polly
(Paramount, 1918) offered featherbrain Billie Burke being mistaken
for a German spy but, of course, being saved at the last minute
by secret service agent Thomas Meighan. In Madame Who? (Paramount, 1918) Bessie Barriscale was branded a spy, but later proved
the accusation to be false by tracking down and capturing the real
culprits. In the Fred Niblo-directed The Marriage Ring (Paramount,
1918), Prussian spies attempted to burn an Hawaiian sugar cane
plantation, a source of vital raw material for the Allied cause.
Universal's Who Was the Other Man? presented Francis Ford as a
secret service agent in pursuit of a German undercover sabotage
unit called the "Black Legion." In the independent film Berlin via
America, Ford was a U.S. agent pretending to be disloyal to America
in order to have an entry into Germany and to be able to smuggle
out information as a member of Baron von Richthofen's Flying Circus. In the ludicrous Madame Spy (Universal, 1918) Jack Mulhall
was a government agent who disguised himself as a woman in order
to lure German spies into a trap.

Westerns also got into the spy game, as in Mr. Logan,
U.S.A. (Fox, 1918), in which Tom Mix, a government undercover
agent, was sent to Arizona to uncover Germans disguised as cowboys who were blowing up tungsten mines. In Lafayette, We Come
(Affiliated, 1918), a composer (E.K. Lincoln) finds out that his
vanished girlfriend (Dolores Cassinelli) was a double agent after a
German spy ring in France, while Fox's For Freedom of the East,
had U.S. and German diplomats match wits in trying to get China
to join their separate causes. In The Claws of the Hun (Paramount,
1918), Charles Ray played a draft dodger who proved his loyalty by
stopping German spies from blowing up his father's munitions plant.
Even Theda Bara got into the medium by portraying a girl trapped
in Germany at the war's outbreak, and held as a spy by the head
of the German secret service, whom she finally kills, in When

Men Desire (Fox, 1919).

Other 1918 spy-adventure movies included Vive la France
(Paramount, 1918) with Dorothy Dalton and Edmund Lowe in his
film debut; Kultur (Fox, 1918) starring Gladys Brockwell; and The
Great Love (D. W. Griffith, 1918), a film dealing with a Canadian
soldier whose English girl friend, when he is away at the front,
marries a man who is really a German spy.   D. W. Griffith directed several movies with war themes, including Intolerance (1916)
and Hearts of the World (1918), but The Great Love was his sole
spy feature.   Boy Scouts to the Rescue was a Universal Special,
actually a series of five films, two reels each, which had the Boy
Scouts capturing a German spy.   Though some comedies were produced during the war, only two dealt directly with the field of spying.   Joan of Plattsburg (Goldwyn, 1918) starred Mabel Normand
as a mischevious young girl who catches a German spy ring, and
Huns and Hyphens (Vitagraph, 1918) was a Larry Semon two-reeler
with the comic as a janitor who catches a German spy.   Vitagraph's
1918 A Woman in the Web, which starred Hedda Nova and J. Frank
Glendon, was a drama built around the Russian Revolution and a
plot against the tsar.

With the end of the war, the public quickly tired of spy
movies and 1919's few films of that genre were mostly late theatrical releases, such as Luck and Pluck and When Men Desire,
and Life's Greatest Problem (Film Clearing House, 1919).   The
latter was a photoplay about sabotage in a shipyard and starred
J. Stuart Blackton.   The Allan Dwan-directed The Dark Star (Paramount, 1919) showcased Marion Davies and told of spies trying to
pilfer a valuable jewel, "The Dark Star."   A comedy, 23 1/2
Hours' Leave (Paramount, 1919), directed by Henry King, told
of a private (Douglas MacLean) in a training camp going AWOL and
capturing a spy ring.   It was remade in 1937 by Grand National,
and the latter version featured James Ellison.

As the Great War ended and the Roaring Twenties took over,
the reaction against war-like subjects resulted in reduced numbers
of spy films being produced.   The global conflict had left the movie-

going public with such a great distaste of war pictures that even romantic dramas which relied on a spy motif were affected. No better example of this is there than The Love Light (United Artists, 1921), a Mary Pickford vehicle, in which the American starlette played a young Italian girl who marries a man who, unknown to her, is a German spy. Later in the story she learns of her mistake and that her husband was the cause of her brother's death. The spy met his end by falling to his death over a cliff. The Love Light, no better nor worse than many other Mary Pickford films, proved to be one of America's Sweetheart's less popular movies. The same year also saw Crane Wilbur and Ben Lyon in David Belasco's old stage melodrama, The Heart of Maryland, which dealt with espionage during the Civil War. The film was produced by Vitagraph and in 1927 Warner Bros. remade it, this time starring Dolores and Helene Costello. Another 1921 film, The Great Impersonation, released by Famous Players-Lasky, concerned German spies in England during the war.

Eternal Peace, an obscure 1922 release, was in three episodes, each dealing with German spies, and in 1923, The Silent Command for Fox, had an ex-navy captain (Edmund Lowe) joining a group of spies (Martha Mansfield, Bela Lugosi, et al.) in order to thwart their plans to explode the U. S. Navy's Atlantic Fleet and to bomb the Panama Canal. The Warrens of Virginia (Fox, 1924) was another vehicle about Civil War spying, and had its hero (Wilfred Lytell) about to be hanged for his crime when he is saved by the coming of the end of the war. No less thrilling was The Story Without a Name (Paramount, 1924) which focused on an international spy's attempt to capture a device which emitted electronic death rays.

By the middle of the decade, spy films were still a relatively sparse commodity in comparison to other types of films. New Lives for Old (Famous Players-Lasky-Paramount, 1925) was a complicated film with Betty Compson as a cabaret dancer obtaining information on a German spy (Theodore Kosloff) during the war. Later he returns to haunt her when she has married a wealthy

American (Wallace MacDonald). In the serial, Sunken Silver
(Pathé, 1925) spying was incidental to a plot that had a secret
service agent (Walter Miller) become involved with a group searching for a pirate treasure lost off the Florida coast in 1804.

Two quality spy dramas were released in 1926, The Great
Deception (First National) and Mare Nostrum (MGM). The former
dealt with a double agent (Ben Lyon) who worked for the Germans
but was loyal to Britain, while the latter film starred matinee idol
Antonio Moreno as a sea captain whose love for an exotic spy
(Alice Terry) caused him to betray his homeland and, indirectly,
to cause the death of his son. In Secret Orders (FBO, 1926)
Evelyn Brent played a girl in World War I working for the U.S.
secret service, who ended up having to combat her husband (Harold
Goodwin), employed by the Germans. Another Civil War spy film
came in Hands Up! (Famous Players-Lasky-Paramount, 1926) which
saw Raymond Griffith as a Confederate spy and Marian Nixon and
Virginia Lee Corbin as two Northern sisters who both loved him and
whom he also loved. The film's surprise ending has the girls
saving him from being hanged and all three migrating to Salt Lake
City where they settled down and received the blessing of the Latter
Day Saints! In the movies, especially where spies were concerned,
anything was possible!

Convoy (First National, 1927) found a young girl's (Dorothy
Mackaill) life nearly ruined because she was involved unknowingly
with a German spy (Lowell Sherman), while The Forbidden Woman
(Pathé, 1927) starred Jetta Goudal as an exotic spy for the Sultan
of Morocco who weds a French colonel (Victor Varconi) to obtain
information from him. For a rare change in the cinema, the spy
(Goudal) is not only caught and sentenced to death, but is not rescued in time. She dies in front of a firing squad. In the ten-chapter serial On Guard (Pathé, 1927), a man (Cullen Landis) about to
commit suicide is persuaded to join a group of international spies
and assist them in placing their people in the U.S. army. Later
with the aid of a patriotic girl (Muriel Kingston) the man double-
crosses the spies and helps to round them up. Hotel Imperial

(Famous Players-Lasky-Paramount, 1927) was a Pola Negri vehicle in which Hungarian spies helped to free their land from Russian control, and The Lady in Ermine (First National, 1927) had its star, Corinne Griffith (who also produced the film) play an 1810 Italian countess who saves her husband (Einar Hansen) from execution for spying.

The Desert Bride (Columbia, 1928) dealt with espionage and conflict between the French army and Arab nationalists with Betty Compson in the middle, and Legion of the Condemned (Paramount, 1928) starred Gary Cooper as a disillusioned soul who joined the French Foreign Legion after his love (Fay Wray) was found with a German officer. Incidentally, this latter B movie used much footage from Wings (Paramount, 1927). In The Mysterious Lady (MGM, 1928), the prestige star of the cinema, Greta Garbo, was a Russian spy who falls in love with an Austrian captain (Conrad Nagel) from whom she had to steal important documents. As was the standard case of the day, love triumphed over all, even including the welfare of state. The serial, The Chinatown Mystery (Syndicate, 1928), starred Joe Bonomo as a secret service agent who was out to help a girl (Ruth Hiatt) who possessed the secret formula for producing artificial diamonds from the wicked "Sphinx" (Francis Ford).

There were a number of screen comedies produced during the 1920s that relied on a spy plot premise to evoke laughter. In The Better 'Ole (Warner Bros., 1926) Sydney Chaplin played a British sergeant caught in the mechanisms of infiltration intrigue on the front lines; in Do and Dare (Fox, 1922), reliable box office champ Tom Mix found himself arrested as a spy in South America. The Weber and Fields comedy, Friendly Enemies (PDC, 1925), had the duo cast as German immigrants who take opposing sides when the Great War comes. Buster Keaton's feature The General (United Artists, 1928) had him working as a Confederate spy, and the Mack Sennett-produced The Goodbye Kiss (First National, 1928) took place in Europe in World War I and had a coward (Matty Kemp) after being shamed by his girl (Sally Eilers) being ferreted out as a German spy and saving his pals from being killed by the enemy.

A racial comedy <u>Ham and Eggs at the Front</u> (Warner Bros.,
1927) had two black soldiers (Tom Wilson, Heinie Conklin) involved
with German spies (William J. Irving, Myrna Loy--the latter as the
black waitress Fifi) at the front.   <u>Heart Trouble</u> (First National,
1928) was a Harry Langdon vehicle in which he was turned down
for military service in the First World War for various reasons.
Wanting to enlist so as to impress his girl (Doris Dawson) he became a hero by discovering a German base off the U.S. coast,
which he destroyed, and then freed a captured American soldier
and rounded up a bunch of German spies.   The popular team of
Wallace Beery and Raymond Hatton starred in <u>Now We're in the</u>
<u>Air</u> (Paramount, 1927) as two daffy soldiers who are shipped over
the enemy lines in a runaway balloon and are honored as heroes by
the Germans who then send them back to spy on the Allies, the
latter almost shooting them.   <u>Riley of the Rainbow Division</u> (Anchor,
1928) concerned two buddies (Creighton Hale, Al Alt) in a military
training camp who capture a balloon-load of spies, and <u>Top Sergeant</u>
<u>Mulligan</u> (Anchor, 1928) told of two more army buddies (Wesley
Barry, Wade Boteler) who fall for the same girl, she turning out
to be a male German spy in disguise!   <u>Spuds</u> (Pathé, 1927) had
Larry Semon as a man who saves his buddy (Edward Hearn) from
being executed after being betrayed by local spies.   Clearly, as
the Roaring Twenties reached a conclusion, filmmakers and the
public alike were looking back nostalgically to the good old war days
when an enemy was an enemy that could be identified and conquered,
unlike the fast-approaching, more intangible Depression.

With the coming of sound, every genre of film was explored
ad nauseum, but the spy picture received only a light rehash.   <u>True</u>
<u>Heaven</u> (Fox, 1929) told of a British soldier (George O'Brien) in
Belgium who falls in love with a cafe singer (Lois Moran), who is a
German spy.   <u>Only the Brave</u> (Paramount, 1930) had Gary Cooper
mixed up in Civil War spying, and <u>Renegades</u> (Fox, 1930) was a
mixed-up Foreign Legion tale which cast Myrna Loy as a spy who
betrays a French officer (Warner Baxter).   <u>Inside the Lines</u> (RKO,
1930) was about two double agents (Betty Compson and Ralph Forbes)

stranded on Gibraltar, and The Case of Sergeant Grischa (RKO,
1930) was a poignant tale of a Russian army officer (Chester Morris) who is arrested for spying and then executed through military
injustice.   Another racial comedy, Anybody's War (Paramount, 1930),
starred the Two Black Crows (George Moran and Charles E. Mack)
in a World War I tale of German spies.   From abroad, came the
German-made Dreyfus (1930) which starred Fritz Kortner, and
examined the infamous late 19th-century Dreyfus case in which an
innocent French army captain was accused of being a German spy.

During the height of the Depression, few American-made spy
movies were produced.   There were too many other topical subjects
to depict on the screen, ranging from the breadlines to the boot-
leggers.   Those few genre entries that did appear blended a heady
dose of romanticism, sophistication, and cynicism, such as Josef
von Sternberg's Dishonored (Paramount, 1931), starring Marlene
Dietrich as an alluring Viennese prostitute-turned-spy.   In the following year, Greta Garbo made her indelible mark as the exotic
femme fatale queen of the spies, Mata Hari (MGM, 1932).   Overseas, Alfred Hitchcock came to the fore in thriller films with The
Man Who Knew Too Much (Gaumont-British, 1934) the first of a
string of successful ventures under his helm which brought a new
suspense and a tense pace to the field.   Back in America, Marion
Davies appeared in the lavish but trivial nonsense, Operator 13
(MGM, 1934), which purported to be a sincere, if romantic, Civil
War spy caper.

However, it was the English who, like the Germans in the
1920s under Fritz Lang and other Berlin filmmakers, created a
taut new standard for the spy film, injecting new life and dimensions into this shopworn field.   In 1935 Leslie Howard starred as
a British nobleman who helped the French aristocrats during their
revolution in The Scarlet Pimpernel (United Artists), the best of
all the screen adaptations of the Baroness Orczy novel.   (Three
years later Barry K. Barnes starred in a weak sequel, Return of
the Scarlet Pimpernel, United Artists, 1938.)   One of the master-
pieces of the spy film genre was Alfred Hitchcock's The Thirty-Nine

Steps (Gaumont-British, 1935), followed the next year by his The
Secret Agent (Gaumont-British, 1936). Spy 77 (First Division,
1936) was the tale of a girl (Greta Nissen) in the Italian Alps who
is torn between her country and her love for an Austrian enemy
agent (Don Alavarado), the age-old operative dilemma of the stage
and screen.

The Firefly (MGM, 1937) told in musical terms of Napoleon's
conquests and featured Jeanette MacDonald and Allan Jones, the
latter introducing Rudolf Friml's "The Donkey's Serenade," while
Dolores Del Rio headlined Lancer Spy (20th Century-Fox, 1937), a
far more conventional account of a girl in love with a counter-spy
(George Sanders).   Victor Seastrom remade Under the Red Robe
(20th Century-Fox, 1937), harkening back to the richly-loaded
espionage days of Cardinal Richelieu and the church's suppression
of the Huguenots in France.   Another Alfred Hitchcock classic appeared in 1938, The Lady Vanishes (Gaumont-British), a feature
that has retained its vitality over decades of reissues.

With the American public newly shocked by the uncovering
of fifth columnists operating an intensive spy network in the U. S. A.,
Hollywood took its cue and came out with Confessions of a Nazi Spy
(Warner Bros., 1939), one of the movie industry's first attempts
to delineate in semi-documentary style the evils of the far-reaching
Third Reich.   Less exploitive and far less effective was the programmer series entry, The Lone Wolf Spy Hunt (Columbia, 1939),
a forerunner of the myriad of cheaply-produced features in the
1940s which would detail America's fight against the Axis enemy.
Nurse Edith Cavell (RKO, 1939) was a retelling of the famed World
War I nurse (Anna Neagle) who sacrificed her life to help the Allied
cause, remaining a humanitarian in concept and deed to the end.
Charlie Chan in Panama (20th Century-Fox, 1940) dispatched the
popular Oriental sleuth to a leading Latin American trouble spot,
the Panama Canal Zone, where agents from all nations were constantly vying for supremacy at all levels.

With the spreading of World War II to the American shores,
the Hollywood film industry took up the call to arms by producing

a steady stream of films depicting patriotism and heroism of the Allies while showing the dastardly deeds of the enemy. International Lady (United Artists, 1941) had alluring spy Ilona Massey involved with government agent George Brent who was trying to break up the spy ring of which she was a member. Paris Calling (Universal, 1941) made use of the fall of France for its tale of partisans, as did Underground (Warner Bros., 1941), the latter set in Nazi-plagued Germany. In the Three Stooges comedy, Dutiful but Dumb (Columbia, 1941), the trio come into a foreign country as photographers, and end up nearly being shot as spies. The two-reeler was one of the first World War II attempts at spy spoofing.

By 1942 Pearl Harbor was a thing of the bitter past, and America was at war. The Nazis were now the U. S. 's total enemy. In All Through the Night (Warner Bros., 1942) Manhattan gangster Humphrey Bogart and his gang track down a group of fifth column-ists operating in the metropolis, and in Across the Pacific (Warner Bros., 1942), Bogart pretends to join the Axis in order to catch their espionage unit leader (Sydney Greenstreet). In Black Dragons (Monogram, 1942) madman Bela Lugosi worked as a Japanese spy, and in Cairo (MGM, 1942), Jeanette MacDonald was engaged in a musical spy spoof. One of the period's best loved stories and topical films was also a tight, compact spy drama: in Casablanca, made in 1942 at Warners, director Michael Curtiz wove a fitting web of romance and espionage, which has made it one of the most popular films of all time. In Enemy Agents Against Ellery Queen (Columbia, 1942), the final entry in that cheap series, the detective (William Gargan) was on the track of spies in America, while in Invisible Agent (Universal, 1942) Jon Hall used his power of invisibility against the Nazis.

The British-made The 49th Parallel (Columbia, 1942) told of Nazi seamen trying to reach a Canadian island after their U-boat was sunk, and Lucky Jordan (Paramount, 1942) found gangster Alan Ladd deciding to go straight after seeing the vicious activities of a group of Nazi agents working in the U. S. Alfred Hitchcock's Saboteur (Universal, 1942) had an innocent man (Robert Cummings)

accused of sabotage in a munitions factory, and Secret Agent of
Japan (20th Century-Fox, 1942) found soldier of fortune Preston
Foster associating with Japanese spies in Singapore.   Two Sher-
lock Holmes films also worked for the red, white, and blue cause;
in Sherlock Holmes and the Voice of Terror (Universal, 1942),
Holmes (Basil Rathbone) discovered the terrible forecaster of mili-
tary disaster in Britain, and in Sherlock Holmes and the Secret
Weapon (Universal, 1942) he (again Rathbone) put an end--so it
seemed--to Moriarty's (Lionel Atwill) working for the Germans.
Spy Ship (Warner Bros. , 1942) had a U. S. female fifth columnist
(Irene Manning) selling secrets to the enemy, and This Gun for
Hire (Paramount, 1942) found tough guy Alan Ladd as a gunman out
to get the agents who doublecrossed him.   In To Be or Not to Be
(United Artists, 1942), Ernst Lubitsch tried to guide his stars (Jack
Benny, Carole Lombard) through a black comedy about the war, only
to find that the public was shocked at a picture that displayed such
"bad taste. "

At the other end of the movie entertainment spectrum, the
serials also reached their peak of spy adventure derring-do in 1942.
The choice of chapter plays ranged from Captain Midnight (Columbia)
to Don Winslow of the Navy (Universal) to Junior G-Men of the Air
(Universal) to The Secret Code (Columbia).   As was standard
practice in this film form, the heavies were extra bad Germans,
and the heroes were superhuman good guys; the plots were obvious,
but the action sequences and the special effects lent a special ambiance that no critic could successfully argue against.

By 1943, the spy genre was already old hat to the new generation of movie viewers, and the number of such entries tapered
off to a marked degree.   The year lead off with a very tepid Stan
Laurel and Oliver Hardy comedy, Air Raid Wardens (MGM, 1943).
On a more serious but equally superficial note there was Above
Suspicion (MGM) with Joan Crawford and Fred MacMurray as newlyweds in Europe who agree to embark on a spy mission.   In Background to Danger (Warner Bros. , 1943), George Raft was pitted
against the Nazi operatives in Turkey, and in Fallen Sparrow (RKO,

1943), John Garfield survived the Spanish Civil War to be tormented
on the home front by pursuing Axis employees. Hangmen Also Die
(MGM, 1943) was a quality comedown from director Fritz Lang's
superior Man Hunt (20th Century-Fox, 1941), in its telling of the
assassination of a high Nazi official in Prague. Northern Pursuit
(Warner Bros., 1943) had Errol Flynn combating collaborationists
in the Canadian wilderness. The Lady Has Plans (Paramount, 1943)
reflected America's growing confidence against the enemy: the war
could be taken lightly as in this scatterbrained comedy with Paulette
Goddard and Ray Milland in backlot Lisbon. Paul Lukas repeated
his stellar stage role in Watch on the Rhine (Warner Bros., 1943),
a story which reminded filmgoers how gullible noncombatants could
be about the seriousness of the confrontations on the European bat-
tlefronts. Sherlock Holmes in Washington (Universal, 1943) presented Holmes (Basil Rathbone) and Watson (Nigel Bruce) with the
problem of how to recover a top secret microfilm hidden in a
matchcover before Moriarity (George Zucco) got hold of it and
handed it over to the enemy. In Passport to Suez (Columbia, 1943),
the Lone Wolf (Warren William) was at odds with Nazis intent on
obtaining control of the vital Suez Canal.

Lovely Hedy Lamarr appeared to little advantage with Paul
Henreid, Sydney Greenstreet, and Peter Lorre in The Conspirators
(Warner Bros., 1944), an empty imitation of Casablanca, and in
Charlie Chan in the Secret Service (Monogram, 1944) the first in
the poverty row studio's new series, the Chinese detective worked
for the government, much to the enemy's chagrin. The Hour Before
the Dawn (Paramount, 1944) found a loyal British pacifist (Franchot
Tone) falling for an alluring Nazi spy (Veronica Lake) and Ministry
of Fear (Paramount, 1944), directed by Fritz Lang, had innocent
Ray Milland framed into a bizarre espionage plot. A British film,
Secret Mission (General Film Distributors, 1944), had a team of
British commando spies in an Anglo invasion of France, while in
the cheapie Waterfront (Producers Releasing Corp., 1944) Nazi
agents (John Carradine, J. Carrol Naish) attempt to scare German
Americans into aiding the Nazis by threatening their relatives overseas.

The last year of the war understandably produced only a handful of spy dramas. Confidential Agent (Warner Bros. , 1945) rehashed the Graham Greene tale of a Spanish Civil War fighter (Charles Boyer) on a mission to England. The House on 92nd Street (20th Century-Fox, 1945) was an excellent, trend-setting semi-documentary film on the F. B. I. 's tracking down and capturing of a ring of enemy spies operating in New York. Thereafter, all spy films owed something to the underplayed realism technique established by Louis de Rochemont in that well-modulated release. First Yank into Tokyo (RKO, 1945) exploited the dropping of atom bombs in Japan, by tacking on the news-shattering events to a standard operative account, whose only novelty was having the hero (Tom Neal) undergo permanent plastic surgery to transform his Occidental features into Oriental style. Another quickie, Tokyo Rose (Paramount, 1945), told the story of the notorious American-born woman who broadcast for the Japanese. A well-done but sparsely-budgeted film, Paris-Underground (United Artists, 1945), had Constance Bennett and Gracie Fields aiding the Allies and ending up being imprisoned in a German prison camp. Unfortunately this feature came too late in the game to have any impact on a war-weary public.

With the end of active hostilities late in 1945, the barrage of spy-oriented features came to a slow halt. Alfred Hitchcock's Notorious (RKO, 1946) told of a girl in World War II South America who marries a Nazi spy (Claude Rains) but who aids an American agent (Cary Grant), while in 13 Rue Madeleine (20th Century-Fox, 1946) James Cagney starred as an underground commando leader in Paris during the war. This latter picture, like Paramount's O. S. S. (1946), with Alan Ladd, gave the filmgoing public an education in the ostensible procedures of the Office of Strategic Services, which had been created during the war by Colonel William "Wild Bill" Donovan. Golden Earrings (Paramount, 1947) had an agent (Ray Milland) joining with Marlene Dietrich and a group of tattered gypsies to do espionage work, and The Stranger (RKO, 1947) contained some aspects of the repercussions from the

spy game, with a government agent (Edward G. Robinson) out to
snare a Nazi war criminal (Orson Welles) hiding out in a small
American hamlet.   Arch of Triumph (United Artists, 1948) with
very little artistic or commercial success, regaled viewers with
the plight of partisans and passportless individuals in pre-occupation Paris.   Jacques Tourneur's Berlin Express (RKO, 1948)
was part of the late 1940s neo-realism movement, with its tale of
(counter)espionage and killings filmed on-the-spot in war-torn
Europe.   The world had grown up a great deal and now demanded
even its pap entertainment garnered with dabs of (pseudo) reality.

    The Iron Curtain (20th Century-Fox, 1948) was another
watershed mark in the annals of the spy films.   A decade earlier
filmmakers had launched a hot and heavy attack on the danger of
enemy sympathizers insinuating their way into the fiber of American
life.   Now in the late 1940s with the cold war reaching an early
zenith, Hollywood felt itself obliged to inform the filmgoer about
the Communist threat.   The Iron Curtain dealt with Russian espionage activity in 1943 Canada, giving the public a gentle introduction to the brutal truth: Red agents were running rampant in the
U. S. A.

    With the coming of the 1950s, the focus of the spy drama
shifted almost completely to the cold war and the supposed efforts
of Communism to take over the world.   I Was a Communist for the
F. B. I. (Warner Bros. , 1951) picked up where Woman on Pier 13
(RKO, 1949) left off, revealing the corruptive influence of Soviet
disciples in the American democracy.   Senator McCarthy's flamboyant attack on alleged American-born Communists was reaching
its peak, and Hollywood obliged by giving the public the well-made
I Was a Communist for the F. B. I., seemingly snatched from the
book of life.

    Concurrent with the focus on the Communist threat, came a
new cycle of spy films.   World War II had already become nostal-
gia--what with the intervening Korean War--and the public was
ready for another batch of espionage thrillers.   Hollywood willingly
obliged.   A comedy My Favorite Spy (Paramount, 1951) featured

Bob Hope thrust into an international intrigue plot which also
starred his favorite lady, Hedy Lamarr. I Was an American Spy
(Allied Artists, 1951) was a cheap throw-back to World War II
days and told of a brave woman (Ann Dvorak) aiding the people as
the Japanese took over the Philippines. A much sturdier drama
was the British-made Odette (United Artists, 1951) in which that
veteran of spy films, Anna Neagle, portrayed a relative of Winston
Churchill held captive by the Nazis. Sealed Cargo (RKO, 1951)
told a war story of German offensive ships operating off the coast
of Newfoundland.

By 1952, the spy screen drama was again booming. Errol
Flynn's Against All Flags (Universal, 1952) told a buccaneer yarn
of a British officer in the 19th century who infiltrated and broke
up a pirate gang. (The film was remade in 1967 by the same
company as King's Pirate.) Big Jim McLain (Warner Bros., 1952)
told a much more topical story of two U.S. agents (John Wayne,
James Arness) investigating Red activity in Hawaii, while Diplomatic Courier (20th Century-Fox, 1952) had glamour star Tyrone
Power out to avenge a friend's murder, while becoming involved
in international intrigue. The highly-regarded Decision Before
Dawn (20th Century-Fox, 1952) found director Anatole Litvak guiding
Oscar Werner, Richard Basehart, et al., through a grim, sad tale
of a conscientious human being, a German no less, deciding that it
would be best for his country if he performed an Allied spy mission, so that perhaps the war would end that much sooner. More
colorful, but still rooted in reality (it was based on a true case)
was Five Fingers (20th Century-Fox, 1952) about an Albanian valet
(James Mason) who photographed top secret British documents and
sold them to the Germans in World War II. Operation Secret
(Warner Bros., 1952) was a regressive example of production-line
filmmaking, relating underground activities in Second World War
France. A most unique motion picture was The Thief (United
Artists, 1952), a movie without dialogue set largely in New York
City and dealing with that staple of 1950s spy films, a loyalty-
twisted atomic scientist (Ray Milland). The near-classic Walk

East on Beacon (Columbia, 1952) shot on location in Boston, re-
told the step-by-step F. B. I. capture of a Communist spy ring.
Dangerous Agent (Borderie, 1952) was a French imitation of American thrillers and came to U. S. television some 13 years after it
was made.   It was about a secret agent (Eddie Constantine) who
broke up a gang of international racketeers.   It is "important" only
because it foreshadowed a mass series of poor spy dramas to pour
out of Europe in succeeding years, though the majority would not
be made until the middle of the next decade when the James Bond
craze had hit.

The Man Between (United Artists, 1953) was the usual Carol
Reed sombre approach to a meaty subject.   Here, a shady crook
(James Mason) in East Berlin risks his life to save a girl from
the Communists, while the European-lensed Man on a Tightrope
(20th Century-Fox, 1953) concerned itself with the lives of those
in a small traveling circus troupe and their daring plan to escape
from behind the Iron Curtain.   The synthetic, poorly-received
Never Let Me Go (MGM, 1953) also dealt with an escape-to-the-
free-West plot, this time featuring newspaperman Clark Gable
determined to smuggle his ballerina wife (Gene Tierney--her
dancing equalled her Russian "accent") out of the U. S. S. R.   A
lighthearted approach to the East-West conflict was presented in
Mr. Potts Goes to Moscow (Allied Artists, 1953), a British-produced lark about a plumber (George Cole) amuck in intrigue-filled
Russia.

Clark Gable was involved with espionage again in the im-
probably cast and badly-guided World War II occupied Holland tale,
Betrayed (MGM, 1954), in which Lana Turner battled with Victor
Mature for the unconvincing histrionics awards.   The Daughter of
Mata Hari (Regent, 1954) was an Italian-French mishmash that almost did in the femme fatale tradition with its sloppy production
values and silly premise.   Much more successful in technical execution was the German-made Canaris-Master Spy (1954), which told
of the high-ranking German general who met his downfall by participating in an anti-Hitler plot.   (Recent documentation reveals that

this romanticized officer was far less a decent human being than it
originally seemed.) Filmed in Berlin in CinemaScope, Night People
(20th Century-Fox, 1954) revolved around cold war espionage and
the people mixed up in it. The same studio also that year churned
out Hell and High Water, whose widescreen process and special
effects could not redeem the shoddy plotline and acting, as Richard
Widmark, Bella Darvi, and others are involved in a U.S. submarine
mission to the Arctic.

The Prisoner (Columbia, 1955) was a harsh study of Communist interrogation tactics, while The Scarlet Coat (MGM, 1955)
was a rare excursion--gorgeously decked out--into the American
revolutionary war period and the perfidy of Benedict Arnold. Spy
Chasers (Allied Artists, 1955) was an asinine Bowery Boys caper
involving you-know-what. A film based on a long-running television
series, Foreign Intrigue (United Artists, 1956) overworked its study
of a trenchcoated hero combatting underhanded forces on the Continent. The same year Alfred Hitchcock remade, but did not overly
improve, The Man Who Knew Too Much (Paramount, 1956).

The cheapie Girl in the Kremlin (Universal, 1957) had Zsa
Zsa Gabor as twins, one of them being Stalin's mistress. Operation
Conspiracy (Republic, 1957) was a British effort about an agent
combatting Reds seeking nuclear information, and the French-made
Operation Abduction (1957) told of a spy hunt for a gang who had
kidnapped the inventor of a new type of fuel. Orders to Kill (United
Artists, 1958) was a mature study of an American undercover man
ordered to Franch to kill an alleged traitor, and the bout of conscience he undergoes. The Quiet American (United Artists, 1958)
attempted to be a solid recitation of the semi-profound Graham
Greene book of a well-meaning American meddler loose in Indochina,
while The Two-Headed Spy (Columbia, 1958) reverted to the 1930's
to detail the elaborate foresight used by the British to place an
agent within the high German military circles years before the
Second World War erupted. A refreshing twist in the genre was
presented in Alfred Hitchcock's North by Northwest (MGM, 1959)
enhanced by Cary Grant's superior performance, and the artful use

of unique backdrops.

The 1960s arrived with little attempt by filmmakers to touch upon new approaches to the spy genre.   Andre de Toth directed the heavy-handed Man on a String (Columbia, 1960) which claimed to be the true story of Boris Morros, a counterspy in the Cold War (his cover being a film producer).   Ernest Borgnine provided plenty of ham in the title role.   Our Man in Havana (Columbia, 1960) was a leaden spy spoof of a vacuum cleaner salesman who is pushed into becoming a British agent.   The picture was yet another example of a Graham Greene book going awry on screen.   Who Was That Lady? (Columbia, 1960) offered the husband and wife team of Tony Curtis and Janet Leigh in a soggy rendition of a middling Broadway comedy which asked the audience to be more naive than the stars, with Curtis and pal Dean Martin out to fool the former's jealous wife (Leigh) by pretending to be secret agents.

In 1961, 20th Century-Fox delved into its television series vaults and issued two features from its NBC video series "Five Fingers."   The titles were Dossier and The Judas Goat.   The next year two more titles were issued from the same origin, Temple of the Swinging Doll and Thin Ice.   This medium-transfer was proving to be a profitable gambit, and the procedure would be used more frequently as the decade progressed.   The Risk (Kingsley International, 1961) was a tense tale of spies on the trail of a scientist who has discovered a cure for a dreaded disease, while The Secret Ways (Universal, 1961) was a would-be thriller about the smuggling of a man from behind the Iron Curtain.   In Ça Va Etre Ta Fête (Belmont Chaillot, 1961) Eddie Constantine played yet another secret agent, but still of the silent, beefy breed, who is pursued by a crime network in Lisbon, while in Me Faire Ça à Moi! (Ares, 1961) he is a reporter hoaxed onto a ship to combat spies, but is really a government decoy.

By 1962 there was an upsurge in the number of films issued with the spy motif.   The public was seeking escapism fare, and even if the espionage action yarns were allegedly geared to present day "true cases" or harked back to the nostalgia-tinged World War

II era for their "it-really-happened" escapades, the vicarious excitement of people engaged in extraordinarily hazardous activity was
a break from life's plodding routines.   The Counterfeit Traitor
(Paramount, 1962) was a perfect example of the factually-oriented
story "enhanced" for the screen, but for a change the embellish-
ments were subtle enough not to distort the realism of the 1940s
Scandinavian counteragent (William Holden) who journeys into the
depths of Germany on a special assignment.   The stark and shrill
The Manchurian Candidate (United Artists, 1962) caused considerable
excitement among the critics and the filmgoers, with its improbable
but possible tale of a robot-like brainwashed Communist operative
who is used as a deadly sniper.   The British continued to produce
their unpretentious little programmers dealing with espionage, as
Dead Man's Evidence (Bayart-Lion, 1962) and The Traitors (Rank,
1962) demonstrated.   From France came The Hideout (Hoche-
Miracle, 1962), which featured Marcel Mouloudji as a saboteur in
World War II who took refuge in a friend's mental institution to
escape the Germans at the war's end, and after his friend's death
could convince no one that he was not insane.   Comment Qu'elle
Est! (Borderie Films, 1962) had the ever-popular agent Eddie Constantine, aided by the French secret service on the trail of a master
spy, and Lemmy pour les Dames (Borderie, 1962) again offered the
same actor as agent Lemmy Caution vacationing on the Riviera and
running into the mysterious wives of three diplomats, a secret laboratory, espionage and murder.   A French-Italian-Japanese co-
production Who Are You? (Gala, 1962) told the true story of Richard
Sorge (Thomas Holtzmann), a spy who worked for and had the confidence of Russia, Germany, and Japan--all at the same time!   An
American cheapie Spy Squad (Riviera, 1962) was also known as Capture That Capsule.

  The highwater mark of the spy genre occurred with the unheralded appearance of Dr. No (United Artists, 1963).   Nothing
could, would, or wanted to be the same thereafter.   Ian Fleming's
James Bond novels had been delighting the public for several years,
gaining even more popularity when it was bandied about that President

John F. Kennedy was an ardent admirer of literature's slick, suave
killer, agent 007. With Sean Connery in the "hero" role, <u>Dr. No</u>
brought sadism-sex-violence-high living to a new peak of screen
perfection. As Ian Johnson wrote in a survey article for the
British <u>Films and Filming</u>, "Identifying our snob sex, and violent
wish-thinking with Bond is a good purgative. But make no mistake
about it, Bond is as much a thug as his opponents beneath his be-
guiling charm. The only difference is he is on our side." In
the past, secret agents, particularly from "civilized" Western
countries, had never been sanctioned by their government sponsors
(at least not ostensibly) to kill. Nevertheless, James Bond, so
the public was constantly told, was licensed to kill by M. I. 5! As
one magazine writer analyzed this necessary adjunct to the cold
war mechanism, James Bond "... found it part of his profession
to kill people. He had never liked doing it and when he had to
kill he did it as well as he knew how and forgot about it. As a
secret agent who held the rare double-0 prefix--a license to kill
in the Secret Service--it was his duty to be as cool about death as
a surgeon. If it happened, it happened. Regret was unprofessional--
worse, it was death-watch beetle in the soul."

     The remarkable box office success of <u>Dr. No</u> caused its pro-
ducers, Harry Saltzman and Cubby Broccoli to open their money
belts and turn out several more installments of the Ian Fleming
series for the hungry public. Meanwhile, before the Bond craze
caught the other filmmakers with their pocketbooks down, there
appeared such conventional entries as the British-produced <u>A Face
in the Rain</u> (Embassy, 1963) which had Rory Calhoun recounting his
World War II espionage experiences in Italy. There was <u>Master
Spy</u> (Grand National, 1963) about a scientist (Stephen Murray) from
the East who seeks refuge in the West but becomes embroiled in a
desperate spy game. <u>Ring of Spies</u> (Lion, 1963) was based on
the actual, astounding Portland Case, about the police rounding up
a highly efficient espionage net operating in England. More serious was <u>The Mind Benders</u> (AIP, 1963), involving both the test of
a person's will and espionage. The salacious <u>The Prize</u> (MGM,

1963), from the Irving Wallace novel, dealt with a libido-obsessed group of prize winners congregating in Stockholm, only to have Communist double-dealing play a strong hand. Spies-a-Go-Go (1963) was a clinker about the Russians trying to pass themselves off as cowpokes and infect America with diseased rabbits. The French did A Toi de Faire, Mignonne (Films Borderie, 1963) a Lemmy Caution (Eddie Constantine) drama, which had Lemmy working for the U.S. secret service, being assigned by the F.B.I. to discover why a female agent was killed and why a top American scholar had been kidnapped.

With the release of United Artists' second James Bond epic, From Russia with Love (1964), the cinema spy craze really began. The new type of screen spy tended to be more of a super secret agent, working for a government against the often unspecified (and certainly unmotivated) evils of the "other side." He usually spent a good deal of time charging in and out of bed with one or more inarticulate, but beautiful bikini-clad girls, some of whom were agents for the evil ones. His weapons were a conglomeration of weapons which were a distinct throwback to the fantastic movie serials of the 1930s. The films themselves tried--so hard and usually so unsuccessfully--to be wonderful tongue-in-cheek excursions, mocking the bureaucracy of the Establishment and the red tape of the cold war. At the same time they pandered to the middle class' secret disavowal of conventional values about sex, sadism, mayhem, and general amoral behavior.

While From Russia with Love was mopping up at the box office and instigating a cinematic cycle that took the rest of the decade to dissipate, the other espionage films of the years included Hide and Seek (Universal, 1964), a would-be kidding British feature about a professor who is the target for kidnapping by a spy network; Stop Train 349 (Allied Artists, 1964), which found Sean Flynn involved with Russians trying to search a Berlin train for a defector; The 36 Hours (MGM, 1964), a World War II spy thriller produced on a lavish scale; Shadow of Fear (Butchers, 1964) about a man (Frank Maxwell) and a girl (Clare Owen) who found themselves as decoys for the M. I. 5; Claude Chabrol's French super spy entry <u>Code Name:</u> <u>Tiger</u> (Gaumont/Procefi, 1964), which told of a fast acting agent (Roger Hanin) protecting a French diplomat's wife and daughter; and <u>The Spy I Love</u> (1964), another French film, with Virna Lisi involved with agents stealing an atomic device.   Another French-produced Nick Carter film, <u>Nick Carter Va Tout Casser</u> (Florida/ Chaumaine/Filmstudio, 1964), starred Eddie Constantine in the title role of John R. Corryell's literary character, who in this installment tracks down Chinese spies who have commandeered an anti-flight weapon.   Nadia Gray appeared as a Mata Hari-type operative in an erotic espionage film, the German-made <u>The Secret</u> <u>Weapon</u> (Boldt, 1964).

By the middle 1960s, television was offering several highly-popular spy series, including "The Man from U. N. C. L. E. " with Robert Vaughn, David McCallum, and Leo G. Carroll, and its short-lived spin-off, "The Girl from U. N. C. L. E. " with Stefanie Powers in the title role.   "I Spy, " with Bill Cosby and Robert Culp, a pathfinding project with a white and black actor star team, debuted in 1965 and from Britain came the long-lasting "The Avengers" and "Secret Agent. "

The highlight year of the new spy film wave was 1965, culminating with the two smash boxoffice James Bond thrillers, <u>Thunderball</u> and <u>Goldfinger</u>, both released by United Artists.   The other landmark entry of the year was Paramount's <u>The Spy Who Came in</u> <u>from the Cold</u>, derived from one of the genre's leading writers, John Le Carre.   The grim drama, starring Richard Burton, Claire Bloom, and Oscar Werner, had the audacity to confront the phenomenal Bond screen rage by depicting in such gritty detail that it had to be true, the tremendously dreary existence endured by the very unglamourous real life operatives, who are usually friendless, unthanked, worn out creatures, desperately searching for a safe hiding place from the world of cold war espionage with which they so chivalrously involved themselves without much fore-thought.   <u>Morituri</u> (20th Century-Fox, 1965) had for its message that Germans in World War II could be and were sensitive, caring human beings too. Operation Crossbow (MGM, 1965) was an expensive misfire that sought to glorify the earnest work of commando-style operatives in the Second World War; the nonsensical Carry on Spying (Governor, 1965) relied on smutty laugh-getting situations to spoof the genre. Michael Caine starred in The Ipcress File (Universal, 1965), which, taking its cue from The Spy Who Came in from the Cold presented a commonplace Cockney scoundrel, Harry Palmer, as the star of what would be a trio of series entries. Masquerade (United Artists, 1965) was an upper-crust send-up of the spy films, but so adroitly handled that it caught the public's fancy.

There was an avalanche of cheap spy thrillers in 1965, mostly shot in Europe, and then hastily dubbed for the English-language countries.   They were so nondescript and enervating that by sheer quantity alone they nearly killed the genre before the end of the decade.   A couple of U.S. financed features, The Fat Spy (Magna, 1965) with Jack E. Leonard, and The Return of Mr. Moto (20th Century-Fox, 1965) were lackluster on all scores.   From Europe came the unheralded The Second Best Secret Agent in the Whole Wide World (Embassy, 1965), with Tom Adams as a hip, but human super agent, involved with guns, girls, and corpses in the protection of a valued scientist.   With the Vietnam war esculating, a few filmmakers made Saigon the site of their films, such as Operation CIA (Allied Artists, 1965), which offered burly and hairy Burt Reynolds as secret agent Mark Andrew out to discover why a message was never delivered to the Saigon embassy and finding a Viet Cong plot to kill the U.S. ambassador.

Jean-Luc Godard's Alphaville (Athos Film, 1965) won some acclaim for its offbeat treatment of blending the spy and science fiction genres--foreshadowing a trend for the 1970s--with Lemmy Caution (Eddie Constantine) dispatched to the "outer countries" to combat a computerized society.

Among the plethora of cheap carbon-copy James Bond super agent films to pour forth from Europe in 1965 were Secret Agent Fireball (The Spy Killers in Britain; Lion), with agent Fleming

(Richard Harrison) determined to aid two Soviet scientists who have
fled with valuable microfilm and are being pursued by Commie
agents.   Feu à Volonte (Faites Vos Jeux, Mesdames) (Speva/Hes-
peria/Cine-Alliance) told of F. B. I. operative Mike Warner (Eddie
Constantine) who rescued a 17-year-old scientist; Nick Carter et le
Trefle Rouge (Chaumaine/Parc/Filmstudio) had federal agent Nick
Carter (Eddie Constantine) recovering a batch of stolen rockets
loaded with a deadly gas.   Other miniature screen entries from
France were: L'Homme de Mykanos (CFFP, 1965); Mission Spe-
ciale à Caracas (CFFP, 1965); Coplan FX 18 Casse Tout (CFFP,
1965); Pleinis Feux sur Stanislas (CICC, 1965) with Alkam Marceau; L'Espion à l'Affut (Griffon, 1965); Furia à Bahia pour OSS
117 (Gaumont/PAC, 1965); and Operation Dorathee (Optamix/Roit-
feld Activités Cinematographiques, 1965), a comedy.   One of the
better productions of this species of cheapies exported from France
was L'Honorable Stanislas, Secret Agent (Licorna/Ital-Gama, 1965)
with Jean Marais well in control of his characterization as a suave
upper-crust playboy dragged into the spy business and acquitting
himself well for his employers.

From Italy came Spla Spione (Colt, 1965), a tepid spoof
with Lando Buzzanca; Agente 777 Mission Summergana (FIDA, 1965);
Agente S3S Massacre in the Sun (Filmar, 1965); Asso di Picche
Operazione Contro-Espionaggio (Filmar, 1965); From 077 Intrigue
in Lisbon (Filmes, 1965); Spies Kill in Silence (Filmes, 1965);
2 + 2 Mission Hydra (Golden, 1965); James Tont, Operation Two
(Panda, 1965), another cinematic dig at the genre with Lando
Buzzanca and directed by Bruno Corbucci; Agent 777 (Protor, 1965);
Spies Love Flowers (Romane, 1965), directed by Umberto Lenzi;
Mark Donen, Agent Z-7 (Operation Rembrandt) (United, 1965); with
Lang Jeffries and Laura Valenzuela and directed by Giancarlo Romi-
telli; and Agent Howard: Seven Minutes to Die (United, 1965),
starring Paul Stevens and Betsy Bet with Ramon Fernandez directing.
Most of these Italian (as well as the French) quickies, were hastily
dubbed and shoved directly onto American television, bypassing the
action double bill theatrical market which had a surfeit of such

features to offer (un)willing patrons.

The only puzzle to potential viewers of the many, many co-productions in the spy film field that appeared in 1965 was the myriad of title changes as the finished product jumped from country to country in its scattered release pattern.   Among such films were Agent 01 Against Fantômes (Apolo, 1965), with Brad Harris, Roberto Camardiel, and Jose Marco, with Richard Jackson directing, being an Italian-Spanish-German co-production as was Jerry Land--Spy Chaser (Orduna, 1965) which Juan Orduna directed.   Spain, Italy, France, and West Germany joined together to make Agent 333, Passport to Hell (AS, 1965) with Sergio Sollima directing, and Agent Z 55, Desperate Mission (AS, 1965).   Spy Chase (Midega, 1965) was a German-French-Italian film, while FBI Agent, Operation Oceano (Coperfilm, 1965) was made by Spain and France.   Spain and Italy joined for Agent OS 14 (C.E.C., 1965), Operation Poker (Alococer, 1965), and Onu Agent Marc Nato (Atlantida, 1965) with Perla Christal, Luis Davila, and Alberto Dalbis.

Solo Spanish super spy features of 1965 included Agent 077, Mission Bloody Mary (Epoca, 1965); Paris-Istanbul: With No Return (Epoca, 1965); Agent 003, Operation Atlantida (Fisca, 1965) Mission Lisbon (Hesperia, 1965), with Brett Halsey, Fernando Rey, and Jeanne Valeria; and 007--But Dial Code Number First (IFI, 1965), a comedy with Cassen and Enconito Palo.   The best that can be said for most of these European entries, from whichever country, was that it kept many hundreds of technicians and actors employed for a spell.

The dizzy spy cycle continued unabated into 1966, with each producer outbidding the next to assemble a more stellar cast for the director to manipulate within the crazy shenanigans of an obtuse plot.   Typical of the mishmashes that often resulted were Bang, Bang You're Dead! (AIP, 1966; also known as Our Man in Marrakesh) and I Spy, You Spy, which featured Tony Randall as a clumsy hotel architect mixed up with murderous spies and a lovely liar (Senta Berger) in a cast that included Wilfrid Hyde-White, Terry-Thomas, and Herbert Lom.   A little more adroit was A Man Could

Get Killed (Universal, 1966), which relied on the exuberant charms of Melina Mercouri. In the inadvertently funny category was Alfred Hitchcock's minor league Torn Curtain (Universal, 1966) which paired Julie "Mary Poppins" Andrews with Paul "Hud" Newman for diminishing returns in a synthetic Iron Curtain espionage caper. Since the theatrical film market was so thoroughly saturated with spy flicks, several filmmakers thought it high time to make elaborate take-offs of the genre in a deliberately funny manner. Unfortunately most of them were incontestibly boring: The Glass Bottom Boat (MGM, 1966) with Doris Day; The Last of the Secret Agents? (Paramount, 1966) with the "comedy" team of Mary Allen and Steve Rossi; and That Man in Istanbul (Columbia, 1966) with Horst Buchholz. A continuing trend was to splice together segments from teleseries episodes and palm them off onto the theatrical market. The most successful practitioner of this subterfuge was MGM with its "The Man from U. N. C. L. E. " series which spawned such scissor and paste features as One Spy too Many, The Spy with My Face, and To Trap a Spy, all 1966. From "Blue Light" came I Deal in Danger (20th Century-Fox, 1966) featuring Robert Goulet and Christine Carere in a World War II setting. Seeing the video episodes on the big screen, despite the much publicized additions of previously unseen outtakes and specially shot new adult footage, only magnified the generally shoddy character of the merchandise.

Many of 1966's spy film releases were again cheapies from abroad. From France came Cartes sur Table (Speva/Cine-Alliance, 1966), with Eddie Constantine battling the Red Chinese; Le Judoka Agent Secret (Francis Ameni, 1966), featuring a judo-expert agent, Avec la Peau des Autres (Montfort, 1966); Le Reseau Secret (Nelson, 1966); and Big Blow in Her Majesty's Service (Atlantia, 1966), a French-Italian-Spanish co-production with Michelle Lup directing star Richard Harrison. Spain produced Agent End--Final Mission (Balcazar, 1966) with Mino Guerrima directing; A Thief for a Spy (Balcazar, 1966) with Lando Buzzanca and Teresa Gimpera; Agent Z55 (Gonzales, 1966) with Jerry Cobb and Maira Mohos; 087 Apocalyptic Mission (Estela, 1966), Spies Kill Silently (Estela, 1966),

and Espia NDD (Halcon, 1966) all featuring Sancho Garcia, Enrique
Avila, and Francisco Ariza.   Japan scheduled The Killing Bottle with
Nick Adams for export, but it took another two years for the fea-
ture to make its way to U. S. television.

In the U. S. , Columbia launched its Matt Helm series starring
sleepy-eyed martini drinker Dean Martin, and found a market for
The Silencers and Murderers' Row, both released in 1966.   With
its reliance on low-brow double entendre humor, catch-all sets and
casting, the Matt Helm property was no match for the ever-con-
tinuing James Bond, which, while it had no new offering for 1966,
was retaining its audience loyalty by re-issuing a double bill pairing of Dr. No and From Russia with Love.   A number of American-
financed foreign titles hit the drive-in market, including Montgomery
Clift's final film The Defector (Warner Bros. , 1966), which treaded
heavily on the sombre, cynical path established by The Spy Who Came
in from the Cold.   England continued with its modestly produced
batch of espionage films, including City of Fear (Planet, 1966),
about a Canadian journalist (Robert Maxwell) who is sent to Budapest to cover a news story and becomes implicated in a plot to
use him as an exchange hostage for a U. S. S. R. spy, and The Runaway (Columbia, 1966), dealing with an ex-Soviet spy who escapes
to South America and 24 years later returns to England to find his
horrendous past catching up with him.

By 1967 even the man in the street, if he thought about
such (to him) mundane matters, was wondering when the spy movie
cycle would end.   It had infiltrated every aspect of his life (from
television programming, to underwear and liquor merchandising) and
he wanted a change of pace.   However, filmmakers still had a few
more entries to offer.   Twentieth Century-Fox launched what seemed
to be a promising series involving Derek Flint (James Coburn) in
In Like Flint (1967) but it died after the follow-up entry in the
series.   Doris Day insisted she could be a sophisticated screen
farceur and flopped in her second spoof of the genre, Caprice (20th
Century-Fox, 1967).   Dean Martin came back as Matt Helm in The
Ambushers (Columbia, 1967), the weakest of the series, while the

same studio offered the sturdy, but neglected British-made The
Deadly Affair (1967), featuring James Mason and Simone Signoret.
Much-heralded was the costly Casino Royale (Columbia, 1967),
which wanted to josh the super agent gambit but almost ruined
James Bond as a viable film property forever. Agent 007 was
not really helped by the authentic thing, for You Only Live Twice
(United Artists, 1967) had science fiction splendor but little of the
distinctive suave sarcasm that usually abounded in past screen
efforts starring Sean Connery. Telefeatures, the new salvation
of the dying new medium (television), still saturated the market,
with paste-ups including two more from the "U. N. C. L. E." files:
The Karate Killers (MGM, 1967), and The Spy with the Green Hat
(MGM, 1967). There was also Code Name: Heraclitus (Universal,
1967), Asylum for a Spy (Universal, 1967), The Scorpio Letters
(MGM, 1967), and Some May Live (RKO, 1967).

    From Europe came Residencia para Espias (Danchez les
Gentlemen) (Hesperia, 1967), about a U.S. secret agent, Dan Layton (Eddie Constantine), who believes a colonel's wife heads a spy
ring in Istanbul; Agent Sigma 3 (Europix, 1967) with Jack Taylor
and Silvia Solan; Secret Code: Kill Maller (Europix, 1967) with
Lang Jeffries and Helga Line; Operation Mystery (Europix, 1967)
with Mark Damon and Seine Sen; The Was Won in Switzerland
(Castroro, 1967), a World War II spy drama; No Roses for Agent
117 (Dama, 1967), an Italian feature with John Gavin, Margaret
Lee, and Curt Jurgens; Coplass Sauve Sa Peau (CFPP, 1967), directed by Yves Boisset; and Agente Z-55 Mission Coleman (Balcazar, 1967), a Spanish-Italian co-production, directed by Miguel
Iglesias. The Walter Reade group released a comedy spy drama in
the U. S. , written, produced, directed by, and starring Jamie Uys,
called After You Comrade (Continental, 1967).

    By 1968 everyone admitted the spy movie fad was swiftly
coming to a close. Telefeatures still clung to the spy motif, but
few good theatrical films did. Dean Martin made his final Matt
Helm film, The Wrecking Crew (Columbia, 1968). Other spy
dramas included the poor A Dandy in Aspic (Columbia, 1968), the

World War II-oriented In Enemy Country (Universal, 1968) and the underrated Sebastian (Paramount, 1968). The final films culled from the "U. N. C. L. E. " series made their appearance; The Helicopter Spies (MGM, 1968) and How to Steal the World (MGM, 1968). There was Koroshi (ITC, 1968), culled from the "Secret Agent" series, and Hawaii Five-0 (Universal, 1968), a telefeature pilot for the long-running series. From Britain came The Limbo Line (London Independent, 1968), with Craig Stevens, which was shunted almost directly to television, as was The Cape Town Affair (20th Century-Fox, 1968) with Claire Trevor, produced in South Africa.

The barrage of Continental spy features was nearly over. From Spain came Agente Sigma (Estela, 1968) and from Italy came Red Dragon (Woolner Bros. , 1968). Assignment to Kill (Warner Bros. , 1968) was a multi-nation co-production with Patrick O'Neal, Herbert Lom, Joan Hackett, Eric Portmann, and Peter Van Eyck, dealing with a $15 million dollar conspiracy (making the film more an international heist yarn than a spy entry).

Even if the over-all quality of spy features was not high, at least the number of shoddy ones decreased in 1969. Among the better theatrical espionage action pictures of the year were Otley (Columbia, 1969), a spoof with Tom Courtenay; Alfred Hitchcock's dragging Topaz (Universal, 1969); the over-ambitious The Chairman (20th Century-Fox, 1969) with Gregory Peck; and the ludicrous but full of action Where Eagles Dare (MGM, 1969) with Richard Burton and Clint Eastwood. Several telefeatures were also good spy dramas, including Destiny of a Spy (Universal, 1969) and Daughter of the Mind (20th Century-Fox, 1969), the latter starring Ray Milland, Gene Tierney, and Don Murray.

Few spy motion pictures appeared in 1970. James Bond returned, not very successfully, in the person of George Lazenby in On Her Majesty's Secret Service (United Artists, 1970), while John Huston offered the disappointing The Kremlin Letter (20th Century-Fox, 1970). Others included the perversely inept The Looking Glass War (Columbia, 1970) and the lackadaisical Matchless (United Artists, 1970). A sole telefeature, Foreign Exchange

(Halsan, 1970) contained the spy motif for stay-at-home small
screen watchers.

Screen spies fared little better in 1971, with such poor
entries as Catch Me A Spy (Rank, 1971) and The Delta Factor
(American Continental, 1971). From television came Vanished
(Universal, 1971), Bette Davis as Madame Sin (ITC, 1971), and
Curt Siodmak's Hauser's Memory (Universal, 1971).

The seemingly indestructible James Bond returned to the big
screen with Diamonds Are Forever (United Artists, 1972) and
wooed a sizeable boxoffice take, more for the sake of nostalgia
than for any innovations the elaborate production with Sean Connery
had to offer. The other few theatrical features delving into the
overworked genre were The Groundstar Conspiracy (Universal,
1972) and the very sloppy The Saltzburg Connection (20th Century-
Fox, 1972). On television there was Assignment: Munich (ABC,
1972) and The Delphi Bureau (Universal, 1972), the latter a forerunner to an eight segment teleseries featuring Anne Jeffreys.

What of the future of the spy film genre? The prospects look
grim indeed for the traditional spy thriller. Even the formerly
avante-garde (now Establishment) James Bond series is delving far
afield in order to insure boxoffice success for the upcoming Live
and Let Die (United Artists, 1973). Not only is there a new agent
007 (Roger Moore) but producers Harry Saltzman and Albert "Cubby"
Broccoli have "black angled" the plot and much of the pitch of the
latest Ian Fleming adventure to take advantage of the black action
movie cycle. James Bond will be battling a black crime kingpin.
(The public reaction to this newest United Artist 007 release, will
greatly shape the direction of the next Bonder on United Artists'
docket, The Man with the Golden Gun.) Pushing in another direction, a few enterprising pornography producers have blended the
skin flick with the spy thriller, as in The Black Tarantula (European Films, 1972), but there is a limit to how much espionage can
transpire within the bedroom.

One avenue of filmed spy adventure that has not been explored very deeply by filmmakers is the blend of science fiction

and the espionage actioner. This Island Earth (Universal, 1955)
and Danger: Diabolik (Paramount, 1968) are two subtle forerunners.
The former, commended as a sturdy futuristic study, and the latter,
dismissed as a cheap copy of the commercially disastrous comic-pop
art mockery Modesty Blaise (20th Century-Fox, 1966), unfortunately
inspired no producer to more carefully blend the two genres for a
commercial success. But with the growing reliance on sophisticated
electronic eavesdropping and photographing devices, as well as the
appearance of totally self-reliant robots, the need for human spies
will disappear, as happens in THX 1138 (Warner Bros., 1971).

Of one thing moviegoers can be sure, no longer will the few-
to-be-produced spy features (and teleseries) be able to rely on the
secure bromide of using a bomb-scarred (East) Berlin for scenic
backdrop. The Communist-controlled sector, like the Western
sector, has undergone a startling renovation process in recent
years, making the settings of The Man Between (United Artists,
1953) and The Spy Who Came in from the Cold (Paramount, 1965)
quite historical.

463 GREAT SPY PICTURES
(with full credits and précis)

A TOI DE FAIRE, MIGNONNE (Prodis, 1963) 93 min.

Director, Bernard Borderie; based on the novel by Peter Cheyney; screenplay, Bernard Borderie, Marc-Gilbert Sauvajon; music, Paul Misraki; camera, Henri Perrin; editor, Christian Gaudin.

Eddie Constantine (Lemmy Caution); Christian Minazzoli (Carletta); Gaia Germani (Geraldine); Elga Andersen (Valerie); Noël Roquevert (Welmer); Philippe Lemaire (Gront); and: Henry Cogan.

Lemmy Caution (Constantine), a U.S. agent, is sent to Europe to discover the cause of the death of a female agent and the whereabouts of a kidnapped scientist, the latter proving to be the leader of a spy group. As always, Constantine spends more time chasing "les dames" and bulldozing his adversaries than in the pursuit of more refined espionage methods.

U.S. tv title: Your Turn, Darling.

ABOVE SUSPICION (MGM, 1948) 93 min.

Producer, Victor Saville; associate producer, Leon Gordon; director, Richard Thorpe; based on the novel by Helen MacInnes; screenplay, Keith Winter, Melville Baker, Patricia Coleman; art director, Cedric Gibbons, Randall Duell; set decorator, Edwin B. Willis, Hugh Hunt; music, Bronislau Kaper; assistant director, Bert Spuring; sound, J. K. Burbridge; special effects, Warren Newcombe; camera, Robert Planck; editor, George Hively.

Joan Crawford (Frances Myles); Fred MacMurray (Richard Myles); Conrad Veidt (Hassert Seidel); Basil Rathbone (Sig von Aschenhausen); Reginald Owen (Dr. Mespelbrunn); Richard Ainley (Peter Galt); Ann Shoemaker (Aunt Ellen); Sara Haden (Aunt Hattie); Felix Bressart (Mr. A. Werner); Bruce Lester (Thornley); Johanna Hofer (Frau Kleist); Lotta Palfi (Ottillie); Cecil Cunningham (Countess); Alex Papana (Man in Paris); Rex Williams (Gestapo Leader); Hans von Morhart (Schmidt); William Yetter (Hauptman); Steve Geray (Anton); William "Wee Willie" Davis (Hans); Ludwig Stossel (Herr Schultz); Ivan Simpson (Porter); Henry Glynn (Chauffeur); Eily Malyon (Manageress); Matthew Boulton (Man); Arthur Shields (Porter); Marcelle Corday (Maid); Frank Lackteen (Arab

43

Vendor); Charles deRavenne (Chasseur); Andre Charlot (Cafe Man-
ager); Frank Arnold (Poet); George Davis (Proprietor); Jack Chefe
(Coatroom Attendant); Felix Basch (Guide); Edit Angold (German
Woman); Lisl Valetti (Nazi Girl); Paul Weigel (Elderly Man); Otto
Reichow (Gestapo Voice); Frank Reicher (Colonel Gerold); Peter
Seal, Nicholas Vehr (Colonel Gerold's Aides); Henry Victor (German
Officer); Egon Brecher (Gestapo Official); Walter O. Stahl (Police-
man); John Rice, Hans Furberg, Albert d'Arno, Erno Verebes
(Gestapo); Steven Muller, Frank Brand, Frederick Bauer (German
Boys); Heather Thatcher, Jean Prescott (English Girls); Sven-Hugo
Borg, Walter Bonn (German Guards); Harold Hensen, Peter Law-
ford, Barry Heenan, David Lennox, Sam McCullough, Oliver Mur-
dock, George Aldwyn, Michael Chudley, Horace Pressel, Oliffe
Oland, Edwin Mills (Boy Students); Greta Dupont (Barmaid); Captain
John Van Eyck (Gestapo in Book Store); Tony Caruso (Italian Border
Sentry); Frederick Giermann (German Border Guard); Louis Donath,
Julius Cramer (Gestapo in Schultz's Laboratory).

Fred MacMurray, Joan Crawford, Ludwig Stossel, Lisa Golm in
Above Suspicion (MGM, 1943).

     Shortly before the outbreak of World War II, American
newlyweds (Crawford and MacMurray) find themselves drafted by
the British secret service to turn their planned Germany honeymoon into an espionage mission. They are required to obtain the

secret plans to the Germans' new magnetic mine weapon. The trail
leads to Paris and then to Salzburg where unfortunately they attract
the suspicions of Gestapo chieftain Sig von Aschenhausen (Rathbone).
   At the time this film trifle was soundly rapped by most free-
thinking critics. Howard Barnes (New York Herald-Tribune) wrote,
"There are so many spies in Above Suspicion that it is hard to keep
track of them. There are so many floral, musical, and crypto-
graphical passwords in the film's plot that the whole show becomes
a sort of super treasure hunt." As to the movie's stars, Barnes
was equally blunt, "Unfortunately, neither Joan Crawford nor Fred
MacMurray look quite bright enough to unravel the tangled skeins of
this screen melodrama."
   On the plus side, both Crawford and Above Suspicion were
far sounder than anyone had any right to expect from the ex-flapper
star or from the glossiest of Hollywood's studios where social conscience was a subject bandied at the commissary luncheon table but
not on screen. Compared to Crawford's much more fanciful Reunion in France (1942), Above Suspicion was more realistic in its
approach to the global conflict and to the people fighting for their
conflicting senses of right and wrong.
   The camp highlight of the film occurs when Crawford and
MacMurray masquerade as an elderly couple in order to escape
over the border to the Allied lines.

ACCIDENTAL SPY   see   MR. STRINGFELLA SAYS NO

ACROSS THE PACIFIC (WB, 1942) 98 min.

   Producer, Jerry Wald, Jack Saper; director, John Huston;
based on the serialized story Aloha Means Goodbye by Robert Carson; screenplay, Richard Macaulay; art director, Robert Haas, Hugh
Reticker; music, Adolph Deutsch; gowns, Milo Anderson; orchestrator, Clifford Vaughan; assistant director, Lee Katz; dialog director, Edward Blatt; makeup, Perc Westmore; montages, Don Siegel;
sound, Everett A. Brown; special effects, Byron Haskin, Willard
Van Enger; camera, Arthur Edeson; editor, Frank Magee.
   Humphrey Bogart (Richard "Rick" Leland); Mary Astor
(Alberta Marlow); Sydney Greenstreet (Dr. H. P. C. Lorenz);
Charles Halton (A. V. Smith); Victor Sen Yung (Joe Totsuiko); Ro-
land Got (Sugi); Lee Tung Foo (Sam Wing On); Frank Wilcox (Cap-
tain Morrison); Lester Mathews (Canadian Major); Paul Stanton
(Colonel Hart); John Hamilton (President of Court Martial); Tom
Stevenson (Tall Thin Man); Monte Blue (Dan Morton); Kam Tong
(T. Oki); Chester Gan (Captain Higoto); Richard Loo (First Officer
Mijyuma); Keye Luke (N. Y. K. Clerk); Spencer Chan (Chief Engineer
Mitaudo); Rudy Robles (Filipino Assassin); Bill Hopper (Orderly);
Frank Mayo (Trial Judge Advocate); Garland Smith, Dick French,
Charles Drake, Will Morgan (Officers); Roland Drew (Captain Hark-
ness); Jack Mower (Major); Eddie Dew (Man); Frank Faylen (Barker);
Ruth Ford (Secretary); Eddie Lee (Chinese Clerk); Dick Botiller

(Waiter); Beal Wong (Usher); Philip Ahn (Man in Theatre); Anthony Caruso (Driver); James Leong (Nura); Paul Fung (Japanese Radio Operator); Gordon De Main (Dock Official).

The reteaming of Bogart, Astor, Greenstreet and director Huston did not live up to its predecessor (The Maltese Falcon), but on its own this film is an engaging World War II melodrama, not damaged too severely by its over-indulgent salute to American patriotism and anti-Japanese sentiment.

Marshalled out of the U.S. Army, Rick Leland (Bogart) is rejected for service in the Canadian artillery. At Halifax he boards the Japanese ship "Genoa Maru" bound for Yokohama via New York and Panama. Aboard the freighter are Alberta Marlow (Astor), a girl of dubious background, and Dr. Lorenz (Greenstreet), a rotund gentleman who openly endorses the Japanese culture. Only when the ship docks in New York is it revealed that Bogart is actually a secret agent trailing the nefarious Greenstreet. Once underway again, Bogart and Greenstreet engage in a cat-and-mouse game, in which the former allows the Axis agent to gain false information concerning military installations at the Canal Zone. In Panama, Astor disappears and Bogart, hot on her trail, finds her and her father (Blue) held prisoners by Greenstreet. Resourceful Bogart rescues them and is able to prevent a Japanese bomber plane from destroying the Canal Locks. In a rather simplistic finale (though better than the usual melodramatics of airfield confrontations in films), Bogart takes Greenstreet into custody when the latter decides against completing his act of hari-kari.

Bogart's restrained performance in Across the Pacific demonstrated an important factor usually ignored by producers of spy pictures: undercover agents do not have to act in so obvious a manner that even a fool, let alone the enemy, would quickly discern their real mission.

ACTION IMMEDIATE [TO CATCH A SPY] (Gaumont, 1956)   105 min.

Director, Maurice Labro; based on the novel by Paul Kenny; adaptation, Frederic Dard; dialog, Jean Redon, Yvan Audouard; music, G. Van Parys; camera, Jean Leherissey.

With: Henri Vidal, Nicole Maurey, Jacques Daqmine, Barbara Laage.

After an Orly Airport robbery, undercover agents search for important stolen rocket plans, leading them to Switzerland and Italy. La Saison Cinématographique branded this French-made effort, "A poor espionage film, without vigor or rhyme...."

[Facing page] Philip Ahn and Humphrey Bogart in Across the Pacific (WB, 1942).

ACTION IN ARABIA   (RKO, 1944)   90 min.

Producer, Maurice Geraghty; director, Leonide Moguy; screenplay, Philip MacDonald, Herbert Biberman; art director, Albert S. D'Agostino, Al Herman; set decorator, Darrell Silvera, Claude Carpenter; music, Roy Webb; music director, C. Bakaleinikoff; assistant director, Ruby Rosenberg; sound, Richard Van Hessen; special effects, Vernon L. Walker; camera, Roy Hunt; editor, Robert Swink.

George Sanders (Gordon); Virginia Bruce (Yvonne); Lenore Aubert (Mounirah); Gene Lockhart (Danesco); Robert Armstrong (Reed); Alan Napier (Latimer); H. B. Warner (Rashid); Rafael Storm (Hotel Clerk); Robert Anderson (Chalmers); Andre Charlot (Leroux); Jamiel Hasson (Kareen); Shusheila Shkari (Arabian Dancer); Edmund Glover (Under Secretary); Maurice Brierre (Drunker Customer); Peter Seal (Husky Attendant); Marcel de la Brosse (French Croupier); John Hamilton (Mr. Hamilton); Michael Ansara (Hamid); Jacques Lory (Arab Beggar); Keith Lawrence (Arab Porter); Francis

George Sanders, Lenore Aubert, H. B. Warner, and Andre Charlot in Action in Arabia (RKO, 1944).

Revel (Rug Peddler); Eric Perge (Gendarme); Ed Gering (Karl);
Frederick Brunn (Erlich); Roberta Daniels (Arab Servant); Abdul-
lah Abbas (Arab Guard); Phiroze Nazir (Haroun); Georges Rene-
vant (Prefect of Police); Frank Lackteen (Ali Omar); Mahmud
Sholkhaly (Selim); Kay Dibbs (Servant); Alex Papana (Pilot);
Tony Patton (Husky Attendant); George Sorel (French Surete);
Irene Seidner (Woman on Plane); Bud Wiser (Man); Isaac Pesaro
(Yussef); Frank Arnold (French Gendarme); Buster Brodie (Bald
Headed Guy).

   As World War II progressed, the plotlines of "B" movies
dealing with the global war went steadily downhill.   On screen
George Sanders had been plying his acting craft for years, delin-
eating both sides of the war efforts.   Here he was again an ally,
this time singlehandedly saving Syria from Axis control.   Such
Flash Gordon comic strip type filmfare strained audience credulity,
no matter how low the viewer's critical standards might be in his
urgent desire for escapist screenfare.
   Dashing American news reporter Gordon (Sanders) finds
himself reassigned to a post in Damascus.   In 1941 this arid city
is a hotbed of political intrigue, with both the Allies and the Axis
anxious to curry the support of the powerful desert tribes.   When
newsman Chalmers (Anderson) is stabbed in the camel's market,
glib Sanders senses a hot story, particularly now that he has noted
the arrival of enemy agent Leroux (Charlot) in Damascus.   Before
long, sleuthful Sanders is wondering on just whose side the French
girl Yvonne (Bruce) is on, and how the native Mounirah (Aubert)
fits into the scheme of things.   A rather fanciful finale finishes
this bit of hokum.
   Of no special interest is the inserted atmosphere footage,
which RKO culled from the reels taken years before by Merian
Cooper and Ernest B. Schoedsack.

ADVENTURES OF TARTU (MGM, 1943)   103 min.

   Associate producer, Harold Huth; director, Harold S. Bucquet;
story, John C. Higgins; screenplay, John Mahin, Howard Emmett
Rogers; art director, John Bryon; assistant director, William
Dodd; sound, V. Wilson; music director, Louis Levy; special ef-
fects, Henry Harris; costumes, Rahirs; camera, John J. Cox;
editor, D. Myers.
   Robert Donat (Terrence Stevenson/Jan Tartu); Valerie Hob-
son (Maruschka Brunn); Walter Rilla (Inspector Otto Vogel); Glynis
Johns (Paula Palacek); Phyllis Morris (Anna Palacek); Martin
Miller (Dr. Novotny); Anthony Eustral (Nazi Officer); Percy Walsh
(Dr. Willindorf); David Ward (Bronty); Frederic Richter (Nestor);
John Penrose (Lt. Kranz); Hubert Leslie (Shoemaker); Mabel
Terry Lewis (Mrs. Stevenson); Mike Iveria (Czech Patriot).

   A highly improbable but eminently satisfying espionage adventure thriller that was too quickly relegated to the just-pap-

entertainment-pile by the critics. Its biggest fault, according to
the reviewers, is that it tried (and succeeded too successfully) to
capture the slickness of the Hollywood-made spy actioners.

Not even Errol Flynn at his cinema peak had to cope with
such a preposterous plot, but Donat acquitted himself with fitting
decorum as the ace delayed-bomb expert sent by the British War
Office to Prague to blow up a large Nazi poison gas factory. Within the filmed adventure, Donat's first stopover is Hungary, where
a British agent supplies him with the forged papers of Jan Tartu,
a Rumanian wanted by the Russian police for anti-regime escapades.
This acquired passport permits "refugee" Donat to obtain a safe
conduct pass to proceed to Czechoslovakia. He boards at the home
of Anna Palacek (Morris), discovering that her young adult daughter
(Johns) is actually a fervent underground agent, and that co-boarder
Maruschka Brunn (Hobson), seemingly the toast of the Nazis, is
really an Allied agent.

One of the most telling moments in this film--or in any of
the genre for that matter--occurs when Johns commits an open act
of sabotage in the Skoda Armament factory and she begs Donat to
denounce her to the guards, both realizing that the Germans have
spotted her bit of foul play. Moments later, while Donat winces,
Johns is shot by the guards as an example to the workers.

No one but a carefree child could accept on face value the
finish which has Donat and Hobson escaping aboard a conveniently
unguarded German bomber plane to the safety of England.

AFTER TONIGHT (RKO, 1933)   71 min.

Executive producer, Merian C. Cooper; associate producer,
H. N. Swanson; director, George Archainbaud; story, Jane Murfin;
screenplay, Murfin, Albert Shelby LeVino, Worthington Miner; art
director, Van Nest Polglase, Al Herman; music director, Max
Steiner; song, Steiner; sound, John L. Cass; camera, Charles
Rosher; editor, William Hamilton.

Constance Bennett (Carla/K-14); Gilbert Roland (Captain
Rudi Riber); Edward Ellis (Major Lieber); Sam Godfrey (Franz);
Lucien Prival (Erlich); Mischa Auer (Adjutant Lehar); Ben Hen-
dricks, Jr. (Sergeant Probert); Leonid Snegoff (Private Muller);
Evelyn Carter Carrington (Frau Stengel); John Wray (Major Mitika);
Vera Lewis (Anna Huber, Cleaner); William Wagner (Overcoat
Spy); Edward Keane (Intelligence Officer); William von Brincken
(Captain--Officer of the Day); Adrienne D'Ambricourt (Woman);
Hans Furburg (Man); Herman Bing (Railroad Ticket Clerk); George
Davis (Frenchman); Frank O'Connor (Officer on Train); Selmer
Jackson (A Spy); Julie Haydon (Hysterical Nurse); Frank Reicher
(Major--Medical Officer); Hooper Atchley (Contact Who's Captured);
Landers Stevens (Major); Major Sam Harris (German Officer);
Virginia Weidler (Olga, Carla's Niece).

Fading superstar Bennett was indulging her artistic fancy
in After Tonight, but nevertheless, the film is illustrative of the

early 1930s concept of the still glamorous spy game in which reality, according to the photoplays, had the slightest of accidental roles. What might have been entertaining fare emerged as "torpid screen drama" (New York Times) and "just another trite variation of an old formula" (New York World Telegram).

First World War Russian operative Carla (Bennett), known as K-14, plies her craft in intrigue-drenched Vienna, unruffled by the seeming necessity to don a new disguise at a moment's notice. At one point she is a cabaret singer, then a humble seamstress (sewing secrets into colleagues' clothes) and still later a Red Cross nurse behind the Austrian front passing information on to confederates through a hidden panel in a peasant's cottage. Bennett's chief nemesis is handsome Austrian officer Rudi Riber (Roland), assigned to seal the information leak, who refuses to believe that his new loved one could be Miss Duplicity herself. In a storybook finish, the two lovers reunite after the war at a Swiss train depot, able to rekindle their burning romance without the tiresome distraction of playing war games.

Unlike Mata Hari (1932) or Dishonored (1931), which focused mostly on the luminous qualities of the femme fatale spy in question, After Tonight beamed a good deal of its attention on the mechanics of the spying system. Unfortunately the approach, like the performances, was juvenile and hackneyed.

AGAINST ALL FLAGS (Universal, 1952)   C 83 min.

     Producer, Howard Christie; director, George Sherman; story, Aeneas MacKenzie; screenplay, MacKenzie, Joseph Hoffman; art director, Bernard Herzbrun, Alexander Golitzen; set decorator, Russell A. Gausman, Oliver Emert; costumes, Edward Stevenson; makeup, Bud Westmore; assistant director, John Sherwood, Phil Bowles, James Welch; sound, Leslie I. Carey, Joe Lapis; special camera, David S. Horsley; dialog director, Irwin Berwick; camera, Russell Metty; editor, Frank Gross.
     Errol Flynn (Brian Hawke); Maureen O'Hara (Spitfire Stevens); Anthony Quinn (Roc Brasiliano); Alice Kelley (Princess Patma); Mildred Natwick (Molvina MacGregor); Robert Warwick (Captain Kidd); Harry Cording (Gow); John Alderson (Harris); Phil Tully (Jones); Michael Ross (Swaine); Bill Radovich (Hassan); Paul Newlan (Crop Ear Collins); Lewis Russell (Oxford); Arthur Gould-Porter (Lord Portland); Olaf Hytten (King William); Lester Mathews (Sir Coudsley); Tudor Owen (William); Maurice Marsac (Captain Moisson); James Craven (Captain Hornsby); James Fairfax (Barber); James Logan (Captain Robert); Keith McConnell, Michael Ferris (Quarter-masters); Emmett Smith (Captain Black Death); Buzz Henry (Pirate Rider); Larry Chance (Lookout); Ed Hinkle (Pirate); Bruce Lansburg (Officer of the Watch); Charles Fitzsimmons (Flag Lieutenant); Renee Beard (Archimedes); Maralou Gray (Harem Girl); Carl Saxe, Chuck Hamilton (Pirate); Dave Kashner (Flogger); Mike Lally (Ad Lib Pirate); Ethan Laidlaw (Ad Lib Townsman).

This feature is one of the few examples of spying in the
swashbuckling days, and it starred the greatest of all the screen
swashbucklers, Errol Flynn. Unfortunately the film was made
during the sunset days of Flynn's movie-starring period, with his
changeover from Warner Bros. to Universal becoming a very sad
move.

The plot dealt with an 18th-century British naval officer
(Flynn) disguised as a deserter who infiltrates a Madagascar stronghold of pirates led by Roc Brasiliano (Quinn) and Spitfire Stevens
(O'Hara). Flynn joins the buccaneers in a raid on the ship of the
emperor of India, concealing the identity of one of its passengers--
the emperor's daughter (Kelly)--so she will not be mishandled by
her captors. Later Flynn sabotages the pirates' cannon guarding
the harbor, rescues Kelly, and then sails off with O'Hara, leaving
the Mediterranean trade route clear for the British merchant fleet.

Made in lackluster fashion on the Universal soundstages and
at Palos Verdes on the Pacific coast, Against All Flags proved to
be poor competition for the popularity of the well-established television medium. Universal remade the story in 1967 as King's
Pirate with Doug McClure in Flynn's old role. It was an even
lesser effort.

AGENT 8 3/4 see HOT ENOUGH FOR JUNE

AGENT FOR H. A. R. M.   (Universal, 1966)   C 84 min.

Producer, Joseph F. Robertson; associate producer, Edward
F. Abrams, Jack Bartlett; director, Gerd Oswald; screenplay,
Blair Robertson; music, Gene Kauer, Douglas Lackey; assistant
director, David Marks; sound, Ken Carlson, Don Harrold; special
effects, Harry S. Wollsman; camera, James Crab; editor, D. E.
Rollins.

Mark Richman (Adam Chance); Wendell Corey (Jim Graff);
Carl Esmond (Professor Janos Steffanic); Barbara Bouchet (Ava
Vestok); Martin Kosleck (Malko); Rafael Campos (Luis); Alizia
Gur (Mid-Eastern Contact); Donna Michelle (Marian); Robert Quarry
(Borg); Robert Donner (Morgue Attendant); Steve Stevens (Billy);
Marc Snegoff (Conrad); Horst Ebersberg (Helgar); Chris Anders
(Schloss); Ray Dannis (Manson); Ronald Von (Police Lieutenant);
Robert Christopher (Police Officer).

"Fooey ... here we go again ... still another anemic James
Bond imitation" (New York Times).

Because Professor Janos Steffanic (Esmond) has escaped
from behind the Iron Curtain and taken asylum in the U. S. to continue his research (an antidote for a poisonous spore from outer
space that turns humans into green fungus), Jim Graff (Corey),
chief of H. A. R. M. (Human Aetiological Relations Machine), assigns
Adam Chance (Richman) to protect the scientist. Corey is particularly worried because Esmond's assistant has been murdered,

and it looks as if enemy agents are congregating on the California
coastal region with the express purpose of grabbing the professor's
secret data.

AGENT 38-24-36   see   UNE RAVISSANTE IDIOTE

AIR RAID WARDENS   (MGM, 1943)   67 min.

        Producer, B. F. Zeidman; director, Edward Sedgwick; screen-
play, Martin Rackin, Jack Jevne, Charles Rogers, Harry Crane;
art director, Harry McAfee; set decorator, Alfred Spencer; music,
Nat Shilkret; assistant director, Roland Asher; sound, Douglas
Shearer; camera, Walter Lundin; editor, Irvine Warburton.
        Stan Laurel (Stanley); Oliver Hardy (Oliver); Edgar Ken-
nedy (Joe Bledsoe); Jacqueline White (Peggy Parker); Stephen
McNally (Dan Madison); Nella Walker (Millicent Norton); Donald
Meek (Eustace Middling); Henry O'Neill (Rittenhouse); Howard
Freeman (J. P. Norton); Paul Stanton (Captain Biddle); Robert Em-
mett O'Connor (Charles Beaugait); William Tannen (Joseph); Rus-
sell Hicks (Major Scanlon).

        Nearing the end of their long film careers, Laurel and Hardy
appeared in the feature Air Raid Wardens, their first film at Metro
since Blockheads (1938). It was a typical war-time comedy with the
boys as the wardens of the title who thwart the Nazis from blowing
up a magnesium plant.
        In The Films of Laurel and Hardy (1967), William K. Ever-
son said Air Raid Wardens was "slick and pleasantly moving," but
added that it "offered little cause for enthusiasm." The boys did
carry the plot fairly well, although the extended length (seven reels)
of the picture forced them to repeat too many gags, and an encounter with old screen foe, Edgar Kennedy, from the Hal Roach
days was not as good as expected.
        During the World War II period, light-hearted toying with
the spy genre was largely kept within the short subject field, as
in the Three Stooges Columbia shorts, You Nazty Spy (1940) and I'll
Never Heil Again (1941). Interestingly, Bud Abbott and Lou Costello, who had become the screen's most popular zany team--far and
away eclipsing Laurel and Hardy--made several service comedies,
but none of them attempted to josh the espionage game.

ALIAS THE LONE WOLF   (Columbia, 1927)   6,843 feet

        Producer, Harry Cohn; director, Edward H. Griffith; based
on the novel by Louis Joseph Vance; screenplay, Dorothy Howell,
Griffith; art director, Robert E. Lee; assistant director, Joe Cook;
camera, J. O. Taylor.
        Bert Lytell (Michael Lanyard); Lois Wilson (Eve de Monta-
lais); William V. Mong (Whitaker Monk); Ned Sparks (Phinuit);
James Mason (Popinot); Paulette Duval (Liane Delonne); Ann Brody

(Fifi); Alphonz Ethier (Inspector Crane).

Although Warren William is better known as the dapper Lone Wolf, it was Bert Lytell who originated the part on screen. The latter actor played Vance's gentleman jewel thief five times on film, beginning in 1917. In 1926, with his movie career on the wane, Lytell began working for the still-new Columbia Pictures and made The Lone Wolf Returns. This was followed by Alias the Lone Wolf.

A silent melodrama, Alias the Lone Wolf, was a tongue-in cheek exercise which presented Michael Lanyard (Lytell) in derring-do involving the smuggling of diamonds, crooks, and secret agents, as well as trying to assist a girl (Wilson) find means to avoid paying heavy duties on a diamond pendant. Most of the screen action took place on a trans-Atlantic ocean liner.

While hardly involved with the subject of espionage, Alias the Lone Wolf did demonstrate, as would countless other features over the decades, that government secret agents had other types of assignments beyond capturing spies.

ALL THROUGH THE NIGHT   (WB, 1942)   107 min.

Producer, Jerry Wald; director, Vincent Sherman; story, Leo Rosten, Leonard Spigelgass; screenplay, Spigelgass, Edwin Gilbert; art director, Max Parker; music, Adolph Deutsch; assistant director, William Kissel; orchestrator, Frank Perkins; song, Johnny Mercer and Arthur Schwartz; sound, Oliver S. Garretson; special effects, Edwin B. DuPar; camera, Sid Hickox; editor, Rudi Fehr.

Humphrey Bogart (Gloves Donahue); Conrad Veidt (Hall Ebbing); Karen Verne (Leda Hamilton); Jane Darwell (Ma Donahue); Frank McHugh (Barney); Peter Lorre (Pepi); Judith Anderson (Madame); William Demarest (Sunshine); Jackie Gleason (Starchie); Phil Silvers (Waiter); Wallace Ford (Spats Hunter); Barton Mac-Lane (Marty Callahan); Edward S. Brophy (Joe Denning); Martin Kosleck (Steindorff); Jean Ames (Annabelle); James Burke (Forbes); Ludwig Stossel (Mr. Miller); Ben Welden (Smitty); Charles Cane (Spence); Frank Sully (Sage); Irene Seidner (Mrs. Miller); Hans Schumm (Anton); Sam McDaniel (Deacon); Leo White, Billy Wayne (Chefs); Al Eben (Pastry Chef); Lottie Williams (Flower Woman); Louis Arco, Wolfgang Zilzer, John Sinclair, John Stark, Bob Kimball, Charles Sherlock (Gestapo); Don Turner, Clancy Cooper, Emory Parnell (Cops); Gertrude Carr (Mrs. Novak); Vera Lewis (Mrs. Fogarty); Charles Wilson (Lieutenant); Creighton Hale (Waiter); Regina Wallace, Leah Baird, Mary Servoss (Women); Mira McKinney (Wife); Dick Elliott (Husband); Philip Van Zandt (Assistant Auctioneer); Stuart Holmes (Man); Chester Clute (Hotel Clerk); Hans Joby, Egon Brecher (Watchmen); Henry Victor, Otto Reichow (Guards); Charles Sullivan, Bob Perry, Bud Geary, Dutch Hendrian (Henchmen); Fred Vogeding (Doctor); Carl Ottmar (Lichtig); Chester Gan (Chinese Laundryman); George Meeker, Roland Drew, Ray Montgomery, De Wolfe (William) Hopper, Walter Brooke (Reporters).

At the time of this Warner Bros.-Jerry Wald release, there was much enthusiasm for the studio's ingenuity in thinking to present Damon Runyonesque crooks as patriotic heroes battling the Nazis.   It was a plot ploy which would soon lose its novelty.   Made primarily as a Humphrey Bogart vehicle, All Through the Night contains many stereotyped, but entertaining, performances from the so-called heroes and some genuinely good ones by the players representing the Axis forces.

Bogart was Gloves Donahue, a Broadway gambler who rallies underworld characters to the side of the stars and stripes when the murder of his favorite baker is traced to Nazi agents.   The fifth columnists are in Manhattan, masterminding a plot to blow up a battleship in the East River, south of the Brooklyn Naval Yard, hoping to snafu U. S. troop movement.

Although the motorboat finale stretches credulity, the range of ingredients in this picture is winning.   For diverse "comic" relief there is Gleason as Starchie, Silvers as the hyper-active waiter, Ford as Spats Hunter, and Brophy as Joe Denning.   Most impressive is the Führer-loyal organization operating from Veidt's antiques auction gallery, particularly Anderson as his solemn, deadly assistant.

ALPHAVILLE: UNE ETRANGE AVENTURE DE LEMMY CAUTION (Athos-Film, 1965)   100 min.

Producer, Andre Michelin; director-screenplay, Jean-Luc Godard; assistant director, Charles Bitsch, Jean-Paul Savignac, Hélène Kalouguine; music, Paul Misraki; sound, René Levert; camera, Raoul Courard; editor, Agnes Guillemot.

Eddie Constantine (Lemmy Caution); Anna Karina (Natacha von Braun); Akim Tamiroff (Henry Dickson); Howard Vernon (Professor Leonard Nosferatu); Laszlo Szabo (Chief of Engineer); Michel Delahaye (von Braun's Assistant); Jean-Louis Comolli (Professor Jeckell); Alpha 60 (Itself).

A secret agent goes into the future world of the computerized city, Alphaville, to discover what happened to his predecessor (Tamiroff) and to Professor Nosferatu (Vernon).   Thus a simple plot became one of the most complex spy films ever made.   Since many spy pictures have the ingredients of science fiction, this film is nothing new in that respect.   However, director Jean-Luc Godard's handling of the total production gives it a deliberately ambiguous quality, one that can place it in several categories: a spy drama, science fiction, fantasy, or out-right horror.

Godard's screenplay for Alphaville uses as its central character a second-rate pulp detective, Peter Cheyney's Lemmy Caution, made famous in Europe in seven films starring ex-patriate U. S. actor-singer Eddie Constantine.   All seven movies were made on the cheap and appeared to be outrageous exaggerations of past George Raft movies.

Filmed in and around Paris in night shots, Alphaville gives

Akim Tamiroff and Eddie Constantine in Alphaville (Athos-Film, 1965).

an appearance of the eerie with a great deal of suspension of reality. Godard evidently made the film in a rather tongue-in-cheek manner, for it has more emphasis toward cartoon and camp figure characters than towards spies and espionage, or even science fiction. "What about Flash Gordon and Dick Tracy?" agent Constantine asks an old citizen of Alphaville (Tamiroff), the latter about to enjoy a streetwalker's favors. "All dead," Tamiroff replies. Later Constantine meets von Braun's daughter (Karina), of whom he becomes enamored, and finally he destroys the Alpha 60 computer and its maker by causing the machinery to short-circuit: he has fed it poetry and non sequiturs. ("What is the privilege of the dead?" Alpha 60 asks Constantine in an attempt to discover his mission. "Never to die," replies the agent.) After the destruction of the computer, and most of the inhabitants of Alphaville, Constantine and Karina whom he has taught to remember such previously forbidden words as "Love" and "robin red breast," return to the "outer countries" in his car. The trip from a future galaxy becomes as simple as a drive on the freeway.

Like an old-fashioned serial, Alphaville rings up an innocence and enjoyment that is beyond the realm of serious critique. Certainly the picture is science fiction in that it is set in the future in a heavily computerized society, but its real essence is that of a spy

drama. It is a spy drama set in a far-off time in a far-off place
where the human mind is controlled by a machine, and this cold
calculating piece of metal is destroyed by a super hero of today
who proves that modern man can control his own destiny, even if
he has to invade the future to do so.

THE AMBUSHERS (Columbia, 1967)   C 102 min.

    Producer, Irving Allen; associate producer, Douglas Netter;
director, Henry Levin; based on the novel by Donald Hamilton;
screenplay, Herbert Baker; art director, Joe Wright; music-music
director, Hugh Montenegro; song, Montenegro and Herbert Baker;
costumes, Oleg Cassini; sound, James Flaster, Jack Haynes; special effects, Danny Lee; camera, Burnett Guffey, Edward Colman;
editor, Harold F. Kress.
    Dean Martin (Matt Helm); Senta Berger (Francesca Madeiros);
Janice Rule (Sheila Sommers); James Gregory (MacDonald); Albert
Salmi (Jose Ortega); Kurt Kasznar (Quintana); Beverly Adams
(Lovey Kravezit); David Mauro (Nassim); Roy Jenson (Karl); John
Brascia (Rocco); Linda Foster (Linda); Yumiko Ishizuka, Ulla
Lindstrom, Lena Cederham, Terri Hughes, Kyra Bester, Anna-
bella, Karin Feddersen, Marilyn Tindall, Susannah Moore, Penny
Brahms, Jann Watson, Dee Duffy (Slaygirls); Pepe Callahan (Mexi-
can Sergeant); Alena Johnston (Masseuse); Inga Neilsen (Girl); Ted
Jordan (Male Attendant); Gary Lasdun (Young Doctor); Duke Hobbie
(Main Titles); Alexandra Hay (Secretary); Mary Jane Mangler, Rita
Rogers (Singing Girls); Karen Lee, Chris Cranston, Dee Gardner
(Beer Mug Girls); Erin Leigh (Captain Mayberry); Tim Herbert
(Gil); John Indrisano (Rapist); Bernice Dalton (Nurse); Ron Doyle,
Ron McCavour (Soldiers); Mauritz Hugo (Man); Edith Angold (Mid-
dle Aged Woman); Vincent Van Lynn (Flight Director); John Find-
later (Young Man).

    The Matt Helm cycle reached a new low with this woebegone
entry, brim full of plodding farcical gear, effortful double entendres,
and coarse comedy. "It belongs to the Playboy ethos of 'Look, but
you can't touch' ... full of phoney promises but no real action.
The credit sequence of glamorous girls and sunny beaches is exactly
like flicking through the pages of one of those glossy magazines,
and the film never really develops beyond that" (British Films and
Filming).
    Once more America's top laissez-faire super agent (Martin)
is drawn into protecting his country from the fantastic plot of a
destruction-bent organization that is now snapping U. S. spaceships
out of the sky. When government test pilot Sheila Sommers (Rule)
wanders out of the (Studio backlot) Mexican jungle in a state of
amnesiac shock, Martin turns his investigations to Acapulco and in
particular the hush-hush activities of beer manufacturer Quintana
(Kasznar). At a shindig tossed by Kasznar, Rule recognizes Jose
Ortega (Salmi) as the hijacker of her craft, and the chase is on,
with Francesca Madeiros (Berger) joining the obstacle run to win

possession of the valuable flying disc.

Despite an occasionally bitchy delivery by Rule and hints of villainy by Berger, nothing reaches credibility level in The Ambushers. Even redirecting the series away from espionage spoof into the "adult" adventure category did not generate new life into this tired and stupid attempt.

ANYBODY'S WAR   (Paramount, 1930)   8,117 feet

Director, Richard Wallace; based on the book The Two Black Crows in the A. E. F. by Charles E. Mack; screenplay, Lloyd Corrigan; additional dialog, Walter Weems; adaptation, Hector Turnbull; sound, M. M. Paggi; camera, Allen Siegler; editor, Otho Lovering.

George Moran (Willie); Charles E. Mack (Amos Crow); Joan Peers (Mary Jane Robinson); Neil Hamilton (Ted Reinhardt); Walter Weems (Sergeant Skipp); Betty Farrington (Camilla); Walter Mc-Grail (Captain Davis).

The veteran vaudeville team of Moran and Mack who were in blackface long before Amos 'n' Andy trod the boards, were "enjoying" the tail end of their movie career when they turned out this slight effort, dedicated to the proposition that their brand of ethnic humor pegged to hoary World War I jokes and situations were still good for a few laughs.

Dogcatcher Amos Crow (Mack) of Bufort, Tennessee, and his pal Willie (Moran) finagle their way into the U.S. army and are soon at the front lines in France. Mary Jane Robinson (Peers), daughter of a hometown aristocrat, narrowly succeeds in disentangling herself from a romance with serviceman Davis (McGrail) who is unmasked as a German spy. The bucolic duo find time to rescue Peers' true love (Hamilton) and even save the day for the Allies.

APPOINTMENT IN BERLIN   (Columbia, 1943)   77 min.

Producer, Samuel Bischoff; director, Alfred E. Green; story, B. P. Fineman; screenplay, Horace McCoy, Michael Hogan; art director, Lionel Banks, Walter Holscher; set decorator, George Montgomery; music, Anthony Collins; music director, Morris W. Stoloff; assistant director, Milton Carter; sound, Ed Bernds; montage special effects, Aaron Nibley; camera, Franz F. Planer; editors, Al Clark, Reginald Browne.

George Sanders (Keith Wilson); Marguerite Chapman (Ilse Preissing); Onslow Stevens (Rudolph Preissing); Gale Sondergaard (Getta van Leyden); Alan Napier (Colonel Patterson); H. P. Sanders (Sir Douglas Wilson); Don Douglas (Bill Banning); Jack Lee (Babe Forrester); Alec Craig (Smitty); Leonard Mudie (MacPhail); Frederic Worlock (von Ritter); Steven Geray (Henri Rader); Wolfgang Z. Zilzer (Cripple); Reginald Sheffield (Miller); Keith Hitchcock (Bobby); Constance Worth (English Girl); Charles Wagenheim (Florist); Felix

Arabesque   59

Basch (Hoppner); Lester Mathews (Air Marshal); Leyland Hodgson
(Joiner); Evan Thomas (Durkin); Montague Shaw (Langly); Nelson
Leigh (Civilian); Gwen Gaze (Girl); Billy Bevan (Barman); Alex-
ander Pollard, Wilson Benge (Bits); Lynton Brent (Practical Artist);
Tom Stevenson (Lieutenant); Gerald Brock (Señor Ortega); Georges
Renavent (Van der Wym); George Cathrey, Wyndham Standing (Bar-
tenders); Frederick Brunn (Gestapo Agent); Walter Bonn (Lazareff);
Alphonse Martell, Jack Chefe (Assistant Croupiers); Marek Windheim
(Croupier); Peter Michael, Fred Kohler, Jr. (S.S. Guards); Robert
Bice, Robert F. Williams (Radio Men); Henry Rowland (Radio
Operator); Art Smith (Dutch Pastor); Arno Frey (Gestapo Captain);
Hank Bell, Victor Travers (Dutchmen); John Meredith (Engineer);
Byron Foulger (Herr Van Leyden); Niels Bagge (Nazi Staff Officer);
Sven-Hugh Borg (Stockholm Waiter); Leslie Denison (Detective).

This "B" picture was ballyhooed as the first American feature
to deal with a Lord Haw Haw type situation.

RAF wing commander GS is outraged at the Munich pact and
his belligerent attitude leads to his being cashiered out of the service. He even spends eighteen months in jail for his unpopular convictions. Only then is it learned that he is actually working for
the British Intelligence Service, establishing an anti-British cover.
Gaining an entree into Axis circles in Berlin he is talked into joining the cause of the Third Reich and is soon broadcasting "The
Voice of Truth" programs to the Allied troops. Actually his propaganda speeches contain coded war maneuver messages for the British
forces. For a change, the hero (Sanders) is sacrificed to accomplish his mission (as is the heroine, Chapman, playing the sister
of Nazi spy Stevens).

Because the picture evolved into just one more behind-enemy-
lines melodrama, it was quickly passed over by the critics, being
chided for its "considerable wishful thinking in its glorification of
the British Intelligence" (New York Herald-Tribune).

Among the supporting cast was Sondergaard as a martyred
British agent, and Sanders' real-life father, H.P. Sanders, making
his film debut by portraying the star's onscreen dad.

ARABESQUE (Universal, 1966)   C   105 min.

Producer, Stanley Donen; associate producer, Denis Holt;
director, Donen; based on the novel, The Cipher, by Gordon Cotler;
screenplay, Donen; assistant director, Eric Rattray; art director,
Reece Pemberton; sound, John W. Mitchell, C. Le Messurier;
music, Henry Mancini; camera, Christopher Challis; editor, Frederick Wilson.

Gregory Peck (David Pollock); Sophia Loren (Yasmin Azir);
Alan Badel (Nejin Beshraavi); Kieron Moore (Yussef); John Merivale (Sloane); Duncan Lamont (Webster); George Coulouris (Professor Ragheeb); Carl Duering (Hassan Jena); Harold Kasket (Moham-
med Lufti); Gordon Griffin (Fanshaw).

Nothing more than "commercial film-making at its mindless, marvelous best," was Life magazine's verdict of this overblown spy caper. One could gawk at "Arabic" Sophia Loren's anatomy filling out her $150,000 Christian Dior wardrobe or gander at director Donen's endless array of pop-ophthalmological happenings, each geared to distract from the hole-ridden plot.

American professor of Egyptology Peck, an exchange instructor at Oxford, is offered $90,000 by London-based Loren to translate a cabalistic hieroglyphic letter, which turns out to reveal a warning of the imminent assassination of the prime minister of a Near East oil country. Is undercover agent Loren for or against Western ideals and how much does she really care for her mysterious keeper (Badel), a nefarious character who wears dark glasses and carries a falcon on his wrist to thwart enemies? None of these basic questions are substantially answered within the film's helter-skelter shenanigans, and for some unexplained reason poor addled, middle-aged Peck just does not seem to care. He is too busy chasing after Loren and away from the various criminal factions out to eliminate him.

Even director Donen realized that his unending utilization of weird and fantastic camera angles would eventually wear thin, and had the good sense to josh the genre a bit. At one point Peck jumps into a London cab and yells at the driver, "Follow that car!" The delighted cabbie retorts, "All my life I've been waiting for someone to say that!" In another scene, Peck is chased across a field by farm machinery a la Alfred Hitchcock's North by Northwest; and for absurd titillation, there is the set-up in which a fully-clothed Peck hides in the shower with au-naturel Loren while her possessive lover (Badel) converses with her unaware.

ARCH OF TRIUMPH   (UA, 1948)   120 min.

Producer, David Lewis; associate producer, Otto Klement; director, Lewis Milestone; based on the novel by Erich Maria Remarque; screenplay, Milestone, Harry Brown; production designer, William Cameron Menzies; art director, William E. Flannery; set decorator, Edward E. Boyle; music, Louis Gruenberg; music director, Morris Stoloff; assistant director, Robert Aldrich; technical advisor, Michel Bernhein; makeup, Gustaf M. Norin; costumes, Edith Head, Marion Herwood Keyes; special effects, Robert M. Moreland; sound, Frank Webster; camera, Russell Metty; editor, Duncan Mansfield.

Ingrid Bergman (Joan Madou); Charles Boyer (Dr. Ravic); Charles Laughton (Haake); Louis Calhern (Morosow); Roman Bohemen (Dr. Veber); Stephen Bekassy (Alex); Ruth Nelson (Madame Fessier); Curt Bois (Tatooed Waiter); J. Edward Bromberg (Hotel Manager); Michael Romanoff (Alidze); Art Smith (Inspector); John Laurenz (Colonel Gomez); Leon Lenoir (Captain, Spanish); Franco Corsaro (Navarro); Nino Pipitone (General Aide); Vladimir Rashevsky (Nugent); Alvin Hammer (Milan Porter); Jay Gilpin (Refugee Boy); Ilia Khmara (Russian Singer); Andre

Marsauden (Roulette Croupier); Hazel Brooks (Sybil); Byron Foul-
ger (Policeman); William Conrad (Pernon, Official); Peter Virgo
(Belansky); Feodor Chaliapin (Scheherazade Chef); Katherine Emory
(Woman); Charles Wagenheim (Small Man).

Charles Boyer and Ruth Warrick in a scene from Arch of Triumph
(UA, 1948) later cut from release prints.

This picturization of Remarque's dignified novel never captured the true ambiance of appeasement-time Europe, nor did it
successfully reflect the author's study of a disenchanted political
refugee tossed about Europe.   Even on a lesser level as just a
conventional love story, the film failed to garner loyal adherents.
As Otis L. Guernsey, Jr. (New York Herald-Tribune) observed,
"Neither he [director Milestone] nor the stars are able to make an
emotion out of a bunch of flowers, a statuette or even a deep sigh,
and the abrupt excursions into melodrama are made no more be-
lievable by the occasional closeup of a gun. "
    Trenchcoated Boyer, in a role once considered the exclusive

cinematic province of Paul Henreid, portrayed Dr. Ravic, formerly
with the Austrian underground. He arrives in Paris of 1938 to join
the throng of stateless persons. Shortly thereafter, he encounters
well-scrubbed street walker Bergman, the latter about to commit
suicide. He aids her in redeeming her life, but when he is deported from France, she drifts back into her old loose ways.
When he later returns to Paris, he finds Bergman and they go to
the Riviera. Once there, however, she meets and has an affair with
playboy Bekassy. Thereafter Boyer is unsuccessful in regaining
Bergman's devotion, but he does succeed in carrying out his revenge on Nazi bigshot Laughton, the German official who had tortured Boyer back in Austria and who had been responsible for the
death of Boyer's fiancée (Brooks).

In some undemonstrated ways, Boyer's character in Arch of
Triumph was a distant foreshadowing of Richard Burton's unglamor-
ous espionage character in The Spy Who Came in from the Cold.
Each of them has been caught between two opposing political forces,
and neither can find the necessary career, political or emotional
safety to carry on a viable existence.

ARIZONA BUSHWHACKERS (Paramount, 1968) C 87 min.

Producer, A.C. Lyles; director, Lesley Selander; story,
Steve Fisher, Andrew Craddock; screenplay, Fisher; art director,
Hal Pereira, Al Roelofs; set decorator, Robert Benton, Jerry
Welch; makeup, Wally Westmore; assistant director, Dale Hutchin-
son; special camera effects, Paul K. Perpae; sound, Joe Edmond-
son, John Wilkinson; camera, Lester Shorr; editor, John F.
Schreiser.

Howard Keel (Lee Travis); Yvonne De Carlo (Jill Wyler);
John Ireland (Dan Shelby); Marilyn Maxwell (Molly); Scott Brady
(Tom Rile); Brian Donlevy (Mayor Joe Smith); Barton MacLane
(Sheriff Lloyd Grover); James Craig (Ike Clanton); Roy Rogers,
Jr. (Roy); Reg Parton (Curly); Montie Montana (Stage Driver);
Eric Cody (Bushwhacker); James Cagney (Narrator).

One of the more pathetic farragos force-fed to action movie
house attendees.

During the Civil War, captured Confederate riverboat gambler
Keel is freed by the Yankees (their prisons are overcrowded) on
condition that he undertake to bring law and order to the West. He
is sent to Colton, Arizona, to become the new sheriff. Unknown to
his benefactors, Keel is actually a Southern spy bent on obtaining
a cache of ammunition and arms from Colton to hand over to the
Rebs. He soon discovers that local seamstress De Carlo is a fellow agent.

Even casting the paltry production values aside, it was a
shattering experience to find oneself debating who had the bigger
paunch (Keel, Donlevy, or Brady), or which of the two female stars
was more embarrassing in her overwrought performance, De Carlo
or Maxwell, the latter complete with a Marie Winsor look and a
Bette "Jezebel" Davis accent.

ASSASSINATION (Butcher's, 1967) C 100 min.

    Producer, Felice Testa Gay; director, Alfonso Brescia;
story, Emil Bridge; screenplay, Lou Strateman, Andy Colbert; art
director, Louis Nadeau; music-music director, Robert Poitevin;
sound, Mike Dodge; camera, Eric Menczer; editor, Sergio Montanari.
    Henry Silva (John/Philip Chandler); Fred Beir (Bob); Ida
Galli (Barbara); Peter Dane (Lang); Billy Vanders (Thomas); Alfredo Varelli (Morrison); Bob Molden (Otto); Karl Menzinger (Hans);
Gunther Scholtz (Senator Grahame); Gert von Zitzweitz (Baron);
John Schoffield (Jack); Helga Braun (Salesgirl).

    Because C. I. A. agent John Chandler (Silva) has been found
guilty of killing a co-worker, he is sentenced to death, and the
"accomplished" execution so announced. However, he is reprieved
on condition that he submit to plastic surgery and take on the
identity of his non-existent brother Philip. As such, he is able
to infiltrate the undercover group which is arranging for the assassination of Senator Grahame (Scholtz), the latter in charge of a
global peace mission planning on a vital Berlin meeting. Meanwhile, Silva's "widow" (Galli) weds co-conspirator Bob (Beir).
Later Silva and Beir are ordered to combat each other by their
sinister chief, with Silva emerging the winner. Then Silva is
taken forcibly to Berlin by the gang who plan to explode the conference room and leave Silva's body as proof of American duplicity. However, Silva proves equal to his opponents and emerges
victorious against the assassins only to meet a new obstacle: a
waiting sniper.
    In this Italian-made violent actioner, "...the general un-
pleasantness of the characters and the snail's pace direction ensure
that one never even begins to care about which double agent is
doing what to whom" (British Monthly Film Bulletin).

ASSIGNMENT ABROAD (Anglo-Amalgamated, 1955) 73 min.

    Producer-director, Arthur Dreifuss; screenplay, Albert
Derr, Ella Sacco; music, Hugo de Groot; art director, John Duetz;
sound, William Huender; camera, Jack Whitehead; editor, Lien
d'Oliveyia.
    Robert Alda (Major Bill Jorgan); Kay Callard (Mrs. Morgan);
Robert Haynes (Toeminah); Indra Kamajozo (Kirono); Lies Franken
(Margriet); Carl Heinz Roth (Von Rundscheig); Teddy Ford (Marina);
Stye van Brandenburg (Link).

    Pulled together from episodes of the "Secret File, U. S. A."
1954 teleseries, the covering premise has Alda relating three adventures to his son as a bedtime story. The segments covered are
set in: 1) Japanese-held Sumatra, 2) German-occupied Holland;
3) post-war Antwerp.
    What seemed fanciful on the small screen became incredible
on the big screen, particularly with the overblown plots and the
undersized demonstration of acting talent.

ASSIGNMENT IN BRITTANY (MGM, 1943) 96 min.

Producer, J. Walter Ruben; director, Jack Conway; based on the novel by Helen MacInnes; screenplay, Anthony Veiller, William H. Wright, Howard Emmett Rogers; art director, Cedric Gibbons, William Ferrari; set decorator, Edwin B. Willis, Edward G. Boyle; music, Lennie Hayton; assistant director, Tom Andre; sound, James F. Gaither, Jr.; special effects, Arnold Gillespie; camera, Charles Rosher; editor, Frank Sullivan.

Pierre Aumont (Captain Metard/Bertrand Corlay); Susan Peters (Anne Pinot); Richard Whorf (Kerenor); Margaret Wycherly (Mme. Corlay); Signe Hasso (Elise); Reginald Owen (Colonel Trane); John Emery (Captain Deichgruber); George Coulouris (Captain Holz); Sarah Padden (Albertine); Miles Mander (Colonel Fournier); George Brest (Henri); Darryl Hickman (Etienne); Alan Napier (Sam Walls); Odette Myrtil (Louis' Sister); Juanita Quigley (Jeannine); William Edmunds (Plehec); Paul Leyssac (The Cure); Almira Sessions (Mme. Perro); Lionel Royce (Von Steffen); Frank Lackteen (Arab Chief); Peter Lawford (Navigator); John Meredith (Pilot); Albert Morin (Arab Mechanic); Alan Schute (Co-Pilot); Stanley Mann, Constant Franke, Robert O. Davis (Orderlies); Ralph Bushman (German Lieutenant); Major Farrell (Jacques); Louise Colombet (Marie); Rex Williams (Sergeant Krulich); Lucien Prival (Major Von Pless); John St. Polis (Old Man in Inn); Duke York (German Private); Horace Carpenter (Yves); Harry Fleischmann (Jules); George Travell (Rochet); Dick Wessel (German Sergeant); Juanita Quigley (Jeannine), Lisl Valetti (Woman Peasant); Alex Papana (Man Peasant); Frank Arnold, Louis Mercier (Fisherman); Hans von Morhart, Paul Kruger (German Privates); Al Masiello, Joseph Marievsky, Joseph Mack, Hector Sarno (Peasants in Cellar); Crane Whitley (Gestapo Lieutenant); Clive Morgan (Commando Officer); Arthur Mulliner, Charles Irwin (Commando Lieutenants); Leyland Hodgson (Commando); Bill Nind (British Lieutenant); George Aldwin (Gunner); Steve Geray (Priest); Morris Ankrum (Stenger); Hans Schumm (German Sentry); Jack Norton (Drunk Peasant).

If anything, this gilded MGM melodrama is remembered as the Hollywood-assembled feature which introduced (Jean-) Pierre Aumont to American audiences. The picture hardly lived up to its extravagant publicity which claimed, "Every second throbs with suspense and danger ... THRILLS COME RIGHT OUT OF THE HEADLINES!--You have read about it! Now see it all with your own eyes!"

Allied Commando Captain Metard (Aumont), having prevented a native uprising in Syria, is handed a new task. He is to replace a Free France traitor, Bertrand Corlay (Aumont), being held captive in England, and return to the latter's hometown to locate the secret Nazi shipping base housed somewhere along the French coast. Among those Aumont encounters at "home" and thereabouts are the traitor's mother (Wycherly), a crippled French patriot-schoolteacher (Whorf), a diabolical Gestapo man (Coulouris), a soft-spoken Nazi (Emery), a British intelligence officer (Owen),

Signe Hasso, Susan Peters, and Jean-Pierre Aumont in <u>Assignment in Brittany</u> (MGM, 1943).

and the two women in his double life, two-timing collaborationist
Elise (Hasso) and loyal De Gaullist peasant girl Anne Pinot (Peters).
There was nothing unique about the well-familiar threads of
screenplay thriller employed in Assignment in Brittany. "It never
finds the depth of meaning it pretends to seek; it has no more
reality than the miniature models used in its commando climax.   As
a drama it is a squeak in a storm" (New York Times).   The film's
basic fairytale approach is exemplified by its blazing cliffhanger
finale, with Aumont and Peters sailing off into the sunset to the
sturdy accompaniment of "La Marseillaise."

ASSIGNMENT K   (Columbia, 1967)   C   97 min.

    Producer, Ben Arbeid, Maurice Foster; director, Val Guest;
based on the novel Department K by Hartley Howard; screenplay,
Guest, Bill Strutton, Foster; art director, John Blezard; music,
Basil Kirchin; music director, John Coleman; costumes, Yvonne
Blake; sound, James Shields; camera, Ken Hodges; editor, Jack
Slade.
    Stephen Boyd (Philip Scott); Camilla Sparv (Toni Peters);
Leo McKern (Smith); Robert Hoffmann (Paul Spiegler); Michael
Redgrave (Harris); Jan Werich (Dr. Spiegler); Jeremy Kemp (Hal);
Jane Merrow (Martine); Vivi Bach (Erika Herschel); David Healy
(David); Dieter Geissler (Kurt); Geoffrey Bayldon (The Boffin);
Carl Mohner (Inspector); Werner Peters (Kramer); John Alderton
(George); Ursula Howells (Estelle); Basil Dignam (Howlett); Joa-
chim Hansen (Heinrich Herschel); Marthe Harell (Mrs. Peters);
Traudi Hochfilzer (Ski Instructress); Friedrich von Thun (Rolfe);
Katharina von Schell (Maggi); Herbert Fuchs (Bavarian Tourist);
Peter Capell (Landlord of Chalet); Heinz Leo Fisher (Joseph); Karl
Otto Alberty (Detective); Helmut Schneider (The Stranger); Fried-
rich von Ledebur (Ski Shop Proprietor); Andrea Allen (Mini Skirt);
Rosemary Reede (English Nurse); Jenny White (Air Hostess); Mia
Nardi (German Nurse); Olga Linden (Night Club Blonde); Alex-
ander Allerson (Model Car Salesman); Alastair Hunter (Doorman);
Gert Widenhofen (Porter).

    Even the usually compassionate New York Daily News was
put off by this hodgepodge conglomeration filmed on location in
England, Austria, and West Germany.   "Assignment K may be impossible to decode.   But its message is clear.   The secret agent
has had his day in the movies, mostly because the moviegoer knows
too much about him."   The producers of this so-called spy film
hoped to clean up at the boxoffice, but its jumbled plot, mediocre
action and overall boredom contributed little to its success other
than guaranteeing bottom half showings on double bills and being
quickly and justly forgotten.
    Boyd ambles through the film as a British toy manufacturer
who uses his frequent trips to Germany to cover for his own small
spy ring.   He becomes a suspect due to his espionage activities and
gets involved with a murder in Munich and a group of counterspies,

one of whom may be his new-found bed partner (Sparv).
Adding insult to injury, the picture was padded out with ski
country footage, filmed in grainy Techniscope.

ASSIGNMENT: MUNICH (MGM/ABC-TV, 1972)   C   100 min.

Director, David Lowell Rich.
Roy Scheider (Jake Webster); Richard Basehart (Major Barney
Caldwell); Lesley Warren (Cathy Lange); Werner Kemperer (Hoff-
man); Robert Reed (Mitch); Pernell Roberts (C. C. Byran); Keenan
Wynn (George); Mike Kellin (Gus).

The pilot telefeature for "Assignment Vienna" (in which
Robert Conrad replaced Scheider), finds Scheider as a wise-lip
Munich saloon owner, and an undercover agent, who skirts the
law to aid the U. S. government find stolen gold worth a cool
$5. 5 million.

ASYLUM FOR A SPY (Universal/Hovuc, 1967)   C   90 min.

Director, Stuart Rosenberg; based on the story by Ellis St.
Joseph, Robert L. Joseph; screenplay, Robert L. Joseph; art di-
rector, John L. Lloyd; makeup, Bud Westmore; special effects,
Ron Roth; camera, Bud Thackery; editor, Howard Epstein.
Robert Stack (Albert Congress); Felicia Farr (Jemy); George
Macready (Jutland); Don Gordon (Harris); J. D. Cannon (Webb);
Albert Paulsen (Avatin); Michael Constantine (Niri); and Victor
Buono, John Hoyt, John van Dreelen, Leon Belasco, George
Michenaud, Vincent Gardenia, Danielle Aubrey, Eva Sorent, Roger
Til, George Nelson, Nadia Posey, Berry Kroeger, Mimi Dillard,
George Horvath, John Francis.

Like several other "features," this film was initially made
by Universal and shown on NBC's "Bob Hope Chrysler Theatre" in
April 1965, in two segments, which were pasted together and
dumped into the limbo of local television programming as a feature,
with its video origins disguised.
The film's plot found C. I. A. agent Albert Congress (Stack),
a former diplomatic attaché in Mexico, now on the skids and hitting
the bottom of the bottle. Suddenly he finds himself being pulled
in several directions: the Soviets think he would make a good
source to siphon off data about which of their citizens plan to defect, the U. S. agents want him to enter a mental hospital and pose
as a patient to locate a spy, while do-gooder rich girl Jemy (Farr)
hopes to reform him.
All in all the padded-out story led only to sheer boredom,
particularly with its soggy dialog (e. g., C. I. A. agent Jutland (Macready): "I'm your country, for better or worse. I'm your country."
Stack: "Leave me alone, you machine-made patriot. ").

ATLANTIC CONVOY (Columbia, 1942)   66 min.

Producer, Colbert Clark; director, Lew Landers; screenplay, Robert Lee Johnson; art director, Lionel Banks; music director, Morris Stoloff; camera, Henry Freulich; editor, James Sweeney.

Bruce Bennett (Captain Morgan); Virginia Field (Lida Adams); John Beal (Carl Hansen); Clifford Severn (Sandy Brown); Larry Parks (Gregory); Stanley Brown (Eddie); Lloyd Bridges (Bert); Victor Kilian (Otto); Hans Schumm (Commander Von Smith); Erik Rolf (Gunther); William von Brincken (Henchman); Eddie Laughton (Radio Operator).

Hans Schumm (second from left), William von Brincken, John Beal, and Victor Kilian in Atlantic Convoy (Columbia, 1942).

With Hollywood at its prolific worst, churning out an apparently endless stream of World War II-derived yarns, even the flimsiest of movies sought to attack some hitherto untouched aspect of the global conflict. Here was the first study of the hazards of the Marine flying patrols guarding the shipping lanes near Iceland. Unfortunately its presentation left a great deal to be desired.

Because he had "deserted" from the Marines when valuable radio blueprints disappeared from his safekeeping, Carl Hansen (Beal) has become a civilian weather scientist stationed at Iceland. The appearance of Marine flying officer Morgan (Bennett) on the scene, along with shipwrecked nurse Lida Adams (Field) and six children--including suspicious Sandy Brown (Severn)--leads to the uncovering of German spies operating from a local fishing boat.

Although the film "...never pretends to be more than a routine bread-and-butter effort, it hardly achieves even that modest level" (New York Times).

ATOMIC AGENT [Nathalie, Agent Secret] (C.F.D.C., 1959) 82 min.

Director, Henri Decoin; screenplay, Pierre Apesteguy, Henri Jeanson, Jacques Robert; music, Georges Van Parys; settings, Robert Clavel; sound, Robert Teisseire; camera, Robert Lefebvre, editor, Claude Durand.

Martine Carol (Nathalie); Felix Marten (Jacques Fabre); Dario Moreno (Dr. Alberto); Noël Roquevert (Pierre Darbon); Jacques Berthier (Jean Darbon); Howard Vernon (William Dantoren); Dany Saval (Pivoine); André Versini (Pellec).

Two bands of spies (Americans and South Americans) are eager to obtain the plans to an atomic motor invented by a brilliant French engineer, leading Gallic law enforcers to intervene to pro- tect this national resource. Meanwhile, mannequin Nathalie (Carol), in love with the inventor, decides to do her own "spying" to un- mask the undercover agents, leaving the path clear for her and her beloved to romance.

"Compared to Brigitte Bardot, Martine (Carol) is a real actress with versatility and talent. She shows it with good results in Nathalie, Agent Secret in which she takes up with a kind of fantasy beauty role which has no incumbent here and was played by Irene Dunne before the war in Hollywood" (Dernieres Nouvelles d'Alasace). On the other hand, France-Soir labeled the picture "A shallow and slap-dash effort."

ATOUT COEUR A TOKIO POUR OSS 117 [Heart Trump for OSS 117 in Tokyo] (Valoria, 1966) C 90 min.

Producer, Paul Cadeac; director, Michel Boisrohd; based on the novel by Jean Bruce; screenplay, Pierre Foucaud, Terence Young, Marcel Mithois; art director, Max Douy; music, Michel Magné; special effects, Gil Delmare; camera, Marcel Grignon; editor, Pierre Gillette.

Frederick Stafford (OSS 117); Marina Vlady (Eva); Henri Serre (Wilson); Inkijinoff (Chief); and: Colin Drake, Tetsuko Yoshimura.

CIA agent OSS 117 (Stafford) is ordered to Japan to break up the secret organization bent on destroying America's interna- tional treaties for Pacific base fortifications.

Since Terence Young, director of Dr. No, From Russia With

Love, <u>Thunderball,</u> collaborated on this Eastmancolor-Franscope production, the similarities between OSS 117 and James Bond are embarrassingly in evidence.   A noticeable cut in production budget also hurt the mounting of this OSS 117 entry.
   British title: <u>Terror in Tokyo</u>.

ATTACK OF THE ROBOTS see CARTES SUR TABLE

AVEC LA PEAU DES AUTRES [To Skin a Spy]   (Valoria, 1966)
C   100 min.

   Producer, Eugene Tucherer; director, Jacques Deray; based on the novel <u>Au Pied du Mur</u> by Gil Perrault; screenplay, José Giovanni, Deray, Georges Bardawil, Franco del Cer; art director, Jean d'Eaubonne, Raymond Gabutti; music, Michel Magné; assistant director, Claude Vital; editor, Henri Lanoe, Vincenzo Tamassi.
   Lino Ventura (Viviani); Jean Bouise (Mageri); Marilu Tolo (Anna); Jean Servais (Lawyer); Adrian Hoven (Friend); Wolfgang Preiss (Chief); Louis Arbessier (Colonel); and Karine Baal, Mino Doro, Charles Regnier, Helen Bahl, Guy Mairesse.

   Just once in a while espionage agents on camera are permitted to demonstrate the human qualities of friendship and compassion--within limited bounds of course.
   Because Mageri (Bouise), heading the French espionage effort in Vienna, is suspected of double dealing, his compatriot Viviani (Ventura) is sent to investigate. Shortly after his arrival in Austria, Ventura finds Bouise missing, assuredly a victim of retaliatory Russian agents. But the kidnapped man has left one clue, a walking stick, which leads to the unmasking of the traitor within the French spy network in Vienna. Meanwhile, Bouise has committed suicide rather than take the chance of talking to his captors, a factor Ventura keeps well in mind when he learns the soon-to-retire Bouise had planned to sell valuable microfilm to the Chinese.   After killing the Oriental agent in question, Ventura returns to Paris and in his report eliminates any hint of his friend's planned perfidy.

THE AVENGERS see THE DAY WILL DAWN

L'AVEU [The Confession] (Paramount, 1970)   C   138 min.

   Producer, Robert Dorfmann, Bertrand Javal; director, Costa-Gavras; based on the book by Lise and Artur London; screenplay, Jorge Semprun; art director, Bernard Evein; sound, William Sivel; assistant director, Alain Corneau; camera, Raoul Coutard; editor, Françoise Bonnot.
   Yves Montand ("Gerard," alias Artur London); Simone Signoret (Lise); Gabriele Ferzetti (Kohutek); Michel Vitold (Smola);

Jean Bouise (Man in Factory); Laszlo Szabo (Secret Policeman); and: Monique Chaumette, Guy Mairesse, Marc Eyraud, Gerard Darrieu, Giles Segal, Charles Moulin, Nicole Vervil, Georges Aubert, Andre Cellier, Pierre Delaval, William Jacques, Henri Marteau, Michel Robin, Antoine Vitez.

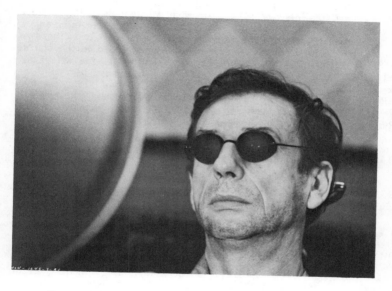

Yves Montand in The Confession (Paramount, 1970).

Breaking a man's resistance through grueling physical and mental indignities is a time-honored regimen of (cold) warfare, well documented in screen espionage thrillers [even in the garbled John Frankenheimer rendition of The Fixer (1968)]. But inducing the victim to intellectually accept his hypothesized guilt as a traitorous collaborator is an avenue of reality only now fully explored in this painstaking screen adaptation of the book by the Czechoslovakian authors Artur and Lise London. Director Costa-Gavras pushes his dramatic documentary style to new, but distractingly repetitive, lengths as he interprets this fragment of political reality for public consumption. Unlike his Academy Award-winning Z (1969), The Confession never generated the same global political controversy or audience interest, and the boxoffice take was far less.

Artur London (Montand), Deputy Minister of Foreign Affairs in the Czechoslovakian Communist government is one day arrested by the secret police and accused of having conspired with Western intelligence agents to overthrow the Russian-backed government of his country.   In order to get this Jewish patriot, who had fought against Franco in Spain and on the side of the Resistance before being captured and sent to a Nazi concentration camp, to confess, he is subjected to brutal interrogation and a maddening ordeal of deprivation and physical abuse.   After several months, interrogator Kohutek (Ferzetti) takes charge of the case and by subtler methods leads Montand into confessing to the trumped-up charges and to testifying at the mock trial, all for what Montand is led to believe is for the good of the Party.   At the trial most of the thirteen defendants are condemned to death, with London and two others sentenced to life imprisonment.   In 1956 he is freed in the course of the country's de-Stalinization process and rejoins his wife Lise (Signoret), one of those who had publically denounced him at the trial.   The couple go to France where they eventually write a book about the trial.   Then in 1968 when London returns to Prague for the publication of his book, he witnesses the city's occupation by Russian tanks.   Was his ordeal all in vain?

BABETTE GOES TO WAR   see   BABETTE S'EN VA-T-EN-GUERRE

BABETTE S'EN VA-T-EN-GUERRE [Babette Goes to War]   (Columbia, 1959)   C   100 min.

Producer, Raoul Levy; director, Christian-Jaque; screenplay, Gerard Oury, Levy, Michel Audraid; music, Gilbert Becaud; art director, Jean André; assistant director, S. Vallin, R. Villette; camera, Armand Thiraid; editor, Jacques Desagneaux.
Brigitte Bardot (Babette); Jacques Charrier (Gerard); Francis Blanche (Schultz); Yves Vincent (D'Arcy); Ronald Howard (Fitzgerald); Pierre Bertin (Duke); René Havard (Louis).

An early Bardot film which kept the well-proportioned star well under wraps throughout the story, eliminating one of her two screen virtues; the other, her famous pout was well in evidence, however.
During the French exodus of 1940 Bardot ends up in England and finds herself sent on a Free French Forces mission; her task: to divert and discredit a top-ranking German general who is involved in the proposed Axis invasion of Britain.   Helping her complete her assignment is French officer Charrier (then BB's real life husband).
Lighthearted comedy has never been Bardot's acting forte and, placed in a generally unfunny presentation, she and the picture went awry before the first reels had even unspooled.

BACKGROUND TO DANGER   (WB, 1943)   80 min.

Producer, Jerry Wald; director, Raoul Walsh; based on the

novel <u>Uncommon Danger</u> by Eric Ambler; screenplay, W. R. Burnett;
art director, Hugh Reticker; set decorator, Casey Roberts; dialog
director, Hugh Cummings; assistant director, Russ Saunders; music,
Frederick Hollander; music director, Leo F. Forbstein; sound, Dolph
Thomas; montages, Don Siegel, James Leicester; camera, Tony
Gaudio; editor, Jack Kilifer.

George Raft (Joe Barton); Brenda Marshall (Tamara); Sydney
Greenstreet (Colonel Robinson); Peter Lorre (Zaleshoff); Osa Mas-
sen (Ana Remzi); Turhan Bey (Hassan); Willard Robertson (Mc-
Namara); Kurl Katch (Mailler); Daniel Ocko (Rashonko); Pedro de
Cordoba (Old Turk); Frank Puglia (Syrian Vendor); Steve Geray
(Rader); Fred Giermann, Alfred Ziesler (Attaches); Ernst Hausser-
man (Clerk); Frank Reicher (Rudick); Curt Furberg (Von Popen);
Jean de Briac (Levantine Porter); Paul Porcasi, George Renavent,
Demetris Emanuel (Turkish Officials); Jean Del Val (Clerk); Kurt
Kreuger (Chauffeur); Charles de Ravenne (Bellboy); Michael Mark
(Night Clerk); Otto Reichow (Mailler's Assistant); William Yetter
(Schneider); Carl Harbaugh (Butler); James Khan (Train Caller);
Charles Irwin (English Traveler); Antonio Samaniego (Policeman);
Rafael Corio (Turkish Husband); Fernanda Eliscu (Turkish Wife);

George Raft and Daniel Ocko in <u>Background to Danger</u> (WB, 1943).

John Piffle (Fat Turk); Irene Seidner (German Mother); Lisa Golm
(German Daughter); Juan Varro, Yeghisha Harout (Turkish Police-
men); Hassan Ezzat (Turkish Conductor); Jerry Mandy (Italian);
Liparit (Wagon Driver); William von Brincken (German Official);
Fred Wolff (Reiger); John Van Eyck (Official); Bob Stevenson (Ger-
man); William Edmunds (Turkish Waiter); Sylvia Opert (Nautch
Dancer); Ray Miller (Chauffeur); Nestor Paiva (Koylan); Dave
Kashner (Man); John Bleifer (Secretary); Charles La Torre (Turk);
Dick Botiller (Plane Announcer); Lou Marcelle (Commentator).

Eric Ambler's novel (Uncommon Danger) deserved a much
better picturization than it received at the hands of producer Jerry
Wald and director Raoul Walsh. "The total entertainment quotient
is very low," reported the New York Herald-Tribune.
U. S. agent Joe Barton (Raft) is sent to Turkey to keep that
country from joining with the Axis powers. In Ankara he meets
Ana Remzi (Massen), a defecting Russian operative, who entrusts
him with secret documents detailing a supposed Russian invasion
of Turkey. Then she is murdered and various international factions turn to Raft to recover the incriminating papers. In his
flight-search, Raft later meets up with alleged Russian agents
Marshall and Lorre as well as Nazi Greenstreet, the latter who
supervises an assortment of evil deeds with the able assistance
of several goons (including Katch). In one violent scene the
henchmen work over Raft within an inch of his life.
At the crux of the Background to Danger misfire was George
Raft, the temperamental star who had rejected roles in Warners'
High Sierra, The Maltese Falcon, and Casablanca, all of which
were eventually played by Humphrey Bogart. Raft accepted the
Ambler story because he felt playing a glorified American hero
would improve his screen image, which might have happened if he
had been more concerned with offering a straightforward performance
with which a viewer could empathize.

BANG, BANG, YOU'RE DEAD! (AIP, 1966) C 92 min.

Executive producer, Oliver A. Unger; producer, Harry Alan
Towers; director, Don Sharp; screenplay, Peter Yeldam; music,
Malcolm Lockyer; assistant director, Barrie Melrose; art director,
F. White; sound, John Brommege, John Payner; camera, John Von
Kotze, Michael Reed; editor, Teddy Darvas.
Tony Randall (Andrew Jessel); Senta Berger (Kyra Stanovy);
Terry-Thomas (El Caid); Herbert Lom (Mr. Casimir); Wilfrid
Hyde-White (Arthur Fairbrother); Gregoire Aslan (Achmed); John
Le Mesurier (George Lillywhite); Klaus Kinski (Jonquil); Margaret
Lee (Samia Voss); Emil Stemmler (Hotel Clerk); Helen Sanguineti
(Madame Couseny); Sanchez Francisco (Martinez); William Sanguineti
(Police Chief); Hassan Essakali (Motorcycle Policeman); Keith Pea-
cock (Philippe); Burt Kwouk (Export Manager).

This British-made feature was called Our Man in Marrakech,

Klaus Kinski (in white suit) in Bang, Bang You're Dead! (AIP, 1966).

before undergoing several title changes in its transition to the States.
On television it is known as I Spy, You Spy. The flow of title
changes is the most imaginative facet of this droopy spoof. Since
no one is ever telling the truth in this "small boy's notion of Middle Eastern intrigue" (New York World Telegram) one is forced soon
to stop paying attention to the convoluted plot and focus on the film's
intrinsic entertainment values, which proves to be a futile exercise.
     No one is quite what he or she appears to be, what with a
bizarre group of unusual types, ostensibly tourists, gathered in
exotic Morocco for a round robin of who-is-spying-on-whom-for-
what? Part of the answer is that one character is carrying two
million dollars to villain Mr. Casimir (Lom), the tidy sum to
be used to swing a crucial United Nations vote in favor of Red
China. Among the offbeat characters are, oil representative Andrew
Jessel (Randall), journalist Kyra Stanovy (Berger), travel agency
executive George Lillywhite (Le Mesurier), salesman Arthur Fairbrother (Hyde-White), and Samia Voss (Lee) as Lom's seductive
mistress ordered to learn whom the courier may be. El Caid
(Terry-Thomas) is the English-educated Arab chief with his own
scimitar to grind.

THE BARON'S AFRICAN WAR   see   SECRET SERVICE IN DARKEST
AFRICA

BEHIND THE IRON CURTAIN   see   THE IRON CURTAIN

BEHIND THE RISING SUN   (RKO, 1943)   88 min.

Director, Edward Dmytryk; based on the book by James R.
Young; screenplay, Emmett Lavery; assistant director, Ruby Rosenberg; art director, Albert S. D'Agostine, Al Herman; set decorator,
Darrell Silvera, Claude Carpenter; music, Roy Webb; music director, C. Bakaleinikoff; sound, Terry Kellum, James G. Stewart;
special effects, Vernon L. Walker; camera, Russell Metty; editor,
Joseph Noriega.

Margo (Tama); Tom Neal (Taro); J. Carrol Naish (Publisher);
Robert Ryan (Lefty); Gloria Holden (Sara); Don Douglas (O'Hara);
George Griot (Boris); Adeline De Watt Reynolds (Grandmother);
Leonard Strong (Tama's Father); Iris Wong (Woman Secretary);
Wolfgang Zilzer (Max); Shirley Lew (Servant); Benson Fong (Jap
Officer); Lee Tung Foo (Dinner Guest); Mike Mazurki (Jap Wrestler).

Like it or not, America was as guilty as any nation of propaganda in World War II; this picture is one of the more blatant examples of how Occidental moviemakers depicted the atrocities
practiced by "Uncle Tojo's dogs," those "slant-eyed monkeys."
Amazingly, now at least, a supposedly savvy trade paper such as
Variety could then evaluate this film as a "good drama of inside
information on the Japanese indoctrination and thinking." Although
direct instances of espionage were not the substance of Behind the
Rising Sun, the brain-washing-training of potential informers played
a major role in the proceedings.

Nipponese-born Neal is educated at Cornell University, then
returns to Japan where his newspaper publisher father (Naish) has
become the Minister of Propaganda for the Emperor. At first Neal
wants to become an engineer and marry his new-found love, low-
caste Margo, an innocent girl educated by the Red Cross. But then
impressionable Neal comes under the heady influence of his country's
warmongers and soon he is so fanatical a nationalist that he quite
willingly gives false testimony which leads to the imprisonment and
torture of friends and family. So appalled is liberal Naish by the
rising tide of military imperialism in Japan and by his son's
dramatic change of heart, that he (Naish) commits hara-kiri. As
for Neal, the script takes a nose dive and has the war-bent youth,
now an air pilot, shot down during one of Doolittle's raids over
Japan.

This exploitation film was prepared by the same team (director Edward Dmytryk--scripter Emmett Lavery) responsible for
the earlier Hitler's Children (1943), a study of mind bending in
Germany. To cover themselves, RKO insisted in its publicity releases that Behind the Rising Sun was really intent on showing that
in Japan there were human beings too.

BERLIN, APPOINTMENT FOR SPIES see BERLINO, APPUNTA-
MENTO PER LE SPIE

BERLIN CORRESPONDENT   (20th-Fox, 1942)   70 min.

Producer, Bryan Foy; director, Eugene Forde; screenplay,
Steve Fisher, Jack Andrews; art director, Richard Day, Lewis
Creben; music director, Emil Newman; camera, Virgil Miller;
editor, Fred Allen.
Virginia Gilmore (Karen Hauen); Dana Andrews (Bill Roberts);
Mona Maris (Carla); Martin Kosleck (Captain Carl von Rau); Sig
Rumann (Dr. Dietrich); Kurt Katch (Weiner); Erwin Kalser (Mr.
Hauen); Torben Meyer (Manager); William Edmunds (Gruber); Hans
Schumm (Gunther); Leonard Mudie (English Prisoner); Hans Von
Morhart (Actor); Curt Furberg (Doctor); Henry Rowland (Pilot);
Christian Rub, Egon Brecher (Prisoners); William Vaughn, Louis
Arco, Arno Frey (Censors); Richard Ryen (Official); Harold F.
Shlickenmeyer, Otto Reichow, Bob Stevenson, William Yetter
(Guards); Frederick Giermann, Rudolf Myzet (Waiters); Emmett
Vogan (Announcer); Robert O. Davis, Abe Dinovitch (Policemen);
John Epper (Searchlight Operator); Lionel Royce (High Official);
Hans Moebus (Sentry); Henry Guttman (Aide to General); Paul
Weigel (Patron); Walter Sande (Reporter); Tom Seidel (Radio Man).

This soggy chestnut dropped out of the overstuffed cornucopia
of World War II adventure flicks and quickly earned the animosity
of the reviewers.   "For what the United Nations are fighting to
stamp out in Germany today is too terribly real and vital to our
future existence to be trifled within cheap melodrama" (New York
Times).   The New York Daily News demanded, "It's high time
Hollywood shelved some of its quaint notions about the workings
of the Gestapo, and long past time for making such melodramatic
balderdash...."
In pre-Pearl Harbor Germany, glib, humorous American
reporter Bill Roberts (Andrews), who also conducts a news commentary program, suddenly finds himself imprisoned by the Third
Reich for his veiled attacks on the regime. He is hustled off to
a concentration camp while a phony Nazi stand-in does his regular
broadcasts. Super hero Andrews not only maneuvers his own
escape from bondage, but in the process he rescues several important scientists from incarceration. The girl in the caper is
Karen Hauen (Gilmore), an unwilling Gestapo spy functionary for
Captain Carl von Rau (Kosleck). She is a lady with a conscience,
for she claims to rue the day when she was tricked into informing
on her very own father.

_____

[Following page]   Dana Andrews and Virginia Gilmore in Berlin
Correspondent (20th-Fox, 1942).

BERLIN EXPRESS (RKO, 1948) 86 min.

Executive producer, Dore Schary; producer, Bert Granet; assistant producer, William Dorfman; director, Jacques Tourneur; story, Curt Siodmak; screenplay, Harold Medford; art director, Albert S. D'Agostino, Alfred Herman; set decorator, Darrell Silvera, William Stevens; music, Frederick Hollander; music director, C. Bakaleinikoff; assistant director, Nate Levinson; sound, Jack Grubb, Clem Portman; choreography, Charles O'Curran; costumes, Orry Kelly; makeup, Gordon Blau; special effects, Harry Perry, Russell A. Cully, Harold Stine; camera, Lucien Ballard; editor, Sherman Todd.

Merle Oberon (Lucienne); Robert Ryan (Robert Lindley); Charles Korvin (Perrot); Paul Lukas (Dr. Bernhardt); Robert Coote (Sterling); Reinhold Schunzel (Walther); Roman Toporow (Lt. Maxim); Peter von Zerneck (Hans Schmidt); Otto Waldis (Kessler); Fritz Kortner (Franzen); Michael Harvey (Sgt. Barnes); Tom Keene (Major); Jim Nolan (Train Captain); Arthur Dulac (Dining Car Steward); Ray Spiker, Bruce Cameron (Huskies); Buddy Roosevelt (M. P. Sgt.); Charles McGraw (Col. Johns); David Clarke (Army Technician); Roger Creed (M. P.); Gene Evans (Train Sgt.); Robert Shaw (R. O. T. Sgt.); Eric Wyland (Clown); Norbert Schiller (Saxophone Player); Merle Hayden (Maja); Bert Goodrich, George Redpath (Acrobatic Team); Richard Flato (Master of Ceremonies); Jack Serailian (Cigarette Maker); Lisl Valetti (German Waitress); Eva Hyde (Ticket Taker); Allan Raye (Corporal); Taylor Allen (Fraulein); David Wold, George Holt, Bill Raisch, Carl Ekberg, Hans Hopf (Germans); Willy Wickerhauser (Frederich); Will Allister (Richard); William Yetter, Jr., Robert Boon (German Youths); Ernest Brengk (Artist); Hermine Sterler (Frau Borne); Rory Mallinson (M. P. Guard); Fernanda Eliscu (German Woman); Curt Furburg (German Bystander); Larry Nunn, Jim Drum (G. I.'s); Fred Spitz (German Civilian); Jack G. Lee (Captain); Hans Moebus (Clerk); Frank Alten (German Steward); Leonid Snegoff (Russian Colonel); James Craven (British Major); Fred Datig, Jr. (American Jeep Driver); William Stelling (American Sgt.); Al Winters (German Peasant).

One of the more authentic post-World War II spy excursions, largely filmed where it happened (in Europe) with the shell-shattered cities of Frankfurt and Berlin as the grim background for a cliff-hanging tale of crass intrigue.

Aboard the Paris to Berlin Express train, a government official is murdered, leading to a manhunt for the killer. Among the passengers involved are U. S. agricultural expert Robert Lindley (Ryan), British schoolmaster Sterling (Coote), German anti-Nazi Perrot (Korvin), his French secretary Lucienne (Oberon), Russian army lieutenant Maxim (Toporow), and world democracy leader Dr. Bernhardt (Lukas). In Frankfurt the travelers are taken into police custody but later released, only to have Lukas mysteriously disappear. He is later found in the hands of a neo-Nazi underground group in an abandoned brewery, paving the way for the unmasking of the double agent.

Paul Lukas, Merle Oberon, Peter von Zerneck (second from right),
and Otto Waldis in Berlin Express (RKO, 1948).

"The whole of the picture is much better than the sum of
its parts" (New York Herald-Tribune). One remembers more
vividly the amoral resignation of the characters and the stark ruins
of Europe's cities, rather than the catch-all thriller plot.

BERLINO, APPUNTAMENTO PER LE SPIE [Berlin, Appointment
For Spies] (AIP, 1966) C 88 min.

Producers, Fulvio Lucisano, Luciano Marcuzzo; director,
Vittoria Sala; screenplay, Romano Ferraro, Adriano Baracco,
Adriano Bolzoni; assistant director, Stefano Rolla; music, Riz
Ortolani; camera, Fausto Zuccoli; editor, Roberto and Renato
Cinquini.
Brett Halsey (Bert Morris); Pier Angeli (Paula Krauss);
Dana Andrews (Colonel Lancaster); Gaston Moschin (Boris); and:
Tania Beryl, Mario Valdemarin, Aldo de Francesco, Marco Origliel-
mi, Alessandro Sperli, Tino Bianchi, Renato Baldini, Luciana
Angiolillo.

Scene: present day Berlin. Both the U.S. and Russian
agents are seeking the formula for the death ray perfected by a

Gaston Moschin and Brett Halsey in <u>Berlino, Appuntamento per le Spie</u> (AIP, 1966).

now deceased Nobel Prize-winning scientist. Each side is convinced the late man's daughter (Angeli) has access to the formula. After she is kidnapped by the Russians, American agent Halsey is dispatched to locate her.

Meantime the Russians are utilizing another ploy. When U.S. Intelligence chief Andrews underwent surgery to have a blinded eye replaced, the Soviets engineered a special coup. A minute transmitting telecamera was inserted in Andrew's eye socket; transforming him into a walking video camera for the enemy camp!

This diverting premise never got off the ground, because its "...effect is lost in the vast maze of perplexing events that segue across the screen" (<u>Variety</u>).

The dubbed version released in the U.S. was retitled <u>Spy in Your Eye.</u>

BETRAYAL FROM THE EAST   (RKO, 1945)   82 min.

Executive producer, Sid Rogell; producer, Herman Schlom; director, William Berke; based on the novel by Alan Hynd; adaptation, Aubrey Wisberg; screenplay, Kenneth Gamet, Wisberg; art director, Albert S. D'Agostino, Ralph Berger; set decorator, Darrell

Silvera, William Stevens; music, Roy Webb; music director, C.
Bakaleinikoff; assistant director, Sam Ruman; sound, Jean L. Speak;
special effects, Vernon L. Walker; camera, Russell Metty; editor,
Duncan Mansfield.
    Lee Tracy (Eddie Carter); Nancy Kelly (Peggy Hamilton);
Richard Loo (Tanni); Abner Biberman (Yamato); Regis Toomey
(Jimmy Scott); Philip Ahn (Kato); Addison Richards (Captain Bates);
Bruce Edwards (Lt. Purdy); Hugh Hoo (Araki); Victor Sen Young
(Omaya); Roland Varno (Kent); Louis Jean Heydt (Marsden); Jason
Robards, Sr. (Hildebrand); Paul Fung (Dr. Kabeneshki); Grace Lem
(Fortune Teller); Edmund Glover (Bit); Fay Wall (Helga); Hermine
Sterler (Keller); Howard Johnson (Wilhelm); George Lee (Bellhop);
Lee Phelps (Immigration Officer); Manuel Lopez (Waiter); Guy
Zanett (Desk Clerk); Manuel Paris (Travel Desk Clerk).

    Despite a prologue and epilogue delivered by famed news-
caster-analyst Drew Pearson, Betrayal from the East lacked sufficient shreds of credibility. Its tale of a carnival barker (Tracy)
who plays along with a trio of dastardly Japanese (Loo, Biberman,
Ahn) out to sabotage the Panama Canal, so he can help Army Intelligence trap the enemy agents, is only extravagant in its silli-
ness. Kelly functions as Peggy Hamilton, an American Mata Hari.

BETRAYED (MGM, 1954) C 108 min.

    Producer-director, Gottfried Reinhardt; screenplay, Ronald
Miller, George Froeschel; music, Walter Goehr; camera, F. A.
Young; editor, John Dunning, Raymond Poulton.
    Clark Gable (Colonel Pieter Deventer); Lana Turner (Carla
van Owen); Victor Mature (The Scarf); Louis Calhern (General Ten
Eyck); O. E. Hasse (Colonel Helmuth Dietrich); Wilfrid Hyde-White
(General Charles Larraby); Ian Carmichael (Captain Jackie Lawson);
Niall MacGinnis (Blackie); Nora Swinburne (The Scarf's Mother);
Roland Culver (General Warsleigh); Leslie Weston (Pop); Christo-
pher Rhodes (Chris); Lilly Kann (Jan's Grandmother); Brian Smith
(Jan); Anton Diffring (Captain Van Stanger); Richard Anderson
(John); Carl Jaffe (Major Plaaten); Wolf Frees (Motorcycle Rider);
Nicholas Bruce (Dietrich's Lieutenant); Theodore Bikel (German
Sergeant); John Wynn, John Singer, Harold Jamison, Basil Appleby
(Paratroopers); Thomas Heathcote, Glynn Houston, John Glen
(Paratrooper Corporals); Kenneth Hyde (Instructor); Peter Martyn
(Freddy Jackson); Mona Washbourne (Waitress); Peter Swanwick
(Fat Major); Ferdy Mayne (Luftwaffe Officer).

    Rather desperately hoping for a bountiful boxoffice, MGM
teamed Gable and Turner for the fourth (and final) time, tossed
in Victor Mature, color, and an expensive mounting, and came up
with Betrayed, a dull tale by any standards. In fact, it proved to
be 53-year-old Gable's final studio feature.
    Set in 1943, a Dutch intelligence officer (Gable) is nimbly
rescued from the advancing Germans and packed off to England by

a Resistance leader known only as "the Scarf" (Mature). In London the authorities decide to cooperate with the Scarf and dispatch Gable to find him. In the search he tumbles for Carla van Owen (Turner) a former Nazi collaborator who now intends to repent for her past misdeeds. After the couple locate the Scarf, the latter's forces begin suffering heavy setbacks. Gable suspects the girl of treachery but he has cause to learn differently before finally leading Turner and the British troops on a secret escape route from besieged Arnhem.

Newsweek magazine accurately termed Betrayed a "clumsy and over-slow paced piece of melodrama." It was painfully clear that audience interest was not with the rather stiff hero (Gable) nor with his uninteresting, overglamorized gal (Turner) but with the flashy character played by pathologically bent Mature. Here was a strong example of star "marquee power" being unable to rescue a badly told story, particularly when it dealt with a genre (spying) that seemed to have run its course for the time being.

THE BETTER 'OLE   (WB, 1926)   8,469 feet

   Director, Charles Reisner; based on the play by Bruce Bairnsfather, Arthur Eliot; adaptation, Reisner, Darryl F. Zanuck; titles, Robert Hopkins; assistant director, Sandy Roth; camera, Ed Du Par, Walter Robinson.
   Syd Chaplin (Old Bill); Doris Hill (Joan); Harold Goodwin (Bert); Theodore Lorch (Gaspard); Ed Kennedy (Corporal Quint); Charles Gerrard (The Major); Tom McGuire (The English General); Jack Ackroyd (Alf); Tom Kennedy (The Blacksmith); Kewpie Morgan (General Von Hinden); Arthur Clayton (The Colonel).

   A retelling of a 1918 Broadway comedy that had been first filmed in 1919 with Charles Rock in the lead. Here Charles Chaplin's brother Syd had a field day portraying Old Bill, the happy-go-lucky British sergeant who has a deuce of a time proving that the major (Gerrard) in his regiment is actually a German spy in collusion with the local innkeeper (Lorch). Before the nine-reel comedy has concluded, Chaplin has been forced to pose as a German soldier, fight an attack against his own regiment, and nearly been shot by the Allies as a spy. But the firing squad unknowingly uses blank cartridges and there is time for conclusive evidence to be presented that clears Chaplin of any traitorous taint.

BIG JIM McLAIN   (WB, 1952)   90 min.

   Producer, Robert Fellows; director, Edward Ludwig; story, Richard English, Eric Taylor; screenplay, James Edward Grand; art director, Al Yvarra; set decorator, Charles Thompson; music director, Emil Newman; assistant director, Andrew McLaglen; camera, Archie Stout; editor, Jack Murray.
   John Wayne (Big Jim McLain); Nancy Olson (Nancy Vallon);

James Arness, Dan Liu, and John Wayne in Big Jim McLain (WB, 1952).

James Arness (Mal Baxter); Alan Napier (Sturak); Veda Ann Borg (Madge); Gayne Whitman (Dr. Gelster); Hal Baylor (Poke); Robert Keys (Edwin White); Hans Conried (Robert Henried); John Hubbard (Lt. Commander Clint Grey); Sara Padden (Mrs. Lexiter); Mme. Soo Yong (Mrs. Nomaka); Dan Liu (Chief of Police); and: Paul Hurst, Vernon McQueen.

Every decade or so political rightist John Wayne becomes involved in a film project which arouses public indignation. The 1960s found him championing America's participation in the Viet Nam War; in 1952 the actor--aided and abetted by his production outfit and distributor Warner Bros.--saw fit to turn out this specious melodrama, which aimed at paying tribute to the fine work of the House Un-American Activities Committee and men "undaunted by the vicious campaign of slander launched against them."

Big Jim McLain opens with a quote from Stephen Vincent Benét's The Devil and Daniel Webster, "Neighbor, how stands the Union?" Then the sophomoric told account gets underway as two FBI special agents (Wayne, Arness) are sent to Hawaii to investigate Communist activity. Checking on a psychiatrist (Whitman) there, one of them (Wayne) falls in love with the doctor's secretary (Olson).

From a local character, the government duo gain knowledge about a party member, and from him they obtain information on people in higher party positions.   When the FBI men try to smoke out the Reds by announcing at a social gathering that they know who the culprits are, the psychiatrist maneuvers to kill Arness via an overdose of truth serum.   Wanting revenge, rugged Wayne employs the Honolulu police to round up the Reds at one of their party meetings.   The case closed, Wayne is free to wed Olson.

The only point engendered by this unsubtle presentation was that Communists are murderous and must be treated in a like manner.   A minor aspect of interest was that real-life Honolulu chief of police Dan Liu played himself in the film, and other islanders were scattered in the cast for "authenticity" purposes.

BILLION DOLLAR BRAIN   (UA, 1967)   C   111 min.

Executive producer, Andre De Toth; producer, Harry Saltzman; director, Ken Russell; based on the novel by Len Deighton; screenplay, John McGrath; art director, Bert Davey; music-music director, Richard Rodney Bennett; production designer, Syd Cain; sound, John Mitchell; camera, Billy Williams; editor, Alan Osbiston.
Michael Caine (Harry Palmer); Karl Malden (Leo Newbegin); Françoise Dorleac (Anya); Oscar Homolka (Colonel Stok); Ed Begley (General Midwinter); Guy Doleman (Colonel Ross); Vladek Scheybal (Dr. Eiwort); Milo Sperber (Basil); Mark Elwes (Birkinshaw); Stanley Caine (G. P. O. Delivery Boy).

Least satisfying of the Len Deighton-derived Harry Palmer (Caine) film trilogy.   "The only fresh aspects of the movie are Helsinki ... and a host of Honeywell electronic calculators ... " (New Yorker magazine).
Having survived the escapades of Funeral in Berlin, the anonymous anti-hero Harry Palmer (Caine) is back in London, eeking out a modest living as a private eye.   But soon, Colonel Ross (Doleman) of M. I. 5 has pressured the disobedient operative back into the spying gambit.   Caine, of the sleepy grin and yawn, thinks he is taking a civilian case when he takes a mysterious package of eggs to Finland.   Once in Helsinki he demands that Anya (Dorleac) direct him to his alleged employer, Dr. Kaarna.   Instead she leads him to fur-coated Leo Newbegin (Malden) who admits he was posing as Dr. Kaarna.   Cockney Caine finds out that the real Kaarna has been killed, and, later, after being drugged by M. I. 5 employees, he realizes that he is being framed for the doctor's murder in order to carry out the agency's latest mission. It develops that Caine's task is to uncover who is in control of a billion dollar computer network, an answer the Russians--led by Caine's old adversary Colonel Stok (Homolka)--are equally eager to have.   Before the fadeout, the path has led to Texas and the stronghold of megalomaniac right winger General Midwinter (Begley) who is launching his elaborate private army attack on Latvia, step number one in his plan to wipe out global Communism.

Caine's nonchalant, seedy Harry Palmer remained his cynical, apathetic self, but the ploy has become sleep-inducing to viewers. The plot of Billion Dollar Brain, incoherent, inconclusive, and far out, led to a grotesquely incredible film, with little suspense and certainly no valid artistic reason for existing.

BIRDS DO IT   (Columbia, 1966)   C   88 min.

Executive producer, Ivan Tors; producer, Stanley Colbert; director, Andrew Marton; story, Leonard Kaufman; screenplay, Arnie Kogen; art director, Mel Bledsoe; set decorator, Don Ivey; music, Samuel Maltovsky; song, Howard Greenfield and Jack Keller; assistant director, James Gordon MacLean; sound, Howard Warren; special effects, Howard Anderson; camera, Howard Winner; editor, Irwin Dumbrille.

Soupy Sales (Melvin Byrd); Tab Hunter (Lt. Porter); Arthur O'Connell (Professor Wald); Edward Andrews (General Smithburn); Doris Dowling (Congresswoman); Beverly Adams (Claudine Wald); Louis Quinn (Sgt. Skam); Frank Nastasi (Yellow Cab Driver); Burt Taylor (Devlin); Courtney Brown (Man); Russell Saunders (Clurg); Julian Voloshin (Professor Neg); Bob Busell (Doorman); Warren Day (Curtis); Jay Laskay (Willie); Burt Leigh (Radar Operator);

Because an alien dust particle ruins a $15 million space rocket launching at Cape Kennedy, government authorities hire Melvin Byrd (Sales) as a "top secret" janitor equipped with self-propelling cleaning utensils to keep the missiles free of damaging dirt. Enemy agents infiltrate the base and determine to get rid of Sales, whom they believe to be a highly-valued U.S. agent. Later, the playful Sales is accidentally negatively ionized, and finds himself able to fly, float, and frolic like a bird. This peculiar body chemical change also makes him irresistible to women, in particular, to Claudine Wald (Adams), the daughter of his project boss, Professor Wald (O'Connell). In a grand demonstration of his new flying capabilities, Sales sees himself pursued by U.S. and enemy operatives, with the Coast Guard on hand to round up the foreign spies. Sales later loses his unique aerial abilities but he retains the affection of Adams.

This daffy feature film debut for the iconoclastic funnyman Soupy Sales may have pleased the kids, but it had little to offer adult viewers.

BLACK DRAGON OF MANZANAR see   G-MEN VS BLACK DRAGON

BLACK DRAGONS (Monogram, 1942)   64 min.

Producer, Sam Katzman; associate producer, Barney Sarecky; director, William Nigh; story-screenplay, Harvey H. Gates; assistant director, Gerald Schnitzer; production manager,

Edward W. Rote; art director, David Milton; sound, Glen Glenn;
camera, Art Reed; editor, Carl Pierson.
     Bela Lugosi (Dr. Melcher/Colomb); Joan Barclay (Alice);
Clayton Moore (Don Martin); George Pembroke (Saunders); Robert
Frazer (Hanlin); Stanford Jolley (The Dragon); Max Hoffman, Jr.
(Kearney); Irving Mitchell (Van Dyke); Edward Piel, Sr. (Wallace);
Bob Fiske (Ryder); Kenneth Harlan (Colton); Joe Eggenton (Stevens);
Bernard Gorcey (Cabby).

     Super economy producers Sam Katzman and Jack Dietz
spared every expense in turning out this "dog," which maliciously
ruined a potentially fine plot premise.
     Dr. Lugosi is a Nazi plastic surgeon who performs opera-
tions on six Japanese Axis agents, causing them to look just like
a sextet of top echelon American industrialists. The latter are
disposed of, and the remodeled Orientals take their place, bent
on sabotage.
     The plot twist, a blatant bit of Allied propaganda, had the
Japanese then imprison Lugosi, stating that the Japs trust no one,
not even the Nazis. Lugosi escapes, remodels his own face, and
arrives in Washington, D. C. , to blithely dispatch his six former
patients, dumping their lifeless bodies on the steps of the closed
Japanese Embassy.

THE BLACK PARACHUTE (Columbia, 1944) 65 min.

     Producer, Jack Fier; director, Lew Landers; story, Paul
Gangelin; screenplay, Clarence Upson Young; art director, Lionel
Banks, Carl Anderson; set decorator, William Kiernan; assistant
director, Robert Saunders; sound, Jack Goodrich; camera, George
Meehan; editor, Otto Meyer.
     John Carradine (General von Bodenbach); Osa Massen (Marya
Orloff); Larry Parks (Michael Lindley); Jeanne Bates (Olga); Jona-
than Hale (King Stephen); Ivan Triesault (Colonel Pavlec); Trevor
Bardette (Nicholas); Art Smith (Joseph); Robert Lowell (Pilot);
Charles Wagenheim (Kurt Vandan); Charles Waldron (Erik Dundeen);
Ernie Adams (Cobbler); Connie Evans, Hazel Boyne (Mountain
Woman); George Magrill, Chuck Hamilton, George Sowards (Moun-
taineers); Charles Faber, Philip van Zandt, Otto Reichow (German
Lieutenants); Harry Semels (Harl); Michel Silva (Peter); Crauford
Kent (Prime Minister); John Eppers, Ted Holley (German Guards);
John Merton (German Senior NCO); William Lawrence (Doctor);
Dick Curtis (Lieutenant); Lynton Brent (Soldier); John Roy, Fred
Lord (German Orderlies); John Forrest (German Junior NCO);
Robert L. Stevenson, John Peters, Louis Arco, Dick Jensen
(Orderlies); Neal Reagan, Herbert Lytton (News Commentators).

     Set in a mythical Balkan kingdom, The Black Parachute was
typical of the Columbia "B" movies of the World War II era. The
American soldier hero (Parks) is parachuted into the Balkan land
to aid the local underground in freeing their king (Hale) who is

being held captive by the Nazis (a bogus monarch is being utilized
to force-feed radioed propaganda messages to the people).   In order
to thwart the rescue plan, Gestapo General von Bodenbach (Carradine) is brought into play.

The focus here was more on physical action than astute
spying by the underground.   Long before he became famous for
The Jolson Story Parks was a sturdy American soldier; Massen
was well cast as the local-girl/love-interest in the underground.
The picture, however, belonged to Carradine, who dominated the
action as the ruthless Gestapo chief routed in the end by a combination of American ingenuity and partisan brawn.

BLINDFOLD (Universal, 1966) C   102 min.

Executive producer, Robert Arthur; producer, Marvin Schwartz;
director, Philip Dunne; based on the novel by Lucille Fletcher;
screenplay, Dunne, W. H. Menger; art director, Alexander Golitzen,
Henry Bumstead; music, Lalo Schifrin; music supervisor, Joseph
Gershenson; costumes, Jean Louis; assistant director, Terry Nelson, Bill Gilmore; camera, Joseph MacDonald; editor, Ted J. Kent.

Rock Hudson and Claudia Cardinale in Blindfold (Universal, 1966).

Rock Hudson (Dr. Bartholomew Snow); Claudia Cardinale (Vicky Vincenti); Guy Stockwell (Fitzpatrick); Jack Warden (General Pratt); Brad Dexter (Harrigan); Anne Seymour (Smitty); Alejandro Rey (Arthur Vincenti); Hari Rhodes (Captain Davis); John Megna (Mario); Paul Comi (Barker).

With Hudson and Cardinale co-starring and Philip Dunne directing-scripting this Panavision-Technicolor outing, very airy escapist fare had to be the order of the day. The result was an unsteady mixture of romantic comedy and adventure, devised to take advantage of the "James Bond" craze. The British Films and Filming reviewer graciously lauded "... a cunning job of substituting entertainment for credibility."

New York playboy-psychologist Dr. Bartholomew Snow (Hudson), who specializes in pampering the minds of the wealthy, had once treated mentally disturbed scientist Arthur Vincenti (Rey). The latter is now engaged on a top level confidential government project and is exhibiting an alarming regression to his prior neurotic state. Thus one morning the C. I. A. man, General Pratt (Warden), has Hudson sidetracked along a horsepath in Central Park and explains that he is needed to cure Rey, but that he must be blindfolded on each visit to the ailing scientist, who is being kept at a Southern bayou hideaway. Soon thereafter Rey's chorus girl sister Vicky (Cardinale), spy ring head Fitzpatrick (Stockwell) and other one-dimensional characters are weaving in and out of the silly plot.

One unusual aspect of Blindfold is that reluctant hero Hudson has a unique means of distracting and overcoming his onscreen adversaries. Because of the professional background of Hudson's movie character, he can play mental games with his less astute and subconsciously fear-ridden oppenents.

THE BLONDE FROM PEKING see LA BLONDE DE PEKIN

LA BLONDE DE PEKIN [The Blonde from Peking] (Paramount, 1968) C 80 min.

Director, Nicolas Gessner; based on the novel by James Hadley Chase; adaptation, Jacques Vilfrid; screenplay, Gesner, Mark Behm; music, François de Roubaix; art director, Georges Peorges Petitot; camera, Claude Lecomte; editor, Jean-Michel Gauthier.

Mireille Darc (Christine); Claudio Brook (Gandler); Edward G. Robinson (Douglas); Pascale Roberts (Secretary); Françoise Brion (Erika); Joe Warfield (Doctor); and: Giorgia Moll, Karl Studer, Yves Elliot, Valery Inkjinoff, Joseph Warfield, Tiny Young, Aime de March, Jean-Jacques Delbo.

When a blonde girl (Darc) suffering from amnesia is found seated on a park bench in Paris, international agents are convinced she is the ex-mistress of a Chinese scientist and may have acquired important nuclear secrets.   Robinson of the CIA hires actor Brook to pose as her husband, hoping to unravel some hard facts.   Brook learns that Darc, the "Blonde from Peking, " is not a spy, but does have access to the rare Blue Grape Pearl which her sister had stolen from the Chinese.   The plot then swerves into a treasure hunt with all parties concerned convening in Hong Kong to capture the valuable jewel.

Since the picture "does not quite have the verve, ironic comic twists or sheer suspense and action flair to bring it off" (Variety), it had to rely on the Robinson marquee lure for its brief U.S. bookings.   The film was typical of the international co-productions of the mid-1960s which disguised a basically simple robbery caper with overtones of global intrigue.

BLOOD ON THE SUN   (UA, 1945)   98 min.

Producer, William Cagney; director, Frank Lloyd; based on a story by Garrett Fort; screenplay, Lester Cole; additional scenes, Nathaniel Curtis; assistant director, Harvey Dwight; technical adviser, Alice Barlow; art director, Wiard B. Ihnen; set decorator, A. Roland Fields; music, Miklos Rozsa; costumes, Robert Martien; makeup, Ernest Westmore; sound, Richard De Wesse; camera, Theodor Sparkuhl; editor, Truman K. Wood, Walter Hanneman.

James Cagney (Nick Condon); Sylvia Sidney (Iris Hilliard); Wallace Ford (Ollie Miller); Rosemary De Camp (Edith Miller); Robert Armstrong (Colonel Tojo); John Emery (Premier Tanaka); Frank Puglia (Prince Tatsugi); Leonard Strong (Hijikata); Jack Halloran (Captain Oshima); Hugh Ho (Kajioka); Philip Ahn (Yomamoto); Joseph Kim (Hayoski); Marvin Miller (Yamada); Rhys Williams (Joseph Cassell); Porter Hall (Arthur Bickett); James Bell (Charley Sprague); Grace Lem (Amah); Oy Chan (Chinese Servant); George Paris (Hotel Manager); Hugh Beaumont (Johnny Clarke); Gregory Gay, Arthur Loft, Emmett Vogan, Charlie Wayne (American Newsmen in Tokyo).

Coming as it did near the very end of World War II, this film smartly turned back to the Japan of the 1920s for its backdrop, to show how early in the game there were already plans of world domination fermenting in the land of the rising sun.   The concept at hand may have been spurious, but its presentation was "hard, tidy and enjoyable" (Time magazine).

Aroused by the vicious murder of American reporter Ollie Miller (Ford) and his wife (De Camp) who first tried to smuggle the audacious Tanaka Plan of world conquest out of Japan, Nick Condon (Cagney), the Yankee editor of a Tokyo newspaper, takes over the mission himself, battling imposing obstacles.   His chief accomplice proves to be noncommittal Iris Hilliard (Sidney), who has suspicious entrees to high political circles.

The most obvious entertainment factor of this two-fisted drama was dynamic Cagney himself, letting out all the stops as he practices jiu-jitsu on his Oriental adversaries. ("It is the most violent workout Mr. Cagney has had since Public Enemy, and it ought to be fine for those who admire a good, ninety-minute massacre"--New Yorker magazine.) But not to be overlooked was the non-pacifist attitude that had swept America in the early 1940s, with the populus craving no-nonsense k. o. punches to be dealt the Axis enemy by any and all Allied representatives, even unauthorized undercover agents such as Cagney's Nick Condon. Illustrating this point is a scene in which Japanese police chief Yamada (Miller) appeals to Cagney's Christian nature in overlooking the untimely deaths of Ford and De Camp. To which an angered Cagney heatedly replies, "Yes. Forgive your enemies. But first--Get even!" Pow!

BRITISH AGENT (WB, 1934)   75 min.

Director, Michael Curtiz; story, H. Bruce Lockhart; screenplay, Laird Doyle; camera, Ernest Haller; editor, Tom Richards.
Leslie Howard (Stephen Locke); Kay Francis (Elena); William Gargan (Medill); Phillip Reed (Gaston La Farge); Irving Pichel (Pavlov); Walter Byron (Stanley); Cesar Romero (Tito del Val); J. Carrol Naish (Commissioner for War); Ivan Simpson (Evans); Gregory Gaye (Kolinoff); Halliwell Hobbes (Sir Walter Carrister); Arthur Aylesworth (Farmer); Doris Lloyd (Lady Carrister); Mary Forbes (Lady Treherne); Alphonse Ethier (Devigny); Paul Porcasi (Romano); Addison Richards (Zvododu); Herbert Bunston (Lord Milner); Marina Schubert (Maria); Tenen Holtz (Lenin); George Pearce (Lloyd George); Thomas Braidon, Basil Lynn, Fred Walton, Winter Hall (Cabinet Members); Walter Armitage (Under Secretary); Wyndham Standing (Englishman); Leonid Snegoff (Russian Diplomat); Edith Baker (Madame Devigny); Joseph Mario (Stalin); Norman Stengel (Radek); Vesey O'Davoren (Secretary); Olaf Hytten (Under Secretary); Frank Lackteen, Robert Wilber, Lew Harvey (Suspects); Corrine Williams (Dora Kaplan); Frank Reicher (Mr. X); Claire McDowell (Woman).

One would hardly expect to have soignée Francis and delicate Howard turning up together in a film set against the lurid backdrop of the social and political upheavals in 1910 Russia, but in the Hollywood of the Thirties anything was possible, including British Agent, very loosely construed from R. H. Bruce Lockhart's autobiographical chronicle published the previous year.
Howard appeared as Stephen Locke, Britain's unofficial emissary to the Russian revolutionary government, hoping to persuade their new leaders not to withdraw from the all important second front in World War I. A quick change of political climate has Howard literally out in the cold, for 10 Downing Street is quite willing to sacrifice Howard (refusing to acknowledge his status) for the sake of appearance. Francis was seen as Elena, the well-garbed secretary of Lenin (Holtz). She was the Cheka spy who placed top priority on her status as a woman in love with Howard rather than on the espionage mission. More sensibly cast were Naish as Trotsky and

Kay Francis and Leslie Howard in <u>British Agent</u> (WB, 1934).

Doris Day and Lilia Skala in <u>Caprice</u> (20th-Fox, 1967).

and Pichel as Stalin.
The fallacy of this "eccentric" feature was to equate the Francis-Howard love tale with the scope of the Russian revolution and the surrounding espionage activity. The film's virtues have been summed up best by John Baxter in Hollywood in the Thirties (1968): "[Director Michael] Curtiz again gives us remarkable sequences; an ambassadorial ball interrupted by a stream of machine gun bullets ripping across the mirrors that line the salon, soldiers raging through the streets in decrepit army trucks, and an odd vignette concerning one of the diplomats who goes out to contact a Russian army officer. Curtiz cuts promptly to the two men walking through a gate as part of a group. The diplomat, smoking nervously, says with a grin, 'Well, Colonel, at least I found you.' The next shot shows them lined up against a wall with the others and executed."

BRITISH INTELLIGENCE   see   THREE FACES EAST

CAIRO   (MGM, 1942)   100 min.

Director, W. S. Van Dyke II; screenplay, John McClain; music, Herbert Stothart; music conductor, Georgie Stoll; choreographer, Sammy Lee; songs, E. Y. Harburg and Arthur Schwartz; art director, Cedric Gibbons; camera, Ray June; editor, James E. Newcom.

Jeanette MacDonald (Marcia Warren); Robert Young (Homer Smith); Ethel Waters (Cleo); Reginald Owen (Mr. Cobson); Mona Barrie (Mrs. Morrison); Lionel Atwill (Teutonic Gentleman); Eduardo Ciannelli (Ahmed Ben Hassan); Dennis Hoey (Colonel Woodhue); Dooley Wilson (Hector); Harry Worth (Bartender); Mitchell Lewis (Ludwig); Frank Richards (Alfred); Rhys Williams (Strange Man); Grant Mitchell (O. H. P. Banks); Bert Roach (Sleepy Man); Larry Nunn (Bernie); Jack Daley (Man in Newspaper Office); Demetrius Emanuel, Jay Novello (Italian Officers); Pat O'Malley (Junior Officer); Selmer Jackson (Ship Captain); Cecil Cunningham (Madame Laruga); Jacqueline Dalya (Female Attendant); Dan Seymour (Doorman); Lorin Raker (Worried Man); Alan Schute (Soldier); Guy Kingsford (Squadron Leader); William Tannen, Michael Butler (Soldiers on Boat); Sidney Melton (Private Schwartz); James Davis (Sergeant); Lee Murray (Messenger); Cecil Stewart (Pianist); Buck Woods (Black); Louise Bates (Mrs. Woodhue); Kanza Omar (Theatre Cashier); Petra R. de Silva (Fat Woman); Ray Cooper (Waiter).

The low budget film that ended MacDonald's MGM tenure was snubbed in its days as an "undistinguishable hybrid" (Variety), but from the perspective of three decades hence, it seems a pleasant enough version of the espionage genre in which the singing star merrily, not clumsily as thought at first, participates in verbal pot shots at her own sacred screen image. For example, at one point, MacDonald is arguing with co-star Young about the relative

merits of northern versus southern California, and the red-headed
luminary reminds her, "And you know what happened when I went
to San Francisco." Later, she is called upon to hit a high C note,
because the vibration will open a secret door panel. She lets loose
an upper register outcry, but nothing happens. With tongue-in-
check she informs her on camera comrades that she must admit
her tone--heaven forbid!--had been offpitch. Had Cairo been
assembled with more production values, the results would have
been far different, but then again, conservative MGM hardly would
have dared to joke about itself and its products in a high priced
picture.

    The rather preposterous storyline has bumpkin newspaper
reporter Homer Smith (Young) being sent to the African battle front
as some kind of honor for his journalistic abilities. In the famous
Egyptian city he meets his life's love, American screen star
Marcia Warren (MacDonald), then in between screen engagements
and singing in a local club. Being oblivious to the actual machinations of the Axis group headed by Atwill, Ciannelli, and Barrie,
Young comes to believe that MacDonald is a Nazi spy.

    MacDonald sings such ditties as "Keep the Light Burning
Bright in the Harbor" and "The Waltz Is Over," while her rambunctious egalitarian black maid (Waters) vocalizes "Buds Won't Bud."

CALLING PHILO VANCE (WB, 1940)   62 min.

    Producer, Bryan Foy; director, William Clemens; based on
the novel by S.S. Van Dine; screenplay, Tom Reed; camera, Lou
O'Connell; editor, Benjamin Liss.

    James Stephenson (Philo Vance); Margot Stevenson (Hilda
Lake); Henry O'Neill (Markam); Ed Brophy (Ryan); Ralph Forbes
(Tom MacDonald); Donald Douglas (Philip Wrede); Martin Kosleck
(Gamble); James Conlin (Dr. Doremus); Edward Raquello (Grassi);
Creighton Hale (Du Bois); Harry Strang (Hennessey); George Irving
(Avery); Richard Kipling (Archer Coe); Wedgwood Nowell (Bris-
bane Coe); Bo Ling (Ling Toy); William Hopper (Hotel Clerk);
George Reeves (Steamship Clerk).

    Warner Bros. dusted off the William Powell-Mary Astor
The Kennel Murder Case (1933) and turned the detective movie
entry into a tale of foreign agents. Now when Archer Coe (Kipling)
is found dead in a bolted and locked room, the problem is more
serious, for airplane designer Kipling has been suspected of selling
plans to the enemy.

    William K. Everson in The Detective in Film (1972) declares
Calling Philo Vance to be "the last good Vance film." Other less
enthusiastic reviewers at the time insisted that the famed screen-
book detective had lost his touch and that despite the addition of an
international cast of characters (Viennese butler, Oriental house-
maid, Italian agent, et al.), the picture was just a standard whodunit, and a pretty flimsy affair at that.

CANARIS--MASTER SPY (Fama F. A. Mainz Film, 1954) 115 min.

Producer, Werner Drake; director, Alfred Weidenmann; story, Erich Ebermayer; screenplay, Herbert Reinecher; art director, Rolf Zehetbauer; music, Siegfried Franz; camera, Franz Weihmayr; editor, Ilse Voigt.

O. E. Hasse (Admiral Canaris); Martin Held (Colonel Heydrich); Barbara Rutting (Irene von Harbeche); Adrian Hoven (Althoff); Wolfgang Preiss (Holl); Peter Mosbacher (Fernandez); Arthur Schröder (von Harbeche); Charles Regnier (Baron Trenti); Franz Essel (Beckman); Herbert Wilk (Degenhard); Alice Treff (Fräulein Winter); Ilse Furstenberg (Frau Ludtke); Oskar Lindner (Gestapo Official); Friedrich Steig (Major Ullmann); Otto Braml (Behrens).

At the outbreak of World War II, Admiral Canaris (Hasse) is head of the German secret service. His arch enemy is Colonel Heydrich (Held), head of the secret police, who remains suspicious of Hasse's motives. In fact, Held persuades Irene von Harbeche (Rutting) to spy on Hasse, promising her that her services just might restore her father to political favoritism. Later Rutting confesses her duplistic role to the understanding Hasse, and he helps her to escape to Spain. Thereafter Hasse joins a group dedicated to removing Hitler from power and having him judged by a lawful court. But England's Chamberlain comes to Munich and the political tide turns too fast for any decisive action against the Führer. When Held is thereafter assassinated in Prague, Hasse considers himself out of danger from within the Third Reich hierarchy. Hitler's conquest of Poland and France, however, inspires Hasse to join with other devoted Germans in a plot to assassinate Hitler. The "conspiracy" fails and Hasse is arrested and hung.

Canaris--Master Spy, released in the U. S. in 1958 as Deadly Decision, never realized its potential as an amazing retelling of the fabulous career of an enigmatic man whose motivations are still being debated. Although some American reviewers noted the picture "Has a certain morbid fascination" (New York Herald-Tribune), most critics were put off by the film's failure to come to terms with the shadowy lead character whose motivations are so ambiguously presented that the tale loses most of its validity. Thus the downfall of Admiral Canaris is not the tragedy intended by the filmmakers.

CANDLELIGHT IN ALGERIA (British Lion, 1944) 85 min.

Director, George King; story, Dorothy Hope; screenplay, Brock Williams, Katherine Strueby; additional dialog, John Clements; camera, Otto Heller, Gus Doisse, Patrick Gay.

James Mason (Alan Thurston); Carla Lehmann (Susan Ann Foster); Raymond Lowell (Von Alven); Enid Stamp-Taylor (Maretza); Walter Rilla (Doktor Mueller); Pamela Stirling (Yvette); Lea Seidl (Senior Sister); Hella Kurty (Maid); Leslie Bradley (Henri de Lange); MacDonald Parke (American); Michel Morel (Commissioner of Police); Albert Whelan (Kadour); Meinhart Maur (Schultz);

Paul Bonifas (French Officer); Harold Berens (Toni); Richard
George (General Mark Clark); Bart Narman (First American Officer); and: John Slater, Berkeley Schultz.

One of those topical espionage studies that became dated
overnight because of the rapidly changing global situation during
the Second World War.

The plot premise concerned the spy intrigue and the hush-
hush surrounding General Mark Clark's (George) secret disembarka-
tion from a British submarine for a meeting of the Allied chiefs of
staffs at a deserted North African coastal site, prior to the Allied
invasion of North Africa.   Tank officer Mason of the British Army
is saddled with the problem of retrieving a telltale photograph of
the castle where the conclave is to be held, a piece of data the
Germans would dearly love to obtain.   Nebraskan Lehmann finds
herself in possession of the snapshot, and it takes all of Mason's
ingenuity, including disguising himself as a native servant, to
arrange her rescue. Mason later wisks Lehmann off to his Casbah
hideaway.

"If not plausible, it's fast, full of wallops and sustained
entertainment" (New York Daily Mirror).

CAPRICE   (20th-Fox, 1967)   C   98 min.

Producer, Aaron Rosenberg, Martin Melcher; associate pro-
ducer, Barney Rosenzweig; director, Frank Tashlin; story, Martin
Hale, Jay Jason; screenplay, Jason, Tashlin; assistant director,
David Silver; music, Frank De Vol; song, Larry Marks; art di-
rector, Jack Martin Smith, Walter Creber; set decorator, Walter
M. Scott, Jerry Wunderlich; costumes, Ray Aghayan; sound, Harry
M. Lendgren, David Dockendorf; makeup, Ben Nye, Harry Maret;
special camera effects, L. B. Abbott, Emil Kosa, Jr.; camera,
Leon Shamroy; aerial camera, Nelson Tyler; editor, Robert Simpson.

Doris Day (Patricia Fowler); Richard Harris (Christopher
White); Ray Walston (Stuart Clancy); Jack Kruschen (Matthew Cutter);
Edward Mulhare (Sir Jason Fox); Lilia Skala (Madame Piasco);
Irene Tsu (Su Ling); Larry D. Mann (Inspector Kapinsky); Maurice
Marsac (Auber); Michael Romanoff (Butler); Lisa Seagram (Mandy);
Michael J. Pollard (Barney); Cherie Foster (Usherette); Romo
Vincent (Stout Man); Penny Antine (Waitress); Roxanne Sprio (Teen-
Age Girl); John Woodjack (Boy); Fritz Feld (Hotel Desk Clerk);
John Bleifer (Doctor); Wayne Lundy (Lieutenant, Swiss Police);
George Wallace, Steve Wayne (Policemen); Madge Cleveland (Wo-
man in Bra); Muriel Landers (Fat Woman); Consuela Neal (Secre-
tary in Personnel Office); Mary Michael (Waitress); Bob Gunner
(Farley); Yutta D'Arcy, Corinna Tsopei (Girls in Hallway); Marsha
Metrinko, Bobbye Whitby, Nancy DeCarl, Claudia Brack, Nadia
Sanders (Models); Leon Shamroy (Himself); Alex Babcock (Himself);
Talya Ferro (Girl in Elevator); Richard Collier (Man in Elevator);
Dick Wilson (Maitre D'); Gina Grant (Wardrobe Mistress); Maurice
Kelly (Choreographer); Jeanette O'Connor (Script Girl); Bert Holland

(Slate Man);   George Beeckman (Police Driver); Danielle Hollender
(Piasco's Granddaughter); Marino Scotoni (Piasco's Grandson).

Having flippered her way through Frank Tashlin's The Glass
Bottom Boat, gauze-filmed Day returned under director Tashlin's
further aegis in an even more absurd espionage lark, hampered by
a joyless plot and inept performances.
Caprice allegedly explicates, while "cutely" spoofing, the
parallels between industrial, criminal, and political espionage.
Patricia Fowler (Day) finds herself a pawn between two hugely
successful cosmetic firms (one in Europe, the other in the U. S.),
both eager to acquire patents on the latest inventions--including a
revolutionary underarm deodorant--of ersatz scientist Stuart Clancy
(Walston). Not content with proceeding on this level, the film
switches mood as it develops that Day is really out to revenge the
death of her Interpol agent father who was slain in the line of duty
(chasing a narcotics ring) on a Swiss ski slope.   Day's antagonist,
Christopher White (Harris), is revealed to be not just a campy
industrial spy, but a double agent also on the narcotics case.
Caprice, courtesy of process shot photography, shifts inco-
herently from Switzerland to the U. S. to Paris, with Day more
often than not amuck in a Jerry Lewis-type farce.   Her best scene,
and one that points up director Tashlin's fascination with the rela-
tionships of the mundane to technical progress, finds Day chomping
away at a container of potato chips, causing an intricate electronic
bugging device to go awry.

CAPTAIN CAREY, U. S. A.   (Paramount, 1950)   83 min.

Producer, Richard Maibaum; director, Mitchell Leisen;
based on the novel by Martha Albrand; screenplay, Robert Thoeren;
art director, Hans Dreier, Roland Anderson; song, Jay Evans and
Ray Livingston; camera, John F. Seitz; editor, Alma McCrorie.
Alan Ladd (Webster Carey); Wanda Hendrix (Giula de Cresci);
Francis Lederer (Barone Rocco de Greffi); Celia Lovsky (Contessa
Francescae Cresci); Angela Clarke (Serafina); Richard Avonde
(Count Carlo de Cresci); Joseph Calleia (Dr. Lunati); Roland
Winters (Acuto); Frank Puglia (Luigi); Luis Alberni (Sandro); Jane
Nigh (Nancy); Rusty Tamblyn (Pietro); George Lewis (Giovanni);
David Leonard (Blind Musician); Virginia Farmer (Angelina); Paul
Lees (Frank); Henry Escalante (Brutus).

This spiritless suspense melodrama is mainly remembered
today for its theme song, "Mona Lisa," by Jay Livingston and Ray
Evans, which won an Academy Award and was made popular by
Nat "King" Cole.   (In the film it is sung briefly by a blind street
singer in the small Italian town where the plotline is set.)
In it, Ladd was the snarling former O. S. S. officer who returns to Italy after the war to find out who was the spy who had
betrayed his combat team during a World War II mission.   In the
tiny Italian town he meets, again, a girl (Hendrix) he had known

in the war, and a wealthy landowner (Lederer) who proves to have had a crucial part in the ignomious betrayal.

A rather vapid film in which Ladd's heroics soon become mundane, and Hendrix, whom Films and Filming termed "one of his tiniest co-stars," had little to do but look lovely. The meatiest assignment went to Lederer.

Captain Carey, U.S.A. is among the relatively few post-World War II features (which includes Foreign Intrigue and Pursued) dealing with the long-standing repercussions resulting from wartime (counter)spying and acts of betrayal.

CAPTAIN MEPHISTO AND THE TRANSFORMATION MACHINE   see THE MASKED MARVEL

CAREFUL, SOFT SHOULDERS   (20th-Fox, 1942)   69 min.

Producer, Walter Morosco; director-screenplay, Oliver L. P. Garrett; art director, Richard Day, Albert Hogsett; camera, Charles Clarke; editor, Nick De Maggio.

Virginia Bruce (Connie Mathers); James Ellison (Thomas Aldrich); Aubrey Mather (Mr. Fortune); Sheila Ryan (Agatha Mathers); Ralph Byrd (Elliott Salmon); Sigurd Tor (Milo); Charles Tannen (Joe); William B. Davidson (Mr. Aldrich); Dale Winter (Mrs. Ipswich).

The still engaging ex-MGM junior star, Bruce, was the chief asset of this filmed quickie, which "goes around in circles to wind up as minor league film fodder ..." (Variety).

Connie Mathers (Bruce), the daughter of a former senator, hangs around the Washington social/political fringes in order to receive her pay for displaying the latest fashions from a modiste shop with a few extra dollars handed her for luring her wealthy pals to the clothing establishment. When World War II comes, the Germans think mercenary Bruce might be a likely pawn for their espionage game. Mr. Fortune (Mather), posing as an American counterespionage official, approaches Bruce, hoping to lure her into "borrowing" secret naval plans via Thomas Aldrich (Ellison)--he being the playboy son of a civilian official.

CARRY ON SPYING   (Warner-Pathé/Anglo Amalgamated, 1964)   87 min.

Producer, Peter Rogers; associate producer, Frank Bevis; director, Gerald Thomas; screenplay, Talbot Rothwell, Sid Colin; assistant director, Peter Bolton; art director, Alex Vetchinsky; music-music director, Eric Rogers; songs, Alex Alstone and Geoffrey Parsons, Eric Rogers; sound, C. C. Stevens; camera, Alan Hume; editor, Archie Ludski.

Kenneth Williams (Desmond Simkins); Bernard Cribbins (Harold Crump); Charles Hawtrey (Charlie Bind); Barbara Windsor (Daphne Honeybutt); Eric Pohlmann (The Fat Man); Eric Barker (The Chief); Dilys Laye (Lila); Jim Dale (Carstairs); Richard Wattis (Cobley); Judith Furse (Dr. Crow); Victor Maddern (Milchmann); Frank Forsyth (Professor Stark); Gertan Klauber (Code Clerk); John Bluthal (Headwaiter); Jill Mai Meredith (Cigarette Girl); Norah Gordon (Elderly Woman); Norman Mitchell (Native Policeman); Angela Ellison (Cloakroom Girl); Hugh Futcher (Scrawny Native); Tom Clegg (Doorman); Renee Houston (Madame); Derek Sydney (Algerian).

It was inevitable that England's long-sustained Carry on film series would turn its attention to the James Bond métier, resulting in an occasionally diverting mockery more intent on the obligatory smutty double entendre than in lampooning a newly-rejuvenated format.

When formula X is stolen from the research lab of the British War Department, B.O.S.H. (British Operational Security) goes into action, fully aware that S.T.E.N.C.H. (Society for Total Extinction of Non-Conforming Humans) is at the bottom of the foul deed. To combat the perilous Dr. Crow (Furse), B.O.S.H., being shorthanded, sends group trainee Williams and his crew of new recruits to Vienna, and then to Algiers. The novices manage to recover formula X from S.T.E.N.C.H.'s agent The Fat Man (Pohlmann) but their success is short-lived.

CARTES SUR TABLE [Attack of the Robots] (Speva/Cine-Alliance/Hesperia, 1965) 95 min.

Producer, Henri Baum; director, Jess Franco; story, Franco; adaptation-dialog, Jean-Claude Carriere; music, Paul Misraki; sets, Jean d'Eaubonne, Carlos Viudes; camera, Antonio Macasoli; editor, Marie-Louise Barberot.

Eddie Constantine (Pereira); Françoise Brion (Lady Cecelia); Sophie Hardy (Cynthia); Fernando Rey (Sir Percy); and: Alfred Mayo, Marcelo Arroita-Jaurequi, Maria Laso.

A formula is developed which turns men into killer robots and agent Pereira (Constantine) and his girlfriend Cynthia (Hardy) are soon combatting both the robots and the Chinese spies who have hijacked the formula.

"The eternal story of the mad scientist who plans to dominate the world and is brought back to reason by the last James Bond look-alike. ...His [Franco] direction is not without merit and yet the spectacle is dull and provides no surprises, even granted there are a few amusing ideas to be found in this yarn" (L'Humanité).

Eddie Constantine in <u>Cartes sur Table</u> (Speva, 1965).

CARVE HER NAME WITH PRIDE (J. Arthur Rank, 1958)   119 min.

Executive producer, Earl St. John; producer, Daniel M.
Angel; associate producer, Hugh Perceval; director, Lewis Gilbert;
based on the book by R. J. Minney; screenplay, Vernon Harris, Gil-
bert; art director, Bernard Robinson; music, William Alwyn; music
director, Muir Mathieson; assistant director, Frederick Stark;
sound, C. P. Stevens, Gordon K. McCallum; special effects, Bill
Warrington, Lionel Banes; camera, John Wilcox; editor, John
Shirley.
Virginia McKenna (Violette Szabo); Paul Scofield (Tony
Fraser); Jack Warner (Mr. Bushell); Denise Gray (Mrs. Bushell);
Alain Saury (Etienne Szabo); Maurice Ronet (Jacques); Anne Leon
(Lillian Rolfe); Sydney Tafler (Potter); Avice Landone (Vera At-
kins); Nicole Stephane (Denise Block); Noel Willman (Interrogator);
Bill Owen (N. C. O. Instructor); Billie Whitelaw (Winnie); William
Mervyn (Colonel Buckmaster); Michael Goodliffe (Coding Expert);
Andre Maranne (Garage Man); Harold Lang (Commandant Suhren).

"Without breaking any new ground, ... [the film] nevertheless stands out as a dignified and absorbing picture" (Variety).
Thanks to a straightforward performance by McKenna in the role

of the real life Violette Szabo, the movie glows as a satisfying tribute to an ordinary girl, full of commonplace fears and emotions, who is uplifted to high dignity by carrying out her wartime spying assignments. The film's detached, almost impersonal style makes Carve Her Name with Pride a far cry from the "similar" screen exercises by Anna Neagle and producer-director Herbert Wilcox decades earlier.

In the late 1930s, British shop assistant Violette Szabo (McKenna), living in a modest London suburb, is hardly touched by the war. Then she weds a French Foreign Legion officer who two years later is killed in action in Africa, leaving her to care for their little girl. Suddenly McKenna resolves to do her bit for the Allied effort and volunteers for a dangerous mission into Occupied France, made feasible because she is half-French and speaks the language well, and because she has always been a physical fitness enthusiast. Her partner on the trek is fellow commando Tony Fraser (Scofield). On her second assignment behind the German lines she is caught and sent to the notorious Ravensbruck concentration camp where after extreme torture and deprivations she stands erect and proud before the firing squad. For her bravery, she is posthumously awarded the George Cross.

CASABLANCA (WB, 1943) 102 min.

Producer, Hal B. Wallis; director, Michael Curtiz; based on the play Everybody Comes to Rick's by Murray Burnett, Joan Alison; screenplay, Julius J. and Philip G. Epstein, Howard Koch; music, Max Steiner; art director, Carl Jules Weyl; assistant director, Lee Katz; makeup, Perc Westmore; songs, Herman Hupfeld, M.K. Jerome, and Jack Scholl; technical adviser, Robert Aisner; gowns, Orry-Kelly; camera, Arthur Edeson; editor, Owen Marks.

Humphrey Bogart (Rick Blaine); Ingrid Bergman (Ilsa Lund Laszlo); Paul Henreid (Victor Laszlo); Claude Rains (Captain Louis Renault); Conrad Veidt (Major Strasser); Sydney Greenstreet (Signor Farrari); Peter Lorre (Ugarte); S. Z. Sakall (Carl); Madeleine LeBeau (Yvonne); Dooley Wilson (Sam); Joy Page (Annina Brandel); John Qualen (Berger); Leonid Kinsky (Sascha); Helmut Dantine (Jan Brandel); Curt Bois (Pickpocket); Marcel Dalio (Croupier); Corinna Mura (Singer); Ludwig Stössel (Mr. Leuchtag); Ilka Gruning (Mrs. Leuchtag); Charles La Torre (Italian Officer Tonelli); Frank Puglia (Arab Vendor); Dan Seymour (Abdul); Lou Marcelle (Narrator); Martin Garralaga (Headwaiter); Olaf Hytten (Prosperous Man); Monte Blue (American); Paul Porcasi (Native); Albert Morin (French Officer); Creighton Hale (Customer); Henry Rowland (German Officer); Richard Ryen (Heinz); Norma Varden (Englishwoman); Torben Meyer (Banker); Oliver Blake (Blue Parrot Waiter); Gregory Gay (German Banker); William Edmunds (Contact); George Meeker (Friend); George Dee (Casselle); Leo Mostovoy (Fydor); Leon Belasco (Dealer).

The cult movie to end all cult movies, Casablanca grows in esteem and popularity with each passing year, aided no doubt in recent years by Woody Allen's take-off play and movie Play It Again Sam.

The classic film is set in 1940 Casablanca, a city which has become a stopping-off point for all sides of the war: the free French, Vichy France, the Nazis, freedom fighters, pacifists, and profiteers. In the latter two categories is Rick Blaine (Bogart) the American owner of "Rick's Café Americain," the haunt of all the divergent groups in the steaming city. Bogart tries to toe the mark between (Vichy) French Captain Louis Renault (Rains) and Nazi Major Strasser (Veidt), but once he comes into possession of two letters of transit from a sleazy black marketeer (Lorre), he finds that all sides are after the letters and him.

Entering this sweltering North African situation are Victor and Ilsa Laszlo (Henreid, Bergman) a European underground leader and his wife, the latter having had a love affair with Bogart in pre-Occupation Paris. Bogart soon finds himself torn between love of Bergman and his hatred for the Axis. Finally his sense of fair play triumphs. He gives Henreid and Bergman the letters of transit which provides their freedom pass to Lisbon. He and Rains then go off into the fog, bound to a Free French port and to join the Allied war cause.

"The problems of the world are not my department," argues ex-patriot American Rick Blaine (Bogart). "I'm a saloon-keeper." But like everyone and everything else in this slickly-directed Michael Curtiz production, surface appearance is far from reality. For example, within the film, 37-year-old Bogart had left the States in a big hurry some years back (probably due to his involvement in a crime) but then ran guns for the Ethiopians in 1935 and fought on the Loyalist side in the Spanish Civil War of 1936. As the slippery Rains is quick to point out, the underdogs may have paid Bogart well in both instances, but the winning side would have paid him much better. Thus beneath Bogart's exterior cynical coldness pounds a heart beating for justice and, as is later shown via Bergman, for romance.

With Bogart's dual nature as the film's focal point, Casablanca spins its complex, multi-faceted plot web, continually re-affirming the fact that during World War II this coastal French Moroccan city was a hotbed of intrigue, corruption, and desperate attempts by individuals to buy freedom. Operating in this ostensibly "neutral" city are several levels of espionage agents, plying their trades with various degrees of diplomacy and success. These operatives range from Rains' Vichy government-endorsed stool pigeons in the Arab marketplaces, to the brutal staff men of visiting Nazi Veidt, to the toadies available to either side for a price, such as the weasel Ugarte (Lorre) or the bulbous Signor Farrari (Greenstreet).

Championing the side of the Allies (and a bit too glamorously at that) is Henreid of the Continental underground and his wife-accomplice Bergman. The latter has not recovered yet from the

intense love affair with Bogart, and she is presented in the cinematic tradition of a distaff partisan/operative who constantly must
reevaluate her sense of loyalty to the cause in balance with her
love for her husband and her romantic memories ("we'll always
have Paris"). Meanwhile, Henreid's arrival sparks the Casablanca
partisans to new peaks of darings, with secret meetings of the
underground interrupted by Rains' police, and murder and mayhem
snowballing from the attempts to speed Henreid and Bergman on
their way to Lisbon and then on to America.

Casablanca is a sturdy if glossy study of how a sense of
fair play and patriotism leads all manner of individuals into the
world of spying and underground work. As the newly-converted
Free France enthusiast Bogart tells watery-eyed Bergman, "... it
doesn't take much to see that the problems of three little people
don't amount to a hill of beans in this crazy world. Someday
you'll understand that. Here's looking at you kid. " With that,
Bogart and Rains wend their way to the Free French garrison at
Brazzaville, to join the countless others who lead the dual lives
of citizen and spy for love of country, ideals, or money.
An interesting aspect of Casablanca, which with its famed
tune "As Time Goes By, " has been termed one of the greatest
romantic screen melodramas ever assembled in Hollywood, is that
its reputation and popularity has survived both the post-World War
II Hollywood neo-realism and the later James Bond sex-and-mayhem screen movements. Iconoclastic cinema reviewer and scholar
Andrew Sarris (Village Voice) is a leading exponent of the theory
that in actuality Casablanca, with its facile depiction of the work-
aday World War II spy and partisan milieu, is actually an anti-
romantic movie; that in practicality, global adventurer Bogart is far
better off and happier going on to new escapades with witty woman-
izer Rains, who can be his comrade in arms, rather than Bogart
having to settle down to the tedium of a regimented life with moody
Bergman.

THE CASE OF SERGEANT GRISCHA (RKO, 1930) 8,261 feet

Producer, William Le Baron; director, Herbert Brenon;
based on the novel Der Streit um den Sergeanten Grischa by Arnold
Zweig; adaptation, Elizabeth Meehan; art director, Max Ree; assist-
ant director, Raoul Spindola, Ray Lissner; sound, John Tribby;
camera, Roy Hunt; editor, Marie Halvey.
Chester Morris (Sergeant Grischa Poprotkin); Betty Compson
(Babka); Alec B. Francis (General von Lychow); Gustav von Seyffer-
titz (General Schieffenzahn); Jean Hersholt (Posnanski); Paul Mc-
Allister (Corporal Sacht); Leyland Hodgson (Lt. Wenfried); Raymond
Whitaker (Alhoscha); Bernard Siegel (Verressjeff); Frank McCor-
mack (Captain Spierauge/Kolga); Percy Barbette (Sgt. Fritz); Hal
Davis (Birkholz).

When initially released, The Case of Sergeant Grischa was

ballyhooed by the studio as a "dramatic masterpiece," reasoning
that any film of the time which departed so radically from the then
popular musical comedy genre had to be considered a sturdy creative
effort.   However, the public did not cotton to the semi-symbolic
presentation, nor was its melancholy story line and bleak ending
easily acceptable to Depression-weary filmgoers.

Taking place in the dark winter of 1917 in a German prison
camp in Poland, the plot revolves around a Russian soldier (Morris) who escapes the compound to see his wife (Compson) and their
newborn child.   After a time he is driven to return to his homeland.   Compson aids Morris by passing him off with the identity
card of a dead soldier.   However, while seeking food, Morris is
captured on the Eastern Front and German commander (von Seyffertitz) condemns him to death as a spy.   After a time Morris' true
identity is established by his nephew (Hodgson) and an advocate
(Hersholt), the latter unsuccessfully trying to have the execution
order reversed.   Posing as a peddler, Compson plans her husband's
escape, but he prefers to place his faith in General von Lychow
(Francis), who after a violent confrontation with von Seyffertitz
sends an order to have the death sentence cancelled.   The telegram,
however, is held up due to a storm, and Morris is executed.

Within The Case of Sergeant Grischa, the subject of spying
is merely a device to put across a strong message of pacifism and,
secondarily, of military reform.   Director Herbert Brenon, who
had done several other anti-war films (e. g. , War Brides, Beau
Geste), put forth with a vehemence the essence of Zweig's novel,
emphasizing the futility of war in his philosophical presentation.

Critics of the day were not overly impressed with the feature.
As the New York Times analyzed, "... it takes a great deal more
than a tragic ending to make a pictorial story dramatic." Many
people found it hard to believe that there could be so much wrangling
over the shooting of a Russian prisoner when the High Command
should have been concerned with more pressing wartime problems.

CASINO ROYALE   (Columbia, 1967)   C   130 min.

Producers, Charles K. Feldman, Jerry Bresler; associate
producer, John Dark; directors, John Huston, Ken Hughes, Val
Guest, Robert Parrish, Joe McGrath; suggested by the novel by
Ian Fleming; screenplay, Wolf Mankowitz, John Law, Michael
Sayers; costumes, Julie Harris; music, Burt Bacharach; choreography, Tutte Lemkow; assistant directors, Roy Baird, John Stone-
man, Carl Mannin; song, Bacharach and Hal David; production designer, Michael Stringer; art director, John Howell, Ivor Beddoes,
Lionel Couch; set decorator, Terence Morgan; titles and montage
effects, Richard Williams; makeup, Neville Smallwood, John O'Gorman; sound, John W. Mitchell, Sash Fisher, Bob Jones, Dick Chris
Greeham; special effects, Cliff Richardson, Roy Whybrow; camera,
Jack Hildyard; additional camera, John Wilcox, Nicolas Roeg; editor, Bill Lenny.

Peter Sellers (Evelyn Tremble); Ursula Andress (Vesper

Lynd); David Niven (Sir James Bond); Orson Welles (Le Chiffre);
Joanna Pettet (Mata Bond); Daliah Lavi (The Detainer); Woody
Allen (Jimmy Bond alias Dr. Noah); Deborah Kerr (Agent "Mimi"
a. k. a. Lady Fiona McTarry); William Holden (Ransome); Charles
Boyer (Le Grand); John Huston (M/a. k. a. McTarry); Kurt Kasznar
(Smernov); George Raft (Himself); Jean-Paul Belmondo (French
Legionnaire); Terence Cooper (Cooper); Barbara Bouchet (Money-
penny); Angela Scoular (Buttercup); Gabriella Licudi (Eliza); Tracey
Crisp (Heather); Anna Quayle (Frau Hoffner); Hermione Baddeley
(Headmistress); Mona Washbourne (Tea Lady); Elaine Taylor (Peg);
Jacqueline Bisset (Miss Goodthighs); Alexandra Bastedo (Meg);
Derek Nimmo (Hadley); Ronnie Corbett (Polo); Colin Gordon
(Hones, the Casino Director); Bernard Cribbins (Taxi Driver);
Tracy Reed (Fang Leader); John Bluthal (Casino Doorman/M. I. 5
Man); Geoffrey Bayldon (Q); John Wells (Quartermaster-Storekeeper);
Duncan MacRae (Inspector Mathis); Graham Stark (Cashier); Richard
Wattis (British Army Officer); Penny Riley (Control Girl); Chic
Murray (Chic); Vladek Sheybal (Le Chiffre's Representative); Jona-
than Routh (John); Percy Herbert (First Piper); Jeanne Roland
(Captain of the Guards); Peter O'Toole (Scottish Piper); Stirling
Moss (Driver) and: Alexander Dore, Arthur Mullard.

James Bond and the world had come a long way since Barry
Nelson portrayed 007 in a quickly-forgotten rendering of Casino
Royale on "Climax" (CBS-TV, October 21, 1954). Later, producers
Charles K. Feldman and Jerry Bresler made what they thought was
the literary coup of the decade by grabbing the screen rights to Ian
Fleming's Casino Royale, a property which they eventually carried
to Columbia Pictures and packaged into a $12 million extravaganza
with five directors, overloaded with uncomfortable guest stars.
"At times, it seemed that the only joke in the film was the impunity
with which the name of James Bond was bandied about" (Andrew
Sarris in The Village Voice). One wit called Casino Royale more
a talent agent than a spy agent show, and most people concluded that
the comic moments were so artificial and the dialog so witless, that
it was a rousing bore. According to the post-mortem consensus, it
was too late in the James Bond craze to find anything left worthwhile
to parody.
        Because S. M. E. R. S. H. is rapidly snowballing in global
powers, the chiefs of the American, British, French, and Soviet
secret services meet to discuss a possible solution. Their conclusion is that Sir James Bond (Niven) must be yanked out of retire-
ment to cope with the problem. After successfully dallying in Scotland with the alleged "widow" (Kerr) of "M" (Huston)--she is out
to sully Niven's good name--the middle-aged 007 returns to London
where he declares that all operatives on this new mission will be
designated "James Bond" or "007" in order to confuse and confound
the ever-watchful enemy. Niven recruits the richest spy (Andress)
in the world, muscular Cooper, and Mata Bond (Pettet), Niven's
daughter by Mata Hari. Each recruit has a special task: Andress
in particular, is to seduce Evelyn Tremble (Sellers), possessor
of an infallible system for winning at baccarat with Sellers eventually

agreeing to go to the Casino Royale and challenging Le Chiffre
(Welles) to a game of baccarat, thus preventing S. M. E. R. S. H.'s
aim to have Welles refill their coffers.   Meanwhile, Pettet is
sent to Berlin to counter S. M. E. R. S. H.'s efforts to force money
from the major powers.   Which still leaves the devilish Dr. Noah
(Allen), who turns out to be the black sheep of the Bond family,
Niven's no-good nephew, Jimmy Bond.   Allen kidnaps Pettet in a
flying saucer, with Niven in hasty pursuit.   The chase leads to the
Casino where Allen maintains his headquarters.   There Niven un-
leashes his special weapon, the Detainer (Lavi), who gains the
upper hand on Allen, even feeding him a time bomb capsule,
causing the bombastic finale: a huge explosion in which everyone
and everything at the Casino is blown to smithereens.
        The few virtues of this overlong, vulgar non-comedy were
Burt Bacharach's score, a few of the elaborate sets used for
idiotic sight gags, and the Berlin spy school sequence.   James
Bond purists and filmgoing realists who sat through Casino Royale
sadly shook their heads and sighed about the good old days when a
spy was a spy was a spy.

CATCH ME A SPY (J. Arthur Rank, 1971)   C 94 min.

        Producer, Steven Pallos, Pierre Braunberger; associate
producer, Ian La Frenais; director, Dick Clement; based on the
novel by George Marton, Tibor Meray; screenplay, Clement, La
Frenais; assistant director, Kip Gowans; art director, Carmen Dil-
lon; music, Claude Bolling; music director, Anthony Bowles;
sound, Derek Ball, Gerry Humphreys; camera, Christopher Challis;
editor, John Bloom.
        Kirk Douglas (Andre); Marlene Jobert (Fabienne); Trevor
Howard (Sir Trevor Dawson); Tom Courtenay (Baxter Clarke);
Patrick Mower (John Fenton); Bernadette Lafont (Simone); Bernard
Blier (Webb); Sacha Pitoeff (Stefan); Richard Pearson (Haldane);
Garfield Morgan (Jealous Husband); Angharad Rees (Victoria);
Isabel Dean (Celia); Robin Parkinson (British Officer); Jonathan
Cecil (British Attache); Robert Raglan (Ambassador); Jean Gilpin
(Ground Stewardess); Bridget Turner (Woman on Plane); Trevor
Peacock (Man on Plane); Clive Cazes (Rumanian on Plane); Ashley
Trevor, Philip Da Costa (Schoolboys); Robert Gillespie (Man in
Elevator); Sheila Steafel (Woman in Elevator); Bunny May (Elevator
Operator); Fiona Moore, Bernice Stegers (Russian Girls); Dinny
Powell, Del Baker (Heavies).

        An antediluvian exercise in the waning spy picture genre.   It
failed to click overseas [a "compendium of comedy-thriller clichés
culled from almost every film from The 39 Steps on ..." (London
Observer)] and has yet to see American theatrical distribution,
despite its production orientation to the English-speaking market.
        French lass Fabienne (Jobert), a games mistress at a boys'
school, finds that her British husband (Mower)--unknown to her, a
Russian agent--has been arrested by the secret police on their

Bucharest honeymoon and will be returned only in exchange for a
London-detained Russian agent (Blier). But she learns Blier is now
dead, so she sets out to find herself a spy suitable for the trade.
Her efforts to snag Baxter Clark (Courtenay) prove fruitless as he
is merely a government functionary, so she turns her full attentions
onto Andre (Douglas), her Bucharest hotel waiter, who is now in
London. It turns out that Douglas has been smuggling Russian
manuscripts to the West and had used Jobert's suitcase as a vehicle. Jobert tumbles for dimpled Douglas and is confounded when
the British actually arrest him, on her prior accusations, and set
him up for the deadly trade.

There are arch jabs at the cinematic presentation of the
espionage game, but Catch Me a Spy wallows in its own cliches,
from the stock casting of Howard (as Jobert's Foreign Office diplomat uncle) onward. "What emerges is a succession of disjointed
scenes with no controlling style or momentum.... It's one of
those films that were obviously more fun to make than they are
to watch" (British Monthly Film Bulletin).

THE CHAIRMAN (20th-Fox, 1969)   C   99 min.

Producer, Mort Abrahams; director, J. Lee Thompson;
based on the novel by Jay Richard Kennedy; screenplay, Ben Mad-
dow; art director, Peter Mullins; music-music director, Jerry
Goldsmith; assistant director, Ferdinand Fairfax; sound, Dudley
Messenger; camera, Ted Moore; editor, Richard Best.

Gregory Peck (Dr. John Hathaway); Anne Heywood (Kay
Hanna); Arthur Hill (Lt. General Shelby); Conrad Yama (The
Chairman); Francisca Tu (Soong Chu); Keye Luke (Professor Soong
Li); Alan Dobie (Air Commodore Benson); Zienia Merton (Ting
Ling); Eric Young (Yin); Burt Kwouk (Chang Shou); Alan White
(Colonel Gardner); Ori Levy (Alexander Shertov).

Even its cast had great difficulty in working up any proper
enthusiasm for this commercial bomb, whose incisive look at Red
China was as synthetic and superficial as the film's alleged coping
with the ramifications of 1960s push button society, super patriotism,
personal and moral commitment to humanity, and technological advances threatening human life. Most of the picture was shot at
Pinewood Studios, in and about London, at Curmdilli, Wales, and
on a brief foray to Taiwan.

Nobel Prize winner and widower Peck is an American teach-
ing at the University of London. He is baffled when his former
instructor (Luke) writes that it would be impossible for Peck to
visit Red China, but the mystery is clarified when the U.S. President and hawkish military attache Hill persuade Peck to undertake
the trip to find out more about a new enzyme being developed there
by Luke which would enable crops to thrive almost anywhere, thus
creating a source of world power for whomever has the secret at
hand. Peck leaves on his trek armed with a Q-23 miniature transmitter embedded in his skull, which permits Allied Intelligence to

carefully monitor his conversations.   Unknown to Peck the internal
device contains an explosive device which can be activated at will
by Hill.   Eventually Peck is presented to Chairman Mao Tse-Tung
(Yang) at the People's Institute of Molecular Biology at Cheng Tu
and is persuaded to work on the enzyme project by being assured
the Chinese Communist Party will share its discovery with the world.
Luke later commits suicide, having bequeathed a coded copy of the
formula to Peck, who in turn is being hunted by Young of Chinese
security.   Just when it seems that Peck cannot escape his pursuers
and London is about to detonate the living bomb (Peck), who comes
to the rescue but a Red Army unit, alerted by Young's henchman
(Kwouk), really a Russian agent.   The supposed irony of the story
occurs when Peck returns to London and finds that the government
authorities intend to classify Luke's research as top secret and sup-
press its humanitarian uses.
    Cue magazine summed up succinctly the criticism of the
film's wishy-washy approach to an intellectual dilemma: "The film is
patently absurd, and what's worse, dull!"
    British release title: The Most Dangerous Man in the World.

CHANCE MEETING   see   THE YOUNG LOVERS

THE CHARGE OF THE GAUCHOS   (FBO, 1928)   5,487 feet

    Director, Albert Kelly; story, Julian Ajuria; screenplay, W. C.
Clifford; titles Garrett Graham; camera, George Benoit, Nick
Musuraca; editor, George Nichols, Jr.
    Francis X. Bushman (Belgrano); Jacqueline Logan (Monica
Salazar); Guido Trento (Monteros); Paul Ellis (Balcarce); Henry
Kolker (Viceroy); Charles Hill Mailes (Saavedra); John Hopkins
(Lezica); Charles K. French (Salazar); Olive Hasbrouck (Mariana);
Mathilde Comont (Aunt Rosita); Jack Ponder (George Gordon); Lige
Conley (Gomez); Gino Corrado (Moreno); Frank Hagney (Goyeneche).

    The once illustrious silent film matinee idol, Francis X.
Bushman, found his career on the nosedive, and considered himself
lucky to obtain even such roles as the lead in this potboiler.   The
Charge of the Gauchos followed the notion that romantic adventure
stories set in far off places (here South America) required a spy--
a female one at that--for flavor and balance.
    Belgrano (Bushman), known as "the Washington of the
Argentine" organizes the populus in direct revolt against their
Spanish rulers, and even with his badly equipped and poorly trained
army manages to beat the enemy.   One of Bushman's staunchest
helpers is Monica Salazar (Logan), the daughter of a Loyalist.   She
not only loves Bushman and the cause, but risks her life to send
the revolutionists valuable secret information.   Logan's luck nearly
runs out when her duplicity is discovered and she is sentenced to
be beheaded.   However, Bushman and his gaucho army come to her
timely rescue and after the revolution the two lovers wed.

CHARLIE CHAN IN PANAMA   (20th-Fox, 1940)   67 min.

Producer, Sol M. Wurtzel; director, Norman Foster; screen-play, John Larkin, Lester Ziffren; camera, Virgil Miller; editor, Fred Allen.
Sidney Toler (Charlie Chan); Jean Rogers (Kathi Lenesch); Lionel Atwill (Cliveden Compton); Mary Nash (Jennie Finch); Victor Sen Yung (Jimmy Chan); Kane Richmond (Richard Cabot); Chris-Pin Martin (Lt. Montero); Lionel Royce (Dr. Rudolf Grosser); Helen Ericson (Stewardess); Jack La Rue (Manelo); Edwin Stanley (Governor Webster); Frank Puglia (Achmed Halide); Addison Richards (Godley); Edward Keane (Dr. Fredericks); Charles Stevens (Native Fisherman); Max Wagner, Allen Davis (Soldiers); Charles Sherlock (Enlisted Man); Eddie Acuff (Sailor); Harold Goodwin (Military Police); Gloria Roy (Hostess); Jimmy Aubrey (Drunken Sailor); Lane Chandler (Officer); Edward Gargan (Attend-ant); Philip Morris (Plainclothesman); Alberto Morin (Hotel Clerk); Joe Dominguez (Policeman).

Joe Dominguez, Victor Sen Yung, Sidney Toler, and Eddie Acuff in Charlie Chan in Panama (20th-Fox, 1940).

One of the best entries in the Sidney Toler "Charlie Chan" series, this 1940 release had Chan (Toler) and Number Two Son

(Sen Yung) flying to the Panama Canal territory to investigate a
murder.   Shortly they confront a group of Axis spies out to blow
up both the Canal and the American fleet stationed there.   Chan
even dons the disguise of a hat vendor.

Smoothly directed by Norman Foster, the film had an excellent cast of red-herrings--all types of spies and sundry suspicious characters lurking about the vital Canal area.   Several scenes
were well-staged, especially the climax set in an old graveyard
with the Axis leader trying to do in Chan, but naturally being out-
witted.   And of course, epigramatic Charlie has the final flowery
words, "Good naval defense is best guarantee for our peace."

CHARLIE CHAN IN SECRET SERVICE   (Monogram, 1944)   63 min.

Producer, Philip N. Krasne, James S. Burkett; director,
Phil Rosen; based on the character created by Earl Derr Biggers;
screenplay, George Callahan; music director, Karl Hajos; art director, Dave Milton; set decorator, Al Greenwood; assistant director, George Moskov; sound, Glen Glenn; camera, Ira Morgan;
editor, Martin G. Cohn.

Sidney Toler (Charlie Chan); Gwen Kenyon (Inez); Manton
Moreland (Birmingham); Arthur Loft (Jones); Marianne Quon (Iris
Chan); Lela Tyler (Mrs. Winters); Benson Fong (Tommie Chan).

After a two-year hiatus, the "Charlie Chan" series, which
had been dropped by 20th Century-Fox in 1942, was revitalized by
poverty-row studio Monogram with Sidney Toler continuing in the
title role.   To instill some topicality into the property, the Chinese
detective is put to solving the murder of an inventor of a new type
of torpedo.   He soon learns that the late scientist had been done
in by foreign agents anxious to obtain the torpedo's plans.

This entry introduced into the series the character Birmingham (Moreland) as Chan's black chauffeur.   Quon made a one-shot
appearance as Chan's daughter Iris, and Fong appeared as still another son, Tommie, who would appear in additional Monogram
entries.

CIPHER BUREAU   (Grand National, 1938)   70 min.

Producer, Franklyn Warner; associate producer-director,
Charles Lamont; story, Arthur Hoerl, Monroe Shaff; screenplay,
Hoerl; art director, Ralph Berger; assistant director, Ralph Slos-
ser; camera, Arthur Martinelli; editor, Bernard Loftus.

Leon Ames (Major Philip Waring); Charlotte Wynters (Helen
Kane); Don Dilloway (Lt. Paul Waring); Joan Woodbury (Therese
Brahm); Tenen Holtz (Simon Horrick); Gustav von Seyeffertitz
(Albert Grood); Walter Bohm (Anton Decker); Si Wills (Lt. Clarke);
Peter Lyn (Lt. Tydall); Jason Robards (Alfred Ellsworth); Joe
Romantini (Robert Wormer); Hooper Atchley (Commander Nash);
Tudor Williams (Norfolk Officer); Carl Stockdale (Judge); Robert

Frazer (Paul's Counsel); Sidney Miller (Jimmy); John Smart (Cas-
lon); Stanley Blystone (Army Lieutenant); Franklyn Parker (Announcer); and: Bud Geary, Bill Stahl, Ray Hanson, Jeanette Noo-
son, Bobby Johnston, Virgil Owens, Duke Shenrer, Ray Mesker,
Bobby Barber.

In late 1938, America was just breathing a sigh of relief
that the foreign spies-on-home-ground-scare was more a false
alarm than a reality (an assumption later proven to be false), but
the U.S. public was freshly interested in the subject of espionage.
Hence such a quickie as Cipher Bureau.

Philip Waring (Ames), group chief of this American undercover branch, is put on the track of a security leak that threatens
to put the plans of a new naval gun into the hands of the enemy
(never named, but they have distinct Teutonic surnames and accents).
Eventually, he latches on to a radio performing piano soloist who
just might be an enemy agent passing along coded messages on the
airwaves.

CLIPPED WINGS (AA, 1953)   65 min.

Producer, Ben Schwalb; director, Edward Bernds; story,
Charles R. Marion; screenplay, Marion, Elwood Ullman; art di-
rector, David Milton; camera, Harry Neumann; editor, Bruce B.
Pierce.

Leo Gorcey (Slip); Huntz Hall (Sach); Bernard Gorcey
(Louie); David Condon (Chuck); Bennie Bartlett (Butch); Renie
Riano (W.A.F. Sergeant Anderson); Todd Karns (Lt. Moreno); June
Vincent (Dorene); Mary Treen (Mildred); Philip Van Zandt (Eckler);
Frank Richards (Dupre); Michael Ross (Anders); Elaine Riley
(Sergeant White); Jeanne Dean (Hilda); Anne Kimbell (Allison).

Still plugging along in their third decade of Bowery Boys
antics, the regular crew (Hall and Leo and Bernard Gorcey) foul
up the Air Force in this entry, and with their innocent buffoonery
do almost as much damage to national security as the spy ring
they encounter.

For those who consider Hall's verbal and facial prattling
an art, the film's highlight becomes the moment when the Neander-
thal-looking comedian is assigned to a W.A.F. barracks by error.

CLOAK AND DAGGER (WB, 1946)   106 min.

Producer, Milton Sperling; director, Fritz Lang; story,
Boris Ingster, John Larkin; screenplay, Albert Maltz, Ring Lard-
ner, Jr.; art director, Max Parker; set decorator, Walter Tilford; costumes, Leah Rhodes; music, Max Steiner; orchestrator,
Hugo Friedhofer; assistant director, Russell Saunders; technical
adviser, Michael Burke; sound, Francis J. Scheid; special effects,
Edwin B. Du Par; camera, Sol Polito; editor, Christian Nyby.

Gary Cooper (Professor Alvah Jesper); Lilli Palmer (Gina); Robert Alda (Pinkie); Vladimir Sokoloff (Polda); J. Edward Bromberg (Trenk); Marjorie Hoshelle (Ann Dawson); Ludwig Stössel (The German); Helene Thimig (Katerin Lodor); Dan Seymour (Marsoli); Marc Lawrence (Luigi); James Flavin (Colonel Walsh); Pat O'Moore (The Englishman); Charles Marsh (Erich); Don Turner (Lingg); Clifton Young (American Commander); Ross Ford (Paratrooper); Robert Coote (Cronin); Hans Schumm, Peter Michael (German Agents); Yola d'Avril, Claire du Brey, Lottie Stein (Nurses); Lynne Lyons (Woman in Bank--Double); Rory Mallinson (Paul); Ed Parker, Gil Perkins (Gestapo Men); Bruce Lester, Holmes Herbert (British Officers); Leon Lenoir (Italian Soldier); Otto Reichow, Arno Frey (German Soldiers); Maria Monteil, Lillian Nicholson (Nuns); Bobby Santon (Italian Boy); Elvira Curci (Woman in Street); Hella Crossley (Rachele); Douglas Walton (British Pilot); Vernon Downing (British Sergeant); Frank Wilcox (American Officer); Michael Burke (O. S. S. Agent).

In World War II, the Office of Strategic Services (O. S. S.) was often forced into recruiting unusual civilians for their espionage missions against the Axis. Such a case was physics Professor Alvah Jesper (Cooper) who near the end of World War II is working on the famed Manhattan Project and is well familiar with the data surrounding nuclear fission. According to O. S. S. Colonel Walsh (Flavin) Cooper would be perfect to analyze the information coming in from O. S. S. agents in Europe. The professor is asked to volunteer for the assignment. He agrees and is sent to Switzerland to find a doctor (Sokoloff), an atomic scientist held by the Nazis. Cooper contacts an Austrian scientist (Thimig) to obtain information on the doctor, but is spotted by a Nazi spy (Hoshelle). Pushing on to Italy he meets a local partisan (Palmer) and is helped by an Allied agent (Alda). Through a carefully manipulated plan, Sokoloff is found and flown to the U. S., with Cooper vowing to return at war's end to claim Palmer.

Cloak and Dagger was among several films (the others included O. S. S. and The Beginning or the End) which directly resulted from the post-war opening of the O. S. S.'s files to Hollywood for a three-week study period. The Warner Bros.' picture was rushed into production under director Fritz Lang: what was intended to emerge as a realistic spy tracking drama, however, became an uneasy blend of romance and outdated patriotism. Thus one finds the film filled with plot contrivances in order to progress the love scenes between Cooper and Palmer (the ads read, "The Moment He Fell in Love Was His Moment of Greatest Danger!"), and instances of forced humanitarianism (Cooper's final speech: "God have mercy on us if we haven't the sense to keep the world at peace"). Homer Dickens in The Films of Gary Cooper (1970) pointed out another weakness of the picture: the performance of Cooper. "He wasn't bad in the role, but his total American demeanor was a bit hard to accept when one knew he wasn't supposed to be detected."

CODE NAME: HERACLITUS (Universal/NBC-TV, 1967) C
104 min.

Director, James Goldstone; screenplay, Alvin Saplinsky.
Stanley Baker (Gannon); Ricardo Montalban (Janacek); Les-
lie Nielsen (Fryer); Signe Hasso (Lydia); Jack Weston (Gerberman);
Malachi Throne (Hoffman); Sheree North (Sally); Don Hammer
(Baldy); Robert Cinder (Macpherson); Kurt Kaszner (Lydia's Husband).

Initially telecast as two segments of the "Bob Hope Chrysler
Theatre," this spy drama had theatrical release in Europe. In it
Baker was cast as an agent investigating the possibility that the
widow (Hasso) of a spy (Kasner) might be herself spying and selling
cold war secrets to the enemy.

CODE NAME: JAGUAR see CORRIDA POUR UN ESPION

CODE NAME: TIGER see LE TIGRE AIME LA CHAIR FRAICHE

COME SPY WITH ME (20th-Fox, 1965) C 85 min.

Executive producer, Alan V. Iselin; producer, Paul M. Hel-
ler; director, Marshall Stone; story, Stuart James; screenplay,
Cherney Berg; music, Bob Bowers; songs, William "Smoky" Robin-
son, Jr. and P.J. Butler; art director, Howard Barker; costumes,
Georganne Aldrich; makeup, Clay Lambert; assistant director,
Charles O. Keen; sound, John W. Barry; camera, Zoli Victor;
editor, Hy Goldman.
Troy Donahue (Pete Barker); Andrea Dromm (Jill Parson);
Albert Dekker (Walter Ludiker); Lucienne Bridou (Linda); Mart
Hulsivit (Larry Claymore); Valerie Allen (Samantha); Dan Ferrone
(Augie); Howard Schell (Corbett); Chance Gentry (Chance); Louis
Edmonds (Gunthe Stiller); Kate Aldrich (Chris); Pam Colbert (Pam);
Gil Pratley (Kieswelter); George Shorican (Pantin); Alston Bair
(Keefer); Tim Moxon (Morgan); Eric Covesly (Karl); Jack Lewis
(Brooks); Peter Finch (Man in Hotel Lobby).

A flimsy, independently-produced clinker whose sole virtue
is its on-location Jamaican scenery. The anemic plot has U.S.
intelligence assign Jill Parson (Dromm) to investigate the death of
two secret agents in the Caribbean. The U.S. spy agency fears
that these murders indicate a threat to the upcoming world leaders
meeting to be held aboard an aircraft carrier stationed in the area.
Ex-beachboy star Donahue performed as Pete Barker, a local charter
boat carrier, with Dekker the enemy chief at bay.

COMMENT QU'ELLE EST!   (Prodis, 1960)   91 min.

Producer director, Bernard Borderie; based on the novel
I'll Say She Does by Peter Cheyney; screenplay, Borderie, Marc-
Gilbert Sauvajon; settings, René Moulaert; music, Paul Misraki;
sound, René Sarrazin; camera, Robert Juillard; editor, Christian
Gaudin.

Eddie Constantine (Lemmy Caution); André Luguet (General
Rupert); Françoise Brion (Martine); Françoise Prevost (Isabelle);
Alfred Adam (Girotti); Renaud Mary (Demur); Robert Berri (Donbie);
Nicholas Vogel (Mayne); Fabienne Dali (Danielle); Jacques Seiler
(Commissioner); Henri Cogan (Mucco).

After a several year lay-off from his Lemmy Caution role-
playing, actor Constantine returned in a new adventure of the
American F. B. I. agent, this time joining with the French Secret
Service in corraling a master spy.
"The precision of comedy, the natural ease and nonchalance
of the director make this film one of the best in the genre.   Constantine has never been so relaxed, natural and less prone to
tricks.... Comment Qu'elle Est! is in every aspect made with care
and remarkably played" (Radio Cinéma).

THE CONFESSION   see L'AVEU

CONFESSIONS OF A NAZI SPY   (WB, 1939)   102 min.

Director, Anatole Litvak; based on material gathered by
Leon G. Turrou; screenplay, Milton Krims, John Wexley; camera,
Sol Polito.

Edward G. Robinson (Ed Renard); Francis Lederer (Schneider);
George Sanders (Schlager); Paul Lukas (Dr. Kassel); Henry O'Neill
(District Attorney Kellogg); Lya Lys (Erika Wolff); Grace Stafford
(Mrs. Schneider); James Stephenson (Scotland Yard Man); Fred
Tozere (Phillips); Sig Rumann (Krogman); Dorothy Tree (Hilda);
Celia Sibelius (Mrs. Kassel); Joe Sawyer (Renz); Lionel Royce
(Hintze); Hans von Twardowsky (Wildebrandt); Henry Victor (Hell-
dorf); Frederick Vogeding (Captain Richter); George Rosener
(Klauber); Robert Daws (Straubel); John Voigt (Westphal); Willy
Kaufman (Grutezwald); William Vaughn (Captain Von Eichen); Jack
Mower (McDonald); Robert Emmett Keane (Harrison); Eily Malyon
(Mrs. MacLaughlin); Frank Mayo (Staunton); Alec Craig (Postman);
Jean Brooks (Kassel's Nurse); Lucien Prival (Kranz); Niccolai
Yoshkin (Man); Bodil Rosing (Anna); Charles Sherlock (Young);
Frederick Burton (U. S. District Court Judge); John Deering (Nar-
rator); Ward Bond (American Legionnaire Thrown out of Bund
Meeting); John Ridgeley (Army Hospital Clerk); Emmett Vogan
(Hotel Clerk); Edward Keane, John Hamilton (F. B. I. Men); Selmer
Jackson (Customs Official); Egon Brecher (Nazi Agent); Martin
Kosleck (Goebbels); Edwin Stanley (U. S. Official).

"Like a real mountain among cardboard foothills. Confessions of a Nazi Spy looms large above the dozens of phony spy pictures of the past decade" (Daily Worker).

Not since the making of Little Caesar, Public Enemy, and Scarface in the early 1930s had one film engendered so much favorable publicity as being the product of earnest civic and patriotic concern by a major filmmaker. The American conscience had been stirred greatly in 1938 when it was publically acknowledged (via courtroom trials) that Axis Fifth Columnists were operating on a large scale within the continental U. S. A. Warner Bros. claimed its feature was "ripped from the headlines" of this spectacular espionage infiltration and the American public took the film's semidocumentary presentation to heart.

The movie opens in Scotland with an elderly lady, a Nazi collaborator, receiving mail from around the globe. When she refuses a stamp collector some of the foreign stamps, he is aroused by her peculiar reaction to refer her activities to the authorities who discover she is a member of an international Nazi spy ring. The action then shifts to the U. S. where a man named Schneider (Lederer) has the Nazi plans to kidnap an American Air Force general. A G-Man, Ed Renard (Robinson), gets on his trail and through the interrogation of Lederer uncovers a nest of Nazis operating in this country. Using Lederer as a link to German-Americans with Third Reich sympathies, the FBI is able to clamp down on the German saboteurs.

Despite its realistic overtones, Confessions of a Nazi Spy reeks with overzealousness. On the one hand it attempts to differentiate between good and bad Germans, but then proceeds to suggest that nearly anyone involved with the U. S. -based German Bunds may be an enemy operative, or at least, a person likely to be a security risk. At the end of the film Robinson states, "After working on this case for so many months I feel as if I had been walking through a madhouse." With such a dastardly spy network as that headed by Lukas, Sanders, Lys, and Tree in the film, one can appreciate G-man Robinson's reaction. This quartet of sinister figures, along with their underlings, represented all that Americans had been told to fear of the Nazis' totalitarianism regime. In contrast, only vaguely through Lederer's character did the picture try to present the other side of the coin: that these Germans believed in their cause and were being as loyal and steadfast in their undercover activities abroad as the FBI agents were in combatting them.

Confessions of a Nazi Spy had a tremendous emotional impact when initially released here. Abroad the reaction was quite different, with the press suggesting that at last America was finally acknowledging what Europe had known for years. Eighteen Latin American and European countries barred showings of this picture. Poland was one country that disregarded the Nazi protests against the movie, and it is claimed that seven threatre operators who showed the picture in Warsaw were hanged following the German occupation. In June 1940 the film was re-released with new explanatory narrative added to bring the storyline up to date.

With its documentary tone, Confessions of a Nazi Spy set the mood for the better spy pictures to come, no longer a genre to be taken lightly as the springboard for whimsical entertainment but the subject of meaty, topical drama.

CONFIDENTIAL AGENT (WB, 1945) 118 min.

Producer, Robert Buckner; director, Herman Shumlin; story, Graham Greene; screenplay, Robert Buckner; dialog director, Jack Daniels; assistant director, Arthur Kueker; art director, Leo Kuter; set decorator, William Kuehl; music, Franz Waxman; music director, Leo F. Forbstein; sound, Oliver S. Garretson; camera, James Wong Howe; editor, George Amy.

Charles Boyer (Denard); Lauren Bacall (Rose Cullen); Katina Paxinou (Mrs. Melandez); Peter Lorre (Contreras); George Coulouris (Captain Curris); Wanda Hendrix (Else); John Warburton (Forbes); Dan Seymour (Mr. Muckerji); George Zucco (Inspector Geddes); Miles Mander (Brigstock); Lawrence Grant (Lord Fetting); Holmes Herbert (Lord Benditch); Art Foster (Chauffeur); Olaf Hytten (Harry Bates); Herbert Wyndham (Fortescue); William Stack (Butler); Herbert Clifton (Jarvis); D. Martin Jones (Detective); Bill Ellfeldt, Leighton Noble (Piano Players); Jack Carter, Stanley Mann (Singers);Arthur Gould Porter (Passenger Flirt); Alec Harford (Bartender); Gordon Richards (Immigration Officer); Keith Hitchcock (Plainclothesman); Charles Knight, Montague Shaw (Customs Officers); Lynne Baggett (Singer); Gerald Hamer (Waiter); Laura Treadwell (White-Haired Woman); James Fowler (Attendant); Grayce Hampton (Woman on Road); Percival Vivian (Man on Road); Rosemary Sharples (Patron); Ruth Vivian (Secretary); Ian Wolfe (Dr. Bellows); Gilbert Allen (London Bobby); Guy Bellis (Butler); Trevor Tremain (Policeman); Creighton Hale (Postman); Brandon Hurst (Lancashire Man on Train); Charles McNaughton, Reggie Sheffield, Cyril Delavanti, Bobby Hale, George Broughton (First Mining Group); Barbara Broughton (Woman Praying); David Hughes, Colin Campbell, Tom Pilkington, Arthur Stenning, Harry Allen, Wilson Benge, Allan Edmiston, Wally Scott, Cyril Thornton, Will Stanton, Ben Webster, George Kirby, Charles Hall, Daniel M. Sheridan, Bob Stephenson, Al Ferguson, Frank Hagney, Frank Leigh (Second Mining Group); Lylian Grene, Marie DeBecker, Hilda Plowright, Clara Reid, Sylvia Andrew, Pat Donison, Mae Roberts, Dorrie Leon (Miners' Wives); Geoffrey Steele (Hotel Clerk); Henry Mowbray (Radigan); Rex Evans (Hanley); Harry Cording, James Logan (Rugged Men); John Rodgers (Seaman); Leyland Hodgson (Freight Officer).

Had Graham Greene's 1939 anti-Fascist thriller been picturized much earlier than 1945, it would have been a far more cogent study of counter-factions struggling in espionage-ridden pre-World War II England, than it actually was.

In 1937, Spanish concert musician turned Loyalist soldier Boyer is sent to England to prevent a shipment of coal from

Art Foster, Victor Francen, Lauren Bacall, and George Coulouris
in Confidential Agent (WB, 1945).

reaching Nationalist hands.   In direct contrast to the usual stereotype, Boyer's spy character is not a glamorous figure, but a life-
beaten middle-aged man who not only has lost his wife and child in
the Spanish Civil War, but has seen his career and ideals gone up
literally in smoke.   He succeeds in his mission, not through any
unique genius on his part but from stubborness and a good dash
of luck.
    To fill out story conventions, Boyer is aided in his tough
task by Bacall, the bored daughter of a British coal tycoon.   At
one point she announces "I hate melodrama," not realizing that she
and her new-found companion (he of the tattered overcoat and bat-
tered hat) are embarking on a full scale "penny dreadful" of their
own, forced to battle the cunning and brawn of Nazi agents Lorre
and Paxinou.
    Despite the good camera work of James Wong Howe, the
slick direction by Herman Shumlin, and the expertise of the Warner
Brothers stock company (Francen, Coulouris, Mander, Seymour,
Zucco, Richards, Wolfe), the final picture did not jell into a
satisfactory whole, as had Greene's exciting book original.   James

Agee of The Nation pinpointed the problem: "It should have been
possible to tell the story in about two-thirds the time taken, without
skipping or slighting anything or seeming at all to hurry; and in
spite of some very good sets and a number of beautiful shots,
Greene's greatest talent--which is, I think, with the look and efflu-
ence of places, streets, and things--is not once even approximated. "

THE CONFORMIST (Paramount, 1970)   C   112 min.

        Producer, Maurizio Ladi-Fe; director, Bernardo Bertolucci;
based on the novel by Alberto Moravia; screenplay, Bertolucci;
music, Georges Delerue; art director, Medo Azzini; costumes, Gitt
Magrini; camera, Vittorio Storaro; editor, Franco Arcalli.
        Jean-Louis Trintignant (Marcello Clerici); Stefania Sandrelli
(Giulia); Gastone Moschin (Manganiello); Enzo Taroscio (Quadri);
Pierre Clementi (Lino Seminara); Dominique Sanda (Anna Quadri);
Christian Alegny (Raoul); Jose Quaglio (Italo); Milly (Marcello's
Mother); Giuseppe Addobbati (Marcello's Father); Yvonne Sanson
(Giulia's Mother); Fosco Giachetti (Colonel); Benedetto Benedetti
(Minister); and: Gino Vagni Luca, Antonio Maestri, Christian
Belegne, Pasquale Fortunato, Marta Lado, Pierangelo Civera, Carlo
Gaddi, Franco Pellerani, Claudio Carpelli, Umberto Silvestri.

        "Not only does the film analyze the roots of Fascism with
X-ray intensity, a theme made popular recently in such films as Z
[1969] and Investigation of a Citizen above Suspicion [1970], but it
also manages to cash in on the 30's revival at the same time.   Indeed, the film could almost be seen as a chamber music version
of Visconti's operatic The Damned [1970]" (Independent Film Journal).
Patriot-traitor, partisan-anti-Resistance; terms no longer seen in
black and white, but now examined with a cerebral firmness that
reveal subversive agents not as amoral James Bond-like robots, but
as conscience-stricken individuals coerced by a variety of factors
into exceptional action.
        Traumatized by a childhood homosexual experience and the
apparent death of his partner (Clementi), Marcello Clerici
(Trintignant) grows to manhood in Mussolini-controlled Italy,
anxious to obtain security and anonymity in adhering to the dictates
of the totalitarian party line.   In 1938 civil servant Trintignant becomes engaged to Giulia (Sandrelli), a girl more sensual than intelligent.   Before they embark on a honeymoon trip to Paris,
Trintignant volunteers his services to the OVRA, the brown shirt
counter-espionage agency, offering to spy upon, and kill if necessary,
his old philosophy professor (Taroscio).   Once in Paris he quickly
falls in love with Anna (Sanda), Taroscio's young wife who soon
spots her suitor as a Fascist spy.   She blandly holds him in con-
tempt while simultaneously engineering the seduction of Sandrelli.
Later Taroscio and Sanda are killed by other OVRA agents, for
Trintignant sits numbly in his car, too frozen with terror to participate in the murders.   Still later, in July, 1943, during the Rome
"celebration" of the downfall of the Fascist regime, Trintignant

wanders through the streets of the city, amazed to have just learned
that his uncultivated wife knew all along about his involvement in
the Paris murders, and even more shocked to come across Clementi,
whom he thought he had indirectly killed many years ago.   The distraught Trintignant denounces Clementi as a Fascist adherent, and
thereafter, finds himself drawn back into his former homosexuality in
his attraction to a young male hustler whom Clementi had just been
importuning.   Unlike his countrymen who are regaining their sense
of perspective, Trintignant's Marcello Clerici is a lost soul, driven
by impulses and personality patterns he can not and will not fathom.

CONSPIRATOR   (MGM, 1950)   87 min.

        Producer, Arthur Hornblow, Jr.; director, Victor Saville;
based on the novel by Humphrey Slater; adaptation, Sally Benson,
Gerald Fairlie; screenplay, Benson; art director, Alfred Junge;
music, John Wooldridge; sound, A. W. Watkins; camera, F. A.
Young; editor, Frank Clarke.

Harold Warrender, Robert Flemyng, and (right) Robert Taylor in
Conspirator (MGM, 1950).

        Robert Taylor (Major Michael Curragh); Elizabeth Taylor

(Melinda Greyton); Robert Flemyng (Captain Hugh Ladhoime); Harold
Warrender (Colonel Hammerbrook); Honor Blackman (Joyce); Mar-
jorie Fielding (Aunt Jessica); Thora Hird (Broaders); Marie Ney
(Lady Pennistone); Wilfrid Hyde-White (Lord Pennistone); Jack
Allen (Ragian); Helen Hayes (Lady Witheringham); Cicely Paget-
Bowman (Mrs. Hammerbrook); Karel Stepanek (Radek); Nicholas
Bruce (Alek); Cyril Smith (Detective Inspector).

  Eighteen-year-old Elizabeth Taylor played her first adult
oncamera role in this film. Her effort was not very successful
but she added decoration to a rather drab and obvious tale. The
film's depiction of British life bore little resemblance to reality,
despite its having been lensed on location in England.

  Naive young Elizabeth weds British army officer Robert
Taylor, little suspecting that her gentlemanly spouse is actually
a Communist agent hopeful of passing along vital military secrets
to the Reds. Although the screenplay made little effort to explicate
Robert Taylor's duplicitous character, the story did have the
courage to avoid a familiar happy finale.

THE CONSPIRATORS (WB, 1944) 101 min.

  Producer, Jack Chertok; director, Jean Negulesco; based on
the novel by Frederick Prokosch; screenplay, Vladimir Pozner, Leo
Rosten; additional dialog, Jack Moffit; art director, Anton Grot; set
decorator, Walter Tilford; music director, Leo F. Forbstein;
assistant director, Reggie Callow; sound, Robert B. Lee; special
effects, William McGann, Willard Van Enger; camera, Arthur
Edeson; editor, Rudi Fehr.

  Hedy Lamarr (Irene Duchatel); Paul Henreid (Vincent Van
Der Lyn); Sydney Greenstreet (Riccardo Quintanilla); Peter Lorre
(Jan Bernaskzky); Victor Francen (Hugh Von Mohr); Joseph Calleia
(Captain Pereira); Carol Thurston (Rosa); Vladimir Sokoloff
(Miguel); Eduardo Ciannelli (General Almeida); Steve Geray (Dr.
Schmitt); Kurt Katch (Lutzge); Gregory Gaye (Anton Wynat); Louis
Mercier (Paulo Leiris); David Hoffman (Antonio); Edward Van Sloan
(Dutchman in Cellar); Jean Jacques du Bois (Bobby Benson); Doris
Lloyd (Mrs. Benson); Phil van Zandt (Gomez); John Arnold,
Michael Gastone, Hal Kelly (Customs Officials); Serge Krizman
(Czech Man); Trudy Glassford (Belgian Girl); Rod De Medici, Jack
Chefe, Eddie Abdo (Immigration Officers); John Bleifer (Polish
Man); George Sorel (Police Officer); Frederick Brunn, Adrian
Droeshout (German Thugs); Roger Neury (Headwaiter); Jacques
Lory (Attendant in Pawnshop); Tony Paton, Dick Botiller, Jay
Novello, Carl Neubert (Detectives); Oscar Loraine (Deschamps);
Christine Gordon (Young Woman); Marguerita Sylva (Older Woman);
Isabelle LaMal (French Woman); Walter Bonn (German); Paul Regas
(Spaniard); Veronica Pataky (Hungarian Woman); Alexander Sacha
(Russian); Billy Roy (Page Boy); Leonid Snegoff, Trevor Bardette
(Men); Sonya Yarr (Russian Woman); Carla Boehm (German Woman);
Leon Belasco (Waiter); Alphonse Martel (Croupier); Frank Reicher

(Casino Attendant); Tony Caruso (Young Fisherman); Pedro Regas, Nick Thompson (Older Fishermen); Paul de Corday (Travel Clerk); Ludwig Hardt (Refugee); Robert Tafur (Policeman); Manuel Lopez (Man on Street); Neyle Marx (Portuguese Boy); Ed Hayns (Hotel Manager); Crane Whitley, Martin Garralaga (Detectives Outside Pawnshop); Harro Meller (General's Secretary); Fred Nurney (Young Attache); Arno Frey (General's Attache); Beal Wong (Japanese Attache); Luis Alberni (Prison Guard); Saul Gorss (Jorge); Art Miles, Robert Barron (Cell Guards); John Mylong (Commandant); Otto Reichow (Slugger); George Macready (Schmitt Con Man); Carmel Myers (Baroness Von Klug); Emil Rameau (Professor Wingby); Leon Lenoir, Erno Verebes, Charles Haefli (Portuguese Fishermen); Louise Lane, Peggy Watts, Buddy Sullivan, John Marlin, Jock Watt, Hans Moebus, Nita Pike, Maurice Brierre, Alex Tamaroff, Sid Dalbrook, Clinton Carey, Paul Bradley, Paul Ravel, Harry Semels, Gertrude Keeler, Fred Fisher, Peggy Watts (Bits).

Having exhausted the environs of Casablanca and Ankara as nests of international intrigue during World War II, Warner Bros. turned to the neutral port of Lisbon for source material and setting. Unfortunately by 1944, the theme of underground agents pitted against guileful Nazis--with surprise good and bad guys popping up all the time--had been overworked. This modestly-received thriller only helped bring the death knell to the genre for the duration.

In spy-plagued Lisbon, Irene Duchatel (Lamarr), wed to Hugh von Mohr (Francen) of the German embassy, is actually employed by the Dutch underground, led by Riccardo Quintanilla (Greenstreet), with Vincent van der Lyn (Henreid)--better known as "The Flying Dutchman"--as its chief heroic partisan. The Portuguese city, or rather the studio's backlot, is crawling with Allied and Nazi agents practicing the usual basic gambits of trickery on each other in such a wearying fashion that the viewer soon tires of the plot ploys. At the turgid finale, Henreid is nobly set to return to Holland, having given languid Lamarr a firm promise that when all this is over....

Director Jean Negulesco dressed up the tattered proceedings with fancy photography, accenting the pseudo-philosophical dialog, and allowed the assemblage of some of Hollywood's slickest screen menaces to romp happily over and through the action. The only new slant to emerge from The Conspirators was the delineation of the exhausting task assigned to the Portuguese police who vainly endeavor to retain a tone of neutrality within their country's borders.

COPLAN FX 18 CASSE TOUT [The Exterminators] (C. F. F., 1965) C 95 min.

Producer, Jean Maumy; director, Ricardo Freda; based on the novel Stop Coplan by Paul Kenny; screenplay, Claude Maroel Richard; art director, Jacques Mawart; music, Michel Magne; camera, Henri Persin; editor, Reny Lichtig.

With: Richard Wyler (Coplan); and: Gil Delamare, Jany Clair, Valeria Ciangotini, Robert Manuel, Maria Rosa Rodriguez,

Jacques Dacqmine, Robert Favart.

Secret agent Coplan (Wyler) is dispatched to investigate the disappearance of two brilliant German nuclear scientists. He is aided in his mission by Israeli agents who are convinced the Egyptians have a part in the kidnapping. It proves that the nefarious organization is constructing a nuclear rocket site at an underground laboratory with plans to destroy New York City, hoping that the Americans will think the attack was Russian-oriented. Movies on TV labeled this a "poor ... espionage thriller."
    U.S. tv title: FX-Superspy.

CORRIDA POUR UN ESPION (Gaumont, 1965)   C   110 min.

Director, Maurice Labio; based on the novel by Claude Rank; screenplay, Rank, Labio, Jean Meckert, Louise Velle; camera, Roger Fellons; editor, Georges Arnstam.
    Ray Danton (Larson); Pascale Petit (Chaton); Roger Hanin (Stewart); Wolfgang Preiss (Captain); Helga Summerfield (Lina); Horst Frank (Scarred Man); Conrado San Martin (Luis).

When it is discovered that the Soviets have placed a Spanish-based American defense installation under television surveillance, secret agent Danton is dispatched to Alicante to rectify the situation. Without a witty script or sufficient budget, the film emerges, to quote La Saison Cinematographique, as "two hours of unwavering tediousness."
    U.S. tv title: Code Name: Jaguar.

COUNT FIVE AND DIE (20th-Fox, 1958)   92 min.

Producer, Ernest Gartside; director, Victor Vicas; based on records of the O.S.S.; screenplay, Jack Seddon, David Pursall; music, John Woolridge; assistant director, Peter Dixon; art director, Den Ashton; makeup, Harold Fletcher; sound, William S. Bland; camera, Arthur Grant; editor, Russell Lloyd.
    Jeffrey Hunter (Captain Bill Ranson); Nigel Patrick (Major Howard); Annamarie Duringer (Rolande Herlog); David Kossoff (Professor Mulder); Claude Kingston (William); Philip Bond (Piet); Rolf Lefebvre (Dr. Faber Radomachey); Larry Burns (Martin, the German Agent); Otto Diamant (Hendryk); Marianne Walla (Karlotta); Beth Rogan (Mary Jane, the Dutch Agent); Arthur Gross (Jan); Robert Raglan (Mill); Peter Prowse (Parrish).

This decent little program filler made in England concerns a British Intelligence unit operating in pre-D-Day London, trying to bluff the Nazis into believing that the major Allied invasion thrust will be spearheaded through Holland. The group, headed by Major Howard (Patrick), operates through a fake documentary film-making company in Soho. Hunter is cast as Captain Bill Ranson,

Jeffrey Hunter, Annamarie Duringer, and Nigel Patrick in Count
Five and Die (20th-Fox, 1958).

an American officer assigned to the case, and Duringer plays a
girl of ambivalent allegiance.
        One of the nicer aspects of Count Five and Die was the
deliberate gray drabness of the film which effectively captured the
grubby, bomb-ridden look of 1944 London. For the record, the
film's title referred to the cyanide capsules that were standard
field equipment for spies.

COUNTER ESPIONAGE (Columbia, 1942) 72 min.

        Producer, Wallace MacDonald; director, Edward Dmytryk;
based upon a work by Louis Joseph Vance; story-screenplay,
Aubrey Wisberg; music director, Morris W. Stoloff; camera,
Philip Tannura; editor, Gene Havlick.
        Warren William (Michael Lanyard); Eric Blore (Jameson);
Hillary Brooke (Pamela); Thurston Hall (Inspector Crane); Fred

Warren William and Stanley Logan in <u>Counter Espionage</u> (Columbia, 1942).

Kelsey (Dickens); Forrest Tucker (Anton Schugg); Matthew Boulton (Inspector Stephens); Kurt Katch (Gustave Sossel); Morton Lowry (Kent Wells); Leslie Denison (Harvey Leeds); Billy Bevan (George Barrow); Stanley Logan (Sir Stafford Hart); Tom Stevenson (Constable Hopkins); Eddie Laughton (Orchestra Leader); Clyde Cook (Huckster); Keith Hitchcock (Williams); Wyndham Standing (Head Waiter); William Von Brincken (Von Ruhoff); William Yetter (Operator); Frank Baker, Herbert Clifton (Squadmen); Eric Wilton (Thomas); Guy Kingsford (Carter); Robert Hale (Newsboy); Heather Wilde (Gertie).

     Another entry in the economy Lone Wolf series.   Once again William portrayed Joseph Louis Vance's debonair jewel thief, this time serving as a secret operative for British Intelligence and trying to ferret out a nest of Nazis in blitzed London.   Aiding the dapper agent was his trustful manservant Jameson (Blore).   Hindering his vital work were Scotland Yard and U.S. investigators, both of whom were unaware of the Lone Wolf's patriotic mission.
     Directed by Edward Dmytryk on the proverbial shoestring

budget, there was little to commend the lumbering programmer beyond William's "pleasant performance" and the injected humor provided by Blore.

THE COUNTERFEIT TRAITOR   (Paramount, 1961) C   140 min.

Producer, William Perlberg; assistant producer, Theodore Taylor; director, George Seaton, based on the book by Alexander Klein; screenplay, Seaton; art director, Tambi Larsen; music, Alfred Newman; sound, Hans Ebel; assistant director, Tom Pevsner; camera, Jean Bourgoin; editor, Alma Macrorie.

William Holden (Eric Erickson); Lilli Palmer (Marianne Mollendorf); Hugh Griffith (Collins); Eva Dahlbeck (Ingrid); Charles Regnier (Wilhelm Kortner); Werner Peters (Bruno Ulrich); Carl Raddatz (Otto Holz); Erica Beer (Klara); Helo Gutschwager (Hans); Ulf Palme (Max Gumpel); Wolfgang Preiss (Colonel Martin Nordoff); Ernst Schröder (Baron von Oldenbourg); Stefan Schnabel (Jaeger); Ingrid van Bergen (Hulda Windler); Holger Hagen (Philip Bowman); Albert Rueprecht (Captain Barlach); Reinhard Kolldenhoff (Colonel Erdmann); Klaus Kinsky (Kindler); Jochen Blume (Dr.

Carl Raddatz, Helo Gutschwager, and William Holden in The Counterfeit Traitor (Paramount, 1962).

Krugman); Max Buchsbaum (Fischer); Peter Capell (Unger); Poul
Reichhardt (Skipper); John Wittig (Sven); Jorgen Reenberg (Poul);
Preben Neergard (Lars); Ejner Federspiel (Professor Björke);
Kai Holm (Gunnar); Erik Schuman (Lieutenant); Martin Berliner
(Porter).

     Once again Hollywood borrowed from fantastic fact to shape
an entertaining action film. Above and beyond the slick presenta-
tion--readily accepted in most quarters--The Counterfeit Traitor
delineated in a somewhat obvious fashion the factors which give
people the courage to become spies, risking their material and
intangible possessions for a cause they believe right, and which
often leads them temporarily to submerge their moral standards to
carry out their espionage tasks.
     In 1942 Eric Erickson (Holden), a naturalized Swede born in
Brooklyn, is an important oil importer in Stockholm. By blackmailing him, British agent Collins (Griffith) is able to persuade
Holden to assist the Allies by supplying them with essential data
on German fuel refineries and troop logistics. In order to do this
Holden is required to insult the Allied cause in public, bypass his
Jewish friends, and boost the grandeur of the Third Reich to one
and all. Soon he is shunned by his family and friends. Holden's
fact gathering assignments lead him to Germany where he recruits
the aid of aristocrat Baron von Oldenbourg (Schröder), friend Otto
Holz (Raddatz), and freedom-dedicated Marianne Mollendorf (Palmer).
A break in the espionage link leads to Palmer's death and to Holden's
near execution, but he manages to escape and, via the Hamburg
and Copenhagen underground, make his way back to Sweden.
     Because of its inordinate length and the pressures of making
a good return on the costly mounting (filming was done on location
in Germany, Denmark, and Sweden), the film contains an over-
balance of synthetic action sequences in relation to the moral
examination of the conscience of a businessman forced into dirty
deeds for a hopefully greater good. Yet there are some very nice
touches woven into the standard cinema trappings. Producer
William Perlberg and director-scripter George Seaton make their
German "monsters" look the way monsters usually look, just like
everyone else, with Holden finding willing helpers from the fatherland because each of them has some very personal axe to grind.
It may have been done before, but the moments on camera in which
the Catholic Mata Hari (Palmer) is tricked at the confessional by a
Gestapo man and later, when Holden's cover is unmasked by a 12-
year-old member (Gutschwager) of the Hitler Youth, are still very
effective cinematic scenes.
     The film concludes on a realistic note, with Holden having
lost both his wife (Dahlbeck), who left him, and a potential other
love (Palmer), who was killed. His only reward: the hope that
his strenuous efforts may have contributed to a quicker end to the
war.

COUNTERSPY (Anglo-Amalgamated, 1953)   68 min.

Producer W. H. Williams; director, Vernon Sewell; story, Julian Symons; screenplay, Guy Elmes, Michael le Fevre; art director, George Haslam; music, Eric Spear; camera, A. T. Dinsdale; editor, G. Muller.

Dermot Walsh (Manning); Hazel Court (Clare); Hermione Baddeley (Del Mar); Alexander Guage (Smith); James Vivian (Larry); Archie Duncan (Jim); Hugh Latimer (Barlow); John Penrose (Paulson).

Accountant Walsh is quite innocently drawn into espionage when he visits the offices of an engineering company to audit the books and is asked by a mysterious woman to retrieve a packet of letters concealed in Penrose's office.   He delivers the letters to the specified address, whereupon he comes upon a corpse in the bath.   A check of the envelope he has been carrying reveals secret plans for jet engines.   His efforts to contact the police are as unsuccessful as his attempts to elude the spies, who draw Walsh's wife Clare (Court) into the misadventure.

"A conventional but quite lively spy thriller, well supplied with action" (British Monthly Film Bulletin).

COWBOY COMMANDOS (Monogram, 1943)   55 min.

Producer, George W. Weeks; director, S. Roy Luby; story, Clark Paylow; screenplay, Elizabeth Beecher; assistant director, Paylow; music, Frank Sanucci; song, Johnny Lange; sound, Lyle Willey; camera, Edward Kull; editor, Roy Claire.

Ray Corrigan (Crash); Dennis Moore (Denny); Max Terhune (Alibi); Evelyn Finley (Joan); Johnny Bond (Slim); Bud Buster (Weiner); John Merton (Fraser); Edna Bennett (Kate); Steve Clark (Bartlett); Bud Osborne (Hans).

The revamped actor trio comprising The Range Busters (Corrigan, Moore, Terhune) were back in Western action again, this time pitted against a new breed of villains, Nazi agents daring to halt the shipments of magnesium from Bartlett's (Clark) mine.   It did not require much perspicacity on the part of the matinee kiddie audience to deduce that Weiner (Buster), Fraser (Merton), Kate (Bennett), and Hans (Osborne) were part of the conspiracy.

To show that its heart was solidly in the right patriotic place, Cowboy Commandos opened with Joan (Finley) stunt riding and then launching into a bond sale plea, speaking right through the camera's eye to the audience.   Later Slim (Bond) entertained with a ditty entitled "I'll Get the Fuehrer Sure as Shootin'."

CRACK-Up (20th-Fox, 1936)   70 min.

Associate producer, Samuel G. Engel; director, Malcolm St.

Clair; story, John Goodrich; screenplay, Charles Kenyon, Sam
Mintz; music director, Samuel Kaylin; songs, Sidney Clare and
Harry Akst; camera, Barney McGill; editor, Fred Allen.
    Peter Lorre (Colonel Gimpy); Brian Donlevy (Ace Martin);
Helen Wood (Ruth Franklin); Ralph Morgan (John P. Fleming);
Thomas Beck (Joe Randall); Kay Linaker (Mrs. Fleming); Lester
Mathews (Sidney Grant); Earle A. Foxe (Operative #30); J. Carrol
Naish (Operative #77); Gloria Roy (Operative #16); Oscar Apfel
(Alfred Kruxton); Paul Stanton (Daniel D. Harrington); Howard C.
Hickman (Major White); Chester Gan (House Boy); Harrison Greene
(Comic at Airport); Lynn Bari (Hostess); Sam Hayes (Announcer at
Airport); Curt V. Fuerberg, Frank Arthur Seales, William von
Brincken (Espionage Agents); Don Brody (Cameraman); Jane Weir,
Almeda Fowler (Sob Sisters); Madge Bellamy (Secretary); Billy
Wayne (Mate); William Benedict (Crumpy); George Offerman, Jr.
(Waiter); Annette Lake (Sauerkraut Woman); Robert E. Homans
(Captain).

    Turned out on the studio backlot with a maximum of speed
for second-bill fodder, this film contained a good cast, a poor plot,
passing direction, and little else. Donlevy was the traitor pilot
who flew the new-styled plane (with its improved propeller thrust
gadget) in its maiden trans-Atlantic crossing from New York to
Berlin (sic), while hero Beck bested the villains in the finale.
Lorre was along as a dimwit who was really a spy for the bad
guys, and Naish passed through the film stuck with the monicker
"Operative 77." The New York Herald-Tribune summed up the
film as "improbable and adolescent. "
    Typical of mid-1930s espionage dramas, Crack-Up only
hinted at the country-of-origin of the villains.

A DANDY IN ASPIC (Columbia, 1968) C 107 min.

    Producer, Anthony Mann; associate producer, Leslie Gilliat;
director, Anthony Mann [died before completion], Laurence Harvey;
based on the novel by Derek Marlowe; screenplay, Marlowe;
assistant director, Jimmy Komisarjevsky; art director, Carmen
Dillon; music-music director, Quincy Jones; titles, Rouxville Pro-
ductions Ltd. ; sound, Peter Davies; camera, Christopher Challis;
editor, Thelma Connell.
    Laurence Harvey (Eberlin); Tom Courtenay (Gatiss); Mia Far-
row (Caroline); Lionel Stander (Sobakevich); Harry Andrews (Fraser);
Peter Cook (Prentiss); Per Oscarsson (Pavel); Barbara Murray
(Heather Vogler); Norman Bird (Copperfield); John Bird (Henderson);
Michael Trubshawe (Flowers); Richard O'Sullivan (Nevil); Geoffrey
Denton (Pond); Geoffrey Lumsden (Ridley); James Cossins (Heston-
Stevas); Calvin Lockhart (Brogue); Geoffrey Bayldon (Lake); Michael
Pratt (Greff); Monika Dietrich (Hedwig); Lockwood West (Quince);
Arthur Hewlett (Moon); Vernon Dobtcheff (Stein); Paulene Stone (Red
Bird).

Laurence Harvey, Tom Courtenay, and Lionel Stander in A Dandy in Aspic (Columbia, 1968).

Russian agent Eberlin (Harvey), who has wormed his way into British Intelligence, has effectively eliminated three of the best English operatives. He is nonplussed when his English superior Fraser (Andrews) orders him to liquidate this unknown assassin. Fortunately--for the moment--Andrews and staff insist that Harvey's contact (Oscarsson) is the chief suspect, but when Oscarsson is murdered, Harvey is sent on a new clue to Berlin where his security partner will be cynical agent Gatiss (Courtenay). The net is drawing tighter and Harvey panics. The Russians repeatedly refuse to grant Harvey asylum, his escape try to East Germany fails, and he has to kill Soviet man Henderson (John Bird) to prevent Courtenay from questioning him and learning the truth about Harvey. Later Courtenay bribes the Russians into revealing the culprit's identity, but to Harvey's relief they insist the trigger man is Copperfield (Norman Bird). The latter is framed and disposed of, Courtenay kills the conniving Russian espionage group head (Stander) in Berlin, leaving a strange about-face and showdown to wind up the picture.

The death of director Anthony Mann before A Dandy in Aspic was completed--Harvey took over as director--created a host of production problems. But the picture had been hamstrung long

before that point by Harvey's wooden performance. There was little
credibility or empathy engendered by his screen character renown
for sartorial elegance and a basic distaste for women (making the
bothersome romance with waif Farrow all the more superfluous).
Much of the other casting reflected the very mechanical nature of
A Dandy in Aspic with such stereotypes as Andrews as the regulation British Intelligence official, and Courtenay as the dispassionate,
ruthless English spy.   Even the arty camera angles could not disguise the déjà vu qualities of nearly everything that transpired,
including yet another guided tour of spy-infested Berlin.   Since
A Dandy in Aspic chose to translate the complex interior action of
the novel--set largely within the lead character's mind, into ex-
ternalized pictorial terms--the basic intellectual dilemma was all
but lost in mundane visual cloak and dagger parading.

DANGER ROUTE   (UA, 1968)   C   95 min.

        Producer, Max J. Rosenberg, Milton Subotsky; associate pro-
ducer, Ted Wallis; director, Seth Holt; based on the novel The

Sylvia Syms and Richard Johnson in Danger Route (UA, 1968).

Eliminator by Andrew York; screenplay, Meade Roberts; music,
John Mayer; song, Lionel Bart; assistant director, Stephen Christian;
costumes, Yvonne Caffin; art director, Don Mingaye; camera, Harry
Waxman; editor, Oswald Hafenrichter.

Richard Johnson (Jonas Wilde); Carol Lynley (Jocelyn); Bar-
bara Bouchet (Mari); Sylvia Syms (Barbara Canning); Diana Dors
(Rhoda); Harry Andrews (Canning); Gordon Jackson (Stern); Maurice
Denham (Ravenspur); Sam Wanamaker (Lucinda).

"Don't expect complete originality from any espionage plot,"
warned critic Frances Herridge (New York Post). "The genre has
been kicked around too often. But this one has tension and surprise
turns all along the way."

Churned out to cash in on the waning spy film craze, Johnson
was cast as a cynical agent, an ex-British commando noted for his
expertise as a top exterminator. Like many another unsung hero of
the global intrigue game, he has had it with his skunky job, and
wants out. But, pleads the upper echelon M.I. 5 officials, there
is just one more job to do. So....

Johnson's new task is to kill a Russian defector currently in
the hands of the FBI. This mission establishes him with four sets
of enemies (the East, the U.S., those who work for both sides, and
some of the British contingent). Along the way there is double-
crossing Lynley and earthy housekeeper Dors.

Above and beyond the asset of Johnson, who would have made
an excellent James Bond, the picture benefits from incisive dialog
and a coating of British crispness.

DANGEROUSLY THEY LIVE   (WB, 1941)   77 min.

Associate producer, Ben Stoloff; director, Robert Florey;
story-screenplay, Marion Parsonnet; art director, Hugh Reticker;
camera, L. William O'Connell; editor, Harold McLernon.

John Garfield (Dr. Michael Lewis); Nancy Coleman (Jane);
Raymond Massey (Dr. Ingersoll); Moroni Olsen (Mr. Goodwin); Lee
Patrick (Nurse Johnson); Christian Rub (Steiner); Roland Drew (Dr.
Murdock); Frank Reicher (Jarvis); Esther Dale (Dawson); John
Harmon (George the Taxi Driver); James Seay (Carl); Frank M.
Thomas (Ralph Bryan); Ilka Gruning (Mrs. Steiner); Gavin Muir
(Captain Strong); Matthew Boulton (Captain Hunter); Arthur Ayls-
worth (Gate Keeper); Ben Welden (Eddie); Cliff Clark (John Dill);
Glen Cavender (Tobacconist); Adolph Milar (Storekeeper); Marijo
James (Reception Nurse); Charles Drake (Joe); Joan Winfield,
Audra Lindley (Nurses); Juanita Stark (Student Nurse); Jack Mower
(Mailman); Leah Baird (Telephone Operator); Sol Gorss (Chauffeur);
Dick Wessell (Grant); Tod Andrews (Craig); Murray Alper (Miller);
Henry Victor (Captain Horst); Henry Rowland (Telegraph Operator);
Ann Edmonds (Secretary); Leslie Denison (Flight Lieutenant Tyler);
Sven Borg (Under-Officer); Spec O'Donnell (Usher); Hans von
Morhart (Man); Lon McCallister (Newsboy).

There were few endorsements for this stock handling of enemy collaborations on the loose in America: "not even remotely subtle film" (New York Times); "moth-eaten spy tale" (New York World-Telegram).

On orders from the British War Office, agent Jane (Coleman) has memorized the detailed plans of Allied ship movements in the Atlantic and is on her way to Halifax with the vital information when she is injured in a car accident in New York. When she awakens at the hospital, she discovers that the Axis subversive group operating in Manhattan is close at hand, intent on gaining the vital information from her. Eminent psychiatrist Dr. Ingersoll (Massey), one of the conspirators, insists that she is suffering from an acute mental disorder and must be placed under his personal care. However, interne Dr. Michael Lewis (Garfield) eventually comes around to believing Coleman's seemingly fantastic tale and aids in her subsequent rescue. Not only are the spies brought to justice, but a covey of German U-boats in the Atlantic are blown up. Democracy and contrived ingenuity win another round!

Because it was standard policy to embellish any Warner Bros. -John Garfield picture with a "message, " Dangerously They Live was set in pre-Pearl Harbor New York, with cocky Garfield convinced at the film's opening that "it can't happen here." He soon sings a different tune about America's political isolationism policies, which, of course, had been changed when the film was made.

DANS CHEZ LES GENTLEMEN   see   RESIDENCIA PARA ESPIAS

DARK JOURNEY (UA, 1937)   82 min.

Executive producer, Alexander Korda; producer-director, Victor Saville; based on the play by Lajos Biro; screenplay, Biro, Arthur Wimperis; camera, George Merinal, Harry Stradling.

Conrad Veidt (Baron von Marwitz); Vivien Leigh (Madeline Goddard); Joan Gardiner (Lupita); Anthony Bushell (Bob Carter); Ursula Jeans (Gertrude); Margery Pickard (Colette); Eliot Makeham (Anatole); Austin Trevor (Dr. Muller); Sam Livesey (Schaffer); Edmund Willard (Chief of German Intelligence); Charles Carson (Head of Fifth Bureau); Phil Ray (Faber); Henry Oscar (Swedish Magistrate); Lawrence Hanray (Cottin); Cecil Parker (Captain of Q Boat); Reginald Tate (Mate of Q Boat); Percy Walsh (Captain of Swedish Packet); Robert Newton (Officer of U-Boat); William Dewhurst (The Killer); Laidman Browne (Rugge); M. Martin Harvey (Bohlau); Anthony Holles (Dutchman).

While World War I is raging on the Continent, Sweden valiantly attempts to retain its neutrality, no matter how many espionage agents ply the streets of Stockholm. One of their number is Madeline Goddard (Leigh) who operates the chic fashion shop known as Chez Madeline. She is actually a French spy who, for the sake of

her country, pretends to be a traitor to France and is selling
"secrets" to Germany. Because of her haute couture profession,
she is able to travel back and forth to France with little difficulty.
Everything is working smoothly until Baron von Marwitz (Veidt)
enters the scene. He is allegedly a Germany Army deserter, but
really is both a ladies' man, and more importantly, the head of
the Kaiser's secret service in Stockholm. It is not long before he
and Leigh meet and fall in love, but almost at the same time he
verifies his suspicions that she is the intelligence leak which must
be finally sealed, particularly now that Germany is planning a big
offensive push that must be kept top secret. Much as Veidt loves
Leigh, he cares for his country more and plots her downfall. She,
in turn, finds a helping hand from Bob Carter (Bushell) a British
secret agent in Stockholm. Bushell realizes that Leigh's only hope
is to put her in the safe custody of the Swedish police, so she is
arrested. But Veidt has one more ploy up his sleeve, leading to
a major encounter between a German U-boat and an English Q boat.

   The chief novelty of this facile production was its locale,
switching the scene of battle to 1918 Stockholm (although the fashions
worn in the picture were very much mid-1930s). It required quite
a complicated plot to maneuver a depiction of the English Q boat
into the action, but once involved it became the most engaging
performer in the film: swift, mysterious and effective.

DARLING LILI (Paramount, 1970) C 136 min.

   Executive producer, Owen Crump; associate producer, Ken
Wales; director, Blake Edwards; screenplay, Edwards, William
Peter Blatty; second unit director, Dick Crockett; director of aerial
sequences, Anthony Squire; assistant director, Mickey McCardle;
production designer, Fernando Carrere; set decorator, Reg Allen,
Jack Stevens; music, Henry Mancini; new songs, Mancini and Johnny
Mercer; French lyrics translated by Danielle Mauroy, Michel Le-
grand; choreographer, Hermes Pan; costumes, Jack Bear (for Julie
Andrews), Donald Brooks; sound, John Carter; aerial camera, Guy
Tabaray; special camera effects, Van der Veer Photo Co., Linwood
G. Dunn, Rex Wimpy; camera, Russell Harlan; editor, Peter Zinner.

   Julie Andrews (Lili Smith); Rock Hudson (Major William
Larrabee); Jeremy Kemp (Kurt von Ruger); Lance Percival (T.C.);
Michael Witney (Youngblood Carson); Jacques Marin (Major Duvalle);
Andre Maranne (Lt. Liggett); Gloria Paul (Crepe Suzette); Bernard
Kay (Bedford); Doreen Keogh (Emma); Carl Duering (Kessler);
Vernon Dobtcheff (Krauss); Ingo Mogendorf (Red Baron).

   In the intervening years since this much touted roadshow film
came and quickly disappeared from view, no two public sources
have agreed over its production costs (ranging from $15 to $20
million and more) or whether the movie is an underrated musical
comedy spoof or just an unsatisfying overblown burlesque. The
public did agree that Darling Lili was generally a colossal bore,
and the bad word of mouth killed the film's revenue prospects in

the later saturation release, when the feature was paired down to
fit on double bills.

> Lili Smith (Andrews): "Goodnight."
>
> Major William Larrabee (Hudson): "I fly at dawn."

Such was the tenor of Darling Lili's extravagant script, as director-
scenarist Blake Edwards led his cast through the bumpy plot of
"romantic absurdities." Andrews is seen as a popular London
music hall singer--the French even decorate her with the Legion
of Honor for her morale boosting--who is providing strategic military information to the Germans on the side. She is assigned to
wheedle data about a new army plane from Eagle Squadron Commander Hudson. While she is courting him, he is falling in love
with her and she becomes jealous of his attention to a French
stripper (Paul). The French believe that Hudson is the military
security leak. Andrews has Paul and, by association, Hudson
arrested by the French, while the Germans decide to eliminate
security risk Andrews. However at the last moment she is saved
by her German contact (Kemp) and by Hudson. After the war
Andrews and Hudson have a joyous reunion upon the London stage.

> Despite the ornate trappings, the parodying of styles and
genres, and the music hall songs, the focus of Darling Lili is
constantly on the pseudo-sentimental attachment of Hudson to
Andrews. Everything else is lost in the shuffle, including the
film's frivolous nods to the Mata Hari legend.

THE DAUGHTER OF MATA HARI see LA FILLE DE MATA-HARI

DAUGHTER OF THE MIND (20th-Fox/ABC-TV, 1969) C 90 min.

> Producer-director, Walter Grauman; based on the novel The
Hand of Mary Constable by Paul Gallico; screenplay, Luther Davis.
> Don Murray (Lauder); Ray Milland (Professor Constable);
Gene Tierney (Lenore); Barbara Dana (Tina); Edward Asner (Wiener);
Pamelyn Ferdin (Mary); Ivor Barry (Cryden); George Macready
(Ferguson); William Beckley (Bessmer); John Carradine (Bosch);
Cecile Ozorio (Devi); Frank Maxwell (General Augstadt); Bill Hick-
man (Enemy Agent); Hal Frederick (Technician); Virginia Christine
(Helga).

> One of the best films ever produced expressly for television,
this tightly engineered melodrama proves that telefeatures can be
of a high calibre. The plot's premise revolves around professor
Milland who believes his young daughter, recently killed in an
automobile accident, is communicating with him from beyond the
grave. It develops that Red agents, including Dana, are using
advanced electronic devices to tip Milland's mind and cause him
to defect to the Communist camp.
> Among the more than competent cast are Tierney as Milland's
invalid wife, Murray as the overly sincere parapsychology authority,
and Asner as a government security man.

Ray Milland and Gene Tierney in <u>Daughter of the Mind</u> (20th-Fox/
ABC-TV, 1969).

DAVID HARDING, COUNTERSPY (Columbia, 1950)   70 min.

      Producer, Milton Feldman; director, Ray Nazarro; based on
the radio program created by Phillips H. Lord; story-screenplay,
Clint Johnson; camera, George E. Diskant; editor, Henry Batista.
      Willard Parker (Jerry Baldwin); Audrey Long (Betty Iverson);
Howard St. John (David Harding); Raymond Greenleaf (Dr. George
Vickers); Harlan Warde (Hopkins); Alex Gerry (Charles Kingston);
Fred Sears (Peters); John Dehner (Frank Reynolds); Anthony Jochim
(Robert Barrington); Jock Mahoney (Brown); John Pickard (McCul-
lough); Steve Darrell (Edwards); Jimmy Lloyd (Burton); Charles
Quigley (Grady); Allan Mathews (Baker).

      An inexpensively-assembled potboiler deriving from the 1942
ABC radio series.   When a naval officer at a U.S. torpedo plant is
killed, Jerry Baldwin (Parker) is assigned to take over the case and
discover whether enemy agents have infiltrated the installation.   Part
of his job calls for romancing the murdered man's widow (Long),

whom he discovers, much to his regret, is one of the spies he and
agent David Harding (St. John) are seeking. Greenleaf was credibly
cast as Dr. George Vickers, one of the spies in disguise.

DAWN EXPRESS see NAZI SPY RING

THE DAY WILL DAWN (General Film Distributors, 1942)   98 min.

Producer, Paul Soskin; director, Harold French; story, Frank
Owen; screenplay, Terence Rattigan, Anatole de Grunwald, Patrick
Owen.
Ralph Richardson (Lockwood); Deborah Kerr (Kari); Hugh
Williams (Colin Metcalfe); Griffith Jones (Gunter); Francis L. Sul-
livan (Wettau); Roland Culver (Naval Attache); Finlay Currie (Al-
stad); Bernard Miles (McAllister); Niall McGinnis (Olaf); Elizabeth
Mann (Gerda); Patricia Medina (Ingrid); Henry Oscar (Milligan);
David Horne (Evans); Henry Hewitt (News Editor).

Breezy young reporter Colin Metcalfe (Williams), who prefers to cover the Ascot races, is sent to "keep an eye on" the
Norwegian situation at the outbreak of World War II. There he
becomes friendly with Kari (Kerr) and her old dad (Currie), a
local fisherman. After the Nazi invasion Williams returns home,
but is persuaded by British Naval Intelligence to return up north
to locate a U-boat base. He is dropped behind enemy lines via
parachute, and soon encounters his chief adversary, skulking Nazi
overlord Wettau (Sullivan).
Although The Day Will Dawn--retitled The Avengers for the
American release--was made with the cooperation of the British
Air Ministry, the War Office, and the Royal Norwegian government
in exile, and despite the generous insertion of newsreel footage to
delineate the British commando assault on the Nazi Norwegian base
on the Lofolen Islands, too much of this picture came across as a
fanciful screen exercise. Granted it was well-intended anti-Fascist
propaganda but like many British features of this vintage it suffered
from a too leisurely exposition and very choppy editing.

DEAD MAN'S EVIDENCE (BLC/British Lion, 1962)   67 min.

Producer, Francis Searle; associate producer, Ryck Rydon;
director, Searle; screenplay, Arthur La Bern; art director, Duncan
Sutherland; music, Ken Thorne; sound, Wally Midner; camera, Ken
Hodges; editor, Jim Commock.
Conrad Phillips (David Baxter); Jane Griffiths (Linda Howard);
Veronica Hurst (Gay Clifford); Ryck Rydon (Fallon); Alex Mackintosh
(Paul Kay); Godfrey Quigley (Inspector O'Brien); Bruce Seton (Colo-
nel Somerset); Harry Webster (Andy); Maureen Halligan (Mrs. Mac);
Laurie Leigh (Pat); Tommy Duggan (Mr. Casey); Frank Siemon
(Barman); Middleton Woods (Kim); Fergus O'Kelly (Night Porter);

Gordon Waine (Hotel Waiter); Sonia Fox (Hotel Receptionist); Alan Barry (Airport Clerk); Robert Marshall (Hotel Barman).

British secret agent Phillips is dispatched to Ireland to identify the body of a frogman washed up on shore. It is believed to be the corpse of another agent, Rydon, who disappeared recently in Berlin, and may have been a defector. Through the intervention of Griffiths the real traitor is unmasked.

A combination of well-planted red herrings and real tension make this one of the better supporting bill items.

DEAD RUN see GEHEIMNISSE IN GOLDENEN NYLONS

THE DEADLY AFFAIR (Columbia, 1966) C 107 min.

Producer, Sidney Lumet; associate producer, Denis O'Dell; director, Lumet; based on the novel Call for the Dead by John Le Carre; screenplay, Paul Dehn; art director, John Howell; music, Quincy Jones; sound, Les Hammond; camera, Freddie Young; editor, Thelma Connell.

James Mason (Charles Dobbs); Simone Signoret (Elsa Fennan); Maximilian Schell (Dieter Frey); Harriet Andersson (Anna Dobbs); Harry Andrews (Inspector Mendel); Kenneth Haigh (Bill Appleby); Roy Kinnear (Adam Scarr); Max Adrian (Adviser); Lynn Redgrave (Virgin); Robert Flemyng (Samuel Fennan); Corin Redgrave (Director); Les White (Harek); June Murphy, Frank Williams, Rosemary Lord (Witches); Kenneth Ivew (Stagehand); John Dimech (Waiter); Julian Sherrier (Head Waiter); Petra Markham (Daughter at Theatre); Denis Shaw (Landlord); Maria Charles (Blonde); Amanda Walker (Brunette); Sheraton Blount (Eunice Scarr); Janet Hargreaves (Ticket Clerk); Michael Brennan (Barman); Richard Steele, Gertan Klauber (Businessmen); Margaret Lacey (Mrs. Bird); Judy Keirn (Stewardess) Royal Shakespeare Company in Scenes from Marlowe's Edward II: David Warner (Edward); Michael Bryant (Gaveston); Stanley Lebor (Lancaster); Paul Hardwick (Young Mortimer); Charles Kay (Lightborn); Timothy West (Matrevis); Jonathan Wales (Gurney); William Dysart, Murray Brown, Paul Starr, Peter Harrison, David Quilter, Terence Sewards, Roger Jones (Nobles).

This frequently by-passed feature admittedly "flattens in a tangle of conventional spy-film tricks" (New York Times), but along the way director Sidney Lumet develops John Le Carre's novel into an admirable depiction of the shabby existence "enjoyed" by members of the espionage networks and by government functionaries. Moreover, The Deadly Affair never falters from being a good old-fashioned thriller.

When top level Foreign Office official Samuel Fennan (Flemyng) commits suicide, agent Dobbs (Mason) is decidedly puzzled, for he had recently validated Flemyng's security clearance. Mason begins to doubt his own judgment, particularly when he perceives that Flemyng's widow (Signoret), a Jew who survived the Nazi concentration camps, proves suspect. His superiors insist he drop the case, which drives Mason to resign from service. On his own he persuades semi-retired Andrews to aid in a private investigation, leading to shocking complications when Schell, Mason's World War II comrade-in-espionage, arrives in town and concludes plans to run away with Mason's wife (Andersson).

Despite being a little too lengthy, improperly paced, and filled with overly serious prattle of morality, pacifism, loyalty, etc., The Deadly Affair nevertheless provides "sheer suspense entertainment" (Cosmopolitan magazine), and benefits from sturdy performances by its international cast. Of special interest is the Hitchcockian murder scene that occurs in the Aldwych Theatre during a performance of Edward II, and the film's fine score by Quincy Jones (and the warbling of its title theme, "Who Needs Forever" by Astrud Gilberto).

DEADLY DECISION see CANARIS--MASTER SPY

THE DEADLY DECOYS see LE GORILLE A MORDU L'ARCH- EVEQUE

DEATH OF A JEW (Cine Globe, 1973) C 93 min.

Director, Denys de la Patelliere; screenplay, Vahe Katcha, de la Patelliere; camera, Alain Levent.

Assaf Dayan (Shimon); Akim Tamiroff (Mehdaloun); Jean Claudio (Kassik).

When originally released in 1970, this Israeli-made feature was entitled Sabra. Its plot is almost as simplistic as its naive thrust. It "... fails to involve the emotions and only mildly stimu- lates intellectually" (Ann Guarino in her 2 1/2 star New York Daily News review).

Within an unidentified Arab country, a young Israeli spy named Shimon (Dayan) is captured and tortured, but still will not talk. Onto the scene comes sly, elderly inspector Mehdaloun (Tamiroff), who wines and dines the youth in the hopes of wooing the information through grand hospitality. Dayan still remains tight-lipped, but the scheme has taken its toll on Tamiroff, who has now grown so appreciative of the good life that he cannot imagine living without it: in his beginning dotage he has acquired a new will for a grand existence, without the necessary means to sustain it.

"Death of a Jew is the kind of film that seems to advance from scene to scene not by an inner necessity, but rather because everybody at a particular time in a particular place finds himself at a loss for what to do next" (Roger Greenspun in the New York Times).

THE DEATH OF ME YET   (ABC, 1971)   C   73 min.

Producer, Aaron Spelling; director, John Llewellyn Moxey; screenplay, A. J. Russell.

Doug McClure (Paul Towers); Darren McGavin (Joe Chalk); Rosemary Forsyth (Sibby Towers); Richard Basehart (Robert Barnes); Meg Foster (Alice); and: Dana Elcar, Steve Dunne, Jean Allison, Allen Jaffe, Sam Edwards, John Kroga, Ivan Bonar.

A "relatively routine 'meller'," (Judith Crist in TV Guide) in which a Russian defector-spy (McClure) is used by a U.S. agent (McGavin) to work against the Soviets, with McGavin pushing McClure on to further acts of espionage because he knows his unwilling accomplice's secrets.

The only real interest in the mediocre melodrama was the Russian reproduction of an American town.

THE DEATHMAKERS see LA PEAU DE TORPEDO

DECISION BEFORE DAWN   (20th-Fox, 1952)   119 min.

Producer, Anatole Litvak, Frank McCarthy; director, Litvak; based on the novel Call It Treason by George Howe; screenplay, Peter Viertel; art director, Ludwig Reiber; orchestrator, Leonid Raab; music, Franz Waxman; sound, Alfred Bruzlin, Roger Heman; camera, Franz Planer; editor, Dorothy Spencer.

Richard Basehart (Lieutenant Rennick); Gary Merrill (Colonel Devlin); Oskar Werner (Happy); Hildegarde Neff (Hilde); Dominique Blanchar (Monique); O. E. Hasse (Oberst von Baker); Wilfried Seyfert (S. S. Man Scholtz); Hans Christian Blech (Tiger); Helene Thimig (Fraulein Schneider); Robert Freytag (Paul); George Tyne (Sgt. Watkins); Adolph Lodel (Kurt); Arno Assmann (Ernst); Loni Heuser (Fritzi); Walter Janssen (Fiedl); Erich Ebert (Freddy); Ruth Brandt (Woman Driver); Liselotte Kirschbaum, Eva Marie Andres (Flak Girls); Aguste Hansen-Kleinmichel (Newspaper Woman); Martin Urtel (Soldier); Otto Friebel (Clerk); Paul Schwed (Wehrmacht Bus Bit); Meta Weber, Henriett Speidel, Ingeborg Luther (Women); Almut Bachmann (Street Car Conductor); Ruth Trumpp (Woman Attendant); Egon Lippert, Gerhard Kittler (Lieutenants); Rainier Geldern (Panzer NCO); Klaus Kinski (Whining Soldier); Von Schmidel (Man); Arnulf Schroder (Old P. W.); Bert Brandt, Erich Jelde, Max Herbst, Klaus Krause, Alex Hohenlohe, Clemens Wildemrod (NCOs); Jasper Gertzen, Ulrich Volkmar, Hans Mohrhard, Kurt Marquardt (P. O. W. s); Jochen Diestelmann, Luitpold Kummer, Heinrich Berg, Dieter Wilsing (Rathskeller Bits); Elfe Gearhart (Bar Maid); Rudolf Heimann (Truck Driver "Leschke"); Werner Fuetterer (von Bülow); Lieselotte Steinweg, Elizabeth Millberg, Ulla Best, Katja Jobs, Eva Maria Hoppe, Maria Landrock, Sonja Kosta (Wehrmacht Girls); Ernst Hoechstaetter (Office Reception Desk); Harald Wolff (Hartmann); Wolfgang Kuhnemann (Clerk in Schleissheim); Walter

Ladengast (Sergeant Deserter); Gerhard Steinberg (Sergeant Klinger);
Peter Luhr (V. Schirmeck); Maria Wimmer (Woman in the Street);
Ursula Voss (Street Car Conductor); Erich Ebert (Freddy).

Within the framework of a clear-cut spy thriller, Decision
before Dawn "tests the tensile strength of your nerves" (New York
Herald-Tribune). But the Anatole Litvak-directed feature is far
more than that, for its semi-documentary approach depicts the
pathetic but exciting saga of a conscious-stricken soldier-turned-
spy operating in the realistic rubble of modern warfare. The dual
aims of Decision before Dawn make it an important entry in the
contemporary espionage film field, with its vivid portrayal of its
subject as a very fragile human being combatting the dire realities
of 20th-century life.
    In the winter of 1945, the American Army is desperate for
men and the military command goes against standard rules against
using German prisoners of war to fulfill undercover missions, in
this case to contact a German commander on the East bank of the
Rhine who is willing to surrender if he can come to terms with the
U. S. forces.   Luftwaffe medic Werner is one of the captured enemy
who volunteers for the assignment, convinced the job at hand will
be easier to handle than fighting for a cause he knows to be wrong.
Another selected German (Freytag) is murdered by fellow prisoners
who condemn the volunteers who are trying to bring the war to an
end.   Eventually American lieutenant Rennick (Basehart), Werner,
and another P. O. W. , Tiger (Blech), head behind enemy lines, and
the operation leads to Munich, Nurenberg, and Manheim, where
Werner is in constant fear of being detected by his own people.
The downbeat conclusion has Werner killed "in the line of duty" with
hardly anyone realizing the sacrifices made by this sensitive idealist
bent on accomplishing his practical goal.
    Sgt. Watkins (Tyne): "Too bad about the kid [Werner]. "
    Lt. Rennick (Basehart): "Yeah. "
    Watkins: "Well, I guess it's no good thinking about it.
After all, he was just another Kraut. "
    A forceful cast emphasized the dramatic points made in
this adaptation of George Howe's novel; particularly with the viable
contrast offered between French underground worker Monique
(Blanchar) and Hilde (Neff), the latter a leftover commodity in
bomb-destroyed Germany.

THE DEFECTOR   (Seven Arts, 1966)   C   101 min.

    Executive producer, Julien Derode; producer-director, Raoul
Levy; based on the novel The Spy by Paul Thomas; adaptation, Jean
Clouzot, Levy; screenplay, Robert Guenette, Levy; art director,
Pierre Guffroy; music, Serge Gainsbourg; sound, Jo de Bretagne;

[Facing page] Oskar Werner in Decision before Dawn (20th-Fox,
1951).

camera, Raoul Coutard; editor, Albert Jurgenson, Roger Dwyre.
      Montgomery Clift (Professor James Bower); Hardy Kruger
(Peter Heinzman); Macha Meril (Frieda Hoffman); Roddy McDowall
(C. I. A. Agent Adams); David Opatoshu (Orlovsky); Christine Dela-
roche (Ingrid); Hannes Messemer (Dr. Saltzer); Karl Lieffen
(Major); Jean-Luc Godard (Orlovsky's Friend); and: Uta Levka.

Montgomery Clift, Roddy McDowall, and Hardy Kruger in The Defector (Seven Arts, 1966).

      In order to receive further government research grants,
American physicist Professor James Bower (Clift) agrees to follow C. I. A. agent Adams' (McDowall) directive to turn his private
visit to East Germany museums into a spy trek, arranging for the
defection of a Russian physicist and providing access to data on the
U. S. S. R.'s space program. In Leipzig Clift is followed by Peter
Heinzman (Kruger), a physicist in the Soviet employ. Kruger soon
learns that the Red scientist in question is dead and that his actual
task is to persuade Clift to defect. Meanwhile, when Clift's local
contact (Messemer) is killed, Kruger tips his hand, but Clift now
insists upon leaving East Germany. Messemer's assistant (Meril)
helps the American to escape across the border to the West.
Thereafter, Kruger "defects" to the West and implores Clift to
assist him to reach America. Naive Clift agrees, but the C. I. A.
knows better, and has counterspy Kruger killed.

In direct opposition to the more recent flippant onscreen treatment of the espionage scene, The Defector employed a straightforward approach, verging on sourness as intellectual amateurs from both sides are maneuvered like pawns by the opposing cold war professionals. Because this was the final film of the late actor Montgomery Clift, the "assembly line" feature received more attention than it warranted, for no aspect of the fragile production managed to come fully to grips with its realistic thesis. At best, Clift's cerebral performance was rated "sad and fascinating and full of grief" (Newsday) and he was the film's sole selling point.

This boxoffice failure was chopped to 68 minutes for much of its European release.

THE DELPHI BUREAU (WB/ABC-TV, 1972)   C   93 min.

Producer, Sam Rolfe; director, Paul Wendkos; screenplay, Rolfe; music, Harper McKay; art director, Eugene Lourie.

Laurence Luckinbill (Gregory); Celeste Holm (Sybil Van Loween); Joanna Pettet (April); Dean Jagger (Keller); Bob Crane (Charlie Taggart); Bradford Dillman (Jamison); Cameron Mitchell (Stokley); David Sheiner (Dobkin).

> From the Capital came a young man
> To uncover some worms in a can.
> So they can him--they frame him
> For Murder--they blame him.
> In turn--he eludes them
> Pursues--then eschews them.
> Till he holds all the strings to their plan.
> The End more or less, Delphian!

The above poem was dragged across the telescreen in the course of this telefeature, line by line, to allegedly advance the plot. It did not. Despite the lackluster nature of this pilot it did sell the ABC series.

Agent Luckinbill of a secret investigative agency, run by a society matron (Holm) and directly answerable to the U.S. President, is dispatched to learn the whereabouts of a stolen fleet of obsolete Air Force planes.

THE DELTA FACTOR (American-Continental, 1971)   C   91 min.

Producer-director, Tay Garnett; based on the novel by Mickey Spillane; screenplay, Garnett; art director, Jack Collis, Ben Resella; assistant director, Dink Templeton; sound, Clem Portman; camera, Ted and Vince Saizis; editor, Richard Farrell.

Yvette Mimieux (Kim Stacy); Christopher George (Morgan); Diane McBain (Lisa Gordot); Ralph Taeger (Art Keifer); Yvonne De Carlo (Valerie); Sherri Spillane (Rosa); Ted De Corsia (Ames); Rhodes Reason (Dr. Fredericks); Joseph Sirola (Sal Dekker); and: Richard Lanni, George Ash, Fred Marsell.

Morgan (George) escapes from a maximum security prison, but is recaptured. His alternatives: return to incarceration (he claims he is innocent of the $40 million theft charge) or to accept a special job. He picks the latter and is soon involved in rescuing a scientist held captive by a Caribbean island dictator. In the course of his mission he is "forced" to wed attractive C. I. A. agent Kim Stacy (Mimieux), his co-worker on the case.

There was surprising little violence or sex in this initially R-rated film (when re-issued the Motion Picture Association of America re-ranked it to PG).

THE DESERT BRIDE   (Columbia, 1928)   5, 400 feet

Producer, Harry Cohn; director, Walter Lang; based on the novel The Adventuress by Ewart Adamson; adaptation, Anthony Coldeway; screenplay, Elmer Harris; art director, Robert E. Lee; assistant director, Max Cohn; camera, Ray June; editor, Arthur Roberts.

Betty Compson (Diane Duval); Allan Forrest (Captain Maurice de Florimont); Edward Martindel (Colonel Sorelle); Otto Matiesen (Kassin Ben Ali); Roscoe Karns (Private Terry); Frank Austin (Beggar).

An overly dramatic rendition of a tried and true theme. Captain de Florimont (Forrest) of the French army intelligence bureau is captured by Arab nationalists while on a spy mission. Thereafter Forrest's faithful sweetheart (Compson) falls into the Arabs' hands, and both she and her lover are tortured by the native leader (Matiesen), but neither will reveal any information. As expected, French troops arrive in time to rescue the brave couple.

DESERT SONG   (WB, 1943)   C   90 min.

Director, Robert Florey; based on the play by Laurence Schwab, Otto Harback, Oscar Hammerstein II, Sigmund Romberg, Frank Nadel; art director, Charles Noir; set decorator, Jack Mc-Conaghy; choreography, Leroy Prinz; assistant director, Art Lueker; camera, Bert Glennon; editor, Frank Magee.

Dennis Morgan (Paul Hudson); Irene Manning (Margot); Bruce Cabot (Fontaine); Victor Francen (Caid Yousseff); Lynne Overman (Johnny Walsh); Gene Lockhart (Benoit); Faye Emerson (Hajy); Marcel Dalio (Tarbouch); Felix Basch (Heinzelman); Gerald Mohr (Haasan); Noble Johnson (Abdel Rahmen); Curt Bois (Francois); Albert Morin (Muhammud); Jack La Rue (Lt. Berten); William Edmunds (Suliman); Wallis Clark (Pajot).

When Desert Song first opened at the Casino Theatre on Broadway on November 30, 1926, critic Richard Watts, Jr. (New York Herald-Tribune) wrote, "The question of how simple-minded the book of a musical comedy can be was debated last night, and the verdict arrived at was 'no end'." The show, however, was nurtured into a 465-performance hit and became a musical comedy perennial. Warner Bros. produced its first picturization of Desert Song in 1929 with John Boles and Carlotta King in the leads; the studio's third rendition in 1953 starred Gordon MacRae and Kathryn Grayson. Version number two, prepared for 1943 release, took advantage of the world situation to update the sand and saber yarn into a Technicolor Allies vs. Axis confrontation, set in 1939 French Africa.

Clean-cut American Paul Hudson (Morgan), who had been a member of the Lincoln Brigade in the Spanish Civil War, arrives in Morocco "one jump ahead of a guy named Franco." He takes a job in a local nightspot as a piano player--all seemingly very harmless. However, his extracurricular activities include donning the costume of El Kohlar and leading the native Riffs against the Nazis who are putting a railroad line through from Dakar to the North African coast.

Besides tinkering with the stage play, eliminating some tunes and adding new numbers (i.e., "Fifi's Song," "Long Live the Night," and "Gay Parisienne"), the screenplay saw fit to take a sharp slap at the pre-war French military caste and its laissez-faire attitude to the double dealings transpiring under their indifferent governmental supervision.

Morgan and Manning, she as a swank Gallic singer named Margot, duet "One Alone" and perform choruses of the title tune. When the inevitable "Song of the Riffs" looms on the soundtrack, even the more topically conscientious viewer found it difficult to worry about the fate of the natives at the hands of the dastardly Germans.

DESTINY OF A SPY (Universal/NBC-TV, 1969) C 100 min.

Producer, Jack Laird; director, Boris Sagal; based on the novel by John Blackburn; screenplay, Stanford Whitmore; music, Ron Graines; sound, Roy Baker; camera, Arthur Grant; editor, Arthur Ludski.

Lorne Greene (Peter Vanin); Rachel Roberts (Megan); Anthony Quayle (Malenden); James Donald (Martin Rolfe); Harry Andrews (Kirk); Patrick Magee (Flack); Patrick Newell (Bates); Raymond Huntley (Pode); Olaf Polley (Trubenoff); Victor Beaumont (Kronig); Janina Faye (Elena); and: Josephine Stuart, Angela Pleasance, Mary Kerridge.

Veteran Russian spy Vanin (Greene) is reassigned from his near-sinecure Moscow post for a sabotage task in London, his mission is to destroy the counter-radar system being developed by British scientist Martin Rolfe (Donald). In order to eliminate his opponent (Donald) and to destroy the man's work, it is necessary for Greene to unravel a cryptic phrase, "I know who the gaunt woman is."

The biggest selling of this London-filmed telefeature was that its star (Greene) was making his first non-"Bonanza" video series dramatic appearance on the small screen in many a year. The results were far from satisfying, leading Daily Variety to suggest, "Lorne Greene should never have left the Ponderosa ... [for this] confused, rambling, old-fashioned tale." The storyline abounded with cliches, particularly stereotyped characterizations of starched, prim British Intelligence agents.

DEUX BILLETS POUR MEXICO   see   GEHEIMNISSE IN GOLDENEN NYLONS

THE DEVIL'S AGENT   (British Lion, 1962)   77 min.

Producer, Emmet Dalton; director, John Paddy Carstairs; screenplay, Robert Westerby; assistant director, Fred Slark; art director, Tony Inglis; music, Philip Green; sound, Liam Saurin, Dal Emanuel; camera, Gerald Gibbs; editor, Tom Simpson.
Peter Van Eyck (George Droste); Marianne Koch (Nora Golden); Macdonald Carey (Mr. Smith); Christopher Lee (Baron von Staub); Billie Whitelaw (Piroska); David Knight (Father Zombary); Marius Goring (General Greenhahn); Helen Cherry (Countess Cosimano); Colin Gordon (Count Dezsepalvy); Niall McGinnis (Paul Vass); Eric Pohlmann (Bloch); Peter Vaughan (Chief of Hungarian Police); Michael Brennan (Horvat); Jeremy Bulloch (Johnny Droste); Walter Gotell (Dr. Ritter); John Cowley (Funnel-Shaped Man); Peter Lamb (Muller); Christopher Casson (Headmaster); Bart Bastable (Cattle Truck Driver); Charles Byrne (Vazlan); Vincent Dowling (Father Farcosc); Adrian Cronin (Young Priest); Robert Lepler (Head Waiter).

Wine salesman George Droste (Van Eyck) is feeling a financial pinch, particularly in keeping up payments on his son's (Bulloch) expensive boarding school education. Then one day an old acquaintance, Baron von Staub (Lee) and the latter's sister (Cherry) invite him to spend a weekend at their lush home in the Soviet zone of Germany. Cherry asks him to deliver a book to Vienna, which leads to Van Eyck's being arrested by Mr. Smith (Carey) of U. S. Intelligence who informs the naive salesman that his East German hosts are Soviet agents. Carey induces Van Eyck to handle some assignments for the Americans, and Van Eyck is soon off to Budapest where he meets co-worker Piroska (Whitelaw). Later, after escaping back to Austria in the company of Hungarian refugee Nora Gulden (Koch), Van Eyck is dispatched to investigate a certain General Greenhahn (Goring) in Berlin, and in the process decides to play both sides against the middle. Van Eyck splits the desired goods between the Americans and Goring, making a tidy profit on the deal. He has become a true professional spy.
"A ragged and episodic affair, which no sooner gets going on one thing than it switches to another, this in no way lives up

to the promise of its cast which, for a B picture, is formidable"
(British <u>Monthly Film Bulletin</u>).

DEVIL'S CHAPLAIN (Rayart, 1929) 5,451 feet

     Producer, Trem Carr; director, Duke Worne; based on the
novel by George Bronson Howard; screenplay, Arthur Hoerl; camera,
Hap Depew; editor, J.S. Harrington.
     Cornelius Keefe (Yorke Norroy); Virginia Brown Faire
(Princess Therese); Josef Swickard (The King); Boris Karloff
(Boris); Wheeler Oakman (Nicholay); Leland Carr (Ivan); George
McIntosh (The Prince).

     Prince McIntosh, fleeing a revolution in his Balkan home-
land, seeks refuge in the U.S., coming under the protection of
American secret service agent Keefe. Not only does Keefe route
the ring of spies out to eliminate the prince, but he wins the love
of princess Faire. A modest blending of the Ruritanian romance
and espionage genre. It should be noted that this film is one of
actor Karloff's earlier screen performances, not available yet for
television showings.

DIAMONDS ARE FOREVER (UA, 1971) C 120 min.

     Producer, Harry Saltzman, Albert R. Broccoli; associate
producer, Stanley Sopel; director, Guy Hamilton; based on the novel
by Ian Fleming; screenplay, Richard Maibaum, Tom Mankiewicz;
music, John Barry, title song, Barry and Don Black; production
designer, Ken Adam; main titles designer, Maurice Binder; assistant
director, Derek Cracknell, Jerome M. Siegel; stunt arranger, Bob
Simmons, Paul Baxley; costumes for Miss St. John, Donfeld; art
director, Jack Maxsted, Bill Kenney; set decorator, Peter Lamont,
John Austin; sound, John Mitchell, Al Overton; visual effects,
Albert Whitlock, Wally Veevers; special effects, Leslie Hillman,
Whitey McMahon; second unit camera, Harold Wellman; camera,
Ted Moore; editor, Bert Bates, John W. Holmes.
     Sean Connery (James Bond); Jill St. John (Tiffany Case);
Charles Gray (Blofeld); Lana Wood (Plenty O'Toole); Jimmy Dean
(Willard Whyte); Bruce Cabot (Sacby); Putter Smith (Mr. Kidd);
Bruce Glover (Mr. Wint); Norman Burton (Leiter); Joseph Furst
(Dr. Metz); David Bauer (Mr. Slumber); Bernard Lee (M); Des-
mond Llewelyn (Q); Leonard Barr (Shady Tree); Lois Maxwell
(Miss Moneypenny); Margaret Lacey (Mrs. Whistler); Joe Robin-
son (Peter Franks); Donna Garratt (Bambi); Trina Parks (Thumper);
David de Keyser (Doctor); Laurence Naismith (Sir Donald Munger).

     After the relatively disappointing <u>On Her Majesty's Secret
Service</u>, producers Harry Saltzman and Albert R. Broccoli moved
mountains to woo recalcitrant actor Sean Connery back to his 007
characterization. They reasoned a return to the formula as before

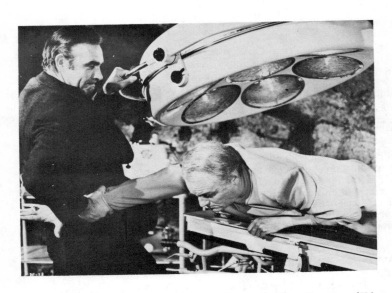

Sean Connery and Charles Gray in Diamonds Are Forever (UA, 1971).

would demonstrate that super spy pictures in general--and the James Bond series in particular--were not outdated commodities at the 1970s boxoffice.   The producers proved somewhat correct, for already (late 1972) Diamonds Are Forever has grossed over $21 million in domestic receipts.

That is not to say that Diamonds Are Forever did not have its inherent problems.   No matter how much production designer Ken Adam gussied up the sets with space age trappings, or how Richard Maibaum and Tom Mankiewicz tinkered with the Ian Fleming book original, the picture had a disturbing déjà vu quality to it. This feel of formula production of the film was not alleviated by director Guy Hamilton (who did Goldfinger) nor by the distracting presence of shapely Jill St. John (as Tiffany Case) and Lana Wood (Plenty O'Toole).   In the case of Hamilton he was urged by the producers to bring the series back along the same course as the mid-1960s series entries, while the very presence of bikini-clad, cooing St. John and Wood only served as a reminder of how inno- cent the double entendre sex gambits in the James Bond series had become in relationship to the available hard core and soft core pornography films of the 1970s.   For the record, the new Bond film had a GP rating.   And most upsetting of all to moviegoers, Connery now at age forty-one, could no longer present a youngish sophisticated rogue oncamera. Time had caught up with the actor as well as the series.

When it is learned that huge quantities of diamonds are being sneaked out of South Africa and stockpiled by a fabulously wealthy racketeer, M (Lee) assigns Bond (Connery) to the case. The trail leads from Amsterdam to Los Angeles and to Las Vegas, where it develops that the mastermind crook is none other than Connery's perennial adversary, arch fiend Blofeld (Charles Gray) who has been utilizing the facilities of twisted recluse gambling club owner Willard Whyte (Jimmy Dean). Gray's plot this time is to use the diamonds to construct a powerful laser, sending it into space with its beam pointed at Washington, D. C. , hoping to blackmail the American government into arranging for global disarmament leaving Blofeld in total power over the world. Connery rises to the occasion and with the aid of the Army launches an attack on Gray's offshore oil-rig operational base. At the successful finish, one finds Connery and St. John enjoying a pleasant trans-Atlantic trip on Dean's ocean liner.

John Brosnan in James Bond in the Cinema (1972) observed, "... the main flaw in the production [Diamonds Are Forever], apart from the over complicated plot, is that everything is played more for laughs instead of thrills and suspense.... Also there is no real sense of menace in the film." Charles Gray's Blofeld was not allowed by the script or direction to be the viable threat that Donald Pleasence's Blofeld had provided in You Only Live Twice, or, for that matter, the less realistic Blofeld played by Telly Savalas in On Her Majesty's Secret Service. Gray's two chief henchmen (Putter Smith, Bruce Glover) emerge as comic sidekicks rather than sinister, deadly forces."

No matter what one's reaction to Diamonds Are Forever may be, the film clearly shows that the age of the onscreen secret agent either super man or drab operative, presented seriously or tongue-in-cheek is fast passing. Possibly, the genre is blending ever more irrevocably into the science fiction field where man, greatly aided by computerized devices, handles all the espionage-strongarm business at hand.

DIMENSION 5 (United Pictures Corp. , 1966) C 88 min.

Executive producer, Fred Jordan; producer, Earle Lyon; director, Franklin Adreon; screenplay, Arthur C. Pierce; assistant director, Joe Wonder; art director, Paul Sylos, Jr. ; set decorator, Ray Blotz; music, Paul Dunlap; camera, Alan Stenvold; editor, Robert S. Eisen.

Jeffrey Hunter (Justin Power); France Nuyen (Kitty Tsu); Harold Sakata (Big Buddha); Donald Woods (Cane); Linda Ho (Nancy Ho); Robert Ito (Sato); David Chow (Stoneface); Lee Kolima (Genghis); and John Lormer, Bill Walker, Virginia Lee, Ken Spalding, Carol Byron, Kam Tong, Tad Horino, John McKie.

Hunter, of the National Intelligence Agency, and his assistant, Nuyen, use their time converter belt to jump ahead three weeks, in order to prevent the Chinese espionage organization, Dragon, from completing its H-bomb destruction of Los Angeles.

"Dismally mounted, sloppily directed piece of spy nonsense, which only needs Batman to complete its comic strip look," was the verdict of the British Monthly Film Bulletin, which also noted, "... this particular American Intelligence Agency seems not averse to some very ungentlemanly torture, even if the apparatus does look innocuously like a hair-drier."

DIPLOMACY (Paramount, 1926)   6,950 feet

Presenter, Adolph Zukor, Jesse L. Lasky; director, Marshall Neilan; based on the play by Victorien Sardou; screenplay, Benjamin Glazer; camera, David Kesson, Donald Keyes.
Blanche Sweet (Dora); Neil Hamilton (Julian Weymouth); Arlette Marchal (Countess Zicka); Matt Moore (Robert Lowry); Gustav von Seyffertitz (Baron Ballin); Earle Williams (Sir Henry Weymouth); Arthur Edmund Carewe (Count Orloff); Julia Swayne Gordon (Marquise de Zares); David Mir (Reggie Cowan); Charles Buddy Post (Baron's Secretary); Mario Carillo (John Stramir); Sojin (Chinese Diplomat); Edgar Norton, Linda Landi (Servants).

A period set-piece derived from Sardou's 19th-century work. It presents a tale of complicity and intrigue long associated with the refined world of diplomacy.   An informal meeting of European powers at Deauville provides ample opportunity for the double dealing of counter-agents of all factions, particularly by Countess Zicka (Marchal), who blithely sells military secrets to Bolshevik employee von Seyffertitz, and casually lays the blame at the feet of innocent Sweet.

DIPLOMATIC COURIER (20th-Fox, 1952)   97 min.

Producer, Casey Robinson; director, Henry Hathaway; based on the novel Sinister Errand by Peter Cheyney; screenplay, Robinson, Liam O'Brien; art director, Lyle Wheeler, John De Cuir; set decorator, Thomas Little, Stuart Reiss; costumes, Eloise Janssen; music director, Lionel Newman; makeup, Ben Nye; sound, W. D. Flick, Roger Heman; special camera effects, Ray Kellogg; camera, Lucien Ballard; editor, James B. Clark.
Tyrone Power (Mike Kells); Patricia Neal (Joan Ross); Stephen McNally (Colonel Cagle); Hildegarde Neff (Janine); Karl Malden (Ernie); James Millican (Sam Carew); Stefan Schnabel (Platov); Herbert Berghof (Arnov); Arthur Blake (Max Ralli); Helene Stanley (Air Line Stewardess); Sig Arno (Chef de Train); Wilfred Dinder (Cherenko); Lee Marvin (M. P. At Trieste); Peter Coe (Zinski); Tyler McVey (Watch Officer); Stuart Randall (Butrick); Dabbs Greer (Intelligence Officer); Carleton Young (Brennan);

Stephen McNally, Karl Malden, and Tyrone Power in Diplomatic Courier (20th-Fox, 1952).

Charles La Torre (French Ticket Agent); Russ Conway (Bill);
Tom Powers (Cherney); Monique Chantal (French Stewardess);
Lumsden Hare (Jacks).

This self-indulgent film wanders about Europe and into the back alleys of cold war double dealing, but since there is a hearty lack of clarity and suspense here, the energy expended on all parts seems wasteful.

Courier Mike Kells (Power) is such an amateur at the sophisticated espionage racket that he is constantly stumbling on his own misjudgments as he attempts to retrieve a vital Russian time-table for the proposed invasion of Yugoslavia. Is Joan Ross (Neal) really a hale and hearty American tourist and is Janine (Neff) really a Red spy? Power is never sure throughout the story, which encompasses unsolved night train murders, muggings in Trieste, and the necessary climatic chase. Chump Power is constantly aghast at the necessity of using extraordinary violence and is astonished to realize that even United States government agents can be as guilty as anyone of duplicity and harsh methods of action and retaliation.

THE DIRTY GAME (AIP, 1966)   91 min.

Executive producer, Richard Hellman; associate producer, Eugene Tucherer; directors, Terence Young, Christian-Jacque, Carlo Lizzani; screenplay, Jo Eisinger; music, Robert Mellin; art director, Roberto Gabriti; H. Weideman; sound, G. Mardiguian; camera, Pierre Petit, Richard Angst, Enrico Menczer; editor, Borys Leurn, Alan Osbistov.

Henry Fonda (Kourlov); Robert Ryan (General Bruce); Vittorio Gassman (Perego); Annie Girardot (Nanette); Bourvil (Laland); Robert Hossein (Dupont); Peter Van Eyck (Berlin C M); Maria Grazia Buccela (Natalia).

Henry Fonda in The Dirty Game (AIP, 1966).

To patly bind together its three divergent stories, The Dirty Game has General Bruce (Ryan) reminiscing about the chain of events involving espionage agents under his jurisdictions, and the situations leading to a meeting with his Russian counterpart on the East-West border in Germany for an exchange of prisoners. The trio of episodes involve agent Gassman in Rome, Soviet agent Girardot in African Somaliland, and West-loyal operative Fonda returning to Berlin after 17 years in the East.

At the end of the film, Ryan snarls in exasperation, "This is a hell of a way to make a living." For most viewers, this strung together international co-venture was a heck of a waste of time, a "low-grade throwback to spying as a gentleman's chess game" (Newsday); "The first law of Iron Curtain spy work is to patch your cracks. Here the seams show all too clearly..." (New York World Journal Tribune).

Also known as The Secret Agents.

DISHONORED (Paramount, 1931) 91 min.

Director-story, Josef von Sternberg; screenplay, Daniel H. Rubin; music, Karl Hajos; camera, Lee Garmes.

Marlene Dietrich (X-27); Victor McLaglen (Colonel Kranau); Lew Cody (Colonel Kovrin); Gustav von Seyffertitz (Secret Service Head); Warner Oland (Colonel von Hindau); Barry Norton (Young Lieutenant); Davison Clark (Court Officer); Wilfred Lucas (General Dymov); Bill Powell (Manager); Ruth Mayhew (Accident Victim); Alexis Davidoff (Officer); William B. Davidson (Firing Squad Officer); Ethan Laidlaw (Russian Corporal); Joseph Girard, Buddy Roosevelt (Russian Officers); George Irving (Contact at Cafe).

Following Der Bläue Angel and Morocco, director Josef von Sternberg further parlayed the Dietrich image into boxoffice with the spy drama, Dishonored. Homer Dickens in The Films of Marlene Dietrich (1968) said, "Mr. Sternberg's taste and ability to elevate a hackneyed script into a visual work are to be admired."

In World War I Vienna the head of the Secret Service (von Seyffertitz) is impressed with the basic integrity of a streetwalker (Dietrich) and enlists her in the Service as a spy, henceforth known as X-27. She is assigned to learn if Austrian General von Hindau (Oland) is really a traitor. Vamping the general, she confirms her superiors' suspicions, whereupon Oland kills himself.

Her next mission is to locate Oland's contact, the clown who gave the general a note from the enemy at a recent masked ball. Meantime she meets an Austrian lieutenant (McLaglen), who is actually H-14, a Russian secret service officer. Finding this out she sets a trap for him but he escapes, and disguised as a Russian maid she goes to the Russian-Polish border and becomes involved with a Russian Colonel (Cody). H-14 later traps X-27, but she escapes and he follows her to Italy where he is captured. Realizing she loves the Russian officer, Dietrich allows him to escape and for her troubles she is executed.

Like the next year's Mata Hari, starring Greta Garbo, Dishonored was nothing more than a glamorized vehicle for its star, allowing the plotline and logic to be jumbled in order to present the screen's new top siren in an exotic light. Years later, director von Sternberg would bemoan the studio's insistence on using

Marlene Dietrich in <u>Dishonored</u> (Paramount, 1931).

<u>Dishonored</u> for the film's release title, insisting that the name tag created a wrong implication. The director reasoned that Dietrich's X-27 was shot in the line of duty, and that she met her fate most honorably and sedately (dressed in the garb of her former profession, and having just applied a fresh dab of lipstick). If anything, the finale of <u>Dishonored</u> illustrates that a female spy could meet her fate just as bravely as any man in the espionage game, even to dying with her boots on.

DR. GOLDFOOT AND THE BIKINI MACHINE   (AIP, 1965)   C
90 min.

Producer, James H. Nicholson, Samuel Z. Arkoff; co-producer, Anthony Carras; director, Norman Taurog; story, James

Hartford; screenplay, Elwood Ullman, Robert Kaufman; art director, Daniel Haller; music, Les Baxter; song, Guy Henric, Jerry Styner; choreography, Jack Baker; sound, Vern Kramer, Jr.; special effects, Roger George; camera, Sam Leavitt; editor, Ronald Sinclair, Fred Feitshans.

Vincent Price (Dr. Goldfoot); Frankie Avalon (Craig Gamble); Dwayne Hickman (Todd Armstrong); Susan Hart (Diane); Jack Mullaney (Igor); Fred Clark (D. J. Pevney); Alberta Nelson (Reject #12); Milton Frome (Motorcycle Cop); Hal Riddle (Newsvendor); Kay Elhardt (Girl in Club); Vincent L. Barnett (Janitor); Joe Ploski (Cook); William Baskin (Guard); Sam and the Ape Men with Diane de Marco (Themselves); Patti Chandler, Sally Sachse, Sue Hamilton, Marianne Gaba, Issa Arnal, Pam Rodgers, Sally Frei, Jan Watson, Mary Hughes, Luree Holmes, Laura Nicholson, China Lee, Deanna Lund, Leslie Summers, Kay Michaels, Arlene Charles (Robots); Annette Funicello, Aron Kincaid, Harvey Lembeck (Guest Stars).

A wacky spoof of spy sagas, mad scientists, and the Keystone Kops. Price is the zany Dr. Goldfoot who invents an electronic duplicating machine for producing beautiful bikini-clad girls who are programmed to seduce wealthy men and urge them to turn over their fortunes to Price. It is Price's nutty assistant Igor (Mullaney) who allows robot Hart to make a pass at secret agent Avalon, which causes the bad doctor's downfall.

"What a mess and what a waste!" was the lofty New York Times' evaluation of this comedy send-up. Had the picture's basic potential been exploited, it might have made lasting impressions. Best scene: the San Francisco cable car chase.

DR. GOLDFOOT AND THE GIRL BOMBS (AIP, 1966) C 86 min.

Producer, Louis M. Heyward, Fulvio Lucisano; director, Mario Bava; story, James Hartford; screenplay, Heyward, Robert Kaufman; music, Les Baxter; song, Guy Hemrick, Jerry Steyner.

Vincent Price (Dr. Goldfoot); Fabian Forte (Bill Dexter); Franco Franchi (Franco); Ciccio Ingrassia (Ciccio); Laura Antonelli (Rosanna); Movana Tahi (Goldfoot's Assistant).

This Italian-made and dubbed sequel to Dr. Goldfoot and the Bikini Machine has Red China and Price teaming to start a war between the U.S. and the Soviet Union by killing a major general and dropping a bomb on Moscow, making each side think the other has committed an act of aggression. US agent (Forte) and Italian doormen (Franchi and Ingrassia) join forces to stop Price, the latter ending up a prison commandant in Siberia.

Directed by the highly regarded Mario Bava, the film should have been much better than it was.

DR. NO (UA, 1963) C 105 min.

Producer, Harry Saltzman, Albert R. Broccoli; director, Terence Young, based on the novel by Ian Fleming; screenplay, Richard Maibaum, Johanna Harwood, Berkely Mather; music, Monty Newman; orchestrator, Burt Rhodes; music director, Eric Rodgers; production designer, Ken Adam; main titles designer, Maurice Binder; animator, Trevor Bond, Robert Ellis; art director, Syd Cain; assistant director, Clive Reed; makeup, John O'Gorman; sound, Wally Milner, John Dennis; special effects, Frank George; camera, Ted Moore; editor, Peter Hunt.

Sean Connery (James Bond); Ursula Andress (Honey); Joseph Wiseman (Dr. No); Jack Lord (Felix Leiter); Bernard Lee (M); Anthony Dawson (Professor Dent); John Kitzmiller (Quarrel); Zena Marshall (Miss Taro); Eunice Gayson (Sylvia); Lois Maxwell (Miss Moneypenny); Lester Prendergast (Puss-Feller); Tim Moxon (Strangeways); Margaret LeWars (Girl Photographer); Reggie Carter (Jones); Peter Burton (Major Boothroyd); William Foster-Davis (Duff); Louis Blaazer (Playdell-Smith); Michele Mok (Sister Rose); Dolores Keaton (Mary); Yvonne Shima (Sister Lily).

John Kitzmiller, Ursula Andress, and Sean Connery in Dr. No (UA, 1963).

"There hasn't been a film like Dr. No since ... when? The
Mickey Spillane thrillers of the middle 'fifties' Dr. No is the headiest
box office concoction of sex and sadism ever brewed in a British
studio, strictly bathtub hooch but a brutally potent intoxicant for
all that. Just as Mike Hammer was the softening up for James
Bond, so Bond is the softening up for ... what? A fascist cinema
uncorrupted by moral scruples? The riot of a completely anarchist
cinema? Dr. No could be the breakthrough to something ... but
what? At one point Bond nonchalantly fires half a dozen shots into
the back of a helpless opponent--the British cinema will never be
the same again" (Richard Whitehall in the British Films and Filming).
    No sooner does British secret service agent 007 (Connery)
arrive in Jamaica to investigate the murder of a fellow agent, than
he becomes the unwilling target of geologist Professor Dent (Dawson)
and Miss Taro (Marshall). Connery survives the assorted deadly
escapades to follow up clues leading to the mysterious Dr. No
(Wiseman). Accompanied by black man Quarrel (Kitzmiller) and
statuesque marine life naturalist Honey (Andress), Connery infiltrates Wiseman's offshore retreat at Crab Key, only to be captured
by the power-hungry madman who informs his prisoners that he is
a member of SPECTRE (The Special Executive for Counter-Intelligence, Terrorism, Revenge and Extortion) using a nuclear-labora-
tory to sidetrack rockets launched from Cape Canaveral. The incarcerated Connery later scampers up a ventilator shaft, dodging
radioactive dangers and shortcircuiting Wiseman's master control
board. Connery and Andress escape aboard a commandeered
speedboat just before Wiseman and the Crab Key base are demolished in a spectacular explosion (in the original book, Dr. No
is buried under a 20-foot pile of bird manure).

    Ian Fleming may have written his James Bond series to be
read while sipping martinis, but from the first of the filmed entries
onward, it was clear that viewers could delightedly chomp through
several bagfulls of popcorn while enjoying each new installment of
the readjusted escapist entertainment. Here was a new breed of
spy, rather distantly related to the trenchcoated character, Richard
Hannay, who wandered across Scottish moors in The Thirty-Nine
Steps (1935), or any of the countless successors in 1940s espionage
screen thrillers who dynamically challenged and conquered the Axis
foe. Actor Connery was presented in such a way as to fulfill most
every Fleming-Bond extravagance. This licensed-to-kill agent is
a sartorial snob and a connoisseur extraordinaire of food, drink,
women, and the high life. In short, Connery is a most muscular
and tanned debonair defender of the faith, who has his tongue
planted well in his cheek.
    One critic quite properly categorized Dr. No as "sadism for
the family," and so it was, garnering over $6.3 million in dis-
tributors' domestic rentals, based on a $1.2 million investment.
With this and all subsequent James Bond screen entries, the prime
gimmick was not the mystery, but the incredible events that happened
along the way (in Dr. No, ranging from the tarantula dropped onto
Connery's bed to the fire-breathing tank dragon utilized by the metal-

handed villain), with Connery operating in increasingly elaborate
settings and utilizing a constantly more staggering variety of
gadgetry-weapons.

DOSSIER   (20th-Fox, 1960)   48 min.

    Producer, Herbert Swope, Jr.; associate producer, Teresa
Calatrese; director, Montgomery Pittman; based on the book Operation Cicero by L. C. Moyzisch; screenplay, Robert Dennis; art director, Duncan Cramer, Ben Hayne; music director, Lionel Newman; camera, Joe MacDonald.
    David Hedison (Victor Sebastian); Luciana Paluzzi (Simone);
Edgar Bergen (Joseph Heidegger); John Williams (Nicolas Constantin); Paul Burke (Robertson); Kurt Kreuger (Van Stappen);
Anthony Eustrel (Strass); Frank Wolf (Radi); and: William Kendis,
Ted Otis.

    One of the segments of the "Five Fingers" video series,
this film was issued as a bottom bill feature in Britain. Its tenuous plot focused on a ventriloquist (Bergen), really an undercover
agent, who in Lausanne becomes implicated with the efforts of East
and West to capture a fabulous list of international spies operating
from both sides of the Iron Curtain.
    "Tired, old cloak-and-dagger tactics which hit a new
low..." was the verdict of the British Monthly Film Bulletin.

THE DOUBLE MAN   (WB, 1967)   C   105 min.

    Producer, Hal E. Chester; director, Franklin J. Schaffner;
based on the novel Legacy of a Spy by Henry S. Maxfield; screen-
play, Alfred Hayes, Frank Tarloff; music, Ernest Freeman;
assistant director, Ron Jackson, William Cartlidge; art director,
Arthur Lawson; camera, Denys Coop; editor, Richard Best.
    Yul Brynner (Dan Slater/Kalmar); Britt Ekland (Gina);
Clive Revill (Frank Wheatly); Anton Diffring (Berthold); Moira
Lister (Mrs. Carrington); Lloyd Nolan (Edwards); George Mikell
(Max); Brandon Brady (Gregori); Julia Arnall (Anna); David Bauer
(Miller); Ronald Radd (General); Kenneth J. Warren (Police Chief);
David Healy (Halstead); Carl Jaffe (Police Surgeon); Frederick
Schiller (Ticket Seller); Douglas Muir (Wilfred); Ernst Walder
(Frischauer); Bee Duffell (Woman on Train); John G. Heller (Bar-
tender).

    When Dan Slater (Brynner) of the C. I. A. learns that his
son has been killed (or murdered) in a Tyrolean Alps ski mishap,
he rushes pell mell into the trap engineered by the Russians who
plan to eliminate him and substitute a plastic surgery-derived lookalike, Kalmar (Brynner), in his stead.
    So much is made of the European skiing locales (on the spot
filming at Arlberg, Stuben, Warth, St. Alban, etc.) that one expects

Yul Brynner and Anton Diffring (center) in The Double Man (WB, 1967).

these sites to have an integral part in the plot, yet the snow scenes emerge as superimposed atmosphere to which the story continually veers solely by contrivance. The few moments of technical excellence (when Brynner confronts "himself") hardly compensate for the oversimplified plot in which every action is overtly telescoped to the viewer.

One of the more explicit denouncements of this unsmart spy feature originated from Renata Adler (New York Times): "The whole form may eventually dissolve, with a double agent chasing himself about in place, into stories of suicide from ambivalent paranoia."

DOWN IN SAN DIEGO (MGM, 1941) 70 min.

Producer, Frederick Stephani; director, Robert B. Sinclair; story, Franz G. Spencer; screenplay, Harry Clork, Spencer; art director, Cedric Gibbons, Gabriel Scognamillo; set decorator, Edwin B. Willis; sound, Douglas Shearer; camera, Paul Vogel; editor, Ben Lewis.

Bonita Granville (Betty Haines); Ray McDonald (Hank Parker); Dan Dailey (Al Haines); Leo Gorcey (Snap Collins); Henry O'Neill

(Colonel Halliday); Stanley Clements (Louie Schwartz); Charles B.
Smith (Crawford Cortland); Dorothy Morris (Mildred Burnette);
Frederic Worlock (Eric Kramer); Robert O. Davis (Henry Sheode);
Hobart Cavanaugh (Telegraph Clerk); William Tannen (Matt Herman);
Ludwig Stossel (Brock); Connie Gilchrist (Proprietress); George
Watts (Sgt. O'Hallihan); Al Trescony (Jimmie Collin); Joe Sawyer
(Dutch); Anthony Ward (Tony); Veda Ann Borg (Cashier); Ralph
Sanford (Man); Ernie Alexander (Sailor); Audrene Brier (Check
Room Girl); George Watts (Desk Sergeant); Ken Christy (Police
Captain Flarrity); Winifred Harris (Lady); Robert Kellard (Bell
Captain); Walter Sande (Sergeant); Hans Von Morhart (Hugo); Cliff
Danielson, James Millican (Sentries); Fredrik Vogeding (Operator);
William Forrest (Naval Intelligence Officer); Paul Newlan (Tough
Waiter); Buster Slaven (Bellhop); Frank Mills (Chauffeur); Franco
Corsaro (Barber); William Yetter (Hugo's Assistant); Jack Norton
(Drunk); James Craven (Flight Commander); Jacques Chapin
(Marine).

Ludwig Stossel, Joe Sawyer, Dan Dailey, and Anthony Ward in
Down in San Diego (MGM, 1941).

The tense world situation is used strictly for diversion in this cavalier minor entertainment. Ex-punk Dailey, now of the Marines, fights his own war against the enemy when Nazi fifth columnists kidnap his sister (Granville) and her pal (McDonald), demanding in exchange for their rescue the delivery of a speedy mosquito boat to their Pacific headquarters. Just to demonstrate where this film's mentality level is, it is the lop-eared dog Spot who ferrets out the saboteur leader.

THE ELUSIVE PIMPERNEL (British Lion, 1950)   C   109 min.

Producer-director, Michael Powell, Emeric Pressburger; based on the novel by Baroness Orczy; screenplay, Powell, Pressburger; camera, Christopher Challis; editor, Reginald Mills.
David Niven (Sir Percy Blakeney); Margaret Leighton (Lady Blakeney); Cyril Cusack (Chauvelin); Jack Hawkins (Prince of Wales); David Hutchinson (Lord Anthony Dewhurst); Robert Coote (Sir Andrew Ffoukes).

This film seemed a good idea at the time: a color remake of the popular The Scarlet Pimpernel (1934) with Niven as the 1950s answer to the late, debonair actor Leslie Howard, cast in the lead role. The British-made feature, a co-venture of Samuel Goldwyn and Alexander Korda, was plagued by production problems (including the necessity of reshooting several reels of footage). Upon release, the filmmakers discovered that post-World War II audiences were not very keen on the product or its subject matter. Niven proved to be a most unsettling Sir Percy Blakeney, Cusack too obvious as ambassador Chauvelin, and Hawkins too rambunctious as the Prince of Wales. Lavish costuming was just no substitute for screen verve, romance, and thrills.

EMBASSY (Hemdale, 1972)   C   90 min.

Producer, Mel Ferrer; director, Gordon Hessler; based on the novel by Stephen Coulter; screenplay, William Fairchild; additional material, John Bird; assistant director, Frank Ernst; production designer, John Howell; art director, Maurice Labbaye Fenykovy; set decorator, Klary Confalonieri; music, Jonathan Hodge; song, Biddu; sound, Joe Christo; camera, Raoul Coutard; editor, Willy Kemplen.
Richard Roundtree (Shannon); Chuck Connors (Kesten); Marie-Jose Nat (Lauré); Ray Milland (Ambassador); Broderick Crawford (Dunninger); Max von Sydow (Gorenko); David Bauer (Kadish); Larry Cross (Gamble); David Healy (Phelan); Karl Held (Rylands); Sarah Marshall (Miss Harding); Dee Pollock (Stacey); Afif Boulos (Foreign Minister); Leila Buheiry (Leila); Gail Clymer (Switchboard Operator); Edmond Rannania (First Man in Black); Mounir Maassri (Michel el Fahdi); Saladin Nader (Roger); David Parker (Tuler); Dean Turner (Clem Gelber); Peter Smith (Cypher Clerk).

This film represents one of the increasingly few contemporary exercises into the espionage-defection métier, with a racial issue loosely grafted onto the story as a token of social consciousness. Gorenko (von Sydow), allegedly a top official in the Russian Foreign Ministry, requests political asylum at the U.S. Embassy in Beirut. Ambassador Milland acquiesces and Shannon (Roundtree) and Dunninger (Crawford) are assigned to expedite the smuggling of von Sydow out of Lebanon. Suddenly a counter-agent pops up at the Embassy, throwing the entire plan out of whack and cascading the plot into a shootout and several decoy maneuvers improvised to implement the departure of badly wounded von Sydow. An ambiguous, diplomatic aboutface rounds off the story.

Aided by several topical twists--black man Roundtree out to beat the white Establishment, von Sydow's son being an incarcerated Soviet poet--director Gordon Hessler guides Embassy into assuming "... a far more interesting resonance than is usual in tales of spy versus spy" (British Monthly Film Bulletin).

ENEMY AGENT (Universal, 1940)   64 min.

Associate producer, Ben Pivar; director, Lew Landers; story, Sam Robins; screenplay, Robins, Edmund L. Hartmann; music director, H. J. Salter; camera, Jerome Ash.

Richard Cromwell (Jimmy Saunders); Philip Dorn (Dr. Jeffrey Arnold); Helen Vinson (Irene Hunter); Marjorie Reynolds (Peggy O'Reilly); Vinton Haworth (Lester Taylor/Lionel Carter); Robert Armstrong (G-Man Gordon); Bradley Page (Francis); Jack LaRue (Alex); Jack Carson (Ralph); Luis Alberni (Calteroni); Henry Victor (Karl the Butler); Abner Biberman (Baronoff); Russell Hicks (Scott); Milburn Stone (Meeker); Charles Williams (Patron in Restaurant); Harry Tyler (Patron); Eddy Waller (Cell Mate); Charles Wilson (Chief); Robert Homans (Doorman); Vic Potel (George the Garageman); Gaylord [Steve] Pendleton (Mickey); Netta Packer (Landlady); Jean De Briac (Barber); Peter Potter (Bob); Ernie Adams (Janitor); Dick Rush (Jailer); Lloyd Ingraham (Barber); Polly Bailey (Woman); Nick Copeland (Waiter); Chuck Morrison (Policeman); Charles Sullivan (Lender); Jessie May Jackson (Young Girl); Brooks Benedict (Head Waiter); James Craig (Drunken College Boy).

This lively little entry caused the New York Times to say, "... it has one of the strangest denouements that you are likely to see in a long time--a scene so ludicrously funny that it alone is almost worth the price of admission." More importantly for the genre, Enemy Agent made its appearance at a time when Europe was engulfed in open hostilities and Axis infiltration of American munition and plane factories seemed far less incredible than it had just a few years before.

At the Fulton Aircraft factory, where the staff is preparing a highly confidential flying fortress, draftsman Jimmy Saunders (Cromwell) is framed by enemy agent co-worker Lester Taylor

Jack LaRue, Fritz van Dongen, Jack Arnold, Helen Vinson, and Bradley Paige in <u>Enemy Agent</u> (Universal, 1940).

(Haworth) as a spy, a ruse that the G-men accept far too easily. But with "waitress" Irene Hunter (Vinson) and drunken "college boys" Carson, Pendleton, and Potter--all government operatives-- on hand, the culprits really do not have a fighting chance.

     Observant viewers noted the utilization of stock footage from <u>Radio Patrol</u> (1937) and background music from <u>Bride of Franken- stein</u> (1935).

ENEMY AGENTS MEET ELLERY QUEEN   (Columbia, 1942) 64 min.

     Producer, Larry Darmour; director, James Hogan; based on the work of Ellery Queen; screenplay, Eric Taylor; camera, James S. Brown, Jr.; editor, Dwight Caldwell.

     William Gargan (Ellery Queen); Margaret Lindsay (Nikki Porter); Charley Grapewin (Inspector Richard Queen); Gale Sonder- gaard (Mrs. von Dorn); Gilbert Roland (Paul Gillette); Sig Rumann (Heinrich); James Burke (Sergeant Velie); Ernest Dorian (Morse); Felix Basch (Helm); Minor Watson (Commodore Bang); John Hamilton (Commissioner Bracken); James Seay (Sergeant Stevens); Louis Donath (Reece); Dick Wessel (Sailor).

Margaret Lindsay and William Gargan in Enemy Agents Meet Ellery Queen (Columbia, 1942).

The swansong entry to this minor Columbia series had a topical plot lackadaisically handled. Diamonds were being smuggled from the Netherlands to the U.S. via Egypt, with Gestapo agents and American officials hunting for the jewels. While carrying the gems into the States, Roland is murdered and detective Gargan and his police inspector father become enmeshed in the case, with the settings jumping from a jewelry shop to an art gallery to an athletic club to a cemetery.

The Ellery Queen character has never had decent screen treatment, though the literature dealing with the detective could have provided a storehouse of solid entertainment. The Columbia series, first with Ralph Bellamy, then William Gargan, was a pedestrian one, slow and mundane, and lacking the snap and spark of the Lone Wolf or Falcon series.

ESPIONAGE   (MGM, 1937)   67 min.

Producer, Harry Rapf; director, Kurt Neumann; play, Walter Hackett; screenplay, Manuel Seff, Leonard Lee, Ainsworth Morgan; camera, Ray June; editor, W. Donn Hayes.

Edmund Lowe (Kenneth); Madge Evans (Patricia); Paul Lukas (Kronsky); Ketti Gallian (Sonia); Skeets Gallagher (Brown); Leonard Kinsky (Burgos); Mitchell Lewis (Sondheim); Barnett Parker (Cordell); Frank Reicher (von Cram); William Gilbert (Turk); Robert Graves (Duval); Charles Trowbridge (Doyle); Nita Pike (Fleurette); Juan Torena (South American); George Sorel (Maitre d'Hôtel); Gaston Glass (La Forge); Egon Brecher (Chief of Police); Max Lucke (Foreign Civilian); Michael S. Visaroff (Foreign Spy); Carlos J. de Valdez (Foreign Officer); Guy d'Ennery, Gordon de Main, Gennaro Curci, Ramsey Mill, Jack Chefe, Walter Bonn, Russell Hicks (Bits); Albert Pollet (French Waiter); Lita Chevret (French Secretary); Jacques Vanaire, Andre Cheron (French Inspectors); Christian J. Frank (French Guard); Eugene Beday (French Gateman); Fred Malatesta (French Pickpocket); Paul Weigel (French Telegraph Man); Carrie Daumery (French Flower Woman); Gino Corrado (Musician); Leo White (Barber); Francesco Maran (Train Guard); Eugene Borden (Doctor); Sven Borg (Masseuse); William von Brincken (Legation Officer); Jean Perry, Robert du Couedic, Albert Moriene (Waiters); Betty Blythe (Passenger); Charles Williams (Simmons); Otto Fries (Driver); George Davis (Bartender); Herbert Corthell (Police Judge); Torben Meyer (Police Inspector); Barbara Leonard (German Telephone Operator).

What commences as a pleasant-boy-meets-girl trifle switches into a no-one-is-who-he-says-he-is bit of shenanigans à la Rome Express (1933). With the shakey European political situation in the mid-1930s, it was easy enough to add espionage overtones to this piece of comedy fluff, based on a successful London play.

Boarding the Orient Express, reporter Evans and novelist-newsman Lowe discover they have no passports and take advantage of a "borrowed" one made out in the name of a married couple. International munitions magnate Lukas, a reserved, esthetic, orderly gentleman, is traveling incognito, buffeted from annoyance in his private car by a bodyguard (Gallagher), who is posing as a St. Louis wet wash tycoon. Also aboard is American-born anarchist Kinsky who wants to kill warmonger Lukas. Evans and Lowe squabble and romance while keeping their eyes peeled for any revelations from Lukas, even following him to his Swiss villa. There it is learned he is about to marry Gallian, and as a wedding gift to her is going into the manufacture of more peaceful products.

ESPIONAGE AGENT   (WB, 1939)   83 min.

Associate producer, Louis F. Edelman; director, Lloyd Bacon; story, Robert Henry Buckner; screenplay, Warren Duff, Michael Fessier, Frank Donaghue; camera, Charles Rosher; editor, Ralph Dawson.

Joel McCrea (Barry Corvall); Brenda Marshall (Brenda Ballard); Jeffrey Lynn (Lowell Warrington); George Bancroft (Dudley Garrett); Stanley Ridges (Hamilton Peyton): James Stephenson (Dr. Rader); Howard Hickman (Walter Forbes); Nana Bryant (Mrs. Corvall); Robert O. Davis (Paul Strawn); Hans von Twardorvski (Dr. Helm); Lucien Prival (Decker); Addison Richards (Bruce Corvall); Edward Stanley (Secretary of State); William Hopper, Glenn Langan (Students); Lionel Royce (Hoffmeyer); Henry Victor (Foreign Official); Lucien Prival (Decker); Lloyd Ingraham (Woodrow Wilson); Chris Martin (Tunisian Guard); Stuart Holmes, John Harron, Fern Barry, Al Lloyd, Eddie Graham, Sally Sage, Alice Connors (Americans); Fred Vogeding, Arno Frey (Men); Sarah Edwards, Lois Chenney, Lottie Williams (Women); Louis Adlon (Youth); Vera Lewis (Militant Woman); Dorothy Vaughan (Stout Woman); Sidney Bracy (Steward); Alex Melesh (Headwaiter); George Irving (Elderly Official); Emmett Vogan, William Worthington, Selmer Jackson (Instructors); John Hamilton (Code Room Instructor); Rolf Lindau (Foreign Agent); Egon Brecher (Detective Larson); Nella Walker (Mrs. Peyton); Jean De Briac (Waiter); Henry Von Zynda (Guard); Billy McClain (Manservant); Winifred Harris (Lady Ashford); Frederick Lindsley (Announcer); Eddie Acuff (Taxi Driver).

While a preamble to the heartier patriotic espionage flicks of the 1940s, Espionage Agent won few endorsements. (". . . [A]n illustrated lecture on the spy menace in the United States . . . but the McCrea-Marshall high-jinks with the enemy spy ring are so ridiculous that the argument itself loses dignity"--New York Times.) Beneath the camouflage of entertainment there were such messages to the American public as There is a difference between pacifistic tolerance and stupidity, and Isolationism is a political policy not a brick wall.

Barry Corvall (McCrea) of the U.S. diplomatic service meets Brenda Ballard (Marshall) in Morocco at a legation function. Unknown to him she is connected with a foreign spy ring who agree to provide her with a faked passport to America if she later supplies them with needed information. McCrea and she fall in love. Once back in the States he completes his courses at the foreign service school in Washington, D.C., and they wed. Suddenly Marshall becomes recalcitrant with her espionage sponsors and they threaten to expose her, but she jumps the gun by informing hubby of her entire shady past. Naturally he must now resign from the service, leaving them both quite free to head for Europe and contact the head of the spy ring in Geneva, for the couple are determined to do their bit for America's safety.

Mingled in this off-the-cuff demonstration of childish counterspying on the Continent, Espionage Agent puts in a heavy plug for the efficiency of the U.S. State Department in its training of America's first line of defense. A liberal amount of newsreel footage was incorporated into the proceedings to give the film a semi-realistic flavor.

LES ESPIONS [The Spies] (Cinedis, 1957)   136 min.

Producer, L. de Mazure; director, Henri-Georges Clouzot;
based on the novel Le Vertige de Minuit by Egon Hostovsky; screenplay, Clouzot, Gerome Geronimi; set designer, Rene Renoux; music,
Georges Auric; camera, Christian Matras.

Martita Hunt (Connie Harper); Vera Cluzot (Lucy); Gabrille
Dorziat (Madame Andree); Curt Jurgens (Alex); Peter Ustinov
(Michael Kiminsky); Sam Jaffe (Sam Rutledge); Gerard Sety (Dr.
Malic); O. E. Hasse (Vogel); Paul Carpenter (Colonel Howard);
Louis Seigner (Valette); Pierre Larquey (Taxi Driver); and:
Georgette Larquey, Jean Brochard, Fernand Sardou.

Because Dr. Malic's (Sety) psychiatric clinic is in financial
difficulties, he is more than intrigued by the bizarre offer of a
man (Carpenter) who calls himself Colonel Howard of the U. S.
Army and requests the doctor to secrete important international
agent Alex (Jurgens) in the clinic for a few days.   Only later does
Sety discover that Jurgens is an atomic scientist whose latest invention has made him the target of both Russia and America.   In
the process of trying to retain his clinic's stability and his own life,
Sety wonders if the five million franc price is worth the cost, especially when a strange new nurse (Hunt) shows up, and Soviet
(Ustinov) versus American (Jaffe) spy derring-do at the clinic gets
'way out of hand.

Although directed by the famed Henri-Georges Clouzot (Wages
of Fear, 1953; Diabolique, 1955) little is known about this feature
across the Atlantic, for it never had American release.   One of
the interesting observations on this modestly-regarded (in Europe)
feature was offered by one of the film's performers, Peter Ustinov.
"Les Espions might have been marvelous but it could never make up
its mind what it was, whether it was Kafka-grim or Kafka-comic.
The idea was a splendid one--a lot of spies who don't know who's
employing them, who are shooting each other and don't know why.
This kind of whimsy appeals to me, because I'm thoroughly sick and
tired of 'serious' spy pictures with people dutifully reporting back
to M. I. 5, or the C. I. A. or the Russian Secret Police. "

THE EXECUTIONER (Columbia, 1970)   C   111 min.

Producer, Charles H. Schneer; director, Sam Wanamaker;
based on a story by Gordon McDonell; screenplay, Jack Pulman;
assistant director, Peter Price; art director, E. W. Marshall;
music-music director, Ron Goodwin; sound, Iain Bruce; camera,
Denys Coop; editor, Roy Watts.

George Peppard (John Shay); Joan Collins (Sarah Booth);
Judy Geeson (Polly Bendel); Oscar Homolka (Racovsky); Charles
Gray (Vaughan Jones); Nigel Patrick (Colonel Scott); Keith Michell
(Adam Booth); George Baker (Philip Crawford); Alexander Scourby
(Professor Parker); Peter Bull (Butterfield); Ernest Clark (Roper);
Peter Dyneley (Balkov); Gisela Dali (Anna).

Despite its ever-changing locales and the crescendos of "sophisticated" turnabouts in plot and characterizations, The Executioner might well have been created directly for television, for it complies with the major dogma of the video medium: do not make any artistic or moral commitment. Somewhere in the outer recesses of this film is a token nod to the dilemma of the 1970s spy film. How can audience interest be maintained in a well-worn genre where the only new plot twists lie in the intellectual areas of deep examination of moral issues involving the cold war professionals? If the film is observed closely, director Sam Wanamaker sneaks in several small doses of his own brand of political philosophy, none of it very positive to the Establishment way of life (e.g., one bureau chief remarks, "It's all a game. It doesn't matter which side wins, as long as it's fun to watch").

British Intelligent agent John Shay (Peppard) narrowly survives destruction in Vienna when Communist counter-espionage ruins his operations. He returns to London positive that a double agent in lurking at M.I.5 headquarters. His bureau secretary girlfriend Polly Bendel (Geeson) removes pertinent files which verify Peppard's assumption and throws suspicion on agent Adam Booth (Michell), with whose wife (Collins) Peppard is having an affair. To unmask the security leak regardless of the cost to friendship and love life, Peppard hikes to Istanbul for corroborating data. Nevertheless, his charges are tossed out by his chief. Later Peppard relies on the testimony of a scientist (Baker) and kills Michell as a spy. He then assumes the dead man's identity and with Collins in tow, keeps the late agent's rendezvous in Athens. There an East-West cat-and-mouse game is played out and the Russians demand that Baker be turned over in exchange for captive Collins. The ironic denouement allows the "right" side to triumph, and although Peppard's suspicions of the malefactors prove to be somewhat offbase, he has engineered a desirable result which merits him a promotion within the Establishment he so despises.

THE EXTERMINATORS   see   COPLAN FX 18 CASSE TOUT

A FACE IN THE RAIN   (Embassy, 1963)   90 min.

Executive producer, Rory Calhoun, Victor Orsatti; producer, John Calley; director, Irvin Kershner; story, Guy Elmes; screenplay, Hugh Butler, Jean Rouverol; art director, Sergio Canevari; music, Richard Markowitz; sound, Verna Fields; camera, Haskell Wexler; editor, Melvin Sloan.

Rory Calhoun (Rand); Marina Berti (Anna); Niall McGinnis (Klaus); Massimo Giuliani (Paolo); and: Peter Zander, Danny Ryais.

American espionage agent Calhoun arrives in German-occupied Pisa, Italy, during World War II to carry out a mission.

Lo and behold he bungles his assignment--spies can be human! In his retreat he takes refuge in the apartment of Berti, whose language professor husband is being detained by the provisional police. Calhoun soon discovers that Berti has an "arrangement" with German officer McGinnis, the latter having agreed to intervene for her husband if she is cooperative at the hearth side. Fugitive Calhoun can only stand by in dismay as the McGinnis-Berti relationship reaches crisis level.

The superior camera work greatly enhances this sensible, offbeat little picture.

FAITES VOS JEUX, MESDAMES see FEU A VOLONTE

THE FALCON'S BROTHER (RKO, 1942) 63 min.

Producer, Maurice Geraghty; director, Stanley Logan; screenplay, Stuart Palmer, Craig Rice; music, Roy Webb; art director, Albert S. D'Agostino, Walter E. Keller; camera, Russell Metty; editor, Mark Robson.

George Sanders (Falcon); Tom Conway (Tom); Jane Randolph (Marcia); Don Barclay (Goldy); Amanda Varela (Carmelita); George Lewis (Valdez); Gwili Andre (Diane); Cliff Clark (Nolan); Edward Gargan (Bates); James Newill (Paul); Charlotte Wynters (Arlette); Andre Charlot (Savitski); Eddie Dunn (Grimes); Mary Halsey (Miss Ross); Richard Martin (Steamship Official); Kay Aldridge (Victory Gown Model/Spanish Girl).

By the middle of the war, the detective hero had fully taken up his country's defense against the Axis powers. George Sanders, however, was demanding an exit from the Falcon series and in order to satisfy him, the RKO mentors hired his look-a-like brother Tom Conway to continue the part. Conway proved to be even more popular than Sanders in the role and kept the Falcon series going for another five years.

This entry found Gay Lawrence (Sanders) meeting his brother Tom (Conway) at a ship docking in New York, only to be informed that Conway has been killed. A quick gander at the corpse tells Sanders the body is not his brother's. The plot then takes off. Conway is being hounded by a Nazi sympathizer whose identity he knows. Joining forces with his brother, Sanders is murdered trying to protect a South American official. Conway then takes patriotism in hand, promising to revenge his brother's death by combatting the Nazis. Ironically, most of the later Falcon films with Conway had little to do with the world situation.

THE FALLEN SPARROW (RKO, 1943) 94 min.

Producer, Robert Fellows; director, Richard Wallace; based on the novel by Dorothy B. Hughes; screenplay, Warren Duff; art

director, Albert S. D'Agostino, Mark Lee Kirk; production designer,
Van Nest Polglase; assistant director, Sam Ruman; music, Roy
Webb; music director, C. Bakaleinikoff; sound, Terry Kellum,
James Stewart; special effects, Vernon L. Walker; camera, Nicholas
Musuraca; editor, Robert Wise.

John Garfield (Kit); Maureen O'Hara (Toni Donne); Walter
Slezak (Dr. Skaas); Patricia Morison (Barby Taviton); Martha
O'Driscoll (Whitney Hamilton); John Banner (Anton); John Miljan
(Inspector Tobin); Hugh Beaumont (Otto Skaas); Bruce Edwards
(Ab Parker); George Lloyd (Sergeant Moore); Russ Powell (Priest);
James Farley (Bartender); Lee Phelps (Cop); Charles Lung (Carlo);
Rosina Galli (Mama); Marty Faust (Chef, Carlo's Cafe); Lillian
West (Receptionist); Miles Mander (Dr. Gudmundson); Edith Evan-
son (Nurse); Bud Geary (Cab Caller); William Edmunds (Papa);
Stella Le Saint (Woman in Street); Nestor Paiva (Jake); Jack Carr
(Danny); Jane Woodworth, Patti Brill, Margie Stewart, Margaret
Landry, Mary Halsey (Bits); Andre Charlot (Pete); Eric Wilton
(Butler); Erford Gage (Roman); Joe King (Desk Sergeant); Al
Rhein (Man); Fely Franquelli (Gypsy Dancer); Mike Lally (Taxi
Driver); Rita Gould (Dot); Sam Goldenberg (Prince François de-
Namur); Billy Mitchell (Porter); Babe Green, George Sherwood
(G-Men); Russell Wade (Flower Clerk); Stanley Price (Caterer).

In real life, actor John Garfield was an ardent political
activist who supported the Loyalist cause during the Spanish Civil
War.   In The Fallen Sparrow he portrayed an American fighting on
the Loyalist side who is captured and tortured by the Nazis, but
who refuses to divulge the information requested of him.   When
drastic interrogation fails, the Germans allow him to escape and
to return to the U.S.   Thereafter, they hound him mercilessly,
driving the mentally shakey American to near insanity.   However,
despite the lure of three contrasting women (O'Hara, Morison,
O'Driscoll) and the omnipresent Slezak, Garfield manages to triumph
both over the Gestapo agents and his own mental fears.

Released in the midst of World War II, with Garfield being
on loan from Warner Bros. to RKO for the production, The Fallen
Sparrow misfired at the boxoffice.   Its Spanish Civil War theme was
too dated in comparison with the then current American involvement
in Europe and Asia and war-weary audiences were hardly seeking
psychological drama for escapist entertainment, even if it involved
Nazis who were subdued by the hero.

Like The Big Sleep the complicated plotline of The Fallen
Sparrow defies logical recitation and remains an engrossing puzzle-
ment.   Today the film is considered a mature and polished psychological spy movie and is quite popular in art house revivals and
on television.

FANTASTIC VOYAGE (20th-Fox, 1966) C 100 min.

Producer, Saul David; director, Richard Fleischer; based on
the story by Otto Klement, Jay Lewis Bixby; adaptation, David

Duncan; screenplay, Harry Kleiner; music, Leonard Rosenman;
assistant director, Ad Schaumer; set decorator; Walter M. Scott;
Stuart A. Reiss; art director, Jack Martin Smith, Dale Hennesy;
special effects, L. B. Abbott, Art Cruickshank, Emil Kosa, Jr.;
camera, Ernest Laszlo; editor, William B. Murphy.

Stephen Boyd (Grant); Raquel Welch (Cora Peterson); Ed-
mond O'Brien (General Carter); Donald Pleasence (Dr. Michaels);
Arthur O'Connell (Colonel Donald Reid); William Redfield (Captain
Bill Owens); Arthur Kennedy (Dr. Duval); Jean Del Val (Jan Benes);
Barry Coe (Communications Aide); Ken Scott (Secret Service Man);
Shelby Grant (Nurse); James Brolin (Technician); Brendan Fitz-
gerald (Wireless Operator).

Barry Coe (center rear), Edmond O'Brien, and Arthur O'Connell
in Fantastic Voyage (20th-Fox, 1966).

As a fascinating contrast to man's current preoccupation with
outer space, this flick imaginatively explores the physical world
of the inner man.   The expertly staged piece of science fiction
garnered two Oscars.   To spice the extended voyage through a man's
circulatory system, a spy element was injected into the screen plot,
with one individual aboard the miniaturized craft out to sabotage
the unprecedented mission.

A brilliant scientist of a country opposed to the U. S. defects
to the Americans.   Then enemy agents cause his almost fatal car

mishap, hoping he will be unable to reveal the secrets of his successful experiments in prolonged miniaturization. Allied Intelligence, with General Carter (O'Brien) at its head, orders the subminiaturization of a technician-filled submarine to be injected into the patient's carotid artery with its destination the injured man's head and the source of the cerebral blood clot. Aboard the shrunken craft are doctors Pleasence and Kennedy, Kennedy's assistant Welch, ship's captain Redfield, and security man Boyd. Because their vessel and they themselves will remain tiny only for a short period, there is a race against time to reach the brain area and have Kennedy apply his laser beam surgery.

So as not to offend audiences, the body organs shown in Fantastic Voyage were constructed in abstract tones with the blood a pale yellow and the inner arteries like underwater marshlands. A highly publicized aspect of this $5 million feature was the continuing sight of shapely Welch floating about in her form-fitting rubberized frogman's suit, a vision as eyefilling as when Jane Russell graced Underwater! (1955) in a tight, red swimsuit.

THE FAT SPY (Magna, 1966) C 75 min.

Producer, Everett Rosenthal; associate producer, Patrick Plives; director, Joseph Cates; screenplay, Matthew Andrews; music, Al Kasha; songs, Jordan Christopher and Chuck Alden; sound, Charles Federmack; assistant director, George Goodman; makeup, Clay Lambert; camera, Joseph Brun; editor, Mort Falleck.
Phyllis Diller (Camille); Jack E. Leonard (Irving/Herman); Brian Donlevy (Wellington); Jayne Mansfield (Junior); Jordan Christopher (Frankie); The Wild Ones (Themselves); Johnny Tillotson (Dodo); Lauree Berger (Nanette); Lou Nelson (The Sikh); Toni Lee Shelley (Mermaid); Penny Roman (Secretary); Adam Keefe (Special Voices); Chuck Alden, Tommy Graves, Linda Harrison, Deborah White, Tracy Vance, Eddie Wright, Tommy Trick, Toni Turner, Jill Bludner, Jeanette Taylor (Treasure Hunters).

Twelve (nondescript) teenagers from Fink University search for treasure on an island off Florida. Involved in the cheap mayhem is spy Leonard, the point of rivalry between Diller and Mansfield, the former winning his heart by using her raucous laugh as a mating call. At the last minute Donlevy replaced George Raft as the cosmetic company owner in this slapdash independent production which saw very limited distribution. "It's from dudsville" was Variety's reaction.

FATHOM (20th-Fox, 1967) C 99 min.

Producer, John Kohn; associate producer, Peter Medak; director, Leslie Martinson; based on the novel by Larry Forrester;

Jack E. Leonard in The Fat Spy (Magna, 1966).

screenplay, Lorenzo Semple, Jr.; art director, Maurice Carter; set decorator, Alan Cassie; music-music director, John Dankworth; titles, Maurice Binder; sound, Jonathan Bates; assistant director, David Tringham; parachute sequences: devised by Ken Vos, aerial camera by Jacques Dubourg; camera, Douglas Slocombe; editor, Max Benedict.

Tony Franciosa (Peter Merriweather); Raquel Welch (Fathom Harvill); Ronald Fraser (Douglas Campbell); Greta Chi (Jo-May Soon); Richard Briers (Timothy); Tom Adams (Mike); Clive Revill (Serapkin); Reg Lye (Mr. Trivers); Ann Lancaster (Mrs. Trivers); Elizabeth Ercy (Ulla); Tutte Lemkow (Mehmed).

Californian dental technician and champ amateur sky diver Fathom Harvill (Welch) is vacationing in Europe when she is abducted in Málaga by Douglas Campbell (Fraser). He informs her that, as head of NATO Intelligence, he requires her assistance in recovering the "Fire Dragon" nuclear trigger device which was lost in the Mediterranean Sea after a bomber plane crash. At least two sets of enemy agents are after the mechanism, Serapkin (Revill) of Red China and Peter Merriweather (Franciosa) of America. Fraser requires Welch to parachute into Franciosa's villa and proceed from there on the recovery mission. A few

Clive Revill and Raquel Welch in Fathom (20th-Fox, 1967).

murders later, Welch is dismayed to learn that "Fire Dragon" is
actually a precious stolen Ming Dynasty treasure and that Fraser
is the real culprit in the robbery caper.

As its chief assets, Fathom had the tantalizing cleavage of
statuesque star(let) Welch and an unpretentious air which made the
extensive and strenuous capering throughout the Spanish countryside
a fine frolic. For a change, here was one entry in the super agent
cycle that did not rely on gadgetry and excessive verbal sexual
innuendoes.

FEU A VOLONTE [Faites vos Jeux, Mesdames] (Speva/Hesperia/
Cine-Alliance, 1965)   88 min.

Director, Marcel Ophuls; story, Jacques Robert; screenplay,
Ophuls, Robert; music, Ward Single; sound, Antoine Petitjean;
camera, Jean Tournier; editor, Louisette Hautecouer.
Eddie Constantine (Mike Warner); Nelly Bendetti (Soledad);
Daniel Ceccalid (Stephane); and: Laura Valenzuela, Luis Davila,
Alfredo Mayo, Enriqueta Canballcina, Dieter Kollesch.

A gang of women spies, led by an ex-Nazi agent, kidnap a
17-year-old atomic scientist and attempt to auction the young genius
off to world powers, but are combatted by F.B.I. agent Mike
Warner (Constantine).

"In order to save this kind of film from total mediocrity a touch of madness and humor, or a particular cleverness in handling the script is needed. Marcel Ophuls hasn't found it necessary to refine and gives us the usual product in all its guaranteed and original stupidity" (Cinéma 65).

LA FILLE DE MATA-HARI [The Daughter of Mata Hari] (Regent, 1954) 92 min.

Director, Carmine Gallone, Renzo Merusi; based on the novel by Cecil Saint-Laurent; screenplay, Merusi, Jean Aurel, Piccini Vitali; art director, Virgilio Marchi; music, Alessandro Casagrande; choreography, Ludmilla Tcherina; camera, Gabor Pogany; editor, Borys Levine.

Ludmilla Tcherina (Elyne); Erno Crisa (Prince Anak); Frank Latimore (Douglas Kent); Milly Vitale (Angela); Enzo Bilotti (Von Hopen); V. Inkyinoff (Naos).

A meandering attempt to update the Mata Hari legend to World War II times, the storyline is a mere excuse for Tcherina, as the daughter of the late, exalted spy, to exercise her ballet expertise. The film is set in 1941 Indonesia where the Dutch are in full retreat from the advancing Japanese forces. Incidentally, Tcherina meets the same onscreen fate as mama.
Television title: Mata Hari's Daughter.

FIRE AT WILL see FEU A VOLONTE

FIREBALL FORWARD (20th-Fox/ABC-TV, 1973) C 93 min.

Producer, Frank McCarthy; director, Martin Chomsky; screenplay, Edmund North; art director, Jack Martin Smith, Bill Malley; music, Lionel Newman; camera, Robert Morrison.

Ben Gazzara (Barrett); Eddie Albert (Colonel Graham); Ricardo Montalban (Jean Duval); Morgan Paull (Sergeant Collins); L. Q. Jones (Major Larkin); Robert Patten (Colonel Avery); Dana Elcar (Colonel Talbot); Anne Francis (Helen Sawyer); Edward Binns (Corps Commander); Curt Lowens (Captain Bauer).

This stodgy telefeature was created to utilize excess footage from the theatrical feature Patton. It told of a World War II general (Gazarra) who is ordered to command a hard-luck division which may have a bad security leak. Among the cameo-studded cast were Patten as a brash colonel, Francis as a hard-boiled lady journalist, Albert playing a kindly intelligence officer, and Montalban as the resolute French guerrilla fighter.

THE FIREFLY (MGM, 1937) C 138 min.

Producer, Hunt Stromberg; director, Robert Z. Leonard; based on the operetta by Otto A. Harbach and Rudolf Friml; adaptation, Ogden Nash; screenplay, Frances Goodrich, Albert Hackett; choreography, Albertina Rasch; art director, Cedric Gibbons; new song, Bob Wright, Chet Forrest, and Friml; music director, Herbert Stothart; sound, Douglas Shearer; camera, Oliver Marsh; editor, Robert J. Kern.

Jeanette MacDonald (Nina Maria Azara); Allan Jones (Don Diego Manrique de Lara / Captain François de Coucourt); Warren William (Colonel de Rougemont); Billy Gilbert (Innkeeper); Henry Daniell (General Savary); Douglass Dumbrille (Marquis de Melito); Leonard Penn (Etienne); Tom Rutherford (King Ferdinand VII); Bele Mitchell (Lola); George Zucco (St. Clair, Chief of French Secret Service); Corbett Morris (Duval); Matthew Boulton (Duke of Wellington); Robert Spindola (Juan); Ian Wolfe (Minister); Manuel Alvarez Maciste (Pedro); Frank Puglia (Pablo); John Piccori (Cafe Proprietor); James B. Carbon (Smiling Waiter); Jason Robards (Spanish Patriot); Alan Curtis (French Soldier); Ralph Byrd (French Lieutenant); Dennis O'Keefe (French Soldier-Admirer);

George Zucco, Harry Worth, and Allan Jones in The Firefly (MGM, 1937).

Maurice Cass (Strawberry Vendor); Sam Appel (Fruit Vendor);
Maurice Black (Pigeon Vendor); Rolfe Sedan (Hat Vendor); Inez
Palange (Flower Woman); Harry Worth (Secret Service Adjutant);
Hooper Atchley, John Merton (French Officers); Stanley Price
(Joseph Bonaparte); Brandon Hurst (English General); Pedro de
Cordoba (Spanish General); Theodore von Eltz (Captain Pierlot);
Lane Chandler (Captain of the Guard); Edward Keane (Colonel, Chief
of Staff); Sidney Bracy (Secretary); Eddie Phillips (Captain); Russ
Powell (Stablehand); Agostino Borgato (Peasant); Robert Z. Leonard,
Albertina Rasch (Cafe Extras).

To provide a proper solo vehicle for their lustrous prima
donna Jeanette MacDonald, MGM would risk nearly anything within
reason. Thus the Otto Harbach-Rudolf Friml operetta The Firefly
(opened December 2, 1912 for a 120-performance Broadway run)
was expanded from the original yarn of an Italian street singer who
poses as a cabin boy to remain near the yachtsman she desires,
into a tale of espionage and romance in Napoleonic Spain. The
public was adequately satisfied by this lavishly mounted sepia-
colored exercise, although there were strong reservations from
critical quarters ("... it is a wearisome offering, pedestrian in
movement, stilted in dialogue, archaic in treatment and a good
sixty minutes too long"--New York World Telegram).
A fiery, popular Spanish dancer Nina Maria Azara (Mac-
Donald) is employed as a spy during the unsettled reign of Ferdinand VII (Rutherford), when the Spanish people, unable to cope
with Joseph Bonaparte (Price) on their throne, rebel and with the
aid of the English led by the Duke of Wellington (Boulton), restore
their king to the monarchy. Working in counterpoint to the carrier
pigeon-using MacDonald is French Intelligence officer Francois
de Coucourt (Jones), who is out to trap the señorita, but instead
wins her heart. MacDonald's noble efforts do help win the battle
of Vittoria for the Spanish-British forces, saving the peninsula
from Napoleonic control, MacDonald-Jones are thus free to pursue
their romantic inclinations.

For MacDonald's first starring vehicle without her ever-
present co-star Nelson Eddy, Metro supplied compact Jones and
had him perform the newly-composed "Donkey Serenade." In the
course of The Firefly, the red-headed MacDonald underwent some
25 costume changes, dance and sang to "Love Is Like a Firefly,"
"When a Maid Comes Knocking at Your Heart," and "He Who
Loves and Runs Away," and performed with Jones, "Sympathy."
Despite a valiant try, MacDonald was not always suitable as the
energetic dancer caught up in the ultra noble (as essayed here) profession of spying. She and Jones frequently lapsed into pretentious
manner, relying on stock inflections and overdramatics. But then,
the ponderous dialog was not much help (e.g.: "I deserve everything you think of me, but I love you just the same").
In short, a little straight operetta goes a long way, particularly in a sumptuously-mounted production that took itself so seriously that Napoleon Bonaparte was reduced in the proceedings to a
virtual extra.

FIRST YANK INTO TOKYO   (RKO,   1945)   82 min.

     Producer, J. Robert Bren; director, Gordon Douglas; story,
Bren, Gladys Atwater; screenplay, Bren; music, Leigh Harline;
music director, C. Bakaleinikoff; assistant director, Sam Ruman;
art director, Albert S. D'Agostino, Walter Keller; set decorator,
Darrell Silvera, Charles Nields; technical advisor, R. Andrew
Smith; sound, John L. Cass; camera, Harry J. Wild; editor,
Philip Martin.

     Tom Neal (Major Ross); Barbara Hale (Abby Drake); Marc
Cramer (Jardine); Richard Loo (Colonel Okanura); Keye Luke
(Haan-Soo); Leonard Strong (Major Nogira); Benson Fong (Captain
Tanahe); Clarence Lung (Major Ichibo); Keye Chang (Captain Sato);
Michael St. Angel (Captain Andrew Kent); Edmund Glover, Robert
Clarke, Johnny Strong, Eden Nicholas, Jimmy Jordan (Prisoners);
Bruce Edwards (Captain Harris); Artarne Wong, Larry Wong
(Koreans); Albert Law (Japanese Pilot); Gerald Pierce (Waist

Clarence Lung (center) and Tom Neal in First Yank into Tokyo
(RKO, 1945).

Gunner); Harry Anderson (Submarine Commander); Ralph Stein
(Bellhop); Dorothy Curtis, Gwen Crawford, Betty Gillette, Frances
Haldern, Ione Reed, Aline Goodwins, Noreen Lee, Bobby La Salle
(Nurses); Russell Hicks (Colonel Thompson); Wallis Clark (Dr.
Langley); John Hamilton (Dr. Stacey); Selmer Jackson (Colonel
Blaine); Thomas Quon Woo, Weaver Levy, George Chung, Spencer
Chan, James Leong (Bits); Joseph Kim (Sergeant Osami); Paul
Fung (Captain Yamanashi); Bob Chinn (Japanese Soldier); Richard
Wang, Tommy Lee (Japanese Sentries); Bo Ching (Dancer); Chet
Verovan (Japanese Soldier); Eddie Luke (Ling Wan); Peter Chong
(Dr. Kai Koon); George Lee (Chinese Captain).

World War II Hollywood filmmakers were naturally anxious
to make their product exploitably topical by ripping events from
the world headlines to sandwich into their screen efforts. First
Yank into Tokyo meretriciously made use of up-to-the-last-minute
newsreel footage of the A-bomb blasts on Japan to bolster the
boxoffice chances of this "fishy little fiction" (New York Times).
Ace U. S. Army pilot Ross (Neal), who had been reared
in Japan, agrees to undergo plastic surgery to Orientalize his
features, so that he may infiltrate behind enemy lines and obtain
needed atomic fission data from Jardine (Cramer), incarcerated in
a Japanese prisoner-of-war camp. Neal is willing to undergo the
drastic operation (doctors advise him that later reversal surgery is
impossible) because he is a resounding American patriot and because his true love, nurse Abby Drake (Hale), is believed to have
been killed in war action. Lo and behold once Nipponese-ized
Neal arrives at the Axis stronghold, whom should he encounter but
Hale, very much alive and well, as serviceman-prisoner Captain
Andrew Kent (St. Clair) can well attest. Whom should the compound
commandant be? Why, none other than Neal's old college buddy
Colonel Okanura (Loo), who distinctly recalls each and every telltale nervous gesture of his one time campus cohort. (Loo even
screens footage of tense Neal on the collegiate football field to
prove his wry point.) The ending is as expected.
In the lengthy history of spy movies, relatively few entries
have focused on the logical use of transracial espionage operatives
to outsmart the opposing force. First Yank into Tokyo, despite
its strong talent-in-the-making production crew, was no inspiration
for continuing the cinema gambit. Super reliance on soundstage
sets for the outdoor scenes did nothing to enhance this very "B"
flick.

FIVE FINGERS (20th-Fox, 1952) 108 min.

Producer, Otto Lang; director, Joseph L. Mankiewicz; based
on the book Operation Cicero by L. C. Moyzisch; screenplay, Michael
Wilson; art director, Lyle Wheeler, George W. Davis; music, Bernard Herrmann; camera, Norbert Brodine; editor, James B. Clark.

James Mason (Cicero); Danielle Darrieux (Anna); Michael
Rennie (George Travers); Walter Hampden (Sir Frederic); Oscar
Karweis (Moyzisch); Herbert Berghof (Colonel von Richter); John
Wengraf (von Papen); Ben Astar (Siebert); Roger Plowden (Mac-
Fadden); Michael Pate (Morrison); Ivan Triesault (Steuben); Han-
nelore Axman (von Papen's Secretary); David Wolfe (Da Costa);
Larry Dobkin (Santos); Nestor Paiva (Turkish Ambassador);
Richard Loo (Japanese Ambassador); Keith McConnell (Johnson);
Jeroma Moshan (Char Woman); Alberto Morin (Butler); Stuart Hall
(British Military Attache); Otto Waldis (Pullman Porter); Frank
Hemingway (Narrator); Leo Mostovoy (Spectator); Sadik Tarlan,
Eghiche Harout (Men); Konstantin Shayne (Proprietor); Marc Snow
(Banker); Martin Garralaga (Butler); Lumsden Hare, Stanley Lo-
gan (M. P. s); Lester Mathews (Under Secretary); Salvador Baguez
(Ship's Captain); Faith Kruger (German Singer); John Sutton (Nar-
rator); Antonio Filauri (Italian Ambassador).

By the early 1950s, Hollywood films were strongly reflecting
the changing mores of post-World War II America, giving more
cognizance to the sociological-political-economic problems plaguing
the country.   A major exception to the neo-realism trend were the
spy films.   As Gordon Gow analyzed in Hollywood in the Fifties
(1971), "Spies, however, were another matter entirely: villains or

Michael Rennie in Five Fingers (20th-Fox, 1952).

heroes by tradition, depending upon which side they represented
(ours or the enemy's), they invariably had a romantic aura. Their
reality was of necessity obscure. They were secret people, and
therefore intriguing. They caused death, to be sure, but their
sneaky activities were usually depicted as quite separate from the
unpleasant stench of battle. " Granting this premise, director
Joseph L. Mankiewicz, nevertheless laced his facile production with
an ingenuous touch of wry wit, not bitterly pessimistic, but recog-
nizing the increasing awareness of moviegoers that in war there
are often no purely good sides, and that those who work the middle
fence are after all practical individuals with a quicker intelligence
than most.

Although set in 1944 Ankara, Five Fingers has an international rather than a regional flavor, with the bulk of its action detailing the clicking away of diplomatic machinery at the various
embassies. Mason excells as the real life spy (with the code
name of "Cicero") serving as valet to the British Ambassador (Hampden) in Turkey, who finds a quick way to make lots of money by
selling Allied war plans to the Germans. Spurring him on in his
lethal activities is Darrieux as the high-born but penniless Polish
countess, who eventually skips out on Mason. Rennie is pictured
as the young British intelligence agent considered a nuisance by
the diplomatic circles, Berghof as the heel-clicking Spanish agent
from Berlin, and Karlweis as Mason's German embassy contact.

The drolly-told caper ends on an ironic note with Mason
stranded in Brazil, having been paid off by the Germans with bogus
loot. The super twist to the whole episode: Mason's espionage
activities did little actual harm, for the German high command did
not quite believe the authenticity of his microfilmed data.

The sophisticated melodrama spawned several imitations,
plus a telefeature (Operation Cicero, 1956) and a video series also
called "Five Fingers. "

THE FORBIDDEN WOMAN (Pathé, 1927)   6, 568 feet

Supervisor, William C. DeMille; director, Paul L. Stein;
based on the novel Brothers; adaptation-continuity, Clara Beranger;
assistant director, Curt Rehfeld; costumes, Adrian; art director,
Mitchell Leisen, Wilfred Buckland; camera, David Abel.

Jetta Goudal (Zita); Ivan Lebedeff (Sheik); Leonid Snegoff
(Sultan); Josephine Norman (Zita's Maid); Victor Varconi (Colonel
Gautier); Joseph Schildkraut (Jean La Coste).

Even for the mid-1920s, this film was an excessively heavy-
handed melodrama, with Goudal mouthing such lines (title cards) as,
"Hate will quicken my woman's wits" and "You will find my hate can
be as deep as my love. "

To expedite the acquisition of confidential military plans, the
Sultan of Morocco (Snegoff) arranges for his exotic spy Zita (Goudal)
to meet Colonel Gautier (Varconi), a meeting which eventually leads
to their marriage. With her new social position, Goudal easily

obtains the needed information which is passed on to Snegoff through
her maid (Norman). Thereafter Varconi is reassigned to Paris.
Goudal follows her spouse only to fall hopelessly in love with
violinist Jean La Coste (Schildkraut), the latter turning out to be
Varconi's younger brother. When the femme fatale realizes her
heart throb can never be hers--Varconi caught his brother in a
compromising situation and demanded he join the Legion in Morocco
--petulent Goudal frames Schildkraut as a spy, but later repents
and admits her own guilt. The firing squad is her just reward.

FOREIGN AGENT (Monogram, 1942) 62 min.

        Producer, Martin Mooney, Max King; director, William
Beaudine; story, Mooney; adaptation, Mooney, John Krafft; song,
Beal Mellette and Bill Anderson; camera, Mack Stengler; editor,
Fred Baine.
        John Shelton (Jimmy); Gale Storm (Mitzi); Ivan Lebedeff
(Okura); Hanz Schumm (Werner); William Halligan (Davis); George
Travele (Nick); Patsy Moran (Joan); Lyly Lattel (Eddie); Herb
Rawlinson (Stevens); Kenneth Harlan (McCall); Jack Mulhall (Editor);
David Clarke (Carl Beck).

        Poverty row Monogram Pictures brought the spy scene home
to Hollywood in this film, whose plot has enemy operatives hustle
to steal a searchlight filter developed by a film studio technician.
As a cover for their underhanded operation, the conspirators establish a phony organization devoted to preaching war resistance.
Because the nest of German-Japanese saboteurs have killed her
inventor dad, actress Mitzi (Storm) and her boyfriend (Shelton)
are drawn into the caper as is radio commentator David (Halligan).
        The resounding patriotic touch is provided by Storm, moon-
lighting as a club singer in the story, when she performs "It's
Taps for the Japs."

FOREIGN CORRESPONDENT (UA, 1940) 119 min.

        Producer, Walter Wanger; director, Alfred Hitchcock; screen-
play, Charles Bennett, Joan Harrison; dialog, James Hilton, Robert
Benchley; set decorator, William Cameron Menzies, Alexander
Golitzen; assistant director, Edmond Bernoudy; special effects, Lee
Zavitz; camera, Rudolph Mate; editor, Otho Lovering, Dorothy
Spencer.
        Joel McCrea (Johnny Jones [later Huntley Haverstock]);
Laraine Day (Carol Fisher); Herbert Marshall (Stephen Fisher);
George Sanders (Scott ffolliott); Albert Bassermann (van Meer);
Robert Benchley (Stebbins); Edmund Gwenn (Rowley); Eduardo
Ciannelli (Krug); Martin Kosleck (Tramp); Harry Davenport (Mr.
Powers); Barbara Pepper (Doreen); Eddy Conrad (Latvian Diplomat);
Charles Wagenheim (Assassin); Craufurd Kent (Toastmaster);
Frances Carson (Mrs. Sprague); Alexander Granach (Valet); Samuel

Adams (Impersonator); Dorothy Vaughan (Jones' Mother); Betty
Bradley (Cousin Mary); Mary Young (Auntie Maude); Jack Rice
(Donald); Jackie McGee, Henry Blair (Children); Rebecca Bohannen
(Sophie); Marten Lamont (Clipper Captain); Barry Bernard (Steward);
Hilda Plowright (Miss Pimm); Gertrude Hoffman (Mrs. Benson);
Jane Novak (Miss Benson); Roy Gordon (Mr. Brood); Bert White,
Thomas Pogue, Jack Voglin, George French (Passengers); William
Stelling, John Meredith, George Cathrey (Flight Officers); Leonard
Mudie (Inspector McKenna); Holmes Herbert (Commissioner ffolliott);
Frederick Sewall (Student); Emory Parnell (John Martin, Captain of
the Mohican); James Finlayson (Dutch Peasant); Hermina Milar
(Little Dutch Girl); Loulette Sablon (Nesta); Douglas Gordon (Taxi
Driver); Colin Kenny (Waiter); Paul Sutton (Male Nurse); Robert C.
Fischer (Manager); Jack Dawson (Schoolmaster); Ken Christy,
Thomas Mizer (Plainclothesmen); June Heiden (Two Year Old);
Terry Kilburn (Boy); Carl Ekberg, Hans Von Morhart (Dutch Police-
men); Otto Hoffman (Telegrapher); Charles Halton (Bradley); Joan
Leslie (Jones' Sister); Paul Irving (Dr. Williamson); Ferris Taylor
(Jones' Father); John T. Murray (Clark); Harry Depp (Uncle
Buren); Meeka Aldrich (Donald's Wife); Willy Castello, Bill Gavier
(Dutch Pilots); Ian Wolfe (Stiles the Butler); Ernie Stanton, Donald

Laraine Day, Joel McCrea, Gertrude Hoffman, Jane Novak, Herbert
Marshall, and George Sanders in <u>Foreign Correspondent</u> (UA, 1940).

Stuart (Newsmen); Colin Kenny (Doctor); Helena Phillips Evans
(Maid); Herbert Evans (English Doorman); Frank Benson (English
Porter); Barbara Boudwin (Barmaid); Louis Borrell (Captain Lanson);
Gino Corrado (Italian Waiter); Elspeth Dudgeon, Gwendolyn Logan
(Spinsters); Eily Malyon (English Cashier); Bunny Beatty (Porter);
John Burton (English Radio Announcer); Raymond Severn (English
Boy); Lawrence Osman, Richard Hammond, Joe O'Brien, Billy
Bester, Billy Horn, Ronald Brown (Eton Boys); Louise Brien
(Secretary); Jack Alfred, George Offerman, Jr. (Copy Boys); E. E.
Clive (Mr. Naismith); Alfred Hitchcock (Man with Newspaper);
Wheaton Chambers (Committeeman).

Many filmgoers consider Foreign Correspondent to be director
Alfred Hitchcock's best American-made feature: an exciting, old-
fashioned thriller which at the same time had the gumption to make
a commentary on the then desperate state of the world. The New
York Herald-Tribune endorsed the film saying, "... it should not
be missed by anyone who cherishes the sheer sorcery of the
medium." An improbable tale? Yes! But highly atmospheric and
extremely entertaining.

Initially Hitchcock planned to base this film on Vincent
Sheean's widely read autobiographical Personal History, but world
events had altered so rapidly that the director had an original
screenplay created instead. The movie's foreword dedicated the
picture "... to those intrepid ones ... those forthright ones who
early saw the clouds of war while many of us at home were seeing
rainbows."

Manhattan crime reporter Johnny Jones (McCrea) is reassigned to cover the European scene in August 1939. His editor
requires a new slant on the war situation because foreign correspondent Stebbins (Benchley) has failed to comprehensively cover the
rapidly changing current events. Soon McCrea is ensnared in a
plot to kidnap an elderly Dutch diplomat (Bassermann) who is
carrying a confidential Allied treaty proviso from London back
to his own country. The Nazi spy ring which takes Bassermann
captive is fronted by Britisher Stephen Fisher (Marshall), father
of heroine Carol (Day), who heads a bogus world peace organization.

William Cameron Menzies' inspired set reconstructions of
European locales--the windmill in particular--did much to enhance
the realness of this movie, and the climactic trans-Atlantic plane
crash is a stunner. But most of all, it is the subtle blend of violence, hairbreadth escapes, and international politics, which makes
this film such a durable entry. The picture is loaded with direct
warnings to America at large, then remaining aloof from the war:
e. g. , beware of peacemakers who show an armed fist, it is the
responsibility of war correspondents to keep uninvolved nations
alerted to actualities.

Foreign Correspondent is one of the most satisfying screen
examples of counter casting to vividly present hard-hearted enemy
collaborators, with such established genteel cinema types as Marshall
and Gwenn (McCrea's would-be killer) quite venal beneath their
placid exteriors.

FOREIGN EXCHANGE   (Halsan/ABC-TV, 1970)   C   73 min.

Executive producer, Harold Cohen; producer, Jimmy Sangster; director, Roy Ward Baker; screenplay, Sangster; assistant director, Roy Batt; art director, Scott Macgregor; music, Philip Martell; music director, Johnny Pearson; camera, Arthur Grant; editor, Spencer Reeves.

Robert Horton (John Smith); Jill St. John (Mary Harper); Sebastian Cabot (Max); Dudley Foster (Leo); Clive Graham (Johns).

Telecast on ABC's "Movie of the Week" as a sequel to The Spy Killer (q. v.), this British-made melodrama retains the three leads from the previous film.   Horton stars as John Smith, who had resigned as a British Secret Service agent to become a detective, but who is persuaded by the intelligence agency to go to Russia to negotiate a spy exchange.   Once there he finds himself ensconced in a political plot and his future looks exceedingly bleak.

FOREIGN INTRIGUE   (UA, 1957)   C   106 min.

Producer, Sheldon Reynolds; associate producer, Nicole Millenaire; assistant producer, John Padovano; director, Reynolds; story, Reynolds, Harold J. Bloom, Gene Levitt; screenplay, Reynolds; assistant director, Tom Younger, Michel Wyn; music, Paul Durand; costumes, Pierre Balmain; Foreign Intrigue concerto, Charles Norman; makeup, Joseph Majinsky; sound, Jean Monchablon; camera, Bertel Palmgren; editor, Lennart Wallen.

Robert Mitchum (Bishop); Genevieve Page (Dominique); Ingrid Tulean (Brita); Frederick O'Brady (Spring); Gene Deckers (Sandoz); Inga Tidblad (Mrs. Lindquist); John Padovano (Tony); Frederick Schrecker (Mannheim); Lauritz Faulk (Jones); Peter Copley (Brown); Ralph Brown (Smith); George Hubert (Dr. Thibault); Nil Sperber (Baum); Jean Galland (Danemore); and: Jim Gerald, John Starck, Gilbert Robin, Valentine Camax, Robert Le Beal, Albert Simmons.

Filmed on location in Europe from Sheldon Reynolds' popular video series, Foreign Intrigue presented a stereotype version of the trenchcoated civilian (in this case agent Mitchum) tumbling about post-war Europe seeking to unravel current events which had their origins in espionage-laden World War II.

When his employer (Galland) dies of a "heart attack" on the French Riviera, Mitchum decides to check into his late boss' mysterious past.   His quest leads him on a picturesque trek through several European cities, with each new stopover revealing more of the real truth about the deceased man's past.   In Vienna there is the widow (Page), a ruthless, ardent woman indifferent to things past.   Next his information hunt leads to Stockholm and pretty Tulean (later known professionally as Ingrid Thulin), and then it is back to Vienna.   The crux of the hazy plotline is that Galland had come into possession of the names of four men in different countries who had been Quislings during the war, and that after the peace he had been blackmailing them.

There was enough plotline for three films in this laborious
production, but the assets of popular star Mitchum, the built-in
attraction of the expanded teleseries format, and the European
location filming gave the picture a boxoffice hypo. The New York
Times rightly pegged it as a "stale melodrama."

FORTY-EIGHT HOURS   see   WENT THE DAY WELL?

THE 49TH PARALLEL   see   THE INVADERS

FRÄULEIN DOKTOR   (Paramount, 1968)   C   104 min.

Producer, Dino de Laurentiis; director, Alberto Lattuada;
story, Vittoriano Petrilli; screenplay, Duilio Coletti, Stanley
Mann, H. A. L. Craig, Petrilli, Lattuada; art director, Mario
Chiari; set decorator, Enzo Eusepi; music, Ennio Morricone;
music director, Bruno Nicolai; costumes, Maria de Matteis; titles,
Lardani; sound, Dragan Grozdanovic; special effects, Dusan Piros;
assistant director, Marcello Aliprandi, Dusan Dimitrijevic, Dorde
Vujovic; camera, Luigi Luveiller; editor, Nino Baragli.

Suzy Kendall (Fräulein Doktor); Kenneth More (Colonel Fore-
man); James Booth (Meyer); Capucine (Dr. Saforet); Alexander Knox
(General Peronne); Nigel Green (Colonel Methesius); Roberto Bisacco
(Hans Schell); Malcolm Novelli (Otto Latemar); Kenneth Poitevin
(Lt. Ernst Wiechert); Bernard de Vries (Lt. Wilhelm von Ober-
dorff); Ralph Nossek (Agent); Michael Elphick (Tom); Olivera
Vuco (Marchioness de Haro); Andreina Paul (Doña Eleña de
Rivas); Silvia Monti (Margarita); Virginia Bell (Doña Julia);
Colin Tapley (General Metzler); Gerard Herter (Captain Munster);
Walter Williams (General von Hindenburg); John Atkinson (Major
Rops); James E. Mishler (General von Ludendorff); Neale Stain-
ton (Sergeant); John Webb (Agent); Joan Geary (Landlady); Aca
Stojkovic (Chemist); Mavid Popovic (Chaplain); Janez Vrhovec
(Belgian Colonel); Bata Paskaljevic, Zoran Longinovic (Wounded
English Soldiers); Dusan Bulajic (Colonel Delveaux); Miki Mikovic
(Blondel); Dusan Djuric (Aide to Ludendorff).

British Intelligence officer Foreman (More) believes a
German spy, known as Fräulein Doktor (Kendall), to be a major
peril to the war effort. Among her deadly accomplishments was
her successful arrangement of the killing of Lord Kitchener. More
sends Meyer (Booth), Kendall's captured co-worker, back to Germany as a counterspy, hoping to track down the elusive lady.
However, German Intelligence Colonel Mathesius (Green) misleads
Booth into thinking Kendall is dead. More is not persuaded by the
deception and follows her new trail to the Belgian front, where she
is posing as a rich Spanish lady organizing a Red Cross mercy
train. Her new goal is to obtain the maps of the Allied offensive

drive.   In a climactic encounter, Booth shoots More, but is himself
killed by German soldiers, leaving Kendall, for the moment, victorious.

Unlike the far less ambitious Stamboul Quest (1934), starring
Myrna Loy, which also dealt with the legendary Fräulein Doktor,
the new rendition was done on a grand scale as a Yugoslavian-
Italian co-production in English; it proved to be a costly flop.   Only
rarely did the attempt to portray a bygone era ring true (as in
the grim moments when the Germans utilize the poison gas in
their trench warfare with the French).   For the most part, Fräulein
Doktor remained a sterile exercise of a remote adventure, with
Kendall unable to provide much scope to her characterization.

Movies and the spy genre had come a long way since Mata
Hari (1932) and Dishonored (1931).   Now the distaff espionage agent
could be presented as a morphine-addicted, amoral lass who thinks
little of seducing and murdering a lesbian doctor (Capucine).   The
film, however, did not quite play cricket with the "established"
facts in the spy's adventurous life.   It was true that Fräulein Doktor, who used beauty and super intelligence to spy, did lead a
charmed existence, but in reality she is thought to have died of
morphine-addiction and insanity in a Swiss hospital, thus providing
her own nasty final downfall.

FRIENDLY ENEMIES (Producers Distributing Corp., 1925)
6, 288 feet

Presenter, A. H. Sebastian; director, George Melford; based
on the play by Samuel Shipman, Aaron Hoffman; screenplay-titles,
Alfred A. Cohn; adaptation, Josephine Quirk; camera, Charles G.
Clark.

Lew Fields (Carl Pfeiffer); Joe Weber (Henry Block); Vir-
ginia Brown Faire (June Block); Jack Mulhall (William Pfeiffer);
Stuart Holmes (Miller); Lucille Lee Stewart (Hilda Schwartz);
Eugenie Besserer (Mrs. Marie Pfeiffer); Nora Hayden (Nora);
Jules Hanft (Frederick Schnitzler); Fred Kelsey (Adolph); Johnny
Fox (Messenger Boy); Edward Porter (Naval Officer).

A fairly serious entry for the dialectic vaudevillains,
Weber and Fields.   Two German immigrants (Weber, Fields) have
become prosperous American residents by the outbreak of World
War I.   Weber is fully behind the American cause, but Fields'
loyalties are divided between his new country and his old homeland.   When German agent Miller (Holmes) persuades Fields to
contribute funds to the Kaiser's cause and the money is used to
place a successful saboteur aboard the troop ship carrying Fields'
son (Mulhall), Fields has a dramatic change of heart.   With the
aid of Weber and secret service agent Hilda Schwartz (Stewart).
the perfidious Holmes is captured.   By the fadeout, the two long-
standing friends are happily agreeing on the virtues of the American way of life.

FROM RUSSIA WITH LOVE   (UA, 1964)   C   116 min.

Producer, Harry Saltzman, Albert R. Broccoli; director,
Terence Young; based on the novel by Ian Fleming; screenplay,
Richard Maibaum, Joanna Harwood; art director, Syd Cain;
Michael White; assistant director, David Anderson; "James Bond"
theme, Monty Arnold; title song, Lionel Bart; orchestral music
composer-conductor, John Barry; makeup, Basil Newall, Paul
Rabiger; costumes, Jocelyn Rickards; titles, Robert Brownjohn,
Trevor Bond; sound, John W. Mitchell, C. Le Mesurier; special
effects, John Stears, Frank George; stunt work arranger, Peter
Perkins; camera, Ted Moore; editor, Peter Hunt.

Sean Connery (James Bond); Daniela Bianchi (Tatiana Ro-
manova); Pedro Armendariz (Kerim Bey); Lotte Lenya (Rosa Klebb);
Robert Shaw (Red Grant); Bernard Lee (M); Eunice Gayson (Sylvia);
Walter Gotell (Morzeny); Francis de Wolff (Vavra); George Pastell
(Train Conductor); Nadja Regin (Kerim's Girl); Lois Maxwell
(Miss Moneypenny); Aliza Gur (Vida); Martine Beswick (Zora);
Vladek Sheybal (Kronsteen); Leila (Belly Dancer); Hasan Ceylan
(Foreign Agent); Fred Haggerty (Krilencu); Neville Jason (Rolls
Chauffeur); Peter Bayliss (Benz); Mushet Auzer (Mehmet); Peter
Brayham (Rhoda); Desmond Llewelyn (Boothroyd); Jan Williams
(Masseuse); Peter Madden (McAdams).

Slick and sick is one way, while "hard-hitting, sexy hokum"
(Variety) is another way to describe this second James Bond screen
adventure which took full commercial advantage of the 007 mania
that was seemingly encircling an entranced globe.

The gambit here involves S. P. E. C. T. R. E. 's master plan,
guided by a scarcely seen but often heard leader called Number
One (really Ernst Stavro Blofeld) to steal the Russian Lektor cipher
machine, put the blame onto the British, and then sell the gadget
back to the Soviets at a huge profit.   The neat strategem, as out-
lined by S. P. E. C. T. R. E. 's Kronsteen (Sheybal), provides for
Russian Tatiana Romanova (Bianchi), working in the embassy at
Istanbul, to "agree" to defect to the British and bring the Lektor
with her, if a particular British operative is sent to escort her.
Since it is assumed 007 (Connery) will be the English agent dispatched, S. P. E. C. T. R. E. is hopeful of providing him with a particularly nasty liquidation to avenge the death of their valued worker,
Dr. No.

John Brosnan in James Bond in the Cinema (1972) points out
that this film "... still remains out of step with the rest of the
series and Bond fans that I've spoken to usually have strong views
concerning it; they either consider it to be the best or the worst.
Also, people who don't normally like Bond films will admit that
they enjoyed this one. " Above and beyond the more than ordinarily
solid plot spun out in From Russia with Love, a good deal of the
viewer's enjoyment derives from the eccentric villains onscreen;
not the science fiction or comic strip variety as in Dr. No but two
dastardly creatures who are real enough in their display of human
vices to be frighteningly three-dimensional.   There is the coldly-

determined hulking dynamo of destruction, blonde Red Grant (Shaw) and the ex-S. M. E. R. S. H. Soviet agent Rosa Klebb (Lenya), a Lesbian-oriented sadist who thrives on such nastiness as using a knife-toed boot to kick her victims to death. With Connery forced to combat these two unsavory characters, the challenges presented are especially exhausting and the activities abounding always very lethal and violent. But, of course, one never really has to guess who will win, but only how Connery will do it.

Part of the delight of From Russia with Love derives from the ever-shifting scenery: from London to the bazaars and embassies at Istanbul, to a gypsy camp outside the Turkish metropolis, to a perilous journey aboard the Orient Express, a climatic speedboat chase near the Gulf of Venice, and the sex-oriented idyllic finale which has Connery and Bianchi gondola-riding in Venice.

A perfect illustration of the outrageous sex-and-mayhem and caustic wit blend that has made James Bond stories so dear to readers and filmgoers, occurs midway in From Russia with Love. Connery and Kerim Bey (Armendariz), the latter a British agent in Istanbul, have just escaped a death trap at the hands of the Bulgars who work for the Russians. After they leave the perilous environs of the gypsy camp, Armendariz swears vengeance on Krilencu (Haggerty), whom he knows to have been responsible for the latest ambush attempt. The two British operatives make their way to the killer's hideout and wait outside the building, with Connery quickly and efficiently assembling his rifle. On the side of the building is a huge billboard advertisement for Bob Hope's Call Me Bwana movie (produced by Harry Saltzman and Albert R. Broccoli). The ad features an oversized picture of voluptuous Anita Ekberg. Armendariz quietly alerts Connery to watch her mouth. Thereafter, two of Armendariz's sons, masquerading as policemen, ring Haggerty's front doorbell. Almost immediately, the two street-watchers spot a light suddenly going on behind the mouth. A small trapdoor opens and a rope is lowered. Connery is about to take aim and shoot, but Armendariz insists on doing the deed himself. He takes a rifle and, balancing it on Connery's shoulder, shoots the escaping Haggerty in the back. Armendariz smiles with satisfaction and Connery, always ready with an amoral quip (heavily laced with obvious Freudian overtones), remarks "She should have kept her big mouth closed." Thus a smart example of the hero and the viewer as well, vicariously enjoying the license to kill with no legal or moral sanctions attached to the act of murder. In fact, as Connery's wisecrack emphasizes, it is one of the rewards of the new-style spy game to regard life, death, sex, luxury, and treachery as casual tidbits on the hearty road of mindless adventure. These removals of conventional strictures on existence are part and parcel of what have made the James Bond oeuvre so thoroughly enjoyed and endorsed by the public.

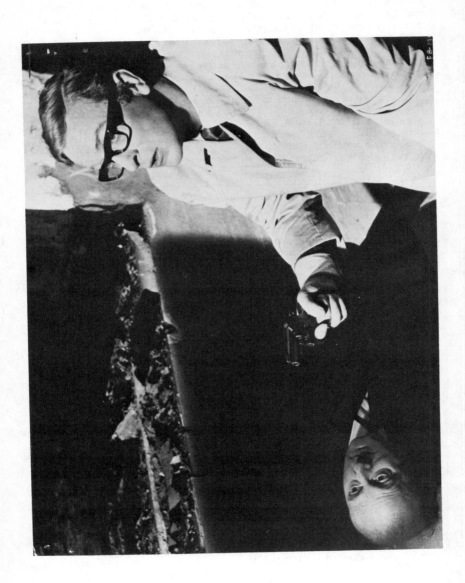

FUNERAL IN BERLIN (Paramount, 1967) C 102 min.

Presenter, Harry Saltzman; producer, Charles Kasher; director, Guy Hamilton; based on the novel by Len Deighton; screenplay, Evan Jones; assistant director, David Bracknell; production
designer, Ken Adam; art director, Peter Murton; set decorator,
Michael White, Vernon Dixon; sound, Peter Davies, Ken Nightingale, Terry Skarrett; makeup, Freddie Williamson; camera, Otto
Heller; editor, John Bloom.

Michael Caine (Harry Palmer); Eva Renzi (Samantha Steel);
Paul Hubschmid (Johnny Vulkan); Oscar Homolka (Colonel Stok);
Guy Doleman (Ross); Rachel Gurney (Mrs. Ross); Hugh Burden
(Hallam); Thomas Holtzmann (Reinhart); Gunter Meisner (Kreutz-
mann); Heinz Schubert (Aaron Levine); Wolfgang Volz (Werner);
Klaus Jepsen (Otto Rukel); Herbert Fux (Artur); Rainer Brandt
(Benjamin); Ira Hagen (Monika); Marte Keller (Brigit); Uschi
Heyer (Bar Girl).

"All that's left to the spy thriller these days is to go one
better than the next man, and Funeral in Berlin piles it on thick
and fast with a plot which has so many twists that even Sherlock
Holmes might have been baffled" (British Monthly Film Bulletin).
Once again Ross (Doleman) of Britain's M.I. 5 drags ex-
Army cop Harry Palmer (Caine) into cold war action, reminding
the Cockney sluffer that his loyalties must be to "Queen, country
and Ross." For £30 a week plus expenses, Caine is ordered to
Berlin, because Military Intelligence has word that Colonel Stok
(Homolka), the Russian intelligence officer in charge of the Berlin
Wall security, is contemplating defection to the West.
"I'm liable to get my head shot off," Caine complains.
"That's your job, Palmer," replies matter-of-fact Doleman.
Once in Berlin, Caine contacts Johnny Vulkan (Hubschmid),
his crony from the old blackmarketeering days who is now a
British agent. The two arrange a talk with Homolka in East Ber-
lin. The rotund Russian's stringent demands are met, including
the foolproof escape supervised by the best man (Meisner) in the
business. Caine obtains the necessary false papers and the price
of the job from the British, only to later find that the contents of
the coffin, the pre-arranged escape vehicle, passed across the
Iron Curtain line is not Homolka, but the dead body of Meisner.
Suddenly the case takes a sharp turn, with both Hubschmid and
an Israeli intelligence group led by Samantha Steel (Renzi) high-
tailing after the false passport papers, since the counterfeit documents contain the coded whereabouts to a fortune confiscated from
Jews by Nazis and now on deposit in Swiss banks.
Unlike the flashy previous entry in this series, The Ipcress
File, directed by Sidney J. Furie, Funeral in Berlin, directed
by Guy Hamilton, is a deadpan study in topicality. Caine's Harry
Palmer remains the very humanized, idiosyncratic spy, complete

[Facing page] Michael Caine in Funeral in Berlin (Paramount,
1967).

with spectacles, Cockney accent, knock-kneed walk, and still very
supercilious and anti-Establishment. His jocular approach is ever
present ("Can't I be Rock Hunter?" Caine asks when being assigned
his new cover as Edmond Dorf, a ladies' underwear salesman),
despite his full realization that his enforced new profession is a
rotten game, that he is quite expendable, and that most of all, as
an espionage agent, he never knows who will be the next person to
do him dirt. Despite these pleasantly quirky qualities, Caine's
Harry Palmer still registers as a minor league James Bond.
There are disturbing character inconsistencies which remind the
viewer anew that Harry Palmer is just a manufactured cinema contrivance. (Our anti-hero suddenly becomes morally conscious in
Funeral in Berlin, refusing to follow M. I. 5's order to eliminate
Hubschmid. Would the negatively-oriented Palmer, always eager
for the fast buck and the quick bed partner, have cared at all about
the fate of his former Nazi war criminal associate?)
     The best moments in Funeral in Berlin occur near the film's
opening when one is treated to a fast-paced over-the-Berlin-Wall
escape.

FURIA A BAHIA POUR OSS 117 [Trouble in Bahia for OSS 117]
(Valoria, 1965)   C   100 min.

        Director, Andre Hunebelle; based on the novel by Jean
Bruce; screenplay, Hunebelle, Pierre Foucaud, Jean Halain; music,
Michel Magné; camera, Marcal Grignon; editor, Jean Feyte.
        Frederick Stafford (OSS 117); Mylene Demongeot (Ann Marion);
Raymond Pellegrin (Leardo); Jacques Richaroldeso (Miguel); Per-
rette Pradier (Consuelo); Anna Anderson (Secretary); Francois
Matthews (Carlo).

        The new OSS 117 (Stafford) carries on his adventures, this
time in Rio de Janeiro and in the heart of the Amazon jungle where
the Indians have cultivated a mysterious plant that a neo-Nazi band
wishes to harness to gain world power.

FX-SUPERSPY see   COPLAN FX 18 CASSE TOUT

G-MEN VS. THE BLACK DRAGON (Republic, 1943)   15 Chapters

        Chapters: (1) The Yellow Peril, (2) Japanese Inquisition,
(3) Arsenal of Doom, (4) Deadly Sorcery, (5) Celestial Murder,
(6) Death and Destruction, (7) The Iron Monster, (8) Beast of
Tokyo, (9) Watery Grave, (10) The Dragon Strikes, (11) Suicide
Mission, (12) Dead on Arrival, (13) Condemned Cargo, (10) Flaming
Coffin, and (15) Democracy in Action.

        Associate producer, W. J. O'Sullivan; director, William Wit-
ney; screenplay, Ronald Davidson, William Lively, Joseph O'Donnell,

Joseph Poland; art director, Russell Kimball; music, Mort Glickman; special effects, Howard Lydecker; camera, Bud Thackery; editor, Edward Todd, Tony Martinelli.

Rod Cameron (Rex Bennett); Constance Worth (Vivian); Roland Got (Chang); Noel Cravat (Ranga); Nino Pipitone (Oyama Haruchi); George Lewis (Lugo); C. Montague Shaw (Nicholson); Allen Jung (Pugi); Forbes Murray (Kennedy); Harry Burns (Tony); Lawrence Grant (Sir John Brooksfield); Edward Keane (Gordon); John Hamilton (Martin); Paul Fung (Japanese Commander); Donald Kirke (Muller); Kenneth Harlan (Lance); Robert Homans (Captain Gorman); Crane Whitley (Burnell); Maxine Doyle (Marie, the Secretary); Ivan Miller (Inspector); Walter Fenner (Williams); Mary Gayless (Matron); Hooper Atchley (Caldwell); Dick French (Norris); Elliott Sullivan (Turner); Charles La Torre (Nick); Tom Seidel (Spencer); Arvon Dale, Charles Flynn (Pilots); William Forrest (Professor Jackson); Virginia Carroll (Nurse); Peter George Lynn (Garr); Pat O'Malley (Gibson); Sam Bernard (Karl); John Wallace (Newman); Ray Parsons (Jones); Stanley Price (Gibbs); Bud Geary (Morse); Eddie Phillips (Heavy); Edmund Cobb (Stewart); Johnny James (Power Company Clerk); Norman Nesbitt (Radio Announcer); Edward Dew (Agent Z-24).

British secret agent Vivian (Worth) joins special U. S. investigator Rex Bennett (Cameron) and Chang (Got) of the Chinese secret service in locating and destroying the sinister Black Dragon Society, led by Oyama Haruchi (Pipitone), a scoundrel smuggled into America from Tokyo.

Pipitone's men wreak havoc on Allied shipping by secretly adding an incendiary ingredient into the surface paint, a scheme the espionage trio soon halt. Later Got pretends to be a Japanese prisoner recently escaped from Manzanar and in the process obtains valuable data on the spy ring, including possession of a useful submarine locator. After Cameron later prevents the sabotage of Boulder Dam, he puts his next defensive ploy into operation, allowing the would-be saboteurs to learn about an allegedly valuable synthetic rubber formula. The enemy agents fall for the bait, leading to the final--it is hoped--destruction of the Black Dragon Society.

Republic pulled no punches in pandering to the baser whims of its patriotic action-hungry audiences. Pipitone played his Oriental villain with appropriate squint-eyed nastiness, and in the course of the 15 chapters, with their train, boat, plane, and car wrecks, the viewer could vicariously fight along with the trio of Allied undercover agents, a threesome who used more brawn than brain, except for attractive Worth, to combat the Black Dragon menace.

The serial was eventually re-edited into a 100-minute television feature version entitled Black Dragon of Manzanar.

DAS GEHEIMNIS DER CHINESISCHEN NELKE [The Secret of the
Chinese Carnation]   (Constantin, 1964)   99 min.

Director, Rudolf Zehetgruber; based on a work by Edgar
Wallace; screenplay, Zehetgruber; music, Miloslav Hurka; camera,
Jan Stallich.
    With: Brad Harris, Horst Frank, Paul Dahlke, Olly
Schoberova, Dietmar Schönherr, Klaus Kinski.

In this pretty weak drama, world powers vie with international underworld forces for control of a professor's revolutionary
new fuel formula, a substance powerful enough to control the
world's economy.

GEHEIMNISSE IN GOLDENEN NYLONS [Deux Billets pour Mexico]
(S. F., 1967)   C   88 min.

Executive producer, René Pigneres; producer, Peter Hahne;
director, Christian-Jaque; based on the novel <u>Dead Run</u> by Robert

Maria Bucella and Peter Lawford in <u>Geheimnisse in Goldenen
Nylons</u> [U. S. tv: <u>Dead Run</u>] (S. F. , 1967).

Sheckley; screenplay, Michel Levine, Christian-Jaque; art director, Jürgen Kiebach; music, Gerard Calvi; sound, Werner Müssig; camera, Pierre Petit; editor, Jacques Desagneaux.

Georges Geret (Carlos); Peter Lawford (Dain); Ira von Furstenberg (Suzanne); Maria Gracia Bucella (Anna); Horst Frank (Manganne); Werner Peters (Bardieff); Jean Tissier (Adelgate); Bernard Tiphaine (Embassy Official); Wolfgang Kieling (Wolfgang); and: Eva Pflug, Wolfgang Preiss, Siegfried Wischniewski, Dean Heyde, Henri Guegan, Alan Collins, Michel Charrel, Roger Treville.

When a gang of hoodlums in Berlin snatch an attaché case containing secret papers, only to be relieved of it by a petty pickpocket (Geret), several factions track the minor crook as he hops from Lucerne to Paris to Vienna in order to sell the valuable dossiers.

This dubbed Continental co-production reached American TV as Dead Run. Despite the cast, especially Geret as a devilishly jovial minor crook, the flaccid script and the stale guided tour of European cities dragged the picture down into mediocrity.

GIBRALTAR [The Spy] (S. F., 1963) 97 min.

Producer, Michel Safra, Serge Silberman; director, Pierre Gaspard-Huit; screenplay, Jean Stelli, Jacques Companeez; adaptation, Robert Thomas, Gaspard-Huit; dialog, Thomas; music, Andre Hossein; sound, Antoine Petitjean; camera, Cecilio Paniagua; editor, Louisette Hautecouer.

Gerard Barray (Frank Jackson); Elisa Montes (Lola); Hildegard Knef (Elinor van Berg); Geneviève Grad (Cathy Maxwell); Bernard Dheran (Harry); Fausto Tozzi (Paoli); Claudio Gora (General Maxwell).

As a cover for his counter-espionage work, British Intelligence member Frank Jackson (Barray) allows himself to fall into the web of Spanish dancer Lola (Montes) in Tangiers. She advises him that a friend will erase his gambling debts if he supplies, in exchange, military information on Allied troop movements in the Mediterranean. Barray proceeds to photograph the required documents from the safe at the British Admiralty's Gibraltar base. He is caught in the act and sentenced to prison, but escapes in order to join the spy ring supervised by Montes' lesbian friend and beauty salon owner Elinor van Berg (Knef).

After a rather slow opening, this English-dubbed French film zooms into action "in the best traditions of spy haute cuisine. The mystic East, complete with sliding panels and subterranean passages, is spread before it.... All this is good stuff and builds up to a tense, well-edited climax calculated to allay the boredom of a wet afternoon" (British Monthly Film Bulletin).

THE GIRL IN THE KREMLIN (Universal, 1957) 81 min.

Producer, Albert Zugsmith; director, Russell Birdwell; story, Harry Ruskin, DeWitt Bodeen; screenplay, Gene L. Coon, Robert Hill; art director, Alexander Golitzen, Eric Orbom; gowns, Bill Thomas; assistant director, Marshall Greene; camera, Carl Guthrie; editor, Sherman Todd.

Lex Barker (Steve Anderson); Zsa Zsa Gabor (Lili/Helga Grisenko/Greta Grisenko); Jeffrey Stone (Mischa Rimilkin); Maurice Manson (Molda/Stalin); William Schallert (Jacob Stalin); Aram Katcher (Lavrenti Beria); Michael Fox (Igor Smetka); Charles Horvath (Igor Smetka); Elena Da Vinci (Olga Smetka); Richard Richonne (Vedeshky); Natalia Daryll (Dasha); Carl Sklover (Rashti); Phillipa Fallon (Nina); Kurt Katch (Commissar); Gabor Curtiz (Dr. Petrov); Peter Besbas (Proprietor in Wine Shop); Franz Roehn (Old Man); Albert Szabo (Truck Driver); Alfred Linder (Tata Brun); Henry Rowland (Policeman); Dale Van Sickel (Cabby); Wanda d'Ottoni (Girl in Sidewalk Cafe); Della Malzahn (Dancer).

A typical quickie Albert Zugsmith production which had a vague topical interest when released, this film from the perspective of some 15 years later is nothing more than espionage hokum.

Barker rushed through the film as an ex-O.S.S. agent who infiltrates the Iron Curtain to entangle with a plot to overthrow Stalin. Gabor was too much of a super-charged personality to ever handle one role at a time competently and was cast in a triple assignment. One part had her as the purported mistress of the Russian chief.

THE GIRL WHO KNEW TOO MUCH (Commonwealth United, 1969) C 95 min.

Producer, Earle Lyon; associate producer, Bill Welch; director, Francis D. Lyon; screenplay, Charles Wallace; music, Joe Green; camera, Alan Stensvold.

Adam West (Johnny Cain); Nancy Kwan (Revel); Robert Alda (Allardice); Nehemiah Persoff (Lt. Crawford); Patricia Smith (Tricia); David Brian (Hal Dixon); Buddy Greco (Lucky); Diane Van Vila (Stripper).

A shoddily-assembled feature concerning club owner-adventurer West who becomes the prime force aiding the CIA in stopping the latest Communist conspiracy, with both crime syndicates and Oriental villains at hand. The only bright stretch to this sleep-inducer is an inserted segment with Van Vila demonstrating her captivating art.

THE GLASS BOTTOM BOAT (MGM, 1966) C 110 min.

Producer, Martin Melcher, Everett Freeman; director,

Frank Tashlin; screenplay, Everett Freeman; art director, George W. Davis, Edward Carfagno; set decorator, Henry Grace, Hugh Hunt; costumes, Ray Aghayan; assistant director, Al Jennings; songs, Joe Lubin and Jerome Howard, Jay Livingston and Ray Evans; music, De Vol; special camera effects, J. McMillan, Johnson, Carroll L. Shepperd; sound, Franklin Milton; camera, Leon Shamroy; editor, John McSweeney.

Doris Day (Jennifer Nelson); Rod Taylor (Bruce Templeton); Arthur Godfrey (Axel Nordstrom); John McGiver (Ralph Goodwin); Paul Lynde (Homer Cripps); Edward Andrews (General Wallace Bleecker); Eric Fleming (Edgar Hill); Dom De Luise (Julius Pritter); Dick Martin (Zack Molloy); Elisabeth Fraser (Nina Bailey); George Tobias (Mr. Fenimore); Alice Pearce (Mrs. Fenimore); Ellen Corby (Anna Miller); Dee J. Thompson (Donna); Robert Vaughn (Napoleon Solo).

This flick has a most looney premise: while on a fishing trip, engineering physicist Bruce Templeton (Taylor) hooks a public relations employee (Day) in his space laboratory, she acting at the time as a mermaid to help her father (Godfrey) who pilots a glass bottom sight-seeing boat. As Day and Taylor become romantically entangled, she becomes embroiled in a faltering plot to steal top secrets from Taylor's plant.

The spy gambit is merely a very loose peg upon which director Frank Tashlin hangs a myriad of varying slapstick sight gags, with Day over-responding with her famed crossed-eyed, slack-jawed double-takes. Best among the strong supporting cast are the overconscientious security guard Homer Cripps (Lynde), who jumps into drag to pursue suspect Day to the ladies room, dictatorial General Wallace Bleecker (Andrews), would-be secret agent Julius Pritter (De Luise), and screeching nosey/neighbor Mrs. Fenimore (Pearce).

This elaborately staged production, which grabbed $4,527,000 in domestic rentals, would have been a much more salutory vehicle for the talents of a Jerry Lewis.

GOLDEN EARRINGS (Paramount, 1947) 95 min.

Producer, Harry Tugend; director, Mitchell Leisen; based on the novel by Yolanda Foldes; screenplay, Abraham Polonsky, Frank Butler, Helen Deutsch; art director, Hans Dreier, John Meehan; set decorator, Sam Comer, Grace Gregory; music, Victor Young, music director, Phil Boutelje; choreography, Billy Daniel; songs, Victor Young, Jay Livingston, and Ray Evans; assistant director, Johnny Coonan; sound, Dan McKay; special camera effects, Gordon Jennings; process camera, Farciot Edouart; camera, Daniel L. Fapp; Alma Macrorie.

Ray Milland (Colonel Ralph Denistoun); Marlene Dietrich (Lydia); Murvyn Vye (Zoltan); Bruce Lester (Byrd); Dennis Hoey (Hoff); Quentin Reynolds (Himself); Reinhold Schunzel (Professor Krosigk); Ivan Tiresault (Major Reimann); Hermine Sterler (Greta

Krosigk); Eric Feldary (Zweig); Fred Nurney, Otto Reichow (Agents);
Gisele Werbiseck (Dowager); Larry Simms (Page Boy); Haldor de
Becker (Telegraph Boy); Gordon Richards, Vernon Downing (Club
Members); Leslie Denison (Miggs); Tony Ellis (Dispatch Rider);
Gwen Davies (Stewardess); Robert Cory (Doorman); Hans von Mor-
hart (S. S. Trooper); Henry Rowland (Peiffer); William Yetter, Sr.,
Henry Guttman (Peasants); William Yetter, Jr., James W. Horne,
Leo Schlesinger (Soldiers); Ellen Baer (Girl); Carmen Beretta
(Tourist); Frank Johnson (Waiter); Mme. Louise Colombet (Flower
Woman); Maynard Holmes (Private); Fred Giermann (Sergeant);
Roberta Jonay (Peasant Girl); Harry Anderson (German Farmer);
Caryl Lincoln (Farmer's Wife); Robert Val, Gordon Arnold, Pepito
Perez (Gypsies); Bob Stephenson, Henry Vroom (S. S. Guards);
George Sorel, Hans Schumm (Policemen); Martha Bamattre (Wise
Old Woman); Antonia Morales (Gypsy Dancer); Jack Wilson (Hitler
Youth Leader); John Dehner (S. S. Man); Howard Mitchell (Naval
Officer); Arno Frey (Major); John Good (S. S. Lieutenant); Jack
Worth, Walter Rode (Nazi Party Officials); Peter Seal (Chief of
Police); John Peters (Lieutenant Colonel); Al Winters (Elite Guard
Colonel); Greta Ullman, Catherine Savitsky (German Wives); Mar-
garet Farrell (Woman); John Gilbreath (Soldier).

After three years of U. S. O. wartime entertaining, Dietrich
returned to Hollywood filmmaking, and Academy Award-winning
Milland was her vis-à-vis in this preposterous bit of cinematic fluff.
Told via flashback aboard a London-to-Paris plane, a British
Intelligence officer (Milland) recounts a bizarre tale to an intrigued
newsman: during one point in the late war he had been held prisoner by the Nazis, who were questioning him about a poison gas
formula. He and his partner (Lester) escape, with Milland remaining on the trail of the formula's inventor, a well-known professor
(Schunzel). Going into the Black Forest, Milland takes cover by
joining a band of wandering gypsies, among whose number is tattered Lydia (Dietrich). She disguises him as a member of their
band and aids him in his efforts to track down the professor. He
eventually obtains the formula for the Allies. Bringing the tale up
to date, Milland tells the reporter that he is now keeping his pledge
to return to Dietrich, who is waiting for him atop the same mountain
she led him to six years before during his undercover mission.
Censorship problems or not (after all Milland and Dietrich
within the tale are living together without benefit of clergy), there
were those who agreed with critic James Agee that Golden Earrings
was a "dreary comedy-melodrama." Most filmgoers, however,
preferred to take the new Dietrich film as an amusing, if fanciful
lark, glad for the opportunity to witness her fabulous gams on
screen once again. The film did focus on a little-known persecuted
group during the war, the gypsies, but too often the scenario allowed
the colorful wanderers to trounce the Gestapo with too easy a flick of
their castinets.

[Facing page] Ray Milland and Marlene Dietrich in Golden Earrings
(Paramount, 1947).

GOLDFINGER (UA, 1964) C 109 min.

Producer, Harry Saltzman, Albert R. Broccoli; director, Guy Hamilton; based on the novel by Ian Fleming; screenplay, Richard Maibaum, Paul Dehn; production designer, Ken Adam; art director, Peter Murton, Michael White, Maurice Pelling; titles designer, Robert Bornjohn; music, John Barry; title song, Barry Leslie Bricusse, and Anthony Newley; assistant director, Fran Ernst; makeup, Paul Rabiger, Basil Newall; action sequences, Bob Simmons; sound, Dudley Messenger, Gordon McCullum; special effects, John Stears, Frank George; camera, Ted Moore; editor, Peter Hunt.

Sean Connery (James Bond); Honor Blackman (Pussy Galore); Gert Frobe (Goldfinger); Shirley Eaton (Jill Masterson); Tania Mallet (Tilly Masterson); Harold Sakata (Oddjob); Bernard Lee (M); Martin Benson (Solo); Cec Linder (Felix Leiter); Austin Willis (Simmons); Lois Maxwell (Miss Moneypenny); Bill Nagy (Midnight); Alf Joint (Capungo); Varley Thomas (Old Lady); Nadja Regin (Bonita); Raymond Young (Sierra); Richard Vernon (Smithers); Denis Cowles (Brunskill); Michael Mellinger (Kisch); Bert Kwouk (Mr. Ling); Hal Galili (Strap); Lenny Rabin (Henchman).

Sean Connery and Honor Blackman in Goldfinger (UA, 1964).

Even the conservative, family-oriented New York Daily News raved in its four star review that Goldfinger was the "best and the wildest" of the James Bond entries to date (and thereafter for that matter). Infused with the directorial energies of series newcomer Guy Hamilton, Goldfinger saw the Ian Fleming property reach its zenith of screen excitement in all cinematic categories: the witty script of Bond regular Richard Maibaum aided by Paul Dehn; the zestiest of John Barry's 007 scores, with the title song by Leslie Bricusse and Anthony Newley sung by Shirley Bassey; and, of immense help, the ever-imaginative production designing of Ken Adam and the editing of director-in-the-making Peter Hunt. Also, of course, there were the most outstanding of the series' villains, Auric Goldfinger (Frobe) and his Oriental henchman Oddjob (Sakata), matched by the brash pulchritude of Pussy Galore (Blackman) and the gold-sprayed Jill Masterson (Eaton).

From the whammo opening pre-credit mini-adventure to the sexual fantasy close out (Connery and Blackman enveloped in a protective parachute cloth), Goldfinger has an abundance of intriguing elements. In the gadget department there is Connery's new Aston-Martin DB-5 automobile, complete with bulletproof glass, fog maker, road slicker, wheel destroyer, two machine guns, and a seat ejector. Avaricious megalomaniac Frobe may have his laser ray gun to level at a horizontally snafued Connery, but bulky Sakata is ever ready with his razor sharp brimmed hat (which eventually does him in). And who is to say who is more appealing in Goldfinger, voluptuous Eaton who ends up a gold-gilted corpse or Blackman, Frobe's sexually ambivalent cohort?

The plot of Goldfinger is a robbery caper on a grand scale with a world domination twist. Frobe, having bought up all private supplies of gold is determined to infiltrate the inner sanctums of the gold bar reserve at Fort Knox and detonate a bomb which will radioactivate the costly ore throwing the Western world economy into a tailspin and, incidentally, making him the richest man around. Along the way there are several unforgettable moments: Frobe playing cards at a swank Miami Beach hotel cabana, unable to resist the merry chance to cheat; the impressive golf match between Frobe and Connery, a battle of words rather than of irons; the gassing of the hoods convened at Frobe's ranch headquarters in America; the spraying of nerve gas over Fort Knox by Blackman's unique flying circus of five beautiful blondes piloting piper cubs; and the race against time within the depository to disconnect the time mechanism from the triggered bomb.

A few sober members of the fourth estate dared to point out that while vicariously relishing Connery's athletic and sexual escapades in Goldfinger, they felt somewhat guilty endorsing such a hedonistic, amoral, violent approach to life. Is this, they wondered, what spying had come to in the depersonalized 1960s?

LE GORILLE A MORDU L'ARCHEVEQUE [The Deadly Decoys]
(Gaumont, 1962) 90 min.

Director, Maurice Labro; screenplay, Antoine Dominique,
Antoine Flachot (pseudonym of Roger Hanin); Jacques Pierre, Labro;
music, Michel Magne; sound, Severin Frankiel; camera, Robert
Lefebvre; editor, Germaine Artus.

Roger Hanin (Le Gorille); Jean Le Poulain (Lehurit); Pierre
Dac ("The Old Man"); Roger Dumas (Louis Lehurit); Huguette Hue
(Jocelyne); Fernand Fabre (General Secretary); James Campbell
(Guémélé); Jose Squinquel (Rapus); Robert Puig (Antoine).

Famous secret agent The Gorilla (Hanin) is ordered to impersonate the killer hired by a commercial organization to assassinate the Secretary-General of the French community in Africa.

"Le Gorille is a personification of brute force, a replica of
Superman. You don't argue with him, you just run away from him.
His adventures are necessarily violent and naive and not very
ethical either. When right triumphs it is only with the help of
bludgeons and fists.... Maurice Labro has chosen to go for comedy
and eliminate all subtlety. The bad guys are incredibly dumb, more
stupid than bad. It's a furious battle between half-wits and there
is no character in which one can perceive the slightest trace of
humanity" (Paris-Presse).

Shot on location.

THE GREAT DECEPTION (First National, 1926) 5,855 feet

Presenter, Robert Kane; director, Howard Higgin; based on
the novel The Yellow Dove by George Gibbs; screenplay, Paul Bern;
camera, Ernest Haller.

Ben Lyon (Cyril Mansfield); Aileen Pringle (Lois); Basil
Rathbone (Rizzio); Sam Hardy (Handy); Charlotte Walker (Mrs.
Mansfield); Amelia Summerville (Lady Jane); Hubert Wilke (General
Von Frankenhauser); Lucien Prival (Von Markow); Lucius Hender-
son (Burton); Mark Gonzales (Maxwell).

The Great Deception is an oversized illustration of how the
average person in 1926 viewed the British upper crust of the World
War I period, and in doing so it reeked with pseudo-veneer.

Taking place during the Great War, the film focused on an
Englishman (Lyon) who was affiliated with the German Secret Service but who was also serving in British Intelligence to which he
was loyal. Lyon was loved by Lois (Pringle) a girl being courted
by Rizzio (Rathbone), the latter a German double agent who suspected Lyon's disloyalty to Germany. Planning to present the Kaiser's
staff with false data, Lyon, Pringle, and Handy (Sam Hardy), Lyon's
loyal mechanic, arrive in Germany. There Rathbone captures
Pringle. She innocently betrays Lyon and he is sentenced to death.
Meanwhile Rathbone nearly convinces Pringle to accompany him on
a new secret mission, but Lyon and Hardy escape in time to rescue

her, and the trio make a hasty departure for England via plane.
The silly plot line did little to recommend the film although
the New York Times commented, "this photoplay possesses an element of mystery and suspense. " The Times went on to say, "The
producers evidently adhere to the idea that fiction is stranger than
truth. " One point of interest within the picture is a sequence in
which a spy is shot in a lofty chamber of the Tower of London and
falls to his death to the wail of bagpipes played by a kilted contingent of Scots. This silent screen gambit predated by some nine
years the similar one of a woman's scream followed by a shrill
locomotive whistle in Alfred Hitchcock's The Thirty-Nine Steps.

THE GREAT IMPERSONATION [Number 1]   (Paramount, 1921)
6, 658 feet

    Presenter, Jesse L. Lasky; director, George Melford; based
on the novel by Edward Phillips Oppenheim; screenplay, Monte M.
Katterjohn; camera, William Marshall.
    James Kirkwood (Sir Everard Dominey/Leopold von Raga-
stein); Ann Forrest (Rosamond Dominey); Winter Hall (Duke of
Oxford); Truly Shattuck (Duchess of Oxford); Fontaine La Rue
(Princess Eiderstrom); Alan Hale (Gustave Seimann); Bertram Johns
(Dr. Eddy Pelham); William Burress (Dr. Hugo Schmidt); Cecil
Holland (Roger Unthank); Tempe Pigott (Mrs. Unthank); Lawrence
Grant (Emperor William of Germany); Louis Dumar (Prince Eider-
strom); Frederick Vroom (Prince Terniloff); Florence Midgely
(Princess Terniloff).

The Great Impersonation [Number 2]   (Universal, 1935)   67 min.

    Producer, Edmund Grainger; director, Alan Crosland; based
on the novel by Edward Phillips Oppenheim; screenplay, Frank
Wead, Eve Greene; music, Franz Waxman; special camera, John
P. Fulton; camera, Milton Krasner; editor, Phil Cahn.
    Edmund Lowe (Baron Leopold Von Ragastein/Sir Everard
Dominey); Valerie Hobson (Lady Eleanor Dominey); Wera Engels
(Princess Stephanie); Henry Mollison (Eddie Pelham); Murray Kin-
nell (Seaman); Leonard Mudie (Mangan); Lumsden Hare (Duke
Henry); Spring Byington (Duchess Caroline); Brandon Hurst (Mid-
dleton); Claude King (Sir Gerald Hume); Esther Dale (Mrs. Un-
thank); Charles Waldron (Sir Ivan Brunn); Ivan F. Simpson (Dr.
Harrison); Frank Reicher (Dr. Trenk); Nan Gray (Middleton's
Daughter, the Maid); Willy Castello (Duval); Priscilla Lawson
(Maid); Pat O'Hara (Chauffeur); Virginia Hammond (Lady Hume);
Thomas R. Mills (Bartender); Tom Ricketts, Frank Terry, Robert
Bolder (Villagers); Lowden Adams (Waiter); Violet Seaton (Nurse);
Dwight Frye (Roger Unthank); David Dunbar, Frank Benson (English
Farmers); John Powers (English Police); Leonid Snegoff (Wolff);
Harry Worth (Hugo); Adolph Milar (German); Larry Steers (Army
Officer); Harry Allen (Parkins); Douglas Wood (Nobleman).

The Great Impersonation [Number 3] (Universal, 1942) 71 min.

Associate producer, Paul Malvern; director, John Rawlins; based on the novel by Edward Phillips Oppenheim; screenplay, W. Scott Darling; art director, Jack Otterson; music director, Harry J. Salter; camera, George Robinson.

Ralph Bellamy (Dominey Von Ragastein); Evelyn Ankers (Muriel); Aubrey Mather (Sir Ronald); Edward Norris (Bardinet); Kaaren Verne (Stephanie); Henry Daniell (Seamon); Victor Zimmerman (Curt); Ludwig Stossel (Dr. Schmidt); Mary Forbes (Lady Leslie); Charles Coleman (Mangan); Rex Evans (Sir Tristram); Charles Irwin (Yardly); Robert O. Davis (Hofmann); Marcelle Corday (French Woman); Olaf Hytten (Tobacconist); Fred Vogeding (Stengel); Fred Giermann (Stamin); Henry Guttman (Hans); Val Stanton (English Porter); Hans von Morhart (Muller); Audrey Long (Anna); Eric Wilton, Hans Herbert (Clerks); Charles Flynn (Nazi Soldier); Napoleon Simpson (Tall Black); Yvette Duguay, Sylvia Arslan (French Children).

This sturdy property derives from the handiwork of Edward Phillips Oppenheim, one of the foremost practitioners of the early 20th-century spy novel. That the story survived three screen renditions over a 20-year span demonstrates yet again how successfully, if mundanely, Oppenheim blended together the requisite ingredients of suspense and action to make a robust thriller.

The initial picturization by Paramount, coming three years after the end of World War I, strove for a Ruritanian effect in its presentation of the two Oxford classmates, Sir Edward Dominey and Baron Leopold von Ragastein (both played by Kirkwood) who meet in German East Africa during the Great War. Von Ragastein is functioning as military commander there, while Dominey has left England post-haste after being suspected of killing a man who interfered with his marriage. Von Ragastein schemes to have Dominey poisoned by the natives, and then by assuming the name of his late lookalike classmate, proceeds to England to spy for the Kaiser. In England he encounters Princess Eiderstrom (La Rue) with whom he had a past affair, and she is distraught to now observe his obvious affection for the lovely Rosamond Dominey (Forrest), leading La Rue to join with German agent Dr. Hugo Schmidt (Burress) to bring von Ragastein/Dominey to task for violating his country's ethics. In a quick turnabout, it develops that it was actually Dominey who had killed von Ragastein back in Africa and he has been secretly combatting England's undercover enemies.

In 1935, Universal released its own rendition of the Oppenheim tale, still situating the account in 1914, although the costumes employed were strictly mid-1930s. The always debonair Lowe inherited Kirkwood's dual role and played it with his usual bored élan, switching with ease from a Teutonic to Oxford accent. There is much more emphasis in version number two on the guilt-stricken backgrounds of both adversaries--Dominey, pictures as an alcoholic, for having supposedly killed his housekeeper's son, and Von Ragastein for having fatally wounded Princess Stephanie's (Engels) husband in a duel. The hashed-over 1935 presentation rated the mild critical dismissal "rather confusing bore" (New York Herald-Tribune).

For its 1942 update, Universal switched The Great Imper- sonation to a World War II setting and into an English versus Nazi spy mold. By this point in the cinema game, viewers were more sophisticated in their approach to spy films--and there were a plethora of espionage movies at the time--that relied so heavily on coincidences and far-fetched situations. Even the attempt to weave topically into the plot by introducing Rudolph Hess' famed Scottish plane trip did not instill pertinence into this haphazardly acted pro- grammer. "Such films," wrote Dorothy Masters in her two star New York Daily News review, "are helping neither the picture in- dustry nor the war effort in letting their heroes play those ex- travagant roles of derring-do."

THE GREAT MANHUNT see STATE SECRET

THE GREAT SPY CHASE (AIP, 1966) 87 min.

Executive producer, Alain Poire; producer-director, Georges Lautner; screenplay, Michel Andiard, Albert Simonin; dialog, Andiard; music, Michel Magne; art director, Jacques D'Ovidio; camera, Maurice Fellous.

Lino Ventura (Lagneau); Bernard Blier (Cafarelli); Francis Blanche (Vassilieff); Mireille Darc (Amaranthe); Charles Millot (Muller); Andre Weber (Rossini); Jess Hahn (O'Brien); Jacques Balutin (Le Douanier); Robert Dalban (Le Camionneur); Michele Marceau (Rosalinde).

Despite the outrageous synchronization, slurred speech, and careless editing of this French-made production, the basic buffoonery of its willing cast stamps the flick with a winning jocularity.

When an important munitions tycoon dies he leaves a top secret document in the possession of his attractive widow (Darc), and agents from both sides of the Iron Curtain scramble to the wake to obtain the valuable papers. In their vain efforts to do away with one another, the operatives bungle the job delightfully, what with dynamiting the water tank over a toilet (triggered, of course, by pulling the chain), putting a scorpion under a pillow, or decorating a ceiling chandelier with spikes and gearing it to fall--obviously at the wrong time.

THE GREAT SPY MISSION see OPERATION CROSSBOW

THE GROUNDSTAR CONSPIRACY (Universal, 1972) C 95 min.

Executive producer, Earl A. Glick; producer, Trevor Wallace;

associate producer, Frank Arrigo; director, Lamont Johnson; based on the novel The Alien by L. P. Davies; screenplay, Matthew Howard; assistant director, Roger Good; art director, Cam Porteous; music, Paul Hoffert; sound, John Guselle; stunt co-ordinator, David Ostere; special effects, Herbert Ewing; camera, Michael Reed; editor, Edward M. Abroms.

George Peppard (Tuxan); Michael Sarrazin (John Welles); Christine Belford (Nicole Bevon); Cliff Potts (Carl Mosely); James Olson (Senator Stanton); Tim O'Connor (Frank Gossage); James McEachin (Bender); Alan Oppenheimer (Joe Hackett); Roger Dressler (Charlie Kitchen); Ty Haller (Henshaw); Anna Hagen (Dr. Jean Plover); Hagen Beggs (Dr. Hager); John Destry Adams (Zabrinski); Milos Zatovic (Dr. Zahl); Don Granberry (Technician); Robin Coller (Secretary); Bob Meneray (M. P. Sergeant); Ed Collier (Nicole's Doctor); John Mitchell, Martin Moore, Richard Sergeant (M. P. s); Don Vance, William Nunn, Peter Lavender, Barry Cahill (Reporters).

While stealing vital information from a top secret American space project, scientist John Welles (Sarrazin) is nearly killed by terrific explosions which rock the installation.   Surgeons piece his shocked mind back together but he has almost no memory, and Tuxas (Peppard), the security agent in charge of the case, cannot dig out of him the nation responsible for sending him on the computer tape theft.   Attractive Nicole Bevon (Belford) is used as bait to loosen Sarrazin's memory, with their every moment together recorded by telecameras and tape machines.   The denouement veers far into left field to (1) reveal the man behind the conspiracy, (2) explicate Peppard's true allegiance, and (3) clarify Sarazzin's actual background.

Based on a modestly circulated novel, The Alien, by L. P. Davies, this film promised little for Universal, other than looking like a refugee telefeature given some theatrical release.   Its adequate screenplay was insufficient to propel the production through very low-key mid-passages, leaving the viewer with the uncomfortable feeling of wondering what all the fuss was about, when all factions were taking so much screen time to settle the situation. Most unsatisfactory of all is the cynical explanation provided for Sarrazin's present plight which ends the film in a depressing manner.   He has become a discarded tool of the new-style espionage game in which man's basic dignity means nothing.

GUNS IN THE HEATHER (Buena Vista, 1968)   C   90 min.

Producer, Ron Miller; associate producer, Hugh Attwool; director, Robert Burler; based on the novel by Lockhart Amerman; screenplay, Herman Groves; art director, Albert Witherick; music, Buddy Baker; sound, Christopher Lancaster; camera, Michael Reed; editor, Peter Boita.

Glenn Corbett (Tom Evans); Alfred Burke (Kersner); Kurt Russell (Rich Evans); Patrick Dawson (Sean O'Connor); Patrick Barr (Lord Boyne); Hugh McDermott (Carleton); Patrick Westwood

(Levick); Eddie Byrne (Bailey); Godfrey Quigley (Meister); Kevin
Stoney (Ernhardt); Shay Gorman (Headmaster); Niall Toibin (Ket-
tering); Ernst Walder (Vollos); and: Robert Bernal, Vincent
Dowling, John Horton, J. G. Devlin, Nicola Davies, Gerry Alex-
ander, Eamon Morrissey, Declan Mulholland, Mary Larkin, Paul
Farrell.

This contemporary espionage thriller, made by Walt Disney,
was told from the point of view of a school boy, and was filmed
entirely in Ireland. After theatrical release abroad, it was cut up
and shown on the weekly Disney teleseries in America.
Seventeen-year-old Rich Evans (Russell), an American
exchange student at a school in Ireland, suddenly learns that his
older brother (Corbett) is not the steel company representative he
seemed to be, but rather a secret agent for the American government. By accident Russell and his friend (Dawson) are drawn
into the case of a defecting Iron Curtain scientist (Walder), who is
being smuggled to America via Ireland. Russell, Dawson, and
Corbett soon find themselves pitted against Communist undercover
officials, with Walder the big prize. Thanks to Russell's skill with
a javelin and Dawson's ability as a glider pilot, Walder's rescue
is insured.

HANDS UP! (Paramount, 1926)   5,883 feet

Presenter, Adolph Zukor, Jesse L. Lasky; director, Clarence
Badger; story, Reginald Morris; screenplay, Monty Brice, Lloyd
Corrigan; camera, H. Kinley Martin.
Raymond Griffith (Confederate Spy); Marion Nixon (The Girl
He Loves); Virginia Lee Corbin (The Other Girl He Loves); Mack
Swain (Mineowner); Montagu Love (Union General); George Billings
(Abraham Lincoln); Noble Johnson (Sitting Bull); Charles K. French
(Brigham Young).

A somewhat wry approach to the rewards in store for a spy,
set in Civil War days. President Lincoln (Billings) dispatches a
messenger to collect a gold cache promised to the Union cause by
a Western mine owner (Swain). Learning of the planned shipment,
General Lee orders a spy (Griffith) to prevent the Union man from
accomplishing his task. Griffith survives many perilous encounters
with Indians and Union soldiers, but while sidetracking the stage-
coach carrying the gold shipment, he is caught and sentenced to be
hanged. But lo and behold, Swain's two daughters (Nixon, Corbin)
protest their love for Griffith and save his life. After the war,
Griffith and the two girls set off for Salt Lake City, determined
to receive the blessings of the Mormon Church in their triangular
love arrangement.

HANGMEN ALSO DIE   (UA, 1943)   131 min.

Producer, Fritz Lang; assistant producer, T. W. Baumfield; director, Lang; story-adaptation, Bertolt Brecht, Fritz Lang; screenplay, John Wexley; art director, William Darling; assistant director, Walter Mayo; music, Hans Eisler; music director, Arthur Guttman; camera, James Wong Howe; editor, Gene Fowler, Jr.

Brian Donlevy (Dr. Svoboda); Walter Brennan (Professor Novotny); Anna Lee (Mascha Novotny); Gene Lockhart (Czaka); Dennis O'Keefe (Jan Horak); Alexander Granach (Alois Gruber); Margaret Wycherly (Aunt Ludmilla); Nana Bryant (Mrs. Novotny); Billy Roy (Beda Novotny); Hans von Twardowski (Heydrich); Tonio Selwart (Haas); Jonathan Hale (Dedic); Lionel Stander (Gabby); Byron Foulger (Bartos); Virginia Farmer (Landlady); Louis Donath (Schirmer); Sarah Padden (Mrs. Dvorak); Edmund MacDonald (Dr. Pilar); Otto Reichow (Gestapo); Eddy Waller (Cab Driver); George Irving (Necval); James Bush (Worker); Arno Frey (Camp Officer); Arthur Loft (Votruba); William Farnum (Viktorin); Reinhold Schuenzel (Ritter); Phil Van Zandt (Officer); Erville Alderson (Liberal Official); Ralph Dunn (Policeman); Emmett Lynn, Lester Sharpe, Emmett Vogan, Billy Benedict (Hostages); Charles Middleton, William Haade (Patriots).

Fritz Lang and Bertolt Brecht built a screenplay about the never discovered assassin of the Reichsaprotektri of Czechoslovakia --better known as "Hangman" Heydrich--who was shot in the streets of Prague in 1942. Filmed under the working title Unconquered, the final version was labeled Hangmen Also Die, and traces the story of the daring killer of Heydrich.

After sniping the Nazi leader, Dr. Franz Svoboda (Donlevy) is taken into hiding by a girl (Lee) and her professor father (Brennan). The latter, along with several other citizen and secret Resistance members, is taken prisoner by the Nazis who demand revenge for the embarrassing killing. In an ironic twist, the partisans are able to frame a Nazi collaborationist as the culprit. Although the Gestapo know the offered villain is innocent of the particular crime, they pretend to have found the killer, to save face.

James Agee said of the film that it "is rich with clever melodrama, over maestoso directorial touches and the sort of querschnitt sophistication for detail Lang always has."

HAUSER'S MEMORY (Universal/NBC-TV, 1970)   C   104 min.

Producer, Jack Laird; director, Boris Sagal; based on the novel by Curt Siodmak; screenplay, Adrian Spies; music, Billy Byers; art director, Ellen Schmidt; production supervisor: Wallace Worsley; assistant director, Weiland Liebske; costumes, Peter

---

[Facing page]   Otto Reichow (center) and Brian Donlevy in Hangmen Also Die (UA, 1943).

Saldutti; makeup, Bud Westmore; camera, Petrus Schloemp; editor,
Frank E. Norris.
David McCallum (Hillel Mondoro); Susan Strasberg (Karen
Mondoro); Lilli Palmer (Anna); Robert Webber (Dorsey); Leslie
Nielsen (Slaughter); Helmut Kautner (Renner); Hans Elwenspoek
(Van Kungen); Peter Capell (Shepilou); Peter Ehrlich (Kucera);
Barbara Lass (Angelika); Gunther Meisner (Koroviev); Otto Stern
(Gessler); Manfred Reddemann (Sorsen); Art Brauss (Bak); Jochen
Busse (Dieter); Barbara Capell (Young Anna).

A telefeature based on Curt Siodmak's novel, <u>Hauser's</u>
<u>Memory</u> was a fitful combination science fiction and <u>spy tale</u>, which
<u>Cinefantastique</u> critic Robert L. Jerome said "faltered ... [only
when it] tried to adapt itself to a spy thriller formula. "
Telling the tale of a dying scientist with the CIA fighting
to save the man's secrets, a young doctor (McCallum) volunteers
to have the scientist's brain fluid injected into his head so as to
preserve the formulas for American use. The result, however,
found McCallum leading a double life which caused him to reject
his own pregnant wife (Strasberg) while meeting the hatred of the
late scientist's spouse (Palmer), herself a Nazi sympathizer.
In many respects, the film was close in kin to another of
Siodmak's novels, <u>Donovan's Brain</u>.

HAWAII FIVE-O (CBS-TV, 1968) C 90 min.

Executive producer, Leonard Freeman; director, Paul Wend-
kos; screenplay, Freeman; camera, Richard Rawlings; editor, Ira
Heymann.
Jack Lord (Steve McGarrett); Nancy Kwan (Rosemary Quog);
Leslie Nielsen (Brent); Andrew Duggan (Miller); James Gregory
(Jonathan Kaye); Khigh Dhiegh (Wo Fat); Lew Ayres (Governor);
and: Zulu, Kam Fong, Philip Ahn, Moah Keen, Wright Esser,
Bill Saito, Baird Miller, Gertrude Flynn.

The telefeature pilot for the long-running video series devoted its time to a study of espionage in scenic Hawaii. When it
is learned that Red Chinese operatives are buzzing about Honolulu,
special law officer Steve McGarrett (Lord) is assigned to the case.
He is particularly interested in tracking down the culprits because
they caused the death of a close friend. Lord's task is to serve
as bait for the baddies and give them false information. To win
the "confidence" of the spies, he must undergo a brutal torture
session.
<u>Daily Variety</u>, like the public, was favorably inclined to the
series' opener: "It's all accomplished with a highly professional
touch. " Lew Ayres, cast as the governor of the state, left the
series after this episode (allegedly due to the smallness of his role)
and was replaced in the regular lineup by Richard Denning.

James Gregory, Jack Lord, and Lew Ayres in Hawaii Five-O
(CBS-TV, 1968).

THE HELICOPTER SPIES (MGM, 1967) C 93 min.

     Executive producer, Norman Felton; producer, Anthony
Spinner; associate producer, Irv Pearlberg, George M. Lehr;
director, Boris Sagal; screenplay, Dean Hargrove; assistant director,
Glenn N. Cook; art director, George W. Davis, James W. Sulli-
van; set decorator, Henry Grace, Hugh Hunt; music, Richard
Shores; title theme, Jerry Goldsmith; sound, Franklin Milton;
camera, Fred Koenekamp; editor, Joseph Dervin, John B. Rogers.
     Robert Vaughn (Napoleon Solo); David McCallum (Illya
Kuryakin); Carol Lynley (Annie); Bradford Dillman (Luther Sebas-
tian); Lola Albright (Azalea); John Dehner (Dr. Kharmusi); Leo G.
Carroll (Mr. Waverly); John Carradine (Third-Way Priest); Julie
London (Laura Sebastian); H. M. Wynant (The Aksoy Brothers);
Roy Jenson (Carl); Arthur Malet (White Hunter); Kathleen Free-
man (Mom); Robert Karnes (Ship's Captain); Barbara Moore (Lisa);
Sid Haig (Alex); Lyzanne Ladua (White-Haired Girl); Thordis
Brandt (Miss Zalamar).

     Still another in "The Man from U. N. C. L. E. " teleseries to
be slapped together for European release, The Helicopter Spies at
best was a poor melodrama in which the U. N. C. L. E. stalwarts
investigate a new and deadly heat ray which has been used to

destroy an African village. The weapon finds its way from the
hands of its wicked Iranian inventor to a safecracker (Dillman)
who lugs it to a Greek Island where he joins a group of mystics,
headed by Carradine, who are impatiently awaiting the arrival of
the millenium.

In commenting on Carradine's performance and the over-all
film, the British Monthly Film Bulletin sighed, "In fact, his [Car-
radine] final silent gesture of resigned despair admirably sums
up the only possible reaction to the whole thing. "

HELL AND HIGH WATER (20th-Fox, 1954) C 103 min.

Producer, Raymond A. Klune; director, Samuel Fuller; based
on a story by David Hempstead; screenplay, Jesse Lasky Jr. , Fuller; art director, Lyle R. Wheeler, Leland Fuller; set decorator,
Walter M. Scott, Stuart A. Reiss; music, Alfred Newman; assistant
director, Ad Schaumer; camera, Joe MacDonald; editor, James B.
Clark.

Richard Widmark (Adam Jones); Bella Darvi (Denis Gerard);
Victor Francen (Professor Montel); Cameron Mitchell (Ski Brodski);
Gene Evans (Chief Holter); David Wayne (Dugboat Walker); Stephen
Bekassy (Neuman); Richard Loo (Fujimori); Peter Scott (Happy
Mosk); Henry Kulky (Gunner McGrossin); Wong Atarne (Chin Lee);
Harry Carter (Quartermaster); Robert Adler (Welles); Don Orlando
(Carpino); Rollin Moriyama (Soto); John Gifford (Torpedo); William
Yip (Ho-Sin); Tommy Walker (Crew Member); Leslie Bradley (Mr.
Aylesworth); John Wengraf (Colonel Schuman); Harry Denny (Mc-
Auliff); Edo Mita (Taxi Driver); Ramsey Williams (Lieutenant);
Robert B. Williams (Reporter); Harlan Warde (Photographer); and:
Neyle Morrow.

More noteworthy for the film's demonstration of the perfected
use of special effects on the widescreen (CinemaScope) than for its
storyline or performances, Hell and High Water is yet another of
the mid-1950s features relegated to the limbo of middling movies
churned out by Hollywood in desperation to combat the competitive
inroads of television.

The rather simplistic storyline--that is, unless one is a
booster of director Samuel Fuller--is mostly an excuse to throw
across the big screen the big action beneath the water's surface.
Within the plot, a group of ideological mercenaries, headed by
Professor Montel (Francen), have information that the Chinese are
building mysterious installations on an island off Alaska.   The
group believes that America is the only possible salvation of the
world, and thus charters a submarine to be skippered by ex-Navy
man Adam Jones (Widmark).   The vessel's mission is to scout the
Chinese site and bring back the information secured for analysis by
U. S. authorities.   Aboard ship are many of Widmark's old Navy
crew, and for a romantic interlude there is Francen's assistant/
daughter Denis Gerard (Darvi).   Before the picture reaches its
conclusion--leading to the explosion of the Chinese atomic energy

fortress--Widmark and his men must combat a Chinese Communist submarine, plus defection from within their own ranks.

THE HEROES OF TELEMARK   (Columbia, 1965)   C   131 min.

Producer, S. Benjamin Fisz; director, Anthony Mann; based on Skis Against the Atom by Knut Hauklid and But for These Men by John Drummond; screenplay, Ivan Moffat; assistant director, Derek Cracknell; music-music director, Malcolm Arnold; art director; Tony Mastus; set decorator, Bob Cartwright, Ted Clements; sound, Ted Mason, Bill Daniels, Gordon McCallum; makeup, Neville Smallwood; stunt advisor, Jerry Crampton; special effects, John P. Fulton; camera, Robert Krasker; editor, Bert Bates.

Kirk Douglas (Dr. Rolf Pedersen); Richard Harris (Knut Straud); Michael Redgrave (Uncle); Ulla Jacobsson (Anna); Roy Dotrice (Jensen); Eric Porter (Terboven); Anton Diffring (Major Frick); Mervyn Johns (Colonel Wilkinson); Barry Jones (Professor Logan); Geoffrey Keen (General Bolts); Jennifer Hilary (Sigrid); Ralph Michael (Nilssen); David Weston (Arne); William Marlowe (Claus); Alan Howard (Oli); John Bolightly (Freddy); Sebastian Breaks (Gunnar); Patrick Jordan (Henrik); Brook Williams (Einar);

Richard Harris, Ulla Jacobsson, and Kirk Douglas in The Heroes of Telemark (Columbia, 1965).

Karel Stepanek (Hartmuller); David Davies (Captain Galtesund);
Faith Brook (Woman on Bus); Elvi Hale (Mrs. Sandersen); Gerard
Heinz (Erhardt); Victor Beaumont (German Ski Sergeant); Philo
Hauser (Businessman); George Murcell (Sturmführer); Russell
Waters (Mr. Sandersen); Jan Conrad (Factory Watchman); Alf
Joint (German Guard on Ferry); Robert Bruce (Major); Brian Jackson (Norwegian Naval Attaché); Paul Hansard (German Official);
Annette Andre (Girl Student); Pamela Conway (Girl in Darkroom);
Grace Arnold, Howard Douglas (Galtesund Passengers); Jemma Hyde
(Businessman's Girl); Joe Powell, Terry Plummer (Quislings).

In 1942 Nazi-occupied Norway, underground leader Knut
Straud (Harris) smuggles a microfilmed message from an agent
in a Nazi factory (deep inside a Norwegian valley) to Dr. Rolf
Pedersen (Douglas). Douglas deciphers the message and finds
that the Germans are producing heavy water, a basic ingredient
required for the manufacture of A-bombs. Douglas and Harris
relay the message to England, and in turn are ordered to parachute within the perimeter of the secret factory and lay the ground-
work for an attack by British commandos. When the English force
is waylaid in an accident, the north country duo decide to complete
the difficult job themselves. They succeed, although in the process
Douglas is captured (he later escapes). Thereafter, the energetic
and determined Germans rebuild the damaged factory and are soon
in operation again, with the British vainly trying to bomb the well-
protected site. After several such Allied attacks, the Nazis decide
to transplant the vital shipment of heavy water back to the fatherland. Douglas and his crew manage to destroy the valuable cargo.

At a reputed cost of $5.6 million, this sumptuously-filmed
feature never caught the public's fancy. As Time magazine analyzed,
"During long debates about love, war and marriage, the drama
loses any sense of immediacy." If one did not know better, one
would think this were another in the long line of Alistair MacLean
espionage adventure yarns, typically long on excitement and short on
characterization, relevancy, and the ironies of warfare. The Heroes
of Telemark garnered most publicity for the continued feuding between
Douglas and Harris during production.

HIDE AND SEEK (British Lion-Abion, 1964)   90 min.

Producer, Hal E. Chester; director, Cy Enfield; story,
Harold Greene; adaptation, Robert Foshko; screenplay, David-
Stone; music, Muir Mathieson, Gary Hughes; camera, Gilbert
Taylor; editor, Thelme Connell.

Ian Carmichael (David Garrett); Janet Munro (Maggie); Curt
Jurgens (Hubert Marek); George Pravda (Frank Melnicker); Hugh
Griffith (Wilkins); Kieron Moore (Paul); Derek Tansley (Chambers);
Esna Cannon (Tea Lady); John Boxer (Secretary); Cardew Robinson
(Constable); Barbara Roscoe (Bride); Tommy Godfrey (Drunken Song-
writer); Lance Percival (Idiot); Julian Gachard (Pompous Man);
Edward Chapman (McPherson); Kynaston Reeves (Hunter); Frederick

Peisley (Cottrell); Charles Lamer (Porter); Una Venning (Mrs. Cromer).

"Rarely has a thriller petered out in such a scrappy manner" (Variety).

Nuclear research scientist David Garrett (Carmichael) encounters Frank Melnicker (Pravda), a long-standing friend from behind the Iron Curtain, at a London chess tournament. Carmichael notices some unorthodox byplays at the match between Pravda and a suspicious looking individual, later divining that the actions pertain to espionage activities. Carmichael follows up the clues which lead him to Maggie (Munro), she claiming that Pravda really handles a refugee escape organization and that she will take Carmichael to see Pravda in Yorkshire to set his mind at ease. It evolves that this is all part of an intricate scheme to sell Carmichael to a Communist country and make it seem he defected of his own free will.

This untidy mixture gussied up with standard spy paraphernalia, including the usual trenchcoated baddies, henchmen in sunglasses, and determined elderly ladies on trains, makes much ado about almost nothing. Carmichael, always noted for his comedy straightman's role, is particularly uncomfortable as the James Bond-type hero.

HIGH SEASON FOR SPIES see   SECHS PISTOLEN JAGEN PROFESSOR Z on page 426

L'HONORABLE STANISLAS, AGENT SECRET (Prodis, 1963) 91 min.

Director, Jean-Charles Dudrumet; screenplay, Michel Cousin, Dudrumet; music, Georges Deleme; camera, Pierre Gueguen.

Jean Maris (Stanislas Evariste Dubois); Genevieve Page (Ursula); Jean Galland (The Colonel); Maurice Teynac (The Dealer); Gaia Germani (Andréa); Noël Roquevert (The Commissioner); Germaine Dermox (Mme. Dubois); and: Michel Seldow, Louis Arbessier.

Stanislas Evariste Dubois (Maris), playboy extraordinaire who dwells in the higher circles of good living, is pressed into the French secret service, chiefly because it is assumed enemy counter-agents would never dream that this bon vivant, whose greatest pleasure is pursuing women, would actually do something constructive with his existence. His cross-continent mission ends in a showdown at the Paris Opera.

Some time before the James Bond trend brought jocularity to the screen's staid approach to spying and the art of espionage, L'Honorable Stanislas, Agent Secret treated the genre with a surprisingly delightful élan, alternating its scenes of the high life with

sequences of action and intrigue.   Ursula (Page) was every bit as enticing as Maris was suave.
Released to American television in 1965 in a dubbed version as The Reluctant Spy.

HOT ENOUGH FOR JUNE   (Rank, 1963)   C   98 min.

Producer, Betty E. Box; director, Ralph Thomas; based on the novel Night of Wenceslas by Lionel Davidson; screenplay, Lukas Heller; art director, Syd Cain; music, Angelo Lavagnino; music director, Muir Mathieson; sound, Don Sharpe; camera, Ernest Steward; editor, Alfred Roome.
Dirk Bogarde (Nicholas Whistler); Sylva Koscina (Vlasta Simenova); Robert Morley (Colonel Cunliffe); Leo McKern (Simenova); Roger Delgado (Josef); John Le Mesurier (Allsop); Richard Pasco (Plakov); Eric Pohlmann (Galushka); Alan Tilvern (Simenova's Assistant); Noel Harrison (Johnnie); Richard Vernon (Roddinghead); Amanda Grinling (Cunliffe's Secretary); Derek Nimmo (Fred); Jill Medford (Lorna); Philo Hauser (Vicek); Gertan Glauber (German Research Man); Frank Finlay (Embassy Janitor); John Junkin (Storeman); John Standing (Washroom Sttendant); Derek Fowlds (Burnt Man); Andre Charise (Waiter); Norman Bird (Labour Exchange Clerk); William Mervyn (Businessman); Igo Meggido, Sandra Hampton (Russian Dancers).

An arch salute to the James Bond cult, which was retitled Agent 8 3/4 when it reached the American shores in mid-1965. The British Films and Filming's reviewer-forecaster rated this effort "only lukewarm--it could have been so much better if writer and director had been more adventurous. "
The picture begins promisingly enough.   A British security man is filing the papers of the late agent 007!   After the amusing appearance of Morley as the bemused spy chief, things start to go downhill.   Unemployed writer Bogarde is referred by the Labour Exchange to a glass manufacturer's office, where his new employer (Morley) offers him a substantial job at a hefty salary.   His first task is to go to Prague on a goodwill errand.   Not until Bogarde arrives in Czechoslovakia does he begin to comprehend that he has innocently joined the ranks of the espionage service.   The Czech police are soon on his trail, but with the aid of his driver (Koscina --actually the local police chief's daughter) he eventually obtains the sanctity of the British embassy.
The would-be madcap antics grind to a stop whenever Bogarde-Koscina engage in romantic moments; too bad, for there seemed so much comedy potential in the premise, and, in some scenes, such as the confrontation of Morley and McKern, in the actual.

HOTEL BERLIN   (WB, 1945) 98 min.

Producer, Louis Edelman; director, Peter Godfrey; based on

the novel by Vicki Baum; screenplay, Jo Pagano, Alvah Bessie; art
director, John Hughes; set decorator, Clarence Steensen; music,
Franz Waxman; orchestrator, Leonid Raab; music director, Leo
Forbstein; assistant director, Claude Archer; technical advisor,
Peter Pohleng; sound, Charles Lang; dialog director, Jack Gage;
camera, Carl Guthrie; editor, Frederick Richards.

Faye Emerson (Tilli Weiler); Helmut Dantine (Martin Richter);
Raymond Massey (Arnim von Dahnwitz); Andrea King (Lisa Dorn);
Peter Lorre (Johannes Koenig); Alan Hale (Herman Plottke); George
Coulouris (Joachim Helm); Henry Daniell (von Stellen); Helen Thimig
(Fran Sarah Baruch); Peter Whitney (Heinrichs); Steven Geray (Klie-
bert); Kurt Krueger (Major Otto Kaunders); Paul Andor (Waiter);
Erwin Kalmer (Dr. Dorf); Dickie Tyler (Number Six); Elsa Heims
(Messenger Woman); Franz Reicher (Fritz); Paul Panzer (Kurt);
John Wengraf (Wolf von Bülow); Ruth Albu (Gretchen); Jay Novello
(Gomez); Torben Meyer (Frank); Johanna Hofer (Frau Plotke);
George Suzanne (Man Pursued); Walter Bonn, Robert Stephenson,
Carl Ekberg, Harold Ramond, Hans Furberg, Hans von Morhart,
Charles Faber (SS Men); Fred Wolff (Air Raid Warden); Kurt Neu-
mann (Lieutenant); Hans Carl Ludwig (Captain); Arne Frey (Officer);
Betty Chay, Yvonne Hekren, Jack Martin, Adolph Milar, Alfred
Stury (Hotel Guests); Wing Goo (Japanese Officer); Leo White
(Printer); Jack Mower (Gustave); Lottie Williams (Anna); Gloria
Paythe, Margaret Story (Women in Air Raid Shelter); Frank Alten
(Floor Warden); George Meader (Furst); Fred Essler (Weyhart
Wolle).

Charles Higham and Joel Greenberg in their Hollywood in
the Forties (1968) label Hotel Berlin, "One of the most extravagant
of all Hollywood war fantasies...." On the other hand, a reviewer
at the time--James Agee (The Nation)--found it "the most heavily
routine of Warner Brothers' political melodramas...."

Grand Hotel authoress Vicki Baum transferred her successful
multi-episode formula to the German capital of 1945, to a hotel
filled with disparate (stereo)types. There is hotel hostess Tilli
Weiler (Emerson); sickly professor Johannes Koenig (Lorre), a
previously eminent scientist and a Gestapo commissioner; German
General Arnim von Dahnwitz (Massey) who participated in the
assassination plot on Hitler and now has the unenviable choice of
committing suicide or being tried by the state for treason; actress
Lisa Dorn (King) enamored of Massey; underground leader Martin
Richter (Dantine), who has escaped from a concentration camp and
is being hidden by former Nazi informer Emerson; and von Stellen
(Daniell), a Gestapo officer bent on going to the United States to
propagandize.

Within its cache of theatrical set pieces, "It is conceivably
a document, but I have my doubts about the art" (New Yorker). A-
midst the myriad of overlapping intrigues, right under the Gestapo's
noses, the best screen moment occurs when exhausted, cynical Lorre
turns his room topsy-turvy hunting for one "good German."

HOTEL RESERVE   (RKO, 1944)   89 min.

Director, Victor Hanbury, Lance Comfort, Max Greene; based on the novel Epitaph for a Spy by Eric Ambler; screenplay, John Davenport; camera, Greene.

James Mason (Peter Vadassy); Lucie Mannheim (Suzanne Koche); Raymond Lovell (Robert Duclos); Julien Mitchell (Monsieur Beghin); Clare Hamilton (Mary Shelton); Martin Miller (Herr Walter Vogel); Herbert Lom (Andre Roux); Frederick Valk (Emil Schimler); Ivan Barnard (Chemist); Valentine Dyall (Walter Skelton); Patricia Medina (Odette Roux); David Ward (Henri Asticot); Hella Kurty (Hilda Vogel); Anthony Shaw (Major Clandon Hartley); Laurence Hanray (Police Commissionaire); Patricia Hayes (Jacqueline).

This well-wrought pre-war thriller about French counter-espionage methods is bolstered by a superior cast, especially Lom as Andre Roux and Medina as his scorned bride.

Set on the Riviera the summer before World War II erupted, the film focuses on a gathering of holiday makers who find themselves enmeshed in a spy hunt being conducted in a particularly severe manner by a French Naval Intelligence officer (Mitchell). Because young Austrian medical student Peter Vadassy (Mason) is first suspected of being the traitor, it rests on him to prove his innocence and find the real culprit among Suzanne Koche's (Mannheim) resort hotel guests.

THE HOUR BEFORE THE DAWN   (Paramount, 1944)   75 min.

Producer, William Dozier; director, Frank Tuttle; based on the novel by W. Somerset Maugham; adaptation, Lesser Samuels; screenplay, Michael Hogan; art director, Hans Dreier, Earl Hedrick; set decorator, Bertram Granger; music, Miklos Rozsa; assistant director, Harvey Foster; sound, Earl Hayman; camera, John Seitz; editor, Stuart Gilmore.

Franchot Tone (Jim Hetherton); Veronica Lake (Dora Bruckmann); John Sutton (Roger Hetherton); Binnie Barnes (May Hetherton); Henry Stephenson (General Hetherton); Philip Merivale (Sir Leslie Buchannan); Nils Asther (Kurt van der Breughel); Edmond Breon (Freddy Merritt); David Leland (Tommy Hetherton); Aminta Dyne (Hertha Parkins); Morton Lowry (Jackson); Ivan Simpson, Boyd Irwin (Magistrates); Donald Stuart (Farmer Searle); Harry Allen (Mr. Saunders); Mary Gordon (Annie); Ernest Severn (Willie); Raymond Severn (Jim as a Boy); Leslie Denison (Captain Atterley); Harry Cording (Sam); Hilda Plowright (Mrs. Merritt); Viola Moore (Maid); David Clyde (Farmer); Tempe Pigott (Mrs. Saunders); Marjean Neville (Evie); Marie deBecker (Amelia); Thomas Louden (Wilmington); Deidre Gale (Emma); Anthony Marsh (Pilot--Lt. Rank); Nigel Horton (Observer Pilot); Otto Reichow (German Pilot); Charles H. Faber (German Co-Pilot).

In a rather drastic mistake, Paramount cast one of its then top stars, Veronica Lake, as a nasty Nazi Fifth Columnist in The Hour Before the Dawn, only slightly based on the W. Somerset Maugham novel. To further complicate the resultant picture, Tone, as the pacifist Britisher who eventually sees his patriotic duty, walked through his part with little more than one passive expression.

Lake, whose beauty and long blonde locks were not overly exposed in this feature, played Dora Bruckmann, a Nazi agent who marries an anti-war English scholar-farmer (Tone) so as to be near a strategic British military airport. She was to aid the Nazis in a planned invasion of Britain. When her husband learns the bitter truth, he murders her and joins the British service.

If anyone was foolish enough to assume that The Hour Before the Dawn contained a shred of truth about the art of spying, he would believe, at least according to Lake's performance, that all it required was to be bitchy and wear a perpetual scowl.

THE HOUSE ON 92ND STREET (20th-Fox, 1945)   88 min.

Producer, Louis de Rochemont; director, Henry Hathaway; based on the story by Charles G. Booth; screenplay, Barre Lyndon, Booth, John Monks, Jr.; art director, Lyle Wheeler, Lewis Creber; set decorator, Thomas Little, William Sittel; music, David Buttolph; music director, Emil Newman; assistant director, Henry Weinberger; sound, W. D. Flick, Roger Heman; special camera effects, Fred Sersen; camera, Norbert Brodine; editor, Harmon Jones.

William Eythe (Bill Dietrich); Lloyd Nolan (Inspector George A. Briggs); Signe Hasso (Elsa Gebhardt); Gene Lockhart (Ogden Roper); Leo G. Carroll (Colonel Hammersohn); Lydia St. Clair (Johanna Schmedt); William Post, Jr. (Walker); Harry Bellaver (Max Coburg); Bruna Wick (Adolphe Lange); Harro Meller (Conrad Arnulf); Charles Wagenheim (Gus Huzmann); Alfred Linder (Adolph Klaen); Renee Carson (Luise Vadja); Rusty Lane (Admiral); John McKee (Dr. Arthur C. Appleton); Edwin Jerome (Major-General); Elisabeth Neumann (Freda Kazel); Salo Douday (Franz von Wirt); Paul Ford (Sergeant); William Adams (Customs Officer); Lew Eckles (Policeman); Tom Brown, Frank Jackson, George Shelton (Internes); Alfred Ziesler (Colonel Felix Strossen); Frank Kreig (Ticket Clerk); Edgar Deering (Cop); E. G. Marshall (Morgue Attendant); Reed Hadley (Narrator); J. Edgar Hoover, Baron von Genin, Dr. Hans Thomson (Themselves).

Louis de Rochemont, producer of the March of Time short subject film series, commenced a new trend for the post-World War II American cinema with the semi-documentary style of this espionage study. Relating the story of a young German-American (Eythe) aiding the FBI in routing a nest of Nazi spies in wartime New York, the picture was a fairly realistic study of the FBI at work.

The film's premise was based on an actual FBI case involving

Harry Bellaver (left) in The House on 92nd Street (20th-Fox, 1945).

the spy hunt for Axis agents who were attempting to steal vital data
on the atomic bomb experiment.   To enhance the quality of verisimili-
tude, director Hathaway filmed much of the feature on location in
Manhattan, utilizing a stentorian narrative device to bind the episodes into a coherent "factual" whole.   The finished product seemed
so real to many moviegoers, that it was frequently accepted as a
recitation of pure documented fact.

Hasso was especially impressive as the ruthless Nazi agent
who headed a Nazi contingent, ruled over by the mysterious "Mr.
George. "

HOW TO STEAL THE WORLD (MGM, 1968) C 89 min.

Executive producer, Norman Felton; producer, Anthony
Spinner; associate producer, George M. Lehr, Irv Pearlberg; di-
rector, Sutton Roley; screenplay, Norman Hudis; assistant director,
David Tringham; art director, Fred Carter; production designer,
Wilfred Shingleton; title theme, Jerry Goldsmith; camera, Robert
Hauser; editor, Peter Tanner.

Robert Vaughn (Napoleon Solo); David McCallum (Illya Kury-
akin); Barry Sullivan (Robert Kingsley); Eleanor Parker (Margitta);
Leslie Nielson (General Maximilian Harmon); Tony Bill (Steven
Garrow); Mark Richman (Mr. Webb); Daniel O'Herlihy (Professor

David Garrow); Leo G. Carroll (Alexander Waverly); Albert Paulsen (Dr. Kurt Erikson); Hugh Marlowe (Grant); Ruth Warwick (Mrs. Garrow); Inger Stratton (Anna Erikson); Richard Bull (Captain Gelser); Edgar Stehli (Veeth); Amy Thomson (Miss Carla); David Hurst (Jan Vanovech); Anella Barsett (Dr. Naomi Fisher); Arthur Hanson (Paul Mackie); Barbara Moore (Lisa Rogers).

The last of "The Man from U. N. C. L. E. " segments to be pasted together for theatrical release abroad, this film was one of the better entries. The British Monthly Film Bulletin reflected, "But though it follows the by now almost traditional pattern, it is less humorous and bizzarely exuberant than its predecessors, and one suspects that the series is now moving from camp Bond to straightforward thriller. "

When U. N. C. L. E. agent Sullivan and European General Nielsen disappear, followed by the abduction of five leading scientists, Solo (Vaughn) and Kuryakin (McCallum) jump onto the hot trail which leads them from Hong Kong to the Himalayan headquarters of Sullivan.

I ACCUSE! (MGM, 1958) 99 min.

Producer, Sam Zimbalist; director, Jose Ferrer; based on the book Captain Dreyfus--A Story of Mass Hysteria by Nicholas Halasz; screenplay, Gore Vidal; art director, Elliot Scott; music, William Alwyn; music director, Muir Mathieson; costumes, Elizabeth Haffenden; camera, F. A. Young; editor, Frank Clarke.

Jose Ferrer (Alfred Dreyfus); Anton Walbrook (Major Esterhazy); Viveca Lindfors (Lucie Dreyfus); Leo Genn (Major Picquart); Emlyn Williams (Emile Zola); David Farrar (Mathieu Dreyfus); Donald Wolfit (General Mercier); Herbert Lom (Major DuPaty de Clam); Harry Andrews (Major Henry); Felix Aylmer (Edgar Demange); Peter Illing (Georges Clemenceau); George Coulouris (Colonel Sandherr); Carl Jaffe (Colonel von Schwarzkoppen); Erich Pohlmann (Bertillon); John Chandos (Drumont); Ernest Clark (Prosecutor); Anthony Ireland (Judge); and: John Phillips, Laurence Naismith, Michael Hordern, Keith Pyott, Ronald Howard, Charles Gray, Michael Anthony, Arthur Howard, Michael Trubshawe.

Seven years after the German-made Dreyfus (1930), which starred Fritz Kortner, Grete Mosheim, Albert Bassermann, and Oscar Homolka, Hollywood made The Life of Emile Zola, which won Joseph Schildkraut an Academy Award as best supporting actor for his performance as Captain Alfred Dreyfus. Twenty-one years later director-star Jose Ferrer journeyed to England to film a CinemaScope rendition of the infamous Dreyfus affair. That fascinating case which had rocked 1890s France and startled the world, revealed a stiffling atmosphere of French military hierarchy bungling, political over-expediency, and rampant anti-Semitism in the French governmental bureaucracy. Unfortunately, Ferrer's I Accuse! was an antiseptic evocation of the facts, marred irrevocably by his own

Jose Ferrer in I Accuse! (MGM, 1958).

pretentiously martyred performance. Only Viveca Lindfors (as the
wife Lucie) emerged as a human being trying to cope with the base
injustices of life. Almost lost in the shuffle of the "unstirring"
I Accuse! were the ramifications inherent when a spy under pressure thrusts his traitorous acts onto an innocent bystander--and
nearly gets away with it!

In 1894 Alfred Dreyfus (Ferrer), a captain on the General
Staff of the French Army, and a Jew, is suspected of treason.
Secret military documents have come into the Germans' possession
via an agent known only as "D." Fearful of the rising French
indignation over the security leakage, Ferrer, on very slight evidence, is made a scapegoat and sent before a court-martial. Because he never believes he could be condemned for a crime he did
not commit, Ferrer is traumatized to find himself judged guilty
and sentenced to life imprisonment on Devil's Island. Meanwhile,
Ferrer's wife (Lindfors) and his brother (Farrar) are determined
to reveal the mockery of the conviction and appeal to France's most
influential citizens for succor, including novelist Emile Zola (Williams), statesman Clemenceau (Illing), and lawyer Demange (Aylmer). Later, Major Count Ferdinand Esterhazy (Walbrook) is
discovered to be the actual spy and is sent to trial on Farrar's
accusations, but the anxious military maneuver to have Walbrook
acquitted. The outraged Williams writes an open letter to the
French President entitled "I Accuse." On the basis of this plea
for justice, Ferrer is called for a new trial, found guilty again,
but on the President's insistence, the dishonored and broken soldier
is pardoned. Years later, Ferrer is proven conclusively innocent
and is rewarded with the Legion of Honor.

I DEAL IN DANGER   (20th-Fox, 1966)   C   89 min.

Executive producer, Walter Grauman; producer, Buck Hough-ton; director, Grauman; screenplay, Larry Cohen; music, Lalo Schiffrin, Mullendore; assistant director, Ray Taylor, Hans Sommer, Wolfgang Von Schiber; sound, Karsten Ultrick; music director, Lionel Newman; special camera effects, Karl Baumgartner, Erwin Lange; camera, Sam Leavitt, Kurt Grigoleit; editor, Jason Bernie, Dolf Rudeen.

Robert Goulet (David March); Christine Carere (Suzanne Duchard); Donald Harron (Spauling); Horst Frank (Luber); Werner Peters (Elm); Eva Pflug (Gretchen Hoffman); Christiane Schmudtmer (Ericka); John Van Drellan (von Lindendorf); Hans Reiser (Richter); Margit Saad (Baroness); Peter Capell (Eckhardt); Osman Ragheb (Brunner); John Aderson (Gorleck); Dieter Eppler (Stolnitz); Dieter Kirschlechner (Becker); Manfred Andrae (Dr. Zimmer); Alexander Allerson (Kraus); Paul Glawton (Submarine Pilot).

John Alderson, Robert Goulet, and Werner Peters in I Deal in Danger (20th-Fox, 1966).

Taped together from the initial three episodes of the short lived "Blue Light" teleseries (ABC-TV, January 1966), the story told of Goulet, an American who was the last remaining agent of an Allied spy ring in World War II known as The Blue Light.   By posing as a Nazi sympathizer, he has worked his way up into the higher echelons of the German Intelligence department.   Goulet's main objective here was to destroy the secret submarine missile manufactury plant at Grossmünchen.   Needless to say he succeeded.

"Without resorting to a single Bondsian or Flintsian gimmick, Goulet is quite adequate in his role" (New York Herald-Tribune).

I MARRIED A COMMUNIST   see   THE WOMAN ON PIER 13

I SPY, YOU SPY   see   BANG, BANG, YOU'RE DEAD!

I WAS A COMMUNIST FOR THE F. B. I.   (WB, 1951)   84 min.

Producer, Byron Foy; director, Gordon Douglas; based on the experiences of Matt Cvetic as told to Pete Martin in the article I Pose as a Communist for the FBI; screenplay, Crane Wilbur; art director, Leo K. Kuter; camera, Edwin DePar; editor, Folmer Neumann.

Frank Lovejoy (Matt Cvetic); Dorothy Hart (Eve Merrick); Philip Carey (Mason); Dick Webb (Crowley); James Millican (Jim Blandon); Ron Hagerthy (Dick Cvetic); Paul Picerni (Joe Cvetic); Frank Gerstle (Tom Cvetic); Russ Conway (Frank Cvetic); Hope Kramer (Ruth Cvetic); Eddie Norris (Harmon); Kasia Orzazekski (Mrs. Cvetic); Ann Morrison (Miss Nova); Konstantin Shayne (Gerhardt Eisler); Roy Roberts (Father Novac); Paul McGuire (McIntyre); Douglas Evans (Chief Agent); Janet Barrett, Karen Hale (Secretaries); Joseph Smith, Jim O'Gatty (Goons); Frank Marlowe (Worker); Miss Ross (Forman); Lenita Lane (Principal); Alma Mansfield (Teacher); Ann Kimball, Paula Sowl (Students); Charles Sherlock, Grace Lenard (Couple); Eric Neilsen (Jackie); Roy Engle (Jackie's Father); Bill Lester (Brown); John Crawford (McGowan); Ernest Anderson, Sugarfoot Anderson (Black Men); Johnny Bradford (Dobbs); Jimmy Gonzales (Brennan); David MacMahon (Masonvitch); Phil Tully (Irish Mick); Howard Negley (Union Chairman); Bobby Gilbert, James Adamson (Pickets); Mary Alah Hokanson, Mildred Boyd (Women); George MacGrill (Man); Barry Reagan (Officer); Hugh Sanders (Garson); Lyle Latell (Cahill); Chuck Colean (Brakeman); William Bailey, Paul Bradley, Buddy Shaw, Dick Gordon (Lawyers); William Forrest (Senator Wood); Bert Moorhouse (Senator Gray).

In the heat of the Senate Un-American Committee hearings, Jack Warner felt compelled to demonstrate his studio's right-thinking by producing this lesson in American patriotism which was geared to be an alarm clock for others.   The finished product was promoted with the same major thrust as the studio's decade-earlier Confessions of a Nazi Spy, although the Communist one lacked the intrinsic merits of the earlier film, what with the overloaded

Frank Lovejoy, Philip Carey, and Richard Webb in I Was a Communist for the F.B.I. (WB, 1951).

screenplay which had the Commies depicted as individuals who eat caviar, guzzle champagne, and boast of the good life they will have after taking over America.

Lovejoy as Matt Cvetic moved stone-faced through this cinema verité chronicle of a Pittsburgh steel worker who, in co-operation with the F.B.I., joins the local Red cell in order to report on the scope of the Communist threat in the Pennsylvania area. The action swings into gear when Gerhardt Eisler (Shayne), the Communist leader in America, arrives in the steel town to foment strike violence and racial hatred. The tension occurs because Lovejoy cannot reveal his true political feelings to his family, particularly his patriotic brother and his own son. The romantic speculations revolve around Lovejoy's association with card-carrying school-teacher Eve Merrick (Hart), a gal who sees the light of democracy and is saved from Communist reprisal by Lovejoy (who kills two

Red thugs to do it).
    The real life Matt Cvetic died in Hollywood on July 26, 1962, at the age of 53.   During his years of undercover work, he joined some 75 Communist front organizations, attended about 2000 meetings, and gave the F. B. I. some 1000 names.

I WAS A SPY   (Gaumont-British-Fox, 1933)   83 min.

    Producer, Michael Balcon; director, Victor Saville; story, Martine McKenna; screenplay, W. P. Lipscomb.
    Madeleine Carroll (Marthe Cnockhaert); Herbert Marshall (Stephan); Conrad Veidt (Commandant); Gerald du Maurier (Doctor); Edmund Gwenn (Burgomaster); Donald Calthrop (Cnockhaert); Eva Moore (Canteen Ma); Nigel Bruce (Scottie); May Agate (Mme. Cnockhaert); Martita Hunt (Aunt Lucille); George Merritt (Captain Reichmann); Anthony Bushell (Otto).

Madeleine Carroll in I Was a Spy (Garumont-British-Fox, 1933).

In 1933 the British film industry was showing a new spark of life and this entry was one of the better new crop, demonstrating the English knack for instilling immediacy to yet another "true" retelling of World War I espionage bravery.

In 1915 occupied Roulers, Belgium, nurse Marthe Cnockhaert (Carroll), the daughter of a cafe proprietor (Cathrop), is persuaded to join the Allied cause by hospital worker Stephan (Marshall), leading to the blowing up of a German ammunition dump and the destruction of some vital military maneuvers by the Kaiser's troops.   For the good of the cause, Carroll is later forced to surrender to the enemy so that Marshall's life may be spared and he can continue his worthy partisan efforts.

The solid cast included burgomaster Gwenn, doctor du Maurier, and commandant Veidt.   Nine minutes were trimmed from the original 92 minute running time when I Was a Spy played its U. S. release engagements in 1934.

I WAS AN AMERICAN SPY   (AA, 1951)   85 min.

Producer, David Diamond; director, Lesley Lelander; based on the story I Was an American Spy and the novel Manila Espionage by Claire Phillips, Myron B. Goldsmith; screenplay, Sam Roeca; music, Edward J. Kay; song, Arthur Hammerstein and Dudley Wilkinson; camera, Harry Neumann; editor, Philip Cahn.

Ann Dvorak (Claire Phillips); Douglas Kennedy (John Phillips); Richard Loo (Colonel Masamoto); Leon Lontok (Pacio); Chabing (Lolita); Gene Evans (Boone); James Leong (Ho Sang); Leo Abbey (Torres); Freddie Revelala (Zig Zag); Philip Ahn (Captain Arito); Marya Marco (Fely); Escolastico Baucin (Memerto); Toshi Nakaki, Jerry Fujikawa, Weaver Levy (Japanese Guards); Lisa Ferraday (Dorothy); Howard Kumagai (Kamuri); Celeste Madamba (Pressa); Andres Lucas (Siggy); Frank Jenks (Mac); Gil Herman (Lieutenant); George Fields (Harmonica Player); Dennis Moore (Sgt. Borden); Kei Thing Chung (Native Newsboy); Richard Bartlett (American Soldier); Riley Hill (Thompson); Lane Nakano (Advance Guard); Bret Hamilton (G. I.); Ed Sojin Jr., Li Sun (Japanese Soldiers); Wong Artarne, Eddie Lee (Japanese M. P. s); Remedos Jacobe (Woman Clerk); William Yip (General Saito); William Yakota (Admiral); Frank Iwanaga (Submarine Officer); Harold Fong, Harry Hamada (Japanese Lieutenants); Lane Bradford (Driver); John Damler (Soldier); Jack Reynolds (U. S. Sergeant); Angel Crux (Mashito); William Tannen (U. S. Army Captain).

The real life adventures of Mrs. Phillips during the World War II Japanese occupation of Manila received strictly routine handling.   Only Dvorak's intense performance in the title role gave the flick a resonance of interest.

The narrative is encompassed by General Mark W. Clark's spoken foreword and by an epilogue presentation of the Freedom Medal to Mrs. Phillips.   As Manila is about to fall to the onpressing Japanese, Dvorak weds soldier John Phillips (Kennedy) only to have

him be captured and die in the notorious Bataan death march.
Thereafter she teams with Boone (Evans) to wage guerrilla warfare on the Oriental occupation force, using as her base a nightclub she operated in Manila. (Dvorak "sings" "Because of You.")
The Japanese eventually connect the enemy operative known as "Miss
Highpocket" with Dvorak and arrest her. Just before she is to be
marched in front of the firing squad, Evans engineers her rescue.
    In their zeal to enliven the cheap melodramatics of I Was
an American Spy, the studio had the Japanese presented as big
blabbermouths who were pretty much just a bunch of fools. The
picture's perverse highlight occurs during the Nipponese's interrogation of Dvorak with Colonel Masamoto (Loo) obliging the woman's
request for water by ordering a water hose shoved down her
throat.

ICE STATION ZEBRA (MGM, 1968) C 152 min.

    Producer, Martin Ransohoff, John Calley; associate producer,
James C. Pratt; director, John Sturges; based on the novel by
Alistair MacLean; screenplay, Harry Julian Fink; art director,
George W. Davis, Addison Hehr; set decorator, Henry Grace,
Jack Mills; music-music director, Michel Legrand; sound, Franklin
Milton; technical adviser, Captain John M. Connolly; special visual
effects, J. McMillan Johnson, Carroll L. Shepphird, Clarence
Slifer; optical effects, Robert R. Hoag; special effects, H. R. Mil-
lar, Sr., Ralph Swartz, Earl McCoy; camera, Daniel L. Fapp;
additional camera, John M. Stephens, Nelson Tyler; editor, Ferris
Webster.
    Rock Hudson (Commander James Ferraday); Ernest Borgnine
(Boris Vaslov); Patrick McGoohan (David Jones); Jim Brown (Cap-
tain Leslie Anders); Tony Bill (Lt. Russell Walker); Gerald S.
O'Loughlin (Lieutenant Commander Bob Raeburn); Alf Kjellin
(Colonel Ostrovsky); Murray Rose (Lieutenant George Mills); Ted
Hartley (Lieutenant Jonathan Hansen); Ron Masak (Paul Zabrinczski);
Joseph Bernard (Dr. Jack Benning); Michael Mikler (Lieutenant
Courtney Cartwright); Sherwood Price (Lieutenant Edgar Hackett);
Lee Stanley (Lieutenant Mitgang); Jonathan Lippe (Russian Major);
Lloyd Nolan (Admiral Garvey); John Orchard, William O'Connell
(Survivors); Ted Kristian (Wassmeyer); Jim Dixon (Earl McAuliffe);
Boyd Berlind (Bruce Kenner); David Wendell (Cedric Patterson);
Ronnie Rondell, Jr. (Lyle Nichols); Craig Shreeve (Gafferty);
Michael Grossman (Kohler); Wade Graham (Parker); Michael Rougas
(Fannovich); Jed Allan (Peter Costigan); Lloyd Haynes (Ebson);
Buddy Garion (Edward Rawlins); T. J. Escott (Lieutenant Carl
Mingus); Buddy Hart (Hill); Gary Downey (Lorrison); Robert Carlson
(Kelvaney); Don Newsome (Timothy Hirsch); Jim Goodwin (Survivor);
Bill Hillman (Philip Munsey); Dennis Alpert (Gambetta).

[Facing page] Ann Dvorak and Richard Loo (officer) in I Was an
American Spy (AA, 1951).

        A capsule containing reconnaissance photographs of American
and Russian bases is erroneously ejected from a Soviet satellite and
is known to have landed near Zebra, the British North Pole weather
station.   Both sides secretly intend to grab the vital container
which has been recovered by a worker, now stranded in a storm
near the station.   Meanwhile the U. S. nuclear submarine "Tiger-
fish" is dispatched from Scotland with orders to proceed to the
North Pole.   Aboard are British agents David Jones (McGoohan)
and Boris Vaslov (Borgnine), the latter a Russian defector, with
orders to retrieve and destroy the capsule.   During the trek to
its destination, the sub is sabotaged, with blame shifting from
Borgnine to Marine captain Leslie Anders (Brown).   Once at the
polar cap, sub captain James Ferraday (Hudson) leads an expedi-
tion through a raging storm to the weather station where several
of the crew are found dead.   Just as the capsule is located, a
contingent of Russian paratroopers, led by Colonel Ostrovsky
(Kjellin), drop into the area.   Borgnine is caught and shot by
McGoohan for attempting to turn over the container to the Soviets,
but later Hudson releases the capsule to the Soviets, and then
electronically destroys it as it is being hoisted by balloon to a
recovery plane.   A fake public announcement is later issued
describing the incident as a fine act of international cooperation.

        Producer Martin Ransohoff had acquired the rights to Alis-
tair MacLean's novel in 1964, planning it first as a Gregory Peck
vehicle (filming started, but was abandoned), and then later as a
picture to star Laurence Harvey.   When the super Panavision color
film did get underway, Hudson was headlining the wobbly production,
which could not overcome its basic structural fault.   "Alistair
MacLean's adventure stories, grounded in circumstances frequently
preposterous and usually fantastic, just about manage to remain
within the realms of credibility when read on the printed page, but
attempts to translate them to the screen rarely seem to succeed....
[I]t may be, more simply, that the camera's critical eye reveals
the misconceptions behind the original thinking" (British Monthly
Film Bulletin).

        One is aware that director John Sturges (and the viewer) is
in for a bumpy trip almost from the start of Ice Station Zebra, with
such simplistic dialog as Admiral Garvey (Nolan) asking eager
beaver Hudson, "Jim, just how much do you know about Ice Station
Zebra?"   The roadshow attraction opened to icy reviews.   Said
Pauline Kael (New Yorker), "perhaps there was a good spy adventure story buried in the verbal mush."   Viewers were as unim-
pressed with the studio soundstage ice flow scenes as with the high
school level dramatics of the all-male cast.   There were not even
any stomach turning widescreen effects to relieve the general
tedium.   The potentially diverting game of who-is-the-real-spy?
sunk with the obvious red herrings.

IN ENEMY COUNTRY   (Universal, 1968)   C   106 min.

        Producer-director, Harry Keller; story, Sy Bartlett; screen-

play, Edward Anhalt; art director, Alexander Golitzen, John Beck-
man; assistant director, Burt Astor; music, William Lava; sound,
Walden O. Watson, Clarence Self; camera, Loyal Griggs; editor,
Russell Schoengarth.

Tony Franciosa (Charles); Anjanette Comer (Denise); Guy
Stockwell (Braden); Paul Hubschmid (Friedrich); Tom Bell (Ian);
Michael Constantine (Ladislo); Harry Townes (General Marchois);
Milton Selzer (Bartowski); Patric Knowles (General Lloyd-Griffis);
Tige Andrews (Nicholay); Emile Genest (General Grieux); Lee
Berger (Mical); Virginia Christine (Frau Grilden); Harry Landers
(Pilot); Gerald Michenaud (Polish Boy); Ivor Barry (Air Marshall
Evelyn); Eugene Dynarski (Capek); Simon Scott (General Jomar).

Guy Stockwell, Anthony Franciosa, and Tom Bell in In Enemy
Country (Universal, 1968).

This minor league World War II espionage film, made more
than two decades after the events it depicts, quickly became sidetracked from its potentially rapid pacing by periodic, ponderous
discussions of moral dilemmas and ironic facts of life.

In 1939, Parisian Denise (Comer) of French Intelligence
weds Baron Friedrich von Wittenberg (Hubschmid) and returns with
him to Germany. Four years later agent Charles (Franciosa), the
American Braden (Stockwell), and British operative Ian (Bell), slip

into Germany and with the help of Polish agent Ladislo (Constantine), infiltrate the slave labor crew at an ordnance factory near Kiel where the Nazis are producing a new type of torpedo. With Comer as their contact, information is passed along to London of the factory's location, and Allied bombers destroy it. Franciosa and Stockwell survive the various skirmishes and load a torpedo prototype aboard a waiting Allied plane. Their job is done.

In Enemy Country was chopped to 81 minutes for its European release.

IN LIKE FLINT (20th-Fox, 1967) C 114 min.

Producer, Saul David; associate producer, Martin Fink; director, Gordon Douglas; screenplay, Hal Fimberg; art director, James Martin Scott, Dale Hennesy; set decorator, Walter M. Scott, James W. Payne; opening montage-titles, Richard Kuhn; assistant director, David Hall; music, Jerry Goldsmith; song, Goldsmith and Leslie Bricusse; sound, Samuel Goode, David Dockendorf; special camera effects, L. B. Abbott, Art Cruickshank, Emil Kosa; camera, William Daniels; editor, Hugh J. Fowler.

James Coburn (Derek Flint); Lee J. Cobb (Cramden); Jean Hale (Lisa); Andrew Duggan (President Trent); Anna Lee (Elisabeth);

James Coburn and Jean Hale in In Like Flint (20th-Fox, 1967).

Hanna Landy (Helena); Totty Ames (Claire); Steve Inhat (Carter);
Thomas Hasson (Avery); Mary Michael (Terry); Diane Bond (Jan);
Jacki Ray (Denise); Herb Edelman (Russian Premier); Yvonne Craig
(Natasha); Buzz Henry (Austin); Henry Wills (Cooper); Mary Meade
French (Hilda); S. P. Lear, Sr. (Bill Lear); and: Erin O'Brien,
Ginny Gan, Eve Bruce, Inge Jaklyn, Kaye Farrington, Thordis
Brandt, Inga Neilsen, Marilyn Hanold, Pat Becker, Lyzanne La Due,
Nancy Stone.

By the time of the sequel to Our Man Flint (1966), the theatrical film market was so glutted with James Bond-like entries
that it would have been nigh impossible for even an extremely
talented production team to come up with a refreshing slant on the
007 formula. In Like Flint was hampered by an already established
characterization-situation set-up, by a dumpy plot, and most of
all by the uninspired directing of Gordon Douglas, no substitute for
the craftsmanship of Daniel Mann on Our Man Flint. (Twentieth
Century-Fox obviously had no faith in the finished product for there
were big production hassles over editing and promotion, with producer Saul David cancelling his studio contract and leaving Fox in a
huff.) Largely because of its major studio distribution and the
public's fond memory of the spanky Our Man Flint, In Like Flint
undeservedly grabbed $5 million at the distributors' domestic rentals
window.

When U. S. President Treng (Duggan) is kidnapped by what is
later learned to be a female undercover organization and a plastic
surgery lookalike put in his place, Cramden (Cobb) of ZOWIE dispatches unreliable but available super agent Derek Flint (Coburn) to
turn the tide on the embarrassing situation. The clues lead first
to a Virgin Island health resort and then to a camouflaged secret
island which is really an elaborate rocket-launching base in the best
007 tradition.

Once again the ogling of shapely pulchritude proved to be
the chief occupation of Coburn on screen, with only uneasy excursions into karate battles with the enemy. Obviously everyone concerned was desperate for new laugh-provoking situations, leading to
the farcical happenstance of having Coburn in leotards dancing with
Russian ballerinas and Cobb parading about in drag. The soundest
contribution to the picture was provided by L. B. Abbott and Art
Cruickshank who devised the special effect explosions which climaxed
the tedious proceedings.

IN SAIGON, SOME MAY LIVE see SOME MAY LIVE

INNOCENT BYSTANDERS (Paramount, 1972) C 111 min.

Producer, George H. Brown; director, Peter Collinson;
based on the novel by James Munro (Mitchell); screenplay, James
Mitchell; assistant director, Clive Reed; art director, Maurice
Carter; music, John Keating; song, Hurricane Smith; sound, Bill

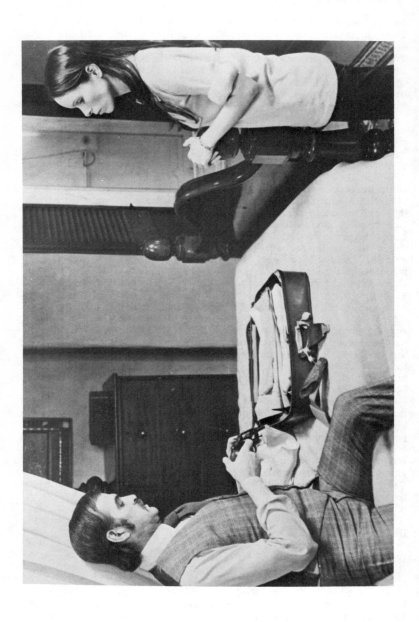

Daniels, Gordon K. McCallum; special effects, Pat Moore; camera, Brian Probyn; editor, Alan Pattilo.

Stanley Baker (John Craig); Geraldine Chaplin (Miriam Loman); Dana Andrews (Blake); Donald Pleasence (Loomis); Sue Lloyd (Joanna Benson); Vladek Sheybal (Aaron Kaplan); Derren Nesbitt (Royce); Warren Mitchell (Omar); Ferdy Mayne (Marcus Kaplan); John Collin (Asimov); Frank Maher (Daniel).

This is one of the increasingly rare recent excursions into the espionage genre. It met with almost total indifference from the seemingly saturated movie-going public. "...[I]t will keep the uncritical intrigued for a while" was the mild reaction of the generally easily-pleased New York Daily News. Clearly, in the effort of today's film producers to eschew the James Bond approach, there is a tremendous uncertainty about how to inject new life into the overplayed spy picture. This creative problem is compounded by the present world situation in which war, fifth columnists, double agents, and all the paraphernalia of fomenting international unrest and one-upmanship is held in hearty disfavor by the masses.

At the urging of Blake (Andrews), head of the American secret service, Loomis (Pleasence), top man in Britain's Department K, agrees to put three agents on the job of tracing former Russian scientist Aaron Kaplan (Sheybal) who acquired his release from a Siberian prison camp by betraying his colleagues. Pleasence assigns Royce (Nesbitt) and Joanna Benson (Lloyd) as a team, and also hands the same task to John Craig (Baker). The latter was the department's top agent until his last mission broke his spirit. Baker is intent upon proving his usefulness and hustles off to New York where he prevents the killing of Sheybal's brother (Mayne) and at the same time takes innocent bystander Miriam Loman (Chaplin), Mayne's ward, as hostage in order to drag information from Mayne about Sheybal's present whereabouts. The trail leads to Kutsk in Turkey and a shootout among the double agents and the pawn in question, Sheybal.

Innocent Bystanders has more than its share of sadism-- seemingly "essential" for today's entries--and while it avoids parodying the Ian Fleming spin-offs, it fails to establish any new ground or methods in unspooling its complex plotline. The mechanical direction and the formula script fail to expound satisfactorily on Baker's character weakness (i.e., past events have made him unsure of himself with women) and fail as well to avoid passing salutes to mankind's sense of guilt about the shaky world situation.

INSIDE THE LINES (RKO, 1930) 76 min.

Producer, William Le Baron; director, Roy J. Pomeroy; based on the play by Earl Derr Biggers; screenplay, Ewart Adamson;

[Facing page] Stanley Baker and Geraldine Chaplin in Innocent Bystanders (Paramount, 1972).

dialog, John Farrow; art director, Max Ree; sound, George Ellis; camera, Nick Musuraca.

Betty Compson (Jane Gershon); Ralph Forbes (Eric Woodhouse); Montagu Love (Governor of Gibraltar); Mischa Auer (Amahdi); Ivan Simpson (Capper); Betty Carter (Lady Crandall); Evan Thomas (Major Bishop); Reginald Sharland (Archie); William von Brincken (Chief, Secret Service).

Betty Compson and Ralph Forbes in <u>Inside the Lines</u> (RKO, 1930).

A girl (Compson) and her fiancé (Forbes) separate in Germany at the beginning of World War I and later meet at the British fortress at Gibraltar. Both are German spies, she posing as the daughter to a friend of the Governor of Gibraltar (Love) and he as a British officer.

Compson attempts to obtain the plans to the harbor's mine fields but finds that Forbes has taken the charts for his own use. She later tries to dissuade him from helping to destroy the British fleet. At this point her supposedly trusted Hindu servant Amahdi (Auer) denounces her as Operator Number 49, a traitor to Germany. The Hindu threatens to kill the girl but is shot by Forbes. The couple then discover that both are actually double agents for Britain, and with the British fleet saved, they can reunite in love and the British cause.

Inside the Lines proved to be such a sadly simple film, that the New York Times' reviewer quipped, "It would not have been surprising if the cameraman and the director had stepped before the lens and declared themselves in the pay of Great Britain, almost everyone else did. "

THE INTELLIGENCE MEN (J. Arthur Rank, 1964) C 104 min.

Producer, Hugh Stewart; director, Robert Asher; story, Peter Blackmore; screenplay, S. C. Green; R. M. Hills; music, Philip Green; camera, Jack Asher; editor, Gerry Hambling.

Eric Morecombe (Himself); Ernie Wise (Ernie Sage); William Franklyn (Colonel Grant of M. I. 5); April Olrich (Madame Petrovna); Gloria Paul (Gena Garlotti); Richard Vernon (Sir Edward Seabrook); David Lodge (Stage Manager); Jacqueline Jones (Karin); Terence Alexander (Reed); Francis Matthews (Thomas); Warr Mitchell (Prozoroff); Brian Oulton (Laundry Basket Man); Michael Peake (Simister Stranger); Peter Bull (Phillipe); Tutte Lemkow (Seedy Schlect Agent); Rene Sartoris (Siegried Dancer); Graham Smith (Evil Owl Dancer); Dilsy Rosser (Girl in Cinema); Johnny Briggs (Boy in Cinema); Ely Counsell (Girl in Cucaracha); Gerald Holy (Carlos); Joe Melia (Conductor); Marianne Stone (Woman in Lift); Jill Curzor (French Girl); Alexis Checnakov (Rostov); Laurence Herder (Ivan).

The top vaudeville-television team of Morecombe and Wise made their transition to feature films with this weary, "occasionally amusing spoof" (Variety), which suffered from a "chaos of flat gags (all of which fall flatter for being in colour)" (London Observer).

With an Anglo-Russian trade agreement about to be signed, it is essential that no tomfoolery occur which might prevent it. Colonel Grant (Franklyn) of M. I. 5 and in turn Morecombe enlist a big jerk named Ernie Sage (Wise) to help England in her hour of need--a sad mistake for all concerned.   Wheeler and Woolsey-- where are you?

INTERNATIONAL LADY (UA, 1941) 102 min.

Producer, Edward Small; associate producer, Stanley Logan; director, Tim Whelan; story, E. Lloyd Sheldon, Jack DeWitt; screenplay, Howard Estabrook; music director, Lud Gluskin; camera, Hal Mohr; editor, Grant Whytock.

George Brent (Tim Hanley); Ilona Massey (Carla Nilson); Basil Rathbone (Reggie Oliver); Gene Lockhart (Sidney Grenner); George Zucco (Webster); Francis Pierlot (Dr. Rowan); Martin Kosleck (Brunner); Charles D. Brown (Tetlow); Marjorie Gateson (Mrs. Grenner); Leyland Hodgson (Moulton); Clayton Moore (Sewell); Gordon DeMain (Denby); Frederic Worlock (Sir Henry); Jack Mulhall (Desk Clerk); Ralph Dunn (Don); Robert Fiske (Head Waiter); Selmer Jackson (Colonel); John Dilson (Decoding Expert); William Forrest (Official).

Martin Kosleck and Ilona Massey in International Lady (UA, 1941).

      Released in the early war period, this film bore a strong plot resemblance to Adventure in Diamonds (Paramount, 1940), also starring George Brent.   In this effort, however, Massey played charming Carla Nilson, a Nazi agent based in London who is sent to assist Nazi collaborators in the U.S. and is trailed there by FBI agent Brent and Scotland Yard man Rathbone.   In America Massey utilizes a musical code to transmit vital information to the Nazis across the ocean.

      The plot thickens (and diverges) as love sets in between Massey and Brent, leaving Rathbone to bow out of the romantic triangle gracefully.   In the end the lady gives up the Axis cause and is forgiven for her past sins, making Massey one of the most quickly exonerated espionage workers in world history.

      A high grade "B" film, International Lady often got top-of-the-bill bookings when issued, due mainly to its stars, and the nifty top supporting cast: Lockhart and Zucco as Nazi leaders,

Pierlot as a doctor producing explosives for the bad guys. Bosley
Crowther (New York Times) termed the picture "just one prolonged
cliche. " However, like many films of the period it now has become fashionably campy, particularly the unsubtle delineation of the
contrasting spy hunt methods employed by lackadaisical Brent and
the more enterprising Rathbone, the latter hamming it up drolly with
a series of disguises.

THE INVADERS [The 49th Parallel] (Columbia, 1942) 123 min.

     Director, Michael Powell; story, Emeric Pressburger; dia-
log, Rodney Ackland, Pressburger; music, Ralph Vaughn Williams;
camera, Frederick Young.
     Leslie Howard (Philip Armstrong Scott); Raymond Massey
(Andy Brock); Laurence Olivier (Johnnie); Anton Walbrook (Peter);
Glynis Johns (Anna); Finlay Currie (The Factor); Eric Portman
(Lt. Hirth); Niall MacGinnis (Vogel); Ley On (Nick the Eskimo);
Charles Victor (Andreas); Raymond Lovell (Lt. Kuhnecke); John
Chandos (Lohrmann); Basil Appleby (Jahner).

     Ostensibly a propaganda study of the vicious qualities of
Nazis, the Michael Powell film came across as a stark and
effective escape thriller in which ideological factions took a subordinate role. (After all, would not most people of whatever
political persuasion do most anything to survive?) The utilization
of many star players in unassuming performances heightened the
film's commerciality.
     When their craft is sunk near the Hudson Bay area of the
Canadian coast, six surviving members of a raiding German U-boat
make their way ashore and begin their trek across the alien territory, hoping for some support from the inland pockets of German
settlers. Leading the arrogant pack is Lieutenant Hirth (Portman)
who brutally shoots anything in his way--Canuck trappers, Eskimos,
animals. His group has a sharp setback regarding the potential
might of the Third Reich when they chance upon the German-
descended Hutterite agricultural community in Manitoba, meeting
with indifference or downright hostility from Peter (Walbrook) and
the other farmers. Portman has his just deserts: just as he is
skipping over the U.S. border he is shot by AWOL Canadian soldier
Andy Brock (Massey).
     This film was started in April 1940 on location in Canada
and England, and required 18 months to complete. Its $100,000
budget, supplied by the British government, was stretched to com-
pletion, largely due to the volunteer services of the actor contingent,
who worked on their scenes as each became available. Howard was
particularly effective as vacationing novelist Philip Armstrong Scott
who witnessed the "ruthlessness" of the Germans first hand as they
destroy his art treasures, as was Olivier as the French Canadian
Johnnie whose reluctant patriotism was shipped into shape by his
interaction with the Germans.

INVISIBLE AGENT (Universal, 1942)   81 min.

Producer, Frank Lloyd; associate producer, George Waggner; director, Edwin L. Marin; screenplay, Curtis Siodmak; assistant director, Vernon Keays; special effects, Joan Fulton; camera, Les White; editor, Edward Curtiss.

Ilona Massey (Maria); Jon Hall (Raymond); Sir Cedric Hardwicke (Stauffer); Peter Lorre (Ikito); J. Edward Bromberg (Heiser); Albert Bassermann (Dr. Schmidt); John Litel (Gardiner); Matt Willis, Marty Faust (Killers); Alberto Morin (Free Frenchman); Henry Guttman (Storm Trooper); Holmes Herbert (Sir Alfred Spencer); Wolfgang Zilzer (von Porten); Ferdinand Munier (Bartender); Keye Luke (Surgeon); Eddie Dunn, Hans Schumm, Philip Van Zandt (S. S. Men); John Burton (R. A. F. Flyer); Lee Tung-Foo (General Chin Lee); Milburn Stone (German Sergeant); Michael Visaroff (Verihen); Walter Tetley (Newsboy); Pat West (Taxi Driver-German); Leslie Denison (British Radio Operator); William Ruhl, Otto Reichow (Gestapo Agents); Pat McVey (German); John Holland (Secretary to Spencer); Wally Scott, Bobby Hale (English Tommies); Mabel Colcord (Housekeeper); Charles Flynn, Phil Warren, Paul Bryar, John Merton (German Soldiers); Lee Shumway (Brigadier General); Henry Zynda (Colonel Kelinski); Ferdinand Schumann-Heink (German Telephone Operator); Victor Zimmerman, Bill Pagan (Storm Troopers); Lane Chandler, Duke York, Donald Curtis (German Sentries); Charles Regan (Ordinance Car Driver); Sven Hugo-Borg (German Captain); James Craven (Ship's Radio Operator).

During the World War II years, Universal turned out much pap entertainment aimed at war-weary audiences. Although much of this type of film fare was far from classic, most was at least mediocre or above. An exception to this rule was Invisible Agent, which save for its special effects is pure junk.

The studio grafted a topical twist to its quickly deteriorating series of films based on H. G. Wells' novel, The Invisible Man, and came up with this time-waster. Here Hall is a printshop owner, the grandson of the original invisible man (played by Claude Rains in the 1933 film), who is bugged by Nazis wanting his invisibility formula. Following the Pearl Harbor attack Hall volunteers for Allied service. His mission: to take a huge dose of the invisibility formula and then parachute into Berlin to obtain a top secret list of Nazi-Japanese spies working abroad.

Only a few of the supporting players gave this film any weight at all, particularly Hardwicke and Bromberg as Gestapo agents, and Lorre as a Japanese secret police officer. Typical of shoddy World War II fodder films, the enemy was depicted as lame-brained, a distortion as far from the truth as was Hitler's fantasy of the perfect Aryan race.

This unhappy mixture of Topper and Confessions of a Nazi Spy was labeled by the New York Sun "as obvious a breach of taste as the screen has produced. "

THE IPCRESS FILE   (Universal, 1965)   C   108 min.

Executive producer, Charles Kasher; producer, Harry Saltzman; associate producer, Ronald Kinnoch; director, Sidney J.
Furie; based on the novel by Len Deighton; screenplay, Bill Cana-
way, James Doran; art director, Peter Murton; music, John Barry;
assistant director, Fred Slark; camera, Otto Heller; editor, Peter
Hunt.

Michael Caine (Harry Palmer); Nigel Green (Dalby); Guy
Doleman (Ross); Sue Lloyd (Jean); Gordon Jackson (Carswell);
Aubrey Richards (Radcliffe); Frank Gatliff (Bluejay); Thomas Bap-
tiste (Barney); Oliver MacGreevy (Housemartin); Freda Bamford
(Alice); Pauline Winter (Charlady); Anthony Blackshaw (Edwards);
Barry Raymond (Gray); David Glover (Chilcott-Oakes); Stanley
Meadows (Inspector Keightley); Peter Ashmore (Sir Robert);
Michael Murray (Raid Inspector); Anthony Baird (Raid Sergeant);
Tony Caunter (O. N. I. Man); Charles Rea (Taylor); Ric Hutton
(Records Officer); Douglas Blackwell (Murray); Richard Burrell
(Operator); Glynn Edwards (Police Station Sergeant); Zsolt
Vadaszffy (Prison Doctor); Joseph Behrmann, Max Faulkner, Paul
S. Chapman (Prison Guards).

Harry Saltzman, co-producer of James Bond pictures, here
launched a new spy series. However, the central character is
based on Len Deighton's writing and is very much an anti-hero:
unscrupulous, insubordinate, a "trickster, perhaps with criminal
tendencies," but quick-witted and with initiative. He has his own
downbeat philosophy (cheating the Establishment) and priorities
("girls, books, music and cooking--but I like girls best!").

When a British Central Intelligence agent is killed and the
scientist he is guarding is kidnapped, the bureau turns to a most
unlikely replacement, Harry Palmer (Caine). The bespectacled,
trench-coated, flabby-waisted Caine is an undisguised opportunist
who while a British sergeant in Berlin had been caught plying the
black market trade and was offered the alternative of jail or becoming a British counterspy. The latter choice seemed more
attractive at the time, that is until Caine was informed of the low
pay scale, the dangers involved and, most dehabilitating of all,
the drab, unglamourous, plodding daily routing of an espionage
agent. Caine's government director is Ross (Doleman) of Military
Intelligence, while forthright Dalby (Green) is his direct superior,
canny Scotsman Carswell (Jackson) his partner, and chipper Jean
(Lloyd) his co-worker.

Once Caine and Jackson stumble upon a piece of recorded
tape with the word "Ipcress" inscribed on it, neither of their lives
is worth dirt. Soon Jackson is slain and Caine is grabbed by the
enemy camp for a brainwash session. The denouement has its
appropriately special twist, but rest assured Caine's Harry Palmer
emerges alive, if shaken, to carry on in further screen adventures.

There are a few obvious credibility gaps in The Ipcress File
(e. g. , the extended brainwash scenes are rather unmotivated saved
for the opportunity to present the viewer with a sadist's delight),

but the picture on the whole is sufficiently terse and tough to stand on its own. It "... manages to be witty without making undue fun of itself" (the New Yorker). Particularly commendable in this deliberate mishmash of double dealing about a brain drain is the boisterous approach of director Sidney J. Furie and the thoughtful, if occasionally arbitrary, Techniscope-color camera angles of cinematographer Otto Heller.

THE IRON CURTAIN (20th-Fox, 1948)   87 min.

Producer, Sol C. Siegel; director, William A. Wellman; based on the memoirs by Igor Gouzenko; screenplay, Milton Krims; art director, Lyle Wheeler, Mark Lee Kirk; set decorator, Thomas Little; music, Dmitri Shostakovich, Serge Prokofieff, Aram Khachaturian, Nicholas Miakovsky; music director, Alfred Newman; assistant director, William Eckhardt; makeup, Ben Nye; costumes, Bonnie Cashin; sound, Bernard Fredrick, Harry M. Leonard; special effects, Fred Sersen; camera, Charles C. Clarke; editor, Louis Loeffler.

Dana Andrews (Igor Gouzenko); Gene Tierney (Anna Gouzenko); June Havoc (Karanova); Berry Kroeger (Grubb); Edna Best (Mrs. Foster); Stefan Schnabel (Ranev); Nicholas Joy (Dr. Norman); Eduard Franz (Major Kulin); Frederick Tozere (Colonel Trigorin); Noel Cravat (Bushkin); Christopher Robin Olsen (Andrei); Peter Whitney (Winikov); Leslie Barrie (Editor); Mauritz Hugo (Leonard Loetz); John Shay (Sergeyev); Victor Wood (Captain Class); Anne Curson (Helen Tweedy); Helena Dare (Mrs. Kulin); Eula Morgan (Mrs. Trigorin); Reed Hadley (Commentator); John Ridgely (Policeman Murphy); John Davidson (Secretary); Joe Whitehead (William Hollis); Michael J. Dugan (Policeman); Harry Carter (Fairfield); Robert Adler (Wilson); Arthur E. Gould-Porter (Mr. Foster); Matthew Boulton (Inspector Burns).

For mainly self-serving reasons, Hollywood felt obligated to stir up the post-World War II American conscience about the growing menace of the Communist infiltration on the North American continent. The facts in the 1946 Igor Gouzenko case were ostensibly the basis for this cloak and sickle tale, which 20th Century-Fox proudly announced as "The most amazing plot in 3300 years of recorded espionage." The studio released the film in simultaneous saturation bookings to 500 theatres throughout the U. S. A. The New York Herald-Tribune commended the picture's "provocative ideological chord," but qualified that it "does not stack up well as propaganda or entertainment." When Bosley Crowther (New York Times) dared to suggest in a review editorial that The Iron Curtain was more fancy than fact, it created a Fox-produced furor that gave the picture far more publicity than it warranted. The picture's main problems were that it sacrificed credibility for marquee allure and replaced semi-documentary logic with contrived cinematic pap.

Set in 1943 Ottawa, Canada, the film depicts the exploits of Russian embassy code clerk Igor Gouzenko (Andrews) who has a

Stefan Schnabel, Noel Cravat, Frederick Tozere, and Dana Andrews in The Iron Curtain (20th-Fox, 1948).

sudden pang of conscience at the sinister espionage activities being conducted by his countrymen under the guise of international diplomacy. Prodded by his pregnant wife (Tierney), he becomes an accomplice of the West in unraveling the far-reaching spy network headed by Ranev (Schnabel). Andrews' professed noble goal is to create a better world for his new-born child.

The Iron Curtain was a goldmine of right wing propaganda, depicting in heavy-handed terms the spectrum of ruthless Reds and fellow travelers. The performances of Havoc, Kroeger, and others as Commie operatives were more comic than real.

Television title: Behind the Iron Curtain.

ISTANBUL EXPRESS (Universal/NBC-TV, 1968) C 93 min.

Producer, Richard Irving; associate producer, Jerrold

Freedman; director, Irving; screenplay, Richard Levinson, William
Link; assistant director, Burt Astor; art director, John J. Lloyd;
set decorator, John McCarthy, Perry Murdock; music, Oliver Nel-
son; music supervisor, Stanley Wilson; costumes, Grady Hunt;
sound, Robert Bertrand; camera, Benjamin H. Kline; editor, Richard
G. Wray.
 Gene Barry (David London); Senta Berger (Mila Darvos);
John Saxon (Cheval); Tom Simcox (Leland McCord); Mary Ann Mob-
ley (Peggy Coopersmith); Werner Peters (Dr. Lenz); Donald Woods
(Shepperd); John Marley (Capel); Norma Varden (English Lady);
Moustache (Gustav); and: Jack Kruschen, Emile Genest.

 When art dealer Barry boards the Orient Express in Paris,
he is told by his assistant Mobley that his next mission--for he is
an American secret agent--is to go to an international auction in
Istanbul and purchase important documents for the U.S. government. Aboard the crack express train heading for Istanbul are
several other espionage agents eager to eliminate Barry. At one
point he is drugged and injected with a truth serum. In Venice he
is almost eliminated by Berger's chief henchman, while in Belgrade he misses the train because his contact is shot and he must
fly on to the next stop. In Istanbul he completes his mission.
 Made expressly for U.S. television, this film did fairly well
when telecast (October 22, 1968), pulling a 34 per cent share of
the viewing audience with a 19.5 Nielsen rating. Abroad the entry
was shown as a theatrical feature and was panned as an unsatisfactory refugee from television's wasteland. "The script follows
a more familiar route, taking in all the cliches of glossy espionage
thrillers, and including a number of characters whose only justifica-
tion for making the trip is to be on hand to extricate the hero from
the most unlikely difficulties in the most unlikely places" (British
Monthly Film Bulletin).
 One of the production's biggest deficits was Barry himself,
who seemed so self-impressed with his alleged charms that he failed
to offer the necessary élan.

THE JERUSALEM FILE (MGM, 1972) C 96 min.

 Executive producer, Anton von Kassel; producer, Ram Ben
Efraim; associate producer, Mark Greene; director, John Flynn;
screenplay, Troy Kennedy Martin; assistant director, Isaac Yeshu-
run; art director, Peter Williams; music, John Scott; sound, Der-
rick Leather; special effects, Jacob Neumann; camera, Raoul
Coutart; additional camera, Brian Probyn; editor, Norman Wanstall.
 Bruce Davison (David Armstrong); Nicol Williamson (Profes-
sor Lang); Daria Halprin (Nurit); Donald Pleasence (Major Samuels);
Ian Hendry (General Mayer); Koya Yair Rubin (Barak); Zeev Revah
(Raschid); David Smader (Herzen); Jack Cohen (Altouli); Isaac
Neeman (Yussof); Ori Levy (Captain Ori); Arie Elias (Informer);
Itzik Weiss (Barak's Brother); Yona Elian (Raschel); Yossi
Werzanski (Alex); Johnnie Phillips (Lieutenant); Gabi Eldor (Hospital

Receptionist); Yael Duryanoff (Lang's Secretary); Moshe Yanai
(Officer); Pink Wigoder (Student); Ali Mohammad Hasan (Fuad);
Samih Mohammad Najib (Achmed); Salah Darwish (Security Officer).

"... [T]he picture's complicated political plot is muddled and
confusing, leaving an audience with less than a full understanding
of the motivations of the characters" (New York Daily Mirror).
Even the introductory explanation printed on screen does not clarify
the plotline.
       Just after the decisive Six Day War, American archaeology
student David Armstrong (Davison) and his Arab friend Raschid
(Revah) are sitting at a Jerusalem cafe when they are fired upon
from a passing car.   Davison revives at a hospital where Major
Samuels (Pleasence) of the city's security police wants information
to halt the violent power play between competing Arab-Jewish
groups.   Davison remains silent, planning to leave Israel as soon
as he is well, but Professor Lang (Williamson) convinces the youth
to accompany him to some new desert excavations.   Through Williamson's mistress, Israeli student Nurit (Halprin), Davison becomes
involved as a liaison between rival Arab student factions.   Williamson warns Davison not to become further implicated, but the Israel
police subtly encourage his participation, hoping he will innocently
lead them to the Arab guerrillas.   Davison's misguided idealism
is shattered when he witnesses the wanton killing of various youth
supporters.
       Thanks to a continually baffling script and its pseudo-jaded
point of view (i. e., espionage and subversive activities should be
left to the experienced and corrupted who know full well what a dirty
game is all about), The Jerusalem File moralizes from an obviously quicksand point of view.   Authentic Israeli backgrounds are
not enough to carry this murky thriller at the boxoffice, as the
producers quickly discovered upon the film's release and hasty
disappearance.

JET PILOT (Universal, 1950; 1957)   C   122 min.

       Producer, Jules Furthman; director, Josef von Sternberg;
screenplay, Furthman; art director, Albert S. D'Agostino, Feild
Gray; set decorator, Darrell Silvera, Harley Miller; costumes,
Michael Woulfe; aerial camera, Philip C. Cohran; camera, Winton
C. Hoch; editor, James Wilkinson, Michael R. McAdam, Harry
Marker, William M. Moore.
       John Wayne (Colonel Shannon); Janet Leigh (Anna); Jay C.
Flippen (Major General Black); Paul Fix (Major Rexford); Richard
Rober (George Rivers); Roland Winters (Colonel Sokolov); Ivan
Triesault (General Langrad); Hans Conried (Colonel Matoff); Denver
Pyle (Mr. Simpson); Joyce Compton (Mrs. Simpson); Perdita
Chandler (Georgia Rexford); John Bishop (Major Lester Sinclair);
Elizabeth Flourney (W. A. F. Captain); Jack Overman, Ken Tobey,
Harry Lauter (Sergeants); Vince Gironda, Armand Tanny (Muscle
Men); Ruthelma Stevens, Lois Austin (Saleswomen); Ruth Lee

(Mother); Alan Dinehart, III (Fresh Kid); Phil Arnold (Bellboy);
Tom Daly (Hotel Clerk); Keith McConnell (Bartender); Herbert
Lytton, Nelson Leigh (F.B.I. Men); Al Murphy, Mike Lally, Theo-
dore Rand, Joey Ray (Waiters); Smoke Whitfield (Henry); Jane
Easton, Dorothy Abbott, Janice Hood (Girls); Allen Matthews (Head-
waiter); Darrell Huntley (Officer); Billy Vernon (Drunk); Gene Roth
(Sokolov's Batman); Jimmy Dime, Paul Bakanas (Russian Security
Men); Michael Mark (Russian General); Greg Barton, Jack Shea
(M.P.s); Gene Evans (Airfield Sergeant); Bill Erwin (Sergeant--
GAC); Richard Norris, Dave Ormond (Russian Interrogators);
Mamie Van Doren, Barbara Freking (WAAFs); Wendell Niles
(Major); Bill Yaeger (Captain); John Morgan (Lieutenant); Joan
Jordan, Joan Whitney (WAC Sergeants); Sylvia Lewis (WAC Cor-
poral); Paul Frees (Lieutenant Tiompkin).

Roland Winters, John Wayne, and Janet Leigh in Jet Pilot (Universal,
1957).

        Produced by Howard Hughes and directed by Josef von Stern-
berg in a wide screen process, Jet Pilot, first out in 1950, should
have been a sensation.   Instead, after a public preview, producer
Hughes withdrew the film and re-cut it, adding additional footage.
It was finally released in 1957 and received both poor notices and
mediocre returns.   The end product, hopelessly outdated, was

frankly so poor that star Wayne preferred to forget it and von Sternberg demanded his name be withdrawn in connection with the film.

Based on a ludicrous screenplay, Wayne was cast as Colonel Shannon, an Air Force commander in Alaska whose base is invaded by a female Soviet pilot (Leigh). Claiming to escape from her country to avoid punishment for disobedience, the girl is taken into custody for further interrogation. The American government decides that Wayne should show the girl the luxuries of the capitalistic way of life, hoping that she will be induced to give up Soviet secrets regarding their air power. Washington soon changes its mind but in the meantime the colonel has fallen in love with the girl and they marry. Wayne has no idea that she is a spy, but when he discovers her true colors, he decides to become a counterspy and they go to Russia where Leigh finally realizes she truly loves her American husband. Together they steal Soviet air secrets and escape back to America in a Soviet jet plane.

John Baxter in The Cinema of Josef von Sternberg (1971) asserts that "Sternberg struggled, often with remarkable success, to instill into this story some of the qualities for which his earlier films were famous." But with the antediluvian storyline and the inept performances, there was little to recommend this butchered feature. Since 1957-1958 the film has been effectively shelved by Hughes. It ranks with the equally enervating The Iron Petticoat (1956) as two of the worst offshoots of the Ninotchka premise.

JOAN OF OZARK (Republic, 1942)   80 min.

Associate producer, Harriet Parsons; director, Joseph Stanley; screenplay, Robert Harari, Eve Greene, Jack Townley; art director, Russell Kimball; music director, Cy Feurer; choreography, Nick Castle; songs, Mort Greene and Harry Revel; Dave Ringle and Fred Meinken; camera, Ernest Miller; editor, Charles Craft.

Judy Canova (Judy Hill); Joe E. Brown (Cliff Little); Eddie Foy, Jr. (Eddie McCabe); Jerome Cowan (Philip Munson); Alexander Granach (Guido); Wolfgang Zilzer (Kurt); Anne Jeffreys (Marie Lamont); Otto Reichow (Otto); H. H. von Twardowski (Hans); William Dean (Karl); Paul Fung (Yamatako); Donald Curtis (Jones); George Eldredge (Chandler); Olin Howlin (Game Warden); Ralph Peters (Window Cleaner); Chester Clute (Salesman); Emmett Lynn (Hillbilly Driver); Tyler Gibson (Zeke); William Sundholm (Si); William Worth (Clem); Robert Cherry (Young Hillbilly); William Nestell (Joe); William Vaughn (German Radio Operator); Kam Tong (Japanese Commander); Eric Alden, Ralph McCullough, Cyril Ring (Reporters); Harry Hayden (Mayor Fadden); Gladys Gale (Mrs. Fadden); Charles Miller (Mr. Graham); Laura Trendwell (Mrs. Graham); Lloyd Whitlock (Colonel Ashley); Nora Lane (Mrs. Ashley); Bob Stevenson (Hillbilly); Peppy Walters, Peanuts Walters (Specialty Dancers); Jason Robards, Ernest Hilliard, Dick Keene (Theatrical Agents); Bobby Stone (Newsboy); Bud Jamison (Cop); Bert Moorhouse (Drunk); Fred Santley, Pat Gleason, Charles Williams (Representatives); Horace B. Carpenter (Mountaineer); Joan Tours, Sally

Cairns, Eleanor Bayley, Billie Lane, Jane Allen, Ruby Morie, Kay Gordon, Aileen Morris, Jean O'Connell, June Earle, Patsy Bedell, Pearl Tolson, Jeanette Dickson, Helen Seamon, Barbara Clark, Mary Jo Ellis, Midgie Dare, Audreno Brier, Maxine Ardell (Dancers).

Otto Reichow, Hans von Twardowski, Jerome Cowan, and Alexander Granach in Joan of Ozark (Republic, 1942).

Two of the screen's wilder buffoons provide a double dose of tomfoolery, on a small scale, as they become innocently intertwined with Axis subversives operating in New York City.

When the Ozark's vocal delight, Judy Hill (Canova), accidentally shoots a carrier pigeon carrying a top level message from a spy ring, she immediately becomes a national heroine, receiving all sorts of promotional offers. Theatrical agent Cliff Little (Brown) hikes out to her rural abode to convince her to headline a Manhattan nightclub show, persuading the countrified thrush to accept his offer by pretending that he is a G-man and needs her help on a vital security mission. Agent H-20 (as Brown calls her) cannot decline a patriotic call to arms and is soon ensconced at New York's Club 79, which just happens to be a front for a nest of Nazi collaborators led by slick Philip Munson (Cowan).

For those who may tire of Brown's wide-mouthed hamming, there is pigtailed Canova's singing-yodeling of "Backwoods Barbecue," "The Lady at Lockheed," and "Wabash Blues." The film's young producer was none other than gossip columnist Louella Parsons' offspring.

THE JUDAS GOAT (20th-Fox, 1960) 49 min.

Producer, Herbert Swope, Jr.; associate producer, Teresa Calatrese; director, Gerald Mayer; based on the book Operation Cicero by L. C. Moyzisch; screenplay, Jerry Devine; art director, Duncan Cramer, George Van Martin; music director, Lionel Newman; camera, Wilfrid M. Cline; editor, Daniel A. Nathan.

David Hedison (Victor Sebastian); Luciana Paluzzi (Simone); Margaret Lindsay (Socialite); Vladimir Sokoloff (Peter Vestor); Paul Burke (Robertson); Kitty Mattern (Countess); Frank De Kova (Landau); Al Szabo (Bruno); Violet Rensing (Anna); John Graham (Wilson); and: Dorothy Sydney, Bobby Slade, Gregg Dunn, Peg Fellows, Willy Kaufman.

Another mini-feature distilled from the "Five Fingers" teleseries. The Judas Goat dealt with the unmasking of a character who continually led groups of fleeing Hungarian refugees into the waiting hands of Communist guards.

The best to be said of this film was the cameo bit of a dizzy socialite, played to perfection by veteran Lindsay.

JUNIOR G-MEN OF THE AIR (Universal, 1942) 12 Chapters

Chapters: (1) Wings Aflame, (2) The Plunge of Peril, (3) Hidden Danger, (4) The Tunnel of Terror, (5) The Black Dragon Strikes, (6) Flaming Havoc, (7) The Death Mist, (8) Satan Fires the Fuse, (9) Satanic Sabotage, (10) Trapped in a Blazing Chute, (11) Undeclared War, and (12) Civilian Courage Conquers.

Associate producer, Henry MacRae; director, Ray Taylor, Lew Collins; screenplay, Paul Huston, George H. Plympton, Griffin Jay; additional dialog, Brenda Weisberg; camera, William Sickner.

Billy Halop (Ace Holden); Gene Reynolds (Eddie Holden); Lionel Atwill (The Baron); Frank Albertson (Jerry Markham); Richard Lane (Don Ames); Huntz Hall (Bolts Larson); Bernard Punsley (Greaseball Plunkett); Gabriel Dell (Stick Munsey); John Bleiffer (Beal); Eddie Foster (Comora); Noel Cravat (Monk); John Bagni (Augar); Paul Phillips (Dick Parsons); David Gorcey (Double Face Barker); Eddy Waller (Jed); Paul Bryar (Oriental Chemist);

Frankie Darro (Jack); Fred Burton (Colonel); Jack Arnold (Flyer);
Mel Ruick (Official); Jay Novello (Dogara); Angelo Cruz (Ito);
Lynton Brent (Sergeant); Pat O'Malley (Conductor); Guy Kings-
ford, Win Wright (Soldiers); Jimmy O'Gatty (Alien Jap American);
Joey Ray (Man); Bill Moss, Bill Hunter, Charles McAvoy (Police-
men); Dick Thane (Patrolman); Rico de Montez (Jap Clerk); Edward
Colebrook (Uamatka); Rolland Morris, William Desmond (Customers);
Guy Usher (Senator); Bert Freeman (Scientist); Hugh Presser
(Lieutenant-State Guard); Heenan Elliott (Watchman); Ben Wright
(Corporal); George Sherwood (Instructor); Billy Benedict (Blackie);
Ken Lundy (Newsboy).

     Many of the Dead End Kids/Little Tough Guys had cavorted
in Universal's serial Sea Raiders (1941). In this film serial on
Junior G-Men, they now played a return match in combatting enemy
agents threatening America's democracy. This time the culprits
were enemy collaborators, the Order of the Black Dragonfly, which
had its headquarters in a camouflaged farm.

THE KARATE KILLERS (MGM, 1967) C 92 min.

     Executive producer, Norman Felton; producer, Boris Ingster;
associate producer, Irv Pearlberg; director, Barry Shear; story,
Ingster; screenplay, Norman Hudis; assistant director, Bill Finne-
gan; art director, George W. Davis, James W. Sullivan; set deco-
rator, Henry Grace, Dick Pefferle, Don Greenwood, Jr.; music,
Gerald Fried; title theme, Jerry Goldsmith; sound, Franklin Mil-
ton; camera, Fred Koenekamp; editor, William B. Gulick, Ray
Williford.
     Robert Vaughn (Napoleon Solo); David McCallum (Illya Kury-
akin); Curt Jurgens (Carl von Kesser); Joan Crawford (Amanda
True); Herbert Lom (Randolph); Telly Savalas (Count de Fanzini);
Terry-Thomas (Constable); Kim Darby (Sandy True); Diane McBain
(Margo True); Jill Ireland (Imogen True); Leo G. Carroll (Alex-
ander Waverly); Danielle De Metz (Yvonne True); Irene Tsu
(Reikko); Jim Boles (Dr. True); Philip Ahn (Sazami Kyushu);
Arthur Gould-Porter (Magistrate); Rob Okazaki (Police Inspector);
Maria Lennard (Show Girl); Lindsay Workman (Leading Scientist);
Rick Traeger (Hotel Clerk); Frank Arno (Chief Fireman); Julie
Ann Johnson, Sharon Hillyer (U.N.C.L.E. Girls); William Burn-
side (Bartender); Gloria Neil (Stewardess); William Bryant (Tech-
nician); Jason Wingreen, Grant Woods (Engineers); Dick Crockett,
Paul Bailey, Jerry Summers, Fred Stromsor (The Karate Killers).

     It's U.N.C.L.E. vs T.H.R.U.S.H. again, with the prize
being a secret process for extracting gold from sea water.
T.H.R.U.S.H. operatives liquidate the inventor (Boles) and his
glamorous wife (Crawford), but not before vital clues have been
passed on to their four daughters (Darby, McBain, Ireland, De
Metz); the chase leads from Italy to London to the Tyrol and then
on to Tokyo and a geisha house where the formula is finally recovered.

Despite the marquee lure of Joan Crawford (who has a very small role in the proceedings), this is one of the less appetizing compendiums of "The Man from U. N. C. L. E. " teleseries episodes. "The pace remains fast enough, but the villains are less picturesque, the girls less gorgeous and the cracks less wise" (British Monthly Film Bulletin). What seemed passable on the small screen, broken up by frequent commercials, was blatantly production-line James Bond imitation when unreeled on the big screen.

KING OF THE MOUNTIES (Republic, 1942)   12 Chapters

Chapters: (1) Phantom Invaders, (2) Road to Death, (3) Human Target, (4) Railroad Saboteurs, (5) Suicide Dive, (6) Blazing Barrier, (7) Perilous Plunge, (8) Electrocuted, (9) Reign of Terror, (10) The Flying Coffin, (11) Deliberate Murder, and (12) On to Victory.

Associate producer, W. J. O'Sullivan; director, William Witney; based on characters created by Zane Grey; screenplay, Ronald Davidson, Joseph Poland, William Lively, Joseph O'Donnell, Taylor Cavan; music, Mort Glickman; special effects, Howard Lydecker; camera, Bud Thackery.
Allan Lane (Sergeant King); Gilbert Emery (Commissioner); Russell Hicks (Marshal Carleton); Peggy Drake (Carol Brent); George Irving (Professor Brent); Abner Biberman (Admiral Yamata); William Vaughn (Marshal Von Horst); Nestor Paiva (Count Baroni); Bradley Page (Blake); Douglass Dumbrille (Harper); William Bakewell (Ross); Duncan Renaldo (Pierre); Francis Ford (Collins); Jay Novello (Lewis); Anthony Warde (Stark); Norman Nesbitt (Radio Announcer); John Hiestand (Lane); Allen Jung (Sato); Paul Fung (Jap Bombardier); Arvon Dale (Craig).

Republic really loaded the dice in this serial, with Lane of the Canadian Mounties battling enemy sympathizers from all three Axis nations, headed by Nazi Vaughn, Japanese Biberman, and Italian Paiva. Here the enemy is using a new plane called the Falcon to bomb Canada. Only the experimental plane detector devised by Professor Irving can halt this merciless attack and the enemy is determined to grab control of the contraption. A rousing finale situated inside a reactivated volcano climaxed this hearty exercise in free world strong-arm tactics outdoing enemy sabotage.

KING'S PIRATE   see   AGAINST ALL FLAGS

KISS THE GIRLS AND MAKE THEM DIE (Columbia, 1966)   C 105 min.

Executive producer, Salvatore Argento, Dino Maiuri; producer, Dino De Laurentiis; director, Henry Levin; story, Maiuri;

screenplay, Jack Pulman, Maiuri; music, Mario Nascembene; song,
Nascembene and Howard Greenfield; assistant director, Giorgio
Gentili, Gianni Cozzi; art director, Mario Garbuglia; set decorator,
Emilio D'Andria; special effects, Augie Lohman; music director,
Robert Pregadio; costumes, Maria De Matteis, Piero Gherardi;
sound, Luciano Welich; camera, Aldo Tonti; editor, Ralph Kemplen,
Alberto Gallitti.

Dorothy Provine (Susan); Michael Connors (Kelly); Raf Val-
lone (Ardonian); Terry-Thomas (Janes/Lord Aldric); Margaret Lee
(Grace); Oliver MacGreevy (Ringo); Nicoletta Rangoni (Sylvia);
Sandro Dori (Omar); Beverly Adams (Karin); Marilu Tolo (Gioia);
Seyna Seyn (Wilma Soong); Jack Gwillim (British Ambassador);
Michael Audley (Major Davis); Nerio Bernardi (Papal Envoy); Andy
Ho (King); K. Wang (Kasai); H. Thoren (Kruger); Edith Peters
(Maria).

"Bring a friend, but leave your brain behind, " was Newsday's
warning about this production filmed in Italy and Rio de Janeiro.
The premise for this dubbed spy spoof was a bit too far-
fetched for credible joshing: Brazilian madman Vallone is determined to launch a satellite that will emit cobalt rays, causing all
of mankind except himself and a bevy of fast-freeze beauties to
lose their sex drive. His "rationale"? He intends to forestall
the population explosion, while at the same time starting his own
new master race. Out to stop this obvious lunatic is CIA agent
Connors, who sports a Silver Cloud Rolls Royce and relies to a
great extent on his bumbling chauffeur Terry-Thomas.
Hardly noted for its plot subtleties, the film did offer
lovely location photography and an exciting fight scene atop the
Christ of the Andes statue in Rio de Janeiro.

KNIGHT WITHOUT ARMOUR (UA, 1937)   107 min.

Producer, Alexander Korda; director, Jacques Feyder; based
on the novel Without Armour by James Hilton; adaptation, Frances
Marion; screenplay, Lajos Biro, Arthur Wimperis; music, Miklos
Rozsa; music director, Muir Mathieson; assistant director, Imlay
Watts; set designer, Lazare Meerson; technical adviser, Roman
Gou; sound, A. W. Watkins; special effects, Ned Mann; camera,
Harry Stradling; editor, Francis Lyon.

Marlene Dietrich (Alexandra); Robert Donat (A. J. Fotherin-
gill); Irene Vanburgh (Duchess); Herbert Lomas (Vladinoff); Austin
Trevor (Colonel Adraxine); Basil Gil (Axelstein); David Tree
(Maronin); John Clements (Poushkoff); Frederick Culley (Stanfield);
Lawrence Hanray (Forrester); Dorice Fordred (Maid); Franklin
Kelsey (Tomsky); Lawrence Kingston (Commissar); Hay Petrie
(Station Master); Lyn Harding (Bargeman); Raymond Huntley (White
Officer); Miles Malleson (Drunken Red Soldier); Peter Evan Thomas
(General Andreyevitch).

While residing in pre-World War I St. Petersburg as a

translator, young Britisher Donat composes an article which irritates the Czar's regime. He is consequently told to leave the country within 48 hours. Only then does he learn that his close friend (Culley) is a British Secret Service agent. Culley is a persuasive man who convinces Donat to pass along messages to members of the revolutionary movement against the Czarist regime. Donat and others are caught and sent to Siberia, but in the upheaval of the Revolution the Reds release Donat and he becomes a minor functionary at Kalinsk. Countess Alexandra (Dietrich), daughter of the former Minister of the Interior (Lomas) reenters Donat's life. Soon he has fallen in love with her and together they make their way to the border, attempting to sidestep confrontations with the opposing Red and White armies.

When released in the U.S., the elaborately-mounted feature was rapped by critics who branded it artistically as imitation Josef von Sternberg and no better than a lengthy paeon to the gaunt beauty of Dietrich. One Continental reviewer likened <u>Knight Without Armour</u> to a Drury Lane musical rendering of the Russian Revolution.

At times reminiscent of the hero of Jules Verne's <u>Michael Strogoff</u>, Donat acquitted himself well in this period piece, striking a good balance between appearing at first to be a timorous voyeur of life and then, when given the opportunity, blossoming forth as a patriot, chivalrous lover, and resourceful adventurer, all standard ingredients for the proper pre-World War II espionage agent.

KOROSHI (ABC-TV, 1968) C 90 min.

Director, Peter Yates, Michael Truman; screenplay, Norman Hudis.

Patrick McGoohan (John Drake); Yoko Tani (Ako/Miho); Ronald Howard (Sanders); George Coulouris (Controller); and: Maxine Audley, Kenneth Griffith, Amanda Barrie, Joe Garrison, Robert Lee, Mona Chang.

Composed of two unseen-in-America segments of the "Secret Agent" teleseries, this film debuted on ABC-TV as a telefeature. It told of British agent John Drake (McGoohan) jetting to Tokyo to investigate a series of high-level political murders. The segments were filmed on location in Tokyo.

THE KREMLIN LETTER (20th-Fox, 1970) C 121 min.

Producer, Carter De Haven, Sam Wiesenthal; director, John Huston; based on the novel by Noel Behn; screenplay, Huston, Gladys Hill; assistant director, Gus Agosti, Carlo Cotti; production designer, Ted Haworth; art director, Elven Webb; set decorator, Dario Simone; music-music director, Robert Drasnin; costumes, John Furniss; sound, Basil Fenton-Smith, Renato Cadueri; camera, Ted Scaife; editor, Russell Lloyd.

Richard Boone (Ward); Bibi Andersson (Erika Boeck); Max
von Sydow (Colonel Vladimir Kosnov); Patrick O'Neal (Lt. Com-
mander Charles Rone); Orson Welles (Aleksei Bresnavitch); Ronald
Radd (Potkin); Nigel Green (Janis, alias "The Whore"); Dean Jagger
(The Highwayman); Lila Kedrova (Madame Sophie); Barbara Parkins
(B.A.); George Sanders (The Warlock); Raf Vallone (The Puppet
Maker); Michael MacGinnis (Erector Set); Anthony Chinn (Kitai);
Guy Deghy (Professor); John Huston (Admiral); Fulvia Ketoff
(Sonia); Vonetta McGee (Negress); Marc Lawrence (Priest); Cyril
Shaps (Police Doctor); Christopher Sanford (Rudolph); Hana-Maria
Pravda (Mrs. Kazar); George Pravda (Kazar); Ludmilla Dudarova
(Mrs. Potkin); Dimitri Tamarov (Ilya); Pehr-Olof Siren (Reception-
ist); Daniel Smid (Waiter); Victor Beaumont (Dentist); Steve Zach-
arias (Dittomachine); Laura Forin (Elena); Saara Rannin (Mikhail's
Mother); Rune Sandlunds (Mikhail); Sacha Carafa (Mrs. Grodin).

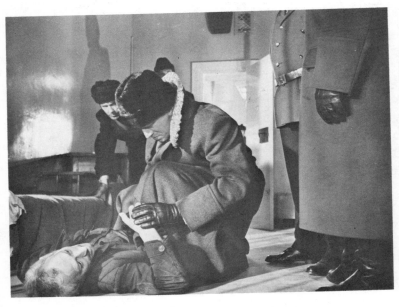

Stavros Tornes (body), Sandor Eles, and Max von Sydow in The
Kremlin Letter (20th-Fox, 1970).

The ads for The Kremlin Letter enticingly read, "Officially,
Russia has no brothels; no drug trade; no black market; no disco-
theques; no homosexual hangouts; officially, five American agents
do not exist; officially there is no Kremlin Letter."

From this rather exciting beginning, once-capable director John Huston took Noel Behn's novel (Huston co-scripted the film with Gladys Hill) and made it into what <u>Films in Review</u> called "drivel made incomprehensible."

A group of U. S. Intelligence workers (O'Neal, Sanders, Green, Parkins) are assigned to find a treaty which an American official erroneously signed with the Soviet Union. This treaty concerns an alleged agreement by the United States to help Russia to eliminate China's nuclear power. Once in Russia, the group is led from official to official, but for all their derring-do, they are never sure who has the elusive treaty, or if any of them will survive the escapade.

The film is filled with gratuitous brutality, especially on the part of the Russian (counter) agents, and unnecessarily convoluted plot trailings, making the viewer feel that all the undercover agents are doing is playing a losing game of blind man's bluff. One of the sadder portions of the film was observing Sanders, in the very twilight of his career, appearing as a "drag queen."

LADIES MAN   see   LEMMY POUR LES DAMES

THE LADY HAS PLANS (Paramount, 1942)   77 min.

Associate producer, Fred Kohlmar; director, Sidney Lansfield; story, Leo Birinski; screenplay, Harry Tugend; camera, Charles Lang; editor, William Shea.

Ray Milland (Kenneth Harper); Paulette Goddard (Sidney Royce); Roland Young (Ronald Dean); Albert Dekker (Baron von Kemp); Margaret Hayes (Rita Lenox); Cecil Kellaway (Peter Miles); Addison Richards (Paul Baker); Edward Norris (Frank Richards); Charles Arnt (Pooly); Hans Schumm, Hans von Morhart (Germans); Genia Nikola (German Maid); Gerald Mohr (Joe Scalsi); Lionel Royce (Guard); Thomas W. Ross (Abner Spencer); Arthur Loft (Mr. Weston); Paul Phillips, Warren Ashe (G-Men); Lee Shumway (Cop); Terry Ray, Charles de Ravenne (Taxi Drivers); Mel Ruick (Announcer); Keith Richards, Hans Furberg, George Dobbs (Hotel Clerks); Louis Mercier (Bellhop); Yola d'Avril (Chambermaid); Wolfgang A. Zilzer (German Clerk--Baron's Office); Hans Joby, William Yetter, Adolph Milar (German Officials); Francisco Maran (Hotel Manager); Jean Del Val (Bartender); Martin Garralaga (Maitre D'); Richard Webb (Information Clerk at Hotel); Bruce Wyndham (German); Ray Flynn (Man).

Not much more than "an amusing skit" (<u>Christian Science Monitor</u>), offering a bit of levity on the grim war situation and counting heavily on Goddard's physical allure to make ends meet at the boxoffice. The premise for this pipedream comedy drama soon wore too thin for comfort.

Newspaper legwoman Sidney Royce (Goddard) arrives in Lisbon to assist bureau chief-radio commentator Kenneth Harper (Milland)

Hans von Morhart, Margaret Hayes, Edward Norris, Albert Dekker, and Addison Richards in The Lady Has Plans (Paramount, 1942).

who is unaware that she is of special interest to many travelers in that city of international intrigue. Since she is believed to be the red-haired German undercover agent (Hayes) due in Lisbon with the latest plans for a U.S. Navy aerial torpedo stenciled on her back, Nazi Baron von Kemp (Dekker) flirts with her, and British diplomat Ronald Dean (Young) is forever trying to get her undraped and have a peak at the drawings. Naturally Hayes, who had been detained by the F.B.I. in New York, appears on the scene, leading to the capture of Milland-Goddard by the angered Germans. But all ends happily, strictly to formula.

THE LADY VANISHES (Gaumont-British, 1938)   97 min.

        Producer, Edward Black; director, Alfred Hitchcock; based on the novel The Wheel Spins by Ethel Lina White; adaptation, Alma Reville; screenplay, Sydney Gilliatt, Frank Launder; music, Louis Levy; sets, Alec Vetchinsky, Maurice Carter, Albert Jullion; sound, Sidney Wiles; camera, Jack Cox; editor, Alfred Roome, R.E. Dearing.
        Margaret Lockwood (Iris Henderson); Michael Redgrave (Gilbert); Paul Lukas (Dr. Hartz); Dame May Whitty (Miss Froy);

Googie Withers (Blanche); Cecil Parker (Mr. Todhunter); Linden
Travers (Mrs. Todhunter); Lary Clare (Baroness); Naunton Wayne
(Caldicott); Basil Radford (Charters); and: Emil Boreo, Zelma
Vas Dias, Philippe Leaver, Sally Stewart, Catherine Lacey,
Josephine Wilson, Charles Oliver, Kathleen Tremaine.

Linden Travers and Naunton Wayne in The Lady Vanishes (Gaumont-
British, 1938).

"If it were not so brilliant a melodrama, we should class it
as a brilliant comedy" (New York Times). There is no diminution
of the action from the start to the finish of the British-made The
Lady Vanishes as it opens on a deliberately commonplace note and
moves steadily to a high pitch of hairbreadth tension before the
effervescent denouement. As such, Alfred Hitchcock's masterpiece
is "diabolically suspenseful, impishly humorous, breath-taking and
vigorous" (New York World Telegram).
    Skittish debutante Iris Henderson (Lockwood) is on her way
home to England from a Balkan vacation. ("I've been everywhere,
done everything. What is there for me but marriage.") Aboard
the train she becomes further acquainted with charming Miss Froy
(Whitty), a tweedy elderly governess, who is returning to England
after a six-year assignment. In the course of the railroad trip, the
old lady disappears. Lockwood is insistent upon finding her, particularly when the other passengers deny ever having seen the
missing woman. It develops that individuals Lockwood turns to for

succor, including Prague brain surgeon Dr. Hartz (Lukas), are part of a lethal spy ring, and that dear Whitty ("Froy--rhymes with toy") is actually a counter-espionage agent. The only person to side with Lockwood and to insist that she is not losing her mind is itinerant musician/scholar Gilbert (Redgrave) who readily helps her with the bewildering puzzle. The couple eventually find themselves and others sidetracked on a spur line with the spies determined to liquidate them all. At last glance, Whitty has ducked out the coach car window, confiding the secret coded message (bars of a pop tune) to Redgrave, in case she should not make it back alive to report to Scotland Yard.

The Lady Vanishes is filled with marvelous moments that make seeing it again and again a still satisfying experience. For any viewer unacquainted with the ramifications of the film's plot, the story's establishing clues may easily slip by unnoticed (e.g., the local musician serenading plump, white-haired matron Whitty; the flower box falling on Lockwood at the train station, etc.). As a political reflection of British (and American) pacifistic non-intervention feelings, there are the two comic British cricketers Caldicott (Wayne) and Charters (Radford) whose only interest is rushing back to England in time to catch some of the test matches at Manchester. For the Continental flavor there is dapper but deadly Lukas. And to tease the filmgoer into sharing the heroine's exasperation and frustration with proving Whitty's existence, there are such moments as the bit of proof on the dining car window being erased when the train passes through a tunnel; or later, Lockwood's observation that the "nun" is decked out with high heel shoes.

Everyone knows--or claims he does--that a spy may be anyone of any type, age, or description. However, there is a highly disarming quality about discovering a genteel sexagenarian who could be one's dear grandmother, engaged in deadly escapades with the spunk, ingenuity, and verve of the heartiest of operatives. Best of all, Whitty's Miss Froy is a full-bodied character, who has a sense of perspective ("You shouldn't judge any country by its politics") and a delicious quality of wry humor (asked if she is a spy, the old woman replies "I think that's a disagreeable word").

LAISSEZ TIRER LES TIREURS (FIDA, 1964) 90 min.

Producer, Jacques Roitfeld; director, Guy Lefranc; story, Michael Lebrun; screenplay, Lebrun, Gilles Morris Dumoulin; music, Georges Delerue; settings, Louis Le Barbenchon; sound, Raymond Gauguier; camera, Henri Persin; editor, Monique Kirsanoff.

Eddie Constantine (Jeff Gordon); Daphne Dayle (Elizabeth); Maria Grazia Spina (Corinne); Guy Tréjan (Philippe Martin); Jean-Jacques Steen (Pascaud); Patricia Viterbo (Patricia); Colette Teisseidre (Sonia); Gerard Darrieu (Raoul); Henri Lambert (Marco); Nino Ferrari (Andersen); and: Pierre Lecomte, Raymond Jourdan, Willy Braque, Jean-Paul Drean, Philippe Guégan, Jan Valmorie, Jean-Marc Allegre, Hubert de Lappanent.

The underworld steals a U. S. missile-tracer with plans to sell it to a foreign power, but agent Jeff Gordon (Constantine) steps in to recover it. A miniature spinoff from the James Bond genre, but without the budget or performers to back up the imitation.

"Apparently one never gets tired of seeing Eddie Constantine do the same number for years and years. Responsibility is seldom his when the film is more insipid than usual, for he takes up his mission of certified brawl and irresistible charmer with utmost seriousness. Laissez Tirer les Tireurs aims at laughs rather than thrills. Gags come by the dozen in a well directed ballet where blows fly aplenty but are harmless enough. It's a film for all seasons" (L'Humanité).

LANCER SPY (20th-Fox, 1937) 84 min.

Associate producer, Samuel G. Engel; director, Gregory Ratoff; story, Martha McKenna; screenplay, Philip Dunne; art director, Albert Hogsett; music director, Arthur Lange; camera, Barney McGill; editor, Louis Loeffler.

Dolores Del Rio (Fraulein Dolores Daria); George Sanders (Baron Kurt von Rohback/Lt. Michael Bruce); Peter Lorre (Major Sigfried Gruning); Virginia Field (Joan Bruce); Sig Rumann (Lt. Col. Gotffried Hollen); Joseph Schildkraut (Prince Ferdi zu Schwarzwald); Maurice Moscovich (General von Meinhardt); Lionel Atwill (Colonel Fenwick); Luther Adler (Schratt); Fritz Feld (Fritz Mueller); Lesther Mathews (Captain Neville); Carlos J. de Valdez (von Klingen); Gregory Gaye (Captain Freymann); Joan Carol (Elizabeth Bruce); Holmes Herbert (Dr. Aldrich); Clyde Cook (Orderly); John Burton (Lieutenant); Herbert Evans, Victor Kolberg (Sergeants); David Clyde, Neil Fitzgerald (Orderlies); Fredrik Vogeding (Danish Boat Captain); Kenneth Hunter (Commandant); Claude King (Captain); Olaf Hytten (Barber); Ian MacLaren (Plainclothesman); Dave Thursby (Sentry); Boyd Irwin, Sr. (Surgeon); Paul Weigel (Hotel Manager Schreiber); Frank Reicher (Admiral); Egon Brecher (Bendiner); Elisabeth Frohlich (Farmer's Wife); Lynn Bari (Fenwick's Companion); Adia Kurnetzoff (Major Domo); Michael S. Visaroff (Referee); Leonard Mudie (Statesman); Hans Joby (Waiter); Bert Sprotte (Conductor); Walter Bonn (Officer on Train); Greta Meyer (Woman on Train); Hans von Morhart (Intelligence Officer); Frank Puglia, Feodor Chaliapin, Jr. (Monks); Frederick Gehrmann, Arno Frey (Soldiers); Bud Geary (Captain's Aide); Major Sam Harris (Officer at Party).

Made as a vehicle to exploit George Sanders as a screen hero, the film's chief assets are the presenting of the actor in the first of his many Prussian-Nazi roles and the offering of the beautiful Dolores Del Rio in a variety of lovely costumes. Other than that, Lancer Spy, which was Gregory Ratoff's first film directing chore, was a "B" film with "A" aspirations.

Sanders played the dual part of Baron Kurt von Rohback, a German imprisoned in England during World War I, and Lt. Michael

George Sanders, Fredrik Vogeding, Fritz Feld, and Bud Geary in
Lancer Spy (20th-Fox, 1937).

Bruce of the British Naval department, who is assigned to go behind German lines to impersonate his look-a-like von Rohback.
Eventually the vipers, led by Lorre and Rumann, comprehend the
deception and use siren Del Rio to vamp the British and learn the
truth.   The girl, however, falls in love with Sanders and is then
torn between her loyalty to country and job with her new found
romance.
         Many critics were duly impressed with Sanders' sweeping the-
atricalism, far more than they were with the film itself. "The cliches
are as familiar as last year's hat, and the dialogue as uninspiring"
(New York Herald-Tribune). The Keystone cops-like finale in which
the Germans use bloodhounds to track the fleeing Sanders, did
nothing to inspire praise for Lancer Spy. The New York World-
Telegram blasted it as a "nursery exercise in espionage and counter-
espionage."

LAST MESSAGE FROM SAIGON see OPERATION C. I. A.

THE LAST OF THE SECRET AGENTS? (Paramount, 1966)   C
90 min.

Producer, Norman Abbott; associate producer, Mel Tolkin;
director, Abbott; story, Abbott, Tolkin; screenplay, Tolkin; assist-
ant director, Francisco Day; art director, Hal Pereira, Roland
Anderson; set decorator, Robert Benton, James Payne; music,
Peter King; songs, Lee Hazlewood; Neal Hefti; King, Abbott, and
Tolkin; choreographer, Andre Tayir; sound, Harold Lewis, John
Wilkinson; camera, Harold Stine; editor, Otho Lovering.

Marty Allen (Marty Johnson); Steve Rossi (Steve Donovan);
John Williams (J. Frederick Duval); Nancy Sinatra (Micheline);
Lou Jacobi (Papa Leo); Theo Marcuse (Zoltan Schubach); Sig Ru-
man (Professor Werner von König); Carmen (Baby Mae Zoftig);
Larry Duran, Remo Pisani (Them); Connie Sawyer (Florence); Ben
Lessy (Harry); Wilhelm Von Homburg, Loren Ewing (G. G. I. Men);
Aida Fries (Belly Dancer); Harvey Korman (German Colonel);
Mark G. Baker (Wardrobe Man); Eddie Carroll, Eddie Donno (Slate
Boys); Philip Salcombe (Englishman); Hoke Howell (Man in Adolph
Hitler Uniform); Allen Durlin Jung (Kurawa from Japan); Louise
Colombet, Paul C. R. Deville (Elderly French Peasants); Phyllis
Ann Davis (Attractive Young Lady); Henry Dar-Boggia (Conductor);

Steve Rossi, Larry Duran, and Marty Allen in The Last of the
Secret Agents? (Paramount, 1966).

Chester A. Hayes (Organ Grinder); Thordis I. Brandt (Fred Johnson); Kathy Martin (Duval's Lovely Companion); Tommy H. Lee (Montgomery); Almira Sessions, Madge Blake (Middle-Aged Ladies); Don H. Keefer (Handsome Spy); Joe Devlin (Waiter); Paul Daniel (Milkman); Susan Jean (Girl Spy); Emanuel Thomas (Frogman); John Sterling (Second Story Man); Matty Jordan (Italian Man); William Yip (Chinese Man); Charles La Torre (Frenchman); Victoria Carroll (Female Approaching Umbrella); Makee K. Blaisdell (King); Kay Hughes (Book Ends); Alain Mehrez (French Boy); Edy Williams (Producer's Girl Friend); Mike H. deAnda (Robust Frenchman); Mark Harris, Scott Elliott (Distinguished Englishmen); Robert Goodwin (Ngumba Nurumbru); George Dega (Boris Tulchinsky); Ray Dannis (Man on TV); Ed Sullivan (Himself).

In Cannes, J. Frederick Duval (Williams), the head of the global police organization known as G. G. I. (Good Guys Institute), invites handymen Marty Johnson (Allen) and Steve Donovan (Rossi) to join the outfit and help smash an international art-theft ring called THEM, a nefarious group led by Zoltan Schubach (Marcuse). G. G. I. provides the dim-witted duo with one weapon, a wondrous gadget-loaded umbrella which saves their necks on many occasions.

This abysmal parody on the espionage genre was as far removed from the enjoyable antics of an Abbott and Costello session as from the zaniness of an Olsen and Johnson outing. Most critics agreed that fright-wigged Allen and bland-faced Rossi were more dull than offensive. Rossi's rendition of the song "You Are," from the movie, as recorded on Musicor Records, did become a pop hit.

LAST TRAIN FROM MADRID (Paramount, 1937) 85 min.

Producer, George M. Arthur; associate producer, Hugh Bennett; director, James Hogan; story, Paul H. Fox, Elsie Fox; screenplay, Louis Stevens, Robert Wyler; music director, Boris Morros; camera, Harry Fischbeck; editor, Everett Douglass.

Dorothy Lamour (Carmelita Castillo); Lew Ayres (Bill Dexter); Gilbert Roland (Eduardo de Soto); Karen Morley (Helene Rafitte); Lionel Atwill (Colonel Vigo); Helen Mack (Lola); Robert Cummings (Juan); Olympe Bradna (Maria Ronda); Anthony Quinn (Captain Ricardo Alvarez); Lee Bowman (Michael Balk); Jack Perrin, Harry Semels (Guards); Frank Leyva (Chauffeur); George Lloyd (Intelligence Officer); Louise Carter (Rosa Delgado); Hooper Atchley (Martin); Stanley Price (Clerk); Francis McDonald (Mora); Stanley Fields (Avila); Sam Appel (Warden); Henry Brandon (Radio Announcer); Maurice Cass (Waiter); Harry Worth (Gomez); Bess Flowers (Saleswoman); Evelyn Brent (Woman); Tiny Newland (Turnkey); Charles Middleton (Warden); Harry Woods (Government Man); Alan Ladd (Extra).

Manufactured as a classy "B" movie with an impressive cast of contract players, The Last Train from Madrid looks like a combination of <u>Grand Hotel</u> and <u>Shanghai Express</u>, though on an abbreviated scale. It was heavily advertised as the first American-made feature to deal with the then current Spanish Civil War. However, in a typical Hollywood manner, it took no political sides; instead it concentrated on melodramatic episodes in the lives of a number of persons leaving on a final train from war-torn Madrid.

With espionage and political intrigue the crux of the story, but still kept at a minimum, the movie had an interesting set of characters heading to Valencia from Madrid. Among the passengers were fugitive Roland, pacifist army deserter Cummings, orphan Bradna who clings to flip newsman Ayres, prostitute Mack, Roland's sweetheart (Lamour), and baroness Morley.

The picture is never more than slick claptrap, but quite enjoyable on its minor, predictable scale.

LEGION OF THE CONDEMNED (Paramount, 1928)   7,415 feet

Presenter, Adolph Zukor, Jesse L. Lasky; producer, William A. Wellman; associate producer, E. Lloyd Sheldon; director, Wellman; story, John Monk Saunders; screenplay, Saunders, Jean De Limur; assistant director, Richard Johnston; titles, George Marion, Jr.; camera, Henry Gerrard; editor, Sheldon, Alyson Shaffer.

Gary Cooper (Gale Price); Fay Wray (Christine Charteris); Barry Norton (Byron Dashwood); Lane Chandler (Charles Holabird); Francis McDonald (Gonzalo Vasques); Voya George (Robert Montagnal); Freeman Wood (Richard DeWitt); E. H. Calvert (Commandant); Albert Conti (Von Hohendorff); Charlotte Bird (Celeste); Toto Guette (Mechanic).

Cooper and Norton are among the young men joining a French flying escadrille known as "The Legion of the Comdemned," a World War I version of the French Foreign Legion where men can escape from past crimes or even boredom, since the price is nearly always death on a dangerous mission. It develops that Cooper, once a reporter, had been so shocked by Wray's conduct in consorting with the German nobility that he hastened to join the Legion. Suddenly he is confronted with his assigned plane passenger, none other than Wray, who explains that all along she has been a French secret agent, and that now she is embarking on a job behind enemy lines. As events work out, Cooper is able to rescue her from death in front of a German firing squad.

This obvious rehash of <u>Wings</u> was publicized as the first of many productions to co-star the new screen team of Cooper and Wray. They never caught on with the public, and this silent feature, with its romanticism balanced by a lack of realism was mostly considered just fast-moving escapist fare.

LEMMY POUR LES DAMES (Prodis, 1962)   95 min.

Director, Bernard Borderie; based on an unpublished novel

by Peter Cheyney; screenplay, Borderie, Marc-Gilbert Sauvajon;
music, Paul Misraki; settings, Rino Mondellini; sound, René Sara-
zin; camera, Armand Thirard, Gilles Bonneau; editor, Christian
Gaudin.

Eddie Constantine (Lemmy Caution); Françoise Brion (Marie
Christine); Claudine Coster (Françoise); Elaine d'Almeida (Sophie);
Yvonne Monlaur (Claudia); Guy Delorme (Mirko); Jacques Berthier
(Dr. Nollet); Robert Berri (Donbie); Lionel Roc (Hugo); Paul
Mercey (Commissioner).

While vacationing on the Côte d'Azur, F.B.I. agent Lemmy
Caution (Constantine) fights the blackmailers of diplomats who have
been using them to obtain state secrets.

"Our friend Lemmy is back surrounded with beautiful broads
and his usual scotch whiskey. ... There is the usual mish-mash
with all the obligatory accessories" (Cinéma 62).

LICENSE TO KILL   see   NICK CARTER VA TOUT CASSER

THE LIFE OF EMILE ZOLA (WB, 1937)   116 min.

Executive producer, Jack L. Warner; producer, Hal B. Wal-
lis; supervisor, Henry Blanke; director, William Dieterle; story,
Heinz Herald, Geza Herczeg; screenplay, Herald, Herczeg, Norman
Reilly Raine; music, Max Steiner; music director, Leo Forbstein;
assistant director, Russ Saunders; art director, Anton Grot; set
decorator, Albert C. Wilson; dialog director, Irving Rapper; gowns,
Mil Anderson, Ali Hubert; makeup, Perc Westmore; camera, Tony
Gaudio; editor, Warren Lowe.

Paul Muni (Emile Zola); Gale Sondergaard (Lucie Dreyfus);
Joseph Schildkraut (Captain Alfred Dreyfus); Gloria Holden (Alex-
andrine Zola); Donald Crisp (Maître Labori); Erin O'Brien-Moore
(Nana); John Litel (Charpentier); Henry O'Neill (Colonel Picquart);
Morris Carnovsky (Anatole France); Louis Calhern (Major Dort);
Ralph Morgan (Commander of Paris); Robert Barrat (Major Walsin-
Esterhazy); Vladimir Sokoloff (Paul Cézanne); Harry Davenport
(Chief of Staff); Robert Warwick (Major Henry); Charles Richman
(M. Delagorgue); Dickie Moore (Pierre Dreyfus); Rolla Gourvitch
(Jeanne Dreyfus); Filbert Emery (Minister of War); Walter Kings-
ford (Colonel Sandherr); Paul Everton (Assistant Chief of Staff);
Montagu Love (Cavaignac); Frank Sheridan (van Cassell); Lumsden
Hare (Mr. Richards); Marcia Mae Jones (Helen Richards); Florence
Roberts (Madame Zola); Grant Mitchell (Georges Clemenceau);
Moroni Olsen (Captain Guignet); Egon Brecher (Brucker); Frank
Reicher (M. Perrenx); Walter O. Stahl (Senator Scheurer-Kestner);
Frank Darien (Albert); Countess Iphigenie Castiglioni (Madame
Charpentier); Arthur Aylesworth (Chief Censor); Frank Mayo
(Mathieu Dreyfus); Alexander Leftwich (Major D'Aboville); Paul
Irving (La Rue); Pierre Watkin (Prefect of Police); Holmes Herbert
(Commander of Paris); Robert Cummings, Sr. (General Gillian);

Harry Worth (Lieutenant); William von Brincken (Schwartzkoppen).

The screenplay as well as the (supporting actor) performance of Joseph Schildkraut won Academy Awards for this illustrious and well-received feature film. "It is great because it has captured the throb of human experience in a memorable biography, beautifully filmed and magnificently acted" (New York Herald-Tribune).

In the course of depicting the life of Emile Zola (Muni) (1840-1902), the William Dieterle-directed picture focused a good deal of screen time on the French writer's participation in securing a new trial for the wrongly-accused Captain Alfred Dreyfus (Schildkraut) who had been made the scapegoat in a military scandal. After the innocent Schildkraut is sentenced to and sent to Devil's Island, Muni rose to the championship of this oppressed Jewish French officer. His highly-publicized newspaper editorial "J'Accuse," printed after the actual culprit, Major Esterhazy (Barrat) had been finally tried, judged, but acquitted, caused Muni to flee the country in 1898 and live in exile in England until a change of regimes in France both pardoned him and freed the suffering Schildkraut.

A flat, reworking of the infamous Dreyfus case was the subject matter of a 1958 feature I Accuse! (q. v.).

The real life Dreyfus died in 1935 at the age of 75, having outlived all other participants in this shocking scandal.

LIGHTNING BOLT (Woolner, 1967)   C   96 min.

Director, Antonio Margheriti (Anthony Dawson); screenplay, Alfonso Belcazar, Jose Antonio de la Loma; art director, Juan Alberto Soler; music, Riz Ortolani; camera, Riccardo Pallottana.

Anthony Eisley (Harry Sennett); Wandisa Leigh (Patricia); Folco Lulli (Rethe); and: Diana Lorys, Jose Maria Caffarel, Ursula Parker, Oreste, Paletta, Paco Sanz, Renato Montalban.

When a number of U.S. moon rockets explode in mid-air after launching from Cape Kennedy, secret agent Eisley (nicknamed in the picture Goldman because of his unlimited expense account) is assigned to investigate the situation in Miami, assisted by his comely helper (Leigh). This Italian-made programmer, originally called Operazione Goldman ("Operation Goldman") was hastily dubbed into English and shoved onto the double-bill market, hoping that the marquee "name" of Anthony Eisley (former star of video series "Hawaiian Eye") would draw some boxoffice receipts. As Variety pegged the film, "Unfoldment of the film's incredible plot premise is professional and rapid, if still standard and uninspired spy fare." It should be noted that the Italian-made studio sets to represent Florida locale are above par.

THE LIQUIDATOR (MGM, 1966)   C   104 min.

Executive producer, Leslie Elliot; producer, Joe Pennington;

director, Jack Cardiff; based on the novel by John Gardner; screenplay, Peter Yeldham; music, Lalo Schifrin; song, Peter Collender
and Schifrin; costumes, Elizabeth Haffenden, Jean Bridges; camera,
Ted Scaife; editor, Ernest Walter.

    Rod Taylor (Boysie Oakes); Trevor Howard (Mostyn); Jill
St. John (Iris); Wilfrid Hyde-White (The Chief); Akim Tamiroff
(Sheriek); Gabriella Licudi (Coral); Eric Sykes (Griffen); David
Tomlinson (Quadrant).

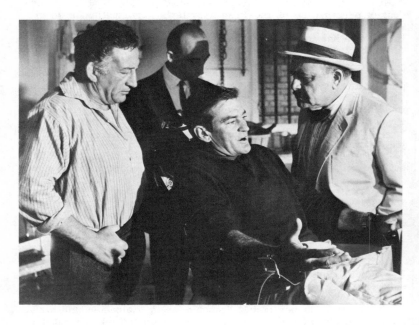

Henri Cogan, Daniel Emilfork, Rod Taylor, and Akim Tamiroff in
The Liquidator (MGM, 1966).

    "What's the price of loyalty these days?" inquires one
British Intelligence department official.
    "Oh, about 6,000 a year, with expenses--and a bit of crum-
pet on the side," replies another.
    This conversation exemplifies the ambience of this English-
made feature. Britisher Hyde-White has concluded that his counter-
espionage division would have a far easier time of it if security
suspects were killed rather than investigated. Second in charge,
Mostyn (Howard), agrees and suggests that an Australian ex-soldier
named Boysie Oakes (Taylor)--they were army pals during the World
War II-Paris liberation days--be hired for the task. Even after the
non-violent Taylor is surfeited with Howard's hatchetman training

he finds himself unable even to contemplate the thought of killing.
Therefore, he hires a free lance assassin, Griffen (Sykes), to do
his onerous field work.   The ploy proves so successful that Taylor
even contemplates having Sykes eliminate Hyde-White, Howard,
et al., so he can be free of the job, but a Riviera weekend with
Howard's shapely secretary (St. John) pushes the unwilling executioner into the environs of real villains, leading to a full scale
shootout.

Three best selling novels based on John Gardner's Boysie
Oakes character had already been published by the time of this
film's delayed release--legal squabbles held up distribution for
many months--with MGM initially planning to spin the project into
a series.   But the premier entry came and went so quietly that
all sequel plans were scuttled.   "... [The] note of the picture is
too craven to be farcical," noted The London Observer, and because
no one involved in The Liquidator dared to push its premise to its
Kind Hearts and Coronets potential, the film emerged as just another James Bond spoof on the Dean Martin sex-and-booze level.

THE LONE WOLF SPY HUNT (Columbia, 1939)   67 min.

Associate producer, Joseph Sistrom; director, Peter Godfrey;
based on a work by Louis Joseph Vance; screenplay, Jonathan Latimer; art director, Lionel Banks; music director, Morris Stoloff;
camera, Allen G. Siegler; editor, Otto Meyer.

Warren William (Michael Lanyard); Ida Lupino (Val Carson);
Rita Hayworth (Karen); Virginia Weidler (Patricia Lanyard); Ralph
Morgan (Gregory); Tom Dugan (Sergeant Devan); Don Beddoe (In-
spector Thomas); Leonard Carey (Jameson); Ben Welden (Jenks);
Brandon Tynan (Senator Carson); Helen Lynd (Marie Templeton);
Irving Bacon (Sergeant); Jack Norton (Charlie Fenton, the Drunk);
Marc Lawrence (Heavy Leader); James Craig (Butler).

Joseph Louis Vance's debonair jewel thief, Michael Lanyard,
alias The Lone Wolf, came to the screen as early as 1917 and
several actors, including Bert Lytell, Jack Holt, and Francis
Lederer, played the role before dapper Warren William took over
the part with The Lone Wolf Spy Hunt (1939).   William had been a
top Broadway leading man before coming to the talkies in 1932.
(Under his real name, Warren Krech, he had appeared with Pearl
White in the 1923 serial Plunder.)
Although the Columbia series was low-budgeted, the William
entries were always spirited and well paced, considering the general level of such detective entries.   The Lone Wolf Spy Hunt told
of an espionage ring operating in the nation's capital.   The group
kidnap William to force him into aiding them in stealing a secret
anti-aircraft plan from the War Department.   Lupino was good as
William's feather-headed girl friend and Hayworth was quite exotic
and lovely as Karen, an alien agent.   Precocious Weidler did a
fine job as William's quick-tongued daughter, although the character
did not reappear in any subsequent entries of the series.

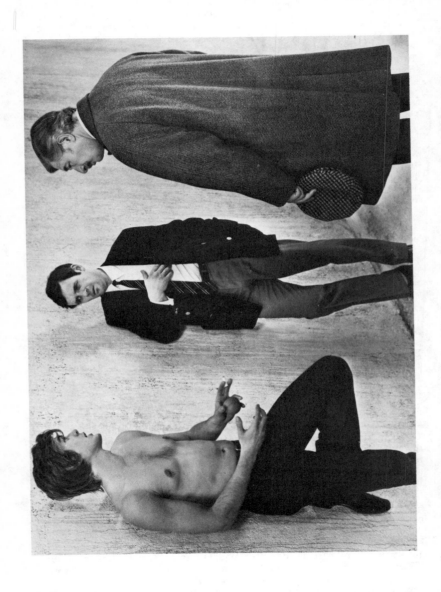

THE LOOKING GLASS WAR   (Columbia, 1970)   C   107 min.

Executive producer, M.J. Frankovich; producer, John Box; associate producer, William Kirey; director, Frank R. Pierson; based on the novel by John Le Carre; screenplay, Pierson; art director, Terry Marsh; set decorator, Henry Federer; music, Wally Scott; sound, Buster Ambler; camera, Austin Dempster; editor, Willy Kemplen.

Christopher Jones (Leiser); Pia Degermark (The Girl); Ralph Richardson (Leclerc); Anthony Hopkins (John Avery); Paul Rogers (Haldane); Susan George (Susan); Ray McAnally (Starr); Robert Urquhart (Johnson); Maxine Audley (Babs Leclerc); Anna Massey (Sarah); Frederick Jaeger (Captain Lansen); Paul Maxwell (C. I. A. Man); Timothy West (Taylor); Vivien Pickles (Carol); Peter Swanwick (Peerson); Cyril Shaps (Detective); Michael Robbins (Truck Driver); Guy Deghy (Fritsche); David Scheur (Russian Officer); John Franklin (Pine); Linda Hedger (Taylor's Child); Nicholas Stewart (Small Boy).

John Le Carre's novel replayed the author's favorite thesis of the futility and frustration of the whole cold war game, and the espionage adjunct in particular. Visualizing this cerebral novel required a surer hand than that of director Frank R. Pierson whose simplified screenplay opted for invented action episodes that were both contrived and pointless. "Espionage is a devious enough business without a studied, elliptical and sketchy screen treatment rendering it even more so and a spy protagonist who sticks out like a sore thumb" (New York Times).

After a furtive encounter at the Berlin airport, a disgruntled, nondescript British agent (West) sets out for home on foot--his department cannot afford transportation. He winds up dead at the side of a snowbound highway in Finland with the "vital" roll of microfilm (of a suspected Russian missile site in East Germany) lying unnoticed in the white ice. Police defector Leiser (Jones), anxious to remain in England, although not so keen anymore on his British girlfriend (George), agrees to undertake vigorous combat and intelligence training so that he may sneak into East Germany and check out the alleged rocket base for the English. Jones' courage begins to fail him when he is forced to kill a guard just after crawling through the barbed wire frontier into Red Germany. When he later remains on the shortwave transmitter too long, allowing the Germans to pinpoint his secret position, his mission superior (Rogers) concludes that Jones is a goner and abandons contact. The youth, alone and panicky near Kalkstadt, chances upon a German girl (Degermark) who offers willing aid. Together they view the transportation of missiles through the town and then rush to contact the British, but the alerted Germans trace them and the duo are gunned down. Agent West's lost microfilm is later found

[Facing page]   Christopher Jones, Anthony Hopkins, and Paul Rogers in The Looking Glass War (Columbia, 1970).

in Finland by a group of children who innocently play with it, letting
it stream in the wind.

Among the more glaring faults of this botched picture was
allowing James Dean lookalike Jones to parade through the East
German segments resembling a hippie tourist more than a secret
agent.   Also jarring were the sudden unrealistic appearance of
glamorous Degermark and the inexplicable necessity of verifying
the Communist missile launcher, when the Reds were openly
pulling their weapons through the German streets.

Distilled or not, The Looking Glass War retained a few
choice observations on present day spying.   Leclerc (Richardson),
as head of the moribund intelligence department in London, is so
eager to convince his political superiors that he and his antiquated
unit are still important that he zealously participates in cooking up
this improbable operation, engulfing it with complicated dressing,
all for the sake of appearance.   Even when Jones has transmitted
accurate data on the Russian military activity in East Germany,
no one back in London wants to believe the facts, preferring to
discount it as a phony counter-espionage planting.   In short, says
author Le Carre, the present day espionage bureaucracy is existing
in a rarefied atmosphere far from the world of reality and necessity.

LUCKY JORDAN   (Paramount, 1942)   84 min.

Associate producer, Fred Kohlmar; director, Frank Tuttle;
story, Charles Leonard; screenplay, Darrell Ware, Karl Tunberg;
art director, Hans Dreier, Ernst Fegte; camera, John Seitz; editor,
Archie Marshek.

Alan Ladd (Lucky Jordan); Helen Walker (Jill Evans); Shel-
don Leonard (Slip Moran); Mabel Paige (Annie); Marie McDonald
(Pearl); Lloyd Corrigan (Ernest Higgins); Russell Hoyt (Eddie);
Dave Willock (Angelo Palacio); Miles Mander (Kilpatrick); John
Wengraf (Kesselman); Charles Cane (Sergeant); George F. Meader
(Little Man); Virginia Brissac (Woman with Little Man); Al M.
Hill, Fred Kohler, Jr. (Killers); Jack Roberts (Johnny); Clem
Bevans (Gas Station Attendant); Olaf Hytten (Charles, the Servant);
William Halligan (Miller, the Gateman); Kitty Kelly (Mrs. Maggotti);
George Humbert (Joe Maggotti); Dorothy Dandridge (Maid at Holly-
hock School); Paul Phillips, Joseph Downing (Stick-Up Men); Danny
Duncan (Clerk in Cigar Store); Carol Hughes (Girl in Back Room);
Ralph Dunn (Army Guard); Kenneth Christy (Sergeant); Edward
Earle, Jack Baxley (Men); Edwin Miller (Officer); John Harmon
(Mug with Big Ears); Edythe Elliott (Secretary); Jimmy O'Gatty
(Mug); John Hamilton, Roy Gordon (Colonels); Albert Ferris, Crane
Whitley (Gardeners); Otto Reichow (Nazi Hood); Ralph Dumke
(Sergeant); Kirk Alyn (Pearl's Boy Friend); Frederick Giermann
(Bulky Gardener); Arthur Loft (Hearndon); Frank Benson (Cab
Driver); Ronnie Rondell (Florist); Terry Ray (Sentry); Elliott Sul-
livan, Bud McTaggart, Keith Richards (Soldiers); Sara Berner
(Helen); William Forrest (Commanding Officer); Paul Stanton (Draft

Official); Virginia Farmer (Lady); Ethel Clayton (Woman); Georgia
Backus (Saleslady in Toy Shop); Harold Minjir (Clerk in Flower
Shop); Marcella Phillips, Alice Kirby, Yvonne DeCarlo (Girls);
Harry V. Cheshire (Garden Gatekeeper); Ralph Peters (Brig
Sergeant).

Following the lead of Warner Bros., which successfully
combined the gangster and spy genres in All Through the Night
(1942), Paramount turned out Lucky Jordan as a vehicle for its
new male star, Alan Ladd, as well as introducing actress Helen
Walker to the screen.

In this "highly entertaining and unpretentious film" (Films
and Filming), Ladd was cast as the title character, a punk who
has no patriotic feelings and goes AWOL from the Army, taking
a canteen hostess (Walker) with him. Returning to the big city
and his old haunts, he finds rival gangster Slip Morgan (Leonard)
has taken over his territory and his moll (McDonald).

Stealing a briefcase loaded with money from Leonard, Ladd
hides out with an old crone (Paige) who pretends to be his mother.
When she is manhandled by a Nazi group working with Leonard in
a plot to blow up American supply ships, Ladd awakens to the situation and decides he hates the Nazis. He patriotically routs the
fifth columnists out of their respectable Long Island flower garden.
By assisting the police in capturing the villains, Ladd is pardoned
and wins the love of the abducted hostess.

Under the steady hand of director Tuttle, Lucky Jordan
proved to be a high grosser, insuring the actor's continued popularity as the sharp personification of the 1940s good-bad cinema
hero. As in Humphrey Bogart's All Through the Night, this patriotic feature demonstrated that even the underworld can perceive
the rightness of the Allied cause, and, more patently, that Axis
infiltrators are no match for the physical might of right-thinking
Americans (law abiders or not).

MA AND PA KETTLE ON VACATION (Universal, 1953)   75 min.

Producer, Leonard Goldstein; director, Charles Barton;
story-screenplay, Jack Henley; art director, Bernard Herzbrun,
Robert Boyle; camera, George Robinson; editor, Leonard Weiner.
Marjorie Main (Ma Kettle); Percy Kilbride (Pa Kettle); Ray
Collins (Jonathan Parker); Bodil Miller (Inez Kraft); Sig Rumann
(Cyrus Kraft); Barbara Brown (Elizabeth Parker); Ivan Triesault
(Henri); Oliver Blake (Geoduck); Teddy Hart (Crowbard); Peter
Brocco (Mr. Wade); Jay Novello (Andre); Jean De Briac (Chef
Chantilly); Larry Dobkin (Farrell); Harold Goodwin (Harriman);
Jack Kruschen (Jacques); Rita Moreno (Soubrette).

The Ma and Pa Kettle series was one of the sociological
quirks of post-World War II America which was grossing Universal
about $2.5 million per entry. In this sixth installment of rural
U.S.A.'s most famous married couple, the scripters had Ma (Main)

and Pa (Kilbride) engaged in undercover work for the F.B.I.   After
all, whom would the enemy least suspect other than this bucolic
couple?

Main and Kilbride maneuver a Parisian trip in the company
of their snooty in-laws (Collins-Brown) and because of a baggage
mixup find themselves holding some items foreign agents are determined to recover.   Along the way Kilbride ogles the Eiffel Tower
and some French postcards, while Main has a workout at a Gallic
cafe where she becomes an unwitting part of an apache dance act.

MADAME SIN   (ITC/ABC-TV, 1972)   C   90 min.

Producer, Julian Wintle, Lou Morheim; co-producer, Scotia
Barber; director, David Greene; screenplay, Greene, Barry Orringer;
costumes, Edith Head.

Bette Davis (Madame Sin); Robert Wagner (Anthony Lawrence);
Denholm Elliott (De Vere); Gordon Jackson (Cavendish); Dudley Sut-
ton (Monk); Catherine Schell (Barbara); Pik-sen Lim (Nikko); Paul
Maxwell (Connors), and: David Healy, Al Mansini, Alan Dobie, Roy
Kinnear, Charles Lloyd Pack, Fred Middlemass, Arnold Diamond.

Made on a $1.2 million budget and shot on location in Scot-
land, this heavily tongue-in-cheek project was made to follow in the
footsteps of the Sax Rohmer and Edgar Wallace thrillers, with Davis
as a slant-eyed master villainess/fiend, who, like Fu Manchu, is
out to dominate the world.

Its fantastic plotline offered Madame Sin (Davis) convincing a
grief-stricken CIA agent (Wagner) that the CIA was responsible for
the death of his girlfriend.   She then persuades him to assist her in
stealing a Polaris submarine, a tidy little treasure which she plans
to resell to an enemy power for $1 billion.   Unfortunately for Wag-
ner's welfare, he goes along with her plan, and eventually learns
that it was really Davis who killed his gal.   For his efforts, he
meets his own end much sooner than he anticipated.

Well-acted, and laced through with such futuristic weapons
as a sting ray and a brain probe machine, and depicting an underground spying system that would have pleased Dr. Mabuse, Madame
Sin was above par television fare.   Davis was always larger than
life in her title role, proving to be one of the most fanciful villains
ever to come on the small or large screen.

MADAME SPY   (Universal, 1934)   70 min.

Director, Karl Freund; based on the German film Unter
falsche Flagge and its screenplay by Johannes Brandt, Joseph
Than, Max Kemmick; adaptation, William Hulburt; camera, Norbert
Brodine.

Nils Asther (Captain Franck); Douglas Walton (Karl); Fay
Wray (Maria); John Miljan (Weber); Robert Ellis (Sulkin); Edward
Arnold (Schultz); David Torrence (Seefeldt); Oscar Apfel (Pahlke);

Vincent Barnett (Peter); Stephen Alden Chase (Petroskie); Rollo
Lloyd (Baum); Noah Beery (Filipow); A. S. Byron, Arthur Wanzer
(Chemists); Ferdinand Schumann-Heink (Cafe Owner); Herbert Hol-
combe (Orderly); Reginald Pasch (Dumb Guy); Ruth Fallows (Lulu);
Mabel Marden (Rose); Robert Graves, Anders Van Haden (Detec-
tives); Edward Peil, Sr. (Garage Proprietor); Werner Plack (Con-
ductor); Albert J. Smith (Lackey); Philip Morris (Russian Officer);
Eddy Chandler (Austrian Officer); Henry Grobel (Austrian Aviator);
Jerry Jerome (Russian Aviator).

The well-received 1932 German film Unter falsche Flagge
inspired Universal's Carl Laemmle to produce an English-language
rendition. Everything seems to have been lost in the transition,
for despite the relatively superior mounting (including a scene at
the Czar's winter palace) and a display of remarkable camera
angles, "the story has such poor substance and continuity that it
is frequently ludicrous" (New York Herald-Tribune).

During World War I, German intelligence officer Franck
(Asther) is returning from the front on an Austrian hospital train
when he falls in love with "nurse" Maria (Wray). She is actually
a clever Russian spy known in the trade as B-24. Schultz (Arnold)
and Weber (Miljan) are the Austrian spy experts assigned to plug
the security leak.

Madame Spy demonstrates one ingenious, if far-fetched, bit
of spy modus operandi. Dictation recorded on a phonograph record
is hidden by superimposing pop tunes. Later the extraneous music
is washed away by dipping the disc into a bath of chemicals.

MADAME SPY (Universal, 1942) 63 min.

Associate producer, Marshall Grant; director, Roy William
Neill; story, Clarence Upton Young; screenplay, Lynn Riggs, Young;
camera, George Robinson; editor, Ted J. Kent.

Constance Bennett (Joan Bannister); Don Porter (David Bannister); John Litel (Peter); Edward S. Brophy (Mike Reese); John
Eldredge (Carol Gordon); Nana Bryant (Alicia Rolf); Selmer Jack-
son (Harrison Woods); Jimmy Conlin (Winston); Edmund MacDonald
(Drake); Nino Pipitone (Miro); Cliff Clark (Inspector Varden);
Johnny Berkes (Hotel Clerk); Billy Wayne (Driver's Helper); Pat
West (Driver); Reid Kilpatrick (Announcer); William Gould (Min-
ister); Phil Warren (Reporter); Anne O'Neal (Woman); John Dil-
son (Proprietor); Thornton Edwards (Foreign Cab Driver); Irving
Mitchell (Man); Sidney Miller (Newsboy); Alexander Lockwood,
Frank Marlowe, Charles Sherlock, Pat Costello (Cab Drivers);
Gerald Pierce (Page Boy); Eddie Coke, Jack Gardner (Attendants);
Rico de Montez (Filipino Servant); Grace Hayle, Mira McKinney,
Norma Drury (Red Cross Women).

Less than a decade after After Tonight (1933), one-time
movie star Bennett had sunk with still considerable charm and style
into programmer work, emoting in such celluloid fodder as this film.

Chic Joan Bannister (Bennett) weds a war correspondent (Porter) and they honeymoon in Shanghai and South America. Returning to Manhattan, she soon is hobnobbing with Peter (Litel) and other alien undesirables, leading her baffled (not very bright for a reporter) spouse to the wrong conclusions. Yup! She is working incognito for the good guys.

MAKE YOUR OWN BED (WB, 1944) 81 min.

Producer, Alex Gottlieb; director, Peter Godfrey; based on the play by Harvey J. O'Higgins, Harriet Ford; screenplay, Frances Swann, Edmund Joseph; art director, Stanley Fleischer; set decorator, Clarence Steensen; music, H. Roemheld; music director, Leo F. Forbstein; sound, Charles Lang; assistant director, Les Guthrie; special effects, Willard Van Enger; camera, Robert Burks; editor, Clarence Kolster.

Jack Carson (Jerry Curtis); Jane Wyman (Susan Courtney); Alan Hale (Walter Whittle); Irene Manning (Vivian Whittle); George Tobias (Boris Murphy); Robert Shayne (Lester Knight); Tala Birell (Marie Guber); Ricardo Cortez (Fritz Allen); Marjorie Hoshelle (Elsa); Kurt Katch (Paul Hassen); Harry Bradley (Mr. Brooking); William Kennedy (FBI Man).

Jack Carson and Jane Wyman in Make Your Own Bed (WB, 1944).

This film gambit of blending bedroom farce, spy melodrama, and a burlesque on the topical theme of the servant shortage just did not jell.

When wealthy war plant owner Hale finds it difficult to hire new domestics, he talks lame-brained private detective Carson into taking a job as a butler by convincing the obtuse gumshoe that enemy agents are infiltrating the secrets of his war plant. Besides, says Hale, neighbor Tobias is making a pass at Hale's wife (Manning). Carson's fiancée (Wyman), who has been introduced as the detective's wife, goes along on the mission disguised as the new maid of the Hale household. Just to keep Carson-Wyman on the job, Hale hires four radio actors to be fake Nazi agents. Naturally, as it turns out, they are for real, and hence the complications of the plot.

THE MAN BETWEEN (British-Lion/UA, 1953)   101 min.

Producer, Carol Reed; associate producer, Hugh Percival; director, Reed; story, Walter Ebert; screenplay, Harry Kurnitz; music, John Addison; music director, Muir Mathieson; art director, Andre Andrejeiv; camera, Desmond Dickenson; additional camera, Hans Schneeberger; editor, A. S. Bates.

James Mason in The Man Between (British-Lion/UA, 1953).

James Mason (Ivo Kern); Claire Bloom (Susanne Mallison);
Hildegarde Neff (Bettina); Geoffrey Toone (Dr. Martin Mallison);
Aribert Waescher (Halendar); Ernst Schroeder (Olaf Kastner);
Dieter Krause (Horst); Hilde Sessak (Lizzi); Karl John (Inspector
Kleiber).

Having examined post-World War II Vienna in The Third
Man (1950), director Carol Reed turned his cinematic attention to
bomb-torn Berlin in the occupation years following the Second World
War, offering an absorbing political drama as stark in its contents
as the rubble-strewn locales and its survival-clinging characters.
The film neatly delineates the battle of wits between the East and
the West with the Red Zone police attempting to halt the trafficking
of human bodies into the West Zone.

Susanne Mallison (Bloom), the naive young sister of Dr.
Martin Mallison (Toone), a British army doctor working at the
Berlin Refugee Reception Centre, pays a visit to her brother and
German sister-in-law (Neff). Bloom is arrested by the East
German police, however, when she accidentally wanders into the
Communist sector during a sightseeing excursion. She gravitates
to an East Berlin lawyer turned black marketeer, Ivo Kern (Mason),
not knowing that he once was wed to Neff or that he had been an
honorable person before Nazism ended his world of justice and
freedom. Meanwhile Communist official Halendar (Waescher) is
blackmailing Mason into luring defecting Olaf Kastner (Schroeder),
a friend of Toone, back to the East. As time passes, Mason re-
sponds to Blooms' engaging innocence and finds his lost conscience
by helping her to return to the West. In the daring escape he loses
his life.

As Reed's cameraman Desmond Dickenson effectively probes
the dingy Berlin jungle glazed over by cold war tensions, the viewer
quickly perceives the factors driving individuals to desperate partisan measures--on both sides of the political fence--in order to allow loved ones the chance at freedom or to survive themselves.
Unfortunately the pat outline of the story and its political-vs. -
romantic dichotomy destroys some of the potential suspense. In
addition, Mason does emerge as too much the glamorous rogue,
selfish but possibly too irresistible for the starkness of the surrounding film.

A MAN CALLED DAGGER (MGM, 1968) C 86 min.

Executive producer, M.A. Ripps; producer, Lewis M. Hor-
witz; director, Richard Rush; idea, W.L. Riffs; screenplay, James
Pearlman, Robert S. Weekdey; music, Steve Allen; art director,
Mike McCloskey; assistant director, Steve Bernhardt; sound, Franklin Milton; camera, Leslie Kovacs; editor, Len Miller.

Paul Mantee (Dick Dagger); Terry Moore (Harper Davis);
Jan Murray (Rudolph Koffman); Sue Ann Langdon (Ingrid); Eileen
O'Neill (Erica); Maureen Arthur (Joy); Leonard Stone (Karl Rainer);
Richard Kiel (Otto); Mimi Dillard (Girl in Auto); Bruno Ve Sota
(Dr. Gulik).

This film's producers may have supplied the hero with fantastic weapons that would have had Bond and Flint drooling with envy, but someone forgot that a passable plot and at least high school level acting are necessary for a picture's well-being. The miscasting of Murray as the arch villain was almost equalized by the ineptness of both Mantee and veteran ingenue Moore.

U.S. secret agent Mantee and fellow worker Moore investigate the flow of ex-Nazi scientists into the States. It seems that Murray, a former SS member and concentration camp commandant who now operates a meat-packing plant, is engineering a neo-Nazi attempt to take over the world.

THE MAN CALLED FLINTSTONE (Columbia, 1966) C 90 min.

Producer-director, Joseph Barbera, William Hanna; screenplay, Harvey Bullock, Ray Allen; additional story material, Barbera, Hanna, Warren Foster, Alex Lorry; music, Marty Paich, Ted Nichols; songs, John McCarthy and Doug Goodwin; art director, Bill Perez; animation director, Charles A. Nichols; sound, Richard Olson, Bill Getty; production supervisor, Howard Hanson; camera, Charles Flekd, Roy Wade, Gene Borghi, Bill Kottey, Norman Stainback, Dick Blundell, Frank Parrish, Hal Sheffman, John Pratt; editor, Milton Krear, Pat Foley, Larry Cowan, Dave Horton.

Voices of: Alan Reed (Fred Flintstone); Mel Blanc (Barney Rubble); and: Jean Vander Pye, Gerry Johnson, Don Messick, Janet Waldo, Paul Frees, Harvey Korman, John Stephenson, June Foray.

American television's favorite Stone Age family, "The Flintstones," came to the big screen in this full-length animated feature--with fine pastel colored backgrounds--complete with Fred and Wilma, their baby Pebbles, and the household pets, Dino the dinosaur and Hoppy the kangaroo. To add a timely appeal to the outing, the Neanderthal domestics became involved with spies. "Unfortunately, the fun gets much too frantic and cluttered with James Bond riggings, which don't enhance such unsophistication" (New York Times).

Because Fred Flintstone is mistaken for secret agent Rock Slag, Flintstone and his wife Wilma, along with neighbors Barney and Betty Rubble, head to Paris, set to encounter SMISH enemy agents, particularly the Green Goose and double operative Tanya.

The attention catcher of this comic strip entry was always its presentation of prehistoric life in contemporary terms, but here the premise wore very thin, occasionally buoyed by such lively musical numbers as "Spy Type Guy." The children-oriented picture was released as a special week-end matinee attraction.

A MAN COULD GET KILLED (Universal, 1966) C 99 min.

Producer, Robert Arthur; associate producer, Ernest

Wehmeyer; director, Ronald Neame, Cliff Owen; based on the novel
Diamonds for Danger by David Esdaile Walker; screenplay, Richard
Breen, T. E. B. Clarke; music, Bert Kaempfert; music supervisor,
Joseph Gershenson; assistant director, Douglas Green, Robert Fiz;
art director, John De Cuir; set decorator, Giuseppe Chevalier;
sound, Waldon O. Watson, William Russell; camera, Gabor Pogany;
editor, Alma Macrorie.

James Garner (William Beddoes); Melina Mercouri (Aurora
Celeste da Costa); Sandra Dee (Amy Franklin); Tony Franciosa
(Steve-Antonio); Robert Coote (Hatton-Jones); Gregoire Aslan (Flori-
an); Roland Culver (Dr. Mathieson); Cecil Parker (Sir Huntley
Frazier); Brenda De Banzie (Mrs. Mathieson); Niall MacGinnis
(Ship's Captain); George Pastell (Laszlo); Martin Benson (Politanu);
Peter Illing (Zarick); Arnold Diamond (Milo); Daniel Vargas (Os-
man); Eric Demain (Max); Conrad Anderson (Heinrich); Nello Paz-
zafini (Abdul); Pasquale Fasciano (Carmo); Nora Swinburne (Lady
Frazier); Ann Firbank (Miss Nolan); Jenny Agutter (Linda Frazier);
Isabel Dean (Miss Bannister); Biuliano Raffaelli (Ludmar); Yamili
Humar (Rosa); and: Pontifex, Jonas Braimer, D. A. Segurd, E.

James Garner, Tony Franciosa, and Roland Culver in A Man Could
Get Killed (Universal, 1966).

Cianfanelli, M. Bevilacqua, M. R. Caldas, O. Acursio, J. Paixio,
A. Costa, L. Pinhao, G. Dusmatas, V. Teixeira, C. DiMaggio,
C. Calisti, C. Perone, P. Solvay, M. Tempesta, S. Minoi, R.
Castelli, R. Alessandri, G. Maculani, G. Lipari, K. Goncalves.

While not the same calibre as Topkapi (1964), this film
sported a lively Mercouri, who sparkles as the Portuguese femme
fatale out for the fast buck the easy way. The pasquinade blithely
runs in small circles with repetitiousness the chief obstacle in its
entertainment path. The dual direction of Ronald Neame and Cliff
Owen obviously hindered the overall effect.
William Beddoes (Garner) arrives in Lisbon where he is
mistaken for a C. I. A. agent. In reality, he is a bank official
negotiating a business deal which requires close cooperation between the English and Americans. Thus he is lodged at the British
Embassy where urbane Ambassador Sir Huntley Frazier (Parker)
insists he does not want to know details of Garner's secret. The
perplexed American is quickly launched into a nightmare of skulking
underworld types, including Auroya Celeste da Costa (Mercouri), the
wayward widow of a Lisbon spy-smuggler, and Steve Antonio (Franciosa),
whom skittish Dee insists is not a Portuguese smuggler but actually
an ex-G. I. from Seattle, Washington. Before long, dazed Garner
is engulfed in a plot to steal industrial diamonds and negotiable bonds
worth millions, with the scene shifting from Lisbon to the Portuguese
coast.

THE MAN FROM O. R. G. Y.   (Cinemation, 1970)   C   92 min.

Producer, Sidney Pink; director, James A. Hill; based on
the novel by Ted Mark; screenplay, Mark; music, Charles Bernstein; sound, Jack Reed; camera, Jose F. Aguayo.
Robert Walker (Steve Victor); Steve Rossi (Luigi); Slappy
White (Vito); Louisa Moritz (Gina Moretti); Lynn Carter (The Madam); and: Mark Hannibal, Michel Stany, Mary Marx, Jan Bank,
Shannon O'Shea.

This would-be spoof on spy pictures, the Mafia, porno-
graphic exploitation films, and a wide variety of other things, lost
its potential sharp focus by trying to satirize too much within its
loosely-constructed frame.
Steve Victor (Walker) of O. R. G. Y. (Organization for Rational
Guidance of Youth) is hired to trace the proper legatees of a $15
million estate. His only clue is that three girls in question each
has tattooed on her bottom the image of a grinning golfer, and that
most likely they are still employed in one of the many whorehouses
dotting the French-Spanish coastline. The Mafia is interested in
Walker's case, because they will be the legal recipients of the
estate if the girls are not found.
The film made its solidest impression with the zany sequences devoted to female impersonator Lynn Carter as a mercenary
Madam who did a repertory of standard routines (including Marlene

Dietrich, Hermione Gingold, Phyllis Diller and Bette Davis).
Originally released as The Real Gone Girls.

MAN HUNT (20th-Fox, 1941) 102 min.

Associate producer, Kenneth Macgowan; director, Fritz Lang;
based on the novel Rogue Male by Geoffrey Household; screenplay,
Dudley Nichols; art director, Ricard Day, Wiard B. Ihnen; music,
Alfred Newman; costumes, Travis Banton; set decorator, Thomas
Little; camera, Arthur Miller; editor, Allen McNeil.
Walter Pidgeon (Captain Thorndike); Joan Bennett (Jerry);
George Sanders (Quive-Smith); John Carradine (Mr. Jones); Roddy
McDowall (Vaner, the Cabin Boy); Ludwig Stossel (Doctor);
Heather Thatcher (Lady Risborough); Frederic Worlock (Lord Ris-
borough); Roger Imhof (Captain Jensen); Egon Brecher (Whiskers);
Holmes Herbert (Farnsworthy); Fredrik Vogeding (Ambassador);
Lucien Prival (Umbrella Man); Herbert Evans (Reeves); Edgar
Licho (Little Fat Man); Eily Malyon (Postmistress); John Rogers
(Cockney); Lester Mathews (Major); Arno Frey (Police Lieutenant);
Keith Hitchcock (London Bobby); Otto Reichow, Bob Stephenson,
William Haade (Sentries); Adolph Milar (Pigeon Man); Sven Borg
(First Mate); Hans Joby (Tracker); Douglas Gerrard (Policeman);
Cyril Delevanti (Cab Driver); Clifford Severn (Cockney Boy);
Charles Bennett, Bobbie Hale (Costermongers); Frank Benson (Cab
Driver); Walter Bonn (Harbor Police); Carl Ekberg (Hitler); Knud
Kreuger, Olaf Hytten (Secretaries); Carol Ottmar (Harbor Police);
William Vaughn (Chief Harbor Police); Virginia McDowall (Post-
mistress' Daughter); Bruce Lester (Co-Pilot); Richard Fraser
(Navigator).

Of director Fritz Lang's 1940s spy stalker pictures, Man
Hunt is the sturdiest and best remembered screen exercise.
Having muffed his opportunity to kill Hitler at Berchtes-
garden, British hunter Captain Thorndike (Pidgeon) is captured and
tortured by the Gestapo. He escapes and makes his way back to
London, but only one step ahead of the pursuing, determined Nazis.
Lang successfully utilized unique camera angles and low key
lighting for melodramatic effects, hoping to reestablish his film
reputation as an unusual director, by proving his point with this
project. The feature has some unusual highlights, such as the
Nazi agents chasing Pidgeon through dark, dank and ill-lit underground passages. As an ironic twist, the only one in London who
stands ready to assist the beleagued Pidgeon is streetwalker Bennett. She later gets killed for her trouble.
In their surface enjoyment of the suspense and action, many
viewers at the time failed to note the parallel between Pidgeon's
failure to shoot Hitler and his subsequent efforts to make amends
with England's initial appeasement policy toward the Third Reich and
its later valiant effort to stem the Nazi tide. There were many
other propaganda angles to this picture, but none as debilitating as
those laced into the director's previous Hangmen Also Die (q.v.).

THE MAN IN THE LOOKING GLASS   (International Television Corp.,
1968)   C   91 min.

Steve Forrest (John/Eddie); Yvonne Furneaux (Selna); Bernard Lee (Travis); Sue Lloyd (Cordella); Ken Warren (Security
Boss); John Carson (Nevell); Frank Wolff (Martin).

This film is one of two telefeatures (Mystery Island was the
other) released to U.S. television from the British video series
"The Baron," which starred Forrest and Lloyd.   In this outing,
Forrest was an art dealer masquerading as a gangster in order to
thwart the theft of Britain's crown jewels by foreign agents.

MAN ON A STRING   (Columbia, 1960)   92 min.

Producer, Louis de Rochemont; associate producer, Louis
de Rochemont III, Lothan Wolff; director, Andre de Toth; based
in part on the book Ten Years a Counterspy by Boris Morros, with
Charles Samuels; screenplay, John Kafka, Virginia Shaler; art di-
rector, Carl Anderson; set decorator, James M. Crowe; sound,
Lambert Day; orchestrator, Arthur Morton; assistant director,
Eddie Salta, Jean Hoerler; camera, Charles Lawlor, Jr., Albert
Benitz, Gayne Rescher, Pierre Poincarde; editor, Al Clark.
Ernest Borgnine (Boris Mitrov); Kerwin Mathews (Bob
Avery); Colleen Dewhurst (Helen Benson); Alexander Scourby
(Vadja Kubelov); Glenn Corbett (Frank Sanford); Vladimir Sokoloff
(Papa); Fredrich Joloff (Nikolai Chapayev); Richard Kendrick (In-
spector Jenkins); Ed Prentiss (Adrian Benson); Holger Hagen
(Hans Grünwald); Robert Iller (Hartmann); Reginald Pasch (Otto
Bergman); Carl Jaffe (People's Judge); Eva Pflug (Rosnova);
Michael Mellinger (Detective).

The record may confirm that much of this compressed yarn,
based on Boris Morros' autobiography, was a recreation of grim
reality, but the picture suffered from an "awkwardness in writing
and performance that doesn't much help the story's credibility" (Cue
magazine).   The on-location lensing in Los Angeles, New York,
Berlin, and Moscow gave the project more stability than the television fare deserved.   Gratuitous tripe abounded; characters mouthed
such sentiments as "In this [espionage] business you have to forget
every human feeling except your love for your country."
Russian-born composer and Hollywood music director-producer
Boris Mitrov (Borgnine) is pressured into becoming a Soviet agent
to save the life of his aged father left behind in the U.S.S.R.   Borgnine's conscience eventually comes to the fore and he confesses to
the F.B.I. which, in turn, employs him as a counter-agent, with
Mathews designated as his assistant.   The extravagant story moves
back and forth between the East and West with a climactic chase in
the mazes of spy-ridden East Berlin.   Scourby functions as the chief
of Russian espionage in the U.S., with Dewhurst as Scourby's solid
mistress.   The film concludes with Borgnine's rehabilitation and

subsequent acclaim by both the Central Bureau of Intelligence and
the United States government and people.

MAN ON A TIGHTROPE   (20th-Fox, 1953)   105 min.

Producer, Robert L. Jacks; associate producer, Gerd Oswald;
director, Elia Kazan; story, Neil Paterson; screenplay, Robert E.
Sherwood; music director, Franz Waxman; art director, Hans H.
Kerhnert, Theodore Zwirsky; costumes, Ursula Maes; makeup,
Arthur Schramm, Fritz Seyfried; assistant director, Hans Tost;
sound, Martin Mueller, Karl Becker; camera, George Krause;
editor, Dorothy Spence.

Fredric March (Karel Cernik); Terry Moore (Tereza Cernik);
Gloria Grahame (Zama Cernik); Cameron Mitchell (Joe Vosdek);
Adolphe Menjou (Fesker); Robert Beatty (Barovic); Alex D'Arcy
(Rudolph); Richard Boone (Krofta); Pat Henning (Konradin); Paul
Hartman (Jaromir); John Dehner (The Chief); Mme. Brumbach
(Mme. Cernik); Hansi (Kalka); the Birnbach Circus (The Cirkus
Cernik); Dorothea Wieck (Duchess); Philip Kenneally (Sergeant);
Edelweiss Malchin (Vina Konradin); William Castello (Captain);
Margaret Slezak (Mrs. Jaromir); Peter Beauvais (S. N. B. Captain);
Robert Charlebois (S. C. B. Lieutenant); Gert Frobe, Rolf Naukhoff
(Police Agents).

In the early 1950s, anti-Communist films were at the zenith
of their popularity. Man on a Tightrope graphically recounted the
plight of (March), the heir of a long line of Czechoslovakian circus
owners, who finds that when the Communists take over the country,
he is deprived of ownership of his rickety big top. He then determines to get his small family troupe through to the Western border.
The plot crisis revolves around March's fear that Joe Vosdek
(Mitchell), the lion tamer lover of his daughter (Moore), is really
a Communist sympathizer. At the same time March is playing a
game of wits with suave Red investigator Fesker (Menjou), and is
trying to cope with the growing antagonism of his young second
wife (Grahame), who mistakes his underplayed attitude to the Communists as a sign of mounting weakness. Man on a Tightrope
climaxes with the daring escape to freedom by March's troupe, and
the unveiling of the actual Red agent. A downbeat finale gives the
film a quite substantial tone.

Directed on location in Bavaria with an actual circus troupe
(Birnbach Circus), director Elia Kazan gauged his storyline well
and his efforts met with good critical reviews. Newsweek called
the film "a highly atmospheric and timely melodrama, jammed with
talent ... an absorbing picture." Unfortunately, the progressive
competition of television, as America's favorite indoor sport, kept
the picture from the popularity it deserved.

[Facing page]   Adolphe Menjou in Man on a Tightrope (20th-Fox,
1953).

THE MAN OUTSIDE   (London Independent Producers, 1967)   C
98 min.

    Producer, William Gell; director, Samuel Gallu; based on the
novel Double Agent by Gene Stackleborg; screenplay, Gallu; addi-
tional dialog, Julian Bond, Roger Marshall; art director, Peter
Mullins; music-music director, Richard Arnell; sound, Stephen
Dalby; camera, Gilbert Taylor; editor, Tom Noble.
    Van Heflin (Bill Maclean); Heidelinde Weis (Kay Sebastian);
Pinkas Braun (Rafe Machek); Peter Vaughan (Nicolai Volkov);
Charles Gray (Charles Griddon); Paul Maxwell (Judson Murphy);
Ronnie Barker (George Venaxas); Linda Marlowe (Dorothy); Gary
Cockrell (Brune Parry); Bill Nagy (Morehouse); Larry Cross
(Austen); Archie Duncan (Detective Superintendent Barnes); Wil-
loughby Gray (Detective Inspector); Christopher Denham (Detective
Sergeant); Rita Webb (Landlady); Carole Ann Ford (Cindy); Carmel
McSharry (Olga); John Sterland (Spencer); Alex Marchevsky (Mik-
hail); Paul Armstrong (Gerod); Hugh Elton (Vadim); Derek Baker
(Gerod's Assistant); Frank Crawshaw (Drunken Hick); Roy Sone
(Albert); Harry Hutchinson (Caretaker); Gabrielle Drake (B. E. A.
Girl); Carol Kingsley (Barmaid); Martin Terry (Gambling Club Bar-
man); Anna Willoughby (Boutique Attendant); Suzanne Owens
(Attendant).

    Because he stubbornly remains loyal to one of his men who
has "defected" to East Berlin (the operative was actually kidnapped
by the Communists), C. I. A. agent Bill Maclean (Heflin) is ordered
from his Germany post back to London where he is officially discredited and removed from service.   At liberty he is soon approached
by his Macedonian working acquaintance, George Venaxas (Barker),
who offers to go into partnership with him on a plan to hand over to
the C. I. A., for $50,000, Rafe Machek (Braun), the Soviet secret
police's number two man, who is anxious to defect to the West.
Barker is shot, and when Heflin refuses to return Braun to the
Russians, the latter, under Nicholai Volkov's (Vaughan) personal
direction, frame Heflin for a murder which set the London police
on his trail.   At a later date Heflin agrees to complete the trade
of Braun for the cash with his ex-boss (Maxwell).   The money is
to be supplied by Charles Griddon (Gray), the latter in charge of
a businessmen's anti-Red fund.   Braun eventually reaches safe hands,
but only after several killings.   As for Heflin, he finally refuses
either to accept the cash payment or to be reinstated in the C. I. A.,
having learned that most of this caper was merely a staged situation to prove Gray's disloyalty.
    Fifty-seven year old Heflin was far enough removed from
his former glamour star status to essay the crumpled, baffled undercover agent who finds that he can still rise to the occasion when
the chips are down, but realizes as well that he is too cynically
seasoned to carry on in the spy business any further.   Throughout
the screenplay, there are diverse potshots at both the inefficiency
of the bureaucratic C. I. A. and, more sharply, at the innocent
apple pie Americans whose tax monies finance this department's

global stunts. Sadly this dual bill item, filmed in Techniscope and color in London reeked of banality in too many places, precluding its deliberately brittle message on spying from capturing either critical or audience support.

THE MAN WHO KNEW TOO MUCH [number 1] (Gaumont British, 1934) 84 min.

Producer, Michael Balcon; associate producer, Ivor Montagu; director, Alfred Hitchcock; story, Charles Bennett, D. B. Wyndham-Lewis; screenplay, A. R. Rawlinson, Bennett, Lewis, Edwin Greenwood; additional dialog, Emlyn Williams; set decorator, Alfred Junge, Peter Proud; music, Arthur Benjamin; music director, Louis Levy; camera, Curt Courant; editor, H. St. C. Stewart.

Leslie Banks (Bob Lawrence); Edna Best (Jill Lawrence); Peter Lorre (Abbott); Frank Vosper (Ramon Levine); Hugh Wakefield (Clive); Nova Pilbeam (Betty Lawrence); Pierre Fresnay (Louis Bernard); Cicely Oates (Nurse Agnes); D. A. Clarke Smith (Binstead); George Curzon (Gibson); and: Celia Lovsky.

THE MAN WHO KNEW TOO MUCH [number 2] (Paramount, 1956) C 120 min.

Producer, Alfred Hitchcock; associate producer, Herbert Coleman; director, Hitchcock; story, Charles Bennett, D. B. Wyndham-Lewis; screenplay, John Michael Hayes, Angus McPhail; sets, Hal Pereira, Henry Bumstead, Sam Comer, Arthur Krams; music, Bernard Herrmann; songs, Jay Livingston and Ray Evans, Arthur Benjamin and Wyndham-Lewis; assistant director, Howard Joslin; costumes, Edith Head; sound, Franz Paul, Gene Garvin; special effects, John P. Fulton; camera, Richard Mueller; editor, George Tomasini.

James Stewart (Dr. Ben McKenna); Doris Day (Jo McKenna); Brenda de Banzie (Mrs. Drayton); Bernard Miles (Mr. Drayton); Ralph Truman (Buchanan); Daniel Gelin (Louis Bernard); Mogens Wieth (Ambassador); Alan Mowbray (Val Parnell); Hillary Brooke (Jan Peterson); Christopher Olsen (Hank McKenna); Reggie Nalder (Rien, the Assassin); Richard Wattis (Assistant Manager); Noel Willman (Woburn); Alix Talton (Helen Parnell); Yves Brainville (Police Inspector); Carolyn Jones (Cindy Fontaine); Abdelhaq Chraibi, Lou Krugman (Arabs); Betty Baskcomb (Edna); Leo Gordon (Chauffeur); Patrick Aherne (English Handyman); Louis Mercier, Anthony Warde (French Police); Lewis Martin (Detective); Gladys Holland (Bernard's Girl Friend); John O'Malley (Uniformed Attendant); Peter Camlin (Headwaiter); Albert Carrier (French Policeman); Ralph Heff (Henchman); John Marshall (Butler); Eric Snowden (Special Branch Officer); Edward Manouk (French Waiter); Donald Lawton (Desk Clerk); Patrick Whyte (Special Branch Officer); Mahin S. Shahrivar (Arab Woman); Alex Frazer (Man); Allen Zeidman (Assistant Manager); Milton Frome, Walter Gotell (Guards); Frank Atkinson, Liddell Peddieson, Mayne Lynton, John Barrard (Workmen in

Taxidermist Shop); Alexis Bobrinsky (Foreign Prime Minister);
Janet Bruce (Box Office Woman); Naida Buckingham (Lady in the
Audience); Clifford Buckton (Sir Kenneth Clarke); Barbara Burke
(Girl Friend of the Assassin); Pauline Farr (Ambassador's Wife);
Harry Fine (Edington); Wolf Priess (Aide to Foreign Prime Min-
ister); George Howe (Ambrose Chappell, Sr.); Harold Kasket (But-
ler); Barry Keegan (Patterson); Lloyd Lamble (General Manager
of Albert Hall); Enid Lindsey (Lady Clarke); Janet Macfarlane
(Lady in Audience); Leslie Newport (Inspector at Albert Hall);
Elsa Palmer (Woman Cook); Arthur Ridley (Ticket Collector); Alma
Taylor (Box Office Woman); Guy Verney (Footman); Peter Williams
(Police Sergeant); Richard Wordsworth (Ambrose Chappell, Jr.).

Doris Day and James Stewart in The Man Who Knew Too Much
(Paramount, 1956).

        When Alfred Hitchcock's British-made thriller The Man Who
Knew Too Much (1934) was exhibited in the United States, the New
York Herald-Tribune applauded it as "shrewd, ominous and dynamic
melodrama." Twenty-two years later the now American-based
director remade the well-remembered feature, utilizing color,
VistaVision, and the marquee lure of stars James Stewart and
Doris Day. The new edition grossed a respectable $4.1 million in
domestic receipts. Comparing the two works, Hitchcock states,

"Let's say that the first version is the work of a talented amateur and the second was made by a professional."

In the 1956 rendition the story opens in Marrakech, Morocco (instead of St. Moritz, Switzerland as in the original) where an American surgeon (Stewart), his wife (Day) and son (Olson) (in the 1934 production the child was a girl) are on vacation. There they meet a friendly British couple (Miles, de Banzie) and a mysterious Frenchman (Gelin). The latter is stabbed in a market place, and before dying, he tells the surgeon he is a French agent and gives the details of a projected political assassination in London.

The amiable Britishers turn out to be foreign agents who kidnap Olson, causing Stewart and Day to head for London to retrieve their offspring and, if possible, to stop the assassination plot. In a typical Hitchcockian grand finale, the film goes to Albert Hall and a performance of the London Symphony Orchestra. At a strategic point, when cymbals crash, a bullet is to kill a visiting prime minister. The surgeon and his wife, however, thwart the murder scheme and rescue their hostaged son.

Made in the typical verbose Hitchcock manner, the production was called "lavish" and the settings "unusual," by the Saturday Review, while the Nation said Stewart and Day turned in "perfect studio performances." "Que Sera" ("Whatever Will Be, Will Be") sung by Day within the film, and since utilized as her trademark tune, won the Oscar as best song of the year. Largely because of its overblown production values and length (120 minutes), the 1956 version has not held up well over the years.

THE MAN WHO NEVER WAS (20th-Fox, 1956)   C   103 min.

Producer, Andre Hakim; director, Ronald Neame; based on the novel by Ewen Montagu; screenplay, Nigel Balchin; music, Muir Mathieson; camera, Oswald Morris.

Clifton Webb (Lt. Commander Ewen Montagu); Gloria Grahame (Lucy); Robert Flemyng (George Acres); Josephine Griffin (Pam); Stephen Boyd (O'Reilly); Andre Morell (Sir Bernard Spilsbury); Laurence Naismith (Admiral Cross); Geoffrey Keen (General Nye); Michael Hordern (General Coburn); Moultrie Kelsall (The Father); Cyril Cusack (Taxi Driver); Joan Hickson (Landlady); William Russell (Joe); Richard Wattis (Shop Assistant); Allan Cuthbertson (Vice-Admiral); Terence Longden (Larry); Brian Oulton (Lt. Jewell); Ronald Adam (Adams); Miles Malleson (Scientist); and: Gibb McLaughlin, Peter Williams, Michael Brill, John Welsh, Cecily Paget-Bowman, Robert Brown, Everley Gregg, Lloyd Lamble, Gordon Bell, Wolf Frees, Gerhard Puritz, D. A. Clarke-Smith.

In 1943, after the tide-turning African campaigns, the British must persuade the Germans that Greece, not Sicily, is their next battle target. To do so, the body of a purported British major is staged to wash up on the Spanish shoreline, complete with a briefcase containing revealing letters to Generals Alexander and Eisenhower.

Robert Flemyng and Clifton Webb in The Man Who Never Was (20th-
Fox, 1956).

Because this extraordinary caper is based on fact, there is
a strong tinge of reality to the proceedings, but the injected romantic nonsense involving Lucy (Grahame) as the non-existent girlfriend of the bogus corpse and the prissy performance of be-
whiskered Webb as the British Naval Intelligence mastermind, drag
down the film's overall effect. Boyd appears as the Nazi spy from
Dublin posted to England by German Intelligence to verify the spurious major's credentials. The most effective performance is offered
by Kelsall as the father of a man who has just died of pneumonia,
asked to release his son's body for a plot that cannot be revealed.
     The CinemaScope-color feature spawned the shortlived tele-
series (1966) featuring Robert Lansing and Dana Wynters.

THE MANCHURIAN CANDIDATE (UA, 1962) 126 min.

Executive producer, Howard W. Koch; producer, George
Axelrod, John Frankenheimer; director, Frankenheimer; based on
the novel by Richard Condon; screenplay, Axelrod; assistant director,
Joseph Behm; dialog coach, Thom Conroy; art director, Richard
Sylbert, Philip J. Jefferies; set decorator, George R. Nelson;

costumes, Moss Mabry; makeup, Bernard Ponedel, Jack Freeman,
Ron Berkeley; music-music director, David Amram; special effects,
Paul Pollard; camera, Lionel Lindon; editor, Ferris Webster.
    Frank Sinatra (Bennett Marco); Laurence Harvey (Raymond
Shaw); Janet Leigh (Rosie); Angela Lansbury (Raymond's Mother);
Henry Silva (Chunjim); James Gregory (Senator John Iselin);
Leslie Parrish (Jocie Jordan); John McGiver (Senator Thomas
Jordon); Khigh Dhiegh (Yen Lo); James Edwards (Corporal Melvin);
Douglas Henderson (Colonel); Albert Paulsen (Zilkov); Madame
Spivy (Berezovo's Lady Counterpart); Barry Kelley (Secretary of
Defense); Joe Adams (Psychiatrist); Lloyd Corrigan (Mr. Gaines);
Whit Bissell (Medical Officer); Mimi Dillard (Melvin's Wife);
Anton Van Stralen (Officer); John Laurence (Gossfeld); Tom
Lowell (Lembeck); Richard La Pore (Mavole); Nicky Blair (Silvers);
Nick Bolin (Berezovo); William Thourlby (Little); Irving Steinberg
(Freeman); John Francis (Haiken); Robert Riordon (Nominee);
Reggie Nalder (Gomel); Miyoshi Jingu (Miss Gertrude); Anna Shin
(Korean Girl); Bess Flowers (Gomel's Lady Counterpart).

    This film illustrates in a vivid manner the premise that
transforming man into a mindless robot could make him the most
deadly spy-saboteur imaginable.   An intriguing corollary, only
hinted at here, is whether a sophisticated piece of steel machinery
could be devised as a total substitute for a human agent, and
whether THIS maneuverable unit of equipment could or would turn
against its captor-master as did Raymond Shaw (Harvey) in The
Manchurian Candidate.
    American Army sergeant Shaw returns from duty in the
Korean War with a Congressional Medal of Honor.   However, the
alleged deeds of bravery which earned Harvey his citation exist
only in the minds of the sergeant and his platoon, because all of
them had been captured by the Communists, totally brainwashed,
and then returned to the Allied lines, unaware of the triggered
response patterns established within Harvey (which have conditioned
him to kill without memory and hence with no guilt feeling).   Harvey
establishes himself as a journalist and soon is transferred from
his Communist manipulator to his American operative, who turns
out to be his own power hungry mother (Lansbury).   (This diabolical woman has sinister plans of her own, which go above and
beyond her staunch Communist Party affiliations, for she intends
to launch her puppet-like right-wing senator husband (Gregory) into
the White House.)   Meanwhile, Major Bennett Marco (Sinatra)
verifies with other soldiers the nightmarish reality of his own hazy
Korean War memories, leading to an Army investigation and
Sinatra's dogged trailing of Harvey, the latter having already killed
several people.   Sinatra soon pieces together the far-reaching plot
and rushes to a Madison Square Garden presidential rally--hopefully
in time to prevent a national tragedy.
    One review aptly labeled The Manchurian Candidate as a
"pastiche Meet John Doe, Nothing Sacred, and The Maltese Falcon,
with a dash of Dr. Fu Manchu."   Time magazine was of the opinion,
"It tries so hard to be different that it fails to be itself."   But the

majority opinion, including those of its entranced viewers, rated
the John Frankenheimer-directed feature as "an insolent, heartless thriller" (London <u>Sunday Times</u>) and "as perfect a shibboleth
picture as could be imagined" (New York Post).

    Above and beyond the garish, frightening plot, <u>The Man-
churian Candidate</u> benefits from a quartet of startling performances
from players who have never been as good on screen before or
since. Lansbury was Oscar-nominated for her emotionally and
politically castrating mother figure. Almost as effective were
Sinatra as the querulous good guy G. I. , Leigh as the non-sequitor-
spouting chick he meets along the way, and of course, Harvey in
a tightly constrained piece of acting as the dehumanized machina
ex deus.

MARE NOSTRUM [Our Sea] (MGM, 1926)   9, 894 feet

    Producer-director, Rex Ingram; based on the novel by
Vicente Blasco-Ibáñez; adaptation, Willis Goldbeck; production
manager, Joseph C. Boyle; art director, Ben Carre; camera, John
F. Seitz; editor, Grant Whytock.

Antonio Moreno and Alice Terry in <u>Mare Nostrum</u> (MGM, 1926).

Uni Apollon (The Triton); Alex Nova (Don Esteban Ferragut); Kada-Abad-El-Kader (His son, Ulysses); Hughie Mack (Carogal); Alice Terry (Freya Talberg); Antonio Moreno (Ulysses Ferragut); Mlle. Kithnou (His Wife, Dona Cinta); Michael Brantford (Their Son, Esteban); Rosita Ramirez (Their Niece, Pepita); Frederick Mariotti (Toni, the Mate); Madame Paquerette (Dr. Fedelmann); Fernand Mailly (Count Kaledine); Andre von Engelman (Submarine Commander).

Filmed on location in Madrid, Naples, Pompeii, Peastrum, Marseilles, and Monte Carlo, this adaptation of Blasco-Ibañez's novel relates a contemporary spy drama in terms of classic literature. Certainly a very mature film for its day, Mare Nostrum is a sturdy spy film accentuated by excellent photography by John F. Seitz and beautiful Mediterranean location shots.

The storyline follows Captain Ulysses Ferragut (Moreno), the last of a famous Spanish seafaring family, who meets Freya (Terry) a beautiful German spy operating in Pompeii. The captain views her as a living personification of Amphitrite, goddess of the sea, whom he had worshipped as a child. Realizing his love for her, Terry uses Moreno's knowledge of the Mediterranean to help German submarines to fuel. The couple part in Naples where Moreno learns that his son (Brantford) has been killed on a torpedoed liner. He now vows revenge on the Axis, and commits his ship "Mare Nostrum" to the Allied cause. Moreno rejects Terry when he learns of her duplicity, and she is eventually shot by the French as a spy. In the climactic battle, Moreno and his crew destroy a German submarine, but the "Mare Nostrum" is sunk and Moreno dies with it.

Not only was Mare Nostrum a haunting story of love, betrayal, and revenge that pulled few punches, it was also a fine presentation of the Wilhelmstrasse spy system used during World War I. Most importantly, Mare Nostrum emerged as one of the very rare spy dramas that is also a poetic film classic.

MARIE-OCTOBRE (Lopert, 1960) 98 min.

Producer, Lucien Viard; director, Julien Duvivier; based on the novel by Jacques Roberts; screenplay, Duvivier, Roberts; dialog, Henri Jeanson; art director, Georges Wakhevitch; sound, Antoine Archinbaud; music, Jean Yatove; camera, Robert Lifebre; editor, Marthe Poncin.

Danielle Darrieux (Marie-Octobre); Bernard Blier (Julien Simon); Robert Dalban (Leon Blanchet); Paul Frankeur (Lucien Marinval); Jeanne Fusier-Gir (Victorine); Paul Guers (Father Yves le Gueven); Daniel Ivernel (Robert Thibaud); Paul Meurisse (Renaud Picart); Serge Reggiani (Antoine Rougier); Noel Roquevert (Etienne Fandasmme).

What is the fate of (counter) spies after their jobs are done? Do they walk off into the sunset and live happily ever after? Marie-Octobre is one of the few films based on such speculation.

Fourteen years following the end of World War II, Marie-Octobre (Darrieux), an alumna of a French Resistance group, invites surviving members of her unit to a reunion. The guests assemble at her country estate where she announces that she knows now that one of them betrayed their leader to the Nazis, causing his death.

This well-acted but talky film unfolds on a single set, making it a static whodunit; its implications are often buried beneath the verbage.

U.S. television title: Secret Meeting.

THE MASKED MARVEL (Republic, 1943)   12 Chapters

Chapters: (1) The Masked Crusader, (2) Death Takes the Helm, (3) Dive to Doom, (4) Suspense at Midnight, (5) Murder Meter, (6) Exit to Eternity, (7) Doorway to Destruction, (8) Destined to Die, (9) Danger Express, (10) Suicide Sacrifice, (11) The Fatal Mistake, and (12) The Man Behind the Mask.

Associate producer, W. J. O'Sullivan; director, Spencer Bennett; screenplay, Royal Cole, Ronald, Davidson, Basil Dickey, Jesse Duffy, Grant Nelson, George Plympton, Joseph Poland; music, Mort Glickman; special effects, Howard Lyndecker; camera, Reggie Lanning.

William Forrest (Crane); Louise Currie (Alice Hamilton); Johnny Arthur (Sakima); Rod Bacon (Jim Arnold); Richard Clarke (Frank Jeffers); Anthony Warde (Mace); David Bacon (Bob Barton); Bill Healy (Terry Morton); Howard Hickman (Warren Hamilton); Kenneth Harlan (Officer); Thomas Louden (Matthews); Eddie Parker (Meggs); Duke Green (Spike); Dale Van Sickel (Kline); Wendell Niles (Newscaster); Lester Dorr (Reporter).

Far more entertaining than Universal's serials Don Winslow of the Navy (1942) and Don Winslow of the Coast Guards (1943), Alan G. Barbour in Days of Thrills and Adventure (1970) ranks this chapterplay favorably: "The action sequences were first rate, and once again the special effects dazzled the eye."

World War II enemies provided the chief menace and foils for an action-packed serial. Because of the steady stream of sabotage on vital war industries, the World-Wide Insurance Company enlists the help of the Masked Marvel to combat former Japanese envoy Sakima (Arthur) who is suspected of engineering these undercover attacks.

The serial was adapted into a 100-minute television feature, entitled: Captain Mephisto and the Transformation Machine.

MASQUERADE (UA, 1965)   C   102 min.

Producer, Michael Relph; director, Basil Dearden; based on the novel Castle Minerva by Victor Canning; screenplay, Relph,

William Goldman; music, Philip Green; song, Green and Norman
Newell; production designer, Don Ashton; costumes, Beatrice Daw-
son; makeup, Harry Frampton; camera, Otto Heller; editor, John
D. Guthridge.

Cliff Robertson (David Frazer); Jack Hawkins (Colonel
Drexel); Marisa Mell (Sophie); Michel Piccoli (Sarrassin); Bill
Fraser (Dunwoody); Christopher Witty (Prince Jamil); Tutte Lem-
kow (Paviot); Keith Pyott (Gustave); Jose Burgos (El Mono);
Charles Gray (Benson); John Le Mesurier (Sir Robert); Roger Del-
gado (Ahmed Ben Fa'id); Jerold Wells (Brindle); Felix Aylmer
(Henrickson); Denis Bernard (King Ahmed); Ernest Clark (Minister);
David Nettheim (Photographer); Anthony Singleton (His Assistant);
Norman Fisher (Bishop); Eric Blyth (General); James Mossman
(Himself).

Jose Burgos, Michel Piccoli, and Cliff Robertson in Masquerade
(UA, 1965).

This picture was passed over lightly by the public but was
cheered by several seasoned critics. "The chief asset is a mood
of light derision which is admirably sustained" (Gordon Gow, British
Films and Filming). Judith Crist (New York Herald-Tribune)
acknowledged that the final half of Masquerade, in which the satirical
brunt switches from a spy lampoon to a debunking of the lengths to

which people go for greed, had especial merit for exhibiting
"... the courage of its convictions that through brain or brawn or
sheer good luck, crooks can, on occasion, get away with their
crime." Almost a decade after its initial release, cinemaphiles
fondly invoke treasured moments from this production in which
joshing allusions to its cinematic forebears abound and romance
and moralizing never step in the way of the cheeky narrative.

Colonel Drexel (Hawkins) is ordered by the British Foreign
Office to thwart a plot being hatched that would bring to the throne
of Ramaut, a Near East state, powers inimical to British oil in-
terests. Hawkins just happens to remember David Frazer (Robertson), his junior officer in the World War II desert campaigns, and
finds that the unsuccessful adventurer--energetic, but gullible--is
agreeable to flying to Costa Blanca, Spain, to guard the 13-year-
old heir to Ramaut, until the youth comes of age and can officially
sign the British agreement. Meanwhile Hawkins has a change of
heart, having once and for all tired of his spineless superiors, become contemptuous of the mealy-mouthed super patriots, and totally
disgusted by the reptilian types in the British government who crave
only money. On the time-honored theory that if you cannot beat
them, join them, he craftily diverts the government scheme to his
own aggrandisement--and successfully at that!

Mixed into the twisting, recherché plot of this mock thriller,
are a circus filled with vicious clowns, a cobwebby castle, a dis-
integrating suspension bridge over a rocky gorge, a peculiar vul-
ture, the devastating sickie Sophie (Mell), and, of course, the precocious Prince Jamil (Witty). Robertson undergoes perils that
would have exhausted Pearl White, only to find himself odd man
out once again and no match for the unscrupulous, latter day
Lawrence of Arabia, Hawkins.

THE MASTER PLAN (Grand National, 1954)   78 min.

Producer, Charles A. Leeds; director, Hugh Raker; story,
Harold Bratt; adaptation, Donald Bull; screenplay, Raker; art
director, Scott Macgregor; music, De Wolfe; camera, Johnah
Jones; editor, Jim Connock.
Wayne Morris (Major Brent); Tilda Thamar (Helen); Norman
Wooland (Colonel Cleaver); Mary Mackenzie (Miss Gray); Arnold
Bell (General Goulding); Marjorie Stewart (Yvonne); Laurie Main
(Johnny Orwell).

American Morris is dispatched to investigate the leak of
confidential information from the Anglo-American military headquarters. But his superiors overlooked his vulnerability: because
of a wartime injury he is subject to periodic blackouts. As such
he is an easy prey for enemy agents who, via hypnosis, induce
him to photograph military files in his care.
Had the production team sustained credibility in the last
part of this low-budget effort, it might have been an engaging, if
minor, exercise in spydom, exhibiting a seldom detailed wrinkle in
the espionage game.

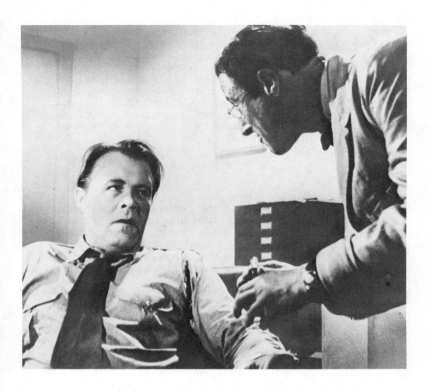

Wayne Morris and Norman Wooland in <u>The Master Plan</u> (Grand
National, 1954).

MASTER SPY (Grand National, 1962)   74 min.

        Producer, Maurice J. Wilson; director, Montgomery Tully;
based on the story <u>They Also Serve</u> by Gerald Anstruther, Paul
White; screenplay, <u>Wilson</u>, Tully; assistant director, David Tring-
ham; art director, Harry White; music, Ken Thorne; music director,
Philip Martell; sound, J. Bramall; camera, Geoffrey Faithfull;
editor, Eric Boyd Perkins.
        Stephen Murray (Boris Turganev); June Thorburn (Leila);
Alan Wheatley (Paul Skelton); John Carson (Richard Colman); John
Brown (John Baxter); Jack Watson (Captain Foster); Ernest Clark
(Dr. Pembury); Peter Gilmore (Tom Masters); Marne Maitland
(Dr. Asafu); Ellen Pollock (Dr. Morrell); Hugh Morton (Sir Gilbert
Saunders); Basil Dignam (Richard Horton); Victor Beaumont (Petrov);
Derek Francis (Police Inspector); Hamilton Dyce (Airport Controller).

On a visit to Britain as a delegate to a scientific conference,
Murray requests and eventually receives political asylum.   The
English officials are not as gullible as first appears, for Murray
has been planted to force feed false information to the Russians via
Wheatley from his new strategic base at Barfield.   Comely assistant Thorbrun, completely in the dark as to Murray's real double
agent nature, stumbles upon the machinations of her boss and
Wheatley, leading to dire consequences narrowly averted.   The
British next have Murray arrested, tried for treason, and sentenced to prison, planning to engineer his escape so that he may
return to the Iron Curtain stronghold and again serve the West.
        The tepid finale robs this modest production of its possible
entertainment bite.

MATA HARI (MGM, 1932)   91 min.

        Director, George Fitzmaurice; screenplay, Benjamin Glazer,
Leo Birinski; dialog, Doris Anderson, Gilbert Emery; sound,
J. K. Brock; camera, William Daniels; editor, Frank Sullivan.
        Greta Garbo (Mata Hari); Ramon Novarro (Lt. Alexis
Rosanoff); Lionel Barrymore (General Serge Shubin); Lewis Stone
(Andriani); C. Henry Gordon (Dubois); Karen Morley (Carlotta);
Alec B. Francis (Caron); Blanche Frederici (Sister Angelica);
Edmund Breese (Warden); Helen Jerome Eddy (Sister Genevieve);
Frank Reicher (The Cook, a Spy); Sarah Padden (Sister Teresa);
Harry Cording (Ivan); Gordon De Main (Aide); Mischa Auer (Exe-
cuted Man); Michael Visaroff (Orderly); Cecil Cunningham (Gambler).

        The legend of Mata Hari (1876-1917, real name Gertrud
Margarete Zelle) has long intrigued filmmakers as a potent movie
subject.   The Germans produced Die Spionin (1921) with Asta Nielsen as the Malaysian dancer; later there was Mata Hari, die Röte
Tanzerin (1927) with Magda Sonja; followed by Mata Hari, the Red
Dancer (Briskin, 1928).   The most famous of the lot, however,
was MGM's well-produced rendition in 1932 starring the prestigious
Greta Garbo.   The George Fitzmaurice-directed feature did nothing
to dispel the growing romanticism surrounding the executed German
spy.   In fact it froze, for a decade or more thereafter, the image
of the operative as a glamourous, quixotic creature.   A disservice
to the spy profession?   Perhaps, but Garbo-Mata Hari was a
cinematic milestone for the genre and set an image that only the
advent of Ian Fleming's James Bond and The Spy Who Came in from
the Cold (Paramount, 1965) truly banished to the realm of historical
set pieces.
        As delineated by aloof Garbo, Mata Hari was a German spy
posing as an exotic dancer in Paris during 1910.   Her major mission was to pass along data on Allied military movements to her

---

[Facing page]   Lewis Stone, Ramon Novarro (second left), and
Greta Garbo in Mata Hari (MGM, 1932).

German superiors.   She encountered a Russian aviator (Novarro),
with whom she had a standard affair, unaware that he possesses the
Soviet messages to the Allies that she must obtain.   Finding out he
has the documents, she spends a diverting night of passion with
him, while her espionage cohorts copy the papers.   Thereafter,
her former lover, General Shubin (Barrymore), who had aided her
many times in the past in exchange for her special favors, learns
of her affair with Novarro (which has proceeded beyond the line
of duty) and he threatens to turn her in as a traitor.   Naturally,
she shoots him. Novarro then returns to Russia where he is shot
down in action and blinded.   Later Garbo is caught and Novarro
is called to testify at her trial.   Rather than allow her blinded
lover to learn the despicable truth of her past, Garbo pleads guilty
and is subsequently shot, taking her punishment in the most stoic,
brave manner imaginable.

This movie is often ridiculed for such famous lines of dialog, as when Novarro says in his accented voice, "What's the
mata, Mata?" Nevertheless, the film was--and still is for some--
an entertaining projection of the average man's romanticized notion
of what the spy game was, or should be, really like.   Although
the film effectively showed the dismal fate awaiting recalcitrant
agents--e.g., the murdering of hesitant German agent Carlotta
(Morley)--filmgoers chose only to remember the dramatically
satisfying martyred finale to the life of Mata Hari.   Within the
film's finale, Garbo has a brief but touching reunion with Novarro
(he is brought to her jail cell, thinking it part of a hospital).
Thereafter the notorious female spy calmly bids farewells to her
nun attendants and bravely walks out to meet her end in front of
the firing squad.

The life and legend of Mata Hari was not put to rest after
the Garbo interpretation, but later served as the basis for such
films as the subdued rendition made with Jeanne Moreau in 1965
France, and as the foundation of a Broadway musical in the late
1960s that never made it to New York.

MATA HARI: AGENT H 21   (Filmel-Films du Carrose/Simar, 1965)
95 min.

Director, Jean Louis Richard; screenplay, François Truffaut,
Richard; music, George Delerue; camera, Michel Kelber; editor,
Kenout Pettier.
Jeanne Moreau (Mata Hari); Jean-Louis Trintignant (Fran-
çois); Frank Villard (Pettetier); Claude Rich (Julien); Marie Du-
bois (Frances); Georges Riquier (Ludovic); and: Albert Remy,
Henri Garlin, Hella Petri.

Recounting the by-now familiar tale of Dutch born Gertrud
Zelle (Moreau) who, billed as Mata Hari, becomes somewhat of a
Parisian sensation with her Malaysian dance act. During World War
I she serves as an effective German spy, only to be eventually
caught by the French military and shot as a traitor.   Coming in

the midst of the James Bond cycle, this entry was a throwback to the old-fashioned spy tale so popular in the 1930s. However, with the very modern screenplay by Truffaut and the economic acting style of Moreau there emerged little relationship between this espionage exercise and the more famous Greta Garbo rendition.

MATA HARI'S DAUGHTER   see   LA FILLE DE MATA-HARI

MATCHLESS   (UA, 1967)   C   104 min.

Executive producer, Dino de Laurentiis; producer, Ermanno Donati, Luigi Carpentieri; director, Alberto Lattuada; story, Donati; screenplay, Lattuada, Mario Pierotti, Luigi Malerba, Jack Pulman; art director, Vincenzo del Prato; set decorator, Gisella Longo; music, Piero Piccioni, Gino Marinuzzi, Jr.; costumes Piero Tosi, Cesare Rovatti, Forquet; sound, Luciano Welisch; special effects, Guy Delecluse; assistant director, Antonio Brandt; camera, Sandro d'Eva; editor, Franco Fraticelli.

Patrick O'Neal (Perry "Matchless" Liston); Ira von Furstenberg (Arabella); Donald Pleasence (Andreanu); Henry Silva (Hank Norris); Nicoletta Machiavelli (Tipsy); Howard St. John (General Shapiro); Sorrell Booke (Colonel Coolpepper); Tiziano Cortini (Hogdon); Andy Ho (O-Chin); Elizabeth Wu (O-Lan); Giulio Donnini (Professor); M. Mishiku (Li-Huang); Jacques Herlin (O-Chin's Doctor); Valery Inkijinoff (Hypnotizer).

"Italian gadget-happy spy spoof" (New York Daily News) not enhanced by either restauranteer-cum-player O'Neal, the majesty of jet set actress von Furstenberg, or by the badly mixed blend of cinematographic elements.

New York Herald-Tribune foreign correspondent Perry "Matchless" Liston (O'Neal) escapes from the clutches of the Red Chinese through a fortuitously acquired magic ring which makes him invisible at will. Once back in the U.S. he joins the American secret service. His first case is to locate master criminal Andreanu (Pleasence), whose closely guarded formula could endanger the world. O'Neal dodges sadistic Hank Norris (Silva), who wants the special ring, and makes his way to London where he joins co-worker Arabella (von Furstenberg). The two insinuate their way into Pleasence's Northumberland castle, steal Pleasence's key to the Frankfurt bank safe containing the formula, and depart for Germany. Their elaborate heist plan works. Later in Hamburg harbor, representatives of the U.S., Russia, and China gather to await the delivery of the formula. However, capricious O'Neal has a sudden change of heart, deciding to dump the formula and the magic ring into the drink.

This film is one of the more absurd and inexcusable examples of the spaghetti spy series, unrelieved by its moments of cynicism (e.g., O'Neal remarks that since half the world is spying on the other half, why not join them) or by such silly humor

Patrick O'Neal, Nicoletta Machiavelli, and Ira von Furstenberg in Matchless (UA, 1967).

as the beautiful spy Wu advising O'Neal, "Call me. I'm in the code book." The film's bottom of the barrel caper occurs in the Frankfurt bank vault scene where O'Neal emerges nude and very much alone.

ME FAIRE ÇA A MOI (Marceau-Cocinor, 1961) 95 min.

Director, Pierre Grimblat; based on the novel by Jean-Michel Sorel; screenplay, Grimblat, Claude de Givray; music, Michel Legrand; settings, Jacques Chalvet; sound, William Sivel; camera, Michel Kelber; editor, Françoise Javet.

Eddie Constantine (Eddie MacAvoy); Bernadette Lafond (Annie); Rita Cadillac (Mercedes); Henri Cogan (Trognon); Jean-Louis Richard (Nonoche); Mick Besson (Titi); Pierre Grasset (Martin).

Newsman Eddie MacAvoy (Constantine) is made a pawn by the Deuxième Bureau, who use him to transport a secret document to Marseilles, hoping this rugged decoy will bring out from hiding the opposing international espionage forces.

"Try to get out of the rules which constrict a genre and you will hear all the heavy thinkers accuse you of conceit. Pierre Grimblat has tried to bring something new to the Constantine image. ... Grimblat has made his character less arbitrary and given us some situations bordering, although timidly, on nonsensical humor.... Me Faire Ça à Moi has the inconvenience of being only a series of sequences without visual or dramatic cohesion, but all these defects can be forgiven if you think of the ending..." (Cinema 61).

THE MIND BENDERS (AIP, 1963)   101 min.

Producer, Michael Relph; director, Basil Dearden; screenplay, James Kennaway; music, Georges Auric; music director, Muir Mathieson; art director, James Mirahan; costumes, Anthony Mendleson; makeup, Harry Frampton; assistant director, Basil Rayburn; sound, Robert T. MacPhee, Gordon K. McCallum; camera, Denys Coop; editor, John D. Guthridge.

Dirk Bogarde (Dr. Henry Longman); Mary Ure (Oonagh Longman); John Clements (Major Hall); Michael Bryant (Dr. Tate); Wendy Craig (Annabelle); Harold Goldblatt (Professor Sharpey); Geoffrey Keen (Calder); Terry Palmer (Norman); Norman Bird (Aubrey); Roger Delgado (Dr. Jean Bonvoulois); Edward Fox (Stewart); Terence Alexander (Coach); Georgine Moon (Persephone); Teresa Von Hoorn (Penny); Timothy Beaton (Paul); Edward Palmer (Porter); Christopher Ellis (Peers); Elizabeth Counsell, Anthony Singleton (Students at Station); Pauline Winter (Mother); Philip Ray (Father); Rene Seton, Ashik Devello (Indian Students); Robin Hawdon (Student in Oxford); Terence Edmond (Student at Party); Ian Dewar (Crowd Ringleader); Saggy (The Dog).

To prove the meaty thesis that man's mind can be twisted by laboratory techniques because the advancements in science now sacrifice human guinea pigs, the filmmakers have decked out their proposition with assorted entertainment overtones. What starts in the best English cinema thriller fashion, shifts to high grade science fiction and then slides into trivial soap opera. In short, The Mind Benders "opens up a little more than it can properly chew in an art sense" (New York Post).

When Professor Sharpey (Goldblatt) suddenly heaves himself under a passing train at Oxford station, a briefcase is found near the body containing £1,000. British agent Major Hall (Clements) investigates the strange circumstances and concludes that the elderly scientist may have been a traitor, passing along military secrets to the enemy. Along comes Goldblatt's young assistant, Dr. Henry Longman (Bogarde) who insists that his late mentor was not guilty of any knowing treason, that he had been engaged in space physiology experiments on the reduction of sensation, and having used himself as a subject, became a "soulless, mindless, will-less thing." To demonstrate his theory, Bogarde voluntarily submits

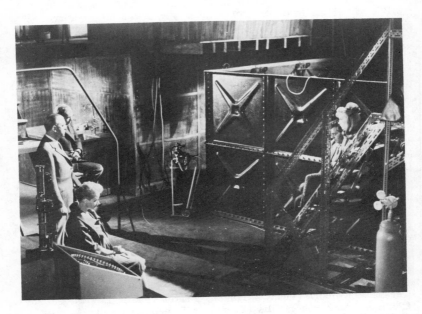

Mary Ure (left), John Clements (rear left), Dirk Bogarde (right), and Wendy Craig in The Mind Benders (AIP, 1963).

to the isolation test. True enough, Bogarde soon passes over the mental brink, becoming a distraught, brainwashed individual alien to his past self. He cavorts with strumpet Annabelle (Craig), abuses his wife (Ure), and seems lost to any recovery until the shock of participating in the emergency delivery of Ure's baby restabilizes his mind.

MINISTRY OF FEAR (Paramount, 1944)   85 min.

Producer, Seton I. Miller; director, Fritz Lang; based on the novel by Graham Greene; screenplay, Miller; art director, Hans Dreier, Hal Periera; set decorator, Bert Granger; music, Victor Young; assistant director, George Templeton; sound, W. C. Smith; camera, Henry Sharp; editor, Archie Marshek.

Ray Milland (Stephen Neale); Marjorie Reynolds (Carla Hilfe); Carl Esmond (Willi Hilfe); Hillary Brooke (Mrs. Bellaire, #1); Percy Waram (Prentice); Dan Duryea (Cost/Travers); Alan Napier (Dr. Forrester); Erskine Sanford (Mr. Rennit); Thomas Louden (Mr. Newland); Aminta Dyne (Mrs. Bellaire, #2); Mary Field (Miss

Penteel); Byron Foulger (Mr. Newby); Lester Mathews (Dr. Morton); Helena Grant (Mrs. Merrick); Grayce Hampton (Lady with Floppy Hat); Ottola Nesmith (Woman at Admission Gate); Connie Leon (Lady Purchaser of Cake); Jessica Newcombe (Cake Booth Lady); Evelyn Beresford (Fat Lady); Frank Dawson (Vicar); Anne Curson (Lady with Children); Harry Allen (Delivery Man); Cyril Delevanti (Railroad Agent); Eric Wilton, Colin Kenny, Boyd Irwin (Scotland Yard Men); Bruce Carruthers (Police Clerk); Frank Leigh, Francis Sayles, Edmond Russell (Men); Arthur Blake (Officer); Edward Fielding (Executive); Wilson Benge (Air Raid Warden); David Clyde (English Bobby); Clive Morgan, George Broughton (Men in Tailor Shop); Olaf Hytten (Tailor Shop Clerk); Hilda Plowright (Maid to Mrs. Bellaire, #2); Leonard Carey (Porter).

Mary Field, Ray Milland, and Byron Foulger in Ministry of Fear (Paramount, 1944).

Based on Graham Greene's taut novel, Paul M. Jensen in The Cinema of Fritz Lang (1969) ranks this film as "a crisp and efficiently made thriller with no pretension to intellectual content ... filled with uncertainty."

Stephen Neale (Milland) is released from the Lembridge Asylum in England after a two-year stay. At a second-rate little carnival he wins a cake which immediately launches him into a complex, nefarious Nazi espionage plot, tied into a heisted microfilm, a homicide, a train wreck, and phoney seances. As Milland

becomes further involved in this mayhem, he and his friend are
led to believe he is still insane.

Although director Lang dismisses this effort ("I saw it
recently on television, where it was cut to pieces, and I fell
asleep"), it is essentially a good psychological thriller--atmos-
pheric, and above all, engrossing to most viewers.

A MISSION FOR MR. DODD   see   VORSICHT, MISTER DODD

MISSION OF DANGER   (MGM, 1959)   C   79 min.

Producer, Adrian Samish; director, George Waggner, Jacques
Tourneur; based on the novel Northwest Passage by Kenneth Roberts;
screenplay, Gerald Drayson Adams; music, Raoul Kraushaar; camera, William Spencer, Harold W. Wellman; editor, Ira Heymann,
Frank Santillo.

Keith Larsen (Major Robert Rogers); Buddy Ebsen (Hank
Marriner); Don Burnett (Langdon Towne); Taina Elg (Spy); Philip
Tonge (General Amherst); and: Alan Hale, Patrick Magnee, Adam
Williams, Sandy Kenyon.

Culled from the "Northwest Passage" teleseries (1957-1959)
this entry displays all the ineptness of that inexpensively mounted
period series, including minuscule sets, banal dialog, and oversimplified characterizations.

In 1759 when the French are threatening to take Quebec,
Americans Major Robert Rogers (Larsen) and Hank Marriner
(Ebsen) set out to kidnap a French general (Tonge) from a forest
fort and obtain needed troop movement information from him.   The
colonial team encounter a lady (Elg) whom they think to be a
French agent, but she turns out to be working for the British and
supplies them with data helpful in the approaching battle of Quebec.

MISSION TO HELL   see   DER SPION, DER IN DIE HOLLE GING

MISSION TO HELL WITH SECRET AGENT X15   see   DER SPION,
DER IN DIE HOLLE GING

MR. MOTO'S LAST WARNING   (20th-Fox, 1939)   71 min.

Producer, Sol M. Wurtel; director, Norman Foster; based
on the character created by John P. Marquand; screenplay, Philip
Macdonald, Foster; camera, Virgil Miller; editor, Norman Colbert.

Peter Lorre (Mr. Moto); Ricardo Cortez (Fabian); Virginia
Field (Connie); John Carradine (Donforth); George Sanders (Eric
Norvel); Joan Carol (Mary Delacour); Robert Coote (Rollo); Mar-
garet Irving (Madame Delacour); Leyland Hodgson (Hawkins); John

Davidson (Hakim); Tera Shimada (Fake Mr. Moto); Georges Renavent (Admiral Delacour); E. E. Clive (Commandant); Holmes Herbert
(Bentham); C. Montague Shaw (First Lord of Admiralty).

By 1939 even middle-of-the-road Hollywood executives decided that open hostility to the Axis powers was a fitting attitude
to be reflected in the studios' products. Thus wily Mr. Moto took
up the allied cause in <u>Mr. Moto's Last Warning</u>. Ironically only a
year later the successful Fox series was halted because of increased anti-Japanese feelings.

In this, the sixth entry in the series, Moto thwarts a scheme
to blow up a detachment of the British Navy entering Port Said.
Hoping to blame the French for the disaster, Axis agents Cortez
and Sanders plan to cause such international tension that war would
be declared.

MR. POTTS GOES TO MOSCOW (AA, 1953) 93 min.

Producer-director, Mario Zampi; story-screenplay, Jack
Davies, Michael Pertwee; music, Stanley Black; camera, Stanley
Pavey; editor, Giulio Zampi.

George Cole (center) in <u>Mr. Potts Goes to Moscow</u> (AA, 1953).

George Cole (George Potts); Oscar Homolka (Zekov); Nadia
Gray (Tania); Frederick Valk (Rakov); Geoffrey Summer (Pike);
Wilfrid Hyde White (Sir Hubert Wells); Ernest Jay (Professor Lay-
ton); Richard Wattis (Barnes); Michael Medwin (Smedley); Frederick
Leister (Prime Minister); Henry Hewitt (Minister of Health); Gibb
McLaughlin (Schoolmaster); Michael Balfour (Sailor); Hal Osmond
(Waiter); Charles Goldner (Gaston); Ronnie Stevens (Aubrey);
Eleanor Summerfield (Cecilia); Irene Handl (Mrs. Tidmarsh);
Phyllis Morris (Mrs. Tweedy); Myrtle Reed (Air Hostess); David
Hurst (Professor Deutsch); Bernard Rebel (Professor Trubiev);
Olaf Pooley (Professor Roblettski); Ronald Adam (Barworth Con-
troller); Edwin Styles (Superintendent); Kynaston Reeves (Director);
and: Walter Horsburgh, Anthony Shaw, Tim Turner, Ina De La
Haye.

      This film represents a male variation of Mrs. 'Arris Goes
to Paris with an espionage angle thrown in for added measure.
Had the direction been livelier the picture would have been much
funnier and the digs at the international bomb race a lot more
effective.
      English sanitary engineer George Potts (Cole) acquires
atomic energy documents when a briefcase mix-up occurs. He
proceeds to Moscow believing that he is carrying the plans for a
new plumbing device and that the Russians, Zakov (Homolka) in
particular, are anxious to make use of his plumbing skills, hence
the Soviets' offer of a yearly stipend, a fully equipped laboratory,
and the run of Russia.
      U. S. television title: Top Secret.

MR. STRINGFELLA SAYS NO (NPFD, 1937)   77 min.

      Producer, Brandon Fleming, Reginald Gottwaltz; director,
Randall Faye; screenplay, Fleming, Faye.
      Neil Hamilton (Jeremy Stringfella); Claude Dampier (Mr.
Piper); Muriel Aked (Mrs. Piper); Kathleen Gibson (Miss Piper);
Marcelle Roget (Marta); Franklin Dyall (Count Hokans); Peter
Gawthorne (Prime Minister).

      This episodic film has clean-cut Hamilton as an American
in England who becomes tangled with a German spy ring.
      Reissue title: Accidental Spy (1948).

MISTER V see PIMPERNEL SMITH

MRS. POLLIFAX--SPY (UA, 1971)   C 110 min.

      Producer, Frederick Brisson; associate producer, Charles

Forsythe; director, Leslie Martinson; based on the novel The Un-
expected Mrs. Pollifax by Dorothy Gilman; screenplay, C. A. Mc-
Knight [pen name for Rosalind Russell]; art director, Jack Polin;
set decorator, William Kuehl; music-music director, Lalo Schifrin;
costumes, Noel Taylor; titles, Don Record; sound, Everett A.
Hughes; technical adviser, Dino Ajeti; camera, Joe Biroc; editor,
Phil Anderson.
     Rosalind Russell (Emily Pollifax); Darren McGavin (Johnny
Farrell); Nehemiah Persoff (General Berisha); Harold Gould
(Colonel Nexdhet); Albert Paulsen (General Perdido); John Beck
(Sergeant Lulash); Dana Elcar (Carstairs); Don Diamond (Bookshop
Proprietor).

Rosalind Russell and Darren McGavin in Mrs. Pollifax--Spy (UA,
1971).

    A very mature Rosalind Russell as a distaff James Bond?
Hardly likely one would think. One of the film's difficulties was
uncertainty about where the fantasy wishing of Russell the scenarist
(under the name of C. A. McKnight) and Russell the 60-year-old
superstar leaves off and the wish-fulfillment of character Emily
Pollifax begins. The stringent production values and the rapid
story deterioration are further deficits that the picture cannot
overcome.
    American matron Mrs. Emily Pollifax (Russell) contacts the

C. I. A. to volunteer her services as a spy, explaining that now she is widowed and her children grown up, she is both eager for the job and very much expendable. Department executive Carstairs (Elcar) suggests that Russell would be useful to pose as a typical tourist and accomplish a hopefully simple assignment in Mexico City. Russell accepts the job with glee. Her prearranged bookshop owner contact seemingly never materializes in Mexico City, but her persistence soon results in her being drugged and taken along with C. I. A. agent Johnny Farrell (McGavin) to a mountain stronghold in Albania. While McGavin, who has injured his leg, remains a despondent prisoner, Russell thrives on their perilous plight, planning to turn the Albanian guards against the Chinese Communist commanders allowing for her and McGavin to escape. Not only do they make good their flight, but Russell discovers among her effects a bit of microfilm that the Chinese Reds had been so very anxious to obtain.

MODESTY BLAISE (20th-Fox, 1966)   C   119 min.

Producer, Joseph Janni; associate producer, Norman Priggen, Michael Birkett; director, Joseph Losey; based on the comic strip created by Peter O'Donnell, Jim Holdaway; screenplay, Evan Jones; assistant director, Gavrik Losey, Claude Watson; production designer, Richard MacDonald; costumes, Bumble Dawson; art director, Jack Shampan; music, John Dankworth; camera, Jack Hildyard; additional camera, Dave Boulton; editor, Reginald Beck.
Monica Vitti (Modesty Blaise); Terence Stamp (Willie Garvin); Dirk Bogarde (Gabriel); Harry Andrews (Sir Gerald Tarrant); Michael Craig (Paul Hagan); Scilla Gabel (Melina); Tina Marquand (Nicole); Clive Revill (McWhirter/The Sheik); Rosella Falk (Mrs. Fothergill); Joe Melia (Crevier); Lex Schoorel (Walter); Silvan (The Great Pacco); Jon Bluming (Hans); Roberto Bisacco (Enrico); Saro Urzi (Basilio); Giuseppe Pagnelli (Friar); Alexander Knox (Minister); Michael Chow (Wang) Marcello Turilli (Strauss); John Karlsen (Oleg); Robin Fox (Doorbell Ringer).

Many theories have been propounded to explain the abysmal failure of Modesty Blaise--an "op-art tangle" (Newsweek)--based on the exceedingly popular comic strip invented in 1962 by Peter O'Donnell for the London Evening Standard. Director Joseph Losey has offered his own rationale: "The picture has been exploited, in my opinion, and in the opinion of many of the people who were involved in it, in a most incredibly wrong way. The audience was told that this was a woman who was 'more dangerous than the male' ... a kind of female James Bond. To exploit it sensationally, vulgarly as something it isn't, obviously gets the wrong audience, and obviously precipitates a certain kind of unthinking critical response. If it's just another one in the series of what I consider these filthy pictures, filthy in their effect, and abominably made and styleless--this, part of their effect and success--then of course it won't work...." (On another occasion, when queried whether

Monica Vitti and Terence Stamp (upright) in <u>Modesty Blaise</u> (20th-Fox, 1966).

<u>Modesty Blaise</u> was indeed a send-off for the James Bond thing,
Losey admitted he had only attended a screening of one James
Bond film and, at that, had left before it was half over.)
  Countering the frequent charge that <u>Modesty Blaise</u> is unsub-
stantial film fare from any critical viewpoint, James Leahy in The
<u>Cinema of Joseph Losey</u> (1967) defends the film as follows: "<u>This</u>
lack of substance is to some extent more apparent than real, the
result of its lack of formal narrative structure; its range of mood,
of effect, of reference, make it a work which grows richer and
more complex on repeated viewings." Yet another observer of this
mod, mock, and often perverse actioner, has said that the real
mystery of <u>Modesty Blaise</u> is to fathom the plot, the inaudible jokes,
the editing, the Dada touches, the gadgetry, and the bizarre decor.

  Superwoman Modesty Blaise (Vitti) has somewhat wearied of
being the "queen of international adventure" with its accompanying
elegance and luxury derived from years of crime. Nevertheless,
she turns an almost willing hand to assist the baffled British government with restabilizing a Middle East crisis, which involves arch
villain Gabriel (Bogarde) and a cache of diamonds. On Vitti's
commando team is Cockney sidekick Willie Garvin (Stamp), and

among their opponents is the ebullient hatchet lady Mrs. Fothergill (Falk) who neatly strangles her almost willing victims between her thighs.

Sandwiched into this maze-like plot are sturdy examples of exotic preciousness, symbolized by elegant sybarite Bogarde, a man who flaunts a white waved wig, pastel parasols, goldfish-laden drinks, and ships that puff multi-colored smoke, and by "hip" but antiseptic Vitti always bounding on camera in a weird new costume. There are also leaden digs at the British establishment, an antique life style staggering in an ambivalent modern world where the enemy can be a camp figure like Bogarde, who shoots down manned government rockets without a wrinkle of conscience but becomes fanatically depressed about tucking into a lobster dinner after recalling that a late, lamented henchman is now at the ocean bottom and may have been the crustacean's own earlier meal.

MOON PILOT (BV, 1962) C 98 min.

Co-producer, Bill Anderson; associate producer, Ron Miller; director, James Neilson; based on the serialized story by Robert Buckner; screenplay, Maurice Tombragel; assistant director, Joseph L. McEveety; music, Paul Smith; songs, Richard M. Sherman and Robert B. Sherman; art director, Carroll Clark, Marvin Aubrey Davis; set decorator, Emile Kuri, William L. Stevens; costumes, Bill Thomas; makeup, Pat McNalley; sound, Robert D. Cook; camera, William Snyder; editor, Cotton Warburston.

Tom Tryon (Captain Richmond Talbot); Brian Keith (Maj. Gen. John Vanneman); Edmond O'Brien (McClosky); Dany Saval (Lyrae); Bob Sweeney (Senator Henry McGuire); Kent Smith (Secretary of the Air Force); Simon Scott (Medical Officer); Bert Remsen (Agent Brown); Sarah Selby (Celia Talbot); Dick Whittinghill (Colonel Briggs); Tommy Kirk (Walter Talbot).

This flippant fantasy from the Walt Disney production mill, while a direct descendant of that studio's goldmine, The Absent-Minded Professor (1961), was actually a message film, containing an unanxious spoof of man's excessive preoccupation with reaching various celestial stopovers before anyone else beats him to it. Interestingly, Moon Pilot grossed far less than the usual Disney family-oriented comedy feature.

When a chimpanzee astronaut returns from a space trip a bit goofy, his human counterparts are naturally reluctant to volunteer as crew of a later voyage. Astronaut Richard Talbot (Tryon) finds himself assigned to the mission and on his three-day leave to visit his mother on the West Coast he encounters foreign-accented Lyrae (Saval), who he is soon convinced is a spy. Federal security agent McClosky (O'Brien) is thrown into the case, and advises Tryon to give Saval a free rein so that she will tip her hand without endangering any of the secrets from McCord Air Force Base. It turns out Saval is actually from the planet Beta Lyrae beyond Andromeda, come to Earth to offer suggestions for

Tom Tryon and Edmond O'Brien in <u>Moon Pilot</u> (Buena Vista, 1962).

the modification of the U.S. space rocket. Instead, she makes a
few alterations of her own, turning Tryon's spacecraft into a honeymoon rocket.

MORITURI [The Saboteur: Code Name Morituri] (20th-Fox, 1965)
116 min.

Producer, Aaron Rosenberg; associate producer, Barney
Rosenzweig; director, Bernhard Wicki; based on the novel by
Werner Jörg Lüdecke; screenplay, Daniel Taradash; music, Jerry
Goldsmith; assistant director, Joseph Silver; art director, Jack
Martin Smith, Herman A. Blumenthal; sound, Garry Harris, David
Rockendorf; camera, Conrad Hall; editor, Silver.
Marlon Brando (Robert Crain); Yul Brynner (Captain Müller);
Janet Margolin (Esther); Trevor Howard (Colonel Statter); Martin
Benrath (Kruse); Hans Christian Blech (Donkeyman); Wally Cox
(Dr. Ambach); Max Haufler (Branner); Rainer Penkert (Milkereit);
William Redfield (Baldwin); Oscar Beregi (Admiral); Martin Brandt
(Nissen); Charles DeVries (Kurz); Carl Esmond (Busch); Martin
Kosleck (Wilke); Norbert Schiller (Steward); Robert Sorrells
(German Crew Member); Rick Traeger (Crew Member); Ivan

Triesault (Lt. Brandt); Henry Hermann-Cattani (Walzenredt); Robert
Kino (Captain Hatsuma); Eric Braeden (Radio Operator); Manfred
Lating (Lutz); Dr. Harold Dyrenforth (Cornelson); Wilhelm Von
Homburg, Paul Baxley, Henry Rowland, Roy Sickner, Gunter
Weishoff, Norbert Siegfried, Heinz Brinkmann, Rick Weber (Crew
Members); Tommy Webb, Marvin Press, Sam Javis, Eugene Dy-
narski, John Logan, Harold Goodwin, David Manley, Gregg Barton,
Hal Bokar, Frank London, James Goodwin, Buck Kartalian, Roy
Jenson, Rusty Wescoatt (Members of U.S. Merchant Marine); Rol-
lin Moriyama (Japanese Tug Pilot); George Takei (Junior Officer);
Gil Stuart, Keith McConnell (Englishman); John Regis (Crewman);
William White (Williams); George Zaima (Executive Officer).

Yul Brynner, William Redfield, and Martin Benrath in Morituri
(20th-Fox, 1965).

This novel, downbeat World War II spy thriller strove to
humanize what had become a stereotyped image of the German
militarist. Unfortunately, director Bernard Wicki, hampered by
severe scripting and post-filming cutting and politicizing, was unable to come to grips with his tenuous subject. Potential filmgoers were so put off by the film's title (translated, "Those who
are about to die") that 20th Century-Fox hastily retagged the picture The Saboteur: Code Name Morituri or just The Saboteur.

Regardless of the marketing ploy, the black and white feature died on the projector. Audiences just were not turned on by the plight of sympathetic Germans in a wartime crisis.

In mid-1942 India, Robert Crain (Brando), an anti-Nazi German demolition engineer who had fled the fatherland, is contacted by a British Intelligent agent (Howard) and urged to pose as a member of the SS. Brando is to board a blockade runner loaded with a strategic cargo of 7000 tons of crude rubber and scuttle the ship before it completes its Tokyo-to-Bordeaux run.

"Why me?" asks the Teutonic-accented Brando.

Howard quickly reminds neutralist Brando that he is in the British protectorate under a forged passport and could be packed back to Germany, stating that "The Gestapo penalties for deserters are somewhat more theatrical than ours." After Brando reluctantly agrees to undertake the assignment, Howard wryly remarks, "In your case I can't say I'm bothered by any moral nausea."

Once aboard the German merchant ship "Ingo," Brando finds his task all the more complex, taking into account that the vessel's Captain Müller (Brynner) has gone sour on the Third Reich, and has taken to drink upon learning that his son was decorated for sinking a hospital ship. Several days out to sea, the "Ingo" picks up survivors from a torpedoed Allied boat, including Jewess Esther (Margolin) who is made a prisoner, but proves of sacrificial use to Brando's sabotage plans.

THE MOST DANGEROUS MAN IN THE WORLD   see   THE CHAIRMAN

MURDER IN THE AIR   (WB, 1940)   55 min.

Director, Lewis Seiler; screenplay, Raymond Schrock; art director, Stanley Fleisher; dialog director, Harry Seymour; camera, Ted McCord; editor, Frank Magee.

Ronald Reagan (Brass Bancroft); John Litel (Saxby); Lya Lys (Hilda Riker); James Stephenson (Joe Garvey); Eddie Foy, Jr. (Gabby Watters); Robert Warwick (Dr. Finchley); Victor Zimmerman (Rumford); William Gould (Admiral Winfield); Kenneth Harlan (Commander Wayne); Frank Wilcox (Hotel Clerk); Owen King (George Hayden); Dick Rich (John Kramer); Charles Brokaw (Otto); Helen Lynd (Dolly); Jeffrey Sayre (Prescott, the Radio Man); Carlyle Moore, Jr. (Sunnyvale Radio Operator); Cliff Clark (Police Chief); Ed Stanley (Congressman Courtney Rico); Selmer Jackson (Captain Riddel); John Hamilton (Hargrave); Alexander Lockwood, Garland Smith (Navigation Officers); Alan Davis (Lt. Bell); Jack Mower (Chemist); Claude Wisberg (Bellboy); John "Skins" Miller (Taxi Driver); Julie Stevens (Nurse); Frank Mayo (Dr. Delby); Paul Panzer (Hans); John Deering (Radio Announcer); Richard Clayton, Paul Phillips (Sailors); David Newell (Man); Lane Chandler (Flagship Radio Officer); Charles Marsh (Sunnyvale Radio Officer); Wedgwood Newell (Admiral); Charles Sherlock (Orderly); Mike

Lally (Operative); Reid Kilpatrick (Radio Operator).

As a follow up to <u>Smashing the Money Ring</u> (1939) Warners pushed out this 55-minute quickie, allegedly distilled from the facts of the Dies Senate Committee hearings then underway. The would-be spy thriller soon got sidetracked in its own minor melodramatics. "In or out of focus, this picture is not worth worrying about" (<u>New York Post</u>).

F.B.I. head Saxby (Litel) assigns agent Brass Bancroft (Reagan) to infiltrate an espionage gang who is known to be planning to steal the Navy's newly-developed inertia projector (a gismo that stops the operation of any sort of engine for miles around). Gabby Watters (Foy) was around for wisecracks and sultry Hilda Riker (Lys) to provide a femme fatale element. The finale had its own element of unintended comedy as the government men aim the in-ertia projector on the fleeing spies.

MURDERERS' ROW (Columbia, 1966) C 108 min.

Producer, Irving Allen; associate producer, Euan Lloyd; director, Henry Levin; based on the novel by Donald Hamilton; screenplay, Herbert Baker; assistant director, Ray Gosnell; art director, Joe Wright; set decorator, George R. Nelson; music, Lalo Schifrin; songs, Tommy Boyce and Bobby Hart; Schifrin and Howard Greenfield; costumes, Moss Mabry; choreography, Miriam Nelson; sound, Charles J. Rice; special effects, Danny Lee; cam-era, Sam Leavitt; editor, Walter Thompson.

Dean Martin (Matt Helm); Ann-Margret (Suzie); Karl Malden (Julian Wall); Camilla Sparv (Coco Duquette); James Gregory (Mac-Donald); Beverly Adams (Lovey Kravezit); Richard Eastham (Dr. Norman Solaris); Tom Reese (Ironhead); Duke Howard (Billy Or-cutt); Jacqueline Fontaine (Singer at Matt Helm's Wake); Ted Hart-ley (Guard); Marcel Hillaire (Captain Devereaux); Corinne Cole (Miss January); Robert Terry (Dr. Rogas); Dino, Desi, and Billy (Themselves).

The second entry in the Matt Helm series features Martin in his regulation Las Vegas slouch as the reluctant espionage super agent who prefers girl-peeping to spying, and tussling with any of his "Slaygirls" to confronting the wiry enemy.

The plot has Big O assigning master villain Julian Wall (Malden) to destroy Washington, D.C., as step one in a new plot to gain world domination. Malden kidnaps scientist Dr. Norman Solaris (Eastham) to force the latter to reveal the secrets of the Helio-Beam, but Martin jogs to the Riviera and back to the States to dispatch Malden and his thugs and save the nation's capital.

<u>Time</u> magazine argued that <u>Murderers' Row</u> "... shouldn't happen to reindeer" but the more favorably disposed <u>Village Voice</u> observed, "Even the sloppiness of the production works in the con-text of casualness Dean Martin has so painstakingly established with his impreciseness and off-timing."

Dean Martin and Camilla Sparv in <u>Murderers' Row</u> (Columbia, 1966).

There was a noticeable pacing letdown in this production.
Martin's supply of wisecracks were not as blue or funny as before,
and "swinger" Ann-Margret (despite a plush discotheque scene) was
no substitute for leading lady Stella Stevens.   Even Malden appeared
noticeably bored with his bad guy role.   The gimmicks were less
extravagant in <u>Murderers' Row</u>, what with simple motorized rafts,
bugged harmonicas, a giant crane, explosive broaches, rocket-launching cigarettes, and this time a delayed-action automatic gun.

MY FAVORITE BLONDE   (Paramount, 1942)   78 min.

Associate producer, Paul Jones; director, Sidney Lanfield;
story, Malvin Frank, Norman Panama; screenplay, Don Hartman,
Frank Butler; art director, Hans Dreier, Robert Usher; camera,
William Mellor; editor, William Shea.
Bob Hope (Larry Haines); Madeleine Carroll (Karen Bentley);
Gale Sondergaard (Mme. Stephanie Runick); George Zucco (Dr.
Hugo Streger); Victor Varconi (Miller); Lionel Royce (Karl); Crane
Whitey (Ulrich); Otto Reichow (Lanz); Charles Cain (Turk O'Flahaty);
Walter Kingsford (Dr. Faber); Erville Alderson (Sheriff); Harry
Hollingsworth (Irish Cop); Richard Elliott (Backstage Doorman);

Dooley Wilson (Porter); Bing Crosby (Man Giving Directions); Milton Parsons (Mortician); Tom Fadden (Tom Douglas); Fred Kelsey (Sam); Edgar Dearing (Joe); Leslie Denison (Elvan); Robert Emmett Keane (Burton); Addison Richards (Herbert Wilson); Matthew Boulton (Colonel Ashmont); Wade Boteler (Conductor); William Forrest (Colonel Raeburn); Carl Alfalfa Switzer (Frederick); Edward Hearn (Train Official); Leyland Hodgson (English Driver); Mary Akin, Jack Luden (Spectators); Ed Peil, Sr., Dick Rush (Cops); Monte Blue, Jack Clifford (Cops at Union Hall); Art Miles (Cop Outside Union Hall); Dick Elliott (Backstage Doorman); Max Wagner (Man with Truck); William Irving (Waiter); Charles R. Moore (Pullman Porter); Dudley Dickerson (Red Cap); Charles McAvoy (Brakeman); Arno Frey (Male Nurse); Lloyd Whitlock (Apartment Manager); George Hickman (Elevator Boy); Joe Recht, Rex Moore, Gerald A. Pierce, Allan Ramsey, Johnny Erickson, David McKim (Newsboys); Frank Mills (New York Taxi Driver); Frank Marlowe, Mike Lally (Chicago Taxi Drivers); Vernon Dent (Ole the Bartender); Sarah Edwards (Mrs. Weatherwax); Paul Scardon (Dr. Higby); Alice Keating, Betty Farrington, Nell Craig (Women); Rose Allen (Outraged Woman); Minerva Urecal (Frozen-Faced Woman); Eddie Dew, George Turner, Kirby Grant, William Cabanne (Pilots).

Madeleine Carroll, Lionel Royce, and Victor Varconi in My Favorite Blonde (Paramount, 1942).

Inaugurating a new title series, Hope was mostly without Crosby (save for a fun cameo bit) in this popular "fast and zigzaggy thriller farce" (New York Times) which returned the pugnacious wit to the world of crooks and newly-turned spies.

The ski-jump nosed comedian was cast as Larry Haines, a down-and-out vaudevillian who takes second billing to his popular stage partner, Percy the Penguin. Hope is accompanying the animal to Hollywood where the latter has a promising film career in the works, but the cross-country trek soon takes second priority to Hope's involvement with blonde British agent Karen Bentley (Carroll), who is smuggling vital information across the continent to a Los Angeles destination. Fearful that the data hidden in a broach will fall into the hands of the pursuing Nazis (Zucco, Royce, Sondergaard), Carroll plays up to vain Hope, luring the cowardly Casanova into chaperoning her to California.

The New York Herald-Tribune found My Favorite Blonde "One of the best screen comedies of the season...." The film is set in pre-Pearl Harbor days with Hope's on-camera reactions to the cloak and dagger derring-do as a reflection of how middle America then felt about the European war. It was standard practice for Hope vehicles to blend farce and slapstick, with sharp repartée usually having the upper edge. Between the wild chases and murder aboard the westbound train, in and about Chicago, and at the Los Angeles air field, Hope and company make monkeys of the Nazis and have ample opportunity to rib the clichéd elements of the espionage genre.

(1) Carroll: "I'm being followed by two men in black!"

Hope: "You're sure they're not two men in white?"

(2) Carroll: "Do you know what it feels like to be watched and hounded every second?"

Hope: "I used to, but now I pay cash for everything."

(3) Later Carroll admits to being a British agent. Hope quips, "Too late sister. I've already got an agent...."

MY FAVORITE BRUNETTE (Paramount, 1947) 88 min.

Producer, Daniel Dare; director, Elliott Nugent; screenplay, Edmund Beloin, Jack Rose; art director, Hans Dreier, Earl Hedrick; song, Jay Livingston and Ray Evans; music director, Robert Emmett Dolan; assistant director, Mel Epstein; special effects, Gordon Jennings; camera, Lionel Lindon; editor, Ellsworth Hoagland.

Bob Hope (Ronnie Jackson); Dorothy Lamour (Carlotta Montay); Peter Lorre (Kismet); Lon Chaney (Willie); John Hoyt (Dr. Lundau); Charles Dingle (Major Simon Montague); Reginald Denny (James Collins); Frank Puglia (Baron Montay); Ann Doran (Miss Rogers); Willard Robertson (Prison Warden); Jack LaRue (Tony); Charles Arnt (Crawford); Garry Owen, Richard Keane (Reporters); Anthony Caruso ("Raft" Character); Matt McHugh ("Cagney"); George Lloyd (Prison Guard--Sergeant); Jack Clifford (Prison Guard--Captain); Ray Teal, Al Hill (State Troopers); Boyd Davis

(Mr. Dawsen); Clarence Muse (Man in Condemned Row); Helena
Evans (Mabel); Roland Soo Hoo (Baby Fong); Jean Wong (Mrs.
Fong); Charley Cooley (Waiter); John Westley (Doctor); Ted Rand
(Waiter Captain); Tom Dillon (Policeman); Harland Tucker (Room
Clerk); Reginald Simpson (Assistant Manager); James Flavin (Mac,
the Detective); Jim Pierce, Budd Fine (Detectives); John Tyrrell
(Bell Captain); Joe Recht (Newsboy); Bing Crosby (Executioner);
Alan Ladd (Detective).

Bob Hope and Dorothy Lamour in My Favorite Brunette (Paramount,
1947).

Made in the typical Hope satirical manner, My Favorite
Brunette was a good take off on the Raymond Chandler/Dashiell
Hammett detective thriller. In it Hope played a bumbling baby
photographer who has aspirations of becoming a famous detective
like a floor-mate (Ladd) in his office building.
    While detective Ladd is away, Hope accidentally assumes

his identity and becomes involved with a pretty damsel (Lamour) who hires him to locate her missing uncle (Puglia) who has been kidnapped after coming to America on a secret mission. The inexperienced sleuth is entrusted with a secret plan for a uranium mine, which is just the item a group of nefarious foreign agents are hellbent to obtain. Going through many perils--and only accidentally getting out of any of them--Hope is convicted of Puglia's murder, only to be vindicated at the last moment, and best of all, to win Lamour's esteem and love.

Breezily directed, My Favorite Brunette was full of stock villains and situations, with Hope dominating the action as the perennially confounded gumshoe. Lorre as a vicious enemy agent and Chaney as his dim-witted assistant offered quite amusing performances in this excellent tongue-in-cheek exercise.

MY FAVORITE SPY (RKO, 1942) 87 min.

Producer, Harold Lloyd; director, Tay Garnett; story, M. Coates Webster; screenplay, Sig Herzig, William Bowers; music, Roy Webb; music arranger, George Duning; music director, C. Bakaleinikoff; songs, Johnny Burke and Jimmy Van Heusen; assistant director, James A. Anderson; camera, Robert De Grasse; editor, Desmond Marquette.

Kay Kyser (Himself); Ellen Drew (Terry Kyser); Jane Wyman (Connie); Robert Armstrong (Harry Robinson); Helen Westley (Aunt Jessie); Ish Kabibble (Ish); William Demarest (Flower Pot Cop); Una O'Connor (Cora the Maid); Lionel Royce (Winters); Moroni Olsen (Major Allen); George Cleveland (Gus); Vaughan Glaser (Col. Moffett); Hobart Cavanaugh (Jules); Teddy Hart (Soldier); Kay Kyser's Band featuring Harry Babbitt, Sully Mason, Dorothy Dunn, Trudy Irwin (Themselves); Edmund Glover (Selvin); Selmer Jackson (Minister); Dorothy Phillips (Bit at Wedding); Hal K. Dawson (Eberle the Hotel Manager); Chester Clute (Higgenbotham); Matt Moore (Desk Sergeant); Charles Williams, Earle Hodgins, Henry Roquemore (Speakers); Sammy Stein, Larry Lawson, Bud Geary, Fred Graham (Marines); Bert Roach (Bit in Park); Barbara Pepper ("B" Girl); Frank Hagney (Bit in Kelly's); Sammy Finn (Dave); Murray Alper (Kay's Driver); Harold Daniels (Madman); Ralph Stanford (Theatre Cop); Ed Deering (Cop -Tag Writing Sergeant); Al Hill (Cooper); Louis Adlon (Lefty); Tony Marrill (Bit in Allen's Office); Harold Kruger (Jail Inmate); Stan Blystone (Turnkey); Vince Barnett (Kay's Driver #2); Carli Elinor (Phillips); Jack Norton (Drunk); Roy Gordon (Major Updyke); William Ruhl (Major Allen's Friend);Walter Reed (Nightclub Patron); John James (Recruit); William Forrest (Captain); Pat Flaherty (Recruit); Bobby Barber (Man in Park); Kit Guard (Henchman).

Since this film was produced by comedian Harold Lloyd it was no accident that bucolic bandleader Kyser was asked to cavort in the style of the bespectacled cinema funnyman. Kyser's mousy imitation was thin and unhep, magnified by a flimsy script full of

Tonio Selwart, Francis L. Sullivan, Mike Mazurki, Bob Hope, and
Marc Lawrence in My Favorite Spy (Paramount, 1951).

tired gags and situations. Worst of all, Kyser and his band were
alloted only two production numbers.

On his wedding day to Terry (Drew), a name mix-up causes
Kyser to be inducted into the Army where he is soon transferred
from recruit instruction detail to the intelligence division. Because
his top secret work involves night duty and cooperating with blonde
agent Connie (Wyman), Drew misunderstands and stalks back home
to mother. By sheer luck Kyser emerges from the ordeal as a
hero by trapping the spies in an abandoned theatre and pinning them
under a stage curtain. At the windup, the baton waver is off on a
belated honeymoon with his duly repentant bride.

MY FAVORITE SPY (Paramount, 1951)   93 min.

Producer, Paul Jones; director, Norman McLeod; story-
adaptation, Edmund Beloin, Lou Breslow; screenplay, Edmund
Hartmann, Jack Sher; additional dialog, Hal Kanter; art director,
Hal Pereira, Roland Anderson; music, Victor Young; camera, Victor
Milner; editor, Frank Bracht.

Bob Hope (Peanuts); Hedy Lamarr (Lili Danielle); Francis
L. Sullivan (Brubaker); Arnold Moss (Tasso); John Archer (Hender-
son); Luis Van Rooten (Hönig); Stephen Chase (Bailey); Morris
Ankrum (General Fraser); Angela Clark (Gypsy Fortune Teller);
Iris Adrian (Lola); Frank Faylen (Newton); Mike Mazurki (Monara);
Marc Lawrence (Ben Ali); Tonio Selwart (Crook); Suzanne Dalbert
(Barefoot Maid); Ralph Smiley (El Sarif); Joseph Vitale, Abdullah
Abbas (Firemen); Nestor Paiva (Fire Chief); Laura Elliott (Maria);
Mary Murphy (Manicurist); Torben Meyer (Headwaiter); Charles
Cooley (Man); Jack Chefe, Rolfe Sedan, Michael A. Cirillo, Dario
Piazza (Waiters); Henry Hope, William C. Quealy (Patrons); Jerry
Lane, Marie Thomas (Cafe Patrons); Michael Ansara, Don Dunning
(House Servants); Norbert Schiller (Dr. Estrallo); Roy Roberts
(Johnson); William Johnstone (Prentice); Jack Pepper, Herrick Her-
rick, Jimmie Dundee, Jerry James, Lee Bennett (FBI Men); Roger
Creed (Photo Double); Peggy Gordon, Suzanne Ridgway, Charlotte
Hunter, Sethma Williams, Patti McKaye (Dancers); Ivan Triesault
(Gunman); Crane Whitley (Willie); Geraldine Knapp (Maid with
Towels); Eugene Borden (Manager); Sue Casey, Dorothy Abbott
(Pretty Girls); Monique Chantal (Denise); Ralph Byrd, George
Lynn (Officials); Sayre Dearing (Dealer in Gambling Room); Jean
DeBriac, Steven Geray (Croupiers); Nancy Duke, Mimi Berry,
Mary Ellen Gleason, Edith Sheets, Leah Waggner, Carolyn Wolfson
(Girls in Gambling Room); Pepe Hern (Bellboy); Alfredo Santos
(Servant); Vyola Vonn (Tara); Lillian Molieri (Girl); Abdullah Abbas
(Egyptian Porter); Henry Mirelez, Tony Mirelez (Shine Boys); Ed
Loredo, Myron Marks (Doormen); Gay Gayle (Flower Girl); Carlos
Conde, Felipe Turich (Porters); Alphonse Martell (Assistant Man-
ager of French Hotel); Alberto Morin (Hotel Employee); Pat Moran
(Little Man); Duke York (Man); Loyal Underwood, Delmar Costello
(Beggars); Rudy Rama (Knife Man); Frank Hagney (Camel Herds-
man); Ralph Montgomery (Grant); Mike Mahoney (Murphy); Michael
Ross, Paul "Tiny" Newlan, Edward Agresti (Tangiers Policemen);
Alvina Temple (Miss Murphy); Fritz Feld (Dress Designer); Roy
Butler (Barber); Jon Tegner (Judo Expert); Bobbie Hail (Tailor);
Charles D. Campbell (Hatter); Helen Chapman (Miss Dieckers);
Joan Whitney (Burlesque Blonde); Howard Negley, Stanley Blystone
(Guards); Billy Engle, Chester Conklin, Hank Man (Comics); Ralph
Sanford (Straight Man); Lyle L. Moraine (Foster).

Having romped through spoofs of various screen genres, Bob
Hope returned to the scene of earlier triumphs (My Favorite Blonde,
They Got Me Covered, etc.) with a new lampoon on the espionage
movie. Douglas McVay in a Focus on Films career study, observed
that My Favorite Spy, in contrast to other middle-years Hope outings,
"proved more lively, mingling farce and wisecracks in proper pro-
portions, with Bob's visual timing for once almost equalling his
vocal...." Not only did this feature boast the comedian in a dual
assignment, but the still lovely Hedy Lamarr was his foil--and a
good one at that.

Because timid burlesque comic Peanuts White (Hope) resembles international spy Eric Augustine (Hope), Peanuts finds

himself entrusted with one million dollars by the U.S. and sent to
Tangiers to purchase an important roll of microfilm.   Once the plot
gets going, Hope charges from each situation to the next one with
his usual abandon, popping off corny, and topical, jokes with tremendous ease.   Although scripters Edmund Hartmann and Jack
Sher loaded this feature with outlandish slapstick, the basic premise
was sound enough for the desired ribbing of the cloak-and-dagger
school of films.   Rotund Sullivan made an excellent master villain.

MY SON JOHN   (Paramount, 1952)   121 min.

    Producer-director-story, Leo McCarey; adaptation, John Lee
Mahin; screenplay, Myles Connolly, McCarey; art director, Hal
Pereira, William Flannery; music, Robert Emmet Dolan; camera,
Henry Stradling; editor, Marvin Coil.
    Helen Hayes (Lucille Jefferson); Van Heflin (Stedman of the
FBI); Robert Walker (John Jefferson); Dean Jagger (Dan Jefferson);
Minor Watson (Dr. Carver); Frank McHugh (Father O'Dowd);
Richard Jaeckel (Chuck Jefferson); James Young (Ben Jefferson);
Nancy Hale, Margaret Wells (Nurses); Todd Karns (Bedford);
Frances Morris (Secretary); Douglas Evans (Government Employee);
Gail Bonney (Jail Matron); Irene Winston (Ruth Carlin); David
Newell (FBI Agent); Erskine Sanford (Professor); Mishka Egan (Man);
David Bond, Eghiche Harout (College Professors); Jimmie Dundee
(Taxi Driver).

    This is one picture Hollywood and most persons involved in
it would prefer to forget.   At the time it received more than its
share of attention because (1) co-star Robert Walker died before
the film was completed, (2) Helen Hayes was making her return to
a major cinema role after more than 17 years, and (3) producer-
director-scenarist Leo McCarey so blatantly overstacked the emo-
tional-logical cards that even the more conservative of the Senator
McCarthy era were not so quietly astounded.   "In effect, McCarey's
picture of how America ought to be is so frightening, so speciously
argued, so full of warnings against intelligent solution of the problem, that it boomerangs upon its own cause and becomes, by mistake, a most vivid demonstration that two wrongs don't make a
right" (Otis L. Guernsey, Jr., in the New York Herald-Tribune).
On the other hand there were responsible people who accepted the
movie's message as gospel.   "It is a film, in fact, that indicates
just what made the United States of America great" (Louisville
Courier-Journal).
    The setting is Anywhere, U.S.A., where wholesome ex-
football players Jaeckel and Young are home visiting their middle-
class parents (grade school teacher Jagger and wife Hayes) before
heading for Korean combat duty.   Hayes is perturbed when her
other son John Jefferson (Walker), a federal agency worker, refuses
to return for the patriotic send-off, and American Legion enthusiast
Jagger is astonished when the overly intellectual Walker does show
up to deliver a commencement address at his alma mater and has

Gail Bonney, Helen Hayes, and Van Heflin in My Son John (Paramount, 1952).

the audacity to smirk at Jagger's "America First" beliefs and to scoff at Jagger's singing of the flag-waving song "Uncle Sammy." Jagger blows his cool and hits Walker with the Bible. When Hayes later finds a key in Walker's trouser pocket which apparently belongs to the apartment of a girl arrested as a Communist spy, Mama immediately concludes he is a Red agent. A hasty trip to Washington to confront her precious son, including a Bible oath swearing session to prove he is a loyal American, does not alter her opinion that F.B.I. man Heflin has the right slant on Walker. Hayes flies into an emotional tizzy and suffers a physical collapse. Walker then has a quick change of heart. Instead of escaping to Lisbon as planned, he decides to confess to the F.B.I., but he is shot by Party members and dies on the steps of the Lincoln

Memorial. A confession he recorded is later played at his college.
In it, Walker admits to being an enemy of America and the servant
of a foreign power, and urges the new graduates to "hold fast to
honor."

THE MYSTERIOUS DOCTOR (WB, 1943)   57 min.

          Director, Ben Stoloff; screenplay, Richard Weil; art director,
Charles Novi; set decorator, Casey Roberts; assistant director,
Wilbur McGaugh; sound, Charles Lang; camera, Henry Sharp;
editor, Clarence Kolster.
          John Loder (Harry Leland); Eleanor Parker (Letty); Bruce
Lester (Lt. Christopher Hilton); Lester Mathews (Dr. Holmes);
Forrester Harvey (Hugh); Matt Willis (Bart Redmond); Art Foster
(Saul Bevan); Clyde Cooke (Herbert); Creighton Hale (Luke);
Phyllis Barry (Ruby); David Clyde (Tom Andrews); Crawford Kent
(Commandant); Stuart Holmes (Peter); Leo White (Headless Man).

Matt Willis and Eleanor Parker in The Mysterious Doctor (WB,
1943).

This tacky programmer is set in the mining district of Kent, England, where the claims of ghosts in the tin mine are pushed aside by the British Army who are intent on obtaining a new flow of the vital metal. The local nitwit, who is blamed for the many production setbacks that occur, is proved finally to be a Nazi loyalist.

THE MYSTERIOUS LADY (MGM, 1928) 83 min.

Director, Fred Niblo; based on the novel Der Krieg im Dunkel ("War in the Dark") by Ludwig Wolff; adaptation-continuity Bess Meredyth; titles Marian Ainslee, Ruth Cummings; assistant director, Harold S. Bucquet; wardrobe, Gilbert Clark; sets, Cedric Gibbons; camera, William Daniels; editor, Margaret Booth.

Greta Garbo (Tania); Conrad Nagel (Karl von Heinersdorff); Gustav von Seyffertitz (General Alexandroff); Albert Pollet (Max); Edward Connelly (Colonel von Raden); Richard Alexander (Aide to the General).

The tattered story was the least credible item of this exotically lensed silent feature which found popular Garbo cast without her standard leading man (John Gilbert) of the day, but still engaged in passionate close-up love scenes, this time with actor Nagel. "None of the actors are able to do much about it save to wander through and hope for something better next time" (New York Times). If the picture had any message, it was that loving and spying just do not mix.

In the days before World War I, mysterious Tania (Garbo) of St. Petersburg conducts a love affair with Austrian captain Karl von Heinersdorff (Nagel) while relieving him of some important state documents. Nagel is later court-martialed and imprisoned for his carelessness, but does escape to pursue Garbo to Russia. There he finds the lovely spy really cares for him. To demonstrate her devotion she realigns herself in accord with Nagel's political loyalties, double-crossing her spy chief General Alexandroff (von Seyffertitz) and passing on documents to Nagel that von Seyffertitz had received from an Austrian traitor. When von Seyffertitz learns of Garbo's deception, she is forced to shoot him. Then the lovers flee Russia and proceed to Austria, first to clear Nagel's name, and then to commence a fresh life.

MYSTERY ISLAND (ATV/ITC, 1967) C 90 min.

Producer, Monty Berman; director, Gordon Flemyng; based on the characters created by John Creasy; screenplay, Terry Nation.

Steve Forrest (John Mannering); and: Sue Lloyd, Derek Newark, John Woodvine, Reginald Marsh.

Adventurer and art dealer John Mannering (Forrest) attempts

to prevent a plot to steal a U.S. spaceship.

This feature was to be part of "The Baron" British teleseries, but was never televised as a segment of the series on
either English or American small screens.

THE NAKED RUNNER (WB, 1967) C 103 min.

Producer, Brad Dexter; director, Sidney J. Furie; based on
the novel by Francis Clifford; continuity, Pat Moon; screenplay,
Stanley Mann; art director, Peter Proud, Bill Alexander; assistant
director, Michael Dryhurst; music, Harry Sukman; orchestrator,
Herbert Spencer; sound, Maurice Askew, Peter Davies; camera,
Otto Heller; editor, Barry Vince.

Frank Sinatra (Sam Laker); Peter Vaughan (Slattery); Dar-
ren Nesbitt (Colonel Hartmann); Nadia Gray (Karen); Toby Robins
(Ruth); Inger Stratton (Anna); Cyril Luckham (Cabinet Minister);
Edward Fox (Ritchie Jackson); J.A.B. Dubin-Behrmann (Joseph);
Michael Newport (Patrick Laker).

Frank Sinatra in The Naked Runner (WB, 1967).

American businessman and widower Sam Laker (Sinatra) resides in London with his 14-year-old son (Newport). Slattery (Vaughan) of British Intelligence, a former Army buddy of Sinatra's, suggests to the marksman American that he would be the perfect hatchet man to liquidate a British spy who has defected to the Communists. Sinatra refuses the commission, but agrees, at least, to deliver a message in Leipzig--where he is to attend the Leipzig Fair with his son--which will aid the underground activities of Karen (Gray), who had befriended Sinatra in World War II. The boy is kidnapped in Leipzig and a Colonel Hartmann (Nesbitt) explains that the child is being held hostage until Sinatra eliminates a particular man in Copenhagen. Sinatra consents, but the would-be victim never appears. Back in Germany, Sinatra is advised that his son has been killed because the mission was not fulfilled. The enraged Sinatra plots his revenge by planning to snipe Nesbitt as he passes along a designated highway mark. The chore completed, he learns that his son is safe, that it was all an elaborate scheme to use him as a pawn. The man in the death car was not Nesbitt, but the defecting spy.

"It's a question of motivation and response" suggests a cold-eyed psychiatrist near the opening of The Naked Runner, referring to the setting-up of Sinatra as a patsy robot executioner. The biggest fallacy of the story is that the viewer is never convinced that all these grandiose measures are necessary to kill an exposed traitor, but are merely a part of the overblown contrivance to thrust a commercial plot into gear. Pauline Kael (The New Republic magazine) termed this boxoffice clinker, "An implausible unconvincing spy story without a single witty idea, and the star's role that of an anxious lifeless mouse."

THE NASTY RABBIT (Fairway-International, 1964) C 85 min.

Producer, Arch Hall (Nicholas Merriwether); director, James Landis; screenplay, Hall, Jim Critchfield; assistant director, David Reed; camera, William Sigmond; editor, Anthony M. Lange.

Mischa Terry (Mischa Lowzoff); Arch Hall, Jr. (Britt Hunter); Melissa Morgan (Cecilia); William Matters (Malcolm McKinley/ Marshall Malouf); Little Jack Little (Maxwell Stoppic); Ray Vegas (Gonzales); John Akana (Colonel Kobayaski); Harold Brizzy (Heinrich Krueger); Sharon Ryker (Jackie); Hal Boker (Gavin); George Morgan (Hubert Jackson); Leslie Kovacs (The Idiot); Pat and Lolly, Vegas, The Archers (Themselves).

A promising premise gone awry. The Russians land a contingent of cowboy-disguised agents on the West Coast with a bacteria-laden rabbit which is to be let loose to destroy America. "... [The production] company which has stressed sex and violence in previous efforts turns to comedy with tragic results" (Variety).

Reissue title: Spies-a-Go-Go.

NATHALIE, AGENT SECRET   see   ATOMIC AGENT

NAZI AGENT   (MGM, 1942)   82 min.

Producer, Irving Asher; director, Jules Dassin; screenplay, Paul Gangelin, John Meehan, Jr.; camera, Harry Stradling; editor, Frank E. Hull.

Conrad Veidt (Otto Becker/Baron Hugh von Detten); Ann Ayars (Kaaren DeRelle); Martin Kosleck (Reicher); Frank Reicher (Fritz); Marc Lawrence (Joe Aiello); Dorothy Tree (Miss Harper); Moroni Olsen (Brenner); Ivan Simpson (Professor Sterling); Sidney Blackmer (Frederick Williams); Pierre Watkin (Grover McHenry); Margaret Bert (Mrs. Dennis); Barbara Bedford (Woman); Mark Daniels, Robert Davis (Cab Drivers); Harry B. Stafford (Elderly Man); Roger Moore (Messenger); Stuart Crawford (Commentator's Voice); Hal Cooke (Clerk); George Noisom (Bellboy); Roland Varno (Bauer); William Tannen (Ludwig, the Chauffeur); William Norton Bailey (Cigar Clerk); Tim Ryan, Walter Byron (Officers); Tom Stevenson (Headwaiter); Christian Rub (Mohr); Hermine Sterler (Mrs. Mohr); Jeff York (Keeler); Jessie Arnold (Landlady); Cliff Danielson (Youth); James Millican (Operator); Philip Van Zandt, George Magrill (Thugs); Joe Yule (Barney); Bernadene Hayes (Rosie); Art Belasco, Charles Sherlock (Detectives); William Post, Jr. (Harry's Voice); Clyde Courtright (Doorman); Polly Bailey (Fat Woman); Joe Gilbert (Sub-Radio Man); Edward Hearn, Jack Daley, Drew Demorest, Wilbur Mack (Reporters); Baldy Cooke (Waiter); Frank Marlowe, Duke York, Ernie Alexander (Sailors); Robert Homans, Russell Simpson (Captains); Ray Teal (Officer Graves); Brick Sullivan (Radio Operator); Roy Barcroft (Chief Petty Officer).

Polished screen miscreant Veidt undertook the dual role gambit in this satisfying movie, which was distinctly superior to the rash of sabotage films deluging the marketplace. "It is a simple, straight-away story, told without noise or flourish..." (New York Times).

Otto Becker (Veidt) is a loyal naturalized American citizen who runs a book shop. His twin brother, Baron Hugh von Detten (Veidt), on the other hand, is a ruthless Nazi party member who serves as German Consul in New York and heads an anti-U.S. sabotage movement. During a quarrel the good brother kills the evil one, adopts his late sibling's identity and sets out to block the fifth columnists' schemes. Veidt's chief accomplice proves to be Ayar, a Nazi agent who fears for her parents' well-being back in the fatherland.

NAZI SPY RING   (Producers Releasing Corp., 1942)   66 min.

Producer, George M. Merrick, Max Alexander; associate producer, Arthur Alexander; director, Albert Herman; story-screenplay, Arthur St. Claire; assistant director, Seymour Roth; music director, Lee Zahler; camera, Eddie Linden; editor, L. R. Brown.

Michael Whalen (Robert Norton); Anne Nagel (Nancy Fielding); William Bakewell (Tom Fielding); Constance Worth (Linda Pavlo); Hans Von Twardowski (Captain Gemmler); Jack Mulhall (James Curtis); George Pembroke (Professor Karl Schmidt); Kenneth Harlan (Brown, FBI Agent); Robert Frazer (John Oliver); Hans Von Morhart (Heinrich); Michael Vallin (Argus); Montague Shaw (Franklyn Prescott); William Costello (Otto); William Yetter (Wolf); Crane Whitley (Ed the FBI Man); George Morrell, Milburn Morante (Waiters); Jack Gardner (Spy with Paper); Ted Adams (Sullivan the Night Guard).

A minor entry from the shoestring P. R. C. film factory, exploiting a war angle with negligible results, unless one counts the unintentional laughs as an asset. "... [I]t fails to create one little bit of suspense, even with all the leering, cruel Nazi faces peeking out of cracked doors at their victims" (New York Daily News).

The Nazis want formula 311, a volatile element that will either intensify the power of gasoline fuel or, if handled incorrectly, blow up everything in the vicinity. As customary, the Axis agents, including Dutch girl Linda Pavlo (Worth), will stop at nothing to achieve their ends. Tom Fielding (Bakewell) is the chemist who can supply the enemy's need and he almost agrees to divulging the formula in order to save his sister (Nagel) and her chemist beau (Whelan).

Also known as Dawn Express.

NEVER LET ME GO (MGM, 1953) 69 min.

Producer, Clarence Brown; director, Delmer Daves; based on the novel Came the Dawn by Roger Bax; screenplay, Roland Miller, George Froeschel; art director, Alfred Junge; music, Hans May; camera, Robert Krasker; editor, Frank Clarke.

Clark Gable (Philip Sutherland); Gene Tierney (Marya Lamarkina); Richard Haydn (Christopher Wellington St. John Denny); Bernard Miles (Joe Brooks); Belita Valentina (Alexandrovna); Kenneth More (Steve Quillan); Karel Stephanek (Commissar); Theodore Bikel (Lieutenant); Anna Valentina (Svetlana Mikhailovna); Frederick Valk (Kuragin); Anton Dolin (Marya's Partner); Peter Illing (N. K. V. D. Man); Robert Henderson (U. S. Ambassador); Stanley Maxted (John Barnes); Meinhart Maur (Lemkov).

In Moscow in 1945, foreign correspondent Gable falls in love with ballet dancer Tierney and they are wed by the American ambassador (Henderson). On their honeymoon the couple meet Britisher Haydn and his Russian wife (Valentina). Thereafter, Haydn is deported from the U. S. S. R. and forced to leave his spouse behind. When the same thing happens to Gable, and diplomatic channels fail

Ann Valentina, Richard Haydn, Gene Tierney, and Clark Gable in
Never Let Me Go (MGM, 1953).

him as they did Haydn, the two purchase a small sailing vessel
and, accompanied by sailor Miles, intend to ferry the wives out of
Russia.   Valentina appears at the rendezvous site on time, but
Tierney has been detained to perform at a hastily ordered ballet
evening in honor of a Russian general.   Gable infiltrates the theatre
security, leaves with Tierney, and after a desperate chase, they
reach safety.

The magic name of Gable was on tap to salvage this highly
implausible adventure.   Gable's character is steeped in the misleading guise of a one-man partisan force, when in reality he is
no more than a latter day Scarlet Pimpernel on a very personal mission.   Tierney's broken English is better than her interpretation of
a ballet dancer.

NICK CARTER CASSE TOUT   see   NICK CARTER VA TOUT
CASSER

NICK CARTER ET LE TREFLE ROUGE   (Columbia, 1965)   85 min.

Director, Jean-Paul Savignac; based on the novel Bombe sur
Table by Claude Rank; screenplay, Savignac, Paul Vechialli; music
Alain Goraguer; camera, Claude Beausoleil; editor, Leila Biro.
Eddie Constantine (Nick Carter); Nicole Courcel (Dora); Jo
Dassin (Jolas); Jeanne Valerie (Cleo); Jacques Herden (Captain);
Jean Ozenne (Professor); and: Marcel Pagliero, Roger Rudel,
Pierre Rousseau, Michel Ruhl, Santesso and Gordon Felio, Graziella
Galvani.

U. S. federal agent Nick Carter (Constantine) goes after the
abductors of rockets loaded with poison gas, which must be recovered at any cost before the gas is set to escape.   A lackluster
entry in the Constantine-Carter series, with the star more inexpres-
sive than usual.

NICK CARTER VA TOUT CASSER [Nick Carter Casse Tout] (Les
Films Fernand Rivers, 1964) 95 min.

Director, Henri Decoin; based on the novel by Jean Marcillac
utilizing the John R. Coryell character; screenplay, Marcillac,
Andre Haguet, Andre Legrand; music, Herrick-Houdi; camera,
Jacques Boutinot.
With: Eddie Constantine (Nick Carter); and: Daphe Dayle,
Paul Frankeur, Vladimir Inkijinoff; Yvonne Monlaur, Charles Bel-
mont.

Nick Carter (Constantine) goes after Chinese spies when they
steal a professor's anti-flight weapon.   The film is livelier than the
usual Nick Carter.
U. S. tv title: License to Kill.

NIGHT PEOPLE   (20th-Fox, 1954)   C   93 min.

Producer-director, Nunnally Johnson; story, Jed Harris,
Thomas Reed; screenplay, Johnson; art director, Hans Kuhnert,
Theo Zwierski; music, Cyril Mockridge; assistant director, Lutz
Hengst; camera, Charles G. Clarke; editor, Dorothy Spencer.
Gregory Peck (Colonel Van Dyke); Broderick Crawford
(Leatherby); Anita Bjork (Hoffy); Rita Gam (Miss Cates); Walter
Abel (Foster); Buddy Ebsen (Sgt. McColloch); Jill Esmond (Frau
Schindler); Casey Adams (Frecerick S. Hobart); Peter Van Eyck
(Petrochine); Marianne Koch (Kathy); Ted Avery (Johnny); Hugh
McDermott (Burns); Paul Carpenter (Colonel Whitby); John Horsley
(Stanways); Lionel Murton (Lakeland); Harold Benedict, Tom Boyd,

T. Schaank, Sgt. Cleary, E. Haffner (Men); Ruth Garcia (Nurse); Peter Beauvais (Driver); A. Faerber (Mr. Schindler); Otto Reichow (Russian Major).

Anita Bjork, Buddy Ebsen, Gregory Peck, and Paul Carpenter in Night People (20th-Fox, 1954).

Ostensibly this Nunnally Johnson production was an elaborate depiction of the shell game as practiced by cold war spies. In practicality it was devised as a facile demonstration of the virtues of the studio's color-CinemaScope process, then still an audience-grabbing novelty. The film's title refers to the belief that the nefarious Russians do all their dirty work after dark.

When the Soviets kidnap a U.S. Army corpsman in Berlin, Lieutenant Colonel Van Dyke (Peck) of counter intelligence must handle the case with dispatch. It seems the Russians are quite willing to trade the nondescript soldier for retired German general Schindler (Faerber) and his English wife (Esmond). (The Reds have a deal to turn the couple over to some SS-type men who want revenge on Faerber for his part in the attempt on the Führer's life in 1944, and on his wife for her past activities as a British spy.) To complicate the delicate situation, the G.I.'s gruff businessman father (Crawford) arrives post haste from Toledo, Ohio, to dictate a few crass terms of his own. Gam is seen as Peck's secretary, with Bjork cast as an ambiguous miss who might just be a double agent.

An unconventional aspect of this very Hollywoodish movie is that the story works itself into a corner, with Peck's ex-pro-football player character finding himself fighting fire with fire-- quite uncharacteristic of the stereotyped forthright disciple of the Free World.

NIGHT TRAIN TO MUNICH   (20th-Fox, 1940)   93 min.

Producer, Edward Black; director, Carol Reed; story, Gordon Wellesley; screenplay, Sydney Gilliat, Frank Launder; art director, Vetchinsky; music director, Louis Levy; camera, Otto Kanturek; editor, R. E. Dearing.

Margaret Lockwood (Anna Bomasch); Rex Harrison (Gus Bennett); Paul Henreid (Karl Marsen); Basil Radford (Charters); Naunton Wayne (Caldicott); James Harcourt (Axel Bomasch); Felix Aylmer (Dr. Fredericks); Wyndham Goldie (Dryton); Roland Culver (Roberts); Eliot Makeham (Schwab); Raymond Huntley (Kampenfeldt); Austin Trevor (Captain Prada); Kenneth Kent (Controller); C. V. France (Admiral Hassinger); Frederick Valk (Gestapo Officer); Morland Graham (Attendant).

This honey of a thriller is one of the outstanding prototypes of the screen spy genre, and, unlike its Hollywood counterparts, is quite free of rancor and exaggeration.

The Nazi invasion of Czechoslovakia is imminent. Axel Bomasch (Harcourt), chief of the Hraska Munition Works and his daughter (Lockwood) are persuaded to leave the country to protect the plant's secrets. On the way Lockwood is captured by the Germans and sent to a concentration camp where she is befriended by Karl Marsen (Henreid). They manage to escape to England and there encounter Gus Bennett (Harrison), a member of a song and dance troupe who is really a British secret service man. Actually, Henreid is Gestapo-linked, a fact which is revealed once Lockwood has led the German to her sought-after father. Harcourt and Lockwood are snatched out of England and taken to Berlin where on threat of Lockwood's being killed, Harcourt agrees to work for the Nazis. Harrison follows in hasty pursuit, infiltrates the inner sanctum of the Third Reich and trails his people aboard the night train to Munich. Everything is righted before the fadeout.

Since the miscreant of this expert spy actioner is known from nearly the start, the focus is on the nip and tuck chase, climaxing in the marvelous cable car shootout, a set piece since imitated many times over (Where Eagles Dare, etc.). The one loophole in the proceedings is the obviousness of Harrison's pose as a Nazi officer which fools his opponents too easily. Caldicott (Wayne) and Charters (Radford), both alumni with Lockwood of the 1938 classic, The Lady Vanishes (q.v.), are on hand again to provide comic relief with their cricket-loving Britisher character- izations.

NO ROSES FOR O. S. S. 117 see PAS DE ROSES POUR O. S. S. 117

NORTH BY NORTHWEST   (MGM, 1959)   C   136 min.

Producer, Alfred Hitchcock; associate producer, Herbert
Coleman; director, Hitchcock; screenplay, Ernest Lehman; music,
Bernard Herrmann; assistant director, Robert Saunders; art director,
William A. Horning, Merrill Pye; set decorator, Robert Boyle,
Henry Grace, Frank McKelvey; sound, Frank Milton; title designer,
Saul Bass; special camera effects, A. Arnold Gillespie, Lee Le
Blanc; camera, Robert Burks; editor, George Tomasini.

Cary Grant (Roger Thornhill); Eva Marie Saint (Eve Kendall);
James Mason (Phillip Vandamm); Jessie Royce Landis (Clara Thorn-
hill); Leo G. Carroll (Professor); Philip Ober (Lester Townsend);
Josephine Hutchinson (Handsome Woman); Martin Landau (Leonard);
Adam Williams (Valerian); Edward Platt (Victor Larrabee); Robert
Ellenstein (Licht); Les Tremayne (Auctioneer); Philip Coolidge
(Dr. Cross); Patrick McVey, Ken Lynch (Chicago Policemen);
Edward Binns (Captain Junket); John Beradino (Sgt. Emile Klinger);
Nora Marlowe (Anna, the Housekeeper); Doreen Lang (Maggie);
Alexander Lockwood (Judge Anson B. Flynn); Stanley Adams (Lt.
Harding); Lawrence Dobkin (Cartoonist); Harvey Stephens (Stock
Broker); Walter Coy (Reporter); Madge Kennedy (Housewife);
Tommy Farrell (Elevator Starter); Jimmy Cross, Baynes Barron
(Taxi Drivers); Harry Seymour (Captain of Waiters); Frank Wilcox
(Weltner); Robert Shayne (Larry Wade); Carleton Young (Fanning
Nelson); Ralph Reed (Bellboy); Paul Genge (Lt. Hagerman); Robert
B. Williams (Patrolman Waggonner at Glen Cove); Maudie Prickett
(Elsie, the Maid); James McCallion (Valet); Sally Fraser, Maura
McGiveney, Susan Whitney (Girl Attendants); Doris Singh (Indian
Girl); Ned Glass (Ticket Agent); Howard Negley (Conductor);
Jesslyn Fax (Woman); Jack Daly (Steward); Tol Avery, Tom Green-
way (Detectives); Ernest Anderson (Porter); Malcolm Atterbury (Man
on Road); Andy Albin (Farmer); Carl Milletaire (Clerk); Olan Soule
(Assistant Auctioneer); Helen Spring (Woman at Auction); Patricia
Cutts, Lucile Curtis, Sid Kane, Hugh Pryor, Charles Postal, Anne
Anderson (Bits); John Damler, Len Hendry (Police Lieutenants);
Sara Berner (Telephone Operator); Bobby Johnson (Waiter); Taggart
Casey (Man with Razor); Bill Catching (Attendant); Dale Van Sickel
(Ranger); Frank Marlowe (Dakota Cab Driver); Harry Strang (Assist-
ant Conductor); Alfred Hitchcock (Man Who Misses Bus).

By the late 1950s there did not seem to be much new cine-
matically to say on the subject of flight and pursuit and mistaken
identity within the context of a screen spy caper. But director
Alfred Hitchcock guided Ernest Lehman's wild tale of a 2000-mile
chase across the northern tier of the U. S. A. into a delectable concoction of thrills, Freudian fantasies, and tomfoolery, that garnered
$6. 31 million in distributors' domestic rentals. In defending the
virtues of the frivolous North by Northwest as a polished exercise,
Robin Wood in Hitchcock's Films (1969) observed, "A light entertain-

Robert Ellenstein, Cary Grant, and Adam Williams in North by Northwest (MGM, 1959).

ment can have depth, subtlety, finesse; it can embody mature moral values; indeed, it seems to me that it must. "

    Debonair Manhattan advertising executive and two time divorcé Roger Thornhill (Grant) is mistaken by an enemy espionage group for George Kaplan, a man who not only does not exist but is essentially a diversion dreamed up by the U.S. Central Intelligence Agency to throw the foreign spy ring headed by Phillip Vandamm (Mason) off the track. A series of fantastic events, including a murder at the United Nations, puts Grant in such a precarious position with the law and the killers that he cannot turn to any established authority for aid. Before long he is heading westward on the Twentieth Century Limited where he becomes involved with the spies' seeming accomplice Eve Kendall (Saint). She later turns out to be a C.I.A. worker. Grant is very nearly eliminated by machine gun sprays from a crop dusting plane and thereafter battles the villains scampering on and about the massive presidential stone faces of Mt. Rushmore.

NORTHERN PURSUIT (WB, 1943)   94 min.

Producer, Jack Chertok; director, Raoul Walsh; based on the story Five Thousand Trojan Horses by Leslie T. White; screenplay, Frank Gruber, Alvah Bessie; dialog director, Hugh Cummings; art director, Leo K. Kuter; set decorator, Casey Roberts; gowns, Leah Rhodes; makeup, Perc Westmore; assistant director, James McMahon; technical advisor, Bruce Carruthers; sound, Stanley Jones; special effects, E. Roy Davidson; camera, Sid Hickox; editor, Jack Killifer.

Errol Flynn (Steve Wagner); Julie Bishop (Laura McBain); Helmut Dantine (von Keller); John Ridgely (Jim Austin); Gene Lockhart (Ernst); Tom Tully (Inspector Barnett); Bernard Nedell (Dagor); Warren Douglas (Sergeant); Monte Blue (Jean); Alec Craig (Angus McBain); Tom Fadden (Hobby); Carl Harbaugh (Radio Operator); Glen Cavender (Workman); Fred Kelsey (Conductor); Herbert Heywood (Farmer); Ben Erway (Immigration Officer); Robert Ashley, Robert Dayne, John Lannon, Jr., Cliff Storey, Eddie Searles (German Ski Troopers); Arno Frey (Submarine Captain); J. Pat Moriarity (Recruiting Sergeant); John Alvin (Orderly); Martin Noble (German Cook); John Forsythe, Robert Kent (Soldiers); Sam Waagenaar (German Assistant Cook); Richard Allord (Preisser); Clay Martin, Bob Gary (Nazi Soldiers); Hugh Prosser (Corporal); Milton Kibbee, George Kirby (Hotel Clerks); Russell Hicks (Chief Inspector); Charles Marsh (Man in Camel's Hair Coat); Arthur Gould-Porter (Little Man on Train); Wallis Clark (Judge); James Farley (Turnkey); Ken Christy (Warden); Paul Irving (Lawyer); George Sherwood (Ticket Seller); Bill Kennedy (Mountie); Richard Allen (Heinzmann); George Lynn (Johnson, the Mountie); Rose Higgins (Alice, Wife of the Mayor); Guy Kingsford (Campbell, the Mountie); James Millican (Army Driver); Joe Herrera, Jay Silverheels, George Urchel (Indians); Joseph Haworth, Jimmy Dugan (Mounties); John Royce (German Aviator).

Canadian Mountie Steve Wagner (Flynn), whose parents were German-born, pretends to defect from the Mounties in order to insinuate himself with a known Nazi saboteur ring. He agrees to guide members of this ring to their predetermined rendezvous spot in the Hudson Bay area. Although Flynn's change of loyalties seems logical to most people, including Nazi contact Ernst (Lockhart), the saboteur leader von Keller (Dantine) insists that Flynn's fiancée (Bishop) serve as hostage on the perilous trek. As anticipated, Flynn must battle the odds at the climax to prevent the Nazis' flight via a waiting bomber plane and save his fiancée at the same time.

Northern Pursuit, like Flynn's Desperate Journey (1942), had many similarities to the trend-setting British-made The Invaders (1942) which had effectively explored the somewhat fantastic but still plausible concept of Nazis disembarking and prowling about Canada. Unfortunately, Northern Pursuit remains a rather paltry product from the Warner Bros. economy production mill.

NOTORIOUS (RKO, 1946) 103 min.

Producer, Alfred Hitchcock; assistant producer, Barbara Keon; director, Hitchcock; screenplay, Ben Hecht; art director, Albert D. D'Agostino, Carroll Clark; set decorator, Darrell Silvera, Claude Carpenter; music, Roy Webb; music director, C. Bakaleinikoff; orchestrator, Gil Grau; gowns, Edith Head; special effects, Vernon L. Walker; assistant director, William Dorfman; sound, John E. Tribby, Terry Kellum; camera, Ted Tetzlaff; editor, Theron Warth.

Reinhold Schunzel and Ingrid Bergman in Notorious (RKO, 1946).

Cary Grant (Devlin); Ingrid Bergman (Alicia Huberman);
Claude Rains (Alexander Sebastian); Louis Calhern (Paul Prescott);
Madame Konstantin (Mme. Sebastian); Reinhold Schunzel ("Dr.
Anderson"); Moroni Olsen (Walter Beardsley); Ivan Triesault (Eric
Mathis); Alex Minotis (Joseph); Wally Brown (Mr. Hopkins); Gavin
Gordon (Ernest Weylin); Sir Charles Mendl (Commodore); Ricardo
Costa (Hupka); Fay Baker (Ethel); Antonio Moreno (Senor Ortiza);
Frederich Ledebur (Knerr); Luis Serrano (Dr. Silva); William
Gordon (Adams); Charles D. Brown (Judge); Ramon Nomar (Dr.
Silva); Peter Von Zerneck (Rossner); Fred Nurney (Huberman);
Herbert Wyndham (Mr. Cook); Aileen Carlyle (Woman at Party);
Harry Hayden (Defense Council); Dink Trout (Court Clerk); Howard
Negley, Frank Marlowe, George Lynn (Photographers); Warren
Jackson (District Attorney); Howard Mitchell (Bailiff); Sandra
Morgan, Lillian West, Leota Lorraine, Beulah Christian, Almeda
Fowler (Women); Garry Owen (Motorcycle Cop); Patricia Smart
(Mrs. Jackson); Candido Bonsato, Ted Kelly (Waiters); Tina
Menard (Maid); Richard Clark, Frank McDonald (Men); Alfredo
De Sa (Ribero); John Vosper, Eddie Bruce, Don Kerr, Ben Erway,
Emmett Vogan, Paul Bryan, Alan Ward, James Logan (Reporters);
Bea Benadaret, Virginia Gregg, Bernice Barrett (File Clerk);
Frank Wilcox (F. B. I. Man).

It is no accident that Ben Hecht's punchy screenplay and
Alfred Hitchcock's fluid direction in this film provide the onlooker
with no clear-cut heroes or villains.   After all, the impolite title
of this set piece refers to Alicia Huberman (Bergman) the heroine.
The nominal hero is U. S. government agent Devlin (Grant), who
professes love for the discredited girl but is still capable of sending
her to wed and bed another man in order to obtain data on the
enemy.   In addition the so-called enemy--represented by Alexander
Sebastian (Rains)--emerges rather sympathetically, as he is portrayed as an understandably pressured pawn between his dominating,
Nazi-oriented mother (Konstantin) and the ring of Third Reich spies.
Hitchcock has been equally acrobatic in preventing Notorious from
falling into any definable screen story category.   The film is both a
pulsating blend of spy and romantic elements as well as a study of
a frightened villain (Rains), who essentially would like to be a
decent chap, but most of all wants to save his own precious neck.
Albert J. LaValley, in his introduction to Focus on Hitchcock (1972),
labels Notorious, "a subjective adventure into morbid eroticism and
primitive fears" that is "quite successful" on those multi levels.
Notorious opens in the spring of 1946 in Miami, Florida,
where Bergman finds herself at loose ends and with a sullied reputation because her father has been convicted as a German spy.   She
meets Grant of the American secret service and they quickly fall in
love.   The scene then shifts to Rio de Janeiro where Grant is
undertaking a dangerous assignment to dig out the facts about a
rumored project being instituted by Rains, a friend of Bergman's
father, and his "ex-" Nazi collaborators.   Partly because Bergman
believes Grant no longer loves her, and partly to demonstrate that
she is a loyal American, Bergman succumbs to Rains' importunings

that she wed him, convinced that by so doing she can learn the truth of Rains' sinister activities. At a celebration party for her marriage, Bergman hands Grant a key to the wine cellar, where he finds samples of uranium ore in shelved bottles. Rains soon grasps the nasty truth about Bergman but dares not kill her openly for fear that his colleagues will take reprisal for his carelessness. Thus Rains and his determined mother slowly poison Bergman, the latter unable to get word of her plight to Grant. At the crucial moment, however, Grant enters the mansion and leads Bergman to safety, leaving Rains to suffer the deadly consequences from his teammates.

NOW IT CAN BE TOLD see THE SECRET DOOR

NURSE EDITH CAVELL (RKO, 1939) 95 min.

Producer, Herbert Wilcox; associate producer, Merrill G. White; director, Wilcox; based on the novel Dawn by Captain Reginald Berkeley; screenplay, Michael Hogan; art director, L. P. Williams; music director, Anthony Collins; special effects, Vernon L. Walker; montage, Douglas Travers; camera, F. A. Young, Joseph H. August; editor, Elmo Williams.

Anna Neagle (Edith Cavell); Edna Mae Oliver (Countess Maron); George Sanders (Captain Heinrichs); May Robson (Mme. Rappard); Zasu Pitts (Mme. Moulin); Sophie Stewart (Miss Watkins); H. B. Warner (Robson); Rex Downing (François Rappard); James Butler (Jean Rappard); Halliwell Hobbes (British Chaplin); Gustav von Seyffertitz (President of Trial Court); Lucien Prival (Lieutenant Schmidt); Rudolph Amendt (Lieutenant Schultz); Bert Roach (George Moulin); Lionel Royce (General Von Erhardt); Will Kaufman (Baron von Wese); Ernest Deutsch (Dr. Schroeder); Frank Reicher (Baron von Bissing); Robert Coote (Bungey); Egon Brecher (Dr. Gunther); Gilbert Emery (Brand Whittlock); Fritz Leiber (Sadi Kirscher); Mary Howard (American Nurse); Richard Dean (Airman Wilson); Martin Kosleck (Pierre); Joseph de Stefani (Manager); Henry Victor (Jaubec); Gui Ignon (Cobbler).

The foreword to this starkly slanted feature states "It is propaganda against WAR, with the pain and suffering visited upon all who are so unfortunate as to come in the way of its destructive forces." To the credit of producer-director Herbert Wilcox, whose 1928 silent rendition of the same story (Dawn, with Sybil Thorndyke) had failed at the roaring '20s boxoffice, Nurse Edith Cavell tried to be objective without sacrificing its inherent poignancy. Variety cautioned that the film was "... historical narrative rather than film entertainment." After a lofty Radio City Music Hall opening, the movie did respectable business around the country, bolstered by the pertinence of the subject matter in the days advancing toward World War II.

In German-occupied Brussels during 1914, Edith Cavell

(Neagle) is head matron at the Berkendale Medical Institute. After aiding her cook's soldier son to escape to neutral frontiers, Neagle finds there are many other hunted Allied servicemen requiring similar assistance. She willingly supplies all the help she can with the able cooperation of a Belgian countess (Oliver). Eventually German Captain Heinrichs (Sanders) apprehends Neagle in the act of treason ("having led recruits to the enemy") and she is sentenced to death. Despite the protests of the U. S. Ambassador (Emery), she is shot by a firing squad on October 12, 1915. Nagel's last words are, "But this I would say, standing before God and eternity. I realize that patriotism isn't enough, I must have no hatred or bitterness towards any one. "

This film represents a remarkable contrast to the stereotyped femme fatale type movie spy tale. It is noteworthy that Nurse Edith Cavell won widespread public endorsement for its relative restraint.

ODETTE (British Lion, 1950/UA, 1951) 123 min.

Producer-director, Herbert Wilcox; based on the book by Jurard Fickell; screenplay, Warren Chetham-Strode; art director, William A. Andrews; sound, Peter Handford; music, Anthony Collins; camera, Max Greene; editor, W. Lewthwaite.

Anna Neagle (Odette); Trevor Howard (Captain Peter Churchill); Marius Goring (Henri); Peter Ustinov (Arnaud); Bernard Lee (Jack); Maurice Buckmaster (Colonel Buckmaster); Marie Burke (Mme. Gliere); Gilles Quiant (Jacques); Guyri Wagner (Interrogator); Wolf Frees (Mayor); Frederick Wendhousen (Colonel); Alfred Schieske (Commandant); Marianne Waller (S. S. Wardress); Catherine Paul (Mother Superior); John Hunter (American Officer); Campbell Gray (Paul); Derrick Penley (Jules).

This English-mounted feature was a letdown from the heights of Nurse Edith Cavell (1939) and the lesser Yellow Canary (1943) turned out by the British team of producer-director Herbert Wilcox and his star-wife Anna Neagle. It was dismissed as "random in construction and obscure in some of its meaning" (New York Times). It had originally been considered as a starring vehicle for Michele Morgan, and was later rejected also by Ingrid Bergman.

Based on the true wartime experiences of Odette Sansom Churchill, the film recounts in too majestic a manner the lady's efforts as a British agent in World War II occupied France. She is caught in 1943 and for the remaining years of the war is imprisoned, tortured, and later shipped to Ravensbruck concentration camp where she is just about to be executed when the Americans arrive on the scene. Howard was cast as Captain Peter Churchill,

[Facing page] Anna Neagle, Hans Schumm, Egon Brecher, and George Sanders in Nurse Edith Cavell (RKO, 1939).

Trevor Howard (second left), Anna Neagle, and Marius Goring (second right) in <u>Odette</u> (British Lion, 1950/UA, 1951).

Winston Churchill's nephew--Neagle's underground superior and later her spouse. Ustinov was seen as Howard's radio operator assistant, later killed by the Germans. Colonel Maurice Buckmaster re-enacted his real life role of the British Intelligence unit's London head.

The major fault with <u>Odette</u> is that throughout the picture Neagle remains ever the genteel English lady, never once submerging her accent, manners, or costumes into the métier of her Gallic base of operation, making her a pretty punk secret agent. (Not that the performance of Goring as the German agent who sported dark glasses and smoked with great flourishes was much more subtle.) In contrast to the controlled viciousness of Nazi interrogator Wagner, Neagle's Odette emerged as just too noble in the prison-torture scenes, despite the fact that the picture was recounting the harrowing reality of agent Odette who never revealed any information to Gestapo, in spite of the pain inflicted upon her.

ON HER MAJESTY'S SECRET SERVICE (UA, 1969) C 140 min.

Producer, Harry Saltzman, Albert R. Broccoli; associate producer, Stanley Sopel; director, Peter Hunt; based on the novel

by Ian Fleming; screenplay, Richard Maibaum; additional dialog,
Simon Raven; production designer, Syd Cain; assistant director,
Frank Ernst; art director, Bob Laing; wardrobe designer, Mar-
jorie Cornelius; set decorator, Peter Lamont; makeup, Paul
Robiger, Basil Newell; stock car sequence director, Anthony
Square; music, John Barry; title song, Barry and Hal David; main
titles designer, Maurice Binder; sound, John Mitchell, Gordon Mc-
Callum; ski camera, Willy Bogner, Jr., Alex Barbey; aerial
camera, John Jordan; stunt arranger, George Leech; special
effects, John Stears; camera, Michael Reed; editor, John Glen.

George Lazenby (James Bond); Diana Rigg (Tracy); Telly
Savalas (Ernst Stavro Blofeld); Ilse Steppat (Irma Bunt); Gabriele
Ferzetti (Marc Ange Draco); Yuri Borienko (Grunther); Bernard
Horsfall (Campbell); George Baker (Sir Hilary Bray); Bernard Lee
(M); Lois Maxwell (Miss Moneypenny); Desmond Llewelyn (Q);
Angela Scoular (Ruby); Catherine Von Schell (Nancy); Dani Sheridan
(American Girl); Julie Ege (Scandinavian Girl); Joanna Lumley

Diana Rigg and George Lazenby in On Her Majesty's Secret Service
(UA, 1969).

(English Girl); Mona Chong (Chinese Girl); Anoushka Hempel
(Australian Girl); Ingrid Black (German Girl); Jenny Hanley
(Italian Girl); Zara (Indian Girl); Sylvana Henriques (Jamaican Girl);
Helena Ronee (Israeli Girl); Geoffrey Cheshire (Toussaint); Irvin
Allen (Che Che); Terry Mountain (Raphael); James Bree (Gumpold);
Virginia North (Olympe); Brian Worth (Manuel); Norman McGlen
(Janitor); Dudley Jones (Hall Porter); John Crewdson (Draco's Heli-
copter Pilot); Josef Vasa (Piz Gloria Receptionist); Les Crawford
(Felsen); George Cooper (Braun); Reg Harding (Blofeld's Driver);
Richard Graydon (Draco's Driver); Bill Morgan (Klett); Bessie
Love, Elliott Sullivan (American Guests); Steve Plytas (Greek Ty-
coon); Robert Rietty (Chef de Jeu).

After a two-year hiatus, James Bond returned to the screen,
with Australian newcomer George Lazenby substituting as a stream-
lined model for recalcitrant actor Sean Connery, and ex-film editor
Peter Hunt directing the intricate proceedings. "This never happened to the other fellow," states Lazenby's perplexed 007 at the
conclusion of the film's standard pre-credit action sequence, and
right he is, for in On Her Majesty's Secret Service, "an attempt,
repeated and strenuous is made to substitute quantities of violence
for quality" (New York Post).

To insure that 007 (Lazenby) will continue to romance and
even perhaps marry his willful jet-set daughter (Rigg), international
rackateer Marc Ange Draco (Ferzetti) offers as a dowry the latest
data on the whereabouts of S. P. E. C. T. R. E.'s Ernst Stavros Blofeld
(Savalas), the arch fiend Lazenby has been trailing for many months.
Lazenby learns that Savalas is anxious to have the title of Count of
the Blofeld family acknowledged by the Royal College of Arms in London. Therefore 007 impersonates the College's director and arrives
at Savalas' stronghold, situated atop Piz Gloria at Lauterbrunne,
Switzerland. Savalas' cover is his Institute of Physiological Research, where, according to the madman's chief henchwoman Irma
Bunt (Steppat), Savalas is the leading authority on allergy cures.
In reality, Savalas is planning to bluff the United Nations into
granting him amnesty and power by threatening bacteriological
destruction of animal and plant life (through his entourage of
specially hypnotized patients--each the daughter of a world leader
and each carrying a deadly disease bomb). Through a series of
spectacular, extended ski slope chases, Lazenby escapes the citadel, rushing to bring back a squad of Ferzetti's men to rescue
Rigg and foil Savalas' latest scheme by exploding the mountain
fortress. But Savalas manages to escape on a bobsled with Lazenby in hot pursuit. Does S. P. E. C. T. R. E.'s number one man die
in the subsequent sled crack-up, and what fate awaits Lazenby
after his marriage to cuddlesome Rigg? These cliffhanging questions are answered in a tacked-on ending that disturbed a great
segment of Bondian enthusiasts.

On Her Majesty's Secret Service followed the Ian Fleming
book original rather closely, eschewing to a great extent the usual
Bond gimmickry and stupendous sets. However, there were too
many deficit ingredients in the picture. For all his macabre

plotting, the bullet-headed, sado-masochistic Savalas was too normal
a figure to give the contest the dimension it required, and no matter how determinedly Lazenby tried, he was unacceptable as a worthy
successor to the much-missed Connery. In contrast, Rigg was an
excellent female foil and a decided virtue to the acting side of the
film. In the X-rated society of the late-1960s which had caught up
with and passed by 007's own code of sex and sin, James Bond
found himself squeezed into conventionality by a traditional marriage
to the leading lady: a sad comeuppance for the once trend-setting
super agent and for the cinema genre itself.

ONE MAN TOO MANY see UN HOMME DE TROP

ONE OF OUR SPIES IS MISSING! (MGM, 1966) C 91 min.

    Executive producer, Norman Felton; producer, Boris Ingster;
associate producer, George M. Lehr; director, E. Darrell Hallen-
beck; story, Henry Selsar; screenplay, Howard Rodman; assistant
director, Wilbur Mosier; art director, George W. Davis, James
Sullivan; set decorator, Henry Grace, Charles S. Thompson, Jack
Mills; music, Gerald Fried; title theme, Jerry Goldsmith; sound,
Franklin Milton; camera, Fred Koenekamp; editor, Henry Berman,
William B. Gulick.
    Robert Vaughn (Napoleon Solo); David McCallum (Illya Kury-
akin); Leo G. Carroll (Mr. Waverly); Maurice Evans (Sir Norman
Swickert); Vera Miles (Madame de Sala); Ann Elder (Joanne Sweet);
Bernard Fox (Jordin); Harry Davis (Alexander Gritsky); Monica
Keating (Olga); Dolores Faith (Lorelei Lancer); Anna Capri (Do
Do); Yvonne Craig (Wanda); Cal Bolder (Fleeton); James Doohan
(Phillip Bainbridge); Ollie O'Toole (Corvy); Anthony Eustrel (Steward);
Richard Peel (Cat Man); Barry Bernard (Pet Shop Owner); Robert
Easton (Texas).

    "The adventures of the men from U.N.C.L.E. have tended
toward science fiction, albeit naturally on a comic-strip level:
happily for me because I think that science fiction contains rather
more imaginative possibilities than the average run-of-the-mill spy
parody which is now looking distinctly tired" (British Films and
Filming).
    When several cats found meowing around Soho Square sud-
denly disappear, the U.N.C.L.E. organization is on guard for any
possible tie-in with the nefarious T.H.R.U.S.H. outfit. Soon the
snooping of Illya Kuryakin (McCallum) in London and the trailing of
Napoleon Solo (Vaughn) to Paris where Madame de Sala (Miles)
runs an haute couture establishment dovetail into an explanation.
Miles has access to a rejuvenation formula (first utilized on cats)
and plans to use the same on retired politician Evans, the latter
bent on ruining England for having had the audacity to turn its
political back on Winston Churchill after World War II.

ONE SPY TOO MANY (MGM, 1966)   C   101 min.

Executive producer, Norman Felton; producer, David Victor; director, Joseph Sargent; screenplay, Dean Hargrove; music, Gerald Fried; title theme, Jerry Goldsmith; art director, George W. Davis, Merrill Pye; sound, Franklin Milton; camera, Fred Koenekamp; editor, Henry Berman.

Robert Vaughn (Napoleon Solo); David McCallum (Illya Kuryakin); Rip Torn (Alexander); Dorothy Provine (Tracey Alexander); Leo G. Carroll (Mr. Waverly); Yvonne Craig (Maude Waverly); David Opatoshu (Kavon); David Sheiner (Parviz); Donna Michelle (Princess Nicole); Leon Lontoc (General Bon-Phouma); Robert Karnes (Colonel Hawks); Clarke Gordon (Claxon); James Hong (Prince Phanong); Cal Bolder (Into Lindstrum); Carole Williams (Receptionist; Teru Shimada (President Sing-Mok); Arthur Wong (General Man-Phang).

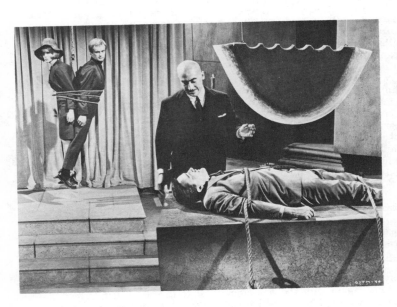

Dorothy Provine, David McCallum, David Sheiner, and Robert Vaughn in One Spy Too Many (MGM, 1966).

"By trying to please everybody, the makers of One Spy Too Many, the third full-length film featuring The Man From U.N.C.L.E. [of television], will succeed in pleasing none. They have tried to mix thrills, comedy, sex, and parody, but have produced a scrappy film whose chief impression is of a send-up which doesn't know what it's sending up" (British <u>Films and Filming</u>).

Alexander (Torn), who has delusions of conquering the world à la Alexander the Great, heists a tankful of the secret "will" gas from the U.S. Army Biological Warfare Division.   U.N.C.L.E. sends agents Napoleon Solo (Vaughn) and Illya Kuryakin (McCallum) after the scoundrel, with Tracey Alexander (Provine) tagging along because she is wed to Torn and wants a divorce.

ONLY THE BRAVE   (Paramount, 1930)   71 min.

Director, Frank Tuttle; story, Keene Thompson; adaptation, Agnes Brand Leahy; dialog, Edward E. Paramore, Jr.; titles, Richard H. Digges, Jr.; sound, J.A. Goodrich; camera, Harry Fischbeck; editor, Doris Drought.

Gary Cooper (Captain James Braydon); Mary Brian (Barbara Calhoun); Phillips Holmes (Captain Robert Darrington); James Neill (Vance Calhoun); Morgan Farley (Tom Wendell); Guy Oliver (General U.S. Grant); John Elliott (General Robert E. Lee); E.H. Calvert (The Colonel); Virginia Bruce (Elizabeth); Elda Voelkel (Lucy Cameron); William LeMaire (The Sentry); Freeman Wood (Elizabeth's Lover); Lalo Encinas (General Grant's Secretary); Clinton Rosemond (Butler); William Bakewell (Young Lieutenant).

This trite excursion into the magnolia-dripped world of the Civil War finds pseudo-Southern gallantry and mock Dixie accents competing for unintended laughs and yawns.

The sight of sweetheart Elizabeth (Bruce) in the arms of a civilian is upsetting enough to Union cavalry office James Braydon (Cooper) to cause him to volunteer for hazardous spy duty.   He is dispatched to the South with a satchel full of false papers which he hopes will lead the Confederate forces astray when Cooper has himself captured and the papers are discovered.   But neither Cooper nor his superiors counted on the hospitality of Virginia belle Barbara Calhoun (Brian) who, much to the chagrin of her volatile suitor Captain Robert Darrington (Holmes), prefers the attention of Cooper, even when he admits his treacherous status. Eventually Cooper "falls" into enemy hands.   They in turn are misled by his documents, and he is about to be shot, when a contingent of Union soldiers fortuitously arrive on the scene.   The Civil War comes to an end and Cooper weds Brian.

ONLY THE COOL   see   LA PEAU DE TORPEDO

OPERATION C.I.A.   (AA, 1965)   77 min.

Producer, Peer J. Oppenheimer; associate producer, Leonard Blair; director, Christian Nyby; story, Oppenheimer;

screenplay, Bill S. Ballinger, Oppenheimer; music, Leonard (Buzz) Blair; gowns, Thelma Nyby; assistant director, Cyril Collick; camera, Paul Dunlap; editor, Joseph Gluck, George Watters.

Burt Reynolds (Mark Andrews); Kieu Chinh (Kim-Chinh); John Hoyt (Wells); Danielle Aubry (Denise Dalbert); Cyril Collick (Withers); Victor Diaz (Professor Yen); William Catching (Frank Decker); Marsh Thomson (Stacey); John Laughinhouse, Frank Estes (American Officers); Chaiporn (Terrorist); Santi (Porter); Juanita (Ming-Tah); Michael Schwiner (Embassy Marine); Robert Gulbranson (Man in Bed); Janet Russell (Girl in Bed).

C. I. A. agent Stacey (Thomson) is killed in Saigon before he can relay important information back to headquarters, and fellow operative Mark Andrews (Reynolds) is dispatched to investigate, using the cover of a professor on a lecture tour. He falls into one trap after another before accomplishing his task--preventing the assassination of the American ambassador.

At least athletic, hairy-chested Reynolds had a field day romping through the thin story which had him beaten up, left to drown, threatened with a cobra, surviving a grenade attack, having his saipan destroyed by an oncoming speedboat, and living through a Viet Cong ambush. All this action is climaxed by an exhausting chase up and down a multi-level hotel during a Chinese New Year celebration. Strangely, there is very little exploitation of the Saigon setting or of the war itself.

This fuzzily photographed (in black and white) feature was later reissued as Last Message from Saigon, trying to exploit the new world interest in Vietnam.

OPERATION CROSSBOW [The Great Spy Mission] (MGM, 1965) C 116 min.

Producer, Carlo Ponti; director, Michael Anderson; story, Duilio Coletti, Vittoriano Petrilli; screenplay, Richard Imrie, Derry Quinn, Ray Rigby; art director, Elliot Scott; music-music director, Ron Goodwin; sound, A. W. Watkins; assistant director, Basil Rayburn; special effects, Tom Howard; camera, Erwin Hillier; editor, Ernest Walter.

George Peppard (Lt. John Curtis); Jeremy Kemp (Phil Bradley); Tom Courtenay (Robert Henshaw); Sophia Loren (Nora); Trevor Howard (Professor Lindemann); John Mills (General Boyd); Richard Johnson (Duncan Sandys); Anthony Quayle (Bamford); Helmut Dantine (General Linz); Richard Todd (Wing Commander Kendall); Lilli Palmer (Frieda); Paul Henreid (General Ziemann); Sylvia Syms (Constance Babington Smith); John Fraser (Flight Lieutenant Kenny); Barbara Rueting (Hanna Reitsch); Patrick Wymark (Winston Churchill); Moray Watson (Colonel Kenneth Post); Richard Wattis (Charles Sims); Maurice Denham (R. A. F. Officer); Karel Stepanek (Professor Hoffer); Allan Cuthbertson (German Technical Examiner); Robert Brown (Air Commodore); Milo Sperber (Waiter); Basil Dignam (English Officer); and: Wolf Frees.

George Peppard, John Mills, and Tom Courtenay (right) in <u>Operation Crossbow</u> (MGM, 1965).

Above and beyond its obvious artistic flaws--no worse than many other less entertaining spy thrillers--this costly but agreeable feature irked the reviewers to an unfathomable degree of distaste. "We feel that the war has been used as the mere backcloth to some modern deed of derring-do that has little significance to us today. No matter what our movies tell us, the war was not a grand adventure" (<u>Saturday Review</u>). "An espionage movie that keeps opening up new doors for its viewers instead of closing them off and sealing them up is in serious trouble, for fresh air and new light are the sure cures for claustrophobia and the deadly enemies of all the tension we crave when we go to a spy movie" (<u>Life</u>). MGM was so taken aback by the adverse critical reaction that after its Radio City Music Hall engagement, the Carlo Ponti production was retitled <u>The Great Spy Mission.</u> The studio rationalized to little effect that the change was required because the potential public was mistaking the film for a medical story, a genre then out of favor with moviegoers.

In December 1942, Whitehall receives reports that the Germans are launching a new secret weapon, a situation which proves true when the V-1 rockets begin devastating London. Word reaches the British that an even more deadly missile is being developed at the German Peenemunde underground base. The English determine to destroy the Nazi buzz bomb production site and train three operatives for the mission. They are parachuted into occupied Holland, posing as German or Dutch scientists, men who have been reported missing. Robert Henshaw (Courtenay) is unmasked by double agent Bamford (Quayle) and is shot. Lt. John Curtis (Peppard) is almost uncovered when the wife (Loren) of the man he is impersonating shows up at his hotel, but he and Phil Bradley (Kemp) overcome the obstacles and reach Peenemunde where they are put to work on the sophisticated production line. Once having radioed the plant's exact location to England, they must provide a guiding light for the Allied bombers, which they do at the cost of their lives. However, the installation is totally demolished.

Director Michael Anderson obviously took his assignment conscientiously, presenting the story from both the Allied and German point of view, and insuring what appeared to be great authenticity of detail and super special effects. Had he pressed harder to instill dimension into his players' characterizations and to smooth out the flow of the episodic plotline, there might have been less carping from all sources. The fact that the wife (Loren) of the film's producer was given co-star billing when she just had a short cameo was not well received by filmgoers. In addition, a host of name performers were spotted in very brief walk-ons--in itself an unsatisfying film gimmick. Continental star Palmer made yet another one of her effective espionage genre appearances, in this case as the realistic undercover worker Frieda, who tosses aside Peppard's sentimental rationalizations and shoots Loren. After all, in the spy game one cannot leave potentially talkative witnesses to spoil one's deceptions.

OPERATION GOLDMAN see LIGHTNING BOLT

OPERATION KID BROTHER (UA, 1967) C 104 min.

Producer, Dario Sabatello; director, Alberto De Martino; screenplay, Paul Levy, Frank Walker; music, Ennio Morricone, Bruno Nicolai; art director, Franco Fontai; set director, Massimo Tavazzi; assistant director, Carlo Moscovini; sound, Deliberti; camera, Alejandas Ulloa; editor, Otello Colangeli.

Neil Connery (Himself); Daniela Bianchi (Maya); Adolfo Celi (Thair Beta); Agata Flori (Mildred); Bernard Lee (Commander Cunningham); Anthony Dawson (Alpha); Lois Maxwell (Max); Yacuco Yama (Yachuco); Guido Lollobrigida (Kurt); Franco Giacobini (Jean); Nando Angelini (Ward Jones); Mario Sonia (Gamma); Anna Maria (Lotte).

Most critics agreed it was not worth the admission price just to see what Sean Connery's brother Neil looked and sounded like in this dubbed Italian-made entry. Buried behind a goatee and an over-careful performance, he proved to be the non-actor he always claimed he was. Even with the bolstering of such James Bond movie alumnae as Lee, Maxwell, Celi (Thunderball), and Bianchi (From Russia with Love), the film was a very weak brew.

The plastic surgeon brother (Neil Connery) of famed 007 is recruited to destroy THANATOS' conspiracy to take over the world's supply of gold. The locale jumps as unevenly as the performers from Monaco to Spain and to the THANATOS headquarters inside a Bavarian castle.

OPERATION MANHUNT (UA, 1954) 77 min.

Producer, Fred Feldkamp; director, Jack Alexander; screenplay, Paul Monash; music director, Jack Shaindlin; camera, Akos Farkas, Benoit Jobin; editor, David Gazalet.

Jacques Aubuchon and Harry Townes in Operation Manhunt (UA, 1954).

With: Harry Townes, Irya Jensen, Jacques Aubuchon,
Robert Goudier, Albert Miller.

This is a little-seen and "unofficial" film continuation of
the events in the life of Igor Gouzenko, the real life character
depicted by Dana Andrews in 20th Century-Fox's The Iron Curtain
(1948).   It was filmed on location in Ottowa, Montreal, and elsewhere in Canada.

Nine years after he has exposed his country's espionage ring
operating in Canada, Gouzenko (Townes), a former Russian code
clerk, is lured from his secluded hiding place by a Soviet agent
who claims he too wants to break with the Soviets.

OPERATION SECRET (WB, 1952)   108 min.

Producer, Henry Blanke; director, Lewis Seiler; story sug-
gestion, Lt. Col. Peter Ortiz; story, Alvin Josephy, John Twist;
screenplay, James R. Webb; music, Roy Webb; orchestrator, Leo
Shuken, Sid Cutner; music director, Ray Heindorf; set decorator,
William T. Kuehl; assistant director, William Kissel; sound,
Oliver S. Garretson; camera, Ted McCord; editor, Clarence
Kolster.

Cornel Wilde (Peter Forrester); Steve Cochran (Marcel
Brevoort); Phyllis Thaxter (Maria); Karl Malden (Major Lautrec);
Paul Picerni (Armand); Lester Mathews (Robbins); Jay Novello
(Herr Bauer); Dan O'Herlihy (Duncan); Ed Foster (Claude); Claude
Dunkin (René); Wilton Graff (French Official); Baynes Barron
(Henri); Philip Rush (Zabreski); Robert Shaw (Jacques); Henry
Rowland (German M. P.); Dan Riss (Sergeant); Gayle Kellogg
(Corporal); John Beattie (Radio Operator); George Dee, Rudy Rama,
Monte Pittman, Tony Eisley, Joe Espitallier, Harry Arnie (Maquis);
Paula Sowl (Hostess); Peter Michael (Legionnaire); Gary Kettler
(Nazi NCO); John Logan (Nazi Soldier); Tom Browne Henry (Monk);
Ted Lawrence (Didot); Don Harvey (Guard); Roy Jenson (Michel);
Craig Morland (British M. P.); Elizabeth Flournoy (Woman Marine);
Harlan Warde (Major Dawson); William Lester (Captain Hughes);
Kenneth Patterson (General); John Nelson (Crewman); William
Slack (Pvt. Korst); Frank Jaquet (Bartender); Larry Winter, Greg
Barton (Sentries); Frances Zucco (Elsa); Len Hendry (Gestapo
Officer); John Marshall (Driver); Charles Flynn (German Civil
Officer); John Pickard (Soldier); Bob Stevenson (Fireman); George
Magrill (Brakeman); Jack Lomas (Engineer); Carlo Tricoli (Old
Peasant); Wayne Taylor (Etienne).

The excessive length (108 minutes) and the constant reliance
on flashbacks were among the many deterrents to the success of
this lukewarm adventure flick criticized for its "comic solemnity"
(New York Herald-Tribune).

The French secret police are conducting a hearing regarding
a murder tied into events that began during World War II.   Each of
the principals relates the events as he chooses to recall them.   The

persons involved include ex-marquis Major Lautrec (Malden), underground worker Maria (Thaxter), Communist agent Marcel Brevoort
(Cochran), Robbins (Mathews) of the British Foreign Office, and
former Gestapo loyalist Herr Bauer (Novello). The finger of guilt
seemingly points to American Peter Forrester (Wilde), who after the
fall of France had been captured by the Germans. He had escaped
to England and joined the U.S. Marines and was later sent to
Germany on a spy mission to find out the real air raid damages at
the Schweinfurt ball-bearing factories. Along the way he also happened to capture Nazi films on the V-1 pilotless bomber and the
Messerschmitt plane.

OPERATOR 13 (MGM, 1934) 85 min.

Producer, Lucien Hubbard; director, Richard Boleslavsky;
based on the story by Robert W. Chambers; screenplay, Harry
Thew, Zelda Sears, Eve Greene; art director, Cedric Gibbons,
Arnold Gillespie, Edwin B. Willis; costumes, Adrian; music, Dr.
William Axt; songs, Walter Donaldson and Gus Kahn; research
director, Gilmore Behmer; camera, George Folsey; editor, Frank
Sullivan.

Marion Davies (Gail Loveless); Gary Cooper (Captain Jack
Gailliard); Jean Parker (Eleanor); Ted Healy (Doc Hitchcock);
Katharine Alexander (Belle); Russell Hardie (Littledale); Henry
Wadsworth (John Pelham); Douglass Dumbrille (General Calhoun);
William Robertson (Captain Chancellor); Hattie McDaniel (Cook);
Fuzzy Knight (Sweeney); Francis McDonald (Denton); William H.
Griffith (Mac); Marjorie Gateson (Mrs. Shackleford); Wade Boteler
(Gaston); James Marcus (Staff Colonel); the Four Mills Brothers
(Themselves); Sam McDaniel (Old Bob); Walter Long (The Groom,
Operator 55); Sidney Toler (Major Allan); Robert McWade (Colonel
Sharpe); Buddy Roosevelt (Civilian); Frank McGlynn, Jr., Wheeler
Oakman (Scouts); Don Douglas (Confederate Officer); Si Jenks
(White Trash); Reginald Barlow (Colonel Storm); Ernie Alexander,
Richard Powell (Confederate Sentries); Belle Daube (Mrs. Dandridge);
Wilfred Lucas (Judge); Bob Stevenson (Guard); Martin Turner (Wick-
man); Frank Burt (Confederate Lieutenant); Wallie Howe (Clergy-
man); William Henry (Young Lieutenant); Martin Turner (Butler);
John Larkin, Poppy Wilde (Party Guests); Richard Tucker (Execu-
tion Officer); Arthur Grant (Chaplin); Sherry Tanzey (Officer); Lia
Lance (Witch Woman); Charles Lloyd (Union Private); DeWitt C.
Jennings (Artillery Man); Sam Ash (Lieutenant); Ernie Adams
(Orderly); Clarence Hummel Wilson (Claybourne); Franklin Parker
(John Hay); Claudia Coleman (Nurse); Sterling Holloway (Wounded
Soldier); Sherry Hall (Army Officer); Douglas Fowley (Union Offi-
cer); Frank Marlowe (Confederate Officer); Fred Warren (Grant);
John Elliott (Robert E. Lee); Frank Leighton (Union Major); James
C. Morton (Secret Service Man).

This was one Marion Davies screen vehicle in which Hearst-
pandering critics were hardly prone to the old cliché, "She never

looked lovelier. " For in much of this period melodrama, Davies romped about the Southern countryside posing as a rambunctious, bright-eyed mulatto laundress à la Topsy.   Later in this haphazardly executed tale the actress returned to her cinema heroine form as a Dixie belle, complete with platinum hair, plucked eyebrows, and an Adrian wardrobe.   She even designed to sing "Once in a Lifetime Love Comes Your Way. " Paramount's Cooper was borrowed for marquee support, and the four Mills Brothers popped up in the picture to provide additional if incongruous consumer bait. Despite everything, the picture was "no great shakes" (New York Herald-Tribune), and was criticized for being a "queer mixture of the realistic and the incredible" (New York Times).

In Civil War days actress Gail Loveless (Davies) is urged to help the Union by becoming a spy. She agrees and disguised as a black servant she is sent South with professional operative Belle (Alexander).   Alexander lodges at a mansion being used as General Stuart's (Dumbrille) headquarters, while Davies is put to work as the officers' laundress.   Alexander's undercover activities are uncovered and although she is sentenced to death, she escapes to the Union lines.   Meanwhile, Davies, who had first met Confederate captain Jack Gailliard (Cooper) while working as the unit's washerwoman, dons the disguise of a Southern belle named Ann Claibourne and stays at Mrs. Shackleford's (Gateson) Richmond home.   Here she again meets Cooper and this time he falls in love with her, unaware she is Operator 13, charged with learning more about Cooper's organization of Southern sympathizers up North. When Davies' ruse is discovered, she escapes with another Union spy.   The latter is shot, but Davies and the pursuing Cooper emerge safe from several near disasters. Cooper eventually bids her fond farewell and returns to the troops in gray.

Even as late as the mid-1930s, it was still a generally held belief by both filmmakers and the public, that a spy picture--particularly one set in historic times or the exotic African deserts-- must be excessively romantic and only accidentally realistic, with more emphasis on glamour than grimness. Operator 13 represented these concepts to the extreme, with unhappy results for all concerned.   Miss Davies thereafter moved over to Warner Bros. for the remainder of her film career.

OPERAZIONE GOLDMAN see LIGHTNING BOLT

AN ORCHID FOR THE TIGER see LE TIGRE SE PARFUME A LA DYNAMITE

ORDERS TO KILL (United Motion Picture Organization, 1958) 111 min.

[Facing page] Marion Davies in Operator 13 (MGM, 1934).

Producer, Anthony Havelock-Allan; director, Anthony Asquith; story, Donald C. Downes; adaptation, George S. George; screenplay, Paul Dehn; music, Benjamin Frankel; camera, Desmond Dickinson; editor, Gordon Hales.

Eddie Albert (Major MacMahon); Paul Massie (Gene Summers); Lillian Gish (Mrs. Summers); James Robertson Justice (Naval Commander); Irene Worth (Leonie); Leslie French (Marcel Lafitte); John Crawford (Kimball); Lionel Jeffries (Interrogator); Sandra Dorne (Blonde); Nicholas Phipps (Lecturer Lieutenant); Anne Blake (Mme. Lafitte); Miki Iveria (Louise); Lathe Bea Gifford (Mauricette); Launce Maraschal (General Nolan); Robert Henderson (Colonel Snyder); William Greene (Mitchell); Selma Vaz Diaz (Patronne); Ralph Nossek (Psychiatrist); Ann Walford (F. A. N. Y.); Boris Rawnsky (Old German Soldier).

On one level this is a Second World War espionage melodrama, yet on another it is a restrained, intelligent study of a man's conscience reshaped by wartime conditions. This tight and tense drama is highly regarded by critics: "smoothly and fastidiously made" (New York Herald-Tribune).

Young American bomber pilot Gene Summers (Massie) finds himself grounded in England and switches to espionage in order to perform a specific job. His chore is to kill a small time Paris lawyer (French) suspected of selling out to the Nazis and providing them with data on the partisan radio operations in France. When Massie reaches Paris he is surprised to find how pleasant a chap the family man French really is, and he has more than second thoughts about performing his task. Later, after the deed is done, it is discovered French was actually innocent.

As with all such films, the sections devoted to the schooling of Massie in the art of killing and surviving in commando fashion are the most absorbing. A major flaw of Orders to Kill is that the finale is rushed a bit too much, not providing the viewer with enough scope on the killer's wavering conscience. The case is overloaded somewhat by having Massie portray such a considerate murderer, who is too conspicuously delicate for the task at hand. A particularly intriguing bit of logic is provided by Resistance agent Leonie (Worth) in the course of convincing Massie of his duty. She reasons that the Third Reich's Goebbels is reputed to be a good father, but like the suspect French is guilty of evil acts. Moreover, Worth insists that pilot Massie would not have turned back from any bombing mission just because a man in the target area, like French, loved and respected his mother.

O. S. S.   (Paramount, 1946)   107 min.

Producer, Richard Maibaum; director, Irving Pichel; screenplay, Maibaum; art director, Hans Dreier, Haldane Douglas; set decorator, Sam Comer, Stanley J. Sawley; music, Daniele Amfitheatrof, Heinz Roemheld; assistant director, John Murphy; technical consultant, Commander John H. Shaheen, USNR, Lieutenant Raphael

G. Beugnon, AUS; sound, Harold Lewis, John Cope; special camera
effects, Gordon Jennings; process camera, Farciot Edouart; cam-
era, Lionel Lindon; editor, William Shea.
    Alan Ladd (John Martin); Geraldine Fitzgerald (Ellen Rogers);
Patric Knowles (Commander Brady); John Hoyt (Colonel Meister);
Gloria Saunders (Mary Kenny--"Sparks"); Richard Benedict (Bernay);
Harold Vermilyea (Amadeus Braun); Don Beddoe (Gates); Onslow
Stevens (Field); Gavin Muir (Colonel Crawson); Egon Brecher (Mar-
cel Aubert); Joseph Crehan (General Donovan); Bobby Driscoll
(Gerard); Julia Dean (Madame Prideaux); Crane Whitley (Arnheim);
Leslie Denison (Lt. Col. Miles); Roberta Jonay (Gracie Archer);
Jean Ruth (Brady's Secretary); Frederick Voltz, Lawson Houghton,
George J. Fannon, Harlan Warde, Fred Zendar, Paul Lees, William
Meader, Albert Ruiz, Charles Victor, Robert Cordell (Trainees);
Catherine Craig (Williams' Secretary); Albert Van Antwerp (Guard);
Frank Ferguson (Research Man); Murray F. Yeats (Tall Man);
Edward Harvey (Mr. Williams); Pat McVey, Tom Schamp (Plains-
clothesmen); Walter S. Pietila (Mansion Attendant); Robert Wegner
(Gateman); James Westerfield (Stout Man); Tom Stevenson (In-
structor); Vern Anders (Sentry); Janna de Loos (Woman Refugee);
Andre Charlot (French Importer); Archie Twitchell (Officer); Will
Thunis (Young Man); George Sorel (Husky Refugee); Jean Del Val
(Conductor); Frank Dae (Scientist); George Barton (Handyman);
Jean Ransome (Elevator Operator); Dorothy Barrett (Brady's
Secretary in London); Ed Kerr (Courier) Herbert Wyndham (Co-
Pilot); Anthony Marsh, Paul Barrett (British Pilots); James Craven
(Jumpmaster); John Bogden (Assistant Jumpmaster); Carl Ekberg,
Leo Schlesinger, Eric Steiner, Eddie Bauer, Walter Rode, Zane
Megowan, Jack Sterling, Bob Templeton, Paul Stupin, Len Hendry
(German Soldiers); Holder Bendixen (German Sergeant); Frederick J.
Waugh (British Non-Com); Robert Cordell (Major at Airport Shack);
Jack Lambert (German Lieutenant); Monica Folts (Little Girl with
Kitten); George Bruggeman (M. P., Non-Com); Rene Dussaq (French
Artillery Officer); John Maxwell (LaFevre); Albert Petit, Paul
Diamond (Resistance Men); Carmen Beretta (Resistance Woman);
Tony Merle (Reynal); Helen Chapman (Resistance Girl); Kathleen
Terry (Operator Next to Kenny); Philip Ahlm (German Officer);
Edmund Porada (German Sergeant--Operator); John Dehner (German
Radar Captain); Jon Gilbreath (German Radar Lieutenant); Henry
Vroom (German Corporal); Peter Michael (German Non-Com); Fred
Kohler, Jr. (Fireman); Jimmie Dundee (Sentry); Joseph Granby
(Engineer); Edward Clark (French Waiter); Renee Randall (Cashier);
Louise Colombet (Old Frenchwoman); Major Fred Darrell (Old
Frenchman); Dorothy Adams (Claudette); John Harmon (Pierre);
Fred Nurney (Major--Courier); Frank Pulliam, Jr. (B-25 Pilot);
George Taylor (Gestapo Plainclothesman); Hans Moebus (Gestapo
Man); Dick Elmore (German Army Private); Gene Garrick (Operator);
Henry Guttman (German Major); Jerry James (Pilot); Byron Poin-
dexter (Co-Pilot); James Andrews (Radio Operator); Carl Saxe,
Roger Creed (S. S. Men); Carl Andre (Colonel Hesiter's Aide);
Jerome Alden (British Non-Com); George Fannon (Marine Captain);
Billy Burt (Lieutenant J. G.); Billy Lechner, Carl Russell, Fred

Datig, Jr. , Frank Chalfant, George Billings, Charles Ferguson (U. S.
Soldiers).

For some time Hollywood had longed for the potentially rich
story material encased within the secret files of the Office of Strategic Services.   In 1946, for a three-week period, the O. S. S.
opened their closed case journals to several moviemakers.   Paramount was among the major studios to survey this now-it-can-be-
told payload, and immediately rushed this Alan Ladd feature into
production on a seven-week shooting schedule, using 30 ex-O. S. S.
heroes as technical advisers and bit players.   O. S. S. was the
first of the new "authentically based" film crop to reach theatrical
distribution.   The pity is that it was a conventional thriller, never
once getting to the depth of the O. S. S. 's real importance, particularly after the on-camera training school sequences merged into
fanciful spy stuff.   Since there were few romantic escapades in
O. S. S. , the film's major concession to reality, Alan Ladd devotees
had little to applaud in this vehicle.

Four disparate civilian types, among the many processed
through the O. S. S. training school, include public relations man
John Martin (Ladd), railroad equipment salesman Gates (Beddoe),
hockey player Bernay (Benedict), and San Franciscan sculptress
Ellen Rogers (Fitzgerald).   By the summer of 1943 the quartet,
known as Team Applejack, is ready to undertake its mission: to
knock out the vital Corbet-Mallons tunnel in occupied France.
Fitzgerald becomes the mistress of German S. S. Colonel Meister
(Hoyt), a relationship which both helps and later hinders her task
and eventually leads to her death in the line of duty.   But Ladd
completes his job and lives to look back with misty eyes on the
human sacrifices required to do the necessary work.

O. S. S. 117 (S. F. , 1963) 110 min.

Director, André Hunebelle; based on the novel O. S. S. 117
Prend le Maquis by Jean Bruce; adaptation, Raymond Borel, Richard
Caron, screenplay, Hunebelle, Pierre Foucaud; music, Michel
Magne; art director, Georges Lévy, Pierre Geffroy; camera, Ray-
mond Lemoigne; editor, Jean Feyte.

Kerwin Mathews (Hubert Bonisseur de la Bath); Nadia Sanders
(Brigita); Henri-Jacques Huet (Renotte); Albert Dagnant (Forestier);
Daniel Emilfork (Sacha); Irina Demich (Lucia); Jacques Harden
(Roos); Roger Dutoit (Mayan); and: André Weber, Michael Jour-
dan, Jean-Pierre Moulinot, Gisèle Grimm, Yvon Chiffre.

The opener of the Hubert Bonisseur de la Bath series was
promoted as "The French answer to James Bond. " "Every once in
a while it promises to round a corner and almost justify the claim,
but unfortunately never quite makes it" (British Monthly Film Bulletin).

American secret service agent Mathews is sent to Corsica to
trace the disappearance of a fellow agent.   He learns that a power-

mad group is constructing a highly effective submarine detector in
their underwater headquarter.   With the aid of his French counterpart (Dagnant) and a Swedish blonde (Sanders) he shoots it out successfully with the conspirators at their subterranean grotto.

O. S. S. 117--DOUBLE AGENT see PAS DE ROSES O. S. S. 117

OTLEY (Columbia, 1968)   C   91 min.

        Executive producer, Carl Foreman; producer, Bruce Cohn
Curtis; director, Dick Clement; based on the novel by Martin Wad-
dell; screenplay, Ian La Frenais, Clement; assistant director,
Dominic Fulford; art director, Carmen Dillon; music-music director,
Stanley Myers; song, Myers and Don Patridge; titles, Paul Huson;
sound, William Trent; camera, Austin Dempster, Brian West; editor,
Richard Best.
        Tom Courtenay (Gerald Arthur Otley); Romy Schneider (Imo-
gen); Alan Badel (Sir Alec Hadrian); James Villiers (Hendrickson);
Leonard Rossiter (Johnston); James Bolam (Albert); Fiona Lewis
(Lin); Freddie Jones (Proudfoot); James Cossins (Jeffcock); James
Maxwell (Rollo); Edward Hardwicke (Eric Lambert); Ronald Lacey
(Curtis); Phyllida Law (Jean); Geoffrey Bayldon (Hewitt); Frank
Middlemass (Bruce); Damian Harris (Miles); Robert Brownjohn
(Paul); Maureen Toal (Landlady); Barry Fantoni (Larry); Bernard
Sharpe (Tony); Paul Angelis (Constable); David Kernan (Ground
Steward); Sheila Steafel (Ground Stewardess); Katherine Parr (News-
agent); Kathleen Helm (Dietician); Ron Owen (Hotel Waiter); Stella
Tanner (Traffic Warden); Jonathan Cecil (Young Man at Party);
Georgina Simpson (Young Girl at Party); Norman Shelley, John
Savident, Ken Parry (Businessmen); Robin Askwith, Kevin Bennett,
Kenneth Cranham (Kids); Robert Gillespie (Policeman); Donald
McKillop (Police Driver); The Herd (Themselves).

        At one time James Mason and George Sanders were con-
sidered to be the most satisfying portrayers of intelligence agents.
For very different reasons Britisher Tom Courtenay in the last
decade has been a perennial choice of casting directors to portray
them (Operation Crossbow, A Dandy in Aspic, Catch Me a Spy).
His boyish look is considered an interesting contrast to his assigned
roles as a hard-hearted, cynical operative. In Otley this on-
camera premise is pushed to the hilt, with the star of Billy Liar
(1963) functioning at his vulnerable best.
        Perhaps just because Gerald Arthur Otley (Courtenay) is so
deliberately geared to be the most unlikely, but still plausible,
candidate for entry into the slick world of spying and double dealing, the character and the overall film lack sufficient audience
identification potential.   The scripters have craftily concocted a
weaving mod script filled with sudden turns, plenty of room for
change of moods and points of view, but are left at the end with
their absurd hero, the clumsy, unsympathetic Cockney outsider

exactly as he was before situations dragged him into the espionage
milieu.   As a freeloading ladies' man, Courtenay's Otley just did
not pass muster.

Parasitic Courtenay takes pot luck among his Portobello
Road antique market acquaintances, accepting the offer to be a
guest at the flat of Eric Lambert (Hardwicke).   During the night
Hardwicke is killed and Courtenay awakens at Gatwick Airport uncertain how he got there, but soon fully aware that in London the
police are convinced he murdered his host.   Suddenly he is kidnapped and interrogated by Hendrickson (Villiers) and Imogen
(Schneider), but he is then set free, only to be recaptured by
another faction headed by dapper Proudfoot (Jones).   Courtenay's
dirty neck is saved merely because Jones' henchman (Rossiter)
discovers that the antique tobacco holder Courtenay filched from
Hardwicke's apartment has a tape-recorded message worth money
to others.   One after another of Courtenay's newly acquired work-
mates proves to be anything but what he appears, and having survived the ordeal, the scalawag decides that his vagabond way of
life is a better deal after all.

OUR MAN FLINT   (20th-Fox, 1966)   C   107 min.

Producer, Saul David; director, Daniel Mann; story, Hal
Fimberg; screenplay, Fimberg, Ben Starr; art director, Jack
Martin Smith, Ed Graves; set decorator, Walter M. Scott, Raphael
Britton; assistant director, David Silver; special action sequence,
Buzz Henry; music, Jerry Goldsmith; sound, Carlton W. Faulkner,
Elmer Raguse; special camera effects, L. B. Abbott, Howard Ly-
decker, Emil Kosa; camera, Daniel L. Fapp; editor, William
Reynolds.

James Coburn (Derek Flint); Lee J. Cobb (Cramden); Gila
Golan (Gila); Edward Mulhare (Malcolm Rodney); Benson Fong
(Dr. Schneider); Gianna Serra (Gina); Sigrid Valdis (Anna); Shelby
Grant (Leslie); Helen Funai (Sakito); Michael St. Clair (Gruber);
Rhys Williams (Dr. Krupov); Russ Conway (American General);
Ena Hartman (WAC); William Walker (American Diplomat); Peter
Brocco (Dr. Wu).

At the subterranean secret meeting headquarters of ZOWIE
(Zonal Organization of World Intelligence and Espionage) it is
reported that the mysterious GALAXY group, headed by a trio of
mad scientists (who else?), is planning to take over the world
(what else?) by controlling the global weather situation.   ZOWIE's
chief, Cramden (Cobb), turns to his trusty computer to run a personnel profile check which reveals that Derek Flint (Coburn) is the
best qualified person to handle the troublesome situation.   Cobb
has serious doubts about this irresponsible, but expert, super secret
agent who idles in luxury with his harem of four exotic international
beauties.   Nevertheless, the computer cannot be wrong.   Coburn's
only mechanical weapon in his contest against the world subversives
is a wonderous cigarette case which has 83 deadly offensive-

defensive functions. Along the path of danger which leads to Rome
and then to a remote volcanic island, Coburn tangles with an assortment of adversaries, none so tricky or beautiful as Gila (Golan).
The public obviously did not mind that Our Man Flint was
merely a snide, perky take-off on James Bond--with a big dash of
Matt Helm thrown in--for the color feature garnered $7.2 million
in distributors' domestic rentals. One of the most enthusiastic
endorsers of Our Man Flint and actor Coburn in particular, was
Judith Crist (New York World Journal Tribune), "Bye, Bye Bond.
Our Man Flint has arrived.... [He has] won our chauvinistic
hearts by out-Bonding James in lean, lanky highly original all-
American fashion and spoofing spies like they've not been spoofed
since."

OUR MAN IN HAVANA (Columbia, 1960) 107 min.

Producer, Carol Reed; associate producer, Raymond Anza-
rut; director, Reed; based on the novel by Graham Greene; screen-
play, Greene; assistant director, Gerry O'Hara; art director, John
Box; camera, Oswald Morris; editor, Bert Bates.
Alec Guinness (James Wormold); Burl Ives (Dr. Hassel-
bacher); Maureen O'Hara (Beatrice Bevern); Ernie Kovacs (Captain
Segura); Noel Coward (Hawthorne); Ralph Richardson ("C"); Jo
Morrow (Milly Wormold); Gregoire Aslan (Cifuentes); Paul Rogers
(Hubert Carter); Maxine Audley (Teresa); Timothy Bateson (Rudy);
Jose Prieto (Lopez); Raymond Huntley (Army Representative);
Maurice Denham (Navy Representative); Hugh Manning (Air Force
Representative).

In the years since Orient Express (1933), some one dozen
of Graham Greene's works had been filmed, often providing diverting screen spy fare. Our Man in Havana, despite Greene's
favorite director (Carol Reed) and a name cast, never made it
off the ground with critics or the public. "What is missed,"
analyzed Films and Filming, "is the subtle toning of the [book]
original: the lightness of touch on the one hand; on the other
the sudden shift, half way through, from farce to ominous drama.
The loss is important; it changes Greene's Our Man in Havana
into something much more ordinary, a classy spy melodrama."
Guinness portrayed a quite ordinary British vacuum-cleaner
salesman, who is persuaded to become a member of M.I. 5's spy
force in Havana. When he is unable to dig up actual espionage, he
creates a bit to impress the home office, leading to lethal implications midst the heavy (counter)-espionage atmosphere of the Cuban
capital.
To the feature's credit, it did highlight an ironic view of
spying which few other films have used. Nevertheless the resulting
picture was basically dull, sort of an inside joke between Reed,
Greene, and the actors, which, on the whole, left out the film's
audience. Then too, any one film which attempts to blend the
diverse acting styles of Guinness, Coward (our man in the West

Indies), Kovacs (the police chief), Richardson (the top officer of
M. I. 5), Ives (an ineffective doctor and possible German spy) and
O'Hara (Guinness' lovely secretary), is begging for trouble.

OUR MAN IN MARRAKECH see BANG, BANG, YOU'RE DEAD!

OUR SEA see MARE NOSTRUM

PACIFIC BLACKOUT (Paramount, 1942)   76 min.

         Producer, Sol C. Siegel; director, Ralph Murphy; story,
Frank Spencer, Curt Siodmak; screenplay, Lester Cole, W. F.
Lipscomb; art director, Hans Dreier, Franz Bachelin; camera,
Theodore Sparkuhl; editor, Thomas Scott.
         Robert Preston (Robert Draper); Martha O'Driscoll (Marty);
Philip Merivale (John Ronnel); Eva Gabor (Marie Duval); Louis
Jean Heydt (Kermin); Thurston Hall (William); Mary Treen (Irene);
J. Edward Bromberg (Pickpocket); Spencer Charteris (Night Watch-
man).

         This entertainment miniature, whose producer projected the
inescapability of U. S. participation in World War II, was presumed
to have more topical importance than it ever aspired to, being released (January 7, 1942) so soon after the Pearl Harbor attack.
Also, the film's title was very misleading, for the story was forced
into a fanciful plot revolving around the elaborately staged blackouts
in West Coast cities when Japanese bombing raids on the American
mainland seemed a distinct likelihood.
         During one of the many blackout rehearsals, Robert Draper
(Preston) escapes from his jailers.   He is the inventor of an
anti-aircraft range finder who has been framed on a murder charge
and sentenced to death.   Now he must prove his innocence.   During
the blackout practice he meets daffy telephone operator Marty
(O'Driscoll) and together they investigate a plot to blow up a
Seattle munitions factory and eventually find that the Axis saboteurs
are connected with the murder that Preston did not commit.
         At the time of its release, there were some persons who
regarded Pacific Blackout as being in poor taste by taking such a
farcical approach to the serious problem of surprise air raids.

PACIFIC RENDEZVOUS (MGM, 1942)   75 min.

         Producer, B. F. Zeidman; director, George Sidney; screen-
play, Harry Kurnitz, P. J. Wolfson, George Oppenheimer; music,
David Snell; camera, Paul Vogel; editor, Ben Lewis.
         Lee Bowman (Lt. Bill Gordon); Jean Rogers (Elaine Carter);
Mona Maris (Olivia Kerlov); Carl Esmond (Andre Leemuth); Paul
Cavanagh (Commander Brennan); Blanche Yurka (Mrs. Savarina);

Russell Hicks (John Carter); Arthur Shields (Professor Harvey Less-more); William Post, Jr. (Lanny); William Tannen (Jasper Dean); Frederic Worlock (Dr. Jackwin); Curt Bois (Kestrin); Felix Basch (Dr. Segroff); Addison Richards (Gordon Trisby); Edward Fielding (Secretary of the Navy); William Tannen (Dean); Eddie Lee, Tommy Lee (Japanese); William Roberts (Operator); Hans von Morhart (German Operator); Frances Carson (Mrs. Hendricks); Michael Visaroff (Colonel Petroff); Edward Earle (Dr. Jackwin's Assistant); Grace Lem (Japanese Woman); Arno Frey (German); Syd Saylor (Navy Recruiting Officer); Tex Brodus (Officer); George Lollier (Marine); Hal Cooke (Orderly); Byron Foulger (Drum Man); Pat O'Malley (Ship's Captain); Phil Tead (Taxi Driver); George Carle-ton (Chaplain); Gayne Whitman (Barini); James Warren (F.B.I. Agent); Bill Nind (Waiter); Milburn Stone (Clerk); Hans Conried (Bellboy); J. Anthony Hughes (Pat Riley); Louis Arco (Assistant German); Henry Rowland (Elevator Boy); Alphonse Martell (Stron-skoff); Joyce Bryant (Girl).

A cornball quickie "on the silly side" (New York Journal American) that for humor turned to the business of decoding enemy messages and gave it the slapstick treatment. "The trouble," wrote Howard Barnes (New York Herald-Tribune) of Pacific Ren-dezvous, "is that they play a dull game of cops and robbers, which has no more reference to the present day than a bad western. Spy thrillers can be very good indeed but it strikes me that at this particular moment they should be very good or left undone."

Foreign correspondent Bill Gordon (Bowman) returns to Washington, D.C., to enlist in the Navy, hoping to be sent into action. Instead he finds himself assigned to cracking the new code being used by the Japanese. He and dizzy debutante Elaine Carter (Rogers) jump in and out of hot water as they uncover a Japanese-German maneuver to relay stolen information to their Pacific-sta-tioned submarines. This data would reveal the exact path to be used by an Allied troop convoy.

As was often the case with World War II exploitation fea-tures, the misleading title of this movie was the most topical and cogent aspect of the film.

PANAMA HATTIE   (MGM, 1942)   79 min.

Producer, Arthur Freed; director, Norman Z. McLeod; based on the play by Herbert Fields, B.G. DeSylva, Cole Porter; screen-play, Jack McGowan, Wilkie Mahoney; songs; Porter; Roger Edens, E.Y. Harburg and Burton Lane; Harburg and Walter Donaldson; choreography, Danny Dare; music director, George Stoll; art di-rector, Cedric Gibbons; camera, George Folsey; editor, Blanche Sewell.

Ann Sothern (Hattie Maloney); Dan Dailey (Dick Bulliet); Red Skelton (Red); Marsha Hunt (Leila Tree); Virginia O'Brien (Flo Foster); Rags Ragland (Rags); Alan Mowbray (Jay Jerkins); Ben Blue (Howdy); Jackie Horner (Geraldine Bulliet); Carl Esmond

(Lucas Kefler); Pierre Watkin (Admiral Tree); Stanley Andrews
(Colonel John Briggs); Lena Horne (Specialty); George Watts (Mac
the Bartender); Lucien Prival (Hans); Joe Yule (Waiter); Duke
York (Bruno); Fred Graham (Naval Policeman); Roger Moore (Spy);
Max Wagner (Guard); Grant Withers (Shore Patrol).

The Broadway musical Panama Hattie, starring Ethel Mer-
man, James Dunn, Arthur Treacher, Rags Ragland, Joan Carroll,
and Betty Hutton, ran for 501 performances in 1940. The movie
rendition was a credit to no one, since it allowed the still prime
vehicle to slip into a meandering not-so-major feature production
for star Sothern. She was asked to rehash her Maisie series'
characterization for the restructured musical, now more a show-
case for the antics of Skelton and Ragland than for the heroine of
the piece, the brassy Hattie Maloney (Sothern), a dame with a
heart of pure gold. To further disconcert those who had witnessed
the Broadway edition, the screen Panama Hattie dropped most of the
Cole Porter score and inserted relief numbers to be crooned by
guest artists Horne and deadpan comedienne O'Brien. For topicality, there was a subordinate let's-capture-the-Axis-spies-in-the-
Panama-Zone gambit tossed in, as undeftly maneuvered as the rest
of the proceedings.

PANAMA PATROL   (Grand National, 1939)   67 min.

Executive producer, Franklyn Warner; producer-director,
Charles Lamont; story, Monroe Shaff, Arthur Hoerl; screenplay,
Hoerl; art director, Ralph Berger; assistant director director, V.O.
Smith; set decorator, Glenn Thompson; sound, Hal Dunbar; camera,
Arthur Martinelli; editor, Bernard Loftus.
Leon Ames (Major Philip Waring); Charlotte Wynters (Helen
Lane); Weldon Heyburn (Lt. Murdock); Adrienne Ames (Lia Maing);
Abner Biberman (Arlie Johnson); Hugh McArthur (Lt. Everett);
Donald Barry (Lt. Loring); John E. Smart (Eli Maing); Lal Chand
Menra (Singh); William Von Brincken (Marlin); Richard Loo (Tommy
Young); Frank Darien (Sam); Paul McVey (Baird); Gerald Mohr
(Pilot); Harry Bradley (Clerk); Philson Ahn (Khantow); Philip Ahn
(Suri); Lew Kelly (Knowles).

This tidy little follow-up to the previous year's Cipher Bureau
has Leon Ames again portraying Army Intelligence officer Philip
Waring. Variety complimented the production team responsible for
having "given polish to a story that is not unusual but technically
the thriller is A-1."
Within its 67-minute framework, Major Philip Waring (Leon
Ames) must postpone his marriage to Helen Lane (Wynters) until
he has solved his latest case, which concerns a nest of Oriental
spies who are engaged in plotting the take-over of the Panama
Canal. Among those embroiled in the caper are Arlie Johnson
(Biberman), an interpreter in the Army Intelligence office, curio
shop dealer Eli Maing (Smart), and Far Eastern femme fatale

Lia Maing (Adrienne Ames--looking very un-Oriental).

PANIC IN THE CITY (Feature Film Corp., 1968) C 97 min.

  Producer, Earle Lyon; director, Eddie Davis; screenplay, Davis, Charles E. Savage; assistant director, William Schwartz; music, Paul Dunlap; art director, Paul Sylos, Jr.; sound, Brad Trask; camera, Alan Stensvold; editor, Terrell O. Morse.
  Howard Duff (Dave Pomeroy); Linda Cristal (Dr. Paula Stevens); Stephen McNally (James Kincade); Nehemiah Persoff (August Best); Anne Jeffreys (Myra Pryor); Oscar Beregi (Dr. Cerbo); Dennis Hopper (Geoff); Gregory Morton (Steadman); and: George Barrows, John Hoyt, Steve Franken, Wesley Lau, Eddie Firestone, Stanley Clements, Eilene Janssen, James Seay, Walter Scott, George Sawaya.

  Produced and quickly sold to American television, this "fair programmer" (Variety) dealt with a man discovered in Los Angeles with the highest dose of radiation poison ever recorded, leading the FBI to investigate a plot to blow up the city and start World War III.
  The film's veteran cast was sparked by a now rare film appearance from Anne Jeffreys.

PARIS AFTER DARK (20th-Fox, 1943) 85 min.

  Producer, Andre Daven; director, Leonide Moguy; based on a story by George Kessel; screenplay, Harold Buchman; art director, James Basevi, John Ewing; music, Hugh W. Friedhofer; assistant director, Bob Herndon; special camera effects, Fred Sersen; camera, Lucien Andriot; editor, Nick De Maggio.
  George Sanders (Dr. Marbel); Philip Dorn (Jean); Brenda Marshall (Yvonne); Madeleine Le Beau (Collette); Marcel Dalio (Luigi); Robert Lewis (Colonel Pirosh); Henry Rowland (Captain Branch); Raymond Roe (George); Gene Gary (Victor); Jean Del Val (Papa Renoit); Curt Bois (Max); Ann Codee (Madame Renoit); Louis Morell (Pickard); John Wengraf (Mannheim); Michael Visaroff (Paul); Frank Lynn (Nazi Agent in Homburg Hat); Simone D'Ambrogio (Servant Girl); Curt Furberg (Anesthetist); Robert Gilbert (Gestapo Agent); George Davis (Barfly); Eugene Borden (Central Committee Member); Henry Le Baubigny (Man); John Beverly, George Sorel, Arno Frey, Walter Bonn (German Detectives); Wolfgang Zilzer (German Radio Announcer); Otto Reicher (German Gestapo Man); Jacques Lory (Blind Man); Christiana Tourneur (Max's Wife); Jack Pullen (Del Val); Paul Weigel (News Dealer); Frank Arnold, Maurice Marsac (French Soldiers); Chavo De Leon (French Gunner); Guy Kingsford (English Pilot); Dick French (Mechanic); Gaston Glass, Richard Ordynski (Soldiers).

  Despite direction by French refugee Moguy and a cast

containing many authentic Gauls, this feature was strictly backlot Hollywood in ambiance. Nor did the production spell out the off-beat implications of one of its major plot premises (i.e., the effect of years in a concentration camp beating down the spirit of a former French patriot, so that when released, he is brainwashed into believing in the alleged invincibility of the Third Reich).

Aristocratic Parisian doctor Sanders secretly works with the French underground, while remaining a confidant of the Nazis. Dorn is the French soldier returning home after two years in a German prison camp, who is amazed to learn that anyone yet dares to fight the Nazis. He is aghast to learn that his wife (Marshall), nurse at Sanders' office, is a leading member of the partisans. The underground's chief goal at the moment is to decelerate production at the Beaumont Factory and to keep the liberation newspaper in print.

By this point of time, the critics, and even the public, were turning a skeptical eye to this sort of patriotic thriller, in which the Allied underground and espionage forces so easily out-maneuvered the particularly blind Germans. "One more underground picture can't do us any harm, or can it?" asked the New York Post. The superabundance of chauvinistic speech-making did not boost the film's stock at the boxoffice, particularly when the tension-building ingredients to Paris After Dark were so placid. Thus it was a particularly forgiving filmgoer who could rally to the cry of such dialog as that delivered by one of the characters, as he goes off to join DeGaulle's forces, "I'll be coming back. I'll be coming back soon, with a couple of million other guys, for a parade down the Champs-Elysées."

PARIS CALLING (Universal, 1941) 95 min.

Producer, Benjamin Glazer; director, Edwin L. Marin; story, John S. Toldy; screenplay, Glazer, Charles S. Kaufman; camera, Milton Krasner; editor, Edward Curtis.

Elizabeth Bergner (Marianne); Randolph Scott (Nick); Basil Rathbone (Benoit); Eduardo Ciannelli (Mouche); Gale Sondergaard (Colette); Lee J. Cobb (Schwabe); Elisabeth Risdon (Madame Jennetier); Charles Arnt (Lantz); Georges Renavent (Butler); William Edmunds (Marceau); Patrick O'Malley (McAvoy); Georges Metaxa (Waiter); Paul Leyssac (Chief of Underground); Paul Bryar (Paul); Otto Reichow (Gruber); Adolph Milar (Gestapo Agent); Marion Murray (Marie); Grace Lenard (Marie); Yvette Bentley (Simone); Marcia Ralston (Renée); Gene Garrick (Wolfgang Schmitt); Pedro de Cordoba (Speaker); Ian Wolfe (Thin Workman); Rosalind Ivan (Mama Picon); Mary Forbes (Lady Guest); Howard Hickman (French General); Ed Emerson (Chauffeur); Harlan Briggs (Papa Picon); Denis Green (English Officer); Charles Wagenheim (French Waiter); Craufurd Kent (British Naval Officer); Fred Vogeding (German Officer); Philip Van Zandt (Thick Workman); Norma Drury (French Lady); Jeff Corey (Secretary); John Bleifer (Workman); Jean Del Val (Peasant); Roland Varno (German Pilot); William Ruhl (Nazi Radio

Operator); Douglas Grant (British Squadron Leader); Eric Lonsdale
(English RAF Lieutenant); John Meredith (English Radio Operator);
Jacques Vanaire (Hotel Manager); Eugene Borden (Aide); Hans Von
Morhart (German Corporal); Gene O'Donnell (English Messenger);
Dick Alexander (German Guard); Alphonse Martel (French Aide--
Gendarme); Arno Frey (Watchman); George Cathrey (RAF Radio
Operator); Ken Nolan (German Sergeant); Eric Alden, Eddie Dew,
William Yetter (Gestapo Men); Joe Kamaryst, Marty Faust, Hans
Fürberg (Men); Pete Sosso (Workman).

William Yetter, Randolph Scott, and Otto Reichow in <u>Paris Calling</u>
(Universal, 1941).

On the way to Bordeaux after the German occupation of Paris,
carefree French aristocrat Bergner has a sudden change of patriotic heart when her mother is killed in a bombing raid. She offers
her services to the Resistance and is soon engaged in undercover
activities--while posing as a piano player in Sondergaard's cheap
waterfront cafe (pounding out specially coded messages on the key-
board). Later Bergner is forced to kill her ex-fiancé (Rathbone),
a Vichy politician who is conspiring to acquire the terms of the
Gaullist surrender. Her knight in shining armor is American
R. A. F. pilot Nick (Scott), who finds himself stranded behind enemy
lines when his teammates pull out of the area. A very stock

thriller finish has the British commandos raid the French coastal
defenses of the Germans.

The Nazi takeover of France was both a historical and emotional catastrophe, neither aspect of which was captured by this
glib rendering, most noted for being the American film debut of
Continental star Bergner. The plot rushes here and there in
search of excitement, but it has nothing new or poignant to say,
relying heavily on its experienced cast to spread a veil of gratuitous
credibility. Most successful in this respect are Cobb as a very
three-dimensional Gestapo official, and Sondergaard, Ciannelli, and
Edmunds as determined Gaullist agents. To the film's slight credit,
it is not entirely anti-German in approach in that it shows a very
humane Third Reich pilot who parachutes out of his craft rather
than bomb defenseless mothers and children.

PARIS UNDERGROUND (UA, 1945) 97 min.

Executive producer, Carley Harriman; director, Gregory
Ratoff; based on the novel by Etta Shiber; screenplay, Boris Ingster,
Gertrude Purcell; producer designer, Nicholai Remisoff; art director, Victor Greene; set decorator, Sydney Moore; music, Alexander Tansman; music supervisor, David Chudnow; assistant director, Ad Schaumer; sound, John Carter; camera, Lee Garmes;
editor, James Newcom.

Constance Bennett (Kitty de Mornay); Gracie Fields (Emmyline Quayle); George Rigaud (Andre de Mornay); Kurt Kreuger (Captain Kurt von Weber); Leslie Vincent (Lieutenant Gray); Charles
Andrew (Father Dominique); Eily Malyon (Madame Martin); Vladimir Sokoloff (Undertaker); Richard Ryan (Mr. Renard).

For its modest approach, Paris Underground was overstated
and slow moving, but it did have the redeeming virtues of a yet
charming producer-star (Bennett) and the offbeat, rousing presence
of Fields. James Agee (The Nation) sized up the film as "mainly
trash, involving enough handsome young men, in various postures of
gallant gratitude, to satisfy Mae West in her prime!"

War makes strange partners, none so seemingly disparate as
frivolous American Kitty de Mornay (Bennett) married to an old
guard French Foreign Office official (Rigaud), and sedate middle-
aged Britisher Emmyline Quayle (Fields) who runs a Paris antique
shop. The German occupation drastically changes both their out-
looks and ways of life, with the two women joining forces to aid
Allied fliers to escape from behind the enemy lines. Each woman
must delve into her own reserve of fortitude and ingenuity as their
daring activities lead them into tense situations and the eventual
necessity of murdering some of their adversaries. Before their
timely rescue by the American army, the distaff partisans are
brave prisoners of the Germans.

Gracie Fields and Constance Bennett in <u>Paris Underground</u> (UA, 1945).

PAS DE ROSES POUR O. S. S. 117 [No Roses for O. S. S. 117] (Valoria, 1968)   C   105 min.

Director, Andre Hunebelle; based on the novel by Jean Bruce; screenplay, Michel Levine, Pierre Foucauld, Jean-Pierre Desagnat, Renzo Cerrato; music, Piero Piccioni; camera, Tonino Delli Colli.

John Gavin (O. S. S. 117); Margaret Lee (Aiche); Curt Jurgens (Major); Luciana Paluzzi (Doctor); Robert Hossein (Saadi); and: Piero Lulli, Rosalba Neri, Guido Alberti, George Eastman.

Disguised as bank robber Chandler, O. S. S. 117 (Gavin) unearths clues which lead him to a powerful criminal organization.   The latter group is bent on fomenting world unrest by killing a diplomat of the UNO, a supervisory organization appointed to bring peace among some tribes in the Middle East.   O. S. S. 117 divides his time between combating the sinister forces and romancing Aiche (Lee).   The actress actually provides the most interesting distractions within the usual stereotyped proceedings.

U. S. tv title: <u>O. S. S. 117--Double Agent.</u>

PASSAGE TO MARSEILLE   (WB, 1944)   109 min.

Producer, Hal B. Wallis; director, Michael Curtiz; based on
the novel Men without Country by Charles Nordhoff, James Norman
Hall; screenplay, Casey Robinson, Jack Moffitt; music, Max Steiner;
assistant director, Frank Heath; art director, Carl Jules Weyl;
makeup, Perc Westmore; special effects, Jack Cosgrove, Edwin B.
Du Par, Byron Haskin, E. Roy Davidson, Rex Wimpy; montages,
James Leicester; song, Steiner and Ned Washington; technical adviser, Sylvain Roberts; camera, James Wong Howe; editor, Owen
Marks.

Humphrey Bogart (Matrac); Claude Rains (Captain Freycinet);
Michele Morgan (Paula); Philip Dorn (Renault); Sydney Greenstreet
(Commandant Duval); Peter Lorre (Marius); George Tobias (Petit);
Victor Francen (Captain Patain Malo); Helmut Dantine (Carou);
John Loder (Manning); Konstantin Shayne (First Mate); Monte Blue
(Second Mate); Corinna Mura (Singer); Eduardo Ciannelli (Chief
Engineer); Vladimir Sokoloff (Grandpere); Charles La Torre
(Lieutenant Lenoir); Hans Conreid (Jourdain); Mark Stevens
(Lieutenant Hastings); Louis Mercier (Engineer); Billy Roy (Mess
Boy); Donald Stuart (Military Driver); Walter Bonn (Prison Official);
Carmen Beretta (Petit's Wife); Diane DuBois (Petit's Daughter);
Jean Del Val (Raoul); Alex Papanao (Lookout); Peter Miles (Jean);
Raymond St. Albin (Medical Officer); Peter Camlin (French Sergeant);
Anatol Frikin (Crazy Convict); Frank Puglia (Older Guard); Harry
Cording (Chief Guard); Adrienne D'Ambricourt (Mayor's Wife); Fred
Essler (Mayor).

Always hoping to repeat a successful screen formula, Warner
Bros. put director Michael Curtiz back in charge of a war story
with an almost identical cast from Casablanca, save that Michele
Morgan replaced Ingrid Bergman. Though Passage to Marseille
was much more brutal than its predecessor, its plot was far more
confused, its dialog less witty, its characters less sympathetic, and
it lacked a great unrequited love theme.

Told in flashbacks, the film recounts the adventures of five
Devil's Island escapees (Bogart, Lorre, Dorn, Dantine, Tobias) who
are picked up by a French freighter on the eve of France's surrender to the Nazis. When the German occupation is announced,
the ship's captain (Francen), a pro-Ally, is forced to fight Commandant Duval (Greenstreet), the latter vowing to turn the freighter
over to the Vichy government when they reach Marseille. Throughout the desperate passage, further flashbacks reveal events in the
escapees' lives which led them to their fate on Devil's Island, and
suggest a vague basis for their turning patriotic and taking the side
of the Allies against the Nazis to save the freighter.

With the newly-potent Bogart marquee name and a heavy
studio publicity campaign, Passage to Marseille was a strong boxoffice winner. Despite the film's paeon to patriotism and the
valiant efforts of French partisans in the underground movement,
James Agee (The Nation) was among those critics registering some
sharp objections to portions of the film, as "when Humphrey Bogart,

on a ship representing France, slaughters the surviving helpless crew of a wrecked plane which represents conquered Germany. Victor Francen is shocked, to be sure; but Bogart is the star, from whom the majority will accordingly accept advice on what to do with Germany."

PASSPORT TO SUEZ   (Columbia, 1943)   71 min.

Producer, Wallace MacDonald; director, Andre de Toth; story, Alden Nash; screenplay, John Stone; music director, Morris W. Stoloff; camera, L. W. O'Connell; editor, Mel Thorsen.

Warren William (Michael Lanyard); Ann Savage (Valerie King); Eric Blore (Jameson); Robert Stanford (Donald Jameson); Sheldon Leonard (Johnny Booth); Lloyd Bridges (Fritz); Gavin Muir (Karl); Lou Merrill (Rembrandt); Frederic Worlock (Sir Roger Wembley); Jay Novello (Cezanne); Sig Arno (Whistler); John Tyrrel, Frank O'Connor (Wembley's Men); Eddie Kane (Gay Man); Stanley Price (Native Cop); Gene Stone (Bartender); Frank Arnold

Jack Rice, Robert Stanford, Warren William, Sheldon Leonard, and Eric Blore in Passport to Suez (Columbia, 1943).

(French Waiter); Carl DeLord, Hercules Mendez, Janet Calionzes
(Greeks); Jack Lee (Drunk); George Chermanoff, Adonis DeMilo,
Tony Abdenour (Turks); Frances Chan (Chinese); Grace Lem
(Woman); Tanya Samova (Russian); Jack Rice (Hotel Clerk); Floyd
Shackelford, Darby Jones (Bellboys); Nick Thompson, Frank Lack-
teen (Launderers); Mal Merrihugh (Chauffeur).

Warren William's last entry in The Lone Wolf detective
series had Michael Lanyard, alias The Lone Wolf (William), and
his trusted valet Jameson (Blore) in Alexandria, Egypt, spying on
the Germans for Great Britain as a part of the latter's North African campaign.   The Germans capture Blore and threaten to kill him
if he does not steal specific documents from the British embassy.
Also involved in the complicated plot is Blore's son (Stanford), who
is in the British Navy, and the boy's girlfriend (Savage), a reporter
double serving as a spy trying to save the Suez Canal from Axis
takeover.
        With The Lone Wolf finally triumphing over the villains, the
film was adequate for the wartime market.   Andre de Toth, later
to direct some top-notch Westerns and melodramas, handled the film
well.   A highlight of the proceedings was a trio of sleazy characters:
Rembrandt (Merrill), Cezanne (Novello), and Whistler (Arno).   In
addition, Leonard was more restrained than usual as a cooperative
cafe owner.

PATRIA   (International Film Service, 1917)   15 chapters

        Chapters: (1) Last of the Fighting Channings, (2) The Trea-
sure, (3) Winged Millions, (4) Double Crossed, (5) The Island God
Forgot, (6) Alias Nemesis, (7) Red Dawn, (8) Red Night, (9) Cat's
Paw and Scapegoat, (10) War in the Dooryard, (11) Sunset Falls,
(12) Peace on the Border or Peace Which Passeth All Understanding,
(13) Wings of Death, (14) Border Peril, and (15) For the Flag.

        Director, the Whartons, Jacques Jaccard; screenplay, Joseph
Vance.
        Irene Castle (Patria); Milton Sills (Donald Parr); and:
Warner Oland, Floyd Buckley, Marie Walcamp, George Maharoni,
Allen Murnane, Dorothy Green.

        For $90,000, an expensive outlay at the time, this 15-chap-
ter serial was mounted by the William Randolph Hearst enterprises
for the express purpose of helping to drag America out of isolationism and into the thick of World War I, a situation President
Woodrow Wilson had been vainly trying to avoid.   Irene Castle who
had attained great fame as the dancing partner of Vernon Castle
was hired to headline this blatant propaganda chapterplay and she

---

[Facing page] Irene Castle and Dorothy Green in Patria (International Film Service, 1917).

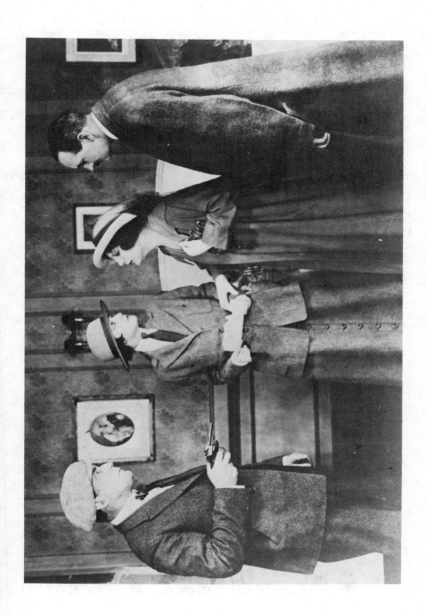

was billed as "the best known woman in America today." In a rather daring display of zealous patriotism, Patria made no bones about naming the villains of the screen piece as the Japanese and Mexicans, two minority groups in America who were often branded as tools of the Kaiser. For many artistic reasons, Patria was never the all-out hit predicted.

Castle was seen as Patria, the last of the "Fighting Channings," and heiress to a large U.S. munitions plant and a huge fortune put aside by her family for the express purpose of providing America with weapons in its time of need. Japan's Baron Huroki and Mexico's Juan de Lima have other plans in mind for the secret trust fund, and only through the astounding perseverence of Castle and Captain Donald Parr (Sills) of the U.S. Secret Service who overcome astounding obstacles, does America remain safe for democracy.

PEARL OF THE ARMY (Pathé, 1916)   15 Chapters

Chapters: (1) The Traitor, (2) Found Guilty, (3) The Silent Menace, (4) War Clouds, (5) Somewhere in Grenada, (6) Major Brent's Perfidy, (7) For the Stars and Stripes, (8) International Diplomacy, (9) The Monroe Doctrine, (10) The Silent Army, (11) A Million Volunteers, (12) The Foreign Alliance, (13) Modern Buccaneers, (14) The Flag Despoiler, and (15) The Colonel's Orderly.

Pearl White in Pearl of the Army (Pathé, 1916).

Director, Edward Jose; screenplay, G. W. McConnell, George
B. Seitz.
With: Pearl White, Ralph Kellard, Marie Wayne, Floyd
Buckley, Theodore Friebus, W. T. Carleton.

The mysterious "Silent Menace" tries to steal defense plans
for the Panama Canal, but in a train wreck the plans are recovered
by White and she foils the Menace each time he attempts to obtain
them.
A highly patriotic serial, the climactic scene had the Menace
trying to lower the U. S. flag and White doing her valiant best to
stop him. (The lowering of the flag was a pre-arranged signal to
start an uprising.)
The finale of this cliffhanger found Pearl's officer lover
(Friebus) cleared of a treason charge and her being honored by
a full dress parade of American troops.
Ten years after the serial's initial release, Pearl of the
Army was re-cut and reissued in a ten-chapter serial format.

LA PEAU DE TORPEDO (Les Films Copernic, 1970) C 93 min.

Producer, Maurice Jacquin; director, Jean Delannoy; based
on the novel by Francis Ryck; screenplay, Jean Cau, Delannoy;
camera, Edmond Sechan.
Stephane Audran (Dominique); Lilli Palmer (Helen); Klaus
Kinski (Torpedo); Michel Constantin (Coster); Jean Claudio (Fedor);
Frederic de Pasquale (Nicholas); Noelle Adam (Laurence); Christine
Fabrega (Sylviane); Georges Lycan (Torpedo II); Catherine Jacob-
sen (Françoise).

Unknown to Dominique (Audran), her Parisian antique shop
owner husband (de Pasquale) is an agent for a foreign spy ring.
Network leader Helen (Palmer) has de Pasquale steal national defense papers and then orders him to drop from sight, along with
co-agent Françoise (Jacobsen). After Audran learns of her husband's multi-duplicities, she shoots him, causing both the police
and Palmer to dog her steps.
Despite the heavy romantic interaction between de Pasquale
and Jacobsen in the course of the story, the feature received a
PG rating in the United States. Boxoffice magazine lauded the
production for being "... replete with subterfuge, intrigue and
other elements dear to the suspense aficionado. "
U. S. release title: Only the Cool; also known as The
Deathmakers.

PICKUP ON SOUTH STREET (20th-Fox, 1953) 80 min.

Producer, Jules Schermer; director, Samuel Fuller; based on
the story by Dwight Taylor; screenplay, Fuller; art director, Lyle
R. Wheeler, George Patrick; set decorator, Al Orenbach; music,

Klaus Kinski in La Peau de Torpedo (Les Films Copernic, 1970).

Leigh Harline; assistant director, Ad Schaumer; camera, Joe Mac-
Donald; editor, Nick de Maggio.
          Richard Widmark (Skip McCoy); Jean Peters (Candy); Thelma
Ritter (Moe); Murvyn Vye (Captain Dan Tiger); Richard Kiley (Joey);
Willis Bouchey (Zara); Milburn Stone (Winoki); Henry Slate (Mac-
Gregor); Jerry O'Sullivan (Enyart); Harry Carter (Dietrich); George
Eldredge (Fenton); Frank Kumagi (Lum); Victor Perry (Lightning
Louie); George Berkeley (Customer); Emmett Lynn (Sandwich Man);
Maurice Samuels (Ped); Farley Baer (Foreigner); Jay Loftin (Li-
brarian); Virginia Carroll (Nurse); Roger Moore (Mr. Victor).

          Ostensibly a gangster film, Pickup on South Street is much
more a study of a particular facet of the American way of life.
Here director Samuel Fuller delineates the world of pickpockets,
petty crooks, pimps, and hustlers, who have their own brand of
morality, one which includes protecting the U.S. from the spread
of Communism.   Unlike the 1942 All Through the Night (q.v.),
which took a rather comic approach to New York gangsters combatting Fifth Columnists, this picture uses an overtone of violence--
particularly counting on star Widmark's tough guy image--to put
across its storyline.

Three-time loser Skip McCoy (Widmark) snatches a purse belonging to Candy (Peters), unaware that her wallet contains microfilm of top secret chemical formulas obtained by a Communist spy ring operating in the New York area. Widmark's crime is observed by two federal agents, including Zara (Bouchey), who have been trailing the naive Peters. Later, Joey (Kiley) tells her girlfriend-worker Peters to get the film back or else. So both Peters and the law enforcers turn to ragamuffin fence Moe (Ritter) to trace sniveling tough guy Widmark's whereabouts--he "lives" in a water-front shack. At first Widmark is willing to do some business with the Red, but after Kiley kills Ritter, Widmark's patriotic conscience comes to the fore, and he turns to the side of the law to track down the Communist culprits.

At the time of this picture's release it was considered a fairly brutal study of the tawdry underworld scene, even with its depiction of the moral conscience of petty crooks who regarded themselves as self-respecting Americans to whom Communism is anathema. Ritter was Oscar-nominated for her contra-casted assignment, while many people wondered why 20th Century-Fox mogul Darryl F. Zanuck ever considered having song-and-dance star Betty Grable play the role of Candy, a part originally ticketed for Shelley Winters. Today, of course, Pickup on South Street has gained a sturdy foothold in the repertory of 1950s cinema as a sterling example of the work of cultist director Fuller.

PIMPERNEL SMITH (UA, 1941)   100 min.

Producer, Leslie Howard; associate producer, Harold Huth; director, Howard; story, A.C. McDonnell, Wolfgang Wilhelm; screenplay, Anatole De Grunewald; camera, M. Greenbaum; editor, Douglas Myers.

Leslie Howard (Professor Horatio); Francis L. Sullivan (General von Graum); Hugh McDermott (David Maxwell); Mary Morris (Ludmilla Koslowski); Raymond Huntley (Marx); A.E. Matthews (Earl of Meadowbrook); Roland Pertwee (Sir George Smith); Manning Wiley (Bertie Gregson); Philip Friend (Spencer); Basil Appleby (Jock MacIntyre); Lawrence Kitchen (Clarence Elstead); David Tomlinson (Steve); Aubrey Mallalieu (Dean); Allan Jeayes (Dr. Breckendorf); Peter Gawthorne (Sidimir Koslowski); Ernest Butcher (Weber); Ben Williams (Graubitz).

"Singapore may fall, but the British can still make melodramas to chill the veins" (New York Times). Director-star Leslie Howard returned to one of his most popular screen characterizations in this updating of The Scarlet Pimpernel, which now had the British star rescuing victims of Nazi Germany rather than revolution-torn 1790s France.

In the summer before World War II began, Cambridge professor Horatio (Howard), an antiquities specialist, has brought a group of students for a field session of artifact digging in Germany, ostensibly to test the Aryan theory of superiority. At first no one links the crotchety, vacant-minded archaeologist with the dashing cool "Mister V" who has been snatching victims from the Gestapo's clutches. Eventually both Howard's adolescent students and the Nazis catch on to his ruse, but Howard politely insists he must undertake one more rescue mission to save a group of scientists and a girl (Morris) being held in a concentration camp.

Since the outcome of this thriller was pretty obvious from the start (Howard the star must emerge successful and very much alive), the story focused on the sharp contrasts of Howard's dual character, as the blundering Germans, under the lead of General von Graum (Sullivan) cope with reality (Mister V) versus appearance (the professor). The plot contained some absurdities, such as Howard's too easy entrance into the concentration camp, but the taut, effective moments more than compensated (especially the scene in which the pursuing Nazis shoot at the elusive Mister V, and apparently miss their target, but then the camera closes in on a seemingly harmless farmyard scarecrow who is dripping real blood). The finale accentuates the strong patriotism then surrounding every aspect of the British way of life. As Howard and his team pass across the frontier into Switzerland, a voice floats across the wind to the stymied German border guards, saying "We'll be back. We'll all be back."

Also known as Mister V.

THE PRESIDENT'S ANALYST (Paramount, 1967) C 103 min.

Executive producer, Howard W. Koch; producer, Stanley Rubin; director-screenplay, Theodore J. Flicker; music, Lalo Schifrin; songs, Barry Maguire, Paul Potash; The Clear Light; production designer, Palo Guzman; assistant director, Kurt Neumann; sound, Robert L. Post, John Wilkinson; costumes, Jack Bear; art director, Hal Pereira, Al Roelofs; set decorator, Robert Benton, Arthur Krams; animation, DePatie-Freleng; special camera effects, Westheimer Company; camera, William A. Fraker; editor, Stuart Pappe.

James Coburn (Dr. Schaefer); Godfrey Cambridge (Don Masters); Severn Darden (Kropotkin); Joan Delaney (Nan Butler); Pat Harrington (Arlington Hewes); Barry Maguire (Old Wrangler); Jill Banner (Snow White); Eduard Franz (Ethan Allan Cocket); Walter Burke (Henry Lux); Will Geer (Dr. Evans); William Daniels (Wynn Quantrill); Joan Darling (Jeff Quantrill); Sheldon Collins (Bing Quantrill); Arte Johnson (Sullivan); Martin Horsey, William Beckley (Puddlians); Kathleen Hughes (Tourist).

Counter counter-espionage is the accepted state of affairs in this fitfully witty exercise about the lunacy abounding in the present-day cold war espionage race. The ultimate scamp in The President's Analyst is none other than the monopolistic telephone company, pointing up the film's satire on American mores in which spying is theorized as "the last refuge of the incurable romantic." The film's jokes ultimately run thin, exposing the underdeveloped

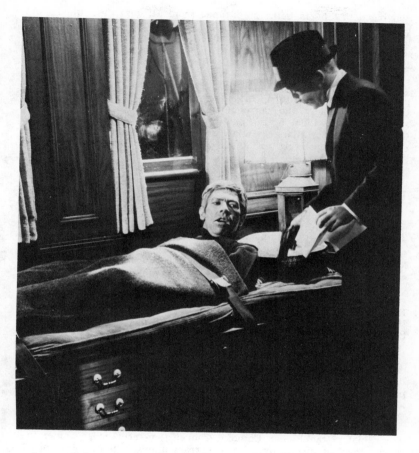

James Coburn in <u>The President's Analyst</u> (Paramount, 1967).

comedy premise.   The press reaction to <u>T. P. A.</u> was mildly un-
favorable and the public politely looked elsewhere for their entertainment.   Brave black comedies are just not likely filmfare for
Americans.
        Neurotic C. I. A. agent Don Masters (Cambridge) agrees that
his swinging New York City psychiatrist Dr. Schaefer (Coburn)
would be a promising candidate to serve as the top secret analyst
to America's President, a troubled man who desperately needs the
opportunity to unburden his mind to someone he can trust.   Before
long Coburn is feeling the strain of his new post.   He begins revealing state secrets in his nightmarish sleep and is almost

convinced that he is being spied upon from all quarters, which, of
course, he is. When he realizes he is about to crack, he plots
his escape, first hiding out with a "typical" New York suburban
family and then by joining a group of wandering hippies. But agents
from all nations are on his trail. The Canadian secret service
team, disguised as a Liverpool rock group, later kidnaps Coburn,
and in turn they are all captured by the Russians, headed by Kropotkin (Darden). In turn, the ultimate baddie and kidnapper is
the phone company who has decided the only way to cope with the
abuse lashed at them by the public, is to take over the country.
Coburn, his gal (Delaney), and Darden manage to destroy the phone
company's headquarters and think they have now saved America.
But have they...?

THE PRISONER (Columbia, 1955) 91 min.

Executive producer, Sydney Box; producer, Vivian A. Cox;
based on the play by Bridget Boland; screenplay, Boland; art director, John Hawkesworth; assistant director, Denis O'Dell; costumes, Julie Harris; makeup, William Pailleton; sound, Dudley
Messenger, Gordon K. McCallum; music, Benjamin Frankel; camera, Reginald Wyer; editor, Frederick Wilson.
        Alec Guinness (The Prisoner); Jack Hawkins (The Interro-
gator); Raymond Huntley (The General); Jeannette Sterke (The Girl);
Kenneth Griffith (The Secretary); Ronald Lewis (The Guard); Gerard
Heinz (The Doctor); Mark Dignam (The Governor); Wilfred Lawson
(The Jailer).

This stark film is anything but the traditional cloak and
dagger movie. Instead, it is an excellent dramatic study that
demonstrates the vicious implications of a situation in which a non-
participant can be mentally tortured into confessing to treasonous
activities. "This is a film that will make you shiver--and think"
(New York Times).
        In an unnamed contemporary European police state, Guinness,
a cardinal of the Roman Catholic Church, is arrested and chief interrogator Hawkins is ordered to extract a full confession from
him that will discredit the Church in the public's eyes. Hawkins
is experienced enough to realize physical persuasion will not serve
his cause, as he and Guinness had worked together years ago in
the Resistance movement and the former is quite aware of the
latter's mettle. Instead Hawkins craftily sizes up the clergyman's
human failing, which proves not to be pride but humility. Over the
months Hawkins relentlessly picks away at Guinness' mental soli-
darity, pushing the prisoner over the brink when he convinces the
weary man of an untenable (half) truth: i.e., Guinness joined the
Church not so much from a pure love of God, but rather to escape
his sordid background (his mother was a fishmonger and a harlot).
Hawkins makes his subject "realize" that his religious calling and
life's work is a mockery. At the shamelessly staged public trial,
Guinness admits to all the stated lies. Instead of being executed

Alec Guinness, Gerard Heinz, and Wilfrid Lawson in The Prisoner (Columbia, 1955).

and becoming a martyr to his flock, he is released to go among his people, a man broken of spirit and will.

The battle of wills between two superior minds, which ends with a disgusted Hawkins not sure who the victor was, is a facet of cold war espionage obviously not geared to satisfy action-hungry moviegoers and thus not considered a very commercial subject for filmmakers. Bridget Boland, who authored the screenplay from her 1954 London play, which co-starred Hawkins, insisted not too successfully that this drama was not based on the then recent events in Hungary concerning Cardinal Mindszenty.

The Prisoner engendered tremendous political-religious antipathy in multi-factioned Europe. In France it was barred from the Cannes Film Festival as being anti-Communist, while in Italy it was branded an anti-Catholic film. In addition, the film was refused entrance at the Venice Film Festival for being a politically dangerous study and was labeled in Ireland as a pro-Communist movie.

THE PRIZE (MGM, 1963) C 136 min.

Producer, Pandro S. Berman; director, Mark Robson; based on the novel by Irving Wallace; screenplay, Ernest Lehman; assistant director, Hank Moonjean; art director, George W. Davis, Urie McCleary; set decorator, Henry Grace, Dick Pefferle; music, Jerry Goldsmith; makeup, William Tuttle; special camera effects, J. McMillan Johnson, A. Arnold Gillespie, Robert R. Hoag; camera, William Daniels; editor, Adrienne Fazan.

Paul Newman (Andrew Craig); Edward G. Robinson (Dr. Max Stratman); Elke Sommer (Inger Lisa Andersen); Diane Baker (Emily Stratman); Micheline Presle (Dr. Denise Marceau); Gerard Oury (Dr. Claude Marceau); Sergio Fantoni (Dr. Carlo Farelli); Kevin McCarthy (Dr. John Garrett); Leo G. Carroll (Count Bertil Jacobssen); Sacha Pitoeff (Daranyi); Jacqueline Beer (Monique Souvir); John Wengraf (Hans Eckart); Don Dubbins (Ivar Cramer); Virginia Christine (Mrs. Bergh); Rudolph Anders (Mr. Bergh); Martine Bartlett (Saralee Garrett); Karl Swenson (Hilding); John Qualen (Oscar); Ned Wever (Clark Wilson); Martin Brandt (Steen Ekberg); Ivan Triesault (Hotel Porter); Grazia Narciso (Mrs. Farelli); Larry Adare (David Garrett); Robin Adare (Amy Garrett); Lester Mathews (BBC News); John Banner (German Correspondent); Teru Shimada (Tokyo Correspondent); Jerry Dunphy (American TV News); Michael Panaieff (French Correspondent); Edith Evanson (Mrs. Ahlquist); Carol Byron (Stewardess); Sam Edwards (Reporter); Gregg Palmer (Swedish Commentator); Donald Ein (Waiter); Anna Lena Lund (Blonde); Peter Bourne (Swedish Man); Queenie Leonard (Miss Fawley); Lyle Sudrow (Swedish Reporter); Anna Lee (American Reporter); Albert Carrier (French Reporter); Gregory Gaye (Russian Reporter); Ben Wright (British Reporter); Erik Holland (Photographer); Sigfried Tor (Swedish Waiter); Gene Roth (Swedish Man); Sven-Hugo Borg (Oscar Lindbloom); Bjorn Foss (Swedish Man); Margareta Lund, Alice Frost, Felda Ein (Swedish Women); Noel Drayton (Police Constable Strohm); Karen von Unge (Receptionist); Birgitta Engstrom (Young Woman); Carl Carlsson (Swedish Visitor); Ike Ivarsen (Swedish Speaker); Carl Rydin, Ronald Nyman (Burly Swedes); Dr. Harold Dyrenforth, Fred Holliday (Swedish Officers); Raanhild Vidar (Swedish Bellboy); John Holland, Mauritz Hugo (Speakers); Peter Coe (Officer); Otto Reichow (Seaman); Robert Garrett, Paul Busch, Danny Klega, Fred Scheiwiller (Deck Hands); Ellie Ein (Bellboy); Sid Raymond (Actor); Britta Ekman, Maiken Thornberg, Maria Schroeder, Jill Carson, Pam Peterson, Sigrid Petterson, Margarto Sullivan (Nudists).

Despite or perhaps because of its myriad artistic and entertainment shortcomings, this hack version of a best-selling pulp novel made money for nearly all concerned, greatly aided by the Newman marquee allure and the highly promoted "nude" sequences. It "plays fast and loose not only with the prestige of the Nobel affair but also with simple conventions of melodrama and with the intelligence of the customers" (New York Times).

Among the recipients gathered in Stockholm to receive their

Nobel Prize Awards are Newman (Literature), Robinson (Physics), Presle-Oury (Chemistry), McCarthy-Fantoni (Medicine). Robinson, who came to Stockholm with his niece (Baker), is kidnapped by his Russian "twin brother," Baker's father. The Communists plan to have the bogus physicist deliver an anti-American acceptance speech, while the real prize winner is shipped behind the Iron Curtain. Because Newman, who has talked with the real physicist, makes some flip, casual remarks at a press conference, the Reds assume he is aware of their hatchet plot, which leads Newman into a rash of intrigue in and about Stockholm, including a chase at a nudist camp. With the attractive assistance of Swedish Foreign office aide Inger Lisa Andersen (Sommer), Newman rescues the real man of science and accompanies him back to the ceremonies just in time to deliver his speech.

In standard Hollywood fashion, with a generous nod to the novel's claptrap contrivances, The Prize is more concerned with pairing off the libidinous players into sparring partners and love matches than in focusing on the more complex intricacies of the enemy agent game. In fact, MGM touted the picture as a "comedy suspense melodrama." The critical furor over this specious movie was nothing compared to the Swedes' reaction to the novel and the subsequent picturization, with their similar undignified renderings of the highly regarded Nobel Prize ceremonies.

THE QUIET AMERICAN (UA, 1958) 120 min.

Producer-director, Joseph L. Mankiewicz; based on the novel by Graham Greene; screenplay, Mankiewicz; art director, Reno Nascimbene, Pierre Guffrey; music, Mario Nascimbene; assistant director, Piero Musetta, Colin Brewer, Giorgio Gentili; makeup, George Frost; sound, Al Thorne; special effects, Rosco Cline, George Schlickin; camera, Robert Krasker; editor, William Hornbeck.

Audie Murphy (The American); Michael Redgrave (Fowler); Claude Dauphin (Inspector Vigot); Georgia Moll (Phuong); Kerima (Miss Hei); Bruce Cabot (Bill Granger); Fred Sadoff (Dominguez); Richard Loo (Mister Heng); Peter Trent (Eliot Wilkins); Clinton Anderson (Joe Morton); Yoko Tani (Hostess); Sonia Moser (Yvette); Phung Thi Nghiep (Isabelle); Vo Doan Chau (Cao-Dai Commandant); Le Van Le (Cao-Dai Pope's Deputy); Le Guynh (Masked Man); Georges Brehat (French Colonel).

Graham Greene's 1956 novel, an acid study of a dangerous American meddler and undercover force in Indo-Chinese politics, was transformed by producer-director-scripter Joseph L. Mankiewicz into a half-hearted tribute to a saintly American boy who dies for his misguided political beliefs (i.e., that some third alternative, neither Communism nor colonialism, is best for the future of Asia). Despite the boxoffice concessions in disguising the film's earnest message, the movie fell on deaf ears. Among the fourth estate who disparaged the picture for one reason or another was the

Michael Redgrave and Audie Murphy in <u>The Quiet American</u> (UA, 1958).

politically aware <u>Films in Review</u>: "The average US audience will not know what this picture is about. As for average audiences in other parts of the world, well, perhaps USIA, CIA, or the State Department, should check on what is on the sound track of the prints distributed abroad. It wouldn't take many changes on the sound track to restore the essence of Graham Greene's anti-Americanism."

    <u>The Quiet American</u> opens in 1952 Saigon where the American's (Murphy) body is found floating in the river on the night of the Chinese New Year. The only one who may have a clue to Murphy's death is the English newsman Fowler (Redgrave). It is known that Murphy, an idealistic graduate student in political science, arrived in Indo-China as part of the American Point Four program. His rarefied political concepts caused him to stray from the rampant Communist versus colonialist/democracy rivalry, and to become

embroiled in a Red-fomented revolution.   As an unwitting collaborationist, do-gooder Murphy comes into direct conflict with the embittered, tired journalist Redgrave, clashing intellectually over
politics and emotionally over Eurasian Phuong (Moll), the girl who
leaves Redgrave for Murphy.
     Filmed at the Cinecitta Studios in Rome with sparse location
work in Vietnam.   Many thought clean-cut Murphy woefully mis-
cast in the lead role of a brash intruder, particularly in contrast
to Redgrave who shone as the cynical world observer, and Dauphin
as intense Inspector Vigot of the French police.

QUIET, PLEASE, MURDER (20th-Fox, 1943)   70 min.

     Producer, Ralph Dietrich; director, John Larkin; story,
Lawrence G. Blochman; screenplay, Larkin; art director, Richard
Day, Joseph C. Wright; camera, Joseph MacDonald; editor, Louis
Loeffler.
     George Sanders (Fleg); Gail Patrick (Myra Blanding); Richard
Denning (Hal McByrne); Lynne Roberts (Kay Ryan); Sidney Black-
mer (Martin Cleaver); Kurt Katch (Eric Pahsen); Margaret Bray-
ton (Miss Oval); Charles Tannen (Hollis); Byron Foulger (Edmund
Walpole); George Walcott (Benson); Bud Geary (Gannett); Frank
O'Connor (Guard in Library); W. R. Deming (Mr. Daly); Arthur
Space (Bance); Lon McCallister (Freddie, the Stack Boy); Chick
Collins (Webley); Harold Goodwin (Stover); Jack Cheatham (Police-
man); Hooper Atchley (Air Raid Warden); James Farley (Detective);
Arthur Thalasso (Air Raid Warden); Mae Marsh (Miss Hartwig);
Monica Bannister (Bit); Fern Emmett (Miss Philbert); Bobby Larsen
(Boy); Minerva Urecal (Housewife); Pat O'Malley (Guard); Jill
Warren (Girl); Bert Roach (Expectant Father); Charles Cane (In-
spector Henderson); Paul Porcasi (Rebescu); Matt McHugh (Taxi
Driver); Theodor von Eltz (Lucas).

     Sanders smoothly essayed a Freudian-oriented art collector
who steals rare volumes, duplicates them, and then blithely sells
the bogus product.   In this nefarious activity he is taken in by
the Nazis who are out to collect a huge art collection culled from
the United States.   With most of its scenes in a few closely con-
fined areas, including the Washington, D. C., library, the Nazis
attempt to eliminate the double-dealing Sanders, only to leave a
trail of corpses in the wake.
     There was much to commend this unpretentious programmer-
chiller, even if "The title is better than the story, which strays from
probability too often" (New York Sun).   It was a rare change for
American filmmakers to portray the Nazis as culture-conscious
citizens of the world, albeit as vicious swine as well.

THE QUILLER MEMORANDUM (20th-Fox, 1966)   C   103 min.

     Producer, Ivan Foxwell; director, Michael Anderson; based

on the novel The Berlin Memorandum by Adam Hall; screenplay,
Harold Pinter; art director, Maurice Carter; music, John Barry;
assistant director, Clive Reed; makeup, W. T. Partteton; special
effects, Les Bowie, Arthur Beavis; camera, Erwin Hiller;
editor, Frederick Wilson.

George Segal (Quiller); Alec Guinness (Pol); Max von Sydow
(Oktober); Senta Berger (Inge); George Sanders (Gibbs); Robert
Helpmann (Weng); Robert Flemyng (Gibbs' Associate); Peter Carsten
(Hengel); Edith Schneider (Headmistress); Gunter Meisner (Hassler);
Robert Stass (Jones); Ernest Walder (Grauber).

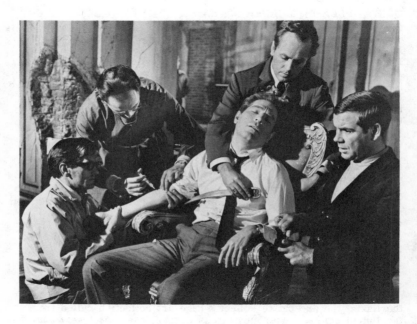

George Segal (center) in The Quiller Memorandum (20th-Fox, 1966).

At the time of release there were few champions for this
feature (which the New York Post derided, "... the picture makes
with spy and counterspy maneuvers that seem commonplace in all
three routines, flight-and-pursuit, chase-and-be-caught, and re-
sistance-despite-drugs"). Rising to the defense were, among others,
Andrew Sarris (Village Voice)--"So masterfully concise that it has
been completely misunderstood"--and Gordon Gow (British Films
and Filming)--"While stirring up many a deep thought upon life and
inhumanity and power and politics, The Quiller Memorandum remains
essentially a rip-snorting thriller, and often the snorts are quite

jolly, to say nothing of the rips." Twentieth Century-Fox had so little faith in the film that they were quite willing to delete all poignant references to the neo-Nazi movements when the feature was exhibited in West Germany and other Continental markets.

Steeped in the direct but ambiguous Harold Pinter screenplay, The Quiller Memorandum follows well in the down-trodden heels of The Spy Who Came in from the Cold in depicting realistically the mundane but dangerous existence of the contemporary spy. Agent Quiller (Segal), like the film, exhibits a strong antipathy to the carryover authority of the old Establishment with its organizational hierarchy, but actor and script also reflect the realization of the necessity of controllers in the helter-skelter modern world playing of espionage. With subtle satire these concepts are reflected in the appearances of Sanders and Flemyng, two Whitehall bigwigs who from their sumptuous safe retreats coldly direct the movements of Segal and other agents by way of matter-of-fact mouthings by Segal's Berlin control contact (Guinness). Guinness establishes the scope of his subordinate's German mission with only a minimum of overt cognizance of the variables and dubious principles at stake. The irony is maintained in the immobile approach of Segal's eventual adversary, the gentlemanly von Sydow.

Segal has been assigned to unearth the headquarters of a neo-Nazi organization running rampant in Berlin. He completes this task knowing full well that despite a temporary setback the militaristic faction will carry on even more strongly in years to come. As a small wheel in a very big machine, Segal abhors his robot-like performance of pre-ordained missions, but he is equally annoyed (and confused) to find that his still very human nature allows him to bypass the capture of German school teacher Berger who is connected with von Sydow. Reflecting on these saturated philosophical aspects of The Quiller Memorandum, critic Gordon Gow theorizes, "Contemporary and provocative as this is, the overall demeanour of the film is quite old-fashioned, making a welcome change from the frenetic trends which by now only Batman can master with a proper show of confidence."

A RAVISHING IDIOT   see   UNE RAVISSANTE IDIOTE

UNE RAVISSANTE IDIOTE [A Ravishing Idiot] (S. N. C., 1964) 108 min.

Producer, Michel Ardan; director, Edouard Molinare; based on the novel by Charles Exbrayat; screenplay, Andre and Georges Tabet; music, Michel Legrand; set designs, Jean Andre, Robert Clavel; sound, Robert Biart; camera, Robert Isnardon.

Brigitte Bardot (Penelope); Anthony Perkins (Harry Compton); Gregoire Aslan (Badga); Andre Luguet (Reginald Dumfrey); Charles Millot (Baianiev); Helene Dieudonne (Mamie); Jacques Monod (Surgeon); Jean-Marc Tennberg (Cartwright); Hans Verner (Farrington);

Paul Demange (Bank Director); Denise Provence (Lady Barbara);
and: Robert Murzeau.

Anthony Perkins, Brigitte Bardot, and Gregoire Aslan in Une
Ravissante Idiote (S.N.C., 1964).

When he is summarily dismissed from his bank post, bumbling Londoner Perkins is innocently led into stealing the plans for
Project Avalance from the home of Luguet, of the British Admiralty.
It develops that the Naval Department is aware of the theft and has
planted false documents with Perkins, hoping to unmask the head of
Soviet espionage in Great Britain.   Abetting Perkins in his seem-
ingly irrational acts is scatterbrained Bardot, an Allied-affiliated
agent posing as a couturière and a Communist party sympathizer.
At the big ball given by Dumfrey, agents from various nations con-
gregate and the phony documents pass from hand to hand.   Bungling
Perkins and Bardot almost ruin the British efforts to capture the
Russian spy head.
This misfire drew little enthusiasm from any quarter.   The
story was set in London but the film was shot in France because
star Bardot was beleagued by British fans.
Also known as Agent 38-24-36.

THE REAL GONE GIRLS see THE MAN FROM O. R. G. Y.

THE RED MENACE (Republic, 1949) 81 min.

Producer, Herbert J. Yates; director, R. G. Springsteen; story, Albert Demond; screenplay, Demond, Gerald Geraghty; art director, Frank Arrigo; music, Nathan Scott; camera, John Mac-Burnie; editor, Harry Keller.

Robert Rockwell (Bill Jones); Hanne Axman (Nina Petrovka); Shepard Menken (Henry Solomon); Barbara Fuller (Mollie O'Flaherty); Betty Lou Gerson (Yvonne Kraus); Lester Luther (Earl Partridge); James Harrington (Marlin Vejac); William J. Lally (Jack Tyler); William Martel (Riggs); Duke Williams (Sam); Kay Reihl (Mrs. O'Flaherty); Royal Raymond (Benson); Gregg Martell (Schultz); Mary DeGolyen (Proprietress); Leo Cleary (Father O'Leary); Norman Budd (Reachi); Napoleon Simpson (Tom Wright); Robert Purcell (Sheriff).

The Communist witch hunt was running rampant and even Republic Pictures, noted for its Westerns and serials, jumped onto the bandwagon with this modest entry, which Cue magazine termed "... frankly propaganda; by no stretch of the imagination can it be termed entertainment." The film was strictly geared to demonstrate, in very heavy-handed style, the calculated chicanery, conniving, and character assassination techniques of Red agents operating in America.

The story opens with Bill Jones (Rockwell) and Nina Petrovka (Axman) fleeing cross-country. It quickly switches into flashback to explain the origin of their plight. Rockwell is an ex-G.I. who was swindled in a housing project scheme; given no redress by an unminding government commission, he falls easy prey to Communist indoctrination, led on by a variety of party workers. When Axman undertakes to teach him the fine points of the Party system, she does not bargain that she will fall in love with the confused chap or that eventually their romance will lead to a mutual reassessment of the values of democracy.

The only satisfying acting performance in The Red Menace is offered by Shepard Menken as Henry Solomon, a disillusioned Jewish poet, who decides that death is the only escape from his involvement with the Communist Party.

THE REDHEAD AND THE COWBOY (Paramount, 1950) 82 min.

Producer, Irving Asher; director, Leslie Fenton; story, Charles Marquis Warren; screenplay, Jonathan Latimer, Liam O'Brien; music, David Buttolph; camera, Daniel L. Fapp; editor, Arthur Schmidt.

Glenn Ford (Gil Kyle); Edmond O'Brien (Dunn Jeffers); Rhonda Fleming (Candace Bronson); Alan Reed (Lamortine); Morris Ankrum (Sheriff); Edith Evanson (Mrs. Barrett); Perry Ivins (Mr.

Barrett); Janine Perreau (Mary Barrett); Douglas Spencer (Perry); Ray Teal (Brock); Ralph Byrd (Captain Andrews); King Donovan (Munroe); Tom Moore (Gus).

Edmond O'Brien and Glenn Ford in The Redhead and the Cowboy (Paramount, 1950).

"... [T]he story has a tight-lipped unfoldment, the terseness being carried to the point of obscurity as both characters and audience are kept in the dark by the step-by-step development" (Variety). For a relatively minor cinematic exercise, The Redhead and the Cowboy enjoyed substantially favorable reviews, enhanced, no doubt, by its still offbeat handling of the spy game set in Civil War times.

Southern sympathizer Candace Bronson (Fleming) is assigned to carry a message through to the leader (Reed) of the Confederate irregulars in the closing days of the Civil War. If she succeeds, the Grays just might get hold of a valuable gold shipment. Gil Kyle (Ford) is a rollicking cowboy who becomes intrigued with redheaded Fleming, but more importantly needs her as a witness to clear himself of a murder charge. He chases after the demure miss as she makes her circuitous tour of the Confederate spy stations. At the same time there comes into sight well-wisher Dunn Jeffers (O'Brien), an undercover Union officer out to corral Reed and hoping to have Fleming lead him to the Reb chief.

THE RELUCTANT SPY see L'HONORABLE STANISLAS, AGENT SECRET

RENEGADES (Fox, 1930)   8,400 feet

Presenter, William Fox; director, Victor Fleming; based on the novel Le Renegat by André Armandy; adaptation-continuity-dialog, Jules Furthman; sets, William Darling; song, Cliff Friend and Jimmy Monaco; assistant director, William Tummel; sound, Arthur L. von Kirbach; costumes, Sophie Wachner; technical adviser, Louis Van Den Ecker; camera, William O'Connell; editor, Harold Schuster.

Warner Baxter (Deucalion); Myrna Loy (Eleanore); Noah Beery (Machwurth); Gregory Gaye (Vologuine); George Cooper (Biloxi); C. Henry Gordon (Captain Mordiconi); Colin Chase (Sergeant-Major Olson); Bela Lugosi (The Marabout); Victor Jory (Officer).

This film is one more of those sand-and-sabre French Foreign Legion dramas, more notable for its fantastic plot than for solid entertainment values. As was then customary, spies were depicted in one-dimensional terms as heartless, self-serving souls.
A quartet of rebellious French Foreign Legionnaires (French officer Baxter, German Beery, American Cooper, and Russian Gaye), attached to Fort Amalfa, Morocco, escape confinement and participate in the defense of a neighboring post. Their actions earn them military honors, but Baxter is overwhelmed by an urge to revenge himself on Eleanore (Loy), a spy who has betrayed him. He installs himself as military leader of a local Arab tribe, has Loy kidnapped, and then made his servant. She in turn plots to win favor with the tribe's leader in order to discredit Baxter. Meanwhile, a change of fortune in the Arab-Foreign Legion conflict causes Baxter to enter the fort under a truce flag. While there, he fully comprehends how despised a renegade he has become, leading him to give up his life to protect the legionnaires when his native followers attack the stockade.
The New York Times rated Renegades as a "muddled and tedious offering."

REQUIEM FOR A SECRET AGENT (PEA/Constantin, 1965) C 105 min.

Director-story, Sergio Sollima; screenplay, Sollima, Sergio Donati; music, Antonio Perez Olea; camera, Carlo Carlini.
Stewart Granger (John "Bingo" Merrill); Daniela Bianchi (Edith); Peter Van Eyck (Oscar Gregory); Guilio Borsetti (Eric); Georgia Moll (Mrs. Bressart); Gianni Rizzo (Alexei); Maria Granada (Betty Lou); France Andrei (O'Brien); and: Wolf Hillinger, Benny Deus.

This intelligently conceived and well-done spy tale was shot on location in Tangiers with excellent color photography. Unfortunately this superior entry received no American theatrical release, being shoved onto the late night U.S. television programming cycle.

Played-out double agent John "Bingo" Merrill (Granger) is called from Berlin to Tangiers where he is hired by a CIA-like agency to combat a group of private mercenaries, whose powerful network arranges political activities, assassinations, and war. At the same time, he is hired by an agent (Borsetti) and a girl (Bianchi) to hunt the network's leader, a former Nazi, who killed the girl's parents.

RESIDENCIA PARA ESPIAS [Dans Chez les Gentlemen] (Hesperia, 1967) C 89 min.

Director, Jess Franco; screenplay, Michel Loggan, Antonio Masasoli.
With: Eddie Constantine (Dan Layton); Anita Hofer, Diana Lorys, Otto Stern, Mari Paz Pondal, Marcelo Arroita-Jauregui.

An internationally co-produced hodgepodge with secret agent Constantine sent to Istanbul where he assumes a colonel's wife is the leader of a spy group, only to discover in the end that the colonel himself is the culprit.

THE RETURN OF MR. MOTO (20th-Fox, 1965) 71 min.

Producer, Robert L. Lippert, Jack Parsons; director, Ernest Morris; based on the character created by John P. Marquand; story consultant, Randall Hood; screenplay, Fred Eggers; assistant director, Gordon Gilbert; art director, Harry White; music, Douglas Gamley; sound, Clive Smith; camera, Basil Emmott; editor, Robert Winter.
Henry Silva (Mr. Moto); Martin Wyldeck (Dargo); Terence Longdon (Jonathan Westering); Suzanne Lloyd (Maxine Powell); Marne Maitland (Wasir Hussein); Harold Kasket (Shahrdar of Wadi Shamar); Henry Gilbert (David Lennox); Brian Coburn (Magda); Stanley Morgan (Inspector Halliday); Peter Zander (Ginelli); Anthony Booth (Hovath); Gordon Tanner (McAllister); Richard Evans (Chief Inspector Marlow); Dennis Holmes (Chapel); Ian Fleming (Rogers); Tracy Connell (Arab); Sonyia Benjamin (The Belly Dancer); Alister Williamson (Maître d'Hotel).

Peter Lorre may have overplayed his understated role of the Japanese sleuth in 20th Century-Fox's late 1930s film series, but there was an individuality and flair to both his character and the B pictures themselves. Now John P. Marquand's intrepid Oriental gumshoe found himself subverted into a James Bond type, still enigmatic but lacking any catchy personal touch. The casual viewer would be hard put to know that actor Silva who plays the role sans special makeup, is portraying a quizzical Japanese detective (the villains even refer to him as "that chink!"). It is little wonder that a projected new Mr. Moto series was shelved after this undistinguished release.

When McAllister (Tanner) of the Beta Oil Company is murdered in London, Mr. Moto (Silva) follows up Interpol's request that he investigate the circumstances. He soon finds out that ex-Nazi Dargo (Wyldeck) was responsible for the crime, and that Tanner had been involved in a plan that would turn over new oil lease agreements between the Shahrdar (Kasket) of Wadi Shamar and Britain to a syndicate who want to control the world's resources. And what was Silva's reward at the finale? A London tour with lovely Maxine Powell (Lloyd). Sic transit gloria.

RETURN OF THE SCARLET PIMPERNEL   (UA, 1938)   86 min.

Producer, Alexander Korda; director, Hans Schwartz; based on the novel by Baroness Orczy; screenplay, Lajos Biro, Arthur Wimperis, Adrian Bruenl; camera, Mutz Greenbaum, L. McLeod.

Barry K. Barnes (Sir Percy Blakeney); Sophie Stewart (Marguerite Blakeney); James Mason (Jean Tallion); Francis Lester (Chauvelin); Anthony Bushell (Sir Andrew ffoukes); Patrick Barr (Lord Hastings); David Tree (Lordy Harry Denning); John Counsell (Sor John Setton); Henry Oscar (Robespierre); Hugh Miller (de Calmet); Allan Jeayes (Judge of the Tribunal); O. B. Clarence (de Marre); George Merritt (Chief of Police); Evelyn Roberts (Prince of Wales); Esnee Percy (Sheridan); Edmond Breon (Colonel Winterbottom); Frank Allenby (Professor Wilkins).

"See the Half-Crazed Robespierre, the Human Killer ... a thousand and one suspense filled nights of betrayal--love--and adventure." So read the ads for this middling sequel to the well-regarded 1935 talkie picturization of Baroness Orczy's novel. The new account was produced on a much lower scale and left a great deal to be desired, especially in recreating the cold, clammy feel of the Reign of Terror.

Return of the Scarlet Pimpernel picks up the threads of the earlier story, in which Sir Percy Blakeney (Barnes) better known as the Scarlet Pimpernel, rescuer of aristocrats from the guillotine, has settled down to life at the British court in regency England. But in Paris, Robespierre (Oscar) is determined to make Barnes pay for his unsolicited gallantry and sets a trap via the persistent Lt. Chauvelin (Lester), in which Barnes' wife (Stewart) will be captured and used to lure the Scarlet Pimpernel back to France.

Barnes was hardly a notable successor to Leslie Howard, unable as he was to capture properly the duality of a man posing as a foppish prissy nobleman hiding a chivalrous, courageous nature. More effective was Mason as Jean Tallion, one of the many threatened with the guillotine. With the oncoming World War II, audiences were hard put to accept a spy character as a romantic hero.

There were too many actual espionage agents lurking in the real world.

REUNION IN FRANCE   (MGM, 1942)   102 min.

Producer, Joseph L. Mankiewicz; director, Jules Dassin; story, Ladislas Bus-Fekete; screenplay, Jan Lustig, Marvin Borowsky, Marc Connelly; music, Franz Waxman; art director, Cedric Gibbons; costumes, Irene; sound, Douglas Shearer; special effects, Warren Newcombe; camera, Robert Planck; editor, Elmo Vernon.

Joan Crawford (Michel de la Becque); Philip Dorn (Robert Croiset); John Wayne (Pat Talbot); John Carradine (Ulrich Windler); Albert Bassermann (General Schröder); Reginald Owen (Schultz); Odette Myrtil (Mme. Montanot); Ann Ayars (Juliette); Moroni Olsen (Grebeau); Henry Daniell (Fleuron); Arthur Space (Henker); Margaret Laurence (Clothilde); J. Edward Bromberg (Thibault); Peter Whitney (Soldier with Candy); Edith Evanson (Genevieve); Morris Ankrum (Martin); Ann Codee (Rosalie); Oliver B. Blake (Hypolite); Ernest Dorian (Captain); Charles Arnt (Honoré); Natalie Schafer (Frau Schröder); George Travell (Jeannot); Howard da Silva (Stregel); Michael Visaroff (Vigouroux); Felix Basch (Pawnbroker); Paul Weigel (Old Man); John Considine, Jr. (Little Boy); Claudia Drake (Girl); Peter Leeds (Boy); Barbara Bedford (Mme. Vigouroux); Basil Bockasta (Delivery Boy); Henry Kolker (General Bartholomae); George Calliga (Monsieur Bertheil); Harry Adams (Monsieur Clemens); Larry Grenier (Monsieru de Brun); Ed Rickard (Chauffeur); Philip Van Zandt (Customer); Louis Mercier (Conductor); Jean Del Val (Porter); Lester Sharpe (Warden); Adolph Milar (Gestapo Agent); Carl Ekberg, Hans Furberg (Soldiers); William Edmunds (Driver); Arno Frey (Guide); Joel Friedkin (Frenchman); Wilda Bieber (Little Girl); Rodney Bieber (Little Boy); Greta Keller (Baroness von Steinkamp); Walter O. Stahl (Baron von Steinkamp); Doris Borodin (Saleslady); Jody Gilbert (Brunhilde); Jack Zeller (Young Man); Edgar Licho (Hawker); Jacqueline White (Danielle); Bob Stevenson (Emile); Gayne Whitman (Maître d'Hotel); George Aldwin (Pilot); Ray de Ravenne (Bartender); Eddie Lee, Tommy Lee (Japs); Muriel Barr, Norma Thelan (Girls in Cafe); Ava Gardner (Girl).

Giddy, richly spoiled Michel de la Becque (Crawford) is blithely unconcerned with the chaos of World War II, for in the well-ordered world of this Paris career woman not even love is taken too seriously. Only gradually does she suspect something is amiss in that her industrial designer paramour Robert Croiset (Dorn) is doing so well in Nazi-occupied France whereas most everyone else is feeling the pinch of the Germans' control. Never much of a patriot, Crawford suddenly is aghast to realize that Dorn's plants are producing weapons for the cause of the Third Reich and that Dorn is hobnobbing with the most elite of the Nazis. A bewildered Crawford is overjoyed now to find a way of showing

her previously undemonstrated loyalties to France and the free
world. American flier Pat Talbot (Wayne) has been downed in
French territory and is being tracked down by the Gestapo. Fate
provides Crawford with the opportunity of helping Wayne reach the
safety of the underground movement and his eventual return to
England. Meanwhile she at last learns that Dorn is not a Nazi
collaborator but that he is secretly sabotaging his own plants' production and is also organizing a new partisan French force to hit
out at the enemy.

The synthetic drama was much criticized at the time for
"making the shallowest drama out of the pith and substance of an
ironic tragedy" (New York Times). And many a critic/viewer
wondered how star Crawford, in the midst of German-occupied
France could acquire such a startling array of Irene-created garb.
Certainly Reunion in France was one of the glossiest and most incredible of the underground-partisan dramas to emerge from the
Second World War era. Its Shirley Temple-like depiction of Nazi
conquest, saboteurs, and internal espionage, would not have made
a sheltered school girl flinch. Its cavalier, unrealistic approach,
however, did make many a moviegoer cringe.

RING OF SPIES (British Lion, 1963)   90 min.

Producer, Leslie Gilliat; director, Robert Tronson; screen-
play, Frank Launder, Peter Barnes; assistant director, Derek
Cracknell; art director, Norman Arnold; sound, Cecil Mason, Red
Law; camera, Arthur Lavis; editor, Thelma Connell.
Bernard Lee (Henry Houghton); William Sylvester (Gordon
Lonsdale); Margaret Tyzack (Elizabeth Gee); David Kossoff (Peter
Kroger); Nancy Nevinson (Helen Kroger); Thorley Walters (Com-
mander Winters); Gillian Lewis (Marjorie Shaw); Brian Nissen (Lt.
Downes); Newton Blick (P.O. Meadows); Philip Latham (Captain
Ray); Howard Pays (P.O. Garton); Cyril Chamberlain (Anderson);
Justine Lord (Christina); Richard Marner (Colonel Monat); Norma
Foster (Ella); Anita West (Tilly); Patrick Barr (Captain Warner);
Edwin Apps (Blake); Derek Francis (Chief Superintendent Croft);
Garry Marsh, Basil Dignam (Members of Lord's); Hector Ross
(Superintendent Woods); Margaret Wood (Superintendent Muriel).

"This more or less factual account of events in the Portland
spy case has rather the effect of a newspaper serialisation, in
which facts and times are carefully recorded, but no one has gone
very far with speculations about how the people concerned might
actually talk and feel" (British Monthly Film Bulletin).
When Warrant Officer Henry Houghton (Lee) is posted home
from the British Embassy in Warsaw for unfitting behavior, he is
reassigned to the records division of the Admiralty's Underwater
Weapons Establishment in Portland. It is not long before Lee is
recruited into the spy ring headed by Gordon Lonsdale (Sylvester),
and soon Lee has convinced Elizabeth Gee (Tyzack), guardian of
the department's secret document safe that Sylvester is a NATO

officer, and that the removal of assorted top level papers from the
safe is quite legitimate. The documents are photographed and
passed by Lee to Sylvester to the Krogers (Kossoff, Nevinson) for
relaying to Moscow. Lee's spendthrift actions about London eventually lead to the roundup and sentencing of the spies.

One of the most infamous espionage capers in recent English
history received a pedestrian outfitting here in this film. A minor
but interesting element of Ring of Spies is the quickly sketched
chronicle of spying which opens the feature, and the melodramatic
final narration which suggests in the best penny dreadful terms that
a spy might well be occupying the next seat in the theatre: "so,
beware!"

THE RISK (Kingsley International, 1961) 81 min.

Producer-director, Roy and John Boulting; based on the
novel A Sort of Traitors by Nigel Balchin; screenplay, Balchin;
additional dialog, Jeffrey Dell, Roy Boulting; music, John Wilkes;
art director, Albert Witherick; assistant director, Basil Rubin;
sound, George Stephenson; camera, Max Greene; editor, John
Jympson.

Tony Britton (Bob Marriott); Virginia Maskell (Lucy Byrne);
Peter Cushing (Professor Sewell); Ian Bannen (Alan Andrews); Ray-
mond Huntley (Sir George Gatling); Thorley Walters (Mr. Prince);
Donald Pleasence (Brown); Spike Milligan (Arthur); Kenneth Griffith
(Dr. Shole); Robert Bruce (Levers); Basil Dignam (Dr. Childs);
Brian Oulton (Director); Sam Kydd (Slater); John Payne (Iverson);
Murray Melvin (Teddy Boy); Andre Charisse (Heller); Geoffrey
Bayldon (Rosson); Margaret Lacey (Prince's Wife); Bruce Wightman
(Phil); Ian Wilson (Pin Table Man).

This meek British entry gained few endorsements when shown
in the United States. "... [T]he tricky and not very substantial
plot with which it is fleshed out attempts to be both comic and
exciting and is often neither" (New Yorker magazine).

A team of British scientists have discovered a method of
stamping out typhus and bubonic plague, but since it could be used
as well to spread the dread diseases, the British government refuses to allow the investigative work to be published. The team
ponders the advisability of defying the Whitehall order, prompted by
an unscrupulous "publisher."

THE RUNAWAY (BLC/Columbia, 1964) 62 min.

Producer, Bill Luckwell, David Vigo; director, Tony Young;
screenplay, John Perceval; additional dialog, John Gerrard Sharp;
assistant director, Clive Midwinter; art director, Don Mingaye;
music, Wilfred Burns; sound, Ken Rawkins; camera, Jimmy Harvey;
editor, Norman Cohen.

Greta Gynt (Anita Peshkin); Alex Gallier (Andrian Peshkin);

Paul Williamson (Thomas); Michael Trubshawe (Sir Roger Clements); Tony Quinn (Professor Hawkley); Wendy Vamals (Tania); Diens Shaw (Russian Agent); Howard Lang (Norring); Ross Hutchinson (Leopold Cleaver); Stuart Saunders (Conway Brockfield); John Watson (Hazleton); John Dearth (Sergeant Hardwick); Leonard Dixon (Constable); Ian Wilson (Caretaker); Arnold Bell, Anthony Pendrell (Staff Officers).

Shortly before the Germans enter Paris in 1940, Polish-born industrial chemist Andrian Peshkin (Gallier), employed as a Russian secret agent, absconds with a large sum of money from the Moscow contingency funds and goes to South America, taking his wife (Gynt) with him. Gynt is the Soviet operative assigned to watch Gallier's every move. Instead she falls in love with him. On the way, the duo is stopped at Trinidad and questioned by British official Thomas (Williamson), who allows them to pass, but confiscates their money. Twenty-four years later, Williamson is now a senior M. I. 5 officer and is ordered to investigate a chemist who has fallen upon knowledge of the ZR 2 formula. The man in question is none other than Gallier.

This attempt to humanize the spy profession went awry. The British Monthly Film Bulletin thought it a "Grotesque spy melodrama, which might almost be a parody if it were not so patently solemn about its hero's predicament. "

SABOTAGE   (Republic, 1939)   69 min.

Associate producer, Herman Schlom; director, Harold Young; screenplay, Lionel House, Alice Altschuler; camera, Reggie Lanning; editor, William Morgan.

Arlene Whelan (Gail); Gordon Oliver (Tommy); Charley Grapewin (Major Grayson); Lucien Littlefield (Eli); Paul Guilfoyle (Borsht); J. M. Kerrigan (Mel); Dorothy Peterson (Edith); Don Douglas (Joe); Joe Sawyer (Gardener); Maude Eburne (Mrs. Hopkins); Horace MacMahon (A. Kruger); Johnny Russell (Matt); Wade Boteler (Cop); Frank Darien (Smitty).

During its test flight, a new bomber crashes, killing three aboard. The government and the civil leaders of the small town where the craft was built are convinced the "accident" was the handiwork of enemy operatives. In fact, the enraged townfolks hastily condemn young aviation engineer Tommy (Oliver), which prompts his dad (Grapewin), a night watchman at the factory and a retired army veteran with the rank of major, to tell the community just what he thinks of their rash, so-called patriotic misjudgments. Grapewin rounds up three pals, including feisty Littlefield, from the old soldiers' home to settle the matter.

Although this bottom of the bill item did not have the courage to brand the country of origin of the agents, it prowled into other moral domains that the major pictures were hesitant to touch (including the point that old people still have usefulness to the world at large).

SABOTAGE SQUAD   (Columbia, 1942)   70 min.

Producer, Jack Fier, director, Lew Landers; story, Bernice Petkere, Wallace Sullivan; screenplay, Petkere, Sullivan, David Silverman; music director, Morris Stoloff; art director, Lionel Banks; camera, Franz F. Planer; editor, William Lyon.

Bruce Bennett (Lt. John Cronin); Kay Harris (Edith Cassell); Eddie Norris (Eddie Miller); Sidney Blackmer (Carlyle Harrison); Don Beddoe (Chief Hanley); John Tyrrell (Robert Fuller); George McKay (Chuck Brown); Robert Emmett Keene (Conrad); Eddie Laughton (Felix); Byron Foulger (Suspect); Edward Hearn (Foreman); Pat Lane (Sam); John Dilson (Mr. Guthrie); Ethan Laidlaw (Strong-Arm Man); Hugh Prosser (Saboteur); Cy Ring (Jefferson); Lester Dorr (Harry); Bill Lally (Cop); Richard Bartell (Gunner); George Magrill (Workman); Al Hill (Police Clerk); Connie Evans (Attendant); Stanley Brown (Clerk); Edmund Cobb (Policeman); Ernie Adams (Customer); Al Herman (Bookmaker); Jack Gardner (Better); Eddie Bruce (Clancy); Brick Sullivan (Cop); Kenneth MacDonald (Medical Examiner); Max Wagner (Recruiting Sergeant).

Byron Foulger, Bruce Bennett, and John Tyrrell in Sabotage Squad (Columbia, 1942).

"While the FBI has been rounding up Nazi saboteurs in bunches, all the B movies have been equipping their villains with German accents and the nefarious schemes to go with them. It's a vicious cycle, which <u>Sabotage Squad</u> pedals a bit further" (<u>PM</u>). The one redeeming factor of this flim is Blackmer as the hissable villain Carlyle Harrison, a doctor who is really the Nazi big shot and a crafty fellow who almost outfoxes Bennett of the F.B.I. Heroine Harris is the manicurist at Keane's tonsorial parlor, the sub-headquarters for the Nazis operatives out to blow up various munitions plants.

SABOTEUR (Universal, 1942) 108 min.

Producer, Frank Lloyd; associate producer, Jack H. Skirball; director, Alfred Hitchcock; story, Hitchcock; screenplay, Peter Viertel, Joan Harrison, Dorothy Parker; set decorator, Jack Otterson; assistant director, Fred Frank; music, Frank Skinner; music director, Charles Previn; camera, Joseph Valentine; editor, Otto Ludwig.

Robert Cummings (Barry Kane); Priscilla Lane (Pat Martin); Otto Kruger (Charles Tobin); Alma Kruger (Henrietta Sutton); Alan Baxter (Freeman); Pedro de Cordoba (Bones, the Human Skeleton); Vaughan Glaser (Philip Martin); Ian Wolfe (Robert, the Butler); Frances Carson (Society Matron); Dorothy Peterson (Mrs. Mason); Billy Curtis (Major, the Midget); Clem Bevans (Neilson); Gus Glassmire (Mr. Pearl); Norman Lloyd (Frank Fry); Marie LeDeaux (Tatania, the Fat Woman); Jeanne and Lynn Romer (Marigold and Annette, the Siamese Twins); Kathryn Adams (Mrs. Brown); Samuel S. Hinds (Foundation Leader); Charles Halton (Sheriff); John Eldredge (Footman); Selmer Jackson (F.B.I. Chief); Emory Parnell (Husband in Movie); Lou Lubin (Man); Will Lee (Worker); Will Wright (Company Official); Murray Alper (Mac, the Deputy-Driver); Jimmy Flavin, Archie Twitchell (Motorcycle Cops--Voices--Seen in Shadow); Margaret Moffat (Neighbor); Hans Conried (Edward); Paul Everton (Bus Man); Pat Flaherty (Navy Man); Barton Yarborough (First F.B.I. Man at Mason's Home); Anita Sharp-Bolster (Esmeralda, the Bearded Lady); Virgil Summers (Ken Mason); Lee Phelps (Plant Police); George Offerman, Jr. (Worker); Harry Strang (Cop); Matt Willis (Deputy); Marjorie Wood (Farmer's Wife); Paul E. Burns (Farmer); Belle Mitchell (Adele, the Maid); Ed Foster (Driver for Saboteurs); William Ruhl (Deputy Marshal); Gene Garrick (Worker); Dick Midgley, Don Cadell (F.B.I. Men); Gene O'Donnell (Jitterbug); Paul Phillips (Driver); Milton Kibbee (Husband in Movie Audience); William Gould (Stranger); Ralph Dunn (F.B.I. Man at Mason's); Jack Arnold (Other Man--in Movie); Margaret Hayes (Wiff--in Movie); Rex Lease (Plant Counterman); Duke York (Deputy); Nancy Loring (Young Mother); Claire Whitney (Wife in Movie Audience); Frank Marlowe (George, the Truck Driver); Alan Bridge (Marine Sgt., M.P.); Norma Drury (Refugee Mother); Charles Sherlock (Barry's Taxi Driver); Jack Gardner (Pat's Taxi Driver); Jack Cheatham

(Detective); Alex Lockwood (Marine); Kernan Cripps (Man in Movie
Audience); Jeanne Trent (Blonde Aircraft Worker); Jim Lucas (Taxi
Driver); Dale Van Sickel (F.B.I. Assistant--Phone Operator);
Walter Miller, Mary Curtis (Midgets); Margaret Ann McLaughlin
(Baby Susie Brown); Kermit Maynard (Cow Hand); Gerald Pierce
(Elevator Operator); Carol Stevens (Deaf Man's Companion); Alfred
Hitchcock (Deaf and Dumb Man Outside Drug Store); Tar, Grey
Shadow, Smokey (Dogs); Cyril Ring (Party Guest); Jeffrey Sayre
(Henchman); Ralph Brooks (Dance Extra).

Robert Cummings and Priscilla Lane in Saboteur (Universal, 1942).

        A minor work in the canon of director Alfred Hitchcock's
American-made features (he even composed the original screen
story), marred both by unfortunate miscasting and by the creator's
blatant self-pilfering from his prior films. Saboteur's redeeming
moment, aside from the circus freak show interlude, occurs atop
the Statue of Liberty where the villain (Lloyd) finds himself suspended in mid-air, clutching vainly at the huge stone: a token
not to America's goddess of democracy who offers no helping hand

to totalitarian adherents.

Barry Kane (Cummings) is a patriotic American worker engaged in post-Pearl Harbor defense production at a Glendale, California, aircraft factory. One day his world is shattered. A mysterious explosive fire breaks out at the plant and after Cummings innocently hands his best friend a fire extinguisher full of gasoline-- killing his pal--the authorities are convinced Cummings is the enemy saboteur. Thereafter, the panic-stricken, handcuffed hero flees the police in order to track down the actual villains. The path leads to the Deep Springs Dude Ranch where he meets the owner's niece (Lane), the only one who believes him innocent. The wholesome twosome proceed cross-country to New York where sinister Charles Tobin (Kruger) and henchman Frank Fry (Lloyd) have blown up a ship launched from the Brooklyn Navy Yard and have further acts of sabotage fully in mind.

THE SABOTEUR: CODE NAME MORITURI see MORITURI

SABRA see DEATH OF A JEW

THE SALZBURG CONNECTION (20th-Fox, 1972)   C   92 min.

Producer, Ingo Preminger; director, Lee H. Katzin; based on the novel by Helen MacInnes; screenplay, Oscar Millard; music, Lionel Newman; art director, Herta Hareiter-Pischinger; assistant director, Gus Agosti, Claude Binyon, Jr., Wieland Liebske; costumes, Lamber Hofer, Jr.; sound, Rolf Schmidt-Gentner, Theodore Soderberg; camera, Wolfgang Treu; editor, John H. Woodcock.

Barry Newman (William Matheson); Anna Karina (Anna Bryant); Klaus-Maria Brandauer (Johann); Karen Jensen (Elissa); Joe Maross (CIA Agent); Wolfgang Preiss (Austrian Detective Zauner); Helmut Schnid, Udo Kier (Spies); Whit Bissell (Publisher); Elisabeth Felshner (Johann's Fiancee); and: Bert Fortell, Alf Beinell, Patrick Jordan, Edward Linkers, Gene Moss, Karl Otto Alberty, Rudolk Bary, Christine Buchegger, Michael Haussermann, Raoul Retzer.

A pity that author Helen MacInnes who has done so much to sustain the spy genre in the publishing field, was dealt yet another disservice by the film industry which turned her recent popular thriller into a junk exercise "erotically limp" (Variety). The picturization of The Salzburg Connection retained none of the book's impact. In fact, the Ingo Preminger production so infuriated the New York critics that they vied to outdo one another in colorfully condemning the "hack rubbish ... unredeemed trivia" (New York magazine). The crowning blow came when Cue magazine charged, "... [it] doesn't even rate a junior G-man's badge."

American attorney William Matheson (Newman) is sent to Salzburg by publisher Bissell to investigate a publishing hoax. While there he stumbles upon a plot by a neo-Nazi group to retrieve from a lake's bottom a chest containing a list of Nazi collaborators and criminals during World War II. Karina's husband is killed for his innocent participation in the venture, while her brother (Brandauer) turns out to be a member of the fascist-bent organization. Before the unwitting "connection" (Newman) that brings together espionage agents from all parts of the world it seems and thereby brings the caper to a close, there is a string of corpses piled about the streets, the Alpine forest, and on ski-lift chairs.

For a supposedly "major" motion picture, there was an unrelenting air of cheapness about the entire production, ranging from the "lifeless looping of location footage" into the storyline to the obviously canned music score.

THE SCARLET CLUE (Monogram, 1945) 65 min.

Producer, James S. Burkett; director, Phil Rosen; based on the character created by Earl Derr Biggers; screenplay, George Callaham; art director, Dave Milton; music director, Edward Kay; assistant director, Eddie Davis; sound, Tom Lambert; camera, William A. Sickner; editor, Richard Currier.

Sidney Toler (Charlie Chan); Benson Fong (Tommy Chan); Mantan Moreland (Birmingham Brown); Helen Devereaux (Diane Hall); Robert Homans (Captain Flynn); Virginia Brissac (Mrs. Marsh); Stanford Jolley (Ralph Brett); Reid Kilpatrick (Wilbur Chester); Jack Norton (Willie Rand); Charles Sherlock (Sgt. McGraw); Janet Shaw (Gloria Bayne); Milton Kibbee (Herbert Sinclair); Ben Carter (Ben); Victoria Fuast (Hulda Swenson); Charles Jordan (Nelson); Leonard Mudie (Horace Carlos); Kernan Cripps (Detective).

Here Biggers' famous Oriental sleuth matched wits with an espionage ring led by a female spy who used invisible gas to kill those who tried to stop her from stealing vital radar plans. Despite several close calls, Chan (Toler) thwarted the spy and saved the day, mostly without the bumbling aid of his chauffeur Birmingham (Moreland) or son Tommie (Fong).

Mostly due to the above-par scripting of George Callahan, this economy entry had some of the quality of the earlier 20th Century-Fox "Charlie Chan" films.

THE SCARLET COAT (MGM, 1955) C 110 min.

Producer, Nicholas Nayfack; director, John Sturges; screenplay, Karl Tunberg; art director, Cedric Gibbons, Merrill Pye; music director, Conrad Salinger; assistant director, Fred Frank; costumes, Walter Plunkett; camera, Paul C. Vogel; editor, Ben Lewis.

Cornel Wilde (Major John Bolton); Michael Wilding (Major John Andre); George Sanders (Dr. Jonathan Odell); Anne Francis

(Sally Cameron); Robert Douglas (Benedict Arnold); John McIntire
(General Robert Howe); Rhys Williams (Peter); John Dehner
(Nathanael Greene); James Westerfield (Colonel Jameson); Ashley
Cowan (Mr. Brown); Paul Cavanagh (Sir Henry Clinton); John Alder-
son (Mr. Durkin); John O'Malley (Colonel Winfield); Bobby Driscoll
(Ben Potter); Robin Hughes (Colonel Tarleton); Anthony Dearden
(Captain DeLancey); Bruce Lester (Colonel Simcoe); Vernon Rich
(Colonel); Charles Watts (Will Potter); Peter Adams (Lieutenant
Blair); Bob Dix (Lieutenant Evans); Wesley Hudman (Captain Shel-
don); Robert Forrest (Stout Man); Tom Cound (English Soldier);
Keith McConnell (Lieutenant); Olaf Hytten (Butler); Phyllis Coghlan
(Woman); Gil Stuart (Officer); Gordon Richards (Mr. Cameron);
Owen McGiveney (Servant); Charles R. Keane, Richard Simmons
(Sergeants); Harlan Warde, John Blackturn (Captains); Leslie Deni-
son (Captain Sutherland); Jim Hayward (Joshua Smith); Rush Wil-
liams (Soldier); Ivan Hayes (Mr. Nyby); Tristram Coffin (Colonel
Varick); Michael Fox (Major Russell); Don C. Harvey (Captain);
Byron Foulger (Man); Barry Regan, Rick Vallin, Ronald Green,
Joe Locke (Lieutenants); Jennifer Raine (Miss Trumbull); Guy
Kingsford (Officer); Richard Peel (Sailor); Dennis King, Jr.

Cornel Wilde, Bobby Driscoll, and John Alderson in The Scarlet
Coat (MGM, 1955).

(Boatswain's Mate); Vesey O'Davoren (Butler); Anne Kunde (Cook); George Peters (Staff Officer); Wilson Benge (Servant); Ethan Laidlaw (Executioner).

Made on a lavish scale, this is one of the few features to depict the American Revolutionary War era, let alone detailing events in the life of the period's most famous spy/traitor, Benedict Arnold (Douglas). Generally unappreciated in its day, The Scarlet Coat did have a few champions, "This is an almost unaccountable lapse into accuracy ... [it] is an entertaining cloak-and-dagger tale" (New York Herald-Tribune).

Wilde was cast as a fictitious American spy who discovered that Arnold, at the time a hero in the Revolutionary War effort, had been brought over to the British cause by British Major John Andre (Wilding). Along the way serpentine doctor Sanders, a Tory, suspects Wilde's true colors, but can convince no one of that fact, until Arnold is found out.

Although exceedingly well-mounted with period deportment and spectacular scenery, director John Sturges (or the budget?) did not allow the novelty of CinemaScope to be properly used with the film's big battle scene. The Scarlet Coat did attempt to demonstrate that spies and counterspies function and react the same in any era of human history.

THE SCARLET PIMPERNEL (UA, 1935) 85 min.

Producer, Alexander Korda; director, Harold Young; based on the novel by Baroness Orczy; adaptation, Robert Sherwood, Arthur Wimperis, S. N. Behrman; camera, Hal Rosson.

Leslie Howard (Sir Percy Blakeney); Merle Oberon (Lady Blakeney); Raymond Massey (Chauvelin); Joan Gardner (Suzanne); A. B. Clarence (Comte de Tournay); Walter Rilla (Armand); Anthony Bushell (Sir Andrew Ffoulkes); Ernest Milton (Robespierre); John Turnbull (Jillyband); Bramwell Fletcher (A Priest); Melville Cooper (Romney the Artist); Nigel Bruce (H. R. H., the Prince Regent); Mabel Terry-Lewis (Comtesse de Tournay); Allan Jeayes (Lord Granville); Edmund Breon (Rene de Grammont); Edmund Willard (Bibot).

Since the Baroness Orczy (Mrs. Montagu Barstow) published her The Scarlet Pimpernel in 1905, the immensely popular novel has often served as film material. Among the silent film renditions were one in 1917 starring Dustin Farnum and another in 1929 featuring Matheson Lang. After the latter, a distinguished Alexander Korda version (which the New York Evening Post applauded for "shaking the moth balls out of history"), there was another cinematic account in 1938 with Barry K. Barnes, and a still later film adaptation in 1950 featuring David Niven, capped by a British video series with Marius Goring. In 1941 producer-director-actor Leslie Howard presented a modernized version entitled Pimpernel Smith (q. v.).

The essential plot of The Scarlet Pimpernel is best summed
up by a poem the foppish Sir Percy Blakeney (Howard) offers as
diverting doggerel at the court of the Prince Regent (Bruce).

"They seek him here, they
seek him there.
The Frenchies seek him everywhere.
Is he in Heaven.   Is he in Hell?
That damned illusive Pimpernel!"

For screen beauty, there was Oberon as the former French actress
wed to Howard, but estranged from him because he believed she
has deliberately betrayed an old friend to the fiendish Robespierre
(Milton).   If only elegant Oberon realized that the effete Howard by
day was really the daring rescuer of French aristocrats by night,
she might not have accidentally led her "simpering" husband into
an almost deadly trap plotted by the unofficial French ambassador
Chauvelin (Massey).   The handsomely mounted tale which begins
in the time of 1792, concludes with a battle of wits between Howard
and Massey at the Lion d'Or.

SCORPIO (UA, 1973) C 114 min.

Producer, Walter Mirisch; director, Michael Winner; story,
David W. Rintels; screenplay, Rintels, Gerald Wilson; music,
Jerry Fielding; art director, Herbert Westbrook; assistant director,
Michael Dryhust; sound, Brian Marshall; camera, Robert Paynter;
editor, Freddie Wilson.

Burt Lancaster (Cross); Alain Delon (Laurier); Paul Scofield
(Zharkov); John Colicos (McLeod); Gayle Hunnicutt (Susan); J. D.
Cannon (Filchock); Joanne Linville (Sarah); Melvin Stewart (Pick);
Vladek Sheybal (Zemetkin); Mary Maude (Anne); Jack Colvin (Thief);
James Sikking (Harris); Burke Byrnes (Morrison); William Smithers
(Mitchell); Shmuel Rodensky (Lang); Howard Morton (Heck Thomas);
Celeste Yarnall (Helen Thomas); Sandor Eles (Malkin); Frederick
Jaeger (Novins); George Mikell (Dor); Robert Emhardt (Man in
Hotel).

"Despite its anachronistic emulation of mid-1960s' cynical
spy mellers, Scorpio might have been an acceptable action programmer if its narrative were clearer, its dialog less 'cultured'
and its visuals more straightforward" (Variety).

After the assassination of an Arab government official,
Laurier (Delon), a C. I. A.-blackmailed figure, pursues Cross (Lancaster) whom he suspects of being a Soviet defector.   The chase
leads from Washington to Europe and a stopover at the Viennese
home of Zharkov (Scofield), a Russian agent who counsels
Lancaster.

THE SCORPIO LETTERS (MGM/ABC-TV, 1966) C 97 min.

Producer-director, Richard Thorpe; based on the novel by

Victor Canning; screenplay, Adrian Spies, Jo Eisinger; assistant
director, Dale Hutchinson; art director, George W. Davis, Addison
Hehr; set decorator, Henry Grace, Jack Mills; music, Dave Cru-
sin; sound, Franklin Milton, Ed Hall; camera, Ellsworth Fredericks;
editor, Richard Farrell.

Alex Cord (Joe Christopher); Shirley Eaton (Phoebe Stewart);
Laurence Naismith (Burr); Oscar Beregi (Philippe Sorieh, alias
Scorpio); Lester Mathews (Mr. Harris); Antoinette Bower (Terry);
Arthur Malet (Hinton); Barry Ford (Bratter); Emile Genest (Garin);
Vincent Beck (Paul Fretoni); Ilka Windish (Miss Gunther); Laurie
Main (Tyson);Andre Philippe (Gian); Harry Raybould (Lodel); Dani-
elle De Metz (Maria).

One of the earliest ABC telefeatures, this stanza concerned
American Joe Christopher (Cord) who is enlisted by the British In-
telligence to take up where a murdered undercover agent left off.
His mission requires that he infiltrate a ring of blackmailers led
by Scorpio (Beregi) as well as learn what bearing a group of
former Resistance men known as the Bianeri have on the case.
For variety sake, the script provided Cord with agent Phoebe
Stewart (Eaton), a member of an overlapping branch of British
Intelligence.

The British Monthly Film Bulletin properly nailed the failing
of this mediocre product: "... it ignores the basic rules of the
spy thriller formula (original gimmicks to frost over the implausi-
bilities and villains mean enough to be worth tracking down in the
first place). Here the criminal organization to be destroyed is
about as threatening as a set of toy poodles, and Alex Cord as the
agent looks more like an irate scoutmaster than an iron man of
action."

SCOTLAND YARD (20th-Fox, 1941) 68 min.

Producer, Sol M. Wurtzel; director, Norman Foster; based
on the play by Denison Clift; screenplay, Samuel G. Engel, John
Balderston; camera, Virgil Miller; editor, Al de Gaetano.

Nancy Kelly (Lady Sandra Lasher); Edmund Gwenn (Inspec-
tor Cork/Sir John Lasher); John Loder (Dakin Barroles); Henry
Wilcoxon (Dakin Barroles #2); Melville Cooper (Dr. Crownfield);
Gilbert Emery (Sir Clive Heathcote); Norma Varden (Lady Heath-
cote); Leyland Hodgson (Henderson); Lionel Pape (Hugh); Lilian
Bond (Lady Constance); Leo G. Carroll (Craven); Frank Dawson
(Kinch the Butler); Eugene Borden (Tony); Edward Fielding
(Pickering); Robert de Bruce (Jeffries); Denis Green (Scott-Bishop);
Jimmy Aubrey (Cockney); Yorke Sherwood (Lorry Driver); Lester
Mathews (Dr. Gilbert); Doris Lloyd (Miss Harcourt); Sidney Bracy
(Train Attendant); Billy Bevan (Porter); Herbert Evans (Footman);
Marga Ann Deighton (Lady Doakes); Leonard Mudie (Clerk); Holmes
Herbert (Dr. Woodward); Reginald Barlow (Messenger); Lilyan
Irene (Maid); John Rogers (Newsboy); Reginald Sheffield (Hat Clerk);
Wright Kramer (Dr. Scott); Forrester Harvey (Air Raid Warden);

Dave Thursby (Laundry Man); Frank Benson (Newsboy).

Denison Clift's crook melodrama which opened on Broadway in 1929 and was made into a 1930 Fox movie, was revamped into a spy drama with negligible results, containing the "usual B-guiling suspense" (New York Times). Its hard-to-swallow masquerade premise was no more convincing this go around than before.

To escape the police, English gentleman robber Wilcoxon joins the army. During the evacuation of Dunkirk his face is mutilated by shrapnel. He is not the only one amazed when plastic surgeons reconstruct his profile into a likeness of Loder, head of London's Mayfair Bank. There is Loder's wife (Kelly) who has been endlessly feuding with her caddish, drunkard husband, and who is amazed at the personality changes in her "spouse." While the real banker is held prisoner by the Germans, the substitute one is used by the enemy to carry out a plan to transfer the bank's gold supply to Axis hands. Gwenn and Emery of Scotland Yard are on hand to bring the intriguers to justice.

SEALED CARGO (RKO, 1951)   89 min.

Producer, Warren Duff; director, Alfred Werker; based on the novel The Gaunt Woman by Edmund Gilligan; screenplay, Dale Van Every, Oliver H. P. Garrett, Roy Huggins; art director, Albert S. D'Agostino; music director, C. Bakaleinikoff; camera, George E. Diskant; editor, Ralph Dawson.

Dana Andrews (Pat Bannon); Carla Balenda (Margaret McLean); Claude Rains (Skalder); Philip Dorn (Conrad); Onslow Stevens (McLean); Skip Homeier (Steve); Eric Feldary (Holger); J. M. Kerrigan (Skipper Ben); Arthur Shields (Dolan); Morgan Farley (Caleb); Dave Thursby (Ambrose); Henry Rowland (Anderson); Charles A. Browne (Smitty); Don Dillaway (Owen); Al Hill (Tom); Lee MacGregor (Lt. Cameron); William Andrews (Holtz); Richard Norris (Second Mate); Kathaleen Ellis, Karen Morris, Harry Mancke (Villagers); Whit Bissell (Schuster); Kay Morley (Wharf Official); Bert Kennedy (Old Seaman); Larry Johns (Mark); George Ovey, Carl Sklover (Men); Bessie Wade (Woman); Bruce Cameron, Ned Roberts (Nazi Machine Gunners); Dick Crockett, Bob Morgan, Wes Hopper (Nazis); Art Dupuis (Bit); Zachary Berger, Bob Smitts, John Royce (Nazi Sailors); Peter Bourne (Lieutenant); William Yetter (German); Geza De Rosner (German Sub Officer); Robert Boon (Sailor with Rating).

During World War II off Newfoundland, Pat Bannon (Andrews), skipper of the fishing ship "Daniel Webster," comes across the shell-riddled squarerigger "Gaunt Woman." The floundering vessel is captained by Skalder (Rains), who requests Andrews to tow the crippled ship to a shore mooring near an isolated village. Belatedly Andrews discovers that Rains' boat is a floating arsenal for the German U-boats plying the North Atlantic. The problem

Eric Feldary and Henry Rowland in <u>Sealed Cargo</u> (RKO, 1951).

becomes how to destroy the floating ammunition depot without harm-
ing the villagers.
        The foreword to <u>Sealed Cargo</u> states that the film is an il-
lustration of "great personal courage by little people" in World War
II.   A good deal of liberties were taken with the Edmund Gilligan
novel, and what should have been an all-male cast movie was di-
luted by the inclusion of such characters as Margaret McLean
(Balenda) a passenger on Andrews' craft who is taken hostage by
Rains.   Among the more effective supporting players were Dorn
and Feldary as Danish crewmen, one of whom is a Nazi agent.

SEBASTIAN (Paramount, 1967)   C   100 min.

        Producer, Herbert Brodkin, Michael Powell; associate pro-
ducer, John Pellatt; director, David Greene; story, Leo Marks;
screenplay, Gerald Vaughan-Hughes; assistant director, Gordon

[Facing page]   John Gielgud and Dirk Bogarde in <u>Sebastian</u> (Paramount, 1967).

Gilbert; production designer, Wilfred Shingleton; art director, Fred
Carter; set decorator, Terence Morgan II; music-music director,
Jerry Goldsmith; song, Goldsmith and Hal Shafer; titles, Richard
Williams Films; sound, H. L. Bird, Gerry Humphreys; camera,
Gerald Fisher; editor, Brian Smedley-Aston.

Dirk Bogarde (Sebastian); Susannah York (Becky Howard);
Lilli Palmer (Elsa Shahn); John Gielgud (Head of Intelligence);
Janet Munro (Carol); Margaret Johnston (Miss Elliott); Nigel Daven-
port (General Phillips); Ronald Fraser (Toby); John Ronane (Jame-
son); Susan Whitman (Tilly); Ann Beach (Pamela); Ann Sidney
(Naomi); Veronica Clifford (Ginny); Jeanne Roland (Randy); Lyn
Pinkney (Joan); Louise Pernell (Thelma); Donald Sutherland (Ameri-
can); Alan Freeman (TV Disc Jockey); Charles Lloyd Pack (Chess
Player); Portland Mason ("Ug" Girl).

Sebastian is not primarily a spy thriller, but it does delve
into the backwater area of the espionage profession, a portion of
the spy network usually glossed over by moviemakers, i.e., the
talented crew of mental gymnasts who work in an intelligence decoding department (tagged here as nothing more than "a kind of
septic tank for all the world's ugly secrets"). Sebastian fizzled
at the boxoffice ("classy pulp" said New Yorker magazine) with
director David Greene's almost accidental, but still pathfinding,
subliminal scene editing going uncommented upon by the press.

Genius Oxford botany professor Sebastian (Bogarde) takes
on a British government post as head of the secret service's deciphering department. Since his staff consists of a roomful of a
hundred (beautiful) decoding girls, it is not long before Bogarde
becomes personally involved with some of his subordinates, all
against the strictures of the Inspector of Security (Gielgud).
There is a former Communist, middle-aged and very sentimental
Elsa Shahn (Palmer) who is led into betraying office secrets to
a left-wing group. Then there is Oxford graduate Becky Howard
(York) whom Bogarde has given a bureau job and allowed to take
the bedside place of his former mistress (Munro). When the
supervisory and political pressures grow too immense, Bogarde
resigns in a huff, but later is induced by Gielgud to return to
tackle a big job, the decoding of a set of seemingly unfathomable
signals transmitted from a new Russian satellite. After surviving
a foreign power trap laid for Bogarde by Munro and enemy agents,
he breaks the code with the timely, if unlikely, assistance of a
rattle being used to pacify his and York's baby boy.

SECHS PISTOLEN JAGEN PROFESSOR Z   see page 426.

THE SECOND BEST SECRET AGENT IN THE WHOLE WIDE WORLD
(Embassy, 1966) C   96 min.

Executive producer, S. J. H. Ward; director, Lindsay Shonteff;
screenplay, Howard Griffiths, Shonteff; music, Bertram Chappell; assistant director, Ernie Lewis; camera, Terry Maher; editor, Ron Pope.

Tom Adams (Charles Vine); Karel Stepanek (Henrik Jacobsen); Veronica Hurst (Julia Lindberg); Peter Bull (Masterman); John Arnatt (Rockwell); Francis DeWolff (Walter Pickering); Felix Felton (Tetchinov); George Pastell (Russian Commissar); Judy Huxtable (Computer Center Girl); Gary Hope (Army Officer); Denis Holmes (Maltby); Billy Milton (Wilson); Carole Blake (Crossword Puzzle Girl); Tony Wall (Sadistikov); Oliver MacGreevy (Russian Commissar); Stuart Saunders (Police Inspector); Paul Tann (Valdimir Sheehee); Shelagh Booth (Governess); John Evitts (Killer); Robert Marsen (August Jacobsen); and: Mona Chong, Michael Godfrey, Julian Strange, Claire Gordon, J.B. Dubin-Behrmann, Sarah Maddern.

Peter Bull (left) and Oliver MacGreevy (center) in The Second Best Secret Agent ... (Embassy, 1966).

Two Danish scientists come close to conning both the British and the Russians into believing that they have perfected an anti-gravity device. They sell the "plans" to both sides.

A far cry from the elaborate James Bond epics, but Adams as Charles Vine, England's number two agent licensed to kill, has the appropriate swaggering style to make his vain, unmannered, impassive character a fitting super hero. Unlike 007, Adams' chief weapon is his flexible gun, but being a very human person, he is not an infallible marksman. The picture is best where there is lots of physical action, and that there is as Adams clashes with Russian assassin Sadistikov (Wall) and engages in the requisite number of homicidal escapades. Arnatt is properly wry as Adams' superior, with Hurst deliberately distracting as the pretty assistant of scientist Henrik Jacobsen (Stepanek).

For the record, the long-winded title song was sung by Sammy Davis.

THE SECRET AGENT (Gaumont British, 1936) 83 min.

Producer, Michael Balcon, Ivor Montagu; director, Alfred Hitchcock; based on the play by Campbell Dixon, adapted from the novel Ashenden by W. Somerset Maugham; adaptation, Alma Reville; dialog, Ian Hay, Jesse Lasky, Jr.; sets, Otto Werndorff, Albert Jullion; costumes, J. Strasser; music, Louis Levy; camera, Bernard Knowles; editor, Charles Frend.

Madeleine Carroll (Elsa Carrington); John Gielgud (Richard Ashenden); Peter Lorre (The General); Robert Young (Robert Marvin); Percy Marmont (Caypor); Florence Kahn (Mrs. Caypor); Lilli Palmer (Lilli); Charles Carson ("R"); and: Michael Redgrave.

Based on selected episodes from Somerset Maugham's "autobiographical" novel and the later Campbell Dixon play adaptation, The Secret Agent had tough sledding on many counts: the hero (Gielgud) is an unwilling worker who bungles his job and along with novice collaborator Carroll suffers unremitting pangs of guilt. Most damaging to the heart of the story is that the film never makes a sufficiently strong case for the necessity of spying or that there is anything worthwhile in Geneva to spy on. The best element of the film is Lorre's performance as the Mexican "General," a homicidal virtuoso who is both wistful and amusing.

Supposedly dead novelist Richard Ashenden (Gielgud) is sent by British Intelligence to Switzerland to slay a troublesome German spy. Elsa Carrington (Carroll), a dilettante who joined the English secret service, is dispatched to Geneva to play Gielgud's wife. By error the wrong person (Marmont) is liquidated via a shove from a mountain peak, leaving a remorseful Gielgud and Carroll (both still libidinous enough to fall in love with one another) to pursue the actual Central Powers agent (Young) through Switzerland and on to Turkey, with a climactic train wreck concluding the spy hunt.

The famed Alfred Hitchcock directorial touch is most evident in the police chase through a chocolate factory, the unlikely headquarters of the spy ring.

SECRET AGENT OF JAPAN (20th-Fox, 1942) 72 min.

Producer, Sol M. Wurtzel; director, Irving Pichel; screenplay, John Larkin; music director, Emil Newman; camera, Lucian

Andriot; editor, Alfred Day.

Preston Foster (Ray Bonnell); Lynn Bari (Kay Murdock); Noel Madison (Saito); Victor Sen Yung (Fu Yen); Janis Carter (Doris Poole); Steve Geray (Alecsandri); Kurt Katch (Trager); Addison Richards (Remsen); Ian Wolfe (Captain Larsen); Hermine Sterler (Mrs. Alecsandri); Selmer Jackson (American Naval Captain); Frank Puglia (Eminescu); Leyland Hodgson, Leslie Denison (English Secret Service Men); Jean Del Val (Solaire); Noel Cravat, Wilfred Hari (Japanese Detectives); Cyril Ring, Harry Denny, Arthur Loft (American Business Men); Florence Shirley (American Woman); Tim Ryan (Bartender); Tom O'Grady (Man at Bar); Al Kikume (Sikh Policeman); Bud Fine (American Detective); Bob Okazaki (Japanese Lieutenant); Don Forbes (Radio Announcer); Daisy Lee (Chinese Landlady); Gino Corrado (Gambler).

Noel Madison, Wilfred Hari, and Preston Foster in Secret Agent of Japan (20th-Fox, 1942).

This feature is noteworthy for being the initial anti-totalitarian feature dealing with Japanese imperialism to come out of World War II Hollywood, focusing on the story behind the stab in the back at Pearl Harbor. For all its whipped-up patriotic overtones, Secret Agent of Japan was a "very mild hate-brew." (The Orientals do

call the hero "American swine," and he in turn labels a Japanese
secret agent, "You son of a rising son.") More importantly, this
film was only a third-rate melodrama "as lurid and fanciful and
cockeyed as a Grade B dragon" (PM).

American Ray Bonnell (Foster) with his fake Swiss passport,
is content to remain in 1941 Shanghai, for he is wanted back in
Ohio on a grand larceny charge. However, when his casino partner (Puglia) is murdered and the Japanese nationalize his club,
Foster experiences pangs of red-white-and-blue, heightened by his
contact with Kay Murdock (Bari) who turns out to be a British
agent with information about the Japs' planned Pearl Harbor attack.
Foster refuses to commit himself to the Allied efforts till almost the
last minute, and by the time he relays the information to the proper
authorities, there is no time to prevent the sneak raid on December
7th in Hawaii.

Even with its topical overtones, Secret Agent of Japan was
a regressive step in the spy films annals, relying enthusiastically
on the very obvious: slinky pearl buyer Bari could be nothing else
but a spy. What modern espionage professional would play such
theatrical games as leaving little white cards (with messages reading "Join the Chinese Army") in unlikely spots at Foster's bar. As
for the depiction of the so-called exquisitely ruthless Japanese agents,
one reviewer of the day noted that they looked more like refugees
from a Chinese hand laundry.

SECRET AGENT X-9 (Universal, 1945) 13 Chapters

          Chapters: (1) Torpedo Rendezvous, (2) Ringed by Fire,
(3) Death Curve, (4) Floodlight Murder, (5) Downgrade, (6) Strafed
by a Zero, (7) High Pressure Deadline, (8) The Sloppy Floor,
(9) The Danger Point, (10) Japanese Burial, (11) Fireworks for
Deadmen, and (12) Big Gun Fusillade.

          Director, Ray Taylor, Lewis D. Collins; story, Joseph
O'Donnell, Harold C. Wire; screenplay, O'Donnell, Patricia Harper;
camera, Maury Gertsman, Ernie Miller.
          Lloyd Bridges (Secret Agent X-9); Keye Luke (Ah Fong); Jan
Wiley (Lynn Moore); Victoria Horne (Nabura); Samuel S. Hinds
(Solo); Cy Kendall (Lucky Kamber); Jack Overman (Marker); George
Lynn (Bach); Clarence Lung (Takahari); Benson Fong (Hakahima);
Arno Frey (Kapitan Grut); Ferdinand Munier (Papa Pierre); Ann
Codee (Mama Pierre); Edward M. Howard (Drag Dorgan); Edmund
Cobb (Bartender); Gene Stutenroth (Yogle); Mauritz Hugo (Garr);
Dick Scott (Miley); Bob Chinn, Angel Cruz, Albert Law (Japanese
Sailors); Jack Cheatham, Carey Harrison (Constables); Stan Jolley
(Trent); Jack Clifford (Pete); James Leong (Japanese Pilot); Robert
Stephenson, Frank Hilliard, Lance Jantzen, Robert Strong, Dan
Stowell (Nazis); Roque Esperitu (Japanese Co-Pilot); George Leigh
(Harper); Larry Wong (Japanese Commander); Heenan Elliott
(Radio Operator); Barry Bernard (Grove); Tony Ellis (James); Nick
Warick (Haney); Henry Wadsworth (Roberts); Robert Lee (Japanese

Operator); Charles Miller (Blanchard); George Reynolds (Wiley);
Luke Chan (Japanese Announcer); Charles Sullivan (Port Guard);
Perc Launders (Messenger); Budd Buster (Mace); John Roy (Lou);
Eddie Hart, Lee Fong, Ed Luke (Sailors); Stanley Price (Duke);
Carey Loftin (Charlie); George Eldredge (Browder); Roger Cole,
Sayre Dearing, Jack Rockwell (Henchmen); Joseph Kim (Saki); Paul
Fung (Kanato); Leon Lontoc (Tichi); John Merton (Parker); George
Chesebro (Test Man); George Chung (Radio Operator on Sub); Beal
Wong (Korakaga); Ted Hecht (Dr. Harold).

Scott Kolk (center) in <u>Secret Agent X-9</u> (Universal, 1937).

Whereas Universal's earlier chapterplay, <u>Secret Agent X-9</u>
(1937) starring Scott Kolk, had concerned itself with the recovery
of the stolen Belgravian crown jewels, the new edition, starring
Lloyd Bridges, focused on the attempts of the Japanese to sneak
an agent into America to obtain a top secret formula for synthetic
fuels.

The operatives involved here include the super human whiz
Secret Agent X-9 (Bridges) of the American secret service, aided
by his Australian (Moore) and Chinese (Luke) counterparts in coping
with the forces of Nabura (Horne) of the sinister Japanese Black
Dragon Intelligence service, a group operating from a base on
neutral Shadow Island off the China coast.

THE SECRET AGENTS   see   THE DIRTY GAME

THE SECRET CODE (Columbia, 1942) 15 Chapters

Chapters: (1) Enemy Passport, (2) The Shadows of the
Swastika, (3) Nerve Gas, (4) The Sea Spy Strikes, (5) Wireless
Warning (6) Flaming Oil, (7) Submarine Signal, (8) The Missing
Key, (9) The Radio Bomb, (10) Blind Bombardment, (11) Ears of
the Enemy, (12) Scourge of the Orient, (13) Pawn of the Spy Ring,
(14) Dead Men of the Deep, and (15) The Secret Code Smashed.

Producer, Larry Darmour; director, Spencer G. Bennett;
screenplay, Basil Dickey, Leighton Brill, Robert Beche; assistant
director, Carl Hiecke; music, Lee Zahler; code lessons, Henry
Lysing; camera, James S. Brown, Jr.; editor, Earl Turner.
Paul Kelly (Dan Barton); Anne Nagel (Jean Ashley); Clancy
Cooper (Pat Flanigan); Trevor Bardette (Jensen); Robert O. Davis
(Thyssen); Gregory Gay (Feldon); Louis Donath (Metzger); Ed
Parker (Berck); Beal Wong (Quito); Jackie Dalya (Linda); Alex
Callam (Hogan); Eddie Woods (Kurt).

Immodestly touted by Columbia as "The Greatest Spy Action
Serial of All Time" ("Super-Secret, Super-Serial, Super-Thrills!")
this propaganda-laden cliffhanger had its share of action episodes,
which according to Alan G. Barbour in Days of Thrills and Adventure (1970) "for Columbia, they were thrill-packed indeed."
Police lieutenant Dan Barton (Kelly) is assigned to smash an
enemy sabotage ring, gaining access to the agents' inner circle by
posing as a disgraced law enforcer. Soon Kelly finds himself in
the precarious position of being hunted by both sides; the federal
government is after him for his "spy activities," while as the
"Black Commando"--the foe of the spy organization--he is the target of the enemy. By the wrap-up the Axis operatives have been
captured and the secret synthetic rubber formula is saved from
enemy hands.
An interesting gimmick of this serial was the utilization at
the end of each chapter of a brief lecture and demonstration on
the cracking of secret codes.

SECRET COMMAND (Columbia, 1944) 92 min.

Producer, Phil L. Ryan; director, Eddie Sutherland; based
on the story The Saboteurs by John and Ward Hawkins; screenplay,
Roy Chanslor; art director, Lionel Banks, Edward Jewell; set
decorator, Robert Priestley; assistant director, Rex Bailey; music,
Paul Sawtell; music director, Morris Stoloff; montages, Aaron
Nipley; sound, Ed Bernds; process camera, David Allen, Ray Cory;
special effects, Robert Wright; camera, Franz F. Planer; editor,
Viola Lawrence.
Pat O'Brien (Sam Gallagher); Carole Landis (Jill McCann);
Chester Morris (Jeff Gallagher); Ruth Warrick (Lea Damaron);
Barton MacLane (Red Kelly); Tom Tully (Brownell); Wallace Ford
(Miller); Howard Freeman (Max Lessing); Erik Rolf (Ben Royall);

Matt McHugh (Curly); Frank Sully (Shawn); Frank Fenton (Simms); Charles D. Brown (James Thane); Carol Nugent (Joan); Richard Lane (Paul).

Pat O'Brien and Carol Landis in <u>Secret Command</u> (Columbia, 1944).

The picture's foreword poured out a few bromides for the war effort, labeling the film a tribute to the men who build American ships, good ships, honest, sturdy ships.... "Eire may be neutral in today's war, but, so far as Pat O'Brien is concerned, there's no question about the sentiments of the Irish, they'll fight

Nazis at the drop of a cliché" (New York Times).
        Naval Intelligence sends ex-foreign correspondent Sam Gal-
lagher (O'Brien) to pilebuck at a large shipyard which is a hotbed
of enemy agent intrigue.   As a cover O'Brien is provided with
F. B. I. operative Jill McCann (Landis) to pose as his wife, plus
two refugee kids (Nugent, Lane) to act as their children.   The ruse
is so convincing that O'Brien's rugged brother Jeff Gallagher (Morris), boss of the night shift unit at the shipyard, thinks his mystify-
ing sibling is up to something very strange.   Because Lea Damaron
(Warrick) was Morris' former gal and had made an overt pass for
O'Brien--before he returned with Landis and kids--the two hot-
tempered sons of Ireland are more often at each other's throats
than trying to save America for democracy by tracking down the
Nazi saboteurs.   The wrap up slug fest has O'Brien tackling the
enemy above and below water as he attempts to disengage a time
bomb set to explode the hull of a new aircraft carrier.

THE SECRET DOOR   (Warner-Pathé, 1962)   71 min.

        Producer, Charles Baldour; associate producer, Robert Hut-
ton; director, Gilbert L. Kay; based on the story Paper Door by
Stephen Longstreet; screenplay, Charles Martin; music, Baldour;
camera, Robert Moss, Aurelio Podriguez.
        Robert Hutton (Joe Adams); Sandra Dorne (Sonia); Peter
Illing (Buergher); Peter Allenby (Edward Brentano); George Pastell
(Antonio); Shirley Lawrence (Gretchen); Bob Gallico (Lt. Ted
Avery); Peter Elliott (Japanese Ambassador); Tony Arpino (Freighter
Captain); James Dyrenforth (Prison Warden); Chris Lawrence (Cap-
tain Hastings); Martin Benson (Edmundo Vara).

        Shortly after Pearl Harbor, safecrackers Joe Adams and
Edward Brentano (Hutton and Allenby) are released from prison
to be trained for the task of photographing Japanese Naval code
records at the Japanese Embassy in Lisbon.   No The Dirty Dozen
this, but like that film, it demonstrated the constructive use of
recalcitrant law breakers in wartime, here for a spy mission requiring expertise that a criminal would best have.
        The British Monthly Film Bulletin endorsed this filmed
caper: "the succession of double-crosses are treated with such
straight-faced elan and economy that the result is quite lively."
        Also known as Now It Can Be Told.

SECRET ENEMIES (WB, 1942)   57 min.

        Director, Ben Stoloff; screenplay, Raymond Schrock; art
director, Hugh Reticker; special effects, Edwin A. Du Par; camera,
James Van Trees; editor, Douglas Gould.
        Craig Stevens (Carl Becker); Faye Emerson (Paula Fengler);
John Ridgely (John Trent); Charles Lang (Jim Jackson); Robert
Warwick (Dr. Woodford); Frank Reicher (Henry Bremmer); Rex

Williams (Hans); Stacy Keach, Victor Zimmerman, Frank Wilcox, Lane Chandler, Lee Powell (Counter Espionage Men); George Meeker (Rudolph); Roland Drew (Fred); Addison Richards (Travers); Cliff Clark (Captain Jarrett); Monte Blue (Hugo); Stuart Holmes (Adolph); Ray Teal (Motor Cop); Ruth Ford (Miss Charlton); Sol Gorss (Joe); Leah Baird (Maid); Jack Mower (Medical Examiner); Frank Mayo (Patrolman's Voice); Marian Hall (Secretary); Ernst Hausman (Bellhop); Rudolf Steinbeck, Robert Stevenson (Spies); Bill Hopper (Ensign); Rolf Lindau (Spy Radio Operator); Harry Lewis (Radio Operator).

Victor Zimmerman (third from left), Rex Williams, Stacy Keach, Sr. (with revolver), and Robert Warwick in Secret Enemies (WB, 1942).

    Labeled a "somewhat sturdier B movie than most" by the New York Times, Secret Enemies was a Warner Bros. bottom bill wartime drama, focusing on the FBI's efforts to clean up a nest of Nazi spies on the homefront. Stevens was serviceable as the federal agent who discovers his girl (Emerson) was a member of the enemy organization he was combatting.

SECRET MEETING   see   MARIE-OCTOBRE

SECRET MISSION   (General Film Distributors, 1942)   94 min.

   Producer, Marcel Hellman; director, Harold French; story,
Shaun Terence Young; screenplay, Anatole de Grunwald, Basil
Bartlett; camera, Bernard Knowles, Cyril Knowles.
   Hugh Williams (Peter Ganett); Carla Lehmann (Michele de
Carnot); James Mason (Raoul de Carnot); Roland Culver (Red Gowan);
Michael Wilding (Nobby Clark); Nancy Price (Violette); Percy Walsh
(Fayolle); Betty Warren (Mrs. Nobby Clark); Nicholas Stuart (Cap-
tain Mackenzie); Karel Stepanek (Major Lang); F. R. Wendhausen
(Von Reichmann); John Salew (Captain Grune); Stewart Granger
(Submarine Lt. Jackson); and: Marcel Hellman, Herbert Lom.

   Three Englishmen and one Fighting French Army Intelligence
member slip into occupied France to discover the strength of Nazi
coastal defense.   Two of the quartet pose as champagne salesmen
and friends of von Ribbentrop, a guise which passes them into
German General Headquarters where they obtain the needed data.
   This rather far-fetched bit of patriotic esoterica pictured
the enemy as particularly dense, and the Allied agents as ever so
spritely and clever.   The highlight of the picture is the demolition
of an expansive underground fortress.

THE SECRET OF THE CHINESE CARNATION   see   DAS GEHEIM-
NIS DER CHINESISCHEN NELKE

SECRET ORDERS   (FBO, 1926)   5,486 feet

   Director, Chet Withey; story, Martin Justice; screenplay,
J. Grubb Alexander; assistant director, Doran Cox; camera, Roy
Klaffki.
   Harold Goodwin (Eddie Delano); Robert Frazer (Bruce Cor-
bin); Evelyn Brent (Janet Graham); John Gough (Spike Slavin);
Marjorie Bonner (Mary, Janet's Friend); Brandon Hurst (Butler);
Frank Leigh (Cook).

   Screen veteran Brent had an athletic workout in this com-
plexly plotted exercise delving once again into the world of sinister spies who populated New York City during World War I.   The
film relied on its Pearl White type heroine to save the day.
   Telegrapher Janet Graham (Brent) weds Eddie Delano (Goodwin) only to later discover he is not a salesman, but a crook.
When he is packed off to jail, she volunteers for the U.S. Secret
Service and is assigned to locate the source leak providing information on troop transport maneuvers.   But it is not all work for
Brent, for she becomes enamored of her superior (Frazer).   Complications arise when Goodwin escapes from prison, comes to New

York, and partners with Spike Slavin (Gough), not knowing the latter
is a German agent.   Meanwhile Brent has discovered that Gough's
cook (Leigh) is a spy, which leads her to Gough's headquarters,
and paves the way for a last minute rescue by Frazer.

SECRET SERVICE   (RKO, 1931)   68 min.

          Director, J. Walter Ruben; based on the play by William
Gillette; screenplay, Gerrit J. Lloyd; adaptation-dialog, Bernard
Schubert; art director, Max Ree; assistant director, James Ander-
son; sound, George Ellis; camera, Edward Cronjager; editor, John
Kitchin.
          Richard Dix (Lewis Dumont); Shirley Grey (Edith Varney);
William Post, Jr. (Lt. Dumont); Gavin Gordon (Archford); Fred
Warren (General Grant); Nance O'Neil (Mrs. Varney); Virginia
Sale (Miss Kittridge); Florence Lake (Caroline); Clarence Muse
(Jonas); Harold Kinney (Howard Varney); Eugene Jackson (Israel);
Frederick Burton (General Randolph); Carl Gerard (Lieutenant
Foray); Gertrude Howard (Martha).

          During the Civil War, Lewis Dumont (Dix) and his brother
Lieutenant Dumont (Post, Jr.) are brought to the headquarters of
General Grant's (Warren) secret service department.   Dix is
ordered to the South to pose as a Confederate officer and worm his
way into the confidence of Richmond's gallant defenders, so the
North may learn of its opponents' weaknesses.   While on the mission, Dix falls passionately in love with Grey, daughter of a Dixie
general.
          Based on the 1895 stage play which starred William Gillette
and the later 1919 silent picture, the new edition seemed outmoded
in 1931.   In fact, observed the New York Times, "Some are likely
to complain that the film has too much love and not enough secret
service."

SECRET SERVICE IN DARKEST AFRICA (Republic, 1943)   15
Chapters

          Chapters: (1) North African Intrigue, (2) The Charred Wit-
ness, (3) Double Death, (4) The Open Grave, (5) Cloaked in Flame,
(6) Dial of Doom, (7) Murder Dungeon, (8) Funeral Arrangements
Completed, (9) Invisible Menace, (10) Racing Peril, (11) Lightning
Terror, (12) Ceremonial Execution, (13) Fatal Leap, (14) Victim
of Villainy, and (15) Nazi Treachery Unmasked.

          Associate producer, W. J. O'Sullivan; director, Spencer Ben-
nett; screenplay, Royal Cole, Basil Dickey, Jesse Duffy, Ronald
Davidson, Joseph O'Donnell, Joseph Poland; music, Mort Glickman; special effects, Howard Lydecker, Jr.; camera, William Bradford.
          Rod Cameron (Rex Bennett); Lionel Royce (Sultan Abou Ben

Ali/von Rommler); Joan Marsh (Janet Blake); Duncan Renaldo
(Pierre LaSalle); Kurt Kreuger (Ernst Muller); Frederic Brunn
(Wolfe); Sigurd Tor (Luger); Alex Montoya (Stoker); Ed Agresti
(French Officer); Emily La Rue (Zara); Erwin Goldi (Colonel von
Raeder); Ralf Harolde (Riverboat Captain); John Royce (German
Lieutenant); Kurt Katch (Hauptmann); Frank Alten (Schloss); Georges
Renavent (Armand); Jack Chefe (French Sentry); William Von
Brincken (Captain Boschert); Eddie Parker (Koche); John Davidson
(Sheik); Frederic Worlock (Sir James Langley); George Sorel (French
Doctor); Eddie Phillips (Bisra); William Yetter (Submarine Comman
dant); Hans von Morhart (Sub Officer); George Lewis (Kaba); Charles
La Torre (Sufi); John Bleifer (Kasar); Walter Fenner (Sheik Fed-
dallah); Anthony Warde (Helzah); Norman Nesbitt (Broadcaster);
Jack La Rue (Hassan); Paul Marion (Abdue); Bud Geary (Black-
smith); George DeNormand (Elmir); Nino Bellini (French Supply
Terminal Officer); Tom Steele (Cameron's Double); Joe Yrigoyen,
Duke Green (Doubles); George Magrill, Ken Terrell (Machine
Gunners).

　　　As a continuation of its popular serial G-Men vs The Black
Dragon (1943), Republic again starred Rod Cameron as athletic
Rex Bennett, one of America's leading undercover agents. This
chapterplay found him combatting the Nazi plot to align the African
Arabs with the Axis cause. The Germans, so Cameron discovers,
have been persuading the natives by using the Dagger of Solomon
and a fake Scroll claimed to be the definite statement of a ven-
erated Moslem leader of antiquity. The action switches from
Berlin to Casablanca where Cameron joins forces with American
correspondent/United Nations secret agent Janet Blake (Marsh) and
French officer Pierre LaSalle (Renaldo). The Allies' primary
nemesis proves to be Baron von Rommler (Royce), head of the
vast Nazi spy complex operating in North Africa.
　　　The serial was later chopped into a 100-minute feature for
television, entitled The Baron's African War.

THE SECRET WAYS (Universal, 1961)   C   112 min.

　　　Producer, Richard Widmark; associate producer, Euan
Lloyd; director, Phil Karlson; based on the novel by Alistair
MacLean; screenplay, Jean Hazlewood; music, Johnny Williams;
music supervisor, Joseph Gershenson; art director, Werner and
Isabella Schichting; assistant director, Erich von Stroheim, Jr.,
Andre Farsch; costumes, Dr. Leo Lei; sound, Kurt Schwarz;
makeup, Rudolf Ohlschmidt; camera, Max Greene; editor, Aaron
Still.
　　　Richard Widmark (Michael Reynolds); Sonja Ziemann (Julia);
Charles Regnier (The Count); Walter Rilla (Jansci); Howard Ver-
non (Colonel Hidas); Senta Berger (Elsa); Heinz Moog (Minister
Sakenov); Hubert von Meyerinck (Herman Sheffler); Oskar Wegro-
stek (The Fat Man); Stefan Schnabel (Border Official); Elisabeth
Neumann-Viertel (Olga); Helmuth Janatsch (Janos); Walter Wilz

(Peter); Raoul Retzer (Special Agent); John Horsley (Jon Bainbridge); Georg Kovary (Language Professor); Adi Berber (Sandor); Jochen Brockmann (The Commandant); Brigitte Brunmuller (Waitress); Reinhard Kelldehoff, Rudolf Rosner (The Count's Men).

Richard Widmark (left) and Walter Rilla (right) in The Secret Ways (Universal, 1961).

      Alistair MacLean's taut novel of espionage adventure received a watery, overlong rendition at the hands of producer-star Widmark who assembled a crew on location in England, Switzerland, and Austria (with Vienna doubling for Budapest locales). The Phil Karlson-directed film was soundly rapped for its "thoroughly out-moded style and a pack of visual cliches" (Variety). One could easily forget that buried within the cinematic fiddle-faddle is a celebration of man's courage for a worthy cause. Universal was not fooled, however, and dumped the film onto the double bill market, packaged with Tammy Tell Me True.
      Cynical American freelance adventurer Michael Reynolds (Widmark) is paid $60,000 in Zurich to induce salty, aging underground leader and university professor Jansci (Rilla) to leave Budapest. Widmark poses as a newsman doing a travel series and penetrates behind the Iron Curtain only to learn that the Hungarian

A. V. O. security forces and the Russian army of occupation are
tough birds to fool. An oversized Szarhaza Prison break is required before Widmark and Rilla can hightail it out of harm's way.
In the course of his adventures Widmark tumbles for Rilla's self-
sufficient daughter Julia (Ziemann) and changes his mind that
"everybody's learned to live by compromises."

SECRETS OF SCOTLAND YARD (Republic, 1944)   71 min.

Executive producer, Armand Schaefer; producer-director,
George Blair; based on the story Room 40, O. B. by Denison Clift;
screenplay, Clift; assistant director, Bud Springsteen; art director,
Russ Kimball; sound, Earl Crain, Sr.; camera, William Bradford;
editor, Fred Allen.
Edgar Barrier (John Usher/Robert Usher); Stephanie Bache-
lor (Sudan Ainger); C. Aubrey Smith (Sir Christopher Pelt); Henry
Stephenson (Sir Reginald Meade); Lionel Atwill (Waterlow); Walter
Kingsford (Roylott Bevan); John Abbott (Mortimer Cope); Frederic
Worlock (Mason); Matthew Boulton (Colonel Hedley); Forrester
Harvey (Alfred Morgan); Bobby Cooper (David Usher); Martin

Richard Ryen, Frank Brand, and Bobby Cooper in Secrets of Scotland Yard (Republic, 1944).

Kosleck (Josef); William Edmunds (Isaiah Thom); Louis V. Arco
(Colonel Eberling); Frederick Giermann (Hans Koebig); Sven-Hugo
Borg (Nazi Messenger); Leslie Vincent (Hardy, the Co-Pilot);
Arthur Stanning (Inspector Collins); Keith Hitchcock (Inspector Cham-
bers); Leonard Carey (Butler); Mary Gordon (Libby, the House-
keeper); Jordan Shelley (Larkworthy, the Pilot); Jack George (Wine
Waiter); Ed Biby (Sir Philip Gough); Arthur Mulliner (Lt. Col.
Jardine); Major Sam Harris (Under Secretary Borden); Eric Wilton
(General Eric Holt); Carey Harrison (British Navy Officer); Larry
Steers (Admiral Langley); William Nind (English Waiter); Carl
Ekberg (German Cook); Antonio Filauri (Waiter); Richard Ryen
(Herr Friedrich Eberling); Frank Brand (Carl Eberling); Nigel
Horton (Official of Communications); Richard Woodruff (Radio Man);
Kenne Duncan (Steward).

This corner-cutting entry is buoyed by a stronger than usual
cast. Barrier portrayed twin brothers, one of whom is killed early
in the film after deciphering a secret Nazi code message. The surviving twin becomes part of the British staff that specialize in un-
scrambling enemy communications, leading to further deaths until
Scotland Yard cracks open the case.

SECRETS OF THE UNDERGROUND (Republic, 1942) 70 min.

Associate producer, Leonard Fields; director, William Mor-
gan; story, Geoffrey Homes; screenplay, Robert Tasker, Homes;
art director, Russell Kimball; set decorator, Otto Siegel; music
director, Walter Scharf; assistant director, Philip Ford; sound,
Fred Stahl; camera, Ernest Miller; editor, Arthur Roberts.
John Hubbard (P. Cadwallader Jones); Virginia Grey (Terry);
Lloyd Corrigan (Maurice Vaughn); Robin Raymond (Marianne Panois);
Miles Mander (Paul Panois); Olin Howlin (Oscar); Neil Hamilton
(Kermit); Marle Shelton (Mrs. Perkins); Ben Welden (Joe); Ken
Christy (Cleery); Dick Rich (Maxie); Pierre Watkin (D. A. Winton);
Eule Morgan (Mrs. Calhoun); George Sherwood (Window Dresser);
Herbert Vigran (Street Photographer); Nora Lane (Woman Clerk);
Charles Williams (Hypo); Bobby Stone (Messenger); Francis Sayles
(Station Agent); Roy Gordon (Mr. Perkins); Connie Evans (Tele-
phone Operator); George Chandler (Lynch the Hotel Clerk); Eddie
Kane (Bradley the Reporter); Joey Ray (Harrison the Reporter); Max
Wagner (Baggage Man); Pauline Drake (Receptionist); Eddy Chandler
(Dan the Detective); Ben Taggart (Bob the Detective).

This film represents a new wrinkle in the spy film field.
The Axis agents are not hellbent after the Allies' latest weapon
invention or out to acquire the master plan of troop maneuvers.
Instead, they are plotting to flood the market with fake war savings
stamps and sabotage the American public's support of Uncle Sam's
war efforts. Unfortunately everything else about the film, which
derived from Phillip H. Lord's radio program "Mr. District Attorney," is very ordinary indeed.

District attorney Hubbard and his fast-talking reporter girlfriend Grey quickly find themselves on the trail of enemy saboteurs
who have forced an artist (Mander) to engrave the phony stamp
plates, if he wants his daughter (Raymond) to remain in good health.
Maurice Vaughn (Corrigan) is not only engaging in an unique profession, as a male modiste, but has suspicious business activities
on the side.

SECHS PISTOLEN JAGEN PROFESSOR Z (International Germania/
Hispaner, A. V. -Films, 1965)   C   92 min.

Director, Jules Coll; screenplay, Coll, Helmuth Harum;
music, Louis Navarro; camera, Mario Pacheco.
Peter Van Eyck (Jack); Letita Roman (Ellen); Antonio Vilar
(Pierre); Klausjurgen Wussow (Johansson); Corny Collins (Jenny);
and: Richard Rubinstein.

Undercover agents and adventurers gamble with death to
obtain a secret metal alloy that might place world domination within the power of the possessor.   The Spanish-Portuguese location
photography was a highlight of the feature.
Television title: High Season for Spies.

SEE VENICE AND DIE   see   VOIR VENISE ET CREVER

LE SERPENT (Les Films la Boetie, 1973)   C   120 min.

Producer-director, Henry Verneuil; based on the novel by
Pierre Nord; screenplay, Verneuil, Gilles Perrault; art director,
Jacques Saulnier; music, Ennio Morricone; camera, Claude Renoir;
editor, Pierre Gillete.
Yul Brynner (Colonel Vlassov); Henry Fonda (Davies); Dirk
Bogarde (Boyle); Philippe Noiret (Berthon); Michel Bouquet (Tavel);
Martin Held (Lepke); Farley Granger (Expert); Virna Lisi (Annabel
Lee); Guy Trejan (Deval); Elga Anderson (Kate); Robert Alda
(Questioner); Natalie Nerval (Tatiana).

"Film has gloss, solid detail and maybe lacks that grain of
personal flair and invention that could have given it a more probing
insight into the eerie game of espionage.   But, as is, it sustains
interest and perhaps with a little tightening would be even more
effective" (Variety).
Colonel Vlassov (Brynner) of the Russian secret police defects to the West, placing himself in the custody of the French
police after alerting the American Embassy.   Before the French
can pry loose from Brynner the names of agents infiltrating into
France, the CIA whisks the valuable prisoner to Washington, where
official Davies (Fonda) directs the questioning.   Brynner's veiled
answers lead to a rash of "suicides" among top level men in

Germany, many of whom could be spies. Appearing on the scene is the mysterious "The Serpent" who proves to be in league with Brynner in a grand Communist plot.

SEVEN DAYS IN MAY (Paramount, 1964) 120 min.

Producer, Edward Lewis; director, John Frankenheimer; based on the novel by Fletcher Knebel, Charles W. Bailey; screenplay, Rod Serling; art director, Cary Odell; set decorator, Edward Boyle; assistant director, Hal Polaire; music, Jerry Goldsmith; sound, Joe Edmondson; camera, Ellsworth Fredericks; editor, Ferris Webster.

Burt Lancaster (General James M. Scott); Kirk Douglas (Colonel Martin Casey); Fredric March (President Jordan Lyman); Martin Balsam (Paul Girard); George Macready (Christopher Todd); Whit Bissell (Senator Prentice); Hugh Marlowe (Harold McPherson); Bart Burns (Arthur Corwin); Richard Anderson (Colonel Murdock); Jack Mullaney (Lieutenant Hough); Andrew Duggan (Colonel "Mutt" Henderson); John Larkin (Colonel Broderick); Malcolm Atterbury (White House Physician); Helen Kleeb (Esther Townsend);

Fredric March, Martin Balsam, Edmond O'Brien, and Malcolm Atterbury (rear) in <u>Seven Days in May</u> (Paramount, 1964).

John Houseman (Admiral Barnswell); Colette Jackson (Bar Girl).

In the same year that saw the release of Dr. Strangelove and Fail-Safe appeared Seven Days in May, equally fantastic and hard to swallow, but closer to possibility when judging the implausible temperament of modern man. Neither the critics nor the public cottoned to this cold sweat session of crushing sub rosa treason in sub rosa fashion. Like the Fletcher Knebel/Charles W. Bailey II original novel, Seven Days in May points a finger of guilt not at individuals but at a way of life. "The enemy is an age," says March's President Jordan Lyman in the picture. "A nuclear age. And out of this comes a sickness.... It happens to have killed man's faith in his ability to influence what happens to him." Herein lies the weak point of the film, for audiences are notorious for wanting their villains spelled out for them in concrete dimensions.

Proceedings against the advice of military advisers, President Jordan Lyman (March) in the year 1974 signs a nuclear disarmament treaty with the Soviet Union, an act highly unpopular with the patriotic elements here and abroad. General Scott (Lancaster), chairman of the Joint Chiefs of Staff, is outraged by this "treasonable" act which will leave America unarmed to fight future wars. In this troubled atmosphere, Lancaster's Marine colonel aide Martin Casey (Douglas) stumbles upon several unexplainable situations which causes him and the country's top administrators a week of total fear and anguish. Douglas has discovered there is a secret Air Force installation in the Texas desert whose existence is unknown to the military hierarchy. After piecing together several puzzling communications between Lancaster and other staff officers, Douglas goes to the White House. "I'm suggesting Mr. President there's a military plot to take over the government." Douglas spells out Lancaster's projected coup d'état in which March would be kidnapped, allowing a new regime to head the government. The would-be revolt, of course, is quelled in the end.

SHADOW OF FEAR   (Butcher's, 1963)   60 min.

Producer, John I. Phillips; associate producer, Ronald Liles; director, Ernest Morris; based on the novel Decoy Be Damned by T. F. Fotherby; screenplay, Liles, James O'Connolly; art director, Wilfred Arnold; music, Martin Stairn; sound, Kevin Sutton; camera, Walter J. Harvey; editor, Henry Richardson.

Paul Maxwell (Bill Martin); Clare Owen (Barbara); Anita West (Ruth); Alan Tilvern (Warner); John Arnatt (Sharp); Eric Pohlmann (Spuoritous); Reginald Marsh (Oliver); John Sutton (Halliday); Colin Tapley (John Bowen); Edward Ogden (Chase); Anthony Wager (Carter); John H. Watson (Baker); Robert Russell (Ransome); John Murray (Scott Endacott); Jack Taylor (Holt); Cecil Waters (Kalik); Mia Karam (Dancey); Eugene Stylianou (Hotel Clerk).

In Baghdad Bill Martin (Maxwell) is asked to deliver a

message to a London contact, unaware that his participation as a
courier will lead to a nightmare existence for him: once it is
learned that he possesses a photographic memory and that he had
glanced at the coded paper, he is the obvious target of all surrounding spies.

SHADOW ON THE LAND (ABC-TV, 1968)   C   100 min.

Producer, Matthew Rapf; director-creator, Sidney Sheldon;
screenplay, Nedrick Young; music, Sol Kaplan; camera, Fred
Koenekamp; editor, Henry Batista.
Marc Strange (Major Shepherd McCloud); Jackie Cooper
(Lt. Col. Andy Davis); John Forsythe (General Bruce); Gene Hack-
man (Reverend); Carol Lynley (Abby Taylor); Janice Rule (Captain
Everett); Mike Margotta (Timothy Willing); Bill Walker (Arnold);
Scott Thomas (Felting); Myron Healy (General Hempstead); Fred-
erick Downs (Drucker); Jonathan Lippe (Lt. Allen); and: Michkey
Sholda, Ronnie Eckstein, Sandy Kevin, Ken Swofford, Kay Stewart,
Paul Sorenson, Paulene Myers.

One of the first telefeatures to serve as a video pilot--in
this case for a product that did not sell--Shadow on the Land told
of a future America, when an iron-fisted dictator rules the country.
He sets out to destroy the underground ring of spies who oppose
his totalitarian rule.   "... [W]hat emerges is just a mediocre
shoot-'em-up, with accent on action instead of realistic, meaningful
characterizations and situations" (Daily Variety).

SHERLOCK HOLMES AND THE SECRET WEAPON (Universal,
1943)   68 min.

Associate producer, Howard Benedict; director, Roy William
Neill; based on the story The Adventure of the Dancing Men by Sir
Arthur Conan Doyle; adaptation, W. Scott Darling, Edward T. Lowe;
screenplay, Lowe, Darling, Edmund L. Hartmann; art director,
Jack Otterson; music director, Charles Previn; camera, Lester
White.
Basil Rathbone (Sherlock Holmes); Nigel Bruce (Dr. Watson);
Kaaren Verne (Charlotte Eberli); Lionel Atwill (Professor Moriarty);
William Post, Jr. (Dr. Franz Tobel); Dennis Hoey (Lestrade);
Phillip Van Zandt (Kurt); George Burr MacAnnan (Gottfried); Holmes
Herbert (Sir Reginald); Henry Victor (Frederick Hoffner); Harold
de Becker (Peg Leg); Paul Fix (Mueller); Robert O. Davis (Braun);
Mary Gordon (Mrs. Hudson); John Burton, Leyland Hodgson, Leslie
Denison, James Craven (Bits); Harry Cording (Brady); Paul Bryar
(Waiter); Vicki Campbell (Aviatrix); Gerard Cavin (Scotland Yard
Man); Guy Kingsford (London Bobby); George Eldredge (Policeman).

SHERLOCK HOLMES AND THE VOICE OF TERROR   (Universal, 1942)   65 min.

Associate producer, Howard Benedict; director, John Rawlins; from the characters created by Sir Arthur Conan Doyle; screenplay, Lynn Riggs, Robert D. Andrews; art director, Jack Otterson; music director, Charles Previn; camera, Woody Bredell.
Basil Rathbone (Sherlock Holmes); Nigel Bruce (Dr. Watson); Evelyn Ankers (Kitty); Reginald Denny (Sir Evan Barham); Montagu Love (General Jerome Lawford); Henry Daniell (Anthony Lloyd); Thomas Gomez (Meade); Olaf Hytten (Fabian Prentiss); Leyland Hodgson (Captain Ronald Shore); Arthur Blake (Crosbie); Harry Stubbs (Taxi Driver); Mary Gordon (Mrs. Hudson); Hillary Brooke (Jill Grandis).

SHERLOCK HOLMES IN WASHINGTON   (Universal, 1943)   71 min.

Associate producer, Howard Benedict; director, Roy William Neill; from the characters created by Sir Arthur Conan Doyle; story, Bertram Millhauser; screenplay, Millhauser, Lynn Riggs; music director, Charles Previn; camera, Lester White; editor, Otto Ludwig.
Basil Rathbone (Sherlock Holmes); Nigel Bruce (Dr. Watson); Marjorie Lord (Nancy Patridge); Henry Daniell (William Raster); George Zucco (Stanley/Moriarty); John Archer (Lt. Peter Merriam); Gavin Muir (Bart Lang); Edmund MacDonald (Det. Lt. Grogan); Don Terry (Howe); Bradley Page (Cady); Holmes Herbert (Mr. Ahrens); Thurston Hall (Senator Henry Babcock); Gilbert Emery (Sir Henry Marchmontt).

When Universal purchased the rights to the Sherlock Holmes character and revived the series with Basil Rathbone and Nigel Bruce--playing Holmes and Watson as they had done two years prior in 20th Century-Fox's Hound of the Baskervilles and The Adventure of Sherlock Holmes--it was astutely decided to update the films, thus giving Holmes adequate new material for sleuthing, including working for the Allied war effort.
Thus Sherlock Holmes and the Voice of Terror centers around Germany's blitzkrieg attack on England and the enemy's persistent radio voice that announces the doom of the tight little island.   Holmes (Rathbone) is called in by Sir Evan Barham (Denny) of the Home Office, to identify the "voice of terror" which is so correctly prognosticating the exact time and place of the Nazi attacks.   Among the characters involved in this entry were a red herring played by Daniell, a Limehouse whore (Ankers), who aided Rathbone in uncovering the terror's identity, and Gomez, as a Nazi sympathizer.   The end found the German invasion fortuitously thwarted and "the voice of terror" captured.   Rathbone then delivered an extended soliliquy on patriotism and faith which would become a standard element of this Universal series.

Sherlock Holmes and the Secret Weapon found Professor

George Zucco, Henry Daniell, Basil Rathbone, and Bradley Page in
Sherlock Holmes in Washington (Universal, 1943).

Moriarty (Atwill) bent on locating the "secret weapon" of the title,
a new bomb-site developed by an inventor (Post, Jr.) whom Holmes
(Rathbone) and Dr. Watson (Bruce) were assigned to protect.   This
time the evil Atwill, working hand in hand with the Axis, tries to
kill Rathbone by draining him of his blood, but his evil deed was
foiled.

   The third entry in the Rathbone-Bruce Universal ventures
into Doyle came with Sherlock Holmes in Washington.   The sleuth
team were on the trail of a microfilm of a highly confidential
government document, which had been hidden in a matchfolder.
Also involved in the action was nemesis Moriarty (Zucco) who was
now masquerading as an art dealer and a highly reputable citizen.
Zucco, who wanted to bargain with the Axis for the information,
followed the valuable matchfolder from person to person, and even
tried to kill a U.S. senator (Hall) along the way.   But once again
the villain is subdued by Rathbone at the climax.

   Although the Sherlock Holmes character had always been
best represented on screen as a period piece, nevertheless the
trio of Universal films dealing with the Baker Street sleuth versus
the Nazis made for viable entertainment, bringing into conflict
opponents of distinctly different eras and opposing codes of operation

and ethics. Here it was a pleasure to view Rathbone, so often
cast as a World War II villain, smoothly committing his oversized
acting art on the side of the Allies, aided by the intrepid bumbler
Bruce, the latter a distinct throwback to the Victorian era.

SHIP AHOY (MGM, 1942) 94 min.

Producer, Jack Cummings; director, Edward N. Buzzell;
story, Matt Brooks, Bradford Ropes, Bert Kalmar; screenplay,
Harry Clork; musical presentation by Merrill Pye; songs, Walter
Ruick; E. Y. Harburg and Burton Lane; Ruick and Margery Cum-
mings; camera, Leonard Smith; editor, Blanche Sewell.
Eleanor Powell (Tallulah Winters); Red Skelton (Merton K.
Kibble); Bert Lahr (Skip Owens); Virginia O'Brien (Fran Evans);
William Post, Jr. (H. V. Bennet); James Cross (Stump); Eddie
Hartman (Stumpy); Stuart Crawford (Art Higgins); John Emery
(Dr. Farno); Bernard Nedell (Pietro Potesi); Tommy Dorsey and
Orchestra (Themselves).

Seemingly the thing to do (in 1942) at MGM was to brush
off once important female stars by installing them in minor spy
spoofs. Jeanette MacDonald was handed Cairo and Eleanor Powell
had her Ship Ahoy. The screen's leading distaff tap dancer was
saddled with a very uninventive Red Skelton as her co-star and a
script that pulled every musical and patriotic cliché imaginable.
The New York Herald-Tribune sneered that Ship Ahoy was "a curious combination of swing and propaganda." Variety was less tact-
ful, calling it an "asinine story and treatment shot off the director's
cuff."
Big band dancer Tallulah Winters (Powell) is about to embark for a Puerto Rico club engagement with Tommy Dorsey's band.
Enemy agent Dr. Farno (Emery) and cohorts posing as F. B. I. men
ask naive Powell to deliver a special package to Puerto Rico.
Emery: "It's not what you've done, but what you can do. If
it were possible for you to perform a great service for your country,
would you do it?"
Powell: "Yes, but...."
Emery: "I don't think it will become dangerous. I think
you're brave enough, ingenious enough to carry it through."
Powell: "I probably won't get much sleep on the way over,
but it will get through.... I feel like Mata Hari. I hope I don't
end up like her." (To complete his persuasive argument, Emery
tells Powell "Anyone can be a spy!")
So Powell nervously boards the S. S. Puerto Rico with her
package (containing a new mine model that the enemy wants to sneak
by customs) and finds on the ocean jaunt that her biggest problem
is none other than Merton K. Kibble (Skelton) the daffy creator of
pulp magazine detective fiction, including the Wonder Lad and
Princess Olga stories. To even out the voyage, Skelton's man
Friday, Skip Owens (Lahr) tumbles for Powell's deadpan pal, Fran
Evans (O'Brien). Once in Puerto Rico, Powell becomes more hip

about the mission and Skelton intensifies his romantic pursuit of her. When she is cornered by Emery and his henchmen aboard their San Juan boat club, she resorts to a tap dance act in which she hoofs out a morse code message to the F.B.I. men in the audience.

SHOCK TROOPS see UN HOMME DE TROP

SHOOT FIRST (UA, 1953) 88 min.

   Producer, Raymond Stross; director, Robert Parrish; based on the novel A Rough Shoot by Geoffrey Household; screenplay, Eric Ambler; music, Hans May; art director, Ivan King.
   Joel McCrea (Lt. Col. Robert Taine); Evelyn Keyes (Cecily); Herbert Lom (Peter Landorski);Roland Culver (Roland); Marius Goring (Hiart); Frank Lawton (Hassingham); Patricia Laffan (Makda); Cyril Raymond (Cartwright); Karel Stepanek (Diss); David Hurst (Lex); Dennis Lehrer (Heimann); Laurence Naismith (Blossom); Megs Jenkins (Mrs. Powell); Robert Dickens (Tommy); Jack Mc-Naughton (Inspector Matthews); Arnold Bell (Sgt. Baines); Irving Ellis (P.C. Wharton); Clement McCallin (Inspector Sullivan).

   "When it comes to spy stories and chases, Geoffrey Household and Eric Ambler are a hard combination to beat" (Variety). This spy film is one of the more underrated genre entries.
   Lt. Col. Robert Taine (McCrea) of the American Army is stationed in Dorset, England, where he contentedly resides with his wife (Keyes). One day while out hunting he mistakes a stranger (Lehrer) for a poacher and lets him have a round of what he thinks is harmless buckshot. The target proves to be very much dead and McCrea (erroneously) believes he killed him. Peter Landorski (Lom) later introduces himself to McCrea stating he is working for M.I. 5--a fact "confirmed" by Roland (Culver) of the secret service--and suggests he knows why Lehrer has disappeared. Thus pressured, McCrea is drawn into undoing a ring of spies in the area, who are stealing atomic secrets. McCrea's efforts to locate the brains of the espionage group nearly causes his court martial and pushes him into one dangerous situation after another, cul-minating in a wax museum confrontation.

THE SILENCERS (Columbia, 1966) C 103 min.

   Producer, Irving Allen; associate producer, Jim Schmerer; director, Phil Karlson; based on the novel The Silencers and Death of a Citizen by Donald Hamilton; screenplay, Oscar Saul; music, Elmer Bernstein; songs, Bernstein and Mack David; choreographer, Robert Sidney; costumes, Moss Mabry; assistant director, Clark Paylow; camera, Burnett Guffey; editor, Charles Nelson.
   Dean Martin (Matt Helm); Stella Stevens (Gail); Daliah Lavi (Tina); Victor Buono (Tung-Tze); Robert Webber (Wigman); James

Gregory (MacDonald); Nancy Kovack (Barbara); Roger C. Carmel
(Andreyev); Cyd Charisse (Sarita); Beverly Adams (Lovey Kravezit);
Richard Devon (Domino); David Bond (Dr. Naldi); John Reach
(Traynor); Robert Phillips, Dirk Evans, Bill Couch, Chuck Hicks,
Gary Lasdun (Armed Men); John Willis (M.C.); Frank Gerstle
(Frazer); Grant Woods (Radio Man); Patrick Waltz (Hotel Clerk);
Pamela Rodgers, Carolyn Neff, Rita Thiel, Barbara Burgess, Gigi
Michel, Jan Watson, Gay MacGill, Marilyn Tindall, Susan Hollo-
way, Victoria Lockwood, Margaret Teele (Slaymates); Mary Jane
Mangler, Margie Nelson, Anna Lavelle, Larri Thomas (Specialty
Dancers); Todd Armstrong, Tom Steele, Myron Cook, Scott Perry,
Richard Tretter, Tom Sweet (Guards); Glenn Thompson, John Da-
heim (Stunt Guards); Tommy Horton, Bruce Ritchey (Hunters); Ray
Montgomery (Agent G); Harry Holcombe (Agent X); Vincent Van Lynn
(Agent Z); Ted Jordan, Robert Ward, Pat Renella (Men); Grace
Lee (Oriental Girl); Carole Cole (Waitress); Inga Neilsen (Statue);
Art Koulias (Engineer); Guy Wilkerson (Farmer); Saul Gorss (Pilot);
Pat Hawley (Eddie, the Bartender); Robert Glenn (F.B.I. Agent);
Frank Hagney (Drunk); Amedee Chabot (Girl); Cosmo Sardo (Bit).

Victor Buono, Stella Stevens, and Dean Martin in The Silencers
(Columbia, 1966).

To kick off its new spy series, Columbia relied on two of Donald Hamilton's novellas for plot substance, realigning the hero's characteristics to fit the widely-established image of lackadaisical star Martin. The movie's Matt Helm is still an unattached free-lance photographer, dragged into working for I. C. E. (Intelligence and Counter Espionage) by group chief MacDonald (Gregory), but that is where any similarity between the author's intent and the studio's delivery ended. Martin's portrayal relies on his tried and true public assets: a sleepy-eyed delivery put across in the casualest of manner, with heavy (pseudo) emphasis on booze, broads, and boorishness. As an added attraction, Martin's Matt Helm occupies an idealized bachelor pad, complete with a motor-ized round bed, swimming pool, and a bevy of "Slaygirls."

It appears that a Far Eastern organization, Big O, with Tung-Tze (Buono) as its American-based head is planning to foment world disorder by diverting missiles from the U. S. 's Alamogordo, New Mexico desert sites to cause widespread destruction and fall-out damage. Can Matt Helm (Martin) prevent this potential dis-aster? With all the dolls, pratfalls, and outrageous repartee along the way, it seems highly unlikely. But Martin survives the death of mysterious dancer Sarita (Charisse), the machinations of Tina (Lavi), and the bumblings of well meaning Gail (Stevens) to finally penetrate Buono's elaborate underground hideaway. Our Mr. Martin does not use judo or karate or kung fu, but Okinawan "te," as well as a gun that fires backwards, coat buttons that are hand grenades, and a little assist from central headquarters all to prove that the American way of life can triumph (sic) once again.

The more serious-minded viewers objected strongly to Martin's somnambulistic manner, complete with his in-jokes about the rat pack, parodying of pop songs, ogling of shapely chicks, and light slaps at the star's own show business image. As to the plot, "It's no story at all, but rather a succession of diffuse, adolescent references to eccentric events" (Newsweek).

But go argue with the American public at large. The Silenc-ers took in $7. 35 million in domestic receipts, insuring more Matt Helm pictures to come.

SMASHING THE SPY RING (Columbia, 1939) 59 min.

Director, Christy Cabanne; story, Dorrell and Stuart Mc-Gowan; screenplay, Arthur T. Horman, the McGowans; camera, Allan Siegler; editor, James Sweeney.

Ralph Bellamy (John Baxter); Fay Wray (Eleanor Dunlap); Regis Toomey (Ted Hall); Walter Kingsford (Dr. Carter); Ann Doran (Madelon Martin); Warren Hull (Phil Dunlap); Forbes Murray (Colonel Scully); Lorna Gray (Miss Loring); Paul Whitney (Mason); John Tyrrel (Johnson); May Wallace (Mrs. Baxter).

"They don't waste any time or footage in these Class B-ers" (New York Post). This film is another example of the gangster thriller plot being switched to the spy genre with fair, predictable results.

Tenacious F. B. I. man John Baxter (Bellamy), aided by assistant Ted Hall (Toomey); is drawn into a tough case. Spies are stealing plans of America's fighting planes and high powered munitions formulas. Bellamy's first clues turn up when his fiancée's (Wray) brother (Hull), another G-man, is killed. There is a scrawl in Hull's notebook and Wray insists the ring Hull is wearing at the time of his death does not belong to him. By posing as airplane mechanics, Bellamy and Toomey learn that spy headquarters may be near the sanitarium operated by Dr. Carter (Kingsford). Imaginative Bellamy uses several ruses to penetrate the agents' headquarters, including faking amnesia, adopting the name of a famous scientist who has a poison gas formula, and having himself committed to Kingsford's hospital.

SOME MAY LIVE [In Saigon, Some May Live] (RKO, 1967) C 100 min.

Executive producer, Philip N. Krasne; producer, Clive Sharp, Peter Snell; director, Vernon Sewell; screenplay, David T. Chandler; assistant director, Anthony Waye; production designer, George Lack; music, Cyril Ornadel; song, Ornadel and Peter Callander; sound, Wally Nelson; camera, Ray Parslow; editor, Gordon Pilkington.

Joseph Cotten (Colonel Woodward); Martha Hyer (Kate Meredith); Peter Cushing (John Meredith); John Ronane (Captain Elliott Thomas); David Spenser (Inspector Sung); Alec Mango (Ducrai); Walter Brown (Major Matthews); Kim Smith (Allan Meredith); Burnell Tucker (Lawrence); and: Edwina Carroll, Paula Li Shiu, Keith Bonnard, Lee Peters, Carol Cleveland.

Colonel Woodward (Cotten) of U. S. Army Intelligence in Saigon has a problem: someone in his office is filching top secret documents to sell to the North Vietnamese. The most likely suspect seems to be department employee Kate Meredith (Hyer) whose husband (Cushing) is known to be linked to the Communists. Drawn into the net of intrigue as a mere pawn is Hyer's child (Smith).

This feature was one of a package of modestly-budgeted, "exploitation" features produced by RKO General for television distribution, none of which were distinguished by any technical or artistic superiority.

THE SONG OF LOVE (Associated First National, 1923) 8,000 feet

Presenter, Joseph M. Schenck; director, Chester Franklin; based on the novel Dust of Desire by Margaret Peterson; adaptation, Frances Marion; camera, Antonio Gaudio.

Norma Talmadge (Noorma-hal); Joseph Schildkraut (Raymond Valverde); Arthur Edmund Carewe (Ramlika); Laurence Wheat (Dick Jones); Maude Wayne (Maureen Desmard); Earl Schenck (Commissionnaire Desmond); Hector V. Sarno (Chandra-lal); Albert Prisco

(Chamba); Mario Carillo (Captain Fregonne); James Cooley (Dr. Humbert).

Talmadge was reputed to be the highest salaried screen actress at the time, and this fanciful film, from her own production unit, satisfied her legion of fans, if not the critics.
Algerian Arab chief Ramlika (Carew) plots to drive out the French and, while engineering this feat, courts dancing girl Noormahal (Talmadge). Since Talmadge only tolerates Carew's advances at the insistence of her uncle (Sarno), she only too willingly lets vital information of Carew's military plans slip out to dashing Raymond Valverde (Schildkraut), unknown to her a French spy. Carew's men eventually attack the French garrison and it is Schildkraut who is on hand to single-handedly stave off the enemy advances. Talmadge arrives on the scene and shoots herself rather than go off with Carew. However, she recovers, and the French troops arrive in time to dispatch the beleaguers.

A SOUTHERN YANKEE (MGM, 1948) 90 min.

Producer, Paul Jones; director, Edward Sedgwick; story, Melvin Frank, Norman Panama; screenplay, Harry Tugend; art director, Cedric Gibbons, Randall Duell; set decorator, Edwin B. Willis, Arthur Krams; music, David Snell; sound, Douglass Shearer, John A. Williams; assistant director, Earl McEvoy; makeup, Jack Dawn; costumes, Valles; special effects, Warren Newcombe; camera, Ray June; editor, Ben Lewis.
Red Skelton (Aubrey Filmore); Brian Donlevy (Curt Devlynn); Arlene Dahl (Sallyann Weatharby); George Coulouris (Major Jack Drumman); Lloyd Gough (Captain Steve Lorford); John Ireland (Captain Jed Calbern); Minor Watson (General Watkins); Charles Dingle (Colonel Weatharby); Art Baker (Colonel Clifford M. Baker); Reed Hadley (Fred Munsey); Arthur Space (Mark Haskins); Addison Richards (Dr. Clayton); Joyce Compton (Hortense Dobson); Paul Harvey (Mr. Twitchell); Jeff Corey (Union Cavalry Sergeant); Cliff Clark (Dr. Cooper); Dick Wessel, Ian MacDonald, John Hilton (Orderlies); Ed Gargan (Male Nurse); David Sharp (Confederate Officer); Frank McGrath (Dispatch Rider); David Newell (Sentry); William Tannen, Stanley Andrews, Roger Moore, Dick Simmons (S.S. Men); Susan Simon (Jenny); Byron Foulger (Mr. Duncan); Paul Newlan (Man with Saber); Howard Mitchell, Paul Krueger, Vic Zimmerman, Chris Frank, James Logan (Men); Marcus Turk, Ralph Montgomery, Walter Merrill (Confederate Soldiers); Ralph Volkie, Steve Bennett, Allen Mathews, William "Bill" Phillips (Soldiers); Ann Staunton (Nurse); Henry Hall (Thadeua Dramman); Lane Chandler, Carl Saxe (Sentries); Weldon Heyburn, Sam Flint, Jack Lee, Forbes Murray (Officers); Harry Cording, Kermit Maynard, John Merton Frank Hagney (Horsemen); Shelly Bacon, Drexle Bobbie Haywood (Boys); Dick Alexander (Bartender); Rod O'Connor (Major Kingsby); Pierre Watkin (Major); Bert Moorehouse (Captain Jeffrys); Bill Kennedy (Lt. Sheve).

Buster Keaton, reduced to being a MGM-paid gag writer for Red Skelton vehicles, turned his own The General (1927) into a property for the redheaded funnyman. The results were less than inspired. In fact, said the New York Times, the picture "... hit the bottom with a sickening thud. "

Simplistic bellboy Aubrey Filmore (Skelton) leaves his St. Louis hotel post to masquerade as the famed Southern spy, the Gray Spider, going behind the enemy lines. Along the bumpy way he encounters Southern gentleman and war profiteer Curt Devlynn (Donlevy), magnolia-scented Sallyann Weatharby (Dahl) and, most important of all, Major Jack Drumman (Coulouris), the latter much more daring than he initially seems.

What did MGM think of this mishmash? They advertised it as a picture in which "Skelton's a spy in a Union suit with a Southern Exposure!"

LE SPIE UCCIDONO IN SILENZIO [The Spy Strikes Silently] (Terra-Filmes Cinematografica-Estela, 1965)   C 95 min.

Director, Mario Caiano; screenplay, Malatesta, Caiano; music, Francesco De Masi; camera, Julio Ortas.
Lang Jeffries (Michel); Emma Danieli (Grace); Andrea Bosic (Rachid); Jose Bodalo (Craig).

The Technicolor-Techniscope backdrop shifts from Beirut to London to Madrid as Scotland Yard agent Jeffries tracks down the murderer of a British scientist (involved in finding a cancer cure). Like many mid-1960s European co-productions this feature had less to do with the art of spying than the title would indicate.

SPIES see SPIONE

THE SPIES see LES ESPIONS

SPIES-A-GO-GO see THE NASTY RABBIT

SPIES IN THE AIR see SPIES OF THE AIR

SPIES OF THE AIR (Associated British, 1939)   77 min.

Director, David Macdonald; based on the play Official Secret by Jeffrey Dell; screenplay, A. A. Rawlinson, Bridget Boland; camera, Bryan Langley.
Barry K. Barnes (Thurloe); Roger Livesey (Houghton); Joan Marion (Dorothy); Basil Radford (Colonel Cairns); Felix Aylmer (Porter); John Turnbull (Sir A. Hamilton); Henry Oscar (Porter);

John Turnbull (Sir A. Hamilton); Henry Oscar (Porter); Wallace
Douglas (Hooper); Hal Walters (Cogswell); Basil Radford (Madison);
Edward Ashley (Stuart); Everly Gregg (Mrs. Madison); Santos
Casani (Foreigner).

Set largely at a British aircraft plant office, the action
centers on the critical government plane construction work being
carried on by Houghton (Livesey) and his crew. Among the contingent at the craft factory is ace aviator Thurloe (Barnes), who
not only is in love with Livesey's wife (Marion) but also has a
special interest in the contents of the plant's confidential safe.
Scotland Yard steps in to save the day.
This modest production, derived from a stage play, was the
first British feature to detail Fifth Columnist activity in World War
II England. The film's producer wishes to use Fifth Column Squad
as the American release title, but author Ernest Hemingway sued
to say that the tag was already too closely associated with one of
his literary works and thus was not usable. Therefore, Spies in
the Air was the name finally selected for the feature when, sliced
down to 62 minutes, it had U. S. distribution.

DER SPION, DER IN DIE HOLLE GING [The Spy Who Went into
Hell] (UCC Films, 1965) C 110 min.

Executive producer, Hans Oppenheimer; director, Maurice
Labro; based on the novel by Claude Rank; adaptation, Maurice
Labro, Jean Meckert; screenplay, Rank; dialog, Louis Velle, Jean
Meckert; art director, Will Schatz, E. Alarcon; music, Michael
Legrand; sound, Gunther Kortwich, Benno Bellenbaum; assistant
director, Jean Hara, Jacques Bourdon; camera, Roger Fellous;
editor, Georges Arnstam.
Ray Danton (Jeff Larson); Pascale Petit (Pilar Perez); Roger
Hanin (Bob Stuart); Helga Sommerfeld (Lina); Horst Frank (Pedro);
Wolfgang Preiss (Captain); Conrado San Martin (Luis); Charles
Regnier (Rios); and: Roberto Rey, Manuel Gil, Grit Bottcher,
Helga Lehner, Mario de Barros, Stanislav Ledinek, Carl Lange.

By means of giant electronic devices, the Soviets have succeeded in transmitting exact television pictures of strategic European NATO bases. A young American FBI agent (Danton) is dispatched to investigate the crisis, his first clue: a Russian fishing
ship anchored outside the territorial waters of Spain. An eminently forgettable German-French co-production.
U. S. tv titles: Mission to Hell with Secret Agent X15; Mission to Hell.

SPION FUR DEUTSCHLAND (DLF-Berlina, 1956) 109 min.

Producer, Kurt Ulrich; director, Werner Klingler; screenplay, Herbert Reinecker; art director, Hanns H. Kuhnert, Paul

Markwitz, Peter Schlewsky; music, Werner Etsbrenner; camera, Albert Benitz.
          With: Martin Held (Erich Gimpel); and: Nadja Tiller, Walter Giller, Gustav Kruth, Werner Peters.

          Erich Gimpel (Held) went to Peru as an engineer in 1936 and there began espionage activity which made him Germany's number one agent abroad during World War II. He was arrested in 1942, taken to the United States, and under a wartime exchange, returned to Germany. He traveled back to the United States on a submarine (ordered by Hitler to spy on the Manhattan Project), but was arrested again in New York, and sentenced to death. Later under the Truman administration he was pardoned. A straight-forward approach to his amazing story.
          U.S. tv title: Spy for Germany.

SPIONE [Spies]   (UFA, 1928)   4,364 meters

          Producer-director, Fritz Lang; screenplay Thea von Harbou, Lang; art director, Otto Hunte, Karl Vollbrecht; music, Werner R. Heymann; camera, Fritz Arno Wagner.
          Gerda Maurus (Sonia); Willy Fritsch (Agent No. 326); Rudolf Klein-Rogge (Haghi); Lupu Pick (Dr. Matsumoto); Lien Deyers (Kitty); Craighall Sherry (Miles Jason); Fritz Rasp (Colonel Jellusic); Louis Ralph (Morrier); Hertha von Walther (Lady Leslane); Paul Horbiger (Franz the Chauffeur); Julius Falkenstein (Hotel Manager); Georg John (Train Conductor); Paul Rehkopf (Stroich); and: Greta Berger.

          With the espionage fever at a high pitch in mid-1920s Europe, Berlin-based director Fritz Lang turned out Spione, a rather complicated melodrama, but one which has become a classic of its kind. Made in a swift, exciting style, with authoritative direction, screenplay, and performances, the silent film stands up very well today, nearly a half century since its initial release.
          Perhaps the chief virtue of the film was Lang's typical master villain, this time called Haghi (Klein-Rogge), the mysterious head of an international spy league, who is the respected manager of a powerful bank, masquerades as a clown in the local circus, and at the same time is actually a trusted agent for the head of the country's Secret Service.
          Within the intricate plot, Agent 326 (Fritsch) is apparently sent by the U.S. to aid the SS in solving the theft of diplomatic documents. Sonia (Maurus, one of Klein-Rogge's agents) is assigned to find out from Agent 326 when a new treaty will be signed. They fall in love and she asks to be removed from the case, but Klein-Rogge refuses. Meanwhile, a Japanese leader, aware spies are after the treaty information, sends three letters, any of which could contain the treaty terms, in an effort to throw Klein-Rogge off the trail. The latter, however, sends a pretty vamp to the Nipponese's home, where she compromises him. Realizing the consequences of

his actions, the diplomat commits suicide. As the film heads to
a finale, Maurus is aboard a speeding train with Agent 326, hoping
to escape from Klein-Rogge. However, the mastermind has the
train wrecked, hoping to eliminate his defecting subordinate. His
plan fails and with Maurus' aid the SS push toward the inevitable
capture.

Paul M. Jensen in The Cinema of Fritz Lang (1969) insists
"Spione is superior to Dr. Mabuse [1922] in almost every respect.
The romantic scenes are less exaggerated, and the acting on the
whole is remarkably reserved and sometimes very adroit. "

After the making of Spione, Mrs. von Harbou novelized the
screenplay. In January 1929 MGM released the Lang film in
America under the title Spies.

THE SPY see GIBRALTAR

SPY CHASERS (AA, 1955) 61 min.

Producer, Ben Schwalb; director, Edward Bernds; screenplay, Bert Lawrence, Jerome S. Gottler; art director, David Milton; music director, Marlin Skiles; assistant director, Edward
Morey, Jr.; camera, Harry Neumann; editor, Lester A. Sansom,
John C. Fuller.

Leo Gorcey (Slip); Huntz Hall (Sach); Bernard Gorcey
(Louie); David Gorcey (Chuck); Bennie Bartlett (Butch); Leon
Askin (Colonel Baxis); Sig Ruman (King Rako); Veola Vonn (Lady
Zelda); Lisa Davis (Princess Ann); Linda Bennett (Little Girl);
Frank Richards (George); Paul Burke (Michael); Richard Benedict
(Boris); Mel Wells (Nick); John Bleifer (Phony Courier).

After two decades in the movie trade, the Bowery Boys had
long since puffed into middle-age, and were obviously running out
of steam in their film programmer series. Backed with the flimsiest of production values they struggled to breathe life into their
annual offering which had repeated their frozen characterizations-
routines formula so often it was hard to tell what was a repeat
of which repeat. Here the gang is involved in helping exiled
Ruritanian King Rako (Ruman) and his daughter (Davis) to return
to their country at a given signal from the counter-revolutionaries.
Even dumb Sach (Hall) eventually catches on that there is a treacherous one among Ruman's skimpy entourage.

SPY FOR GERMANY see SPION FUR DEUTSCHLAND

SPY HUNT (Universal, 1950) 74 min.

Producer, Ralph Dietrich; director, George Sherman; based
on the book Panther's Moon by Victor Canning; screenplay, George

Zuckernn, Leonard Lee; art director, Bernard Herzbrun, Alexander Golitzen; set decorator, Russell A. Gausman, John Austin; music director, Joseph Gershenson; gowns, Bill Thomas; makeup, Bud Westmore; sound, Leslie I. Carey, Corson Jewett; special camera, David S. Horsley; camera, Irving Glassberg; editor, Ted J. Kent.

Howard Duff (Roger Quain); Marta Toren (Catherine Ullven); Philip Friend (Chris Denson); Robert Douglas (Stephen Paradou); Philip Dorn (Paul Kopel); Walter Slezak (Dr. Stahl); Kurt Kreuger (Captain Heimer); Aram Katcher (Georg); Otto Waldis (Gormand); Ivan Triesault (Debron); Jay Barney (Fusek); Carl Milletaire (Ticket Clerk); Antonio Filauri (Telegraph Clerk); Peter Ortiz, Peter Appelquist (Soldiers); Carlo Tricoli (Italian Man); Betty Greco (Italian Girl); Carmela Restivo (Italian Woman); Jack Chefe (Waiter); Rudy Silva (Young Italian Man).

Marta Toren, Ivan Triesault, and Jay Barney in Spy Hunt (Universal, 1950).

Gormond (Waldis), a British Intelligence agent, boards a train bound for Milan, hoping to smuggle microfilmed evidence of an Eastern European political coup to United Nations authorities in Paris. In Milan he passes on the data, secreted in a cigarette, to fellow agent Catherine Ullvan (Toren), who is posing as a foreign correspondent. She in turn boards a Paris-bound express train and stashes the evidence in the collar of one of two panthers that Roger Quain (Duff) has been hired to escort back to the United States for circus use. The rival operatives (Dorn, Douglas, Friend) are

aware of the data's whereabouts and derail the panther-occupied
train car, not expecting that the beasts will work their way loose
and escape into the Swiss mountainside. The opponents gather at
Dr. Stahl's (Slezak's) mountain chalet where a simultaneous wild
animal and spy hunt transpires.

The fabricated thriller with a "wildly confused continuity"
(New York Herald-Tribune) made little impression in the market
place.

THE SPY IN BLACK (Columbia, 1939) 82 min.

Director, Michael Powell; story-screenplay, J. Storer Clouston; scenario, Roland Pertwee; screenplay, Emeric Pressburger;
camera, Bernard Browne.

Conrad Veidt (Captain Hardt); Sebastian Shaw (Ashington);
Valerie Hobson (School Mistress); Marius Goring (Schuster); June
Duprez (Anne Burnett); Athole Stewart (Reverend Hector Matthews);
Agnes Laughlan (Mrs. Matthews); Helen Haye (Mrs. Sedley); Cyril
Raymond (Reverend John Harris); George Summers (Captain Ratter);
Margaret Moffat (Kate); Kenneth Warrington (Commander Denis);
Torin Thatcher (Submarine Officer); Robert Kendall (Admiral);
Grant Sunderland (Bob Bratt); Mary Morris (Chauffeuse).

This "praiseworthy film" (Variety), melodramatic but plausible on a certain level, was a staple of 1950s television showings,
and has gained its own special reputation as a standard-bearer in
the area of spy films. It is particularly remembered for Veidt's
lurking performance.

German submarine captain Hardt (Veidt) is ordered to proceed to the Orkney Islands to meet a school teacher spy (Hobson),
who will provide him with new orders. She instructs Veidt to sink
15 British ships cruising off the coast of Scotland. However, it
is not long before Veidt's suspicions are confirmed, Hobson and
her co-agent Ashington (Shaw), a discharged "traitorous" British
Navy lieutenant, are really working for the English. Veidt's immediate new plan is to frustrate these counterspies.

THE SPY IN THE GREEN HAT (MGM, 1966) C 92 min.

Executive producer, Norman Felton; producer, Boris Ingster;
supervising producer, David Victor; associate producer, Irv Perlberg; director, Joseph Sargent; story, Victor; screenplay, Peter
Allan Fields; assistant director-second unit director, Eddie Saeta;
art director, George W. Davis, James W. Sullivan; set decorator,
Henry Grace, Dick Pefferle, Francisco Lombardo; music, Nelson
Riddle; title theme, Jerry Goldsmith; sound, Franklin Milton; camera, Fred Koenekamp; editor, Ray Williford, Joseph Dervin.

Robert Vaughn (Napoleon Solo); David McCallum (Illya Kuryakin); Jack Palance (Louis Strago); Janet Leigh (Miss Diketon);
Letitia Roman (Pia Monteri); Eduardo Ciannelli (Arturo "Fingers"

Stilletto); Allen Jenkins (Enzo "Pretty" Stilletto); Jack La Rue
(Federico "Feet" Stilletto); Leo G. Carroll (Alexander Waverly);
Ludwig Donath (Dr. Heinrich von Kronen); Joan Blondell (Mrs.
"Fingers" Stilletto); Will Kuluva (Mr. Thaler); Penny Santon
(Grandma Monteri); Vincent Beck (Benjamin Luger); Frank Puglia
(Padre); Maxie Rosenbloom ("Crunch" Battaglia); Vince Barnett
("Scissors"); Elisha Cook (Arnold).

In this outing culled from "The Man from U. N. C. L. E. "
video series, U. N. C. L. E. employees Vaughn and McCallum are
ordered to Sicily to cover a meeting between once-Nazi scientist
Donath and Palance, a T. H. R. U. S. H. operative hiding behind the
cover of being a liquor magnate.   The mad scheme at hand is a
plan to divert the Gulf Stream and throw the world into new chaos.
By this point, the teleseries had planted its entertainment
tongue well in cheek and could light-heartedly toy with the James
Bond idiom.   The show's formula might have been wearing thin
here, but the solid cast of veterans boosted the production into
diverting film fare.

SPY IN THE SKY (AA, 1958) 80 min.

Producer-director, W. Lee Wilder; based on the novel Counter-
spy Express by A. S. Fleischman; screenplay, Myles Wilder; art
director, Nico van Baarle; music, Hugo de Groot; sound, William
Huender; camera, Jim Harvey; editor, Lien d'Oliveyra.
Steve Brodie (Victor Cabot); Andrea Domberg (Alexandrine);
George Coulouris (Colonel Benedict); Sandra Francis (Eva Brendisi);
Bob de Lange (Sidney Jardine); Hans Tiemeyer (Dr. Keller); Her-
bert Curiel (Pepi); Dity Oorthius (Fritzo).

Captive German scientist Dr. Keller (Tiemeyer), engaged on
the Russian satellite program, escapes to the West. He is shadowed
by Pepi (Curiel), who intends to sell the scientist's whereabouts to
the U. S. , and by Colonel Benedict (Coulouris), who will bargain
Tiemeyer's future to the highest bidder.
"This story is full of complications which scarcely compensate for the lengths to which the basically simply plot is stretched"
(British Monthly Film Bulletin).

SPY IN YOUR EYE see BERLINO, APPUNTAMENTO PER LE
SPIE

THE SPY KILLER (Hammer/ABC-TV, 1969) C 73 min.

Executive producer, Harold Cohen; producer, James Sangster;
director, Roy Ward Baker; based on the novel Private i by Sangster;
screenplay, Sangster.
Robert Horton (John Smith); Sebastian Cabot (Max); Jill St.

John (Mary Harper); Eleanor Summerfield (Miss Roberts); Robert Russell (Police Sergeant); Barbara Shelley (Danielle); Donald Morley (Dunning); Douglas Sheldon (Alworthy); Kenneth Warren (Diaman); Philip Madoc (Gar); Lee Montague (Igor).

Sebastian Cabot and Robert Horton in The Spy Killer (ABC-TV, 1969).

Made at the traditionally horror-filled Hammer Studios by the chief horror exponent of the company, James Sangster, this spy thriller had U.S. release on television. Movies on TV calls it "predictable espionage fare."

Sangster's script concerned a private eye (Horton) who is arrested for murder but released on the condition that he locate a book containing the names of secret agents planted inside Red China.   An ex-employee of British Security, the detective finds his life threatened as he becomes more deeply involved in the deadly business of political intrigue and counter-espionage.

Relatively successful, the film spawned a sequel, Foreign Exchange (q.v.), with Horton again as the detective, Jill St. John as his sexy girl, and Sebastian Cabot as his ex-chief, all roles they had performed in the initial entry.

SPY OF NAPOLEON (Twickenham, 1936)   98 min.

Director, Maurice Elvey; based on the novel by Baroness
Orczy; adaptation, Fred V. Herrick, Harold Simpson; camera,
Curt Courant.
Richard Barthelmess (Gerard de Lanoy); Dolly Haas (Eloise);
Frank Vosper (Louis Napoleon III); Francis L. Sullivan (Chief of
Police); Joyce Bland (Empress Eugenie); C. Denier Warren (Nicolet);
Henry Oscar (Hugo Biot); Marjorie Mars (Anna); Brian Buschell
(Philippe St. Paul); Wilfrid Carthness (von Moltke); George Merritt
(Prussian Consul); Stafford Hilliard (News Vendor).

To save his life, Gerard de Lanoy (Barthelmess), a French
aristocrat and political exile, expediently agrees to wed blonde
ballet dancer Eloise (Haas), the illegitimate daughter of Louis
Napoleon (Vosper).   Barthelmess later finds himself attempting to
warn the French emperor not to count on Italian or Austrian aid
in the Franco-Prussian War.
This picturization of a Baroness Orczy book thriller was
made in England and took three years to find U.S. distribution, at
which time Frank J. Nugent (New York Times) complained it was
"a jigsaw puzzle which has not merely been badly assembled, but
misses several key pieces." Ex-silent star Barthelmess regained
none of his former screen prestige with his colorless performance
here.

THE SPY RING (Universal, 1938)   61 min.

Producer, Trem Carr; associate producer, Paul Malvern;
director, Joseph H. Lewis; based on the story by Frank Van Wyck
Mason; screenplay, George Waggner; assistant director, Glenn
Cook; music director, Charles Previn; camera, Harry Neumann;
editor, Charles Craft.
William Hall (Captain Tod Hayden); Jane Wyman (Elaine
Burdette); Esther Ralston (Jean Bruce); Robert Warwick (Colonel
Burdette); Leon Ames (Frank Denton); Ben Alexander (Captain
Don Mayhew); Egon Brecher (Brig. Gen. A.R. Bowen); Paul Sut-
ton (Charley the Chauffeur); Jack Mulhall (Captain Tex Randolph);
LeRoy Mason (Paul Douglas); Harry Woods (Captain Holden); Glenn
Strange (The Champ); Lester Dorr (Radio Operator); Harry Harvey,
Eddie Parker, Pat Gleason (Reporters); Eddie Gribbon, Forrest
Taylor (Sergeants).

"... [T]here is no excuse at this time for a film produced
by a major company--Universal--to be so woefully inexpert technically" (New York World Telegram).   Very careless scripting
made the freelance spies seem dumber than usual, and the insertion of extraneous army camp polo matches to pad out the footage
was another minus factor.
The mysterious death of the inventor of a new weapon (a
simply gadget which can convert any weapon into an emergency

anti-aircraft gun) leads Army Intelligence officer Tod Hayden (Hall) to investigate sultry blonde Jean Bruce (Ralston), who is being very persuasive with civilian Frank Denton (Ames). Another person involved in the caper, set in Washington, D. C. and Monterey, California, is the colonel's daughter (Wyman).

SPY 77 (First Division Exchange, 1936) 76 min.

Director-story-screenplay, Arthur Woods; camera, Cyril Bristow, Jack Parker; editor, E. B. Jarvis.
Greta Nissen (Marchesa Marcella Galdi); Don Alvarado (Valenti); Carl Diehl (Herr Hauptmann von Honbough); C. M. Haldmuller (Herr Oberst von Waldmuller); Austin Trevor (Herr Hauptmann Larco); Wallace Geoffrey (B. 18); Lester Mathews (Colonello Romanelli); Cecil Ramage (Davila); Esme Percy (Bluentzli).

In World War I in the Italian Alps, troops fight to stop the advancing Austrians, and a local girl (Nissen) is torn between loyalty to her country and the love of a man (Alvarado) whom she knows to be a secret enemy agent after an important member of the Austrian Intelligence Department.
The irony of this British B film is that most of the screen time is devoted to Nissen's efforts to decide how best to solve her dilemma, while in the end it is fate which makes a decision over which she has no control.

SPY SHIP (WB, 1942) 52 min.

Director, B. Reaves Eason; based on the novel by George Dyer; screenplay, Robert E. Kent; camera, Harry Newmann; editor, James Gibbon.
Craig Stevens (Ward Prescott); Irene Manning (Pamela Mitchell); Maris Wrixon (Sue Mitchell); Michael Ames (Gordon Morell); Peter Whitney (Zinner); John Maxwell (Ernie Haskell); William Forrest (Martin Oster); Roland Drew (Nils Thorson); George Meeker (Paul); George Irving (Harry Mitchell); Frank Ferguson (Burns); Olaf Hytten (Drake); Jack Mower (Inspector Bond); Keye Luke (Haru).

This rehash of Bette Davis' Fog over Frisco (1934), is still a hokey, hoary melodrama, but now is dressed up with World War II espionage overtones. In its favor, Spy Ship is rather unpretentious.
In the days before Pearl Harbor, heiress-aviatrix Pamela Mitchell (Manning) is a very active participant of the "America Above All" meetings, lecturing against war. Only knowing listeners are aware that her speeches contain secret information about Allied shipping schedules which the misguided debutante is selling to the Nazis. Aggressive, and ever so patriotic, newsman Ward Prescott (Stevens), engaged to Sue Mitchell (Wrixon), suspects something is

John Maxwell, Fred Kelsey, and Craig Stevens in <u>Spy Ship</u> (WB, 1942).

amiss with her half-sister (Manning). It all culminates in a fight between Stevens, the enemy agents, and the police aboard a mysterious Danish ship interned in the harbor.

SPY SMASHER (Republic, 1942) 12 Chapters

Chapters: (1) America Beware, (2) Human Target, (3) Iron Coffin, (4) Stratosphere Invaders, (5) Descending Doom, (6) The Invisible Witness, (7) Secret Weapon, (8) Sea Raiders, (9) Highway Racketeers, (10) 2700° Fahrenheit, (11) Hero's Death, and (12) V...-.

Associate producer, W. J. O'Sullivan; director, William Witney; suggested by the comic character <u>Spy Smasher;</u> screenplay, Ronald Davidson, Norman S. Hall, William Lively, Joseph O'Donnell, Joseph Poland; music, Mort Glickman; special effects, Howard Lyndecker; camera, Reggie Lanning; editor, Tony Martinelli, Edward Todd.

Kane Richmond (Spy Smasher/Jack Armstrong); James Dale

(Twin Brother); Marguerite Chapman (Eve Corby); Sam Flint (Admiral Corby); Franco Corsaro (Durand); Hans Schumm (The Mask); Tristram Coffin (Drake); Tom London (Crane); Paul Bryar (Laslor); John James (Steve); Richard Bond (Hayes); Henry Zynda (Lazar); Robert O. Davis (Colonel Von Kahr); Georges Renavent (Governor); John Buckley (Walker); Crane Whitley (Dr. Hauser); Bob Stevenson (Torpedo Chief); Ken Terrell (Jerry); Cy Slocum (French Private); Marty Faust (Blacksmith); Leonard St. Leo (French Lieutenant); Dudley Dickerson (Porter); Martin Garralaga (Commandant); Carleton Young (Taylor); Pat Moran (Waiter); Jack Arnold (Camera Clerk); Hugh Prosser (Navigator); Jerry Jerome (Burns); Arvon Dale (Thornton); George Lewis (Stuart); Max Waizman (Auto Clerk); Buddy Roosevelt (Lieutenant); Lee Phelps (Jail Guard); William Forrest (Douglas); George Sherwood (Jailer); Hans von Morhart (Captain Gerhardt); John Peters (Sub-Quartermaster); Gil Perkins (Sub-Valve Sailor); Frank Alten (German Officer); Lowden Adams (Headwaiter); Ray Parsons (Livingston); Charles Regan (Cafe Manager); Yakima Canutt (Armored Car Driver).

While the comic strip-based Batman was battling Dr. Daka and his robots in the Columbia serial play, Republic turned out Spy Smasher, based on the Whiz Comics magazine character. It emerged as one of the most popular of the wartime cliffhangers, wherein for a change there was an almost even match between the hero and the arch villain, each employing undercover tactics to win his goals.

The Spy Smasher (Richmond), an American free lance agent in newly occupied France, barely escapes with his life and returns to the U.S., still uncertain of the identity of The Mask (Schumm), head of German spy activities in America. With the aid of his twin brother Jack (Richmond), Spy Smasher battles the enemy and is forced to cope with the Axis' bat plane, a secret ray gun, and other ploys which almost win The Mask his worldly ambitions.

The serial was later adapted into a 100-minute feature for television entitled Spy Smasher Returns.

SPY SMASHER RETURNS   see   SPY SMASHER

THE SPY STRIKES SILENTLY   see   LE SPIE UCCIDONO IN SILENZIO

SPY TRAIN (Monogram, 1943)   61 min.

Producer, Max King; director, Harold Young; story, Scott Littlefield; screenplay, Leslie Schwabacher, Wallace Sullivan, Bert Lytton; art director, Dave Milton; assistant director, Richard Le Strange; camera, Mack Stengler; editor, Martin G. Cohn.
Richard Travis (Bruce); Catherine Craig (Jane); Chick Chandler (Stu); Thelma White (Millie); Evelyn Brent (Frieda);

Gerald Brock (Italian); Fred "Snowflakes" Toones (Porter); Bill
Hunter (Detective); Steve Roberts (Chief Nazi); Warren Hymer
(Herman); and: John Hamilton.

The only emotion this paltry entry stirred up was "a serious state of ennui" (Variety). A travel bag has what is thought to
be important Nazi documents. In reality, it contains a time bomb.
The piece of luggage is ferreted from one train compartment to
another, as the assorted operatives aboard the express train vie
to have a peek at it. Among those journeying on the railway are
reporter Bruce (Travis), photographer Stu (Chandler), dumb dora-
style maid Millie (White), various Nazis (Roberts, Hymer) and
Axis people (Brock), a detective (Hunter), a suspicious damsel
named Frieda (Brent), and, the pro-forma black porter (Toones).

THE SPY WHO CAME IN FROM THE COLD   (Paramount, 1965)
112 min.

Producer-director, Martin Ritt; based on the novel by John
Le Carre; screenplay, Paul Dehn; assistant director, Colin Brewer;
music, Sol Kaplan; costumes, Motley; art director, Edward Marshall;
camera, Oswald Morris; editor, Anthony Harvey.
Richard Burton (Alec Leamas); Claire Bloom (Nan Perry);
Oskar Werner (Fiedler); Peter Van Eyck (Hans-Dieter Mundt); Sam
Wanamaker (Peters); George Voskovec (East German Defense At-
torney); Rupert Davies (Smiley); Cyril Cusack (Control); Michael
Hordern (Ashe); Robert Hardy (Carlton); Bernard Lee (Patmore);
Beatrix Lehmann (President of Tribunal); Esmond Knight (Old Judge);
Walter Gotel (Holten); Tom Stern (C. I. A. Agent); Niall MacGinnis,
George Mikell (German Guards); Scott Finch (German Guide); Kathy
Keeton (Stripper); Richard Caldicot (Mr. Pitt); Marianne Deeming
(Frau Flördke); Michael Ripper (Lofthouse); Henk Mobenberg (Pass-
port Officer); Richard Marner (Vopo Captain); David Bauer (Young
Judge); Michael Ritterman, Edward Harvey (Men in Shop); Nancy
Nevinson (Mrs. Zanfrello); Warren Mitchell (Mr. Zanfrello); Anne
Blake (Miss Crail).

Similar in impact to the book upon which it is based, this
film is a major hallmark in the see-sawing progression of the spy
film, after which nothing could ever realistically be the same again.
For in The Spy Who Came in From the Cold, the glamour of the
secret agent was stripped forever with the ultimate ruthlessness of
the modern methods of espionage. It demonstrated that the real
life spy is as far removed from the world of James Bond as is
the ordinary man on the street.
Ironically this landmark film did not make the boxoffice impact expected. Filmed in a semi-documentary style with very

[Facing page]   Peter Van Eyck (left) and Richard Burton in The
Spy Who Came in From the Cold (Paramount, 1965).

grainy photography and little physical action (until the climax), the
movie was overloaded with "elusive talk, involved explanations,
cryptic references and name dropping" (New York Times). This
pervading note of confusion and desperate grayness bored some
viewers, baffled others, and provided still another faction with peg-
boards to pin assorted political labels to the picture's fragmented
characters and shifting philosophies.

Just before he is to retire from British Intelligence, agent
Alec Leamas (Burton) is recalled from Berlin to London, to explain
why contact man after contact man has fallen victim to Hans-Dieter
Mundt (Van Eyck), the ex-Nazi head of the East German counter-
espionage command. The British control leader (Cusack) assigns
Burton a very dirty task, to turn his now standard state of being
(i.e., a burnt out, embittered, middle-aged man) to good use by
posing as a demoralized drunk ready for defection. It is hoped
that Burton can penetrate and end Van Eyck's scope of operations
in Iron Curtain Berlin. No one involved--least of all Burton--
counts on the strange twist of events that transpire because Van
Eyck's second in charge, the Jew Fiedler (Werner) is fanatically
jealous of his superior. The film ends where it starts--at the
Berlin Wall, with two lost souls, Burton and his warm-hearted,
meek Communist librarian mistress (Bloom), exposed in the no
person's land between opposing political camps. Distraught Burton
is finally forced to make a crucial decision, one that might provide
him with some dignity and purpose in society but also might snuff
out his meager life.
     The Spy Who Came in From the Cold was touted as the most
accurate picture to date permitted by security regulations regarding
espionage activities on both sides of the Atlantic. ("The film makes
you believe it could have happened. And that's the remarkable
thing"--Bosley Crowther, New York Times.) The film was in production for 18 weeks of shooting at the Ardmore Studios in Bray,
Ireland, and at the Shepperton Studios, London, with sequences
lensed in Dublin to simulate divided Berlin.

THE SPY WHO WENT INTO HELL see DER SPION, DER IN DIE
HOLLE GING

THE SPY WITH A COLD NOSE (Embassy, 1968) C 93 min.

     Executive producer, Joseph E. Levine; producer, Leonard
Lightstone; associate producer, Robert Porter; director, Daniel
Petrie; story-screenplay, Ray Galton, Alan Simpson; assistant
director, Colin Brewer; art director, Peter Mullins; music, Riz
Ortolani; titles, Richard Williams; sound, Leslie Hammond, John
Aldred; camera, Kenneth Higgins; editor, Jack Slade.
     Lionel Jeffries (Stanley Farquhar); Laurence Harvey (Dr.
Francis Trevellyan); Daliah Lavi (Princess Natasha Romanova);
Eric Sykes (Wrigley); Eric Portman (British Ambassador); Colin

Blakely (Russian Prime Minister); Denholm Elliott (Pond-Jones); Robert Flemyng (Director of M.I. 5); June Whitfield (Elsie Farquhar); Paul Ford (American General); Bernard Archard (Russian Intelligence Chief); Robin Bailey (M.I. 5 Commander); Nai Bonet (Belly Dancer); Michael Trubshawe (Braithwaite); Bruce Carstairs (Butler); Genevieve (Nightclub Hostess); Glen Mason ("Ark" Assistant); Norma Foster ("Ark" Nurse); Perry Brooks, Trevor Delaney, Steven Morley (Farquhar's Children); Gillian Lewis (Lady Warburton); Wanda Ventham (Mrs. Winters); Amy Dalby (Miss Marchbanks); Tricia De Dulin (Air Hostess); Virginia Lyon (Lift Attendant); Julian Orchard (Policeman); John Forbes-Robertson (M.I. 5 Workshop Director); Arnold Diamond (Agent in Water Wagon); Ex-R.S.M. Ronald Brittain (Commissionaire); Peter Bayliss (Professor); Renee Houston (Lady Blanchflower).

Not nearly as funny as those involved assumed it would be, this spoof of a spoof had to be top drawer to succeed. The very British farce "demonstrates the fallacy of making a movie consisting entirely of character bits" (Village Voice). Only Jeffries as the prize bungling secret agent, eager to jump out of his career rut, handles his acting assignment with aplomb.

Stanley Farquhar (Jeffries) of M.I. 5 hardly seems the prototype of a successful secret agent; but then the bespectacled, balding, paunchy Britisher has spent so many dull years in the secret service low down on the personnel scale, that he has almost given up hope of ever seeing exciting action. However, he hits upon a unique plan to confound the Russians. A miniature radio transmitter is to be placed inside a bulldog named Disraeli--the operation to be performed by upper-crust veterinary surgeon Francis Trevellyan (Harvey) who will be blackmailed into assisting on the project--and the fixed animal to be sent as a goodwill gesture to the Soviet premier. The scheme works and the Russians are aghast by the sudden security leak. They call in espionage expert Princess Natasha Romanova (Lavi) who quickly traces the source of the deception to Jeffries. Meanwhile, Disraeli has fallen ill. If he is X-rayed, the game is up. Jeffries copes with this latest obstacle by winning over Lavi's loyalty and by having her join him and Harvey in a quick trip to Moscow to sidetrack the Russians while Harvey removes the telltale eavesdropping device. So far so good, but the U.S.S.R. has the last recorded word on Jeffries.

THE SPY WITH MY FACE (MGM, 1966) C 86 min.

Executive producer, Norman Felton; producer, Sam Rolfe; associate producer, Joseph Calvelli; director, John Newland; story, Clyde Ware; screenplay, Ware, Calvelli; assistant director-second unit director, E. Darrell Hallenbeck; art director, George W. Davis, Merrill Pye; set decorator, Henry Grace, Robert R. Benton; music, Morton Stevens; title theme, Jerry Goldsmith; sound Franklin Milton; camera, Fred Koenekamp; editor, Joseph Dervin.

Robert Vaughn (Napoleon Solo); Senta Berger (Serena); David

McCallum (Illya Kuryakin); Leo G. Carroll (Alexander Waverly);
Michael Evans (Darius Two); Sharon Farrell (Sandy Wister);
Fabrizio Mioni (Arsene Coria); Donald Harron (Kitt Kittridge); Bill
Gunn (Namana); Jennifer Billingsley (Taffy); Paula Raymond (Di-
rector); Donna Michelle (Nina); Harold Gould (Doctor); Nancy Hsueh
(Wanda); Michele Carey (Maggie); Paul Siemion (Clerk); Jan Arvan
(Waiter).

"... [P]erhaps most garbled, plotwise, of any present entry
on the current spy-melodrama cycle" (Variety).
    Industrious MGM bolstered a "The Man from U. N. C. L. E. "
tele-episode, The Double Affair (NBC, November 17, 1964) with
new footage, especially of scantily clad girls, for its theatrical
release. The plot as such has Napoleon Solo (Vaughn) and Illya
Kuryakin (McCallum) assigned to transport a new vault combination to Switzerland where a closely guarded safe contains a scientific secret of immense global importance. A power hungry organization creates a double for Vaughn, intending to use this ploy
to grab that top level item. Serena (Berger) was the entrapping
operative, Sandy Wister (Farrell) a sexpot, and super calm Alexander Waverly (Carroll) wry as always as the deadpan U. N. C. L. E.
executive.

STAMBOUL QUEST (MGM, 1934) 88 min.

    Director, Sam M. Wood; story, Leo Mirenski; screenplay,
Herman J. Mankiewicz; camera, James Wong Howe; editor, Hugh
Wynn.
    Myrna Loy (Annemarie); George Brent (Beall); Lionel Atwill
(Von Strum); C. Henry Gordon (Ali Bey); Douglass Dumbrille
(General); Rudolf Amendt (Earl); Mischa Auer (Roberts); Robert
Gleckler (Naval Officer); Reginald Barlow, Joseph Sawyer (German
Officers); Christian Rub (Dentist); Judith Vosselli (Maid); Belle
Mitchell (Companion); Harry Schultz (Doorman); Edward Keane
(Waiter); Barlowe Borland (Officer); Theodore Lodi, Anders von
Haden (Conductors); Otto H. Fries (Stewart); Perry Ivins (Man-
ager); Lal Chand Mehra (Turkish Officer); Tito H. Davison (Bell-
hop); Adrian Rosley (Waiter); Russ Powell (Fat German); Hans
Joby, Frank Publia (German Aides); Ralph Fitzsimmons (General);
Hooper Atchley (German Colonel); Max Barwyn, Jamiel Hasson
(Aides); Helen Freeman (Nun).

    "To forestall possible advance objections to another spy
story, let it be said at the outset that the heroine of this film is
not torn between love for her country and unwillingness to betray
her lover. There is a conflict, of course, but happily it does not
center in the traditional dilemma of the traditional cinema Mata

[Facing page] David McCallum in The Spy with My Face (MGM,
1966).

George Brent, Myrna Loy, and C. Henry Gordon in Stamboul Quest (MGM, 1934).

Hari" (New York Times). In her first solo starring role at MGM, Loy sparkled as Annemarie, better known as Fraulein Doktor, the most successful spy in the German service during World War I. Her performance revealed the operative to be resourceful and natural, with no telltale air of obvious mystery and slinkiness.

In 1915 when the German counter-espionage office, headed by pompous Von Strum (Atwill), is concerned with the steady leakage of information regarding the position of mines and other German defenses in the Dardanelles, Loy is sent to investigate. The prime suspect is Ali Bey (Gordon), commander of the Turkish forces, who might well be selling secrets to the enemies. American medical student Beall (Brent), who had been training in Germany prior to the outbreak of the Great War, meets Loy, falls madly in love with her, and accompanies her to Constantinople, where his pervading naiveté creates a special brand of problems.

The intriguing character of Fraulein Doktor was the subject of the French-made Mademoiselle Docteur (1937) directed by Edmond T. Greville, and starring Erich von Stroheim, Dita Parlo, and Claire Luce. In 1969 Paramount released its Fräulein Doktor (q.v.) with Suzy Kendall in the title role.

STATE SECRET   (Columbia, 1950)   97 min.

Producer, Sidney Gilliat, Frank Launder; based on the novel Appointment with Fear by Roy Huggins; screenplay, Gilliat, Launder; music, Muir Mathieson, William Alwyn; art director, Wilfrid Shingleton; language adviser, Georgina Shield; sound, Alen Allen; editor, Thelma Myers.

Douglas Fairbanks, Jr. (Dr. John Marlowe); Glynis Johns (Lisa); Jack Hawkins (Colonel Galcon); Herbert Lom (Theodor); Karel Stepanek (Dr. Revo); Walter Rilla (General Niva); Carl Jaffe (Prada); Olga Lowe (Baba); Therese Van Kye (Teresa); Hans Moser (Sigrist); Eric Pohlmann (Cable Car Conductor); Peter Illing (Macco); Paul Demel (Barber); Anton Diffring (State Policeman).

Douglas Fairbanks, Jr., in State Secret (Columbia, 1950).

Scripted by the team who wrote The Lady Vanishes (1938) and Night Train (1940) (qq. v.) State Secret rises easily above the penny dreadful level with its proper dashes of built-in tension and surprise cat-and-mouse chase. It expertly picks up steam, and leads to a cold sweat conclusion. The film's primary flaw is a glib explanation eliminating all the alternative methods of escape.

Circumstances provide young American surgeon Dr. John
Marlowe (Fairbanks, Jr.) with a deadly secret. The Fascist dictator of Vosnia is dead, a fact which Colonel Galcon (Hawkins) of
the state security force wants suppressed at any cost. As the
frightened runner desperate to escape from the Balkan country,
Fairbanks grabs at straws of help, including the assistance offered
by pert music hall performer Lisa (Johns) and wily black marketeer
Theodor (Lom).

State Secret was filmed on location in Italy. For the American release, the film's title was changed to The Great Manhunt.

THE STORY WITHOUT A NAME (Paramount, 1924) 5,912 feet

Presenter, Adolph Zukor, Jesse L. Lasky; director, Irvin
Willat; based on the novel by Arthur Stringer; screenplay, Victor
Irvin; camera, Hal Rosson.
Agnes Ayres (Mary Walsworth); Antonio Moreno (Alan Holt/
Frederick); Tyrone Power (Drakma); Louis Wolheim (Kurder); Dag-
mar Godowsky (Claire); Jack Lionel Bohn (Don Powell); Maurice
Costello (The Cripple); Frank Currier (Admiral Walsworth); and:
Ivan Linow.

Drakma (Power) an international spy, is after the triangula-
tor--a device emitting electronic death rays--which radio expert
Alan Holt (Moreno) has invented for the American government.
Mary (Ayres), Moreno's girl, destroys the machine before Power
can get it, so the latter kidnaps both the inventor and the girl,
leading to a daring sea rescue by Ayres' father (Currier) and his
crew.
This overly action-packed but naive film focused on an international spy rather than one from a specific country, since by
the mid-1920s, America was in prosperity and feeling pity for the
plight of its one-time World War I foes. As the plotline indicates,
the hero and heroine undergo enough perils to supply several serial
chapters, a credibility fault prevalent in silent spy films.
Photoplay magazine offered a $5,000 prize for anyone sup-
plying the best title to the picture. It has also been known as
Without Warning.

SUBTERFUGE (Commonwealth United, 1969) C 89 min.

Executive producer, Trevor Wallace; producer, Peter Snell;
director, Peter Graham Scott; screenplay, David Whitaker; art
director, Roy Lewthaite; music, Cyril Ormandee; sound, David
Ashley; camera, Roy Feller; editor, Lewthaite.
Gene Barry (Donovan); Joan Collins (Anne); Richard Todd
(Remayne); Tom Adams (Langley); Suzanne Leigh (Donetta); Michael
Rennie (Goldsmith); Marius Goring (Shevik); Scott Forbes (Pannell);
Colin Gordon (Kitteridge).

The rare spy film that appeared in the diminished theatrical
film market of the late 1960s reflected an increased tendency to
rely on a plastic ambiance of cynicism and violent sordidness to
cover over the usual lack of logical plot progression and character
development.   The quickly-mounted Subterfuge was one such example.
Its cast of players rambled through a disconcerting, jumbled storyline that relied on the bromide, "spying is a nasty, confusing business."   It certainly was in this entertainment trifle.
          C. I. A. agent Donovan (Barry), on assignment in England, is
forced to cope with a nefarious double agent.   He and London security chief Kitteridge (Gordon) are uncertain whether the culprit is
woman-chasing Remayne (Todd) or sulking, complaining Langley
(Adams), the latter having comely Anne (Collins) for a wife.
Among the Russians stalking about the banks of the Thames is
Shevik (Goring).
          One of the few points of interest in Subterfuge is Collins'
constantly changing wardrobes and coiffures.

SUNDOWN   (UA, 1941)   90 min.

          Producer, Walter Wanger; associate producer, Jack Moss;
director, Henry Hathaway; story, Barre Lyndon; adaptation, Charles
G. Booth; screenplay, Lyndon; music, Miklos Rozsa; art director,
Alexander Golitzen; special camera, Ray O. Binger; camera,
Charles Lang; editor, Dorothy Spencer.
          Gene Tierney (Zia); Bruce Cabot (Captain Bill Crawford);
George Sanders (Major Coombes); Harry Carey (Dewey); Joseph
Calleia (Pallini); Sir Cedric Hardwicke (Bishop Coombes); Carl
Esmond (Kuypens); Reginald Gardiner (Lt. Turner); Marc Lawrence
(Hammud); Gilbert Emery (Ashburton); Jeni LeGon (Miriami);
Emmett Smith (Kipsang); Dorothy Dandridge (Kipsang's Bride);
Horace Walker (Lecherous Old Man); Edward Das (Pindi); Prince
Modupe (Miriami's Sweetheart); Hassan Said (Arab Reader); Wes-
ley Gale, Jester Hariston (Native Boi); Curtis Nero (Corporal of
Askaris); Al Duval (Magabul); Kenny Washington (Sgt. Kumakwa);
Woodrow Strode (Tribal Policeman); Walter Knox (Father); William
Broadus; (Village Headman); Ivan Browning (Signal Man); William
Dunn (Kipsang's Victim); Tetsu Komai (Kuypens' Shenzi Aide);
Frederick Clark (Ibriham); Darby Jones (Camel Man); Blue Washing-
ton (Askari Veteran); Laurence La Mar (Ehenzi Informer); Frank
Clark, George Lincoln (Airplane Pilots).

          Sundown attempted something different, by taking the spy
motif to the Dark Continent, an area not well covered in films of
that time.   But as the New York Times was quick to point out,
"You can't try to give exalted overtones of meaning for our times
to a slick magazine serial without making both sound rather ridiculous."
          In the bleak African Somali-Abyssinian border land, a short-
staffed British outpost is barely holding its own, and is unequipped
to cope with a Nazi-inspired native uprising.   The six-man Allied

squad includes Major Sanders, sent on from Nairobi headquarters,
local commissioner Cabot, Italian prisoner of war Calleia now serving as the cook (and rather happily at that), Lt. Gardiner, an
alleged Dutch geologist (Esmond), and white hunter Carey. Also
prowling about the desert environs was exotic half-caste Tierney
who just might be in league with the Shensi tribe and the dastardly
Arab leader Lawrence.

The photography of Charles Lang and Ray O. Binger did
much to enhance the production, at times successfully creating
the arid feel of the film's setting.

TARZAN'S DESERT MYSTERY (RKO, 1943)   70 min.

Producer, Sol Lesser; associate producer, Kurt Neumann;
director, William Thiele; based upon characters created by Edgar
Rice Burroughs; story, Carroll Young; screenplay, Edward T.
Lowe; music, Paul Sawtell; music director, C. Bakaleinikoff; art
director, Hans Peters, Ralph Berger; set decorator, Victor Gangelin, Stanley Murphy; assistant director, Clem Beauchamp; camera,
Harry Wild, Russ Harlan; editor, Ray Lockert.

Johnny Weissmuller (Tarzan); Johnny Sheffield (Boy); Nancy
Kelly (Connie Bryce); Otto Kruger (Hendrix); Joe Sawyer (Karl);
Robert Lewery (Prince Selina); Lloyd Corrigan (Sheik); and:
Frank Publia.

Having descended from mighty MGM to a new studio berth
at RKO, the Tarzan series was showing telltale signs of production
penny-pinching. Like the prior year's Tarzan Triumphs, the new
entry had a topical overlay by having the jungle ruler combat the
Nazi menace, here most unconvincingly portrayed by Kruger and
his henchman Sawyer.

The plot is thrown into gear when Jane writes from England
requesting Tarzan (Weissmuller) to ship her a rare malaria serum
to be extracted from particular jungle plants. In his quest for
these obscure plants, Weissmuller and Boy (Sheffield) must cross
the (soundstage) desert. Along the way they engender the dis-
pleasure of German agent Kruger, a situation intensified when they
reach an Arab city and rescue stranded lady magician Kelly from
a death sentence. (It seems she has been framed by the Nazis on
a murder charge, solely because she possesses a confidential message for Sheik Corrigan, informing him that Kruger and Sawyer are
Axis menaces bent on stirring up trouble.) Here the spies meet
a most bizarre end, being thrown to a giant spider by the angered
justice fighter, Tarzan.

TEMPLE OF THE SWINGING DOLL (20th-Fox, 1960)   48 min.

Producer, Herbert Swope, Jr.; associate producer, Teresa
Calabrese; director, Paul Wendkos; based on characters created in
the book Operation Cicero by L. C. Moyzisch; screenplay, Jerry

Devine; art director, Duncan Cramer, George Van Marter; theme music, David Raksin; music director, Lionel Newman; camera, Wilfred M. Cline; editor, Fred Feitshans.

David Hedison (Victor Sebastian); Luciana Paluzzi (Simone Genet); Viveca Lindfors (Mme. Zapote); John Emery (Norman Kingsley); Clu Gulager (Larry Dane); Sterling Holloway (Hayden); Rodolfo Hoyes (Rios); Joan Tabor (Mona); Casey Adams (Randy); Johnny Seven (Tupac); Arline Hunter (Gloria).

Another entry culled for the British theatrical release market from the American teleseries "Five Fingers" (1959-1960). This episode took place in South America with Victor Sebastian (Hedison) a spy fronting as a theatrical agent.

TEXAS TO BATAAN (Monogram, 1942)   55 min.

Producer, George W. Weeks; director, Robert Tansey; story-adaptation, Arthur Hoerl; songs, John King; camera, Robert Cline; editor, Ray Curtis.

John King (Dusty); Dave Sharpe (Davy); Max Terhune (Alibi); Marjorie Manning (Dallas); Budd Buster (Tad); Kenne Duncan (Captain Anders); Escolastico Baucin (Cookie); Frank Ellis (Richards); Carl Mathews (Engel); Guy Kingsford (Miller).

Combining the gangster and (World War II) spy film genres worked nicely in the 1942 All Through the Night (q.v.) and others, so Hollywood decided to mesh together the western and the espionage thriller. The results were often diverting, particularly with the novel sight of ranch-garbed enemy agents being chased by horse-mounted American cowboys and the villains more often than not dispatched to justice with a nifty lasso rather than a speedy bullet from a carbine.

The Range Busters (consisting of King, Sharpe and Terhune) are assigned to accompany a herd of cattle sold by their ranch boss to the Army for delivery in the Philippines. Before leaving the Long Star state, they capture a horde of Japanese spies, but one escapes. Later in a Bataan dive, they come across the former ranch cook (Baucin), and quickly deduce that the Japanese is the elusive enemy operative. The trail next leads back home to Texas where they are amazed to find that one of the seemingly upstanding local citizens is really part of the Axis plot. Later they hear radio news of the Pearl Harbor attack and quickly enlist in the Army.

So that diehard Western fans would not be disappointed, all the standard sagebrush programmer ingredients were present, including the comedy relief of Terhune and his dummy Elmer, and two songs sung by King.

THAT MAN IN ISTANBUL (Columbia, 1966) C 117 min.

Executive producer, Nat Wachsberger; director, Antonio
Isasi; screenplay, Giovanni Simonelli, Luis Comeron, Isasi, R.
Illa; music, Georges Garvarentz; assistant director, Luis Garcia;
camera, Juan Gelpi; editor, Juan Palleja.

Horst Buchholz (Tony Maecenes); Sylva Koscina (Kenny);
Mario Adorf (Bill); Perette Pardier (Elisabeth); Klaus Kinski
(Schenck); Alvaro de Luna (Bogo); Gustavo Re (Brain); Christine
Maybach (Josette); Gerard Tychy (Charly); Augustin Gonzalez
(Jonny); Rocha (Chinese).

"... [G]oofy, not spoofy ... [but] it contains more violent
physical action, of the mindlessly anarchical sort, carried on with
a bumbling delight in violence for its own sake, than we have seen
since Cagney hung up his shoulder holster" (Life magazine). The
critics and public alike (those who still went to the movies) were
surfeited with 007-ish films and it was only the sturdiest of the
cinema species--this was not one--that made any lasting impression.
That Man in Istanbul provided Techniscope-color photography of
Turkey's metropolis and a flamboyant ex-racketeer hero (Buchholz)
who tried harder and still was not even second best in the Bond
super sweepstakes.

When an unidentified gang kidnap a U.S. nuclear scientist
and demand that he build an H-bomb so they can blackmail the
world, American club owner-gambler Tony Maecenes (Buchholz)
and off-duty C.I.A. lass Kenny (Koscina) take on the case, leading
to a self-propelling string of gymnastics in and about the edifices
of Istanbul. Director/co-scripter Antonio Isasi made a valiant
effort to package Buchholz as a frolicsome Mr. Virility, but the
Germanic leading man was not the type. At one point in the proceedings, Buchholz must look directly into the camera and say,
"What! Me worry?" More often than flipping such forced wisecracks, stripped-to-the-waist Buchholz is making it with the various
bikini-clad girls stashed about the film. He calls curvacious
Koscina "Baby Fat," and the dolls are forever "Ciao Tony" as they
disappear from the view of the perpetually unruffled Buchholz. At
least the film kept Buchholz moving from one scrape to another,
grabbing a chance rope to jump free of a car catapulting off a
cliff, dropping from a helicopter onto a speeding train, tackling a
killer underwater without an oxygen mask, zipping through the
women's section of a Turkish bath, and so forth.

THEY CAME TO BLOW UP AMERICA (20th-Fox, 1943) 73 min.

Producer, Lee Marcus; director, Edward Ludwig; story,
Michel Jacoby; screenplay, Aubrey Wisberg; art director, James
Basevi, John Ewing; set decorator, Thomas Little, Al Orenbach;
music, Hugo Friedhofer; music director, Emil Newman; assistant
director, William Eckhardt; sound, W.D. Flick, Harry M. Leonard;
special effects, Fred Sersen; camera, Lucien Andriot; editor, Nick
De Maggio.

George Sanders (Carl Steelman); Anna Sten (Frau Reiker); Ward Bond (Mr. Craig); Dennis Hoey (Colonel Manheim); Sig Ruman (Dr. Baumer); Ludwig Stossel (Mr. Steelman); Robert Barrat (Captain Kranz); Poldy Dur (Helga); Ralph Byrd (Gebhardt); Elsa Janssen (Mrs. Steelman); Egon Brecher (Kirschner); Rex Williams (Richner); Charles McGraw (Zellerbach); Sven-Hugo Borg (Hauser); Kurt Katch (Schonzeit); Otto Reichow (Fritz); Walter O. Stahl (Manheim's Aide); Andre Charlot (Zugholtz); Arno Frey (Krantz's Aide); Sam Wren (Jones); Etta McDaniel (Theresa); Peter Michael (Gertzer); Dick Hogan (Coast Guardsman); Lisa Golm (Saleslady); Wolfgang Zilzer (Schlegel); Charles Tannen (Smith); Eula Guy (Anne, the Nurse); Lane Chandler (Reynolds); Frederick Giermann, William Yetter, John Banner (Gestapo); Pierre Watkin, Forbes Murray (Diplomats); Torben Meyer (Gottwald); George Lynn (Herman); Henry Guttmann (Fiertag); Sigurd Tor (Holtzfeld); Walter Sande (Boatswain's Mate); Frederick Brunn, Albert d'Arno (German Soldiers); Arthur Space, Brice Warren, Hugh Prosser (F.B.I. Men); John Epper (Dispatch Rider); Bob Stephenson (Sentry); Fred Nurney (Ernest Teiker); Jack Lorenz (Marine Sentry); Bud Geary, Fred Graham (Policemen); John Mylong (German Officer); Ruthe Brady (Secretary).

With its lurid title, it would have been near impossible for critics to take this "mild thriller" (New York Times) at face value. Too bad, for it had an entertaining storyline, even if the Nazis were portrayed as far less cunning and tough than reality had proven them. The picture's premise was based on an actual case that occurred in the United States the previous year, with the movie's foreword stating the complete truth surrounding the case was still a government secret.

Sanders was cast as an American who spent much of the pre-World War II years in South America. With the beginning of the global conflict he is called back to the States by the FBI to investigate the activities of a German-American bund which is suspected of harboring enemy agents. Being a dead ringer for the group's leader, he replaces him when the leader is killed. As such he treks to Berlin to infiltrate the intelligence department of the Nazi government. Ironically he is called upon to lead a Nazi invasion off Long Island. To complicate matters, and provide a bit of tension, he is eventually exposed by the dead man's wife (Sten) while at the same time branded as a traitor to his own country.

THEY GOT ME COVERED (RKO, 1943) 95 min.

Producer, Samuel Goldwyn; director, David Butler; story, Leonard Q. Ross, Leonard Spigelgass; screenplay, Harry Kurnitz; music, Leigh Harline; music director, C. Bakaleinikoff; special effects, Ray Binger; camera, Rudolph Mate; editor, Daniel Mandell.

Bob Hope (Robert Kittredge); Dorothy Lamour (Christina Hill); Lenore Aubert (Mrs. Vanescu); Otto Preminger (Fauscheim); Eduardo Ciannelli (Baldanacco); Marion Martin (Gloria); Donald Meek

(Little Old Man); Phyllis Ruth (Sally); Philip Ahn (Nichimuro);
Donald MacBride (Mason); Mary Treen (Helen); Bettye Avery
(Mildred); Margaret Hayes (Lucille); Mary Bryne (Laura); William
Yetter (Holtz); Henry Guttman (Faber); Florence Bates (Gypsy
Woman); Walter Catlett (Hotel Manager); John Abbott (Vanescu);
Frank Sully (Red); Wolfgang Zilzer (Cross); Nino Pipitone (Testori);
George Chandler (Smith); Stanley Clements (Office Boy); Don Brodie
(Joe McGuirk); Arnold Stang (Drug Store Boy); Etta McDaniel
(Georgia); Hugh Prosser (Captain); Donald Kerr (Stage Manager);
Doris Day (Beautiful Girl in Sheet); Lane Chandler, Dick Keene
(Reporters); Edward Gargan, Ralph Dunn (Cops); Merike Boros
(Laughing Woman); Pat Lane (Ballet Dancer); Jack Carr (Comedian);
Bill O'Leary (Tramp); Peggy Lynn (Burlesque Actress); Lillian
Castle (Wardrobe Woman); Greta Meyer (Kathrina); Anne O'Neal
(Woman Patron); Hans Schumm (Schmidt); Henry Victor (Straeger);
Vic Mazetti, Tom Mazetti, Gil Perkins, John Sinclair (Nazis);
George Sherwood (Reporter); Byron Shores (F.B.I. Man); Charles
Legneur (Passenger in Plane).

Two thirds of the exceedingly popular The Road to ... trio
were exported by Paramount to Samuel Goldwyn-RKO for a thin
rehash of My Favorite Blonde (1942). The results were disappointing, as there was no one around to field Hope's quips, and the
action labored in too many critical spots. The very manufactured
finale exposed just how mechanical the entire vehicle was.

Unobservant foreign correspondent Robert Kittredge (Hope)--
he thought the German march into Russia was a local parade--is
fired from his Moscow post and returns to the States determined
not only to regain his job with Amalgamated News Service but also
to cop the Pulitzer Prize in journalism. Hope's big chance arrives
one day in Washington, D.C., when his old Rumanian friend-in-
formant Vanescu (Abbott) tips him off on a German (Preminger)-
Italian (Ciannelli)-Japanese (Ahn) spy link operating in the nation's
capital. Amalgamated's Washington branch supervisor (Lamour)
dubiously aids flip Hope, although she too almost believes her boyfriend a complete fool when she reads that he has married statuesque but dumb burlesque performer Gloria (Martin). (But it proves
to be that the overnight wedding was an Axis plan to discredit Hope
to the American public so that should his tale of intrigue ever
reach print, no one will believe it.) The final slapstick encounter
transpires at a beauty salon with Hope cavorting in and out of the
steam baths.

In accord with the film's unsubtle lampoon of the spy genre,
the triumvirate of espionage agents were hissably sinister and Nazi
enchantress Mrs. Vanescu (Aubert) deliberately overly-sirenish.

THEY MEET IN THE DARK (English Films, 1943) 96 min.

Producer, Marcel Hellman; director, Karel Lamae; story,
Anthony Gilbert; screenplay, Anatole de Grunwald, Miles Malleson;
song, Moira Heath, Ben Frankel; dialog director, Basil Sydney;

camera, Otto Heller; editor, Terrence Fisher.

James Mason (Commander Heritage); Joyce Howard (Laura Verity); Tom Walls (Christopher Child); Phyllis Stanley (Lily Bernard); Edward Rigby (Mansel); Ronald Ward (Carter); David Farrar (Commander Lippencott); Karel Stepanek (Riccardo); Betty Warren (Fay); Walter Gresham (Charlie); George Robey (Pawn-broker); Peggy Dexter (Bobby); Ronald Chesney (Max); Finlay Currie (Merchant Captain); Brefni O'Rorke (Inspector Burrows); Jeanne De Casalis (Lady with Dog); Patricia Medina (Mary the Manicurist); Eric Mason (Benson, the Illusionist); Herbert Lomas (Van Driver); Charles Victor (Pub Owner); Robert Sansome (Petty Officer Grant); Alvar Lidell (Boothby, the Radio Announcer).

Because British naval officer Commander Heritage (Mason) has been bilked by enemy agents into revealing the sailing dates of government ships, he is dismissed from service. He decides to un-ravel the mystery himself, which leads to the Axis headquarters lo-cation at a nightclub and an adjoining dance school/hall for sailors. Involved in the spy hunt are a hypnotist who strangles his victims after obtaining confidential information, a magician, and an insur-ance broker who uses his agency as a blind for spy operations.

This rather hastily-produced venture suffered from choppy editing at least in the American release print. Walls made a sharp impression as the villain. "He is the archetype of all the world's heavies; leering, strutting, showing his teeth, gloating, sneering and making large gestures with the hands. All he needed to com-plete his impersonation was a placard around his neck reading 'I am a spy'" (Baltimore Sun).

THE THIEF (UA, 1952) 85 min.

Executive producer, Harry M. Popkin; producer, Clarence Greene; director, Russell Rouse; screenplay, Greene, Rouse; music, Herschel Gilbert; assistant director, Leon Chooluck; production designer, Joseph St. Amand; camera, San Leavitt; editor, Chester Schaeffer.

Ray Milland (Allan Fields); Martin Gabel (Mr. Bleek); Rita Gam (The Girl); Harry Bronson (Harris); John McKutcheon (Dr. Linstrum); Rita Vale (Miss Philipps); Rex O'Malley (Beal); Joe Conlin (Walters).

On its own terms a rather bold excursion into the realm of a speechless (but not soundless as there is a music score and back-ground noise) picture. "But because the script insists on keeping its people apart from revealing themselves through speech, we are never permitted to understand the motivation of any of them" (Satur-day Review). The film's gimmick disguised the fact that at hand was a rather ordinary spy thriller, using the 1950s favorite hero-villain, the nuclear physicist.

Allan Fields (Milland), a respected scientist and a member of the U.S. Atomic Energy Commission, succumbs to the entreaties

John McKutcheon and Ray Milland in The Thief (UA, 1952).

of the Communists and microfilms secret documents for the Reds'
use.   The espionage trail leads from Washington, D.C., to New
York where the panicky Milland kills F.B.I. agent Harris (Bronson)
atop the Empire State building, and then just as his escape to overseas freedom seems to be in his grasp the guilt-stricken American
gives himself up to the federal authorities.
        The viewer is generally so preoccupied with the technique of
speechless story progression that the obviousness of the characterizations, especially Gabel as the sinister Mr. Bleek, becomes less
obvious.   Gam added an erotic touch as the temptress neighbor of
man-on-the-lam Milland.   The spies of The Thief are, of course,
delineated as acting behind a proverbial wall of silence, what with
telephone signals, notes on back of cigarette wrappers, etc.

THIN ICE   (20th-Fox, 1960)   49 min.

        Producer, Herbert Swope, Jr.; associate producer, Teresa
Calabrese; director, Lamont Johnson; based on the book Operation
Cicero by L.C. Moyzisch; screenplay, Philip MacDonald; music

director, Lionel Newman; theme music, David Raksin; camera, Wilfrid M. Cline.

David Hedison (Victor Sebastian); Luciana Paluzzi (Simone); Peter Lorre (The Colonel); Alan Young (Karel); Brett Halsey (Prince Ahmed); and: Paul Burke, Alan Napier, Peter Brocco, Marc Platt, James Fairfax, Joe Abdullah, Essi Davis, Frank Lucas.

Taken from the NBC teleseries "Five Fingers" (1959-1960), this brief lower-case melodrama was one of four series' segments to be given theatrical release in Britain.

U.S. intelligence agent Victor Sebastian (Hedison) the star of the series, performed as a double agent in a match of wits with Russian master spy Lorre.

13 RUE MADELEINE (20th-Fox, 1946) 95 min.

Producer, Louis de Rochemont; director, Henry Hathaway; screenplay, John Monks, Jr., Sy Bartlett; art director, James Basevi, Maurice Ransford; set decorator, Thomas Little; music, Alfred Newman; music director, David Buttolph; orchestrator, Edward Powell, Sidney Cutner, Leo Shuken; costumes, Rene Hubert; makeup, Ben Nye; assistant director, Abe Steinberg; special camera effects, Fred Sersen; camera, Norbert Brodine; editor, Harmon Jones.

James Cagney (Sharkey); Annabella (Suzanne de Bouchard); Richard Conte (Bill O'Connell); Frank Latimore (Jeff Lassiter); Walter Abel (Charles Gibson); Melville Cooper (Pappy Simpson); Sam Jaffe (Mayor Galimard); Marcel Rousseau (Duclois); E. G. Marshall (Emile); Blanche Yurka (Madame Thillot); Peter Von Zerneck (Karl); Alfred Linder (Hans Feinke); Judith Lowry (Peasant Lady); Richard Gordon, Walter Greaza (Psychiatrists); Ben Low (Hotel Clerk); Roland Belanger (Joseph); James Craven, Edward Cooper (R. A. F. Officers); Alexander Kirkland (Briefing Officer); Donald Randolph (LaRoche); John Morre, Leslie Barrie, Charles Campbell (Psychiatrists-Instructors); Red Buttons, Peter Gowland (Dispatchers); Otto Simanek (German Staff Officer); Mario Gang, Henry Rowland, Martin Brandt, Fred Nurney, Julius Carmer, Albert D'Arno, Dick Wessel, Frederic Brunn, Arno Frey (German Officers); Frank De Langton (Athletic Instructor); Robert Morgan (Telegraph Instructor); Roland Winters (van Duyval); Harold Young (Tailor); William Syran (Detective Inspector, Submarine Plant); Reginald Mason (Communications Chief); Sally McMarrow (Chief Operator); Durant Rice, William Mendrek (Men); Coby Neal (Flyer); Karl Malden (Flyer Bit); Otto Reichow (German Soldier); Jean Val (French Peasant); Reed Hadley (Narrator); James Craven (English Announcer--Voice Only).

A film given far more attention than it was worth, 13 Rue Madeleine (originally called 32 Rue Madeleine) was intended to be a tribute to the Office of Strategic Services (O. S. S.) and its commander, Major General William "Wild Bill" Donovan. Shot on

Sam Jaffe and James Cagney in 13 Rue Madeleine (20th-Fox, 1946).

location in New York City, Quebec, and Boston, at an estimated savings of $150,000 over using studio sets, even before its release the feature came under fire by the man to whom it was made a tribute.

Donovan complained to 20th Century-Fox head Darryl F. Zanuck that the film showed the O.S.S. trespassing into other fields of military intelligence. With the then current release of Paramount's O.S.S. and Warner Bros.' Cloak and Dagger, Fox re-edited the picture to involve all branches of intelligence under the Allied Chiefs of Staff.

The finished product hardly merited all the bother. Dealing with "Secret Intelligence" and its unit "0-77," 13 Rue Madeleine used a newsreel format to introduce 0-77 men Cagney, Abel, and Latimore. [The film's producer Louis de Rochemont, handler of the March of Time short subjects for a decade, had scored a big success with his staged cinema verité The House on 92nd Street (1945), and repeated the documentary techniques here.] The main plot involves the mission of four American espionage workers (Cagney, Annabella, Conte, Latimore) to train and fulfill a mission in occupied France. Their main task is to locate a German rocket bomb building site that must be destroyed before the imminent D-Day invasion. As the quartet push on to their objective, they rub shoulders with partisans and counter-agents. Eventually Cagney is captured by the Nazis who torture him to extract the needed information. However Allied planes bomb the building to wipe out the Gestapo stronghold and prevent Cagney from spilling the confidential data.

While Cagney shone in the early training sequences, he was sorely out of place when posing as a vigorous youngish spy in Nazi-controlled France. Nor did Annabella serve her intended purpose, to supply credible romantic relief. The picture's ending was branded "sheer Hollywood."

THE 39 STEPS (G.F.D., 1935)   81 min.

Producer, Michael Balcon; associate producer, Ivor Montagu; director, Alfred Hitchcock; based on the novel by John Buchan; adaptation-screenplay, Charles Bennett, Alma Reville; additional dialog, Ian Hay; sets, Otto Werndorff, Albert Jullion; costumes, J. Strassner; music, Louis Levy; sound, A. Birch; camera, Bernard Knowles; editor, Derek N. Twist.

Madeleine Carroll (Pamela); Robert Donat (Richard Hannay); Lucie Mannheim (Miss Smith/Annabella); Godfrey Tearle (Professor Jordan); Peggy Ashcroft (Mrs. Crofter); John Laurie (Crofter the Farmer); Helen Haye (Mrs. Jordan); Frank Cellier (Sheriff); Wylie Watson (Mr. Memory).

THE 39 STEPS (20th-Fox, 1960)   C 95 min.

Producer, Betty E. Box; director, Ralph Thomas; based on the novel by John Buchan; screenplay, Frank Harvey; art director, Maurice Carter; music, Clifton Parker; music conductor, Muir Mathieson; costumes, Yvonne Caffin; camera, Ernest Stewart; editor, Alfred Roome.

Kenneth More (Richard Hannay); Taina Elg (Fisher); Brenda de Banzie (Nellie Lumsden); Barry Jones (Professor Logan); Reginald Beckwith (Lumsden); Faith Brook (Nannie); Michael Goodliffe (Brown); James Hayter (Mr. Memory); Duncan Lamont (Kennedy); Jameson Clark (McDougal); Andrew Cruikshank (Sheriff); Leslie Dwyer (Milkman); Betty Henderson (Mrs. McDougal); Joan Hickson (Miss Dobson); Sidney James (Perce); Brian Oulton (Mr. Pringle).

At the time of making The 39 Steps (1935), director Alfred Hitchcock explained his rationale for doing the film "I am out to give the public good, healthy, mental shake-ups. Civilization has become so screening and sheltering that we cannot experience sufficient thrills at first hand. Therefore, to prevent our becoming sluggish and jellified, we have to experience them artificially."

Robert Donat and Madeleine Carroll in <u>The 39 Steps</u> (G. F. D. , 1935).

It was this movie which first brought the highly regarded British-based director to the attention of the American public. <u>The 39 Steps</u> emerges as probably one of the director's most facile English pro-ductions (rivaling <u>The Lady Vanishes,</u> q. v.) and certainly as one of his overall finest pictures in a long career which has turned out some of filmdom's best suspense movies.

    Hitchcock frankly admits that author John Buchan (later Canada's Governor-General) offered a direct inspiration to the film-maker in the art of creating suspense mood, and that he acquired the rights to Buchan's <u>The 39 Steps</u> because he found the novel so ap-pealing for its "understatement of highly dramatic ideas."

    The non-stop action commences in a British music hall where Canadian Richard Hannay (Donat) meets a young woman (Mannheim) in the minor panic following a shot being fired in the theatre. The girl begs to return with him to his apartment. Once there she divulges that she is a government agent after a group bent on smuggling top government secrets out of the country. A short time later Mannheim is murdered and the fleeing Donat learns he is the

Kenneth More (second left), Betty Henderson, and Taina Elg in
The 39 Steps (20th-Fox, 1960).

suspected killer.
        Donat is convinced the only way to clear himself of the homi-
cide charge is to track down the spy plot, and so he heads for Scotland, as per his information-learning session with Mannheim.
Aboard the northbound train he meets a young lady (Carroll) with
whom he carries on a love-hate relationship for the bulk of the picture, as she comes in and out of his life. A stopover with Professor Jordan (Tearle) leads to unexpected complications, and soon
Donat finds himself on the run not only from the police but from
the espionage ring. Eventually Carroll realizes Donat's bizarre
story is true and the duo head back to London, with the climax
occurring at the Palladium Theatre where Mr. Memory (Watson)
is performing his total recall vaudeville act.
        Several scenes in Steps are classics: the murdered Mann-
heim slumping over Donat's bed, revealing the knife sticking out of
her back; the chambermaid chancing upon the woman's body and
letting out a shriek which blends into the screaming whistle of a
locomotive as the plotline leaps onward; the ironic sexual implications of Donat and Carroll handcuffed together and "forced" to spend

a night together in a local inn; or the bizarrely comic moment at
the film's opening when a theatre customer keeps asking "Mr.
Memory," "How old is Mae West?"

A well-made film, which proved popular both in Europe and
the U.S., it was not shown on U.S. television until 1972, and today
still remains a perennial on the art house screening circuit.

All the suavity of the original Steps which had so rightly
laced its suspense with wit, was missing from the Ralph Thomas
update filmed in color. Only a good cast kept this British remake
from sinking into oblivion. The new edition followed the original
storyline closely and even tried to duplicate Hitchcock's thematic
and scene shot breakdowns, but all to little avail. The combination
of Kenneth More and Taina Elg as the new leads could not match the
artful sparring of the ultra professional Donat and Carroll. Then
too by 1960, a lot of spy pictures had come and gone, and a new
approach was sorely needed.

36 HOURS   (MGM, 1965)   115 min.

Producer, William Perlberg; director, George Seaton; based
on the novel Beware of the Dog by Roald Dahl and a story by Carl
K. Hittleman, Luis H. Vance; screenplay, Seaton; music, Dimitri
Tiomkin; assistant director, Donald Roberts; sound, Franklin Milton;
art director, George W. Davis, Edward Carfagno; camera, Philip
H. Lathrop; editor, Adrienne Fazan.

James Garner (Major Jefferson Pike); Eva Marie Saint (Anna
Hedler); Rod Taylor (Major Walter Gerber); Werner Peters (Otto
Shack); John Banner (Ernst); Russell Thorson (General Allison);
Alan Napier (Col. Peter MacLean); Oscar Beregi (Lt. Col. Oster-
mann); Ed Gilbert (Captain Abbott); Sig Ruman (German Guard);
Celia Lovsky (Elsa); Karl Held (Corporal Kenter); Martin Kosleck
(Kraatz); Marjorie Bennett (Charwoman); Henry Rowland, Otto
Reichow (German Soldiers); Hilda Plowright (German Agent); Walter
Friedel (Denker); Joseph Mell (Lemke); John Gilgreen (Lt. Busch);
Joe de Reda, Jeffrey Morris (G.I.'s); Mike Stroka, Chris Anders
(German Officers); Kurt Lander (German Sergeant); James Doohan
(Bishop); Erick Micklewood (British Officer); Richard Peel (Dudley);
Roy Eason (Reynolds); Leslie Bradley (British Announcer); Louis
Sarrano (Portuguese Official); Luis Delgado (Lieutenant); Harold
Dyrenforth (Major General Ungerland); Danny Klega (German Lieu-
tenant); Walter Janowitz (Dr. Metzler); Charles Hradilac (Dr.
Kleiner); Rudolph Anders (Dr. Winterstein); Norbert Schiller (Dr.
Wittelbach); John Dennis (M.P. Guard); Barry Macollum (Bartender);
Roy Jenson (Soldier); John Hart (Perkins); Howard Curtis (Dutton);
Owen McGiveney (Elderly Man); Henry dar Boggia, Rolfe Sedan
(Frenchmen); Kort Falkenberg (Radio Voice); George Dee (French
Informer); Werner Reichow, Paul Busch (Germans); Chic Masi
(Waiter); Charles Bastian (Swiss Soldier); Horst Ebersberg (Swiss
Officer).

There were so many incredible but true spy and counter-intelligence episodes in World War II that it is always difficult to challenge the authenticity of any such caper, no matter how far fetched, in its recreation for the screen. But 36 Hours, expansive and well done, pushes the viewer's credulity to the breaking point with its artificial and slick premise. Moreover, the second half flounders into a lengthy escape-the-dumb-Nazis rut. "It epitomizes the disposable film" (Christian Science Monitor).

On the eve of D-Day, 1944, American Army intelligence officer Jefferson Pike (Garner), who is privy to the top secret Allied invasion plans, is sent to Lisbon to confirm through a German contact that the Nazis still expect the Allies to land their forces in the Calais area. But Garner is betrayed by his man in Spain and instead is whisked off by the Germans to a fake U.S. hospital in Bavaria, near the Swiss border. German psychiatrist Walter Gerber (Taylor) plans to convince Garner that the alleged Allied-won World War II has been over for six years and that Garner is just now recovering from a long bout of amnesia. (Besides performing overnight plastic surgery on Garner to "age" him, the Germans go to elaborate and expensive lengths to transform the prison site into a Yankee hospital installation, complete with American-accented attendants and the "latest" newspapers.) "What do you remember last? For instance what do you remember about the invasion?" Taylor asks the baffled Garner. The doctor has to work fast for the SS, under the prodding of antagonistic Otto Shack (Peters), has given Taylor just 36 hours to prove the effectiveness of his methods. Otherwise, Peters will switch to more orthodox Gestapo ways of persuasion.

36 Hours contains one of the most preposterous ploys ever utilized in the battle of wits between war opponents. In addition, the biggest script flaw is the postulate that the Germans would have entrusted a former Auschwitz inmate (Saint) with the vital job of nursing a top secret prisoner (Garner). Then too, the split factions among the Germans leads to a very convenient denouement.

By the mid-1960s it was exceedingly rare for a major motion picture like 36 Hours to rely on black and white photography, no matter how effectively it captured the exteriors filmed at California's Yosemite National Park.

THIS GUN FOR HIRE (Paramount, 1942) 80 min.

Producer, Richard M. Blumenthal; director, Frank Tuttle; based on the novel by Graham Greene; screenplay, Albert Maltz, W. R. Burnett; art director, Hans Dreier; songs, Frank Loesser and Jacques Press; camera, John Seitz; editor, Archie Marshek.

Veronica Lake (Ellen Graham); Robert Preston (Michael Crane); Laird Cregar (Willard Gates); Alan Ladd (Philip Raven); Tully Marshall (Alvin Brewster); Mikhail Rasumny (Slukey); Marc Lawrence (Tommy); Pamela Blake (Annie); Harry Shannon (Finnerty); Frank Ferguson (Albert Baker); Beradine Hayes (Baker's Secretary); James Farley (Night Watchman); Virita Campbell (Cripple Girl);

Roger Imhof (Senator Burnett); Victor Kilian (Brewster's Secretary); Olin Howland (Fletcher); Emmett Vogan (Charlie); Chester Clute (Mr. Stewart); Charles Arnt (Will Gates); Virginia Farmer (Woman in Shop); Clem Bevans (Old Timer); Harry Hayden (Restaurant Manager); Tim Ryan (Guard); Yvonne De Carlo (Show Girl); Ed Stanley (Police Captain); Eddy Chandler (Foreman); Phil Tead (Machinist); Charles R. Moore (Dining Car Waiter); Pat O'Malley (Conductor); Katherine Booth (Waitress); Sarah Padden (Mrs. Mason); Louise La Planche (Dancer); Richard Webb (Young Man); Frances Morris (Receptionist); Cyril Ring (Waiter); Lora Lee (Girl in Car); William Cabanne (Laundry Truck Driver).

The drastically changing world situation forced Paramount to virtually rewrite Graham Greene's novel This Gun for Hire, transforming the locale to California and switching the lead figure to the cold-blooded killer Philip Raven (Ladd), a nearly heartless creature who detests most people but likes cats and children. The critics and public alike endorsed the final screen product, particularly attracted to the cinema "find" of the year, tough guy Ladd, who in tandem with peekaboo hairstyle star Veronica Lake, made one of the most subtly erotic cinema love teams of the 1940s.

The sinister cat-and-mouse game that comprises most of the running time of This Gun for Hire has hired killer Ladd being double-crossed by his nominal employer, the hefty, epicene Willard Gates (Cregar). The angered Ladd thereafter determines to locate Cregar's big boss and turn the tables on the whole nasty gang. As the story progresses, Ladd becomes enmeshed with lady magician-songstress Ellen Graham (Lake) not knowing that the Los Angeles cop (Preston) pursuing him is her long-standing beau.

Like Humphrey Bogart in All Through the Night (1942), underworld figure Ladd proves that when the chips are down, he is as patriotic as the next American, particularly when his opponent proves to be the dastardly Mr. Big, a master criminal with a spy network throughout America, who sells poison gas formulas to the Axis camp.

THIS LAND IS MINE (RKO, 1943)   103 min.

Producer, Jean Renoir, Dudley Nichols; director, Renoir; screenplay, Nichols; art director, Albert S. D'Agostino, Walter E. Keller; dialog director, Leo Bulgakov; assistant director, Edward Donahue; sound, Terry Kellum, James Stewart; music, Lothar Perl; music director, C. Bakaleinikoff; special effects, Vernon L. Walker; camera, Frank Redman; editor, Frederic Knudtson.

Charles Laughton (Arthur Lory); Maureen O'Hara (Louise Martin); George Sanders (Georgia Lambert); Walter Slezak (Major von Keller); Kent Smith (Paul Martin); Una O'Connor (Mrs. Emma Lory); Philip Merivale (Sorel); Thurston Hall (Major); George Coulouris (Prosecuting Attorney); Nancy Gates (Julie Grant); John Donat (Edmund Lorraine); Frank Alten (Lieutenant Schwartz); Wheaton Chambers (Mr. Lorraine); Cecil Weston (Mrs. Lorraine);

Louis Donath (German Captain); Lillian O'Malley (Woman in Street);
Gordon Clark (Lieutenant); Hans Moebus (German Chauffeur); Jack
Martin (German Captain); Gabriel Lenoff, Philip Ahlm (German
Lieutenants); Albert d'Arno, Rudolph Myzet, Lester Sharpe, Sven
Borg, Nick Vehr, Russell Hoyt, Walter Thiele (German Soldiers);
Louis Arno, Bob Stevenson, Hans Schumn, John Banner, George
Sorel (German Sergeants); Ferdinand Schumann-Heink (Karl); Gus
Taillon (Newsman); Bill Yetter (Otto the German Soldier); Edward
McNamara (Policeman); Otto Hoffman (Printer); Hans von Morhart
(Soldier Who Gets Slapped); John Dilson (Mayor's Secretary);
Ernest Grooney (Priest); George MacQuarrie (Chief of Police);
Tommy Bond (Julian); John Rice, Jack Shea (Burly Cops); Ida
Shoemaker (Woman in Street); Oscar Loraine (Clerk); Joan Bar-
clay (Young Woman); Mildred Hardy, Margaret Fealy (Old Woman);
Linda Ann Bieber (Emily); Lloyd Ingraham (Paper Man on Street).

Unlike the more action-filled The Moon Is Down and Edge
of Darkness, both 1943, which also attempted to extract the
dramatic roots of conflict among patriots, quizlings and occupation
forces, the rather eloquent This Land Is Mine is a tale of conflict
within a man's soul.   His intellectual turmoil is set off by the hor-
rors of World War II.   As an adjunct to the main point of the film,
This Land Is Mine also illustrates just how law-abiding citizens become saboteurs, depicting not just the explosive results, but the
underlying causes.
In a small occupied European town (where everyone speaks
with French accents), the Nazis have taken control under the stern
supervision of Major von Keller (Slezak), aided by the collaborationist mayor (Hall) and by others, such as railroad superintendent
Georgie Lambert (Sanders), who find it expedient to side with the
winning Germans.   Sanders' schoolteacher fiancée, Louise Martin
(O'Hara), of a more patriotic spirit, turns to bumbling, middle-aged
instructor Arthur Lory (Laughton), who until the German occupation
had been firmly tied to his mother's (O'Connor) apron strings.   But
the enemy oppression and the courage of the local Resistance group
headed by O'Hara's brother (Smith), instills a moralist independence
within jellyfish Laughton and he refuses to advance the Nazi cause.
He will not offer fake courtroom testimony.   Thereafter he lectures
his young students on the solid principles of democracy, knowing
full well the fatal consequences for himself.   Meanwhile, Sanders
has committed suicide, the implications of his unpatriotic acts having
taken its toll.
The film's overzealous philosophical approach was understandable, but the uncontrolled hamming of many cast members was
so rampant that one perturbed critic suggested the picture be retitled "This Picture Is Mine."

THIS MAD WORLD   (MGM, 1930)   5, 446 feet

Director, William De Mille; based on the play Terre Inhu-
maine by François Curel; adaptation, Clara Beranger; dialog,

Beranger, Arthur Caesar; titles, Madeleine Ruthven; art director, Cedric Gibbons; sound, J. K. Brock, Douglas Shearer; gowns, Adrian; camera, Peverell Marley, Hal Rosson; editor, Anne Bauchens.

Kay Johnson (Victoria); Basil Rathbone (Paul); Louise Dresser (Pauline); Veda Buckland (Anna); Louis Natheaux (Emile).

This sombre study of the no-nonsense rules of the war game is based on the 1923 French play. French secret agent Paul (Rathbone) sneaks behind German lines to Alsace-Lorraine to carry out an important mission and to also visit his mother (Dresser). At her inn he encounters Victoria (Johnson), the wife of a German general. Rathbone and Johnson embark on a passionate, but short-lived romance, for he admits he was responsible for the death of her nephew. She in turn provides information leading to his arrest, and, in anguish over this betrayal, commits suicide. When the Germans inquire into her death, Dresser denies any knowledge of her son's identity, knowing that he will be shot regardless, and that she must now fulfill his mission.

THREE FACES EAST (Producers Distributing Corp. , 1926) 7, 419 feet

Presenter, Cecil B. De Mille; director, Rupert Julian; based on the play by Anthony Paul Kelly; adaptation, C. Gardner Sullivan, Monte Kattejohn; recording engineer, Clifford A. Ruberg; camera, Peverell Marley; editor, Claude Berkeley.

Jetta Goudal (Miss Hawtree/Fräulein Marks); Robert Ames (Frank Bennett); Henry Walthall (George Bennett) Clive Brook (Valdar); Edythe Chapman (Mrs. Bennett); Clarence Burton (John Ames); Ed Brady (Firking).

THREE FACES EAST (WB, 1930)   71 min.

Producer, Darryl F. Zanuck; director, Roy Del Ruth; based on the play by Anthony Paul Kelly; screenplay-dialog, Oliver H. P. Garrett; camera, Chick McGill; editor, William Holmes.

Constance Bennett (Frances Hawtree/Z-1); Erich von Stroheim (Valdar/Schiller/Blecher); Anthony Bushell (Captain Arthur Chamberlain); William Courtenay Yates);Charlotte Walker (Lady Catherine Chamberlain); Craufurd Kent (General Hewlett); Ulrich Haupt (Colonel); William von Brincken (Kruger the Aide); Paul Panzer ("Kirsch" the Decoy).

BRITISH INTELLIGENCE (WB, 1940)   62 min.

Director, Terry Morse; based on the play Three Faces East by Anthony Paul Kelly; screenplay, Lee Katz; additional dialog, John Langan; music, Heinz Roemheld; camera, Sidney Hickox; editor, Thomas Pratt.

Boris Karloff (Franz Strendler); Margaret Lindsay (Helene von Lorbeer); Maris Wrixon (Dorothy); Bruce Lester (Frank Bennett);

Constance Bennett, William Courtenay, Erich von Stroheim, Anthony Bushell, and William Holden in <u>Three Faces East</u> (WB, 1930).

Leonard Mudie (James Yeats); Holmes Herbert (Arthur Bennett); Winifred Harris (Mrs. Bennett); Lester Mathews (Thompson); John Graham Spacey (Crichton); Austin Fairman (George Bennett); Clarence Derwent (Milkman); Louise Brien (Miss Risdon); Frederick Vogeding (Kugler); Carlos de Valdez (von Ritter); Frederick Giermann (Kurtz); Willy Kaufman (Corporal); Frank Mayo (Brixton); Stuart Holmes (Luchow); Sidney Bracey (Crowder); Jack Mower (Morton); Paul Panzer (Peasant); David Thursby (Mysterious Man); Leyland Hodgson (Lord Seedbury); John Sutton (Officer); Gordon Hart (Doctor); Willy Kaufman (German Corporal); Arno Frey (German Junior Officer); Hans Schumm (German Senior Officer); Henry Von Zynde (German); Sidney Bracy (Club Attendant); Joseph De Stefani, Ferdinand Schumann-Heink (German Officers); Glen Cavender (Under Officer Pfalz); Jack Richardson, Bob Stevenson (Cockney Soldiers); Carl Harbaugh (German Soldier); Morton Lowry (Lt. Borden); Leonard Willey (Captain Stuart).

Anthony Paul Kelly's spy melodrama was first presented on Broadway in 1918, starring Violet Heming, Emmett Corrigan, and Joseph Selman. Its thriller qualities were enhanced by its topical nature and it enjoyed a 335-performance run. Eight years later a rather standard picturization appeared and was considered just

another entry in the burgeoning espionage film genre.   Its plot followed the stage original fairly faithfully: Britisher Frank Bennett
(Ames), a prisoner of war in Germany, is cared for by Fräulein
Marks (Goudal), a German nurse with whom he falls in love.   Later
she is captured in a British raid and it develops she is really Miss
Hawtree of the British secret service.   Thereafter she is dispatched
to the home of George Bennett (Walthall)--Ames' father, the head of
the War Office--with orders to trap a Germany spy named Boelke.
Ames is heartbroken to observe Goudal's apparent infatuation with
servant Valdar (Brook), but it turns out the butler is really the
wanted spy.   After the Armistice, Ames and Goudal plan to wed.
       In 1930, Darryl F. Zanuck produced a remake of Three
Faces East as a starring vehicle for chic Constance Bennett.   To
bolster the film's potential revenue, ex-movie director von Stroheim
("the man you love to hate") was cast as the spy-butler.   Von Stroheim reportedly claimed to have rewritten parts of the film, especially his scenes as the decadent aristocrat in disguise.   This first
talkie rendition magnified the weak points of Kelly's play: i.e.,
it is ever so convenient, but strange, that von Stroheim is able to
so easily maneuver a post in the home of the Lord of the Admiralty.
The New York Times complimented the "agreeable finesse" of director Roy Del Ruth's film, but viewed today, the picture seems
especially lethargic in pacing and obvious in performances.

       Along came World War II and Warner Bros. dusted off
Three Faces East as a property for Karloff who here spies on
people instead of haunting them.   In a bit of unwarranted diplomacy,
Warners chose to retain the World War I setting rather than updating the storyline.   (It did toss in a few bits of contemporane-
ousness by including in the complex screenplay, post facto pro-
phecies about German domination in years to come.)   What resulted
was an "unexciting espionage photoplay" (New York Herald-Tribune)
with Karloff overplaying his role as a supposed Belgium refugee
working in the home of English cabinet minister Arthur Bennett
(Herbert).
       For the record "Three Faces East" was the password for
German spies operating in England; the proper answer in code was
"Forward and back."

THUNDERBALL (UA, 1965) C 125 min.

       Producer, Kevin McClory; director, Terence Young; based
on the novel by Ian Fleming and an original screenplay by Jack
Whittingham, McClory, Fleming; screenplay, Richard Maibaum,
John Hopkins; production designer, Ken Adam; music, John Barry;
"Thunderball" lyrics, Barry and Don Black; art director, Peter
Murton, Michael White; assistant director, Gus Agosti; makeup,
Paul Rabiger, Basil Newall; action sequences, Bob Simmons; sound,
Bert Ross, Maurice Askey; costumes, Anthony Medelson; main
titles designer, Maurice Binder; underwater director, Ricou Brown-
ing; underwater camera, Lamar Boren; camera, Ted Moore; editor,
Peter Hunt.

Sean Connery (James Bond); Claudine Auger (Domino); Adolfo Celi (Largo); Luciana Paluzzi (Fiona); Rik Van Nutter (Felix Leiter); Bernard Lee (M); Martine Beswick (Paula); Guy Doleman (Count Lippe); Molly Peters (Patricia); Desmond Llewelyn (Q); Lois Maxwell (Miss Moneypenny); Roland Culver (Foreign Secretary); Earl Cameron (Pinder); Paul Stassino (Palazzi); Rosa Alba (Madame Boiter); Philip Locke (Vargas); George Pravda (Kutee); Michael Brennan (Janni); Leonard Sachs (Group Captain); Edward Underdown (Air Vice Marshal); Reginald Beckwith (Kenniston).

Sean Connery and Bob Simmons in Thunderball (UA, 1965).

Even though Thunderball from all counts is the least satisfying of the (Sean Connery) James Bond outings, it has proven to be the highest grosser* of the film series to date. Director Terence Young was back at the helm, but through a twist of copyright legal

*Domestic distributors' rentals of the series as of the end of 1972 are as follows (in millions of dollars): Dr. No, $6.3; From Russia with Love, $9.8; Goldfinger, $22.8; Thunderball, $28.3; You Only Live Twice, $20; Casino Royale, $10.2; On Her Majesty's Secret Service, $9; Diamonds Are Forever, $21.

manipulations, it was producer Kevin McClory who found himself
owning the screen rights to an "original story by Kevin McClory,
Jack Whittingham and Ian Fleming" based on the Fleming novel of
the same title.   Expenses were not spared in elaborating the gimmicks within Thunderball, but something was missing, noticeably in
the special characteristics that blended together to make Connery a
breathing super operative, tongue-in-cheek or not.   For the first
time in the movie series, Connery's British agent took a sad back
seat to the free wheeling action about him, with the gismos hogging
the limelight and tying together the spotty action.

    Everything about Thunderball had a "here we go again tone. "
There is the expected snappy pre-credit action interlude (in which
Connery eliminates a deadly widow who proves to be a husky iron
poker-wielding man), a S. P. E. C. T. R. E. boardroom meeting where
Blofeld (not fully seen in this entry) eliminates a negligent subordinate and propounds the plan that S. P. E. C. T. R. E. leader number two--eye-patched Emilio Largo (Celi)--will undertake: to hi-
jack a nuclear bomb-laden NATO Vulcan bomber and blackmail the
Western world into paying a huge ransom; and finally the assignment of 007 to the case by bureau chief M (Lee), accompanied by
the good wishes of M's romantically-inclined secretary Miss Moneypenny (Maxwell) and a briefing on new offensive-defense gadgetry by
the Ministry's arms controller Q (Llewelyn).

    What follows for the bulk of the picture is a tedious sub-
terranean chase, as Celi's crew employ an underwater flying saucer
to tote the hydrogen bomb to Celi's "Disco Volante" vessel headquarters.   Connery eventually follows in pursuit, abetted by Domino
(Auger), the sister of the French observer to the bomber project,
and by Nassau-based Paula (Beswick), with S. P. E. C. T. R. E. killer
Fiona (Paluzzi) out to confound him.   The overextended concluding
battle occurs beneath the water as Connery and a team of U. S.
aqua-paratroopers combat the S. P. E. C. T. R. E. frogmen.

    One novelty in the standardized 007 exploits came at the
end of Thunderball.   Connery's James Bond was allowed no work
respite.   He and Auger did not loll off for a romantic interlude;
instead the adrift couple were hoisted up from their raft to a
passing overhead plane, jerking the hero out of view after an excep-
tionally tiresome chain of adventures.

THE TIGER LIKES FRESH BLOOD   see   LE TIGRE AIME LA
CHAIR FRAICHE

LE TIGRE AIME LA CHAIR FRAICHE [The Tiger Likes Fresh
Blood] (Gaumont/Procefi, 1964)   C   85 min.

    Producer, Christine Gouze-Renal; director, Claude Chabrol;
based on an idea by Antoine Flachot; screenplay, Jean Halain;
music, Pierre Jansen; assistant director, Pierre Gauchet, José
Dagnant; camera, Jean Rabier; editor, Jacques Gaillard.

Roger Hanin (Louis Rapière, Le Tiger); Maria Mauban (Mme. Baskine); Daniela Bianchi (Mehlica); Roger Dumat (Duvet); Mario David (Dobrovsky); Albert Dagnant (General Condé); Sauveur Sasportes (Baskine); Pierre-François Moro (Ghislain); Antonio Passalia (Koubassi); Roger Rudel (Benita); Carlo Nell (Theatre Assassin); Henri Attal, Dominique Zardi (Airport Gunmen); Jimmy Karoubi (Jean-Luc, the Midget); Christa Lang (Dobrovsky's Girl); Guy d'Avout (French Minister); Stephane Audran (Soprano); Charles Audisio (Tenor); Maurice Besson, Michel Charrel, Marcel Maurice Gassouk, Francois Terzion (Inspectors).

A basically simple plot--Turkish minister Baskine (Sasportes) arrives in Paris to negotiate a deal for 40 fighter jets, while a secret organization out to prevent the pact--is embellished by the variety of factions which emerge as the story progresses. Chabrol's French security agent, Le Tiger (Hanin), is far removed from the James Bond "slickness and gadgetry" school. Instead he relies on established army techniques of strike first and ponder later to accomplish his mission. Robin Wood and Michael Walker in their book-length study, Claude Chabrol (1970), observe that throughout the film "Chabrol is working himself into a frenzy over the inanity of his material: assaulting the genre by grotesque over-indulgence. This brings him perilously close to the excruciating over-indulgence of Losey in Modesty Blaise, but Chabrol, unlike Losey, has a sense of humour."

U.S. television title: Code Name: Tiger.

LE TIGRE SE PARFUME A LA DYNAMITE [An Orchid for the Tiger] (Gaumont/Progefi, 1965) C 82 min.

Producer, Dino de Laurentiis, Francisco Balcazar; director, Claude Chabrol; screenplay, Antoine Flachot, Jean Curtelin; music, Jean Wiener; camera, Jean Rabier; editor, Jacques Gaillard.
Roger Hanin (Tigre); Margaret Lee (Pamela Mitchum); Roger Dumas (Duvet); Michel Bouquet (Jacques Vermorel); J.-M Caffarel (Colonel Pontarlier); Georges Rigaud (Commander Damerec); Assad Bahador (Hans von Wunchendorf); Carlos Casaravilla (Ricardo Sanchez); Michaela Cendali (Sarita Sanchez); and: Michel Etcheverry, Claude Chabrol.

The followup adventure of French Secret Service agent Le Tigre (Hanin) is considered to be inferior to the original, what with its bizarre mixing of species and its rather unfathomable plot. The locale skips from Barcelona to the West Indies to the coast of French Guiana as Hanin and his assistant (Dumas) combat the sinister Orchid organization (very Neo-Nazi in its Aryan depiction) and the latter's plot to foment a revolution. However, Robin Wood and Michael Walker in their book Claude Chabrol (1970) rate the plot "quite fascinating" and the feature's offbeat qualities (especially the extraordinary traps laid for the Tiger by villain Bouquet) as having a "good edge on Chair Fraiche."

TO BE OR NOT TO BE   (UA, 1942)   99 min.

Presenter, Alexander Korda; producer-director, Ernst Lubitsch; story, Lubitsch, Melchior Lengyel; screenplay, Edwin Justus Mayer; music, Werner Heyman; art director, Vincent Korda; makeup, Gordon Bau; special camera effects, Lawrence Butler; camera, Rudolph Mate; editor, Dorothy Spencer.
Carole Lombard (Maria Tura); Jack Benny (Joseph Tura); Robert Stack (Lt. Stanislav Sobinski); Felix Bressart (Greenberg); Lionel Atwill (Kawitch); Stanley Ridges (Professor Siletsky); Sig Rumann (Colonel Ehrhardt); Tom Dugan (Bronski); Charles Halton (Dobosh the Producer); George Lynn (Actor-Adjutant); Henry Victor (Captain Schultz); Maude Eburne (Anna the Maid); Armand Wright (Makeup Man); Erno Verebes (Stage Manager); Halliwell Hobbes (General Armstrong); Miles Mander (Major Cunningham); Leslie Dennison (Captain); Frank Reicher (Polish Official); Peter Caldwell (William Kunze); Wolfgang Zilzer (Man in Bookstore); Olaf Hytten (Polonius--in Warsaw); Charles Irwin, Leyland Hodgson (Reporters); Alec Craig, James Finlayson (Scottish Farmers); Edgar Licho (Prompter); Robert O. David (Gestapo Sergeant); Roland Varno (Pilot); Helmut Dantine, Otto Reichow (Co-Pilots); Maurice Murphy, Gene Rizzi, Paul Barrett, John Kellogg (R. A. F. Flyers); Sven-Hugo Borg (German Soldier).

More so than Charles Chaplin's The Great Dictator (1940), To Be or Not to Be is the blackest of black comedy anti-Nazi parodies. America was caught totally off guard by the film. It was a time when the nation's funnybone was simply out of joint and the public was in no mood to laugh at macabre jokes about the war (e. g., a Nazi general quips, "We do the concentrating, the prisoners do the camping"). Then too, the untimely death of the movie's star, Carole Lombard, killed in a plane crash shortly after completing the picture, turned another segment of the potential audience off the movie. Life magazine was one of the rare major sources at the time to objectively assess To Be or Not to Be: "... like an unmixed cocktail it packs a wallop, and its rating as entertainment is high. "
On the eve of World War II, a Polish acting troupe in Warsaw prepare to present a new anti-Nazi melodrama, but the Polish government cancels the show, fearing the play might sharpen the rift between Berlin and Warsaw. Instead, the players, whose stars are Shakespearian specialists Joseph and Maria Tura (Benny and Lombard), a sort of Polish Lunt and Fontanne, present Hamlet. (A running gag has poor Benny never able to complete the famous "To Be or Not to Be" soliloquy without someone in the audience jumping up to leave. Unknown to Benny, these stage lines are usually the cue for Lombard's latest suitor to rush backstage to chat while her husband is busy onstage.)

Meanwhile in London, Polish Air Force pilot Stanislav Sobinski (Stack) and other Polish freedom fighters who have all joined the British Air Force are tricked into providing Axis agent

Professor Siletsky (Ridges) with the names and addresses of relatives back in Warsaw. Stack has given Ridges the name of Maria
Tura (Lombard) with whom he is in love. The young flyer, how-
ever, becomes puzzled when Ridges claims to be unacquainted with
Lombard. After all, she is, according to general consensus,
"Poland's leading actress." Stack reports the matter to British In-
telligence which quickly orders him to Warsaw to recover the list
of names and addresses at any cost. Ridges, it develops, is a
German agent. Back in Poland, Stack obtains the assistance of
Lombard and the troupe to accomplish his complex mission. While
Stack is on the job, Ridges is also busy. He has Lombard arrested.
Later Ridges is corraled by members of the troupe who, dressed
as Nazi soldiers, bring the spy to the theatre where Benny, disguised as the Gestapo chief, Colonel Ehrhardt (Rumann), tricks the
professor into revealing the whereabouts of the list. Growing con-
fident that his disguise is perfect, Benny toys with Ridges (he
struts about and sing-songs "So they call me 'Concentration Camp
Ehrhardt' "), but gives away the show when he questions the man
too much about Lombard's affair with Stack. Thereafter the professor is killed, Benny hastens to Gestapo headquarters at the
Hotel Europejski to rescue Lombard, and eventually after the troupe
don several other disguises (including one actor masquerading as
Hitler), they all manage to flee the country in a stolen plane. Once
over Scotland, the bogus Hitler (Duggan) orders the two German
pilots to jump without parachutes. The troupe then parachutes to
safety. In London the players present Hamlet, but once again at
the crucial moment during the Dane's famous speech, a young naval
officer in the front row rises to leave....
    An interesting sidelight of To Be or Not to Be is that for
a change a film script satisfactorily paved the way for the picture's
amateur spies to assume alien poses. Here it is well established
that the Polish troupe are all versatile stage performers.

TO CATCH A SPY see ACTION IMMEDIATE

TO SKIN A SPY see AVEC LA PEAU DES AUTRES

TO TRAP A SPY (MGM, 1965) C 92 min.

        Producer, Norman Felton; associate producer, Joseph Gant-
man; director, Don Medford; screenplay, Sam Rolfe; assistant director, Maurice Vaccarino; art director, George W. Davis, Merrill Pye; set decorator, Henry Grace, Frank McKelvy; music,
Jerry Goldsmith; sound, Franklin Milton; camera, Joseph Biroc;
editor, Henry Berman.
        Robert Vaughn (Napoleon Solo); David McCallum (Illya Kuryakin);
Patricia Crowley (Elaine May Donaldson); Fritz Weaver (Vulcan);
Luciana Paluzzi (Angela); William Marshall (Ashumen); Will Kuluva

(Mr. Allison); Eric Berry (Alfred Ghist); Victoria Shaw (Gracie
Ladovan); Ivan Dixon (Soumarin); Miguel Landa (Lancer).

The powers behind "The Man from U. N. C. L. E. " teleseries
shrewdly strung together video episodes with scraps of out-takes
and specially shot "adult" footage, throwing the items onto the
theatrical market with good results. To Trap a Spy derives from
the program's premier episode The Vulcan Affair (NBC, September
22, 1964). The critics carped "these are inferior goods, crammed
with tasteless leers and japes, misbegotten direction, poor scripting
and wooden acting" (New York Herald-Tribune); "... it's becoming
harder and harder to spoof Agent 007. He does it so much better
himself" (New York Morning Telegraph).

The newly-independent African state of Western Natumba is
in danger of takeover by W. A. S. P. , a global crime syndicate.
The coup d'état is to be triggered by the assassination of that
country's president (Marshall) at the chemical plant owned by Vulcan (Weaver). With the aid of Elaine May Donaldson (Crowley),
Weaver's one-time college sweetheart, U. N. C. L. E. agents Napoleon
Solo (Vaughn) and Illya (McCallum) save the day.

This entry did benefit from a freshness that would soon
evaporate from the video program. Vaughn is at his flippant,
sexy best, parrying well with calculating egotist Weaver, and in-
teracting smoothly with both vicious Angela (Paluzzi) and house-
wife-cum-spy Crowley. For added verve there is fiendish scientist Alfred Ghist (Berry).

TOKYO ROSE (Paramount, 1945)   70 min.

Producers, William Pine, William Thomas; director, Lew
Landers; story, Whitman Chambers; screenplay, Geoffrey Homes,
Maxwell Shane; assistant director, Bob Meiklejohn; art director,
F. Paul Sylos; set decorator, Glenn Thompson; music, Rudy
Schrager; sound, Frank Webster; camera, Fred Jackman, Jr.;
editor, Howard Smith, Henry Adams.

Lotus Long (Tokyo Rose); Byron Barr (Peter Sherman);
Osa Massen (Greta Swanson); Don Douglas (Timothy O'Brien);
Richard Loo (Colonel Suzuki); Keye Luke (Charlie Otani); Grace
Lem (Soon Hee); Leslie Fong (Wong); H. T. Tsiang (Chung Yu);
Larry Young (Jack Martin); William Challee (Mike Kovak); Chris
Drake (Frank); James Millican (Al Wilson); Al Ruiz (Mel); Blake
Edwards (Joe).

If this badly assembled mini-actioner had been released
earlier, its exploitation value might have justified its existence.
There has yet to be a decent screen treatment of the psychology
underlying the infamous Tokyo Rose or the German-based Lord
Haw Haw, whose behind-the-line propaganda was as destructive as
the battle front work of fellow espionage agents.

G. I. Peter Sherman (Barr) escapes from a Japanese prison
camp with the primary intent of seeking revenge on Tokyo Rose

Lotus Long, Keye Luke, and Byron Barr in <u>Tokyo Rose</u> (Paramount, 1945).

(Long) whose broadcast was indirectly responsible for the death of his service buddy.   Barr concocts a wild scheme in which Long will be kidnapped right under the Nipponeses' noses and taken via submarine to the U.S.

The real life Tokyo Rose, born Miss Toguri in Los Angeles, was freed from Sugamo Prison in Tokyo on October 25, 1946.   The Allied Army of Occupation stated it had insufficient evidence to prosecute her for acts of treason.

TOP SECRET see MR. POTTS GOES TO MOSCOW

TOPAZ (Universal, 1969) C 125 min.

Producer, Alfred Hitchcock; associate producer, Herbert Coleman; director, Hitchcock; based on the novel by Leon Uris; screenplay, Samuel Taylor; assistant director, Douglas Green, James Westman; production designer, Henry Bumstead; set decorator, John Austin; music-music director, Maurice Jarre; costumes, Edith Head; sound, Waldon O. Watson, Robert R. Bertrand; technical advisers, J. P. Mathieu, Odette Ferry; photographic consultant, Hal Mohr; special camera effects, Albert Whitlock; camera, Jack

Hildyard; editor, William H. Ziegler.
        John Forsythe (Michael Nordstrom); Frederick Stafford (Andre
Devereaux); Dany Robin (Nicole Devereau); John Vernon (Rico Parra);
Karin Dor (Juanita de Cordoba); Michel Piccoli (Jacques Granville);
Philippe Noiret (Henri Jarre); Roscoe Lee Browne (Philippe Dubois);
Per-Axel Arosenius (Boris Kusenov); Claude Jade (Michele Picard);
Michel Subor (Francois Picard).

Roscoe Lee Browne and Donald Randolph in Topaz (Universal, 1969).

        Alfred Hitchcock's 1969 entry into film history is based on
the actual exploits of French espionage agent Philippe de Vosjoli,
who was involved with the 1962 "Sapphire" scandals in France, in
which top French officials were found to be Soviet agents, leaking
top French government secrets as well as those of NATO and other

Western organizations, to the Soviets.

Utilizing Leon Uris' encompassing novel as a basis, Hitchcock extracted the aspects of political intrigue and turned them into a slow-moving albeit exceedingly interesting film of spies involved in government activities. The locale shifted constantly between New York, Paris, Russia, Copenhagen, and Cuba. Its plot involved a U.S. agent (Forsythe) and a French counterpart (Stafford) and their efforts to locate those in the Topaz ring, a group high up in the French government suspected of selling secrets to the Eastern powers. Tied into this plot thread were the efforts of the CIA to discover the extent of Russian missile sites in Cuba.

The British Monthly Film Bulletin pegged the essential faults in Topaz as follows: "... the characters begin to proliferate and the plot is nudged forward in a series of rather boringly shot dialogue exchanges as the cold war scene of 1962 is uneasily evoked ... fact vies uneasily with fiction all the way along. The film offers a tantalizing hors d'oeuvre, but the main course seems to have been lost somewhere along the way."

Ironically Hitchcock used only one American name (Forsythe) in Topaz and instead loaded his picture with actors known mainly in Europe for their roles in imitation-cheap, Continental spy thrillers (i.e., Stafford, Vernon, Dor, Robin). The film had only the director's name to carry it at the boxoffice where it enjoyed adequate but hardly exceptional business. While far from top Hitchcock, Topaz is a satisfactory intrigue film which will probably gain in stature with passing years. For it is certainly a good telling of actual historic events as well as a craftsmanlike handling of a complicated, intriguing melodrama.

TORN CURTAIN (Universal, 1966) C 128 min.

Producer-director, Alfred Hitchcock; story-screenplay, Brian Moore; pictorial designer, Albert Whitlock; assistant director, Donald Baer; production designer, Hein Heckroth; set decorator, George Milo, makeup, Jack Barron; music, John Addison; costumes, Edith Head; sound, Waldon O. Watson, William Russell; camera, John F. Warren; editor, Bud Hoffman.

Paul Newman (Michael Armstrong); Julie Andrews (Sarah Sherman); Lila Kedrova (Countess Kuchinska); Hansjörg Felmy (Heinrich Gerhard); Tamara Toumanova (Ballerina); Wolfgang Kieling (Hermann Gromek); Günter Strack (Professor Karl Manfred); Ludwig Donath (Professor Gustav Lindt); David Opatoshu (Mr. Jacobi); Gisela Fischer (Dr. Koska); Mort Mills (Farmer); Carolyn Conwell (Farmer's Wife); Arthur Gould-Porter (Freddy); Alfred Hitchcock (Man in Hotel with Baby on Lap); Gloria Gorvin (Fräulein Mann); Erik Holland (Hotel Travel Clerk).

This Hitchcockian exercise into cold war spy clichés drew the ire of critics and received a rather apathetic welcome from the public, with a relatively minor $6.5 million domestic rental take. "... [T]here is a distracted air about much of the film--as

Julie Andrews and Paul Newman in <u>Torn Curtain</u> (Universal, 1966).

if the master were not really paying attention to what he was doing. Therefore our emotional involvement never grows to the point where it overrules rational disbelief or blocks out those flaws of logic which should not be noticed until we emerge into daylight" (Richard Schickel in <u>Life</u> magazine).

Professor Michael Armstrong (Newman) a top U.S. atomic scientist passes himself off as a defector to East Germany, hoping to uncover a secret antimissile formula that is in the possession of Professor Gustav Lindt (Donath) of Leipzig. Newman and his frosty sweet fiancée (Andrews), she bewildered by his apparent rash of free world disloyalty, traipse behind the Iron Curtain into East Germany, clumsily eliminating a Red agent along the way. Gaining the necessary information, the couple are sneaked out of the country in the costume baskets of a departing ballet troupe.

Perhaps the only credible scene in this rather dull, glossy production, had Newman and Andrews in a crowded theatre filled with Russian SS on their trail. In order to escape the closing net, Newman yells "fire" which stampedes the crowd and allows the duo to make their hasty getaway. One wonders, however, how the word "fire" spoken in English, could cause so much excitement in a non-English speaking theatre?

It was a toss-up which was worse: the casting of Newman and Julie "Mary Poppins" Andrews in top roles, or the sophomoric screenplay by Brian Moore. Certainly never had two such lackluster,

inexperienced undercover operatives deserved less to have the reward of mission completed and being cozily alive at the finale to
boot.

THE TRAITOR (Rank, 1962) 71 min.

Producer, Jim O'Connolly; director, Robert Tronson; idea,
J. Levy, O'Connolly; screenplay, O'Connolly; art director, Bert
Davey; assistant director, John Peverall; music, Johnny Douglas;
sound, Dudley Messenger; camera, Michael Reed; editor, Peter
Borta.

Patrick Allen (John Lane); James Maxwell (Ray Ellis); Ewan
Roberts (Colonel Burlinson); Jacqueline Ellis (Mary); Zena Walker
(Annette Lane); Jeffrey Segal (Dr. Lindt); Ance Padwick (Miss
Lindt); Harold Goowin (Edwards); John Brown (Mason); Sean Lynch
(Porter); Jack May (Burton); Mark Singleton (Vennon).

When a packet of top secret British microfilm is found in
the wreckage of a civilian plane near Munich, Major Ellis (Maxwell)
of NATO Security and investigator John Lane (Allen) are called in to
smoke out the chain of spies operating within the British Foreign
Office.

"It's nicely underplayed with no glamorized cloak-and-dagger
schmaltz, and romance, what there is of it, is held to a reasonable
minimum" (New York Herald-Tribune). Like many another superior
British second feature, this entry got short shrift at the American
boxoffice.

TRIPLE CROSS (WB, 1967) C 140 min.

Executive producer, Fred Feldkamp; producer, Jacques-Paul
Bertrand; associate producer, Georges Cheyko; director, Terence
Young; based on the book The Eddy Chapman Story by Frank Owen;
screenplay, Rene Hardy; assistant director, Christopher Raoux,
Bernard Quatrehomme; music, Georges Garvarentz; camera, Henri
Alekan; editor, Roger Dzoyre.

Christopher Plummer (Eddie Chapman); Romy Schneider (The
Countess); Trevor Howard (Distinguished Civilian); Yul Brynner
(Baron von Grunen); Gert Frobe (Colonel Steinhagen); Claudine
Auger (Paulette); Harry Meyen (Lt. Keller); Jess Hahn (Commander
Braid); Gil Barber (Bergman); Jean-Claude Bercq (Major von Leeb);
Jean Claudio (Sgt. Thomas); Robert Favart (General Dalrymple);
Bernard Fresson (Raymond); Clement Harari (Losch); Georges Ly-
can (Leo); Hubert Noel (von Runstedt's Staff Officer); Howard Ver-
non (Lisbon Embassy Official); Francis de Wolff (German Colonel-
General).

"...[B]y inadvertence, it is a spoof of all the spy movies of
the last 20 years or so" (New York Times).

For robbing a movie theatre, Eddie Chapman (Plummer) is

sent to prison on the Isle of Jersey.   Along comes the Second World
War and the Germans occupy the island.   Crafty Plummer offers
his services as a spy to the Nazis.   Colonel Steinhager (Frobe) is
dubious about Plummer's reliability and puts the Countess (Schneider)
on the case, but finally approves the applicant.   Plummer is sent
to France where under the new name of Fritz Grauman he is trained
by Colonel Baron von Grunen (Brynner).   His "loyalty" verified by
Brynner, Plummer is then parachuted into England where he hastens
to offer his services to British Intelligence in exchange for a complete pardon.   The English arrange a fake explosion of an aircraft
factory which German reconnaissance planes duly photograph.
When Plummer returns to Paris he is decorated with the Iron Cross
for his achievements.   Later he is dispatched to check on the success of the V-1 and V-2 rocket attacks on England.   He succeeds
in misguiding the German rockets from their targets.   When the war
concludes he is given his pardon, only to learn that his criminal
records had been destroyed in an air raid.
        Even though this French-produced picture (made with an in-
ternational cast in England) is based on fact, it emerges as a dull
tangle of incredibility.   (At one point in the picture, Plummer's
character is made to ask, "How the hell did I get mixed up in all
this anyway?")   Despite the novelty of having a mid-1960s feature
dealing with spying in World War II rather than in the contemporary
cold war, every cliché of the genre is present, including spy Plummer's preoccupation with the opposite sex, and monocled Brynner
as a stereotyped disgruntled German somehow involved in the
assassination plot on the Führer.

TROUBLE IN BAHIA FOR O.S.S. 117 see FURIA A BAHIA POUR
O.S.S. 117

TRUE HEAVEN   (Fox, 1929)   5,531 feet

        Presenter, William Fox; supervisor, Kenneth Hawks; director,
James Tingling; based on the story Judith by Charles Edward Mon-
tague; adaptation, Dwight Cummins; titles, Malcolm Stuart Boylan;
assistant director, Lesley Selander; camera, Conrad Wells.
        George O'Brien (Lt. Philip Gresson); Lois Moran (Judith);
Phillips Smalley (British Colonel Mason); Oscar Apfel (German
General); Duke Martin (British Sergeant Major); Andre Cheron
(British Spy); Donald MacKenzie (British Colonel); Hedwiga Reicher
(Madame Grenot); Will Stanton (Gresson's Chauffeur).

        Despite the addition of sound effects, this was still a spy
melodrama of the old screen school, "a mildly entertaining but often
unbelievable espionage romance ... invariably weak during the
dramatic junctures" (New York Times).
        British lieutenant Philip Gresson (O'Brien), on active duty
in World War I Belgium, becomes entranced with cafe entertainer
Judith (Moran), who is soon instrumental in saving his life.

Thereafter, using the cover of a German officer, he is dispatched behind the enemy lines, where he meets Moran, an agent for the Kaiser. Despite her love for O'Brien, she turns him in to the authorities. He is sentenced to be shot, but the Armistice is signed and he is saved.

TRUNK TO CAIRO (American-International, 1967) C 80 min.

Producer, Menahem Golan; associate producer, Michael Kugan; director, Golan; screenplay, Marc Behm, Alexander Ramati; art director, S. Zafrir; music, Duv Seltzerg; assistant director, Jacques Erlich; sound, Zalman Nachligel; song, Geula Gil; camera, Mimish Herbst; editor, Danny Shik.
Audie Murphy (Mike Merrick); George Sanders (Professor Schlieben); Marianne Koch (Helga Schlieben); Hans Von Borsodi (Hans Klugg); Joseph Yadin (Captain Gabar); Gila Almagor (Yasmin); Eytan Priver (Jamil).

Israeli producer-director Menahem Golan who had tremendous international success with his film <u>Sallah</u>, decided to join the James Bond-imitation bandwagon with this premiere made-in-Israel espionage caper. Nothing went right with the project, completed in 1965 but not released in the U.S. until well into 1966 by which time the market was saturated with far superior spy movies.
Mike Merrick (Murphy), a secret service agent, posed as a German undercover agent attempting to sabotage a rocket factory in Cairo. Sanders played a demented German scientist in the employ of the Egyptians, with Koch as his sexy daughter in love with Murphy.
Actually there was nothing real about this film. Israeli location sites were used to depict Cairo and Murphy, complete with his still intact Southern accent, was such a dud as a James Bond disciple that the usually gentle New York <u>Daily News</u> suggested the former Western movie star should "get back on his horse." Sanders' German physicist spoke beautifully accented Queen's English, and seemed extremely blasé about working on a nuclear warhead for use against Israel. His ennui led the <u>New York Post</u> to carp, "If the scientists are as inept as the movie, the world is safe."

THE TWO-HEADED SPY (Columbia, 1958) 93 min.

Executive producer, Hal E. Chester; producer, Bill Kerby; director, Andre de Toth; story, J. Alvin Kugelmass; screenplay, James O'Donnell; art director, Ivan King; sound, Teddy Darvas, A.B. Bradburn; special effects, George Blackwell, Jr.; technical adviser, Colonel Alexander Scotland, O.B.E., Carl Henrich Perle; music, Bernard Schurmann; music director, Muir Mathieson; songs, Peter Hart; camera, Ted Scaife; editor, Raymond Pulton.
Jack Hawkins (Schottland); Gia Scala (Lila Geyr); Erik Schumann (Lt. Reinisch); Alexander Knox (Müller); Felix Aylmer (Cornaz);

Laurence Naismith (General Hauser); Donald Pleasence (General Hardt); Kenneth Griffith (Adolf Hitler); Harriette Johns (Karen Crosher); Edward Underdown (Kallenbrunner); Martin Benson (General Wagner); Walter Hudd (Admiral Canaris); Bernard Foy (Lieutenant); Geoffrey Bayldon (Dietz); Deering Wells (General Merkel); John McLaren (Colonel Hansen); Nada Beale (Eva Fischer); Ian Colin (Colonel Heinz); Victor Woolf (Pawnbroker); Peter Swanick (General Foppe).

Alexander Knox (center) and Jack Hawkins in The Two-Headed Spy (Columbia, 1958).

Despite the misnomer of the title, it is "a jolting, brisk and very well turned out film" (New York Herald-Tribune), demonstrating that the careful planting of a spy within the opponent's camp is not an overnight operation. In fact, the film suggests that while most light-headed individuals are enjoying the fruits of "peace" that follows each major war, the more realistic members of a government are already looking ahead to the next Armageddon. Thus it is a rare spy who can ever enjoy the fool's paradise of the common man, for cynicism, pessimism, and reality must ever be his watchwords for success and survival.

After 25 years of devoted duty as a bogus "German," General Schottland (Hawkins) neatly worms his way into the confidence of the Gestapo hierarchy and even earns the respect of Hitler, a status which makes Hawkins privy to Third Reich secrets badly needed by the Allied forces. Hawkins' accomplices include Lili Geyr (Scala) and Berlin clock merchant Cornaz (Aylmer), with his primary opponents, Müller (Knox) and Lt. Reinisch (Schumann) of the Gestapo.

UN HOMME DE TROP [One Man Too Many] (Artistes Associes, 1967) C 110 min.

Producer, Raymond Froment; director, Costa-Gavras; based on the novel by Jean-Pierre Chabrol; screenplay, Costa-Gavras; dialog, Daniel Boulanger; music, Michel Magne; art director, Maurice Coasson; special effects, René Albouze, Georges Iaconella; camera, Jean Tournier; editor, Christiane Gaudin.

Jean-Claude Brialy (Jean); Bruno Cremer (Cazal); Jacques Perrin (Kerk); Gerard Blain (Thomas); Claude Brasseur (Groubac); Michel Piccoli (Extra Man); Pierre Clementi (Lucien); François Perier (Moryon); Charles Vanel (Passevin); Paolo Fratini (Philippe); Michel Creton (Solin); Claude Brosset (Orif); Nino Segurine (Paco); Med Hondo (Lecocq); Julie Dassin (The Girl).

The cinema, like the publishing industry, has long been guilty of disguising or ignoring the inherent ambiguities of the world of espionage, and imposing instead a black and white dichotomy in which the good guys and the bad guys are quite well defined. Costa-Gavras offered his apology to this standard mistreatment of the spy game in screening this novel by Jean-Pierre Chabrol.

During World War II, French Resistance commandos, under the leadership of Cazal (Cremer), rescue 12 men condemned to death at a German prison camp. After the daring raid they discover they have a 13th man (Piccoli) among them. Because he is wearing German boots, has no identification, and initially refuses to speak, the consensus opinion is to do away with him as a German agent. Later on, just before they are about to execute him, he explains to one of their number (Blain) that actually he is a pacifistic deserter. Thereafter, in a skirmish with the Germans, all the commandos left are killed; only Piccoli escapes death.

Costa-Gavras made this feature in 1966, a picture selected to open the Moscow Film Festival in 1967. It was not until two years later that a dubbed English version, heavily edited, and re-titled Shock Troops was dumped onto the American film market as a double bill entry. The critics were quite unenthusiastic about the production, "If the dramatic-visual quality and explosive, slam-bang speed of the last half of this French-Italian co-production dubbed into English, were matched by dramatic unity, this import might have been fine" (Howard Thompson in the New York Times). Not all the blame can be set at the feet of the distributors, for director Costa-Gavras insisted upon making this film a (sub)conscious tribute to American war and Western pictures, thus somewhat distorting the story's basic message.

UNDER THE RED ROBE   (Goldwyn-Cosmopolitan Dist. Corp., 1923)
9,062 feet

　　　Director, Alan Crosland; based on the novel by Stanley J.
Weyman; screenplay, Bayard Veiller; sets, Joseph Urban; music
score, William Frederick Peters; costumes, Gretl Urban; art titles,
Oscar C. Buchheister Art Title Company; camera, Harold Wenstrom,
Gilbert Warrenton.
　　　Robert B. Mantell (Cardinal Richelieu); John Charles Thomas
(Gil de Berault); Alma Rubens (Renée de Cocheforet); Otto Kruger
(Henri de Cocheforet); William H. Powell (Duke of Orleans); Ian
MacLaren (King Louis XIII); Genevieve Hamper (Duchess de Chevreuse); Mary MacLaren (Anne of Austria); Rose Coghlan (Marie de
Medici); Gustav von Seyffertitiz (Clon); Sidney Herbert (Father
(Joseph); Arthur Housman (Captain La Rolle); Paul Panzer (Lt. in
the French Army); Charles Judels (Antoine); George Nash (Jules
the Innkeeper); Evelyn Gosnell (Madame de Cocheforet).

Alma Rubens in Under the Red Robe (Goldwyn-Cosmopolitan, 1923).

UNDER THE RED ROBE   (20th-Fox, 1937)   82 min.

　　　Producer, Robert T. Kane; director, Victor Seastrom; based
on the novel by Stanley J. Weyman; screenplay, Lajos Biro, Philip
Lindsay, J. L. Hodson; camera, Georges Perinal; editor, James
Clark.
　　　Conrad Veidt (Gil de Berault); Annabella (Lady Marguerite);

Raymond Massey (Cardinal Richelieu); Romney Brent (Marius); Sophie Stewart (Duchess of Foix); F. Wyndham Goldie (Duke of Foix); Lawrence Grant (Father Joseph); Haddon Mason (Count Rossignac); J. Fisher White (Baron Breteuil); Ben Soutten (Loval); Anthony Eustrol (Lt. Brissic); Desmond Roberts (Captain Rivarolle); and: Shale Gardner, Frank Damer, James Regan, Eddie Martin.

Stanley J. Weyman's 1894 novel and 1896 Broadway drama (with William Faversham and Viola Allen) pleased audiences with its intricate blend of costume drama and intrigue set in the days of the wily Cardinal Richelieu who craftily manipulated the power strings of King Louis XIII's France with the Huguenots the chief scapegoats.

The 1923 silent film adaptation, impressively mounted and boasting a high calibre cast, was endorsed far more by the public than the critics. "The story has not been particularly well adapted, for it could be much stronger and more convincing" (New York Times). In this tale of duplicity, disguises, and diplomacy, gallant Gil de Berault (Thomas), in order to save his life, must comply with the request of Cardinal Richelieu (Mantell) that he capture Henri de Cocheforet (Kruger), the latter the alleged head of an anti-monarchy conspiracy. Thomas' mission is hampered by his falling in love with Kruger's sister (Rubens) which leads Thomas to return to Mantell, empty handed but heavy hearted with love. Meantime, the King's brother (Powell) convinces Louis XIII (MacLaren) to rid the court of Mantell's influence. However, Thomas exposes Powell's treachery and as a reward is returned to royal-clergy favor.

The 1937 British-made remake was less elaborate but as convoluted as the original, following the plot in a very solemn tone. The new rendition suffered from the casting of a too mature Veidt as the hell-raising hero and in focusing on the machinations of ruthless, implacible Cardinal Richelieu (Massey), the film ignored too often the action and romantic relief needed to make it a success.

UNDERGROUND (WB, 1941) 95 min.

Producer, Jack L. Warner, Hal B. Wallis; director, Vincent Sherman; story, Edwin Justus Mayer, Oliver H. P. Garrett; screenplay, Charles Grayson; music director, Leo F. Forbstein; music, Adolph Deutsch; art director, Charles Novi; camera, Sid Hickox; editor, Thomas Pratt.

Jeffrey Lynn (Kurt Francken); Philip Dorn (Eric Francken); Kaaren Verne (Sylvia Helmuth); Mona Maris (Fräulein Gessner); Peter Whitney (Alex); Martin Kosleck (Heller); Erwin Kalser (Dr. Francken); Ilka Gruning (Frau Francken); Frank Reicher (The Professor); Egon Brecher (Herr Director); Ludwig Stossel (Herr Müller); Hans Schumm (Heller's Aide); Wolfgang Zilzer (Hoffman); Lisa Golm (Ella the Maid); Roland Varno (Ernest Liebling); Henry Brandon (Rolfe); Lotte Palfi (Mrs. Rolfe); Lionel Royce (Captain); Roland Drew (Gestapo); Robert Davis (Official); Ernest Hausman (Rudd); Carne Whitley, Henry Victor, Hans von Morhart, Otto

Reichow, Bob Stevenson (Gestapo Men); Paul Panzer (Janitor);
Willy Kaufman (Customer); Ludwig Hardt (Clerk); Hans Wollen-
berger (News Vendor); Lester Alden (Herr Krantz); Fred Gier-
mann, Rolf Lindau (Radio Men); Henry Rowland (Paul); John
Piffl (Herr Mazel); Erno Verebes (Head Waiter); Louis Arco (Otto);
Hans Conried (Herman); David Hoffman (Willi); Edith Angold
(Cashier); William von Brincken (Captain Bornsdorff); Norbert
Schiller (Blind Man); Glen Cavender (Man); Louis Alden (Attendant);
Gretl Sherk (Landlady); Carl Ottmar (Official); Arno Frey (Guard);
Walter Bonn (Lieutenant).

Erwin Kalser and Peter Whitney in Underground (WB, 1941).

        Even though it was just one more in the swelling succession
of anti-Nazi pictures, the hard-hitting Warner Bros. sensationalism
touch used by director Vincent Sherman provided Underground with
"the urgency of an overpowering subject" (Variety).   Under the
guise of depicting the heroics of "the world's secret battlefront"
this film offered viewers a bluntly brutal dose of conditions in
Gestapo-dominated Germany.   Hollywood now had no qualms about
showing the Nazis as skunks, and if in order to tap viewers' patriotic emotions it was necessary to make an unsubtle case of the in-
human Germans, so much the better, or so the philosophy of the
day went.

The plot revolves about Third Reich enthusiast Kurt Francken (Lynn) who discovers a new set of values from the heroic efforts of his brother (Dorn), an announcer on the clandestine Resistance radio, and the other underground workers. Among the partisans in wartime Berlin are Fräulein Gessner (Maris), secretary to Heller (Kosleck) of the German secret police, and Sylvia Helmuth (Verne), a sub rosa partisan worker. In the course of the story, several of the underground group are killed, with Lynn's act of redemption creating a stirring, if still downbeat, final note to the tale.

UNDERGROUND   (UA, 1970)   C   100 min.

Producer, Jules Levy, Arthur Gardner; director, Arthur Nadel; story, Marc L. Roberts, Ron Bishop; screenplay, Bishop, Andy Lewis; assistant director, Richard Dalton; art director, Frank White; special effects, Nobby Clark; camera, Ken Talbot; editor, Tom Rolf.

Robert Goulet (Dawson); Danielle Gaubert (Yvonne); Lawrence Dobkin (Boule); Carl Duering (Stryker); Joachim Hansen (Hessler); Roger Delgado (Xavier); Alexander Feleg (Moravin); George Pravda (Menke); Leon Lissik (Sergeant in Bistro); Harry Brooks, Jr. (Panzer Sergeant); Sebastian Breaks (Condon); Nicole Croisille (Bistro Singer); Derry Power (Pommard); Paul Murphy (Jean); Gerry Sullivan (Fosse); Eamonn Keane (Emile); Andre Charise (Gerrard).

This antediluvian entry neither sparked renewed interest in the waning partisan-espionage screen thriller nor impressed the public, which had had quite enough of bearded singing star Goulet's battlefront heroics on the teleseries "Blue Light" (1965).

Because American army officer Dawson (Goulet) had been earlier captured and tortured by the Nazis into naming other members of his espionage ring, including his wife, he is now eager to redeem himself. (Goulet's inconsistently contrived character, however, does not mind causing the death of several French Marquis teammates in the course of his mission.) Goulet's task is to be parachuted into France and spirit away a disillusioned Nazi general (Duering) to England so the British can learn the extent of the Nazis' preparation for the imminent Allied invasion of the Continent. For his cover, Goulet poses as a French baker with Gaubert as his wife.

Made on location in Ireland in 1969. For a late 1960s-produced picture, Underground had very little violence or nudity. One of the few redeeming moments in the film was the spectacular climactic ambush and air rescue from a field lit by gasoline drenched haystacks.

UNDERGROUND AGENT   (Columbia, 1942)   70 min.

Producer, Sam White; director, Michael Gordon; story-screenplay, J. Robert Bren, Gladys Atwater; art director, Lionel

Banks, Jerome Pycha, Jr.; set decorator, George Montgomery;
assistant director, Seymour Friedman, Bud Brill; camera, L.W.
O'Connell; editor, Arthur Seid.
     Bruce Bennett (Lee Graham); Leslie Brooks (Ann Carter);
Frank Albertson (Johnny Davis); Julian Rivero (Miguel Gonzales);
George McKay (Pete Dugan); Rhys Williams (Henry Miller); Henry
Victor (Johan Schrode); Addison Richards (George Martin); Rosina
Galli (Maris Gonzales); Warren Ashe (John Ward); Russel Gaige
(Dr. Fenwick); Crane Whitley (Guiseppe Ormanti); Leonard Strong
(Count Akiri); Hans Conried (Hugo); Hans Schumm (Hans); Sonny
Schulman (Jose); Jovanhy Blake (Elena); Ben Taggart (Police Chief);
Kenneth MacDonald (Clyde); Jayne Hazard (Secretary); Lynton Brent
(Engineer); Lloyd Bridges (Chemist); Oscar "Dutch" Hendrian,
George Magrill (Men); Jack Shay (Hank); Bud Geary (Fred); William
Caldwell, Sandy Sanford, William Stahl (Telephone Men); Ralph San-
ford (Big Guy); Johnny Tyrrell (Assistant).

     Because Axis agents are wiretapping the lines at a top de-
fense plant, government trouble shooter Lee Graham (Bennett) is
called into action.   He may be smart as a spy catcher (he invents
a word scrambler which eliminates the further possibility of
mechanical eavesdropping), but he has a few things to learn about
diplomacy.   Bennett's investigations at the plant accidentally lead
to the firing of Ann Carter (Brooks).   To make amends, he hires
her as his secretary and part of his counter-espionage staff, which
includes Johnny Davis (Albertson), Pete Dugan (McKay), and Miguel
Gonzales (Rivero).   Bennett finds that residing at Henry Miller's
(Williams) boarding house pays double dividends in cracking down on
the enemy gang.
     To promote this junior spy picture, Columbia advertised it
as involved with "Cracking down on the secret ears of the enemy!"

VANISHED   (Universal/NBC-TV, 1971)   C   240 min.

     Director, Buzz Kulik; based on the novel by Fletcher Knebel;
screenplay, Dean Riesne.
     Richard Widmark (President Roudebrush); James Farentino
(Culligan); E. G. Marshall (Ingram); Robert Young (Senator Gannon);
Arthur Hill (Greer); Eleanor Parker (Sue Greer); Skye Aubrey
(Jill); Robert Hooks (Storm); William Shatner (Patrick); Murray
Hamilton (McCann); Larry Hagman (Freytag); Tom Bosley (Cava-
naugh); Stephen McNally (General Palfrey); Sheree North (Beverly);
Robert Lipton (Loomis); Jim Davis (Captain Coolidge); Michael
Strong (Descourcy); Christine Belford (Gretchen Greer); Catherine
McLeod (Grace).

     Given plenty of advertising by NBC as television's first three-
hour telefeature, Vanished presented the simple yarn of intrigue surrounding the disappearance of a top presidential adviser.   Based on
Fletcher Knebel's best-selling 1968 suspense novel, critic Judith
Crist called it "standard stuff in Seven Days in May tradition."

The main asset of the slick but empty production was its large and good cameo guest star-studded cast: Widmark as the president whose chief adviser appears to have been abducted by foreign agents, Young as a slippery old Senator, Marshall as a CIA chief, Farentino as the president's press agent, and realistic bits by several real-life newsmen (Chet Huntley, Herb Kaplow, Martin Agronsky).

THE VENETIAN AFFAIR (MGM, 1967)   C   92 min.

Producer, Jerry Thorpe, E. Jack Neuman; director, Thorpe; based on the novel by Helen MacInnes; screenplay, Neuman; art director, George W. Davis, Leroy Coleman; set decorator, Henry Grace; Lalo Schifrin; camera, Milton Krasner; editor, Henry Berman.

Robert Vaughn (Bill Fenner); Elke Sommer (Sandra Fane); Felicia Farr (Claire Connor); Karl Boehm (Robert Wahl); Luciana Paluzzi (Giulia Almeranti); Boris Karloff (Dr. Pierre Vaugiroud); Roger C. Carmel (Mike Ballard); Edward Asner (Frank Rosenfeld); Joe DeSantis (Jan Arvan); Fabrizio Mioni (Russo); Wesley Lau (Neill Carlson); Bill Weiss (Goldsmith).

Bill Weiss and Robert Vaughn in The Venetian Affair (MGM, 1967).

"...[W]ith scripts like these what makes the film-makers think the customers are going to come back?" (British <u>Films and Filming</u>). This "tepid programmer" (<u>Variety</u>) relied on the box-office value of "The Man from U. N. C. <u>L. E.</u>" telestar Vaughn, the scenic shots of Venice, the peripheral appearance of veteran Karloff, and least of all--or so it seemed from the mistreatment--the popular Helen MacInnes novel of 1963.

After an American diplomat explodes an international conference in Venice, killing all present including himself, seedy New York reporter-photographer Bill Fenner (Vaughn) is detailed to cover the case with his journalist colleague in Venice, Mike Ballard (Carmel). It develops that Vaughn is an ex-C. I. A. man who was dismissed from service when he wed suspicious Sandra (Sommer), whom is now known to have been closely involved with the late U. S. diplomat. Vaughn has been instructed to trace the whereabouts of his ex-wife and to obtain a secret report on the affair prepared by political scientist Dr. Pierre Vaugiroud (Karloff).

To flesh out this hack spy flick, there are Giulia Almeranti (Paluzzi) and Claire Connor (Farr) for decoration, lots of color shots of St. Marks' Cathedral, the Grand Canal, and other Venetian tourist spots, and a plethora of hackneyed dialog (e. g., "How about them? Are they trustworthy? ... When is the killing going to end?" "Sorry about her [re Sommer's murder]; it's a stinking business"). The final insult to viewers is the obnoxious rendition of "Our Venetian Affair" sung over the end titles by a yodeling Julius La Rosa.

P. S. :   Venice failed its screentest as the new spy movie capital.

VERBOTEN!   (J. Arthur Rank, 1958)   87 min.

Producer-director-screenplay, Samuel Fuller; art director, John Mansbridge; set decorator, Glen L. Daniels; music, Harry Sukman; Ludwig van Beethoven, Richard Wagner; assistant director, Gordon McLean; camera, Joseph Piroc; editor, Philip Cahn.

James Best (David Brent); Susan Cummings (Helga); Tom Pittman (Bruno); Paul Dubov (Captain Harvey); Harold Daye (Franz); Dick Kallman (Helmuth); Stuart Randall (Colonel); Steven Geray Mayor); Robert Boon (SS Officer); Sasha Harden (Erich); Anna Hope (Mrs. Schiller); Neyle Morrow (Sergeant Kellog); Joseph Turkel (Soldier); Paul Busch (Guenther); Charles Horvath (Man with the Bald Woman).

This offbeat study of a very different type of partisan underground spy force was put together with skill; it reflected, as Phil Hardy describes in his book <u>Samuel Fuller</u> (1970), "a symmetrical structure of infiltration and betrayal." Largely due to the now fashionable vogue for director Fuller, the film has come in for closer study in recent years.

In post-war Germany, there existed an offshoot of the supposedly suppressed Hitler Youth Group movement, called "the werewolves" whose sole purpose was to loot and kill, and aid escaped

Nazi war criminals. This is sticky for the American forces stationed there who must retain an appearance of peaceful neutrality. To focus in on the situation, the movie relates the growing tension between American G. I. David Brent (Best), his German bride (Cummings), and her 15-year-old brother (Daye)--a member of the werewolves.

VOIR VENISE ET CREVER [See Venice and Die] (Cocinor, 1964) 100 min.

Director, Andre Versini, based on the novel Mission to Venice by James Hadley Chase; screenplay, Jacques Robert, Versini; music, Alain Garaguer; camera, André Germain; editor, Henri Taverna.
Sean Flynn (Michel Nemours); Madeleine Robinson (Mme. Tregard); Karin Baal (Maria Natzka); Ettore Manni (Gueseppe); Hannes Messemer (Carl Natzka); Pierre Mondy (Paul); Jacques Monad (Colonel Vallier); Jacques Dufilho (Cesar); and: Margaret Hunt, Daniel Emilfork.

When a man believed to be a traitor to France disappears in Venice, a cold-blooded adventurer (Flynn) sets out to solve the matter, much to the annoyance of the Italian police. It develops that the missing man is a French secret agent. U. S. television title: Mission to Venice.

VORSICHT, MISTER DODD (Gloria/Divina, 1964) C 98 min.

Producer, Utz Utermann, Claus Hardt; director, Günter Grawert; screenplay, Utermann, Hardt; art director, Willi Schatz, Robert Stratil; music, Franz Grothe; costumes, Inge Ege-Grützner; sound, Walter Rünland; camera, Erich Claunigk; editor, Elisabeth Grothe.
Heinz Rühmann (Mr. Dodd-Marmion); Ernst Fritz Fürbringer (Sir Gerald Blythe); Maria Sebaldt (Miss Parker); Mario Adorf (Buddy Herman); and: Horst Keitel, Robert Graf, Anton Diffring, Harry Wüstenhagen.

A school teacher innocently becomes involved in espionage because he resembles a noted international spy. U. S. tv title: A Mission for Mr. Dodd.

WALK A CROOKED MILE (Columbia, 1948) 91 min.

Producer, Grant Whytock; director, Gordon Douglas; story, Bertram Millhauser; screenplay, George Bruce; art director, Rudolph Sternad; set decorator, Howard Bristol; music, Paul Sawtell; assistant director, Ridgeway Callow; makeup, Norbert Miles; sound, John Carter; camera, Edward Coleman; editor, James E. Newcom.

Louis Hayward (Philip Grayson); Dennis O'Keefe (David O'Hara); Louise Allbritton (Dr. Toni Neva); Carl Esmond (Dr. Ritter von Stolb); Onslow Stevens (Igor Braun); Raymond Burr (Krebs); Art Baker (Dr. Frederick Townsend); Lowell Gilmore (Dr. William Forrest); Philip Van Zandt (Anton Radchek); Charles Evans (Dr. Romer Allen); Frank Ferguson (Carl Bemish); Jimmy Lloyd (Alison); Bert Davidson (Potter); Paul Bryer (Ivan); Howard J. Negley (Feodore); Crane Whitley (Curly); Grandon Rhodes (Adolph Mizner); Keith Richards (Miller); Tamara Shayne (Landlady); Reed Hadley (Narrator).

Dennis O'Keefe, Louis Hayward, and Louise Allbritton in <u>Walk a Crooked Mile</u> (Columbia, 1948).

The promotional ads for this low-budget picture read, "Heart-in-mouth realism ... in the smash-up of a spy ring stealing America's top secrets." At the time there was a good deal of patriotic resistance to the picture's premise: that American scientists could be capable of jumping over to the Communist side, passing along top secret data on the atomic tests. The use of a semi-documentary approach, complete with narration, did not lace the feature with the expected realistic tone, but merely slowed down the basic action.

When it is learned that an American big-wig scientist working on the Lakeview Nuclear Project is in cahoots with Russian atomic spies, a joint effort between O'Keefe of the FBI and Hayward of Scotland Yard is necessary to outwit the traitors.

WALK EAST ON BEACON (Columbia, 1952) 98 min.

Producer, Louis de Rochemont; associate producer, Borden Mace, Lothar Wolff; director, Alfred Werker; suggested by the article The Crime of the Century by J. Edgar Hoover; screenplay, Leo Rosten; additional dialog, Virginia Shaler, Leonard Heideman; art director, Herbert Andrews; music director, Jack Shaindlin; sound, Dodge Cunningham; camera, Joseph Brun; editor, Angelo Ross.

George Murphy (Inspector Belden); Finlay Currie (Professor Kafe); Virginia Gilmore (Millie); Karel Stepanek (Alex); Louisa Horton (Elaine); Peter Capell (Gino); Bruno Wick (Danzig); Karl Weber (Reynolds); Rev. Robert Dunn (Dr. Wincett); Jack Manning (Vincent Foss); Vilma Kurer (Mrs. Ross); Michael Garrett (Terrence); Robert Carroll (Boldany); Ernest Graves (Martin); Rosemary Pettit (Mrs. Martin); George R. Hill (Wilben); Bradford Hatton (Masen); Eva Condon (Landlady); Paul Andor (Melmuth); Lotte

George Murphy in Walk East on Beacon (Columbia, 1952).

Palfi (Mrs. Kafer); Ann Thomas (Philadelphia Suspect); Nancy Heyl
(Mrs. Belden); Suzanne Moulton (Sherry Helden); John Farrell (Taxi
Driver); Stephen Mitchell (Samson).

Hollywood had propelled itself into a new crusade, showing
the insidious menace of Communism in America. Louis de Rochemont, whose The House on 92nd Street (1945) was still revered as
a model of documentary-style entertainment, jumped onto the com-
mercial-political bandwagon. That his latest newsreel-like exposé
was overpraiseworthy of the F.B.I. was understandable if not con-
donable. "As a sketch of sample techniques of espionage and de-
tection, ... it has the curious fascination of a glimpse behind the
door marked 'No admittance' into the complex machinery of political
crime and investigation" (New York Herald-Tribune).
Master foreign spy Alex (Stepanek) is dispatched to the U.S.
to replace American-born espionage agent Martin (Graves), who has
failed to obtain the required data on the U.S. government scientific
project "Falcon." When Graves disappears--he has been hustled
off to Russia aboard a Polish freighter--his wife (Pettit) hurries
to the F.B.I. The federal agency launches an investigation under
the direction of Inspector Belden (Murphy) and uncovers a nest of
espionage in the Boston area where refugee scientist Professor Kafe
(Currie) has been pressured--his son is still in East Germany--into
aiding the Red plot. The trail leads to Washington, D.C., where
fake microfilm of Project Falcon is handed over to the conspirators.

WATCH ON THE RHINE (WB, 1943) 114 min.

Producer, Hal Wallis; director, Herman Shumlin; based on
the play by Lillian Hellman; screenplay, Dashiell Hammett; additional scenes-dialog, Hellman; art director, Carl Jules Weyl; set
decorator, Julia Heron; dialog director, Edward Blat; music, Max
Steiner; music director, Leo F. Forbstein; assistant director,
Richard Mayberry; sound, Dolph Thomas; camera, Merritt Ger-
stad, Hal Mohr; editor, Rudi Fehr.
Bette Davis (Sara Muller); Paul Lukas (Kurt Muller);
Geraldine Fitzgerald (Marthe DeBrancovis); Lucile Watson (Fanny
Farrelly); Beulah Bondi (Anise); George Coulouris (Teck de Bran-
covis); Donald Woods (David Farrelly); Henry Daniell (Phili von
Ramme); Donald Buka (Joshua Muller); Eric Roberts (Bodo Muller);
Janis Wilson (Babette Muller); Helmut Dantine (Young Man); Mary
Young (Mrs. Mellie Sewell); Kurt Katch (Herr Blecher); Erwin
Kalser (Dr. Klauber); Robert O. Davis (Overdorff); Clyde Fillmore
(Sam Chandler); Frank Wilson (Joseph); Clarence Muse (Horace);
Violett McDowell (Belle); Joe Bernard, Jack Mower (Trainmen);
Creighton Hale (Chauffeur); William Washington (Doc); Elvira Curci
(Italian Woman); Anthony Caruso (Italian Man); Michele Fehr (Baby);
Jean DeBriac (Mr. Chabeuf); Leah Baird (Miss Drake); Howard
Hickman (Cyrus Penfield); Frank Reicher (Admiral); Robert O.
Fischer (German Ambassador); Walter Stahl (German Embassy But-
ler); Glen Cavender (German Embassy Servant); Joe deVillard

(Spanish General); Wedgwood Nowell (American Diplomat); Hans Tanzler (German Diplomat); Herma Cordova, Gretl Dupont (Women); Alan Hale, Jr. (Boy); Garry Owen (Taxi Driver); Hans von Morhart (German).

Janis Wilson, Paul Lukas, Eric Roberts, and Donald Buka in Watch on the Rhine (WB, 1943).

Dashiell Hammett adapted Lillian Hellman's Drama Circle Award (1941) play to the screen, with Herman Shumlin repeating his direction of the drama set in pre-Pearl Harbor days. Although the world situation had changed tremendously since the play was written and rather faithfully adapted for the cinema, Watch on the Rhine emerged as a pertinent movie, "documented with tremendous dramatic force and pictorial excitement" (New York Herald-Tribune). Its message still came across loud and clear: some people of good will can be blind and complacent to the barbaric nature of the global tragedy at hand.

The plot centered around European engineer (Lukas) and his family who are visiting his wife's (Davis) mother (Watson) in Washington, D. C. Here a foreign count (Coulouris), a nominal friend of the family, learns that Lukas is really the right-hand man to a

captured European underground leader. The Count demands $10,000
from the engineer for his silence, or he will pass along the information to interested parties at the appropriate Washington delegations
of foreign powers. Realizing he is in a trap, Lukas kills the Count,
says farewell to his family, and returns to Europe to try to obtain
the underground leader's release.

The Hollywood Production Code of the period stated if a
murder was committed on screen, the killer must pay the consequences. The finished screenplay for Watch on the Rhine changed
the Hellman play in that Lukas had to "pay for the crime." When
it came time to shoot the final (new) sequence, star Lukas, who
had headed the Broadway company, refused to materialize on the
soundstage. Thus it was necessary for a new finish to be concocted, in which it is hinted he died in Europe, and his oldest son
(Buka) will follow in his father's footsteps to champion the cause of
freedom.

Very little actual spying occurred within Watch on the Rhine,
although the entire film was based on the subject. The main character (Lukas) was a spy, as were the Axis agents who are searching for him both abroad and in the supposedly neutral environs of
Washington, D.C.

Lukas received an Academy Award for his performance and
Bette Davis, top billed but doing boxoffice duty in the subordinate
role of the wife, drew a very solid characterization as the strong
and noble woman behind the man fighting for his homeland.

WATERFRONT   (Producers Releasing Corp., 1944)   65 min.

Producer, Arthur Alexander; director, Steve Sekely; screenplay, Martin Mooney, Irwin R. Franklyn; music director, Lee
Zahler; art director, Paul Palmentola; set decorator, Harry Reif;
assistant director, Lou Perlof; sound, Arthur B. Smith; camera,
Robert Cline; editor, Charles Henkle, Jr.

John Carradine (Victor Marlowe); J. Carrol Naish (Dr.
Carl Decker); Maris Wrixon (Freda Hauser); Edwin Maxwell (Max
Kramer); Terry Frost (Jerry Donovan); John Bleifer (Zimmerman);
Marten Lamont (Mike Gorman); Olga Fabian (Mrs. Hauser); Claire
Rochelle (Maisie); Billy Nelson (Butch).

A sleezy thriller directed in feeble style. This poverty-row
entry had little to recommend it by way of production values, but
if one could suspend his sense of disbelief there was a wry enjoyment to be had at the sophomoric approach to fifth columnists
running rampant in the U.S.A.

Naish "emoted" as an optometrist trying to force other
German-Americans into aiding the Nazi cause, forcing his point
by reminding recalcitrant helpers that they still had relatives back
in the homeland. Suddenly black-garbed Axis spy Carradine arrives
on the scene, backed by the latest orders from the Gestapo and a
personal urge to obtain Naish's secret black book (of codes and
contact) so that he can acquire his own degree of wealth and power.

John Bleifer and John Carradine in Waterfront (PRC, 1944).

Ironically no one seems to ever get around to spying, being too busy seeking the valuable black book.

WENT THE DAY WELL? (UA, 1942) 93 min.

Producer, Michael Balcon; director, Alberto Cavalcanti; story, Graham Greene; screenplay, John Dighton, Diana Morgan, Angus MacPhail; camera, Wilkie Cooper.

Leslie Banks (Oliver Wilsford); Basil Sydney (Ortler); Frank Lawton (Tom Sturrg); Elizabeth Allan (Peggy); Valerie Allan (Nora Ashton); Marie Lohr (Mrs. Frazer); C. V. France (Vicar); John Slater (German Sergeant); Johnny Schofield (Joe Garbett); Edward Rigby (Preacher); Mervyn Johns (Sims); Muriel George (Mrs. Collins); Thora Hird (Land Girl); Patricia Hayes (Daisy).

Hypothesizing the attempted German airborne invasion of a sparsely populated portion of England, and using a contemporaneous

Our Town format, <u>Went the Day Well?</u> depicts 72 hours in the life
of Bramley Green, a tiny hamlet in the heart of the English countryside. Oliver Wilsford (Banks) was the British-born enemy agent
and Ortler (Sydney) was the baby-killing Prussian.
        Members of the Gloucestershire Regiment were used to
portray the German invaders and the Home Guard.   U.S. title:
<u>48 Hours.</u>

WHAT'S UP, TIGER LILY?   (AIP, 1966)   C   80 min.

        Executive producer, Henry G. Saperstein; associate producer,
Woody Allen; revised screenplay, Allen; music-song, The Lovin'
Spoonful; supervising film editor, Richard Krown.
        With: Woody Allen, Mie Hama, Akiko Wakabayashi, the
Lovin' Spoonful, China Lee.

Woody Allen in <u>What's Up, Tiger Lily?</u> (AIP, 1966).

        How do you turn a modest investment in an already completed
Grade Z Japanese spy thriller into a tidy boxoffice profit?   For a
total of about $66,000, producer Henry G. Saperstein allowed wild
wit Woody Allen to have a cinematic field day--as Allen himself
describes in the picture's foreword--by converting several reels of
an Oriental-produced actioner into an English-dubbed spoof of James
Bond, complete with Jewish jokes, digs at all sacred cows (e.g.,
"Spartan dog! Roman swine! Spanish fly!"), and a "no star cast."

The premise of this reassembled put-on has the Japanese super hero Phil Moskowitz, "lovable rogue," out to save the world from arch villain Shepherd Wong, an egg salad addict ("He who makes the best egg salad can control the world") who has a "chicken on his back."

When the take-off wears thin--and it does--and the non sequiturs lose their effect--and they do--there are inserted song interludes by the rock group, The Lovin' Spoonful.

WHERE EAGLES DARE   (MGM, 1969) C 155 min.

Producer, Jerry Gershwin, Elliot Kastner; director, Brian G. Hutton; based on the novel by Alistair MacLean; screenplay, MacLean; assistant director, Colin Brewer; second unit director, Yakima Canutt; art director, Peter Mullins; set decorator, Arthur Taksen; music-music director, Ron Goodwin; sound, Jonathan Bates; special camera effects, Tom Howard; camera, Arthur Ibbetson; second unit camera, H. A. R. Thompson; editor, John Jympson.

Richard Burton (John Smith); Clint Eastwood (Lt. Morris Schaffer); Mary Ure (Mary Ellison); Patrick Wymark (Colonel Turner); Michael Hordern (Vice-Admiral Rolland); Donald Houston (Christiansen); Peter Barkworth (Berkeley); Robert Beatty (Cartwright Jones); William Squire (Thomas); Derren Nesbitt (Major von Hapen); Anton Diffring (Colonel Kramer); Brook Williams (Sgt. Harrod); Neil McCarthy (MacPherson); Vincent Ball (Carpenter); Victor Beaumont (Colonel Weissner); Richard Beale (Telephone Orderly); Ivor Dean (German Officer); Lyn Kennington (German Woman); Nigel Lambert (Young German Soldier); Michael Rooney (Radio Operator); Ernst Walder (Airport Control Officer); Ingrid Pitt (Heidi).

Every season seems to produce its picturization of an Alistair MacLean book thriller in which the actions of (good or bad) subversive groups are made the focal point, with the (counter)spying reduced to a soft-pedalled adjunct. Distributors' domestic rentals of $7,090,000 prove director Brian G. Hutton's thesis that a "magnificently ludicrous blockbuster" that is a "giant leg-pull" can be vicariously satisfying to audiences, no matter how absurd the characterizations and plotting. Hutton and novelist-scripter MacLean ring into Where Eagles Dare all the gimmicks and tricks of the trade, including a direct steal from the famous Night Train (1940) cable car shootout.

In World War II, a team of seven men, headed by British Major John Smith (Burton) of M. I. 6, are parachuted into the Bavarian Alps with the goal of rescuing a top-ranking Allied officer being held captive by the Germans in the nearly escape proof Schloss Adler. One of the commando group is soon found with his neck broken, forcing Burton to conclude there is a traitor among their number. After joining with agent Mary Ellison (Ure), the group moves to a close-by village to meet barmaid Heidi (Pitt), really an Allied agent, who will insinuate Ure into the almost impregnable

castle.   Later, another of the team is murdered; and the remaining group finds itself having to surrender.   Burton and his American O. S. S. lieutenant (Eastwood) escape and make their way to Schloss Adler via a cable car, leading to double bluff upon double bluff as the Anglo-American combat team completes its mission and makes its way to safety.

With a nod to his prior spaghetti Western screen epics, actor Eastwood again almost single-handedly dispatches the enemy, but good naturedly leaves a fair share of nasties for Burton and Ure to liquidate.   Early on in the film, agent Ure asks nonchalant, over-weight, graying Burton, "Why do you go on these insane missions?" You're getting too old."   He tacitly agrees with her but, in a re-flection of the nonsense that abounds in Where Eagles Dare, Burton merrily proceeds to join the younger, athletic Eastwood in scaling dizzy heights to reach the castle, to give into reckless abandon by toying with his German confreres (at that point Burton is disguised as an officer of the Wehrmacht and sports a fluent German accent), and to confound the enemy and counter agents by pulling ploy after ploy.

For those viewers not glued to the next batch of stunting pranks handled by second unit director Yakima Canutt, there is time to ponder why midst all the snow scenes, not one of the Allied group uses skis or snowshoes, or why in this day of advanced cinema technology, the optics for the film's rear-view projection are so blatantly crude.

WHERE THE BULLETS FLY   (Embassy, 1966)   C   90 min.

Producer, S. J. H. Ward; associate producer, George Fowler; director, John Gilling; screenplay, Michael Pittock; assistant di-rector, Ray Frift; art director, George Lack; music director, Philip Martell; title song, Ron Bridges and Bob Kingston; camera, David Holmes; editor, Ron Pope.

Tom Adams (Charles Vine); Sidney James (Mortuary At-tendant); Dawn Addams (Fiz); Wilfrid Brambell (Train Guard); Joe Baker (Minister); Tim Barrett (Seraph); Michael Ripper (Agent); John Arnott (Rockwell); Ronald Leigh-Hunt (Thursby); Marcus Ham-mond (O'Neil); Maurice Browning (Cherub); Michael Ward (Michael); Bryan Mosley (Connolly); Terence Sewards (Minister's P. A.); Heidi Erich (Carruthers); Suzan Farmer (Caron); Maggie Kimberley (Jac-queline); Julie Martin (Verity); Sue Donovan (Celia); Tom Bowman (Russian Colonel); Patrick Jordan (Russian); Gerard Heinz (Ven-stram); James Ellis (Flight Lieutenant Fotheringham); Charles Hous-ton (Co-Pilot); Tony Alpino (Butler); Michael Balfour (Bandleader); Garry Marsh (Major); Michael Cox (Lieutenant Guyfawkes); Peter Ducrow (Professor Harding); Barbara French (Harding's Secretary); John Horsley (Air Marshal); Michael Goldie (Labourer); Joe Ritchie

[Facing page]   Clint Eastwood, Ingrid Pitt, Mary Ure, and Richard Burton in Where Eagles Dare (MGM, 1969).

(Truck Driver); John Watson (Controller); David Gregory (R. A. F. Sergeant); Roy Stephens (Staff Officer).

Tom Adams (center) in <u>Where the Bullets Fly</u> (Embassy, 1966).

      Midst this labyrinth of red herrings, double dealings, intrigue, and sabotage, there is a modicum of enjoyment for self-indulgent filmgoers, but this sequel to <u>The Second Best Secret Agent in the Whole Wide World</u> (1966) is mostly a tiresome display of 007 child's play.

      A menacing organization headed by Angel (Ripper) is conspiring with the Russians to obtain Spurium Apparatus, a secret invention which permits a plane to fly by nuclear power from a new compact unit. Secret agent Charles Vine (Adams) is assigned to stop this scheme, an order which creates a trail of ammunition wastage and corpses.

WHERE THE SPIES ARE (MGM, 1965) C 113 min.

      Producer, Val Guest, Steven Pallos; associate producer, Frank Sherwin Green; director, Guest; based on the novel <u>Passport</u>

to Oblivion by James Leasor; screenplay, Wolf Mankowitz, Guest; additional scenes, Leasor; art director, John Howell; music, Mario Nascimbene; music director, Alfredo Antonini; sound, A.W. Watkins; camera, Arthur Grant; editor, Bill Lenny.

David Niven (Dr. Love); Françoise Dorleac (Vikki); Nigel Davenport (Parkington); John Le Mesurier (Macgillivray); Ronald Radd (Stanilaus); Cyril Cusack (Rosser); Eric Pohlmann (Farouk); Paul Stassino (Simmias); Geoffrey Bayldon (Lecturer); George Pravda, Gabor Baraker (Agents); Noel Harrison (Jackson); Derek Patridge (Duty Officer); Robert Raglan (Sir Robert); Riyad Ghomieh, Muhsen Samrani (Taxi Drivers); George Mikell (Assassin); Richard Marner (Josef); Basil Dignam (Major Harding); Gordon Tanner (Inspector); Bill Nagy (Aeradio); Alan Gifford (Security).

"In these days of widely assorted, highly spiced, scientifically advanced epics of derring-do in the world of espionage, it is good to come up with an old-fashioned doctor and amateur spy who has never lost his original British cool" (Archer Winston in the New York Post). Had this agreeable British-made feature not appeared midst the barrage of super spy flicks, it would have made its own mark as a realistic but very jovial entertainment, bolstered considerably by Niven's charming performance. The Wolf Mankowitz-Val Guest screenplay took appropriate potshots at the rash of gimmicky James Bond imitation cinema offering, lampooning with a friendly, not arch, point of view (e.g., a disgruntled, incredulous Niven tells his over-enthusiastic secret service outfitter, "If you were one of my patients, I'd have you certified"; and later a fellow agent in the field advises the befuddled Niven, "Take my advice, get rid of that bloody gear and get yourself a good heavy gun").

Because middle-aged, rural practitioner Dr. Love (Niven) was in the British Intelligence during World War II, it is decided to coerce him into returning to the field, knowing that this admirer of vintage sports cars will do most anything for Her Majesty's government in order to receive in exchange a special antique Cord car. Oil treaties in the Middle East are involved, and enemy agents are bent on assassinating the pro-British prince. Vikki (Dorleac) is the scrumptuous Russian operative who switches her loyalties to Niven and the British cause.

WHERE THERE'S LIFE (Paramount, 1947) 75 min.

Producer, Paul Jones; director, Sidney Lanfield; story, Melville Shavelson; screenplay, Allen Boretz, Shavelson; art director, Hans Dreier, Earl Hedrick; set decorator, Sam Comer, Syd Moore; music director, Irvin Talbot; assistant director, Oscar Rudolph; sound, Hugo Grenzback; special effects, Gordon Jennings; process camera, Farciot Edouart; camera, Charles B. Lang, Jr.; editor, Archie Marshek.

Bob Hope (Michael Valentine); Signe Hasso (Katrina Grimovitch); William Bendix (Victor O'Brien); George Coulouris (Krivoc); Vera Marshe (Hazel O'Brien); George Zucco (Paul Stertorius);

Dennis Hoey (Minister of War Grubitch); John Alexander (Mr. Herbert Jones); Victor Varconi (Finance Minister Zavich); Joseph Vitale (Albert Miller); Harry Von Zell (Joe Snyder); Emil Rameau (Dr. Josefsberg); William Edmunds (King Hubertus II); Leo Mostovoy (Minister of Interior Karakovic); Norma Varden (Mrs. Herbert Jones); Ray Atwell (Salesman); Harlan Tucker (Mr. Alvin); Oscar O'Shea (Uncle Phillip); Crane Whitley (Man with Cane); Mary Field, Phyllis Kennedy (Hotel Maids); Fred Zendar (Co-Pilot); Rene Dussaq, Charles Legneur (Officers); Mike Macy (Peasant); Edwin Chandler (Officer); George Bruggaman, George Magrill, Carl Saxe, Tom Costello (Aides); John Mallon, Charles Cooley, Ralph Gomez, Dario Piazza, Otto Reichow, Eugene Stutenroth (Mordians); Floyd Pruitt, Tom Coleman, Jack Clifford, William Haade, John Jennings, Pat Flaherty, Bud Sullivan (O'Briens); Erno Verebes (Peter Gornics); Dorothy Barrett (Model in Window); Edgar Dearing (Desk Sergeant); Ralph Peters, James Dundea, George Lloyd (Cops); Dorothy Barrett (Girl); Hans von Morhart (Karl); Edwin Chandler (New York Policeman); Eric Alden, Len Hendry (Airport Attendants); Guy Kingsford (Mordian Pilot); Lorna Jordan, Letty Light (Salesgirls); Lucille Barkely (Salesgirl); Brandon Hurst (Floor Walker).

Bob Hope and Signe Hasso in Where There's Life (Paramount, 1947).

Internal discord and revolution within a country quite naturally lead to a second front of frantic undercover agents, a situation parodied with very mild success in Where's There Life. "...[T]hose less susceptible to his [Hope] high spirits are likely to be just depressed... " (New York Times).

When the King (Edmunds) of Barovia is shot down and lies
in a state of near death, a successor to the throne must be found,
and at once! By error it is assumed that Hope, a small time New
York City radio disc jockey, is the legitimate heir apparent (the
tangible result of the King's youthful States-side escapades). General Katrina Grimovitch (Hasso) is dispatched to Manhattan to insure that the king-to-be is prepared for his weighty role. However, cowardly but flippant Hope would much rather stay put,
especially since he is about to wed Hazel O'Brien (Marshe) and her
burly cop brother (Bendix) is getting rather persistent and pesty
about questioning Hope's association with on-the-spot Hasso. Just
to make things particularly tough for Hope, there is traitorous Krivoc
(Coulouris) and other adherents of the revolutionary movement,
prowling about New York with the intent of eliminating Hope from
the running.

WHO WAS THAT LADY? (Columbia, 1960) 115 min.

Producer, Norman Krasna; director, George Sidney; based
on the play Who Was That Lady I Saw You With? by Krasna;
screenplay, Krasna; music, Andre Previn; gowns, Jean Louis;
assistant director, David Silver; art director, Edward Haworth;
camera, Harry Stradling; editor, Viola Lawrence.

Tony Curtis (David Wilson); Dean Martin (Michael Haney);
Janet Leigh (Ann Wilson); James Whitmore (Harry Powell); John
McIntire (Bob Doyle); Barbara Nichols (Gloria Coogle); Larry
Keating (Parker); Larry Storch (Orenov); Simon Oakland (Belka);
Joi Lansing (Florence Coogle); Marion Javits (Miss Mellish);
Michael Lane (Glinka); Kam Tong (Lee Wong); William Newell
(Schultz); Mark Allen (Joe Bendix); Snub Pollard (Tattoo Artist).

Back in 1958, Norman Krasna's play Who Was That Lady I
Saw You With?, starring Peter Lind Hayes, Mary Healy, and Larry
Blyden, stretched out its thin comedy premise for a 208-performance
Broadway run. The elaborate film stretched out the anemic plot
device to such a tinsel thin extent that it snapped midway, leaving
the cast and audience to flounder on their own.

When Ann Wilson (Leigh) catches her young chemistry
teacher husband (Curtis) kissing a pretty student in his Columbia
University laboratory, she rightly thinks the worst, and packs her
bags for Reno. But man-about-town television writer Michael
Haney (Martin) steps in to save his pal; he swears Leigh to secrecy
and then tells her a whopper of a lie (i.e., Curtis is working on a
top level spy case for the F.B.I. and the interaction with the telltale girl is all in the line of his secret service duty). Gullible
Leigh is taken in by the Martin-Curtis ploy, but then along comes
real F.B.I. agent Harry Powell (Whitmore) and some actual spies
(Oakland, Storch) from Moscow, and Leigh-Curtis find themselves
up to their pretty necks in helter-skelter espionage miscapering.

The best bits of this nosediving tomfoolery are the scenes

Simon Oakland, Larry Storch, and Tony Curtis in <u>Who Was That</u>
<u>Lady?</u> (Columbia, 1960).

involving the curvaceous dumb-bunny Coogle sisters (Nichols and
Lansing) and the finale in the sub-basement of the Empire State
Building, with the harrassed Leigh-Curtis convinced that they are
imprisoned in the hold of an enemy submarine.

WITHOUT WARNING see THE STORY WITHOUT A NAME

THE WOMAN ON PIER 13 [I Married a Communist] (RKO, 1949)
73 min.

  Executive producer, Sid Rogell; producer, Jack J. Gross;
director, Robert Stevenson; story, George W. George, George F.
Slavin; screenplay, Charles Grayson, Robert Hardy Andrews; art
director, Albert S. D'Agostino, Walter E. Keller; music director,
C. Bakaleinikoff; camera, Nicholas Musuraca; editor, Roland Gross.
  Laraine Day (Nan Collins); Robert Ryan (Brad Collins);
John Agar (Don Lowry); Thomas Gomez (Vanning); Janis Carter
(Christine); Richard Rober (Jim Travis); William Talman (Bailey);

Paul E. Burns (Arnold); Paul Guilfoyle (Ralston); G. Pat Collins
(Charles Dover); Fred Graham (Grip Wilson); Harry Cheshire (Mr.
Cornwall); Jack Stoney (Garth); Lester Mathews (Dr. Dixon);
Marlo Dyer (Evelyn); Erskine Sanford (Clerk); Bess Flowers (Sec-
retary); Charles Cane (Hagen); Dick Ryan (Waiter at Cocktail Bar);
Barry Brooks (Burke); William Haade (Cahill); Iris Adrian (Waitress);
Don Brodie (Drunk); Al Murphy (Jeb); Evelyn Ceder (Girl Friend);
Marie Voe (Striptease Dancer); George Magrill (Tough); Allan Ray
(Man); Louise Lane (Girl); Jim Nolan (Cop).

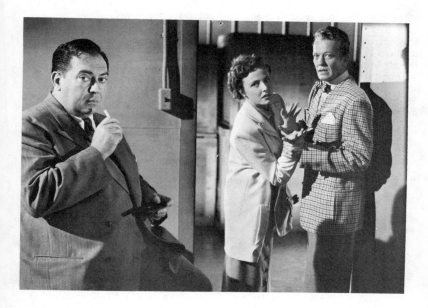

Thomas Gomez, Laraine Day, and William Talman in Woman on
Pier 13 (RKO, 1949).

      In retrospect, one can only ponder at all the fuss over this
picture, which became a political football in the power play changeover of regimes at late 1940s RKO in which Howard Hughes emerged
as the new studio head.   In very overstated terms, the picture
maneuvers a gangster yarn into a blatant study of Communist takeover techniques along the San Francisco docks.   Hughes was among
those who felt that before the picture was doctored (and its title
changed from I Married a Communist), it was too sympathetic a
study of Democracy vs. Communism.
      Brad Collins (Ryan), vice-president of a San Francisco
shipping company, is a tough-as-nails guy, proud of having risen

from dock walloper to top executive. However, he is silent about the fact that in the process he changed his name and broke away from his youthful affiliation with the Communist party. Then Christine (Carter), his ex-girlfriend shows up; her jealousy of Ryan's wife (Day) leads her to bring Vanning (Gomez) and his Red cell henchmen to Ryan's doorstep, implicating Ryan in a dockside labor strike and murder. Meanwhile Carter baits Day's young brother (Agar) into joining the party, but in the process falls in love with him. When Agar later undergoes a political awakening he is murdered, as is Carter after she tells Day the true facts. Later Day is almost eliminated by the Communists, but Ryan sacrifices his life to save her and wipe out the gang.

The Woman on Pier 13 really stacks the deck by exaggerating the extreme ruthlessness of the Reds in disciplining erring/backsliding Party members and by dramatizing the account in such an overly emotional fashion that the picture quickly loses its potential authority. Some politically-oriented reviewers of the day wondered why this film's hero could not have renounced the Party like Louis Budeny and Whittaker Chambers, without a huge Hollywood-style shootout.

WOMEN ARE LIKE THAT see COMMENT QU'ELLE EST!

THE WRECKING CREW (Columbia, 1968) C 105 min.

Producer, Irving Allen; associate producer, Harold F. Kress; director, Phil Karlson; based on the novel by Donald Hamilton; screenplay, William McGivern; art director, Joe Wright; set decorator, Frank Tuttle; music-music director, Hugh Montenegro; song, DeVol; sound, James Z. Flaster, Arthur Piantadosi; karate adviser, Bruce Lee; assistant director, Jerome Siegel; special effects, Paul Stewart; helicopter sequence, Frank Tallman; camera, Sam Leavitt; editor, Maury Winetrobe.

Dean Martin (Matt Helm); Elke Sommer (Linka Karensky); Sharon Tate (Freya Carlson); Nancy Kwan (Yu-Rang); Nigel Green (Count Massimo Contini); Tina Louise (Lola Medina); John Larch (MacDonald); John Brascia (Karl); Weaver Levy (Kim); Wilhelm von Homburg (Gregory); Bill Saito (Ching); Fuji (Toki); Pepper Martin (Frankie); and: Ted Jordan, James Daris, Whitney Chase, Tony Giorgio, Brick Huston, Josephine James, Harry Fleer, James Lloyd, Vincent Van Lynn, Dick Winslow, Harry Geldard, Noel Drayton, Rex Holman, Allen Pinson, J. B. Peck.

Production-wise, this is the most pleasing of the four Matt Helm films, with special emphasis on the Danish scenery, tourist bureau employee Freya Carlson (Tate), and Martin's Sy Devore wardrobe of turtleneck sweater ensembles.

After the hijacking in Denmark of a billion dollars worth of gold bullion, a heist designed to spread financial chaos in the Western world, I. C. E. chief MacDonald (Larch) dispatches girlie photographer Matt Helm (Martin) to remedy the situation pronto, leading to a confrontation with the deadly Count Massimo Contini (Green), his Oriental partner Yu-Rang (Kwan), and his mistress Linka Karensky (Sommer).

Director Phil Karlson, who also did the first in this series, boosted the sagging property with visual techniques (split screen effects) and gadgetry (excessive variations of electronically-devised booby traps), but as Judith Crist (New York magazine) explicated, "The Dean Martin species and sex melanges don't merit discussion; they're the Andy Hardy movies of our time."

Production costs had so mounted on the Matt Helm pictures --countered by diminishing boxoffice returns--that Columbia wisely decided to drop further picturizations of the exploits of the Donald Hamilton character creation.

THE YELLOW CANARY (RKO, 1944)   84 min.

Producer-director, Herbert Wilcox; story, D. M. Bower; screenplay, Miles Malleson, DeWitt Bodeen; art director, W. C. Andrews; music, Clifford Parker; camera, Mase Greene; editor, Vera Campbell.

Anna Neagle (Sally Maitland); Richard Greene (Jim Garrick); Nova Pilbeam (Betty Maitland); Albert Lieven (Jan Orlock); Lucie Mannheim (Madame Orlock); Margaret Rutherford (Mrs. Towcester); Marjorie Fielding (Lady Maitland); Valentine Dyall (German Commander); David Horne (Admiral); Claude Gouley (Major Fothergill).

The fact that 14 minutes were chopped out of the American release print, that half-way through the picture the plot twist is given away, and that the clipped British accents were difficult to comprehend, did not endear this British-made thriller to U.S. audiences. The New York World Telegram criticized the picture for "... operating on the odd notion that confusion is the element that makes a mystery story fascinating." The British were now at their production peak in churning out spy pictures, this being the latest effort from the husband and wife team of producer-director Herbert Wilcox and star Anna Neagle.

High born Britisher Sally Maitland (Neagle) is reputed to be in the employ of the Third Reich--accused of having signalled the Germans during a bomber raid on London. She is asked to leave England and she books passage on a Halifax-bound ship. Aboard, she is romanced by Polish flyer Jan Orlock (Lieven) and is surveilled by British Naval Intelligence officer Jim Garrick (Greene). It develops that the Nazis plan to blow up Allied shipping in Halifax harbor and the announced arrival of suspected "traitor" Neagle leads to trouble in that Nova Scotia town for the aristocratic miss.

The plot springboard for The Yellow Canary was the real life case of blonde Britisher Unity Mitford-Freeman whom Hitler took a fancy to and who may have been a British agent all along. The film's title refers to the little canary in a box received by Neagle, with a message commending her good work for the Führer.

YOU ONLY LIVE TWICE   (UA, 1967)   C   116 min.

Producer, Harry Saltzman, Albert R. Broccoli; director, Lewis Gilbert; based on the novel by Ian Fleming; screenplay, Roald Dahl; production designer, Ken Adam; art director, Harry Pottle; assistant director, William P. Carlidge; second unit director, Peter Hunt; makeup, Basil Newall, Paul Rabiger; sound, John Mitchell; music, John Barry; title song, Barry and Leslie Bricusse; technical advisor, Kikumaru Okuda; aerial unit camera, John Jordan; underwater camera, Lamar Boren; special effects, John Stears; action sequences, Bob Simmons; main titles designer, Maurice Binder; camera, Freddie Young; editor, Thelma Connell.

Sean Connery (James Bond); Akiko Wakabayashi (Aki); Tetsuro Tamba (Tiger Tanaka); Mie Hama (Kissy Suzuki); Teru Shimada (Osato); Karin Dor (Helga Brandt); Lois Maxwell (Miss Moneypenny); Desmond Llewelyn (Q); Charles Gray (Henderson); Tsai Chin (Chinese Girl); Bernard Lee (M); Donald Pleasence (Blofeld); Alexander Knox (American President); Robert Hutton (President's Aide); Burk Kwouk (S. P. E. C. T. R. E. #3); Michael Chow (S. P. E. C. - T. R. E. #4).

Sean Connery in <u>You Only Live Twice</u> (UA, 1967).

The imitations and spinoffs of the James Bond sex and spy

formula continued to pour forth, but audiences remained stubbornly
loyal to the original, even after the disappointing Thunderball (1965),
and even with this "scientifically the most ambitious, sexually the
most routine, scenically one of the best, and in essence a long
step down in the sequel-in-series pictures" (New York Post).   For
a reported $10 million, Albert Broccoli and Harry Saltzman pro-
duced a stunning, gadget-happy, science fiction picture, but it was
far removed from the established, dehumanized world of James Bond.
A pity.

    You Only Live Twice contains two new twists within the series
canon.   James Bond (Connery) is killed--but not for long, and he
"marries."   The story falls into line when an American space capsule launched from Cape Kennedy, Florida, is gobbled up in outer
space by an unidentified craft which proceeds back to earth, but is
lost on the American radar scanners before it lands.   At a specially
convened meeting of the big powers, the U.S. accuses the Russians
of the deed, while the Soviets counter that it must be an American
ploy to provoke trouble.   All of which is just what Ernst Stavro
Blofeld (Pleasence) of S. P. E. C. T. R. E. intended to happen.   The
British member present hastily intervenes, stating that their man in
Singapore is almost sure he spotted a strange object landing in the
Sea of Japan and that the matter is being handled by their Hong
Kong agent, the latter proving to be Connery.   007 is then seemingly killed by the machine-gun bursts of two Chinese assailants,
but it later proves to be a trick to fool Bond's enemies into be-
lieving he is dead.   Soon Connery is sent ashore to Tokyo, relying
on the assistance of Aki (Wakabayashi), secretary to the head (Tamba) of the Japanese secret service.   Through ingenuity and charm
Connery survives a potentially deadly encounter with S. P. E. C. T. R. E. 's
Helga Brandt (Dor).   For her failure to accomplish her task, Dor
suffers the fate of many another careless S. P. E. C. T. R. E. agent--
sudden death, here being unexpectedly dropped into a piranha pool.
Connery eventually traces mysterious shipments of liquid nitrogen
to the vicinity of an extinct volcano which is really the well-armored
headquarters of Pleasence.

    In order to investigate the scene more closely, Connery dons
the disguise of a Japanese fisherman (not very convincingly) and
"marries" Kissy Suzuki (Hama), the latter provided by the Japanese
secret service.   The indomitable British agent makes his entry to
Pleasence's headquarters and even has a long-awaited personal confrontation with the arch villain before he and the Japanese Ninja
Commandos foil Pleasence's attempt to grab another space missile.
The spectacular finale has S. P. E. C. T. R. E. 's Far Eastern headquarters blown to bits, with Connery, Hama, and the others making
a timely escape.

    Even the exotic Oriental flavor (including a Toyota 6T-2000
car) of You Only Live Twice could not hide the letdown in quality
from Goldfinger (1964).   "The gaggy screenplay for this installment
coarsens the style ... the sense of play keeps getting lost" (New
Yorker magazine).   As if to compensate for the dreary supermen
heroics of the carbon copy James Bond movies, in You Only Live

Twice Connery is more than once caught with legendary aplomb
down, and his exploits with women noticeably lean more to whimsy
than leers.
    You Only Live Twice was heavily promoted as the last James
Bond film to star Connery, the latter champing at the bit to try his
acting hand at other types of screen roles.

YOUNG EAGLES (Paramount, 1930)   72 min.

    Director, William A. Wellman; based on the stories The One
Who Was Clever and Sky-High by Elliott White Springs; screenplay-
dialog, Grover Jones, William Slavens McNutt; songs, Ross Adrian
and Lee Silesu; Arthur A. Penn; sound, Eugene Merritt; assistant
director, Charles Barton; camera, A. J. Stout; editor, Allyson
Shaffer.
    Charles Buddy Rogers (Lt. Robert Banks); Jean Arthur (Mary
Gordon); Paul Lukas (von Baden); Stuart Erwin (Pudge Higgins);
Virginia Bruce (Florence Welford); Gordon De Main (Major Lewis);
James Finlayson (Scotty); Frank Ross (Lt. Graham); Jack Luden
(Lt. Barker); Freeman Wood (Lt. Mason); George Irving (Colonel
Wilder); Stanley Blystone (Captain Deming); and: Newell Chase,
Lloyd Whitlock.

    Director William A. Wellman continued his cinematic pre-
occupation with the infant airplane industry during World War I in
this undistinguished entry. "It is a highly incredible narrative
with two good air-fighting episodes and a mass of wild and absurd
incidents" (New York Times).
    American aviator Lt. Robert Banks (Rogers) meets fellow
American Mary Gordon (Arthur) while he is on leave in Paris.
They romance, and he returns to the front. Thereafter in an air
skirmish Rogers grounds Germany's air ace von Baden (Lukas),
known as the Grey Eagle, whom he takes to American Intelligence
in Paris. Rogers is aghast when he is later drugged by Arthur
and Lukas is allowed to escape. Therefore, Rogers reasons that
Arthur is a German spy. Only with feisty Lukas, does the American learn that Arthur is actually a spy for U. S. Intelligence.

THE YOUNG LOVERS (G. F. D., 1954) 96 min.

    Producer, Anthony Haverlock-Allan; director, Anthony
Asquith; screenplay, George Tabori, Robin Estridge; art director,
John Howell, John Box; music director, Benjamin Frankel; camera,
Jack Asher; editor, Frederick Wilson.
    Odile Versois (Anna Szobek); David Knight (Ted Hutchens);
Joseph Tomelty (Moffatt); Paul Carpenter (Gregg); Theodore Bikel
(Joseph); Jill Adams (Judy); David Kossoff (Szobek); John Mc-
Claren (Colonel Margetson); Betty Marsden (Mrs. Forrester); Peter
Illing (Dr. Weissbrod); Peter Dyneley (Regan); Bernard Rebel
(Stefan).

An American, employed at the London embassy, falls in love with the daughter (Szobek) of an Iron Curtain Minister. Both are suspected of subversive activities and are spied upon by both governments.

It was given two stars by the New York Daily News; Movies on TV (1972) noted it was a "... good idea marred by inconclusive, fence-straddling treatment ... some tender, romantic moments...."
U.S. release title: Chance Meeting.

YOUR TURN, DARLING   see   A TOI DE FAIRE, MIGNONNE

ZEPPELIN (WB, 1971)   C 97 min.

Executive producer, J. Ronald Getty; producer, Owen Crump; director, Etienne Perier; story, Crump; screenplay, Arthur Rowe, Donald Churchill; assistant director, Kip Gowans; production designer, Fernando Carrere; art director, Bert Davey; set decorator, Arthur Taksen; music, Roy Budd; sound, Gordon Everett, Colin Le Mesurier; German technical adviser, Dr. Friedrich Sturm; special camera effects, Wally Veevers; camera, Alan Hume; editor, John Shirley.

Michael York (Geoffrey Richter-Douglas); Elke Sommer (Erika Altschul); Peter Carsten (Major Tauntler); Marius Goring (Professor Altschul); Anton Diffring (Colonel Hirsch); Andrew Keir (von Gorian); Rupert Davies (Captain Whitney); Alexandra Stewart (Stephanie); William Marlowe (Anderson); Richard Hurndall (Blinker Hall); Michael Robbins (Cockney Sergeant); George Mikell (German Officer); Clive Morton (Lord Delford); Gary Waldhorn (Harlich); Alan Rothwell (Brandner); John Gill (Meier); Ben Howard (Jamie Fergusson); Arnold Diamond (Major Proudfoot); Bryan Coleman (Colonel Whippen); Ronald Adam (Prime Minister); Frazer Hines (Radio Operator); Ruth Kettlewell (Mrs. Parker); Ray Lonnen (Sergeant Grant).

A labored throwback to the naive spy dramas of the 1920s, this miniature Darling Lili faired badly with both the critics and the public, coming and going without leaving any mark.

In 1915, the British regard it as vital to obtain the airship plans from the Zeppelin works in Friedrichshafen so they may perfect a counter-ship and knock the Germans' Zeppelins (then bombing London) out of the skies. Scotsman York, of Germanic origins, is recruited for the mission, in which he "defects" to the Kaiser's side. Once in Germany he reestablishes his friendship with Goring, the Zeppelin's inventor, and with Sommer, Goring's very young and curvaceous wife. Because German Colonel Diffring and his staff are so intent upon their own plan of landing a Zeppelin in Scotland to heist all the national documents and art treasures stored in an isolated castle, no one seems to pay much mind to the amateurish spy activities of York.

As the British Monthly Film Bulletin complained, "... the

cardboard characters and ridiculous plot are obviously just an excuse for the Panavision shots of the Zeppelin: sailing through the
clouds, engaging in an aerial battle with the fighters, and finally
--though none too soon--burning itself to a cinder."

SPY-ADVENTURE SHOWS ON RADIO

CAPTAIN JAMES ARCHIBALD	(Syndicated, 1930s)
CHANDU, THE MAGICIAN	(ABC, 1949)
CLOAK AND DAGGER	(Syndicated, 1940s)
COUNTERSPY	(ABC, 1942)
DANGEROUS ASSIGNMENT	(NBC, 1950)
THE FBI IN PEACE AND WAR	(CBS, 1944)
FOREIGN ASSIGNMENT	(Syndicated, 1944)
NED JORDAN, SECRET AGENT	(Syndicated, 1940)
SECRET AGENT K-7	(Syndicated, 1938)
SECRET MISSIONS	(Mutual, 1949)
SPECIAL AGENT	(Syndicated, 1945)
THIS IS YOUR ENEMY	(Syndicated, 1940s)
THIS IS YOUR FBI	(ABC, 1945)

SPY-ADVENTURE SHOWS ON TELEVISION

Compiled by Vinnie Terrace

THE ADVENTURER   with: Gene Barry, Robert Morse (Syndicated, 1972)

ASSIGNMENT: VIENNA   with: Robert Conrad, Charles Cloffi (ABC, 1972)

THE AVENGERS   with: Patrick Macnee, Honor Blackman, Diana Rigg, Linda Thorson (ABC, 1966)

THE BARON   with: Steve Forrest, Sue Lloyd (ABC, 1966)

BEHIND CLOSED DOORS   with: Bruce Gordon, Richard Webb (NBC, 1958)

BIFF BAKER, U.S.A.   with: Alan Hale, Jr., Randy Stuart (Syndicated, 1953)

BLUE LIGHT   with: Robert Goulet, Christine Carere (ABC, 1966)

BOLD VENTURE   with: Dane Clark, Joan Marshall (Syndicated, 1958)

CALLAN   with: Edward Woodward (British, 1967)

CASABLANCA   with: Charles McGraw (ABC, 1955)

COUNTERSPY   with: Don Megowan (Syndicated, 1958)

COUNTERTHRUST   with: Tod Andrews, Diane Jergens (Syndicated, 1959)

CRANE   with: Patrick Allen (Syndicated, 1965)

526

THE CRUSADER   with: Brian Keith   (CBS, 1955)

DANGEROUS ASSIGNMENT   with: Brian Donlevy   (Syndicated,
                                    1952)

DOOR WITH NO NAME   with: Grant Richards, Mel Ruick
                                    (NBC, 1951)

DOORWAY TO DANGER   with: Roland Winters, Stacy Har-
                                    ris   (NBC, 1952)

THE DOUBLE LIFE OF HENRY   with: Fred Clark, Red Buttons
    PHYFE   (ABC, 1966)

ESPIONAGE   with: John Gregson, Bradford
                                    Dillman   (NBC, 1963)

FIVE FINGERS   with: David Hedison, Luciana
                                    Paluzzi   (NBC, 1959)

FOREIGN ASSIGNMENT (also: with: Jerome Thor, James Daly,
    Foreign Intrigue; Overseas   Gerald Mohr   (Syndicated, 1951)
    Adventures; Dateline Europe)

FOUR JUST MEN   with: John Conte, Dan Dailey,
                                    Jack Hawkins, Vittorio De Sica
                                    (Syndicated, 1959)

GET SMART   with: Don Adams, Barbara Fel-
                                    don, Ed Platt   (NBC, 1965)

THE GIRL FROM U.N.C.L.E.   with: Stefanie Powers, Noel
                                    Harrison, Leo G. Carroll, Randy
                                    Kirby   (ABC, 1966)

HONEY WEST   with: Anne Francis, John Eric-
                                    son, Irene Hervey   (ABC, 1966)

THE HUNTER   with: Barry Nelson   (Syndicated,
                                    1952)

I LED THREE LIVES   with: Richard Carlson, Virginia
                                    Steffan, John Beradino   (Syndicated,
                                    1953)

I SPY   with: Raymond Massey   (Syndi-
                                    cated, 1956)

I SPY   with: Robert Culp, Bill Cosby
                                    (NBC, 1965)

INTERPOL CALLING   with: Charles Korvin   (Syndicated,
                                    1960)

IT TAKES A THIEF

with: Robert Wagner, Malochi Throne, Fred Astaire, John Russell (ABC, 1968)

MAJOR DELL CONWAY OF THE FLYING TIGERS

with: Ed Peck (DuMont, 1951)

THE MAN CALLED X

with: Barry Sullivan (Syndicated, 1955)

THE MAN FROM INTERPOL

with: Richard Wyler (NBC, 1960)

THE MAN FROM U. N. C. L. E.

with: Robert Vaughn, David McCallum, Leo G. Carroll (NBC, 1964)

THE MAN WHO NEVER WAS

with: Robert Lansing, Dana Wynter, Murray Hamilton, Alex Devion (ABC, 1966)

MARK SABER

with: Tom Conway, Frank Burke (Syndicated, 1952)

MISSION: IMPOSSIBLE

with: Martin Landau, Barbara Bain, Peter Graves, Leonard Nimoy, Greg Morris, Peter Lupus, Linda Day, Leslie Warren (CBS, 1966)

NEW ADVENTURES OF CHARLIE CHAN

with: J. Carrol Naish, James Hong (Syndicated, 1957)

O. S. S.

with: Ron Randell, Lionel Murton (ABC, 1957)

PASSPORT TO DANGER

with: Cesar Romero (Syndicated, 1954)

PENTAGON CONFIDENTIAL

with: Edward Binns, Gene Lyons (CBS, 1953)

SABER OF LONDON

with: Donald Gray (Syndicated, 1957)

SEARCH

with: Burgess Meredith, Doug McClure, Tony Franciosa, Hugh O'Brian (NBC, 1972)

SECRET AGENT

with: Patrick McGoohan (CBS, 1965) [Note: First seen as Danger Man (CBS, 1961); later revamped as The Prisoner (CBS, 1968)

SECRET FILE, U. S. A.

with: Robert Alda, Lois Hensen (Syndicated, 1954)

THE SENTIMENTAL AGENT

with: Carlos Thompson (Syndicated, 1962)

SHADOW OF THE CLOAK

with: Helmut Dantine (DuMont, 1951)

THE THIRD MAN

with: Michael Rennie, Jonathan Harris (NBC, 1960)

TOP SECRET

with: William Franklyn (Syndicated, 1960)

TOP SECRET, U. S. A.

with: Paul Stewart, Gena Rowlands (Syndicated, 1954)

SELECTED BIBLIOGRAPHY OF SPY NOVELS

by T. Allan Taylor

INTRODUCTION

Ever since man's first aggression against his fellow man, the deceptive methods of spying and counterintelligence have fascinated the world. Truly, espionage can be rightly called the "second oldest profession." Its arts have evolved into a complicated, secretive and multifaceted structure, which is, nevertheless, considerably similar in method in all nations of the world. Espionage as a term is usually used to refer to anything and everything associated with the global trading of national secrets. In its strict definition it refers mainly to the use of spies or agents (human or otherwise) to obtain or transmit information. Actually, in reality, this part of the espionage game is merely the tip of an iceberg. Such information as is gleaned through spies must be validated, interpreted and integrated with other similar or even dissimilar information before it becomes useful. For this reason, the term espionage is somewhat narrow, while the terms intelligence or intelligence operations come closer to a fuller description of man's spying on his fellow being.

The particular structure of each nation's intelligence gathering institutions is shaped by both circumstance and the particular personality or government of the nation. Nevertheless, just as with the method of espionage, there is a similar organizational pattern which maintains a fair consistency from country to country and throughout history. This pattern consists basically of a civilian intelligence system, a military intelligence system, a diplomatic network of information gathering, which frequently also acts as a cover for members of the other component parts of the intelligence

531

operation as a whole, and a counter-intelligence agency.

In the United States, the Central Intelligence Agency, or CIA, is the major civilian intelligence bureau, while the Defence Intelligence Agency, or DIA, under the direction of the Secretary of Defense and the Joint Chiefs of Staff, is the military arm of American espionage.   The FBI (Federal Bureau of Intelligence) is responsible for counter-intelligence within territorial United States, while the Bureau of Intelligence and Research for the State Department coordinates diplomatic eavesdropping.   In addition, there is the NSA (National Security Agency), under the Secretary of Defense, which is responsible for cryptoanalysis (code-breaking) and worldwide electronic eavesdropping on foreign communications, and, finally, the Division of Intelligence of the Atomic Energy Commission, busy gathering information about the scientific and nuclear capabilities of other nations.   All these organizations form the USIB (United States Intelligence Bureau), an overview committee, whose chairman is the director of the CIA.   This group reports directly to the National Security Council, which, in turn, reports directly to the President.

Likewise, in Great Britain, there is the division between military intelligence, M. I. 5, and the civilian intelligence operations --the Secret Intelligence Service or SIS, which is also known as M. I. 6, a holdover term from World War II.   Counter-intelligence activities on the home front are mostly handled by Scotland Yard and the Home Office, while overseas counter-intelligence is pursued by the DGI, or the Director of General Intelligence.   The latter institution, however, coordinates closely with the Home Office.   The French Secret Service is called the "Service de Documentation Extérieure et de Contre-Espionage," known for short as SDECE.   Its duties cover both espionage outside France and counter-espionage within.   In addition, there exists the "Direction de la Surveillance du Territoire," or DST, responsible for counter-espionage outside France.   Finally, each of the fighting services have their own intelligence bureaus, commonly known as "Deuxièmes Bureaus," all of which are connected with the Ministry of Defense.

The situation in Soviet Russia is a bit complicated in that

governmental power is split between the state government hierarchy and the Communist Party Organization. The GRU is the chief intelligence directorate of the Soviet Government, and is actually an arm of the Soviet Army subordinate to the Ministry of Defense. The KGB is the intelligence unit within the Secretariat of the Communist Party of the Soviet Union. Both intelligence units are responsible for espionage and counter-espionage within and without the Soviet Union. Similarly, in Nazi Germany, the division between military intelligence, the "Abwehr, " and the intelligence apparatus of the Nazi party, the SS under Himmler, was clearly differentiated. As World War II progressed, the SS, with its subdivisions such as the SD (intelligence gathering agency), and the Gestapo (internal state security agency), gained ascendancy in influence over the "Abwehr. " Much of the internal fighting within the Nazi intelligence institutions is excellently documented in such books as Heinz Hohne's The Order of the Death's Head: The Story of Hitler's OSS (1970) and Ladislas Farago's fascinating account of German espionage in America and Great Britain, The Game of the Foxes (1971). Of the countless other books on German espionage activities during World War II and the Cold War aftermath, one must mention especially those dealing with the spectacular General Gehlen--his own memoirs, The Service (1972), as well as two biographies of him, Gehlen: Spy of the Century (1972), by E. H. Cookridge, and The General Was A Spy (1972), by Heinze Hohne and Herman Zolling. In addition, there are Giles Perrault's Red Orchestra (1968), outlining the story of a spy ring for the Soviet Union operating from the heart of Hitler's headquarters; the memoirs of Walter Schellenberg, head of Hitler's SD agency, Hitler's Secret Service (1971); and Edward Crankshaw's useful paperback, Gestapo (1970). From the Allied point of view there is Major General Sir Kenneth Strong's memoirs as head of Intelligence from the Supreme Allied Command in World War II, Intelligence at the Top (1968).

    There are too many histories of individual intelligence agencies to attempt to cover even a representative number of them, but a few should be mentioned. So far as American intelligence agencies

are concerned, there are several excellent studies of the OSS
(Office of Strategic Services), forerunner of the present CIA. One
is OSS: The Secret History of America's First Central Intelligence
Agency (1972), by R. Harris Smith, formerly a research analyst
for the CIA and at present a lecturer at the University of California.
There are also Cory Ford's biography, Donovan of OSS (1970), the
story of William J. "Wild Bill" Donovan, the man President Roosevelt chose to head the OSS; Stuart Alsop and Thomas Braden's Sub
Rosa: The OSS and American Espionage (1964); and, finally,
chemist Stanley Lovell's revelations of some of the tricks and gadgetry he prepared during his OSS service in Of Spies and Strategems
(1963).   A recently published (1973) controversial study of the CIA
is worth investigating: The Secret Team: The CIA and Its Allies
in Control of the United States and the World by retired Colonel L.
Fletcher Prouty, who was a former liaison officer between the CIA
and the Pentagon.   In addition, the following books add much to the
growing picture of the U. S. intelligence organization and efforts:
CIA: The Inside Story (1961), by Andrew Tully, and Super Spies
(1969) by the same author, the latter dealing mostly with the National Security Agency; The Invisible Government (1964), by David
Wise and Thomas Ross; The Craft of Intelligence (1963), by former
CIA director, Allen Dulles; The Real CIA (1968), by Lyman Kirk-
patrick, a former Deputy Director of the CIA; and, finally, The
American Intelligence Community (1967) by Monro MacClocky, a
retired Air Force general.

        For Britain, the single most important book is Richard
Deacon's History of the British Secret Service (1970).   In addition,
readers should investigate Donald McLachlan's story of naval operational intelligence, Room 39 (1968), as well as John C. Masterman's
long-awaited report, The Double-Cross System in the War of 1939
to 1945, published in 1972 after being declassified by the present
British government.   Lastly, one of the most fascinating books of
recent times on the espionage business, and a fine complement to
Stanley Lovell's book mentioned above, is Colonel R. Stuart Macrae's
story of the development of secret weapons used by the British in

their fight against Hitler, Winston Churchill's Toyshop (1972).

For a basic overall review of the history of espionage, the interested reader should turn to Encyclopedia of Espionage: From the Age of Jericho to the Age of James Bond by Ronald Seth, published in 1973. In addition, The Espionage Establishment (1967), by David Wise and Thomas Ross, is an informative introduction to foreign intelligence systems, with the Soviet Union, Great Britain and Communist China getting the majority of the attention. And for those readers interested in cryptography and code breaking, The Codebreakers (1967), by David Kahn, is a necessity; further reading should include Ladislas Farago's The Broken Seal (1967) and Barbara Tuchman's The Zimmerman Telegram (1958), as well as two basic primers, Lawrence D. Smith's Cryptography (1958), and Helen Games' Cryptoanalysis (1956). Finally, two books investigating the part computers are playing in contemporary espionage and code breaking are Secrets of Electronic Espionage (1966), by John Carroll, and Secret Sentries in Space (1971), by Philip Klass, the latter a study of the development of the space satellite as a means of espionage by both the United States and Soviet Russia. An article by George Siehl, "Cloak, Dust Jacket, and Dagger," appearing in the October 15, 1972, issue of Library Journal is a valuable guide to these and other books on the espionage establishments of the world.

If intelligence operations have fascinated social scientists, historians and biographers, the spy novel, short story, film and play has likewise had a tremendous vogue with the public at large. Spies have had a part to play in all eras and all types of literary endeavor and entertainment. Examples of espionage activities abound from the historical-literary tales of Homer and the Roman poets up to the present day. Alexander Dumas introduced one of literature's most famous "femme fatales" in the person of Milady, Cardinal Richelieu's spy, in his The Three Musketeers, while spies played their parts in the picaresque and historical novels of Sir Walter Scott, James Fenimore Cooper, Edward Bulwer-Lytton, etc.

Spies have had their heyday in drama as well. Such playwrights as Victorien Sardou (Diplomacy), Augustus Thomas

(Shenandoah), William Gillette (Secret Service) and Anthony Paul
(Three Faces East) revolved their plots around themes and person-
ages involved in espionage. In more recent times there has appeared Lillian Hellman's famous Watch on the Rhine, an excellent
play and a film, as well as Norman Krasna's comedy spoof, the
play (and film) Who Was That Lady I Saw You With?

For all its numerous appearances in classical literature,
espionage as a literary ploy is primarily a 20th-century phenomenon.
Certainly, its overwhelming popularity is a modern event. At
present, there are more books (both novels and non-fiction) written
on intelligence operations, espionage and international intrigue than
ever before. Undoubtedly, the two world wars and the resultant
faster pace and the international character of our 20th-century
civilization have been major factors in the unprecedented popularity
of the spy and adventure novel.

In the following bibliography of spy novels, many novels of
adventure and international intrigue have been included as they
border on the area of intelligence activities, or, in some cases,
help round out the picture of a particular author's oeuvre. Many
invaluable sources of information have helped in compiling this
bibliography, and they are listed below.

BIBLIOGRAPHIC SOURCES

American Book Publishing Record cumulative volumes: 1960-1964,
        1965, 1966, 1967, 1968, 1969, 1970, 1971. (R.R. Bowker
        Co.)

Books in Print 1972. (R.R. Bowker Co., 1972)

British Books in Print 1971 (J. Whitaker & Sons, London, 1971)

A Catalogue of Crime, by Jacques Barzun and Wendell Hertig Tay-
        lor (Harper, 1971)

Cumulated Fiction Index, 1945-1960. Comp. by G.B. Cotton and
        Alan Glencross (Assoc. of Assistant Librarians, London,
        1960)

Cumulated Fiction Index, 1960-1969. Comp. by Raymond Ferguson
        Smith (Assoc. of Assistant Librarians, London, 1970. Dist.
        in U.S. by Chicorel Library Pub. Corp., N.Y.)

Fiction Catalog 1960 with yearly supplements to 1972.   (H. W. Wilson Co.)

Library Journal Book Review Annual 1967, 1968, 1969, 1970.
    (R. R. Bowker Co.)

Library Journal (various issues of 1965, 1966 and 1971-1973).
    (R.R. Bowker Co.)

The New York Times Sunday Book Review Sections (various issues
    from 1968 through 1973).   (New York Times Co.)

Paperbound Books in Print cumulative editions (various issues from
    1968 through 1972).   (R. R. Bowker Co.)

Publisher's Weekly (various issues from 1967 through 1973).   (R. R.
    Bowker Co.)

Who Done It?   A Guide to Detective, Mystery and Suspense Fiction
    by Ordean A. Hagen.   (R. R. Bowker Co. , 1969)

AARONS, Edward S.
(see Series 57)

ADAMS, Christopher
Amateur Agent (1964)

ADAMS, Joey
You Could Die Laughing (1968)

ADAMS, Nathan M.
Fifth Horseman (1967)

ALBRAND, Martha
After Midnight (1949)
Call from Austria (1963)
Day in Monte Carlo (1959)
Desperate Moment (1951)
Door Fell Shut (1966)
Endure No Longer (1944)
Hunted Woman (1952)
Linden Affair (1956)
Mask of Alexander (1955)
Meet Me Tonight (1960)
Nightmare in Copenhagen (1954)
No Surrender (1943)
None Shall Know (1946)
Obsession of Emmet Booth (1957)
Remembered Anger (1946)
Rhine Replica (1969)
Story That Could Not Be Told
    (1956)
Wait for the Dawn (1950)
Whispering Hill (1947)
Without Orders (1943)

ALDANOV, Mark
For Thee the Best (1947)

ALDRIDGE, James
Captive in the Land (1963)
The Diplomat (1950)
Statesman's Game (1966)

ALINGTON, Cyril Argentine
Midnight Wireless (1942)

ALLBEARY, Ted
Choice of Enemies (1973)

ALROY, Lionel
Shut Out the Sun (1955)

AMBLER, Eric
Background to Danger (1937)
    (English Title: Uncommon
    Danger)
Cause for Alarm (1939)
Coffin for Dimitrios (1939)
    (English Title: Mask for
    Dimitrios)
Dark Frontier (1936)
Dirty Story (1967)
Epitaph for a Spy (1952)
Intercom Conspiracy (1969)
Journey into Fear (1940)
Judgment on Deltchev (1951)
Kind of Anger (1964)
The Levanter (1972)
Light of Day (1963)
Passage of Arms (1960)
Schirmer Inheritance (1953)
State of Siege (1956) (English
    Title: Night Comers)

AMIS, Kingsley
Anti-Death League (1966)

ANDERSON, Oliver
Random at Random (1959)

ANNE-MURIEL
Rendezvous in Peking (1973)

ANNESLEY, Michael
Agent Intervenes (1944)
Lights That Did Not Fail (1949)
Missing Agent: A Secret Ser-
    vice Story (1938)
Room 14 (1935) (alt. title:
    Fenton of the Foreign Office)
Spies Abounding (1945)

Spies Against the Reich (1940)
Spies in Action (1937)
Spies in the Web (1936)
Spy Corner (1948)
Spy--Counter Spy (1948)
Spy Island (1950)
Suicide Spies (1944)
They Won't Lie Down (1947)
Unknown Agent (1940)
Vanished Vice-Consul (1939)

ANTHONY, Evelyn
The Assassin (1970)
The Legend (1969)
Poellenberg Inheritance (1972)
The Rendezvous (1968)
Stranger at the Gates (1973)
Tamarind Seed (1971)
Valentina (1966)

ARDEN, William
Deal in Violence (1970)
Die to a Distant Drum (1972)

ARDIES, Tom
Pandemic (1973)
This Suitcase Is Going to Ex-
    plode (1972)

ARENT, Arthur
Gravedigger's Funeral (1967)
Laying On of Hands (1969)

ARMSTRONG, Anthony
Room at the Hotel Ambre (1956)
    (English Title: Spies in
    Amber)

ARMSTRONG, Charlotte
Lemon in the Basket (1967)
Seven Seats to the Moon (1969)

ARNOLD, Elliott
Code of Conduct (1970)
The Commandos (1942)
Night of Watching (1967)

ARNOLD, John
I Was a Spy

ARNOLD, Ralph
On Secret Service (1935)

ASH, William
Take-Off (1970)

ASIMOV, Isaac
Caves of Steel (1954)

ATCHESON, George
Peking Incident (1973)

ATLEE, Philip
(see Series 33)

AULLEN, Gilbert
Mysterious Courier (1953)

AVALLONE, Michael
(see Series 25, nos. 1, 2; 44,
    no. 1)

AYER, Frederick
Man in the Mirror (1965)

AYSCOUGH, John
Jacqueline (1918)

BAGGALEY, James
Shadow of an Eagle (1956)

BAGLEY, Desmond
Freedom Trap (1972)
Golden Keel (1964)
High Citadel (1965)
Landslide (1967)
Running Blind (1971)
Tightrope Men (1973)

BAHAREV, I. D.
Winds of April (1965)

BAHR, Jerome
Holes in the Wall: Portraits
    of the Cold War (1970)

BAILEY, Charles W., 2nd, and
    Fletcher Knebel
Seven Days in May (1962)

BAILEY, Henry Christopher
Barry Leroy (1919)

BAKER, Elliott
Pocock & Pitt (1971)

BAKER, William Howard
Brussels Dossier
Departure Deferred (1965)
Dirty Game (1967)
Every Man an Enemy (1966)
Hero Game (1965)
Judas Diary (1969)
Night of the Wolf (1966)
Rape of Berlin
Storm Over Rockall (1965)
Strike North
Traitor! (1967)

BALCHIN, Nigel Marlin
Sort of Traitor (1956)

BALL, John
First Team (1971)

BALLARD, K. G.
Gauge of Deception (1963)

BALLINGER, William Sanborn
Spy at Angkor Wat (1965)
Spy in the Java Sea (1966)
Spy in the Jungle (1965)

BALZAC, Honore de
The Chouans (1829, 1st English
    ed., 1908)

BARLOW, James
Hour of Maximum Danger (1963)
One Half of the World (1957)
The Patriots (1960)
The Protagonists (1956)

BARON, Stanley Wade
End of the Line (1956)

BARR, Robert
Dark Island (1973)

BARRON, Donald
Man Who Was There (1969)
Zilov Bombs (1963)

BARTER, John P.
Secret Place (1952)

BASS, Milton R.
Force Red (1970)

BASSETT, James
Sky Suspended (1968)

BEARE, George
Bee Sting Deal (1972)
Bloody Sun at Noon (1970)
Very Breath of Hell (1971)

BEATY, David
Temple Tree (1971)

BEEDING, Francis
Eleven Were Brave (1941)

BEGBIE, Garstein
Trailing Death: A Romance of
    the Secret Service (1932)

BEHN, Noel
Kremlin Letter (1966)
The Shadowboxer (1969)

BELL, Josephine
The Alien (1964)

BELLAH, James, and Robert G.
    Stimson
Avenger Tapes (1971)

BENCHLEY, Nathaniel
Catch a Falling Spy (1963)
Wake of the Icarus (1969)

BENDER, W., Jr.
Tokyo Intrigue

BENNETT, Arnold
T. Racksole and Daughert
    (1902) (English Title: Grand
    Babylon Hotel)

BENNETT, Kem
Dangerous Knowledge (1957)
Devil's Current (1953)
Rococo and a Bottle of Rum
    (1947)

BENTLEY, John
Pattern for Perfidy (1946)

BENTLEY, Nicholas Clerihew
Floating Dutchman (1951)
Gammon and Espionage (1938)

Third Party Risk (1948)
Tongue-Tied Canary (1949)

BENTON, Kenneth
Spy in Chancery (1973)
Twenty-Fourth Level (1970)

BENZONI, Juliet
Marianne (1970)
Marianne #2: The Eagle and
   the Nightingale (1972)

BERNARD, Jay
Burning Fuse (1970)

BERNARD, Robert
Illegal Entry (1972)

BESTE, Raymond Vernon
The Moonbeams (1961) (English
   Title: Faith Has No
   Country)
Repeat the Instructions (1967)
Seeds of Destruction (1964)

BETTERIDGE, Don
Balkan Spy (1942)
Case of the Berlin Spy (1954)
Contact Man (1960)
Death to the Fifth Column (1939)
Death Under Gibraltar (1938)
Dictator's Destiny (1945)
Double Menace (1954)
Escape of General Gerard (1943)
German Spy (1936)
Gibraltar Conspiracy (1933)
Lady Doctor--Woman Spy (1937)
Moscow Murder (1948)
Not Single Spies (1951)
Package Holiday Spy Case (1962)
Potsdam Murder Plot (1947)
Scotland Yard Alibi
Second Front--First Spy (1944)
Secret Servant (1935)
Secret Weapon (1941)
Siegfried Spy (1940)
Spies Left (1950)
Spies of Peenemunde (1958)
The Spy (1935)
Spy Catchers (1945)
Spy--Counter Spy (1933)
Spy in the Brown Derby (1945)

BICKERS, R. T.
Hellions (1968)
Scent of Mayhem (1968)

BINGHAM, John Michael Ward
Double Agent (1967)

BLACK, Gavin
Bitter Tea (1973)
Time of Pirates (1971)
Wind of Death (1967)

BLACK, Lionel
Bait
Chance to Die
Lady Is a Spy (1967) (English
   Title: Two Ladies in Verona)

BLACKBURN, John
Broken Boy (1962)
Flame and the Wind (1967)
Packed for Murder (1964) (Eng-
   lish Title: Colonel Bogus)
Sour Apple Tree (1958)
Young Man from Lima (1968)

BLACKER, Irwin R.
Chain of Command (1965)
Kilroy Gambit (1960)
Search and Destroy (1966)
To Hell in a Basket (1967)

BLAKE, Nicholas
Whisper in the Gloom (1954)

BLANKFORT, Michael
Behold the Fire (1965)
Widow Makers (1946)

BLASCO IBAÑEZ, Vincente
Mare Nostrum (1919)

BLOODWORTH, Dennis
Any Number Can Play (1973)

BLUM, Ralph
Simultaneous Man (1970)

BLYTH, James
Napoleon Decrees (1914)

BOLAND, John
Counterpol (1963)

Counterpol in Paris (1964)
Disposal Unit (1966)
Operation Red Carpet (1959)
(See also Series 23)

BOLTON, John
Spy Hunters (1940)

BORDEN, Mary
Catspaw (1950)

BOTTOME, Phyllis
Lifeline (1946)

BOULLE, Pierre
Ears of the Jungle (1972)
The Executioner (1961)
Noble Profession (1960)
Not the Glory (1955)

BOURNE, Peter
Fall of the Eagle (1967)

BOWEN, Elizabeth
Heat of the Day (1949)

BOYLE, Kay
Avalanche (1944)

BRADDON, George
Death Doubles Death (1952)
Death in the Picture (1951)
Death Rings No Bell (1951)
Time Off for Death (1952)

BRAIN, L.
It's a Free Country (1966)

BRAND, Max
Phantom Spy (1973)

BRAUN, M. G.
Apostles of Violence (1962)
Operation Atlantic (1964)
Operation Jealousy (1966)
That Girl from Istanbul (1966)

BRETT, J. M.
Cargo of Spent Evil (1966)

BRETT, Michael
Diecast (1963)

BRIDGE, Ann
Dangerous Islands (1963)
Dark Moment (1952)
Emergency in the Pyrenees (1965)
Episode at Toledo (1966)
Julia Involved (1962)
Lighthearted Quest (1956)
Malady in Madeira (1969)
Numbered Account (1960)
Portuguese Escape (1958)
Singing Waters (1946)
Tightening String (1962)

BRIDGES, Victor
Quite Like Old Days (1949)

BRINTON, Henry
Death to Windward (1942)
Purple Six (1962)

BRISTOW, Gwen
Celia Garth (1954)

BRITTAIN, Dan
The Godmakers

BROGAN, D. W.
Stop on the Green Light (1942)

BROGAN, James
Cummings Report (1958)

BROWN, Edward
Penny to Spend (1965)
Vandersley (1969)

BRUCE, Jean
Cold Spell (1967)
Dead Silence (1967)
Deep Freeze (1966)
Double Take (1964)
Flash Point (1965)
High Treason (1967)
Hot-Line (1967)
Last Quarter Hour (1955)
Live Wire (1966)
Photo Finish (1965)
Pole Reaction (1966)
Shock Tactics (1965)
Short Wave (1964)
Soft Sell (1965)
Strip Tease (1968)

Top Secret (1967)
Trouble in Tokyo (1958)

BRUNNER, John
Wrong End of Time (1971)

BRYAN, John
Contessa Came Too (1957)
Man Who Came Back (1959)

BRYDON, S.
Penman's Progress (1969)

BUCHAN, John
Free Fishers (1934)
Greenmantle (1915)
Huntingtower (1922)
Mr. Standfast (1919)
Prince of the Captivity (1933)
39 Steps (1915)

BUCHANAN, James David
The Professional (1972)

BUCHARD, Robert
Thirty Seconds Over New York
  (1969)

BURGESS, Anthony
Tremor of Intent (1966)

BUTLER, Leslie
Recover or Kill (1965)

BUTLER, Richard
More Dangerous Than the
  Moon (1968)

BUTLER, William
Mr. Three (1964)
Spying at the Fountain of Youth
  (1969)

CAIDIN, Martin
Last Fathom (1967)
Mendelev Conspiracy (1969)
(See also Series 61)

CAILLOU, Alan
Alien Virus (1957)
Journey to Orassia (1966)

Marseilles (1964)
Mindanao Pearl (1959)
The Plotter (1960)
Rogue's Gambit (1955)
Swamp Fire (1973)
Who'll Buy My Evil (1966)
(See also Series 56)

CAIN, Cabot
(See Series 7)

CAIN, James Mallahan
Past All Dishonor (1946)

CALLAS, Theo
City of Kites (1955)

CALLISON, Brian
Dawn Attack (1973)
Flock of Ships (1970)
Plague of Sailors (1971)

CANNING, Victor
Bird of Prey (1931) (English
  Title: Venetian Bird)
Black Flamingo (1962)
Burning Eye (1960)
Chasm (1947)
Delivery of Furies (1961)
Doubled in Diamonds (1966)
Firecrest (1972)
Forrest of Eyes (1950)
Girl from the "Turkish Slave"
  (1963)
Golden Salamander (1949)
Handful of Silver (1954) (alt.
  title: Castle Minerva)
House of the Seven Flies (1932)
Limbo Line (1963)
Man from the "Turkish Slave"
  (1954)
Manasco Road (1957)
Melting Man (1969)
Panther's Moon (1948)
Python Project (1967)
Queen's Pawn (1970)
Rainbird Pattern (1973)
Scorpio Letters (1964)
Spy Hung (1971)
Twist of the Knife (1955) (Eng-
  lish Title: His Bones Are
  Coral)

Victor (1972)
Whip Hand (1965)

CARGILL, Leslie
Gestapo Gauntlet (1939)
Man from the Rhine (1943)
Motley Menace (1949)

CARR, John Dickson
Captain Cut-Throat (1955)
Man Who Explained Miracles
    (1963) (2 stories)

CARSTAIRS, John Paddy
Concrete Kimono (1965)

CARTER, Nick
(See Series 52)

CARTER, Youngman
Mr. Campion's Farthing (1969)

CARTLAND, Barbara
Love Is an Eagle (1967)

CARVIC, Heron
(See Series 48)

CASSIDY, Bruce
Operation Goldkill--Code Name:
    Jericho (1967)

CATTO, Max
Banana Men (1967)

CHABER, M. E.
No Grave for March (1952)
So Dead the Rose (1960)
Splintered Man (1955)
Wild Midnight Falls (1968)

CHANCE, John Newton
Commission for Disaster (1964)
Death Under Desolate (1964)
Man In My Shoes (1952)
Night of the Full Moon (1950)

CHANNEL, A. P.
Arctic Spy (1962)

CHARLES, Robert
Arctic Assignment (1966)
Assassins for Peace (1967)

Dark Vendetta (1964)
Fourth Shadow (1966)
Stamboul Intrigue (1968)
Strikefast (1969)

CHASE, James Hadley
This Is for Real (1967)
You Have Yourself a Deal (1966)

CHESTER, Peter
The Traitors (1964)

CHEYNEY, Peter
Adventures of Julia (1954)
Can Ladies Kill? (1938)
Dark Bahama (1950) (alt. title:
    I'll Bring Her Back)
Dark Duet (1942) (alt. title:
    Counterspy Murders)
Dark Hero (1946) (alt. title:
    Case of the Dark Hero)
Dark Interlude (1947) (alt. title:
    Terrible Night)
Dark Street (1944)
Dark Wanton (1948)
Date After Dark (1946)
G Men at the Yard (1953)
Ladies Won't Wait (1951)
Lady, Behave! (1950)
Lady Beware (1950)
Lady in Green (1947)
Lady in Tears (1948)
Sinister Errand (1945)
Stars Are Dark (1943) (alt.
    title: London Spy Murders)
Unhappy Lady (1948)

CHILDERS, Robert Erskine
Riddle of the Sands (1903)

CHILDS, Marquise
Taint of Innocence (1967)

CHITTENDEN, Frank Albert
Four Cornered Story (1951)

CHRISTIE, Agatha
Death on the Nile (1937)
Man in the Brown Suit (1924)
Murder in Mesopotamia (1936)
Murder in the Calais Coach
    (1934) (alt. title: Murder on
    the Orient Express)

N or M? (1941)
Passenger to Frankfurt (1970)
Secret Adversary (1922)
So Many Steps to Death (1954)
  (English Title: Destination
  Unknown)
They Came to Baghdad (1951)

CLARE, John
Passionate Invaders (1965)

CLARKE, Jonathan
Peter and the Lovers (1972)

CLEARY, Jon
Fall of an Eagle (1964)
Forests of the Night (1970)
High Commissioner (1966)
Long Pursuit (1967)
North from Thursday (1969)
Pulse of Danger (1966)
Season of Doubt (1968)

CLEEVE, Brian Talbot
Death of a Bitter Englishman
  (1967)
Escape from Prague (1970)
Vote X for Treason (1964) (alt.
  title: Counterspy)

CLEMENT, Henry
Darling Lili (1970)

CLEMENTS, Eileen Helen
Chair-Lift (1954)
Honey for the Marshall (1960)
Other Island (1956)
Uncommon Cold (1958)

CLIFFORD, Francis
All Men Are Lonely Now (1967)
Another Way of Dying (1969)
Blind Side (1971)
Naked Runner (1966)

CLIFT, Denison Halley
Spy in the Room (1944)

CLOUSTON, Joseph Storer
Beastmark the Spy (1941)
Man from the Clouds (1937)
Simon (1919)

Spy in Black (1917)
(See also Series 39)

COLE, Burt
Funco File (1969)

COLES, Manning
Alias Uncle Hugo (1952)
All That Glitters (1954) (English
  Title: Not for Export)
Among Those Absent (1948)
Basle Express (1956)
Birdwatcher's Quarry (1956)
Brief Candles (1954)
Come and Go (1954)
Concrete Crime (1962) (English
  Title: Crime in Concrete)
Dangerous By Nature (1950)
Death of an Ambassador (1957)
Diamonds to Amsterdam (1949)
Drink to Yesterday (1941)
Duty Free (1959)
Far Traveler (1956)
Fifth Man (1946)
Green Hazard (1945)
Happy Returns (1955) (English
  Title: Family Matter)
House at Pluck's Gutter (1963)
Knife to the Juggler (1953) (alt.
  title: Vengeance Man)
Let the Tiger Die (1947)
Man in the Green Hat (1955)
Night Train to Paris (1952)
No Entry (1958)
Not Negotiable (1949)
Nothing to Declare (1960)
Now or Never (1951)
Search for a Sultan (1961)
They Tell No Tales (1941)
This Fortress (1941)
Three Beans (1957)
Toast for Tomorrow (1940)
  (English Title: Pray Silence)
With Intent to Deceive (1947)
  (English Title: Brother for
  Hugh)
Without Lawful Authority (1943)

COLLINGWOOD, Charles
The Defector (1970)

CONNABLE, Alfred
Twelve Trains to Babylon (1971)

CONNELL, Vivian
Monte Carlo Mission (1954)

CONNELLY, Marc
Souvenir from Qam (1965)

CONRAD, Joseph
Secret Agent (1906)

CONWAY, Troy
(see Series 12)

COOKE, David C.
c/o American Embassy (1967)
14th Agent (1967)

COONEY, Michael
Doomsday England (1968)

COOPER, Brian
Van Langeran Girl (1960)

COOPER, James Fenimore
The Spy (1821)

COPP, De Witt
Pursuit of Agent M (1961)
Radius of Action (1961)

CORBETT, James
Agent No. 5 (1945)

CORDELL, Alexander
Deadly Eurasian (1967)

CORLEY, Edwin
Jesus Factor (1970)

CORRIGAN, Mark
Big Squeeze (1955)
Girl from Moscow (1959)
Lady from Tokyo (1961)
Lady of China Street (1952)
Madame Sly (1951)
Menace in Siam (1959)
Shanghai Jezebel (1951)
Sin of Hong Kong (1957)
Singapore Downbeat (1959)
Sydney for Sin (1956)

CORY, Desmond
Dead Man Falling (1953)
Even If You Run (1972)

Hammerhead (1964) (alt. title:
   Shockwave)
Intrigue (1954)
Name of the Game Is Death
   (1964)
Phoenix Sings (1955)
Pilgrim at the Gate (1958)
Pilgrim on the Island (1961)
Secret Ministry (1951)
Stranglehold (1961)
This Traitor, Death (1952)
Undertow (1962)
(See also Series 35)

COTLER, Gordon
Bottletop Affair (1959)
The Cipher (1961)
Mission in Black (1967)

COULTER, Stephen
Embassy (1969)
Off-Shore (1966)
Stranger Called the Blues (1968)
   (alt. title: Players in a Dark
   Game)
Threshold (1964)

CRABB, Alfred Leland
Mockingbird Song at Chicka-
   mauga (1949)

CRAIG, David
Contact Lost (1970)

CRAIG, William
Tashkent Crisis (1971)
Ultimatum (1970)

CREASEY, John
Days of Danger (1937)
Dead or Alive (1951)
Death by Night (1940)
Enemy Within (1950)
Go Away Death (1941)
Island of Peril (1940)
Kind of Prisoner (1954)
The Menace (1938)
Murder Must Wait (1939)
Panic! (1939)
Peril Ahead (1946)
Sabotage (1941)
Touch of Death (1954)
(See also Series 18)

CROFT-COOKE, Rupert
Barbary Night (1958)

CROSSEN, Kendall Foster
Big Dive (1958)
Tortured Path (1957)

CUNNINGHAM, E. V.
Assassin Who Gave Up His Gun
 (1969)

DA CRUZ, Daniel
Vulcan's Hammer (1967)

DANIEL, Roland
Amber Eyes (1935)
Crimson Shadow (1935)
Deadly Mission (1962)
Double-Crossing Traitor (1959)
Dragon's Claw (1934)
Female Spy (1966)
Green Jade God (1932)
Lady Turned Traitor (1961)
Man Who Sold Secrets (1948)
The Prisoner (1965)
Return of Wu Fang (1937)
Secret Hans (1936)
Secret Service Girl (1966)
Slant Eye (1940)
Snake Face (1936)
Society of the Spiders (1928)
Son of Wu Fang (1935)
Spencer Blair, G-Man (1949)
Undercover Girl (1951)
Wu Fang (1929)
Wu Fang's Revenge (1934)
Yellow Devil (1932)

DANIELS, Norman
Baron of Hong Kong (1967)
Deadly Game (1959)
Hunt Club (1964)
Operation "K" (1965)
Operation "N" (1966)
Operation "T" (1967)
Operation "VC" (1967)
Overkill (1964)
Secret War (1964)
Spy Ghost (1965)
Spy Hunt (1961)

DARK, James
(See Series 45)

DARK, Rex
Channing Affair (1937)
Invisible Hand (1937)
Spy 222 (1940)
Uranian Jewel Case (1939)

DAVEY, Jocelyn
Capitol Offense (1956) (English
 Title: Undoubted Dead)
Killing in Hats (1965)
Naked Villany (1958)
Touch of Stagefright (1960)

DAVIDSON, B.
Andrassy Affair (1966)
Golden Horn

DAVIDSON, Lionel
Menorah Men (1966)
Night of Wenceslas (1960)
Rose of Tibet (1962)

DAVIS, Dorothy Salisbury
Enemy and Brother (1967)

DAVIS, Franklin M.
Kiss the Tiger (1961)
Naked and the Lost (1954)
Secret: Hong Kong (1962)

DAVIS, Howard Charles
Dangerous Twin (1957)
Murder Starts from Fishguard
 (1966)
Renegade from Russia (1959)
Third Assassin (1959)
Waxworks Spies (1962)

DAVIS, Maggie
Rommel's Gold (1971)

DAVISON, Gilderoy
Chessboard Spy
Nest of Spies (1968)
Prince of Spies (1932)
Satan's Satellite (1945)
Spy Who Swapped Shoes
Traitor Unmasked (1932)

DAWSON, James
Hell Gate (1967)

DAY, Gina
Tell No Tales (1967)

DEANE, Norman
Incense of Death (1954)
(See also Series 62)

DEELEY, R.
King's Man (1968)

DEIGHTON, Len
Billion Dollar Brain (1966)
Expensive Place to Die (1967)
Funeral in Berlin (1964)
Horse Under Water (1963)
Ipcress File (1963)

DEKKER, Anthony
Temptation in a Private Zoo
    (1970)

DEKOBRA, Maurice
Chinese Puzzle (1956)
Honeymoon in Shanghai (1946)
    (alt. title: Shanghai Honey-
    moon)
Madonna of the Sleeping Cars
    (1927)
Man Who Died Twice (1954)
Operation Magali (1952)
Poison at Plessis (1953)

DEMBO, Samuel
Kalahari Kill (1964) (alt. title:
    Sands of Lilliput)

DERBY, Mark
Afraid of the Dart (1952) (Eng-
    lish Title: Malayan Rose)
Bad Step (1954) (English Title:
    Out of Asia Alive)
Big Water (1953)
Element of Risk (1952)
Five Nights in Singapore (1961)
Sunlit Ambush (1955)
Womanhunt (1959) (English Title:
    The Tigress)

DESMOND, Hugh
Silent Witness (1963)

DILNOT, George
Counter-Spy (1962)
Secret Service Man (1960)

DIMENT, Adam
Bang, Bang Birds (1968)
Dolly, Dolly Spy (1967)
Great Spy Race (1968)

DINES, M.
Operation-Deadline (1967)

DIPPER, Alan
Paradise Formula (1970)
Wave Hangs Dark (1969)

DOCTEROW, E. L.
Book of Daniel (1971)

DODGE, David
Hooligan (1969)

DOWNES, Donald
Easter Dinner (1960)

DRISCOLL, Peter
White Lie Assignment (1973)

DRUMMOND, Jane
Cable Car (1967)

DUFF, David
Traitor's Pass (1955)

DUNCAN, William Murdock
Cult of the Queer People (1949)

DUNNETT, Dorothy
Murder in Focus (1973)
Murder in the Round (1970)

DURBRIDGE, Francis
Other Man (1958)

DURRELL, Lawrence
White Eagles Over Serbia (1957)

DURSTON, P. E. H.
Mortissimo (1967)

EARLY, Charles
Tigers Are Hungry (1967)

EASTWOOD, James
Chinese Visitor (1965)
Diamonds Are Deadly (1970)
Little Dragon from Peking (1967)

EBERHART, Mignon Good
Wings of Fear (1945)

EDELMAN, Maurice
Call on Kuprin (1959)

EDEN, Dorothy
Waiting for Willa (1970)

EDEN, Matthew
Conquest Before Autumn (1973)
Flight of Hawks (1970)
Gilt-Edged Traitor (1972)

EDWARDS, Anne
Miklos Alexandrovitch Is
    Missing! (1970)

EDWARDS, Paul
(See Series 34)

EGLETON, Clive
Last Post for a Partisan (1971)
Judas Mandate (1972)
Piece of Resistance (1970)

EHRLICH, Jack
The Drowning (1970)

ELLIN, Stanley
House of Cards (1967)

EVANS, Alfred John
All's Fair on Lake Gerda (1958)
V2 Expert (1956)

EVANS, Kenneth
Oasis of Fear (1968)

EVERETT, Bridget
Cold Front (1973)

FADIMAN, Edwin, Jr.
Who Will Watch the Watchers
    (1970)

FALKIRK, Richard
Twisted Wire (1971)

FALLON, Martin
Midnight Never Comes (1966)

FEARING, Kenneth
Clark Gifford's Body (1942)

FELIX, Christopher, and George
    Martin
Three-Cornered Cover (1972)

FENNELL, George
Blood Patrol
Killer Patrol

FENNERTON, William
Lucifer Cell (1968)

FERGUSON, John Alexander
Stealthy Terror (1918)

FIRTH, Anthony
Tall, Balding and Thirty-Five
    (1966)

FISH, Robert L.
Always Kill a Stranger (1967)
Assassination Bureau (1963)
Brazilian Sleigh Ride (1965)
Diamond Bubble (1965)
Hochmann Miniatures (1967)
Isle of the Snakes (1963)
Shrunken Head (1965)
Whirligig (1970)

FISHER, Norman
Walk at a Steady Pace (1971)

FITZGERALD, Kevin
Throne of Bayonets (1952)

FLEISCHMAN, A. S.
Counterspy Express (1954)
Look Behind You, Lady (1963)
Malay Woman (1954)
Shanghai Flame (1951)
Venetian Blonde (1963)

FLEMING, Ian
(See Series 30)

FLEMING, Nichol
Counter Paradise (1969)

FLETCHER, Lucille
Blindfold (1960)

FLOOD, Charles Bracelen
Trouble at the Top (1972)

FOLEY, Rae
Man in the Shadows (1953)

FORBES, Colin
Palermo Affair (1972)

FORBES, Donald
Eleventh Hour (1955)

FORD, Hillary
Bella on the Roof (1965)

FORREST, David
And to My Nephew I Leave the
    Island What I Won Off Fatty
    Horgan in a Poker Game
    (1969)

FORRESTER, Larry
Girl Called Fathom (1967)

FORSYTE, Charles
Diplomatic Death (1961)
Dive into Danger (1962) (alt.
    title: Diving Death)
Double Death (1965)

FORSYTHE, Frederick
Day of the Jackel (1971)
Odessa File (1972)

FOTHERBY, T. F.
Decoy Be Damned

FOWLES, Anthony
Double Feature (1973)

FOX, James M.
Code Three (1953)
No Dark Crusade (1954)

FRANK, Pat
Affair of State (1948)

Forbidden Area (1956)
Seven Days to Never (1957)

FRANKAU, Pamela, with Diana
    Raymond
Colonel Blessington (1969)

FRANKLIN, Charles
Cocktails with a Stranger (1947)
Death in the East (1967)
Escape to Death (1951)
Exit Without Permit (1946)

FRANKLIN, Steve
The Malcontents (1970)

FRAYN, Michael
Russian Interpreter (1966)

FREDE, Richard
Coming Out Party (1969)

FREDMAN, John
Fourth Agency (1968)

FREEMANTLE, Brian
Goodbye to an Old Friend (1973)

FRENCH, Richard P.
Spy Is Forever (1970)

FREUND, Philip
The Spymaster (1965)

FRIZZEL, Bernard
Grand Defiance (1972)

FROST, Frederick
Bamboo Whistle (1937)
Secret Agent Number One (1936)
Spy Meets Spy (1937)

FRY, Pete
Black Beret (1959)
Bright Green Wastecoat (1967)
Gray Sombrero (1959)
Paint-Stained Flannels (1966)
Purple Dressing Gown (1960)
Red Stockings (1962)
Scarlet Cloak (1958)
Thick Blue Sweater (1964)
Yellow Trousers (1963)

FULLERTON, Alexander
Bury the Past (1954)

GADNEY, Reg
Somewhere in England (1972)

GAINES, Robert
Against the Public Interest
    (1959)
Invisible Evil (1963)

GAINHAM, Sarah
Appointment in Vienna (1957)
    (English Title: Mythmaker)
Cold Dark Night (1958)
Place in the Country (1969)
Silent Hostage (1960)
Stone Roses (1959)
Time Right Deadly (1956)

GALLAHUE, John
The Jesuit (1973)

GALLERY, Daniel V.
The Brink

GALWAY, Robert Connington
(See Series 58)

GARDNER, John
(See Series 6)

GARFIELD, Brian
Deep Cover (1971)
Line of Succession (1972)

GARFORTH, John
(See Series 3)

GARNER, William
Deep Deep Freeze (1968)
The Manipulators (1970)
Overkill (1966)
Us or Them War (1969)

GARNETT, Mrs. Robert
    Singleton
Infamous John Friend (1909)

GARTH, David
Three Roads to a Star (1955)

GARVE, Andrew
Ascent of D-13 (1968)
Ashes of Loda (1964)
Hero for Leanda (1952)
Hole in the Ground (1952)
Murder Through a Looking Glass
    (1950) (English Title: Murder
    in Moscow)

GARVIN, Richard M. , and Ed-
    mund G. Addeo
Fortrac Conspiracy (1968)
Talbot Agreement (1968)

GASK, Arthur
Master Spy (1937)
Night and Fog (1951)
Vaults of Blackarden Castle
    (1950)

GASKIN, Catherine
File on Devlin (1965)

GATE, Natalie
Hush Hush Johnson (1967)

GAVIN, Catherine
Devil in Harbour (1968)

GEER, Andrew
Sea Chase (1948)

GEORGE, Jonathan
Kill Day (1970)

GEORGE, Peter
Pattern of Death (1954)

GERARD, Francis
Envoy of the Emperor (1951)
Transparent Traitor (1930)

GERRARE, Wirt
Exploits of Jo Salis, a British
    Spy (1905)
Secret Agent in Port Arthur
    (1905)

GIBBS, George
Yellow Dove (1915) (alt. title:
    Great Deception)

GIBBS-SMITH, Charles Harvard
Caroline Affair (1955) (alt. title:
    Operation Caroline)
Escape and Be Secret (1957)

GILBERT, Michael Francis
Be Shot for Sixpence (1956)
Game Without Rules (1967)
Overdrive (1967)

GILLIGAN, Edmund
Gaunt Woman (1943)

GILMAN, Dorothy
Uncertain Voyage (1967)
(See also Series 50)

GILMAN, William
Spy Trap (1944)

GLASKIN, Gerald M.
Man Who Didn't Count (1967)

GOBLE, Neil
Condition Green: Tokyo (1966)

GODEY, John
Man in Question (1951)

GODWIN, F.
Mission to Samarkind (1964)

GOLDBERG, Marshall
Karamanov Equations (1972)

GOLDMAN, James
Waldorf (1966)

GOODCHILD, George
Q33 (1933)
Q33--Spy Catcher (1937)

GOODFIELD, Jane
Courier to Peking (1973)

GORDON, Donald
Golden Oyster (1968)

GORKI, Maxim
Life of a Useless Man (1907)

GOULART, Ron
Sword Swallower (1968)

GRAEME, Bruce
Drums Beat Red (1963)
Madame Spy (1935)
(See also Series 4)

GRAEME, Roderic
(See Series 5)

GRAHAM, Anthony
Behind the Arras (1964)
The Veetols (1965)

GRAHAM, Winston
Greek Fire (1958)
Night Journey (1968)

GRANT, Richard
Case of the Baronet's Memoirs
    (1960)
Circle of Death (1952)

GRAY, Rod
(See Series 37)

GRAYSON, Richard
(See Series 26)

GREEN, Frederick Lawrence
Ambush for the Hunter (1952)

GREEN, Gerald
Faking It (1972)

GREEN, William M.
Spencer's Bag (1972)

GREENE, Graham
Confidential Agent (1939)
Ministry of Fear (1943)
Orient Express (1933) (English
    Title: Stamboul Train)
Our Man in Havana (1958)
Quiet American (1953)
Third Man (1950)
This Gun for Hire (1936)

GREENE, Harris
Cancelled Accounts (1973)

GRIERSON, Francis Durham
Blind Frog (1955)

GRISWOLD, George
Checkmate by the Colonel (1952)
Gambit for Mr. Groode (1952)
Pinned Man (1942)
Red Pawns (1954)

GRUBER, Frank
Little Hercules (1965)
Twilight Men (1967)

GULYASHKI, A.
Zakhov Mission (1969)

GUNN, Neil Miller
Lost Chart (1949)

GUNN, Victor
Dead Man's Warning (1949)

GUTTERIDGE, Lindsay
Cold War in a Country Garden
    (1971)

HABE, Hans
Devil's Agent (1958) (English
    Title: Agent of the Devil)

HACKFORTH-JONES, Frank
    Gilbert
Fish Out of Water (1954)

HAGGARD, William
Closed Circuit (1960)
The Protectors (1972)
Telemann Touch (1958)
(See also Series 9)

HAIG, Alec
Flight from Montego Bay (1972)
Sign On for Tokyo (1969)

HALL, Adam
Ninth Directive (1967)
Quiller Memorandum (1965)
    (English Title: Berlin
    Memorandum)
Rook's Gambit (1972)
Striker Portfolio (1969)
Warsaw Document (1971)

HALL, Andrew
Frost (1967)

Man in Aspic (1965)

HALL, Patrick
Power Sellers (1969)

HALL, Roger
19. (1970)

HALLIDAY, Leonard
Devil's Door (1959)
Smiling Spider (1955)
Top Secret (1957)

HAMILTON, Donald B.
Date with Darkness (1947)
Murder Twice Told (1947)
Steel Mirror (1948)
(See also Series 46)

HARDY, Lindsay
Faceless Ones (1956)
Nightshade Ring (1954)

HARDY, Ronald
Face of Jalanath (1973)

HARLING, Robert
Endless Colonnade (1958)
Enormous Shadow (1955)

HARMAN, Neal
Case of the Wounded Mastiff
    (1947)
Death and the Archdeacon (1947)

HARRINGTON, William
Jupiter Crisis (1971)

HARRISON, Harry
Daleth Effect (1970)
Montezuma's Revenge (1972)

HART, Carolyn G.
Spy Track (1970)

HART-DAVIS, Duff
Gold Trackers (1970)

HARVESTER, Simon
Arrival in Suspicion (1953)
Bamboo Screen (1955)
Breastplate for Aaron (1949)
Cat's Cradle (1952)

Chinese Hammer (1960)
Copper Butterfly (1957)
Delay in Danger (1954)
Dragon Road (1956)
Epitaph for Lemmings (1943)
Flight in Darkness (1965)
Flying Horse (1964)
Golden Fear (1957)
Hour Before Zero (1960)
Lantern for Diogenes (1947)
Let Them Pray (1942)
Lucifer at Sunset (1959)
Maybe a Trumpet (1945)
Moonstone Jungle (1961)
Obols for Charon (1951)
Paradise Men (1956)
Shadows in a Hidden Land
   (1966)
Sheep May Safely Graze (1950)
Spider's Web (1953)
Tiger in the North (1963)
Traitor's Gate (1952)
Troika (1962)
Vessels May Carry Explosives
   (1951)
Whatsoever Things Are True
   (1947)
Witch Hunt (1951)
Yesterday Walkers (1958)
(See also Series 19)

HARWOOD, Ronald
Guilt Merchants (1969)

HAWTHORNE, John
None of Us Cared for Kate
   (1968)

HAYES, Roy
Hungarian Game (1973)

HAYLES, Kenneth
Purple Sheba (1959)

HEATER, Basil
Naked Island (1968)

HEBDEN, Mark
Errant Knights (1968)
The Eyewitness (1967)
Killer for the Chairman (1972)
Mask of Violence (1970)

HECKSTALL-SMITH, Anthony
Men with Yellow Shoes (1958)

HENDERSON, James
Copperhead (1971)

HEPPELL, B.
Hidden Flame (1965)

HERMAN, Walter
Operation Intrigue (1956)

HERRON, Shaun
Hound and the Fox and the
   Harper (1970)
Miro (1969)
Through the Dark and Hairy
   Wood (1972)

HESKY, Olga
Time for Treason (1968)

HILL, Vincent
Cunning Enemy (1957)

HOBSON, Francis
Death on a Back Bench (1959)

HOCKING, Mary
Ask No Questions (1967)

HODDER-WILLIAMS, Christopher
Egg-Shaped Thing (1967)

HODGE, Jane Aiken
Watch the Wall, My Darling
   (1966)
Winding Stair (1969)

HOFFENBERG, Jack
Thunder at Dawn (1965)

HOLLY, J. Hunter
(See Series 44, nos. 10, 16)

HONE, Joseph
Private Sector (1972)

HONIG, Louis
For Your Eyes Only: Read
   and Destroy (1972)

HOPE, Fielding
Marie Arnaud, Spy (1964)

HOPKINS, Joseph G. E.
Retreat and Recall (1966)

HORLER, Sidney
Dark Danger (1945)
Dark Journey (1938)
Enemy Within the Gates (1940)
Death of a Spy (1953)
High Game (1950)
High Hazard (1943)
Man Who Died Twice (1939)
Man Who Used Perfume (1941)
Man Who Walked with Death
    (1931)
My Lady Dangerous (1932)
Nighthawk Mops Up (1944)
Secret Service Man (1930)
The Spy (1931)
Terror on Tiptoe (1939)
These Men and Women (1931)
They Thought He Was Dead
    (1949)
Tiger Standish Steps On It
    (1940)
The Traitor (1936)

HOSSENT, Harry
Fear Business (1967)
Memory of Treason (1963)
No End to Fear (1959)
Run for Your Death (1966)
Spies Die at Dawn (1958)
Spies Have No Friends (1966)

HOSTOVSKY, Egon
Midnight Patient (1954)

HOTCHNER, A. E.
Treasure (1970)

HOUGH, Stanley Bennett
Mission in Guemo (1953)

HOUSEHOLD, Geoffrey
Arabesque (1948)
Doom's Caravan (1971)
Fellow Passenger (1955) (alt.
    title: Brides of Solomon)
Olura (1965)
Rogue Male (1939)

Rough Shoot (1951)
Time to Kill (1951)
Watcher in the Shadows (1951)

HOWARD, Hartley
Department K (1970)
Eye of the Hurricane (1968)

HOWARTH, David
Across to Norway (1952)
Thieves' Hole (1954)

HOWE, George L.
Call It Treason (1949)

HOYLE, Frederic
Ossian's Ride (1959)

HUGGINS, Roy
Appointment with Fear

HUGHES, Dorothy B.
Fallen Sparrow (1942)

HUMES, Harold Louis
Underground City (1958)

HUNTER, Jack D.
Expendable Spy (1965)
One of Us Works for Them
    (1967)
Spies, Inc. (1969)

HURD, Douglas
Truth Game (1973)

HURD, Douglas, and Andrew
    Osmond
Smile on the Face of the Tiger
    (1970)

HYLAND, Henry Stanley
Green Grow the Tresses-O
    (1959)
Top Bloody Secret (1969)
Who Goes Hang? (1958)

IAMS, Jack
Body Missed the Boat (1947)
Into Thin Air (1952)
Shot of Murder (1950)

IGGALDEN, John
Breakthrough (1964)

INCHBALD, Ralph
Colonel Paternoster (1951)

INNES, Hammond
Angry Mountain (1950)
Levkas Man (1971)
Sabotage Broadcase (1938)
Trojan Horse (1940)

INNES, Michael
Hare Sitting Up (1959)
Man from the Sea (1955)
Secret Vanguard (1940)

JACOBS, Thomas Curtis Hicks
Brother Spy (1940)
Danger Money (1963)
Documents of Murder (1931)
   (English Title: Bronkhurst
   Case)
Elusive Mr. Drago (1954)
Target for Terror (1961)
Tattooed Man (1961)
Traitor Spy (1939)
Woman Who Waited (1954)

JAKES, John W.
Night for Treason (1956)

JAMES, John
Seventeen of Leyden: A Frolic
   Through This Vale of Tears
   (1970)

JAMES, Leigh
Capitol Hill Affair (1968)
Chameleon File (1967)
Pushbutton Spy (1970)

JAMESON, Storm
Before the Crossing (1947)

JASON, Stuart
Kill Quick or Die (1971)

JAY, Charlotte
Arms for Adonis (1960)
Beat Not the Bones (1952)
Brink of Silence (1956) (English

Title: Feast of the Dead)
Yellow Turban (1955)

JAY, Simon
Sleepers Can Kill (1968)

JEFFRIES, Ian
It Wasn't Men (1961)

JENKINS, Geoffrey
Grue of Ice (1962) (alt. title:
   Disappearing Island)
Hunter, Killer (1967)
River of Diamonds (1964)
Twist of Sand (1959)

JOHN, Owen
Beam of Black Light (1968)
Dead on Time (1969)
The Disinformer (1967)
Sabotage (1973)
Shadow in the Sea (1972)
Thirty Days Hath September
   (1966)

JOHNSON, James L.
(See Series 8)

JOHNSON, Stanley
Presidential Plot

JOHNSTON, Ronald
The Stowaway (1966)

JOHNSTON, William
(See Series 47)

JONES, Bradshaw
Crooked Phoenix (1963)
Embers of Hate (1966)
Layers of Deceit (1970)
Private Vendetta (1964)
Tiger from the Shadows (1963)

JONES, Philip
Month of the Pearl (1965)

JOSEPH, George
Curtain Has Lace Fingers (1954)

KAINEN, Ray
Spy Who Came (and Came and
   Came) (1969)

KANE, Harriet T.
Smiling Rebel (1955)

KANE, Henry
Laughter in the Alehouse (1968)

KAVANAGH, Paul
Such Men Are Dangerous (1969)

KAYE, Mary Margaret
Death Walked in Berlin (1955)
Death Walked in Cyprus (1956)
Death Walked in Kashmir (1953)

KELLAND, Clarence Budington
Death Keeps a Secret (1953)
   (alt. title: Spy and Counterspy)

KELLER, Beverly
Baghdad Defections (1973)

KELLY, Michael
Assault (1968)

KEMELMAN, Harry
Monday the Rabbi Took Off
   (1972)

KENNEDY, Milward
Escape to Quebec (1946)

KENYON, Michael
May You Die in Ireland (1965)

KIEFER, Warren
Lingale Case (1972)

KING, James Clifford
Place to Hide (1951)

KINSLEY, Peter
Pimpernel 60 (1968)

KIPLING, Rudyard
Kim (1901)

KIRK, Lydia
Man on the Raffles Verandah
   (1969)

KIRKBRIDE, Ronald
Secret Journey (1965)

KIRST, Hans Helmut
Last Card (1967)
Night of the Generals (1964)
No Fatherland (1970)

KLEIN, Alexander
Counterfeit Traitor (1958)

KNEBEL, Fletcher
Night of Camp David (1965)
Vanished (1968)
Zinzin Road (1966)

KNEBEL, Fletcher, and Charles
   W. Bailey, 2nd
Seven Days in May (1962)

KNIGHT, Leonard Alfred
Close the Frontier (1939)
High Treason (1954)
One Way Only (1956)

KNIGHT, Mallory T.
(See Series 43)

KRASLOW, David, and Robert
   S. Boyd
Certain Evil (1965)

KUNICZAK, W. S.
Sempenski Affair (1969)

KYLE, Duncan
Cage of Ice (1971)
Flight into Fear (1972)
Raft of Swords (1973)

LABORDE, Jean
Calina Olivia

LAFLIN, Jack
Reluctant Spy (1966)
Spy in White Gloves (1965)
Spy Who Didn't (1966)
Spy Who Loved America (1964)

LAMB, Antonia
Lady in the Shadows (1968)

LAMBERT, Derek
Angels in the Snow (1969)

Kites of War (1969)
Red House (1972)

LAMPARD, David
Present from Peking (1965)

LANCASTER, Bruce
No Bugles Tonight (1948)
Secret Road (1952)

LANDON, Christopher Gay
Flag in the City (1954)
Hornet's Nest (1956)
Mirror Room (1960)

LANZOL, Cesare
Serpent of Venice (1970)

LARANY, Daniel
Big Red Sun (1971)

LATHAM, Murray
Even from the Law (1946)

LATHEN, Emma
Murder Against the Grain (1967)

LAUMER, Keith
Star Treasure (1971)

LEASOR, James
(See Series 17)

LE CARRE, John
Call for the Dead (1961)
Looking Glass War (1965)
Murder of Quality (1962)
Small Town in Germany (1968)
Spy Who Came In from the
    Cold (1963)

LEES, Dan
Rainbow Conspiracy (1972)

LEGARET, Jean
Tightrope: A Novel of Intrigue
    in the Paris Underworld
    (1970)

LEJEUNE, Anthony
Crowded and Dangerous (1959)
Duel in the Shadows (1963)

LEONARD, Charles
Fanatic of Fez (1943)
Search for a Scientist (1947)
Secrets for Sale (1950)
Sinister Shelter (1950)
Treachery in Trieste (1951)

LEQUEUX, William Tufnell
Behind the German Lines (1917)
Cipher Six (1919)
Czar's Spy (1905)
Donovan of Whitehall (1917)
England's Peril (1899)
German Spy (1914)
Hushed Up at German Head-
    quarters (1917)
In Secret (1921)
The Intriguers (1920)
Luck of the Secret Service (1914)
Man from Downing Street (1904)
No. 7, Saville Square (1920)
No. 70, Berlin (1916)
Revelations of the Secret Ser-
    vice (1907)
Sant of the Secret Service
    (1918)
Secret Formula (1928)
Secrets of the Foreign Office,
    Describing the Doings of
    Duckworth Drew of the Secret
    Service (1903)
Spy Hunter (1916)
Stolen Statesman (1918)

LESLIE, Peter
Gay Deceiver (1967)
(See also Series 25, no. 3;
    44, nos. 7, 9, 14, 18)

LESLIE, Thane
Yu Malu, the Dragon Princess
    (1967)

LESTER, Frank
Bamboo Girl (1961)
Death of a Frightened Traveler
    (1959)

LEWELLEN, T. C.
Billikan Courier (1968)

LEWIS, Norman
Flight from a Dark Equator (1972)
Small War Made to Order (1966)

LIEBERMAN, Herbert
Eighth Square (1973)

LILLEY, Tom
Officer from Special Branch
(1971)

LITTELL, Robert
Defection of A. J. Lewinter
(1973)

LLEWELLYN, Richard
Bride of Israel, My Love (1973)
But We Didn't Get the Fox
(1969)
End of the Rug (1968)
Night Is a Child (1972)
White Horse to Banbury Cross
(1970)

LORAINE, Philip
Break in the Circle (1951)
Nightmare in Dublin (1964)
(English Title: Dublin
Nightmare)
W. I. L. One to Curtis (1967)

LUARD, Nicholas
Warm and Golden War (1967)

LUDLUM, Robert
Matlock Paper (1973)
Osterman Weekend (1972)
Scarlatti Inheritance (1970)

LYALL, Gavin
Midnight Plus One (1965)
Most Dangerous Game (1963)
Shooting Script (1966)
Venus with Pistol (1969)
Wrong Side of the Sky (1961)

MCCALL, Anthony
Holocaust (1967)
Operation Delta (1966)

MCCLOY, Helen
Goblin Market (1943)

Panic (1944)

MCCUTCHAN, Philip Donald
All-Purpose Bodies (1970)
Hopkinson and the Devil of Hate
(1961)
On Course for Danger (1959)
Poulter's Passage (1967)
Sladd's Evil (1965)
(See also Series 11)

MCCUTCHEON, Hugh
Red Sky at Night (1972)
Suddenly in Vienna (1963)

MCDANIEL, David
(See Series 44, nos. 4, 6, 8, 13,
15, 17)

MCDONALD, Philip
List of Adrian Messenger (1959)

MCDONELL, Archibald Gordon
Crew of the "Anaconda" (1940)
Intruder from the Sea (1953)

MCDOUGALL, Murdoch Christie
Soft As Silk (1957)

MCGERR, Patricia
Is There a Traitor in the House?
(1964)
Legacy of Danger (1970)

MCGIVERN, William Peter
Caper of the Golden Bulls (1966)
Caprifoil (1972)
Choice of Assassins (1963)
Odds Against Tomorrow
Seven File (1956)
Seven Lies South (1960)

MACGOVERN, James
Berlin Couriers (1960)

MACINNES, Helen
Above Suspicion (1941)
Assignment in Brittany (1942)
Decision at Delphi (1960)
Double Image (1967)
Friends and Lovers (1947)
Horizon (1945)
I and My True Love (1952)

Message from Malaga (1971)
Neither Five Nor Three (1951)
North from Rome (1958)
Pray for a Brave Heart (1955)
Rest and Be Thankful (1949)
Salzburg Connection (1968)
Venetian Affair (1963)
While Still We Live (1944)

MACINTYRE, John Thomas
Ashton Kirk, Secret Agent (1916)
Secret Agent: Ashton-Kirk
   (1921)

MACKENNA, Marthe
Arms and the Spy (1942)
Double Spy (1938)
Drums Never Beat (1936)
Hunt the Spy (1939)
Lancer Spy (1937)
Nightfighter Spy (1937)
Set a Spy (1937)
Spy in Khaki (1941)
Spy Was Born (1935)
Spying Blind (1939)
Three Spies for Glory (1950)

MACKENZIE, Andrew Carr
Grave Is Waiting (1957)
Shadow of a Spy (1958)

MACKENZIE, Sir Compton
Extremes Meet (1928)
Three Couriers (1929)
Water on the Brain (1951)

MACKENZIE, Donald
Double Exposure (1963)   (alt.
   title: I Spy)
Night Boat from Puerto Verda
   (1970)
Quiet Killer (1968)

MACKENZIE, Nigel
Fear Stalks the City (1965)
In Great Danger (1959)
Race Toward Death (1963)
Red Light (1950)

MACKINNON, Allan
Assignment in Iraq (1960)
House of Darkness (1947)
Map of Mistrust (1948)

Report from Argyll (1964)
Summons from Baghdad (1958)
   (English Title: Red-Winged
   Angel)

MACLEAN, Alistair
Bear Island (1971)
Caravan to Vaccares (1970)
Fear Is the Key (1961)
Force 10 from Navarone (1968)
Golden Rendezvous (1962)
Guns of Navarone (1964)
Ice Station Zebra (1963)
Night Without End (1967)
Puppet on a Chain (1969)
Secret Ways (1959) (English
   Title: Last Frontier)
When Eight Bells Toll (1967)
Where Eagles Dare (1967)

MCLEAVE, Hugh
Steel Balloon (1964)
Vodka on Ice (1969)

MCLEISH, Dougal
Traitor Game (1968)

MACLEOD, Alison
The Hireling (1968)

MACLEOD, Robert
Iron Sanctuary (1967)
Place of Mists (1970)
Cave of Bats (1966)

MACNEIL, Neil
Spy Catchers (1966)

MCNEILLY, Wilfred
No Way Out (1966)

MACSWAN, Norman
Inn with the Wooden Door (1958)

MACTYRE, Paul
Bar Sinister (1964)
Fish on a Hook (1963)

MACVICAR, Angus
Crouching Spy (1941)
Grey Shepherds (1964)

MADDOCK, Stephen
Date with a Spy (1941)
Overture to Trouble (1946)
Spies Along the Severn (1939)

MAGGIO, Joe
Company Man (1972)

MAGOWAN, Ronald
Funeral for a Commissar (1970)

MAINE, Charles Eric
Never Let Up (1964)

MAIR, George Brown
Death's Foot Forward (1963)
(See also Series 16)

MAKEPEACE, Ann
Mistaken Marriage (1958)

MALLOCH, Peter
Fly Away Death (1958)

MALTZ, Albert
Cross and the Arrow (1962)

MANCHESTER, William
Beard the Lion (1958) (alt. title:
    Cairo Intrigue)

MANDEL, Paul, and Sheila
    Mandel
Black Ship (1969)

MARCHETTI, Victor
Rope Dancer (1971)

MARIN, A. C.
Clash of Distant Thunder (1968)
Rise with the Wind (1969)
Storm of Spears (1971)

MARK, Ted
I Was a Teeny-Bopper for the
    C. I. A. (1967)
(See also Series 24, 40, and 41)

MARKHAM, Robin
(See Series 31)

MARLOWE, Dan J.
(See Series 20)

MARLOWE, Derek
Dandy in Aspic (1966)
Echoes of Celandine (1970)

MARLOWE, Hugh
Passage by Night (1966)

MARLOWE, Stephen
Come Over, Red Rover (1968)
Danger Is My Line (1960)
Jeopardy Is My Job (1961)
Manhunt Is My Mission (1963)
Peril Is My Pay (1960)
Search for Bruno Heidler (1966)
Second Longest Night (1955)
The Summit (1970)
Terror Is My Trade (1958)
Trouble Is My Name (1956)
Violence Is My Business (1958)
(See also Series 21)

MARQUAND, John P.
(See Series 49)

MARS, Alistair
Atomic Submarine (1957) (alt.
    title: Fire in Anger)

MARSH, James J.
Peking Switch (1972)

MARSH, Ngaio
Colour Scheme (1942)
Spinsters in Jeopardy (1953)

MARSHALL, Raymond
Mallory (1950)
Mission to Sienna (1955)
Mission to Venice (1954)

MARTIN, James E.
95 File (1973)

MARTON, George, and Chris-
    topher Felix
Three-Cornered Cover (1972)

MARTON, George, and Tibor
    Meray
Catch Me a Spy (1969)

MASON, Alfred Edward Woodley
Fire Over England (1949)

MASON, Francis Van Wyck
(See Series 10)

MASON, John William
The Saboteurs (1955)

MASON, Michael
71 Hours (1972)

MASTERS, John
Breaking Strain (1967)
Lotus and the Wind (1953)

MATHER, Berkley
Achilles Affair (1959)
The Break (1970)
Gold of Malabar (1966)
Pass Beyond Kashmir (1960)
Spy for a Spy (1968)
The Terminators (1972)

MAUGHAM, Robin
Man with Two Shadows (1959)

MAUGHAM, William Somerset
Ashenden, or, The British
    Agent (1927)

MAXFIELD, Henry S.
Legacy of a Spy (1958)

MAYO, James
Hammerhead (1964)
Let Sleeping Girls Lie (1964)
Shamelady (1966)

MEAD, Shepherd
How to Succeed at Business
    Spying By Trying (1968)

MEADE, Richard
Danube Runs Red (1968)
Lost Fraulein (1970)

MELCHIOR, Ib
Order of Battle (1972)

MENEN, Aubrey
SheLa (1962)

MERCER, Ian
Mission to Majorca (1958)

MERGENDAHL, Charles
Drums of April (1965)

MERLE, Robert
Day of the Dolphin (1969)

MERRICK, William
Packard Case (1961)

MERRIMAN, Henry Seton
Burlasch of the Guard (1903)
The Vultures (1902)

MESSMANN, Jon
(See Series 32)

MEYNELL, Laurence Walter
Dark Square (1941)

MIDDLETON, Ted
Operation Tokyo (1956)

MILLER, Merle
Secret Understanding (1956)

MILLS, Osmington
Traitor Betrayed (1964)

MILLS, Woosman
Dusty Coinage (1953)

MILTON, Joseph
Assignment: Assignation (1964)
Baron Sinister (1965)
Big Blue Death (1965)
Death-Makers (1966)
Man Who Bombed the World
    (1966)
President's Agent (1967)
Worldbreaker (1964)

MITCHELL, James
Red File for Callan (1971)
    (English Title: Magnum for
    Schneider)

MONTAGU, Ewan
Man Who Never Was (1967)

MONTANELLI, Indro
General Della Rovere (1959)

MONTEILHET, Hubert
Return from the Ashes (1963)
  (English Title: Phoenix from
  the Ashes)

MONTROSS, David
Fellow-Travelers (1965)
Traitor's Wife (1962)
Troika (1963) (alt. title: Who
  Is Elissa Sheldon?)

MOORCOCK, Michael
Chinese Agent (1970)

MOORE, Clay
Sensuous Spy (1972)

MOORE, Donald
Highway of Fear (1961)

MOORE, Robin
Country Team (1967)

MORGAN, Bryan
Business at Blanche Capel
  (1953)

MORGAN, Patrick
(See Series 54)

MORLEY, Christopher
Haunted Bookshop (1923)

MORRIS, Jean
Man and Two Gods (1953)

MORRIS, Joe Alex
Bird Watcher (1966)

MORRIS, Thomas Baden
Blind Bargain (1957)

MOSLEY, Nicholas
The Assassins (1967)

MOUNCE, David R.
Operation Cuttlefish (1972)

MOWATT, Ian
Just Sheaffer or Storms in the
  Troubled Heir (1973)

MUDDOCK, Joyce Emerson

Chronicles of Michael Danevitch
  of the Russian Secret Service
  (1897)
Eugene Vidocq: Soldier, Thief,
  Spy, Detective (1895)
In the Queen's Service (1907)

MUNDY, Max
Death Is a Tiger (1960)

MUNDY, Talbot
Black Light (1930)
Caves of Terror (1932)
Devil's Guard (1926)
Nine Unknown (1924)
Om: The Secret of Ahbor
  Valley (1924)
Red Flame of Erinpura (1934)

MUNRO, James
Innocent Bystanders (1970)
Man Who Sold Death (1965)
Money That Money That Can't
  Buy (1967)

MURPHY, Warren
(See Series 15)

MURRAY, William Hutchinson
Appointment in Tibet (1959)
Dark Rose the Phoenix (1965)
Five Frontiers (1959)

MYRER, Anton
Tiger Waits (1973)

NAPIER, Geoffrey
Very Special Agent (1967)

NATHANSON, E. M.
Dirty Dozen (1968)

NEWMAN, Bernard Charles
Centre Court Murder (1951)
Cup Final Murder (1951)
Dangerous Age (1967)
Dead Man Murder (1946)
Death to the Spy (1939)
Evil Phoenix (1966)
Mussolini Murder Plot (1939)
Operation Barbarossa (1956)
Otan Plot (1963)

Papa Pontivy and the Maginot
    Murder (1939) (English
    Title: Maginot Line Murder)
Silver Greyhound (1960)
Spy at No. 10 (1965)
Taken at the Flood (1958)
Travelling Executioners (1964)

NIELSEN, Helen Berneice
Stranger in the Dark (1955)

NIXON, Alan
Attack on Vienna (1972)
Item 7 (1971)

NOEL, Sterling
Few Die Well (1953)
I Killed Stalin (1951)
Run for Your Life (1958)
Storm Over Paris (1955) (alt.
    title: Intrigue in Paris)

NORMAN, Barry
Matter of Mandrake (1968)

NORMAN, Bruce
Hounds of Sparta (1968)

O'BRIEN, Robert C.
Report from Group 17 (1972)

O'BRINE, Padraic Manning
Mills (1969)
Passport to Treason (1955)

O'DONNELL, Peter
(See Series 51)

O'HARA, Kenneth
Double Cross Purposes (1962)
Sleeping Dogs Lying (1962)
Underhandover (1961)
View to Death (1958)

O'MALLEY, Patrick
Affair of Chief Strongheart (1964)
Affair of John Donne (1964)
Affair of Jolie Madame (1963)
Affair of Swan Lake (1962)
Affair of the Blue Pig (1965)
Affair of the Bumbling Briton
    (1965)

Affair of the Red Mosaic (1961)

"OPERATOR Five"
Army of the Dead (1966)
Blood Reign of the Dictator
    (1966)
Hosts of the Flaming Death
    (1966)
Invasion of the Yellow Warlords
    (1966)
Legions of the Dead Master
    (1966)
March of the Flame Marauders
    (1966)
Master of Broken Men (1966)

OPPENHEIM, Edward Phillips
Ambrose Lavendale, Diplomat
    (1920)
Double Traitor (1915)
Envoy Extraordinary (1937)
Exit a Dictator (1939)
For the Queen (1912)
Great Impersonation (1920)
Great Prince Shan (1922)
Illustrious Prince (1910)
Last Train Out (1940)
Light Beyond (1928)
Maker of History (1905)
Man from Sing Sing (1932)
    (English Title: Moran Cham-
    bers Smiled)
Miss Brown of X. Y. O. (1927)
Mysteries of the Riviera (1916)
Mysterious Mr. Sabin (1898)
Pulpit in the Grill Room (1938)
The Secret (1907) (alt. title:
    Great Secret)
Secret Service Omnibus (1932)
Sir Adam Disappeared (1939)
Spies and Intrigues (1936)
Spy Paramount (1934) (Serial
    Title: Man Who Saved the
    World)
The Spymaster (1938)
Strange Boarders of Palace
    Crescent (1934)
The Traitors (1902)
Treasure House of Martin Hews
    (1928)
Zeppelin's Passenger (1918)
    (English Title: Mr. Lessing-
    ham Goes Home)

ORAM, John
(See Series 30, no. 3)

ORCZY, Baroness Emmuska
Spy of Napoleon (1934)
(See also Series 59)

ORGILL, Douglas
Astrid Factor (1968)
Cautious Assassin (1963) (English
   Title: Ride a Tiger)
Journey into Violence (1962)
   (English Title: Death
   Bringers)
Man in the Dark (1965) (Eng-
   lish Title: Days of Darkness)

ORVIS, Kenneth
Night Without Darkness (1967)

OSBORNE, Geoffrey
Power Bug (1968)
Traitor's Gait (1970)

OSBORNE, Helen
My Enemy's Friend (1972)

OSMUND, Andrew, and Douglas
   Hurd
Smile on the Face of the Tiger
   (1970)

OVALOV, Lev
Comrade Spy (1965)
Secret Weapon (1965)

PACE, Eric
Saberlegs (1970)

PAGE, Michael Fitzgerald
Innocent Bystander (1957)

PALMER, John
Cretan Cipher (1965)

PAPE, R.
Boldness By My Friend (1952)
Fortune Is My Enemy (1957)
No Time to Die (1962)

PARKER, Maude
The Intriguer (1952)

Invisible Red (1953)
Secret Envoy (1930)

PARKER, Robert B.
Passport to Peril (1951)
Ticket to Oblivion (1950)

PATTINSON, James
Contact Mr. Delgardo (1959)

PAYNE, Laurence
Spy for Sale (1970)

PEARL, Jack
Our Man Flint (1965)
Plot to Kill the President (1970)

PECK, L.
Touch Pitch (1967)

PENDOWER, Jacques
Traitor's Island (1967)
Widow from Spain (1961)

PENTECOST, Hugh
Golden Trap (1967)

PERRAULT, E. G.
Twelfth Mile (1972)

PERRY, Ritchie
Fall Guy (1972)

PETERKIEWICZ, J.
Isolation (1965)

PETERS, Elizabeth
Dead Sea Cipher (1970)

PETERS, Ellis
Piper on the Mountain (1966)

PETERS, Ludovic
Cry Vengeance (1961)
Double Take (1968)
Snatch of Music (1962)
Tarakian (1963)
Two After Malic (1965)

PHILLIFENT, John T.
(See Series 44, no. 5)

PICARD, Sam
(See Series 53)

PICKERING, R. E.
Himself Again (1967)
Uncommitted Man (1967)

PIERCE, Noel
Messenger from Munich (1973)

PLATT, Kim
Pushbutton Butterfly (1970)

POLLARD, Alfred Oliver
A. R. P. Spy (1940)
Counterfeit Spy (1954)
Dead Man's Secret (1949)
Death Intervened (1951)
Death Parade (1952)
Flanders Spy (1938)
Gestapo Fugitives (1944)
Hidden Cypher (1938)
Homicidal Spy (1954)
Iron Curtain (1947)
Red Target (1952)
Secret Formula (1939)
Secret Pact (1940)
Secret Weapon (1941)
Unofficial Spy (1936)
Wanted by the Gestapo (1942)

PONTHIER, François
Assignment Basra (1969)

POOLE, Frederick King
Where Dragons Dwell (1971)

PORTER, Joyce
Chinks in the Curtain (1967)
Sour Cream with Everything
    (1966)

POSTGATE, Raymond
Ledger Is Kept (1953)

POWELL, Lester
Count of Six (1948)

POYER, Joe
Balkan Assignment (1971)
Chinese Agenda (1972)
North Cape (1969)
Operation Malacca (1968)

PRAEGER, J. Simon
Newman Factor (1973)

PRICE, Anthony
Alamat Ambush (1972)
Labyrinth Makers (1971)

PRIESTLEY, John Boynton
Blackout in Gretley (1942)
Saturn Over the Water (1961)

PROKOSCH, Frederic
The Conspirators (1943)

PUCCETTI, Roland
Death of the Fuhrer (1973)

QUARTERMAIN, James
Book of Diamonds (1972)
Diamond Hook (1970)
Man Who Walked on Diamonds
    (1971)

QUIGLEY, John
Last Checkpoint (1971)

RAINE, R. A.
Wreath for America (1967)

RAINE, Richard
Bombshell (1969)
Corder Index (1967)
Night of the Hawk (1968)

RAMATI, Alexander
Beyond the Mountains (1967)
    (alt. title: Desperate Ones)

RANDALL, A. A.
Flashpoint (1966)
Ride a Tiger (1968)
Suicide Point (1967)
To Catch a Spy (1969)

RATHBONE, Julian
Diamonds Bid (1967)
Hard Out (1968)
Trip Trap (1972)
With My Knives I Know I'm
    Good (1970)

RAVEN, Simon
Brother Cain (1960)

READE, Hamish
Comeback for Stark (1968)

REDGATE, John
Killing Season (1967)

REED, Eliot
Maras Affair (1953)

REEMAN, Douglas
Deep Silence (1968)

REMARQUE, Erich Maria
Arch of Triumph (1946)

RESTON, James, Jr.
To Defend, To Destroy (1970)

REVELLI, George
Commander Amanda Nightingale
    (1969)
Report to War (1971)

REY, H.-F.
Mechanical Pianos (1966)

RHODE, John
Double Florin (1924)

RICHARDS, Clay
Gentle Assassin (1964)

RICHARDS, David
Double Game (1958)

RICHARDS, Francis
Innocent House (1959)

RICHARDS, Paul
(See Series 27)

RICO, Don
(See Series 42)

RIMMER, Robert H.
Zolotov Affair (1967)

ROBERTS, James Hall
February Plan (1967)
Q Document (1964)

ROBERTS, Thomas A.
Heart of the Dog (1972)

ROBERTSON, Colin
Dark Knight (1946)
Dark Money (1962)
Judas Spies (1966)
North for Danger (1952)
Soho Spy (1941)

ROBERTSON, Constance
Golden Circle (1951)

ROBINSON, L. W.
The Assassin (1968) (alt. title:
    With Time Running)

ROHMER, Sax
(See Series 22)

ROMAINS, Jules
Death of a World: Mission to
    Rome (1938)

ROMANO, Deane
Flight from Time One (1972)

ROSENBERGER, Joseph
(See Series 14)

ROSENBLUM, Robert
Mushroom Cave (1973)

ROSSITER, John
Rope for General Dietz (1972)

ROSTAND, Robert
Killer Elite (1973)

ROSTEN, Leo
Most Private Intrigue (1967)

ROTH, Holly
Content Assignment (1954) (alt.
    title: Girl Who Vanished)
Mask of Glass (1954)
The Sleeper (1955)

ROTHBERG, Abraham
Thousand Doors (1965)

ROTHWELL, Henry Talbot
Dive Deep for Danger (1966)

Duet for Three Spies (1967)
Exit a Spy (1966)
No Honour Among Spies (1969)

ROUGVIE, Cameron
Medal from Pamplona (1964)
Tangier Assignment (1965)

ROYCE, Kenneth
My Turn to Die (1958)

RUMANES, George N.
Man with the Black Worrybeads
    (1973)

RUSHTON, Charles
Dark Amid the Blaze (1950)

RUSSELL, Fox
Phantom Spy (1904)

RUSSELL, Victor
Under Control (1951)

RYACK, Francis
Green Light, Red Catch (1973)
Loaded Gun (1970)
Woman Hunt (1972)

ST. CLAIR, Leonard
Fortune in Death (1972)

ST. GEORGE, George
Mauricette (1967)

ST. JOHN, David
Diabolus (1971)
Festival for Spies (1965)
Mongol Mask (1968)
On Hazardous Duty (1965)
One of Our Agents Is Missing
    (1967)
Return from Vorkuta (1965)
The Sorcerers (1969)
Towers of Silence (1966)
Venus Probe (1966)

SALE, Richard
For the President's Eyes Only
    (1971)

SALINGER, Pierre

On Instructions from My Govern-
    ment (1971)

SANDERS, Bruce
Code of Dishonor (1964)
Feminine for a Spy (1967)
To Catch a Spy (1958)

SANDERS, John
Fireworks for Oliver (1965)
Hat of Authority (1966)

SANDFORD, Ken
Dead Reckoning (1955)
Sead Secret (1957)

SANGSTER, Jimmy
Foreign Exchange (1968)
private i (1967)
Touch Gold (1970)
Touchfeather (1969)
Touchfeather Too (1970)

SAPIR, Richard
(See Series 15)

SARASIN, J. G.
Fleur de Lys (1929)
Invasion Coast (1948)
Thunderbolt (1958)

SAVAGE, Richard
The Innocents (1959)

SAWKINS, Raymond
Snow Along the Border (1968)
Snow on High Ground (1967)

SAXTON, Mark
Islar: A Narrative of Lang III
    (1969)

SCHURMACHER, Emile C.
Assignment X: Top Secret
    (1965)

SCOTT, Jack Denton
Spargo (1971)

SCOTT, Reginald Thomas Mait-
    land
Secret Service Smith (1923)

"SEA-Lion" (Bennett, Geoffrey Martin)
Damn Desmond Drake (1953)
Death in Russian Habit (1958)
Desmond Drake Goes West (1957)
Meet Desmond Drake (1954)
Phantom Fleet (1946)

"SEAMARK" (Small, Austin J.)
Mystery Maker (1929)

SEARLS, Hank
Pentagon (1971)

"SECRET Agent X"
City of the Living (1966)
Curse of the Mandarin's Fan (1966)
Death-Torch Terror (1966)
Octopus of Crime (1966)
Servants of the Skull (1966)
Sinister Scourge (1966)
Torture Thrust (1966)

SELA, Owen
Beaver Plot (1973)

SERLING, Robert J.
President's Plane Is Missing (1967)

SETH, Ronald
The Patriot (1954)
Spy Has No Friends (1952)
Spy in the Nude

SEWARD, Jack
(See Series 13)

SHECKLEY, Robert
Game of X (1965)
Dead Run (1961)

SHELDON, Walter J.
Gold Bait (1973)

SHELLABARGER, Samuel
King's Cavalier (1950)

SHERWOOD, John
Mr. Blessington's Imperialist Plot (1951) (English Title: Mr. Blessington's Plot)

Two Died in Singapore (1954)

SHORT, Christopher
Dark Lantern (1961)

SHUB, Joyce L.
Moscow by Nightmare (1973)

SHUTE, Nevil
Mysterious Aviator (1928) (English Title: So Disdained)

SIGEL, Efrem
Kermanshah Transfer (1973)

SILONE, Ignazio
Fox and the Camellias (1961)

SIMMEL, Johannes Mario
Dear Fatherland (1969)
It Can't Always Be Caviar: The Fabulously Daring Adventures of an Involuntary Secret Agent (1965)

SIMPSON, Howard R.
Three-Day Alliance (1972)

SINCLAIR, Michael
Folio Forty-One (1972)
Sonntag (1971)

SINCLAIR, Upton
Story of a Patriot (1920) (English Title: The Spy)
(See also Series 38)

SINSTADT, Gerald
Fidelio Score (1965)
Ship of Spies (1966)

SIODMAK, Curt
Donovan's Brain (1943)

SKIRROW, Desmond
I'm Trying to Give It Up (1969)
It Won't Get You Anywhere (1966)

SLATER, Humphrey
The Conspirator (1948)

SMITH, Don
(See Series 60)

SMITH, Godfrey
Flaw in the Crystal (1954)

SNOW, Charles Horace
Buckhorn Murder Case (1952)

SOUTHCOTT, Audley
Black General (1969)

SPENCER, D. J.
Jing Affair (1965)

SPICER, Bart
Brother to the Enemy (1956)
Burned Man (1966)
Day of the Dead (1955)

SPILLANE, Mickey
Bloody Sunrise (1965)
By-Pass Control (1966)
Day of the Guns (1964)
Death Dealers (1965)
Delta Factor (1968)

STACKELBERG, Gene
Double Agent (1959)

STACPOOLE, Henry De Vere
Man in Armour (1949)

STANLEY, Bennett
Government Contract (1955)

STANTON, Ken
(See Series 2)

STARK, Richard
The Blackbird (1969)

STARNES, Richard
Flypaper War (1969)
Requiem in Utopia (1967)

STARR, Richard
Marinova of the Secret Service
    (1937)
Married to a Spy (1915)

STEIN, Aaron Marc
The Finger (1973)

STEIRMAN, Hy
Strike Terror

STERN, Richard Martin
I Hide, We Seek (1965)
Kessler Legacy (1967)
Search for Tabatha Carr (1960)

STEVENSON, Anne
Relative Stranger (1970)

STEWART, Mary
Airs Above the Ground (1963)
Gabriel Hounds (1967)
Ivy Tree (1966)
Madam, Will You Talk? (1956)
Moon Spinners (1963)
My Brother Michael (1960)
Nine Coaches Waiting (1959)
This Rough Magic (1964)
Thunder on the Right (1958)
Wildfire at Midnight (1961)

STIMSON, Robert G., and James
    Bellah
Avenger Tapes (1971)

STONE, David
Tired Spy (1961)

STONE, Scott C. S.
Dragon's Eye (1969)

STOREY, Michael
Solf in the Middle (1972)

STOU, Peter
Charade (1963)

STRACHAN, Tony Simpson
No Law in Illyria (1957)
Short Weekend (1953)

STRATTON, Thomas
(See Series 44, nos. 11, 12)

STREET, Bradford
In Like Flint (1967)

STUART, Alan
Unwilling Angel (1955)

STUART, Ian
Black Shrike (1961)
Dark Crusader (1965)
Satan Bug (1962)

STYLES, Frank Showell
Traitor's Mountain (1946)

SULZBERGER, C. L.
Tooth Merchant (1973)

SWIGGETT, Howard
Hidden and the Hunted (1950)

SYMONS, Julian
Broken Penny (1953)

TACK, Alfred
Spy Who Wasn't Exchanged
   (1968)

TAIT, William Nelson
On Secret Service (1921)

TALBOT, Hake
Catch Me a Traitor (1966)
Cold Line to Moscow (1968)
Spy in the Hand (1966)

TATE, Warren
Matter of Diplomacy (1970)

TAYLOR, David
Farewell to Valley Forge (1955)
Storm the Last Rampant (1960)

TAYLOR, Ray W.
Doomsday Square

TAYLOR, Thomas
A-18 (1967)

TEILHET, Darwin, and Hilde-
   garde Teilhet
Double Agent (1945)
Rim of Terror (1950)

TELESCOMBE, Anne
The Listener (1960)

THAYER, Charles Wheeler
Checkpoint (1965)

Moscow Interlude (1962)

THOMAS, Leslie
Orange Wednesday (1968)

THOMAS, Paul
Cargo Trouble (1960)
Code Name: Rubble (1967)

THOMAS, Ross
Backup Man (1971)
Cast a Yellow Shadow (1967)
Cold War Snap (1966)
Singapore Wink (1969)
Spy in the Vodka (1967)

THORNE, E. P.
Assignment Haiti (1963)
Caribbean Affair (1967)
Chinese Poker (1964)
Code Word, "Proton" (1968)
House of the Fragrant Lotus
   (1962)
Moscow File (1967)
Zero Minus Nine (1964)

THURSTON, Ernest Temple
Portrait of a Spy (1928)

TICKELL, Jerrald
Villa Mimosa (1960)

TIGER, John
(See Series 28)

TOMPKINS, Peter
Spy in Rome (1964)

TORR, Dominic
Diplomatic Cover (1966)
Mission of Mercy (1969)
Treason Line (1968)

TRALINS, Robert
Chic Chick Spy (1966)
Miss from S. I. S. (1966)
Ring-a-Ding UFO's (1967)

TRANTER, Nigel
Man Behind the Curtain (1959)

TRAVERS, Robert
Apartment on K Street (1972)

TREFUS, Victor
But No Man Seen (1955)

TREGASKIS, Richard
China Bomb (1967)

TREVANIAN
Eiger Sanction (1972)
Loo Sanction (1973)

TREVOR, Elleston
The Shoot (1966)
The V. I. P. (1960)

TRIMBLE, Louis
Tide Can't Wait (1957)

TRUSS, Sheldon
Hidden Men (1959)
Truth About Claire Veryan
    (1957)

TUCKER, Arthur Wilson
The Warlock (1967)

TURNBULL, Patrick
One Bullet for the General
    (1968)

UNDERWOOD, Michael
Shadow Game (1969)
Unprofessional Spy (1964)

UPFIELD, Arthur William
Devil's Steps (1946)

URIS, Leon
Angry Hills (1955)
Topaz (1967)

USHER, Frank Hugh
Man from Moscow (1965)

VAHEY, John George Haslette
Spies in Ambush (1934)

VANCE, Ethel
Escape (1939)
Reprisal (1942)

VAUGHAN, Carter A.

The Wilderness (1959)

VERALDI, Gabriel
Spies of Good Intent (1969)

VERNER, Gerald
Dene of the Secret Service
    (1941)
Faceless Ones (1964)
Ghost Squad (1963)

VERRON, Robert
Fifth Must Die (1949)

VIERTEL, Peter
Love Lies Bleeding (1964)

VON ELSNER, Don Byron
Ace of Spies (1966)
Countdown for a Spy (1966)

VONNEGUT, Kurt, Jr.
Mother Night (1966)

VOSS BARK, Conrad
See the Living Crocodiles (1968)
Shepherd File (1966)

WADDELL, Martin
(See Series 55)

WADE, Robert
Knave of Eagles (1969)

WAGER, Walter
Sledgehammer (1970)
Swap (1972)
Viper Three (1971)

WAINWRIGHT, John
Web of Silence (1968)

WAKEMAN, Frederic
Free Agent (1963)

WALKER, David Esdaile
Diamonds for Danger (1953)
    (English Title: Diamonds
    for Moscow)

WALLACE, Edgar
Adventures of Heine (1919)
Green Rust (1919)

WALLACE, Leslie
The American (1970)

WALSH, James Morgan
Island of Spies (1937)
Man from Whitehall (1934)
Secret Service Girl (1933)
Secret Weapons (1940)
Spies Are Abroad (1933)
Spies from the Skies (1941)
Spies in Pursuit (1934)
Spies in Spain (1937)
Spies Never Return (1935)
Spies' Vendetta (1936)

WALTER, Hugh
Bullet for Charles (1955)

WARD, Henry
Green Suns (1963)

WAUGH, Alec
Mule on the Minaret (1965)
Spy in the Family: An Erotic
  Comedy (1970)

WAYLAND, Patrick
Counterstroke (1964)
Double Defector (1964)
Waiting Game (1965)

WEBSTER, Frederick Annesley
  Michael
Beneath the Mask (1948)

WEEKS, William Rawle
Knock and Wait Awhile (1957)

WEIL, Barry
Dossier IX (1969)

WEINSTEIN, Sol
(See Series 29)

WELCOME, John
Beware of Midnight (1961)
Hard to Handle (1964)
Hell Is Where You Find It
  (1968)
Run for Cover (1959)
Stop at Nothing (1960)
Wanted for Killing (1967)

WEST, Eliot
Man Running (1959)
Night Is the Time for Listening
  (1966)
These Lonely Victories (1972)

WEST, Morris L.
Ambassador (1965)
Tower of Babel (1968)

WEST, Rebecca
Birds Fall Down (1966)

WESTLAKE, Donald E.
Spy in the Ointment (1966)

WEVERKA, Robert
One Minute to Eternity (1960)

WEYMAN, Stanley J.
Long Night (1903)
Red Cockade (1895)
Under the Red Robe (1894)

WHALEY, Francis John
Enter a Spy (1941)

WHEATLEY, Dennis
Black Baroness (1940)
Codeword--Golden Fleece (1951)
Come Into My Parlour (1967)
Contraband (1936)
Curtain of Fear (1953)
Dark Secret of Josephine (1966)
Eunuch of Stamboul (1935)
Faked Passports (1943)
Forbidden Territory (1933)
Golden Spaniard (1938)
Island Where Time Stands Still
  (1954)
Launching of Roger Brook (1947)
Mayhem in Greece
Man Who Killed the King (1951)
Rape of Venice (1963)
Rising Storm (1952)
Scarlet Imposter (1942)
Second Seal (1944)
Shadow of Tyburn Tree (1948)
Sultan's Daughter (1965)
Sword of Fate (1944)
They Used Dark Forces (1963)
Traitor's Gate (1958)
V for Vengeance (1966)

Vendetta in Spain (1961)
Wanton Princess (1966)

WHEELER, Keith
Last Mayday (1970)

WHITE, Alan
Long Drop (1970)
Long Night's Walk (1969)
Long Watch (1971)

WHITE, Ared
Agent B-7 (1934)
Seven Tickets to Singapore
    (1939)
Spy Net (1930)

WHITE, Ethel Lina
Some Must Watch (1934) (alt.
    title: Spiral Staircase)
Wheel Spins (1936) (alt. title:
    Lady Vanishes)

WHITE, Jan Manchip
Nightclimber (1968)

WHITE, Lionel
Crimshaw Memorandum
House on K Street (1965)
Ransomed Madonna

WHITNEY, Alec
Every Man Has His Price: A
    Novel of Industrial Espionage
    (1968)

WHITTINGTON, Harry
(See Series 44, no. 2)

WILKINSON, Burke
Last Clear Chance (1954)
Night of the Short Knives (1964)

WILLIAMS, Alan
False Beards (1963) (English
    Title: Barbouze)

WILLIAMS, Charles
Wrong Venus (1967)

WILLIAMS, David
Agent from the West (1956)

WILLIAMS, Jay
The Witches (1957)

WILLIAMS, Valentine
Okewood of the Secret Service
    (1925)
Spider's Touch (1936)
Three of Clubs (1924)

WILLOCK, Ruth
Street of the Small Steps (1972)

WILMER, Dale
Dead Fall (1954)

WILSON, Ivor
Empty Tigers (1965)
Lilies That Fester (1964)

WINSTON, Peter
(See Series 1)

WOLK, George
Leopold Contract (1970)

WOOD, James Alexander Fraser
Fire Rock (1966)
Friday Run (1970)
Lisa Bastian (1961)
Northern Mission (1954)
Rain Islands (1957)
The Sealer (1960)
Three Blind Mice (1971)

WOODHOUSE, Martin
Blue Bone (1973)
Bush Baby (1968)
Mama Doll (1972)
Tree Frog (1966)

WOODS, Sara
Error of the Moon (1963)

WORMSER, Richard
Torn Curtain (1966)

WUORIO, Eva-Lis
Midsummer Lokki (1967)
Woman with the Portuguese
    Basket (1963)
Z for Zaborra (1966)

WYLIE, D. B.
Joyous Errand (1958)

WYLIE, James
Lost Rebellion (1971)

WYLIE, Philip Gordon
Smuggled Atom Bomb (1965)
Spy Who Spoke Porpoise (1969)

WYND, Oswald
Sumatra Seven Zero (1968)
Walk Softly, Men Praying
    (1967)

YORK, Andrew
(See Series 36)

YOUNG, Edward Preston
Fifth Passenger (1963)

ZARUBICA, Mladin
Scutari (1967)
Year of the Rat (1964)

ZENO
Grab (1970)

ZERWICK, Chloe, and Harrison
    Brown
Cassiopeia Affair (1967)

ZHDANOV, Aleksandr Ivanovich
Shadow of Peril (1963)

1 THE ADJUSTORS (Peter Winston)
1: Assignment to Bahrein (1967)
2: The ABC Affair (1967)
3: Doomsday Vendetta (1968)
4: The Glass Cipher (1968)
5: The Temple at Ilumquh (1969)

2 THE AQUANAUTS (Ken Stanton)
1: Cold Blue Death (1969)
2: Ten Seconds to Zero (1970)
3: Seek, Strike and Destroy (1970)
4: Sargosso Secret (1971)
5: Stalkers of the Sea (1971)
6: Whirlwind Beneath the Sea (1972)
7: Operation Deep Six (1972)

3 THE AVENGERS (John Garforth)
1: The Floating Game (1967)
2: The Laugh Was on Lazarus (1967)
3: The Passing of Gloria Munday (1967)
4: Heil Harris! (1967)

4 BLACKSHIRT Series (Bruce Graeme)
Adventures of Blackshirt (1929) (English Title: Blackshirt Again)
Alias Blackshirt (1932)
Blackshirt Counter-Spy (1938)
Blackshirt Interferes (1939)
Blackshirt Strikes Back (1940)
Blackshirt Takes a Hand (1937)
Blackshirt the Adventurer (1936)
Blackshirt the Audacious (1935)
Calling Lord Blackshirt (1943)
Lord Blackshirt (1942)
Monsieur Blackshirt (1933)
Return of Blackshirt (1927)
Son of Blackshirt (1941)

Sword of Monsieur Blackshirt (1934)
Vengeance of Monsieur Blackshirt (1934)

5 BLACKSHIRT Series (cont. by Roderic Graeme
Amazing Mr. Blackshirt (1955)
Blackshirt Finds Trouble (1961)
Blackshirt Helps Himself (1951)
Blackshirt Meets the Lady (1956)
Blackshirt On the Spot (1963)
Blackshirt Passes By (1953)
Blackshirt Saves the Day (1964)
Blackshirt Sees It Through (1960)
Blackshirt Sets the Pace (1959)
Blackshirt Takes the Trail (1962)
Blackshirt Wins the Trick (1953)
Call for Blackshirt (1963)
Concerning Blackshirt (1952)
Double for Blackshirt (1958)
Paging Blackshirt (1957)
Salute to Blackshirt (1954)

6 BOYSIE OAKES Series (John Gardner)
Air Apparent (1970)
Amber Nine (1966)
The Liquidator (1964)
Madrigal (1968)
Understriker (1965)

7 CABOT CAIN (Cabot Cain)
Assault on Agathon (1972)
Assault on Fellawi (1972)
Assault on Kolchak (1969)
Assault on Loveless (1969)
Assault on Ming (1969)

8 CODE NAME SEBASTIAN Series (James L. Johnson)
Code Name Sebastian (1967)
Handful of Dominoes (1970)
Nine Lives of Alphonse (1968)

9 COLONEL CHARLES RUSSELL

(William Haggard)
The Antagonists (1964)
The Arena (1961)
The Conspirators (1967)
Cool Day for Killing (1968)
Hard Sell (1965)
The Hardliners (1971)
High Wire (1963)
Powder Barrel (1965)
Power House (1967)
Sixth Notch on the Knife (1973)
Slow Burner (1958)
Too Many Enemies (1971) (English Title: Bitter Harvest)
Unquiet Sleep (1962)
Venetian Blind (1959)

10 COLONEL HUGH NORTH
(Francis Van Wyck Mason)
Branded Spy Murders (1932)
Bucharest Ballerina Murders (1940)
Budapest Parade Murders (1935)
Cairo Garter Murders (1938)
Dardanelles Derelict (1950)
Deadly Orbit Mission (1968)
Forgotten Fleet Mystery (1936)
Fort Terror Murders (1931)
Gracious Lily Affair (1957)
Himalayan Assignment (1950)
Man from G-2 (1943)
Maracaibo Mission (1965)
Multi-Million Dollar Murders (1960)
Rio Casino Intrigue (1941)
Saigon Singer (1946)
Secret Mission to Bangkok (1960)
Seeds of Murder (1930)
Seven Seas Murder (1936)
Shanghai Bund Murders (1933)
Singapore Exile Murders (1939)
Spider House (1932)
Sulu Sea Murders (1933)
Trouble in Burma (1962)
Two Tickets to Tangier (1955)
Vesper Service Murders (1931)
Washington Legation Murders (1935)
Yellow Arrow Murders (1932)
Zanzibar Intrigue (1963)

11 COMMANDER SHAW (Philip Donald McCutchan)

All-Purpose Bodies (1970)
Bluebolt One (1962)
Bright Red Business Man (1969)
Dead Line (1966)
Gibraltar Road (1960)
Man from Moscow (1963)
Moscow Coach (1963)
Red Cap (1961)
Screaming Dead Balloons (1968)
Skyprobe (1968)
Warmaster (1963)

12 COXEMAN Series (Troy Conway)
All Screwed Up
Best-Laid Plans
Big Broad Jump
Billion Dollar Snatch
Bite Off More Than You Can Chew
Blow-Your-Mind Job
Cockeyed Cuties (1972)
Come One, Come All (1968)
Cunning Linguist
Good Peace
Had Any Lately?
Hard Act to Follow
Harder You Try, The Harder It Gets
I Can't Believe I Ate the Whole Thing (1973)
I'd Rather Fight Than Swish
It's Getting Harder All the Time
It's Not How Long You Make It
It's What's Up Front That Counts
Just a Silly Millimeter Longer ('69)
Keep It Up, Rod
Last Licks
The Man-Eater
Master Baiter
The Penetrator
Sex Machine
Son of a Witch
Spy Who Came in with the Hots (1970)
Stiff Proposition (1970)
Turn the Other Sheik
Up and Coming (1972)
Wham! Bam! Thank You, Ma'am Affair (1968)
Whatever Goes Up
Will the Real Rod Please Stand Up?

13 CURT STONE Series (Jack
    Seward)
Eurasian Virgins (1968)
Frogman Assassination (1968)

14 DEATH MERCHANT Series
    (Joseph Rosenberger)
1: The Death Merchant (1971)
2: Operation Overkill (1972)
3: The Psychotron Plot (1972)
4: Chinese Conspiracy (1973)
5: Satan Strike (1973)

15 DESTROYER Series (Richard
    Sapir and Warren Murphy)
1: Created, the Destroyer (1971)
2: Death Check (1972)
3: Chinese Puzzle (1972)
4: Mafia Fix (1972)
5: Dr. Quake (1972)
6: Death Therapy (1972)
7: Union Bust (1973)
8: Summit Chase (1973)

16 DR. DAVID GRANT (George
    Brown Mair)
Black Champagne (1968)
Day Khrushchev Panicked (1970)
Girl from Peking (1967)
Kisses from Satan (1965)
Live, Love and Cry (1966)
Miss Turquoise (1964)

17 DR. JASON LOVE (James
    Leasor)
Passport for a Pilgrim (1969)
Passport in Suspense (1967)
Passport to Oblivion (1964) (alt.
    title: Where the Spies Are)
Spylight (1966) (English Title:
    Passport to Peril)
Yang Meridian (1967)

18 DR. PALFREY (John Creasey)
The Blight (1968)
The Depths (1966)
The Drought (1959) (alt. title:
    Dry Spell)
The Executioners (1967)
The Famine (1967)
The Flood (1956)
The Inferno (1965)
The Menace (1938)

The Oasis (1970)
Perilous Country (1966)
Plague of Silence (1958)
The Sleep (1964)
The Smog (1970)
The Terror: The Return of Dr.
    Palfrey (1962)
Touch of Death (1969)
Traitor's Doom (1943)

19 DORIAN SILK Series (Simon
    Harvester)
Assassins Road (1965)
Battle Road (1967)
Moscow Road (1971)
Nameless Road (1971)
Red Road (1967)
Sahara Road (1972)
Silk Road (1963)
Treacherous Road (1966)
Unsung Road (1960)
Zion Road (1968)

20 EARL DRAKE (Dan J. Mar-
    lowe)
Name of the Game Is Death (1962)
One Endless Hour
Operation Breakthrough (1971)
Operation Checkmate (1972)
Operation Drumfire (1972)
Operation Fireball
Operation Flashpoint (1970)
Operation Stranglehold (1973)

21 DRUM BEAT Series (Stephan
    Marlowe)
Drum Beat--Berlin (1964)
Drum Beat--Erica (1967)
Drum Beat--Madrid (1966)
Drum Beat--Martinique (1965)

22 FU MANCHU (Sax Rohmer)
Book of Fu Manchu (1929)
Bride of Fu Manchu (1933) (alt.
    title: Fu Manchu's Bride)
Daughter of Fu Manchu (1931)
Devil Doctor (1916)
Drums of Fu Manchu (1939)
Emperor Fu Manchu (1959)
Hand of Fu Manchu (1917)
Hangover House (1949)
Insidious Dr. Fu Manchu (1913)
    (alt. title: Mystery of Dr.

Fu Manchu)
Island of Fu Manchu (1941)
Mask of Fu Manchu (1932)
Moon Is Red (1954)
President Fu Manchu (1936)
Re-Enter Fu Manchu (1957)
Return of Fu Manchu (1916)
Return of Sumura (1954)
Sand and Satin (1955)
Shadow of Fu Manchu (1948)
Si-Fan Mysteries (1917)
Sinister Madonna (1956)
Sins of Sumura (1950)
Slaves of Sumura (1952)
Sumura (1951)
Trail of Fu Manchu (1934)
Virgin in Flames (1953)

23 GENTLEMEN Series (John
Boland)
Gentlemen at Large (1962)
Gentlemen Reform (1961)
League of Gentlemen (1958)

24 GIRL FROM PUSSYCAT
Series (Ted Mark)
Dr. Nyet (1966)
Girl from Pussycat (1965)
Nude Who Did
Nude Who Never
Nude Wore Black (1967)
Pussycat, Pussycat (1966)
Pussycat Transplant (1968)

25 GIRL FROM U. N. C. L. E.
Series (various authors)
1: The Birds of a Feather
Affair, by Michael Avallone
(1966)
2: The Blazing Affair, by
Michael Avallone (1966)
3: The Cornish Pixie Affair,
by Peter Leslie (1967)

26 GUN COTTON Series
(Richard Grayson)
Cotton Gunston (1936)
Gun Cotton--A Romance of
the Secret Service (1939)
Gun Cotton--Adventurer (1932)
Gun Cotton--Secret Airman
(1939)

27 HOT LINE ESPIONAGE
Series (Paul Richards)
President Has Been Kidnapped
(1971)

28 I SPY Series (John Tiger)
1: I Spy (1965)
2: Masterstroke (1966)
3: Superkill (1967)
4: Mission Impossible (1967)
5: Countertrap (1967)
6: Doomtrap (1967)
7: Death-Twist (1968)

29 ISRAEL BOND "OY-OY-7"
(Sol Weinstein)
Loxfinger (1965)
Matzohball (1966)
On the Secret Service of His
Majesty the Queen (1966)
You Only Live Until You Die
(1968)

30 JAMES BOND "007" (Ian
Fleming)
Casino Royale (1953)
Diamonds Are Forever (1956)
Doctor No (1958)
For Your Eyes Only (1960)
From Russia With Love (1957)
Goldfinger (1959)
Live and Let Die (1954)
Man With the Golden Gun (1965)
(English Title: Golden Gun)
Moonraker (1955) (alt. title:
Too Hot to Handle)
Octopussy (1966)
On Her Majesty's Secret Ser-
vice (1964)
Spy Who Loved Me (1962)
Thunderball (1962)
You Only Live Twice (1964)

31 JAMES BOND "007" (cont.
by Robin Markham)
Colonel Sun: A James Bond
Adventure (1968)

32 JEFFERSON BOONE: HANDY-
MAN (Jon Messmann)
Bullet for the Bride (1972)
Moneta Papers (1973)

33 JOE GALL (Philip Atlee)
Canadian Bomber Contract
  (1971)
Death Bird Contract (1966)
Fer-de-Lance Contract (1970)
Green Wound (1963)
Ill Wind Contract (1971)
Irish Beauty Contract (1966)
Judah Lion Contract (1972)
Kiwi Contract (1972)
Paper Pistol Contract (1971)
Rockabye Contract
Silken Baroness
Skeleton Coast Contract
Spice Route Contract (1973)
Star Ruby Contract (1967)
Trembling Earth Contract
  (1969)
White Wolverine Contract (1971)

34 JOHN EAGLE: EXPEDITOR
  (Paul Edwards)
1: Needles of Death (1973)
2: Brain Scavengers (1973)
3: Laughing Death (1973)

35 JOHNNY FEDORA (Desmond
  Cory)
Dead Man Alive
Fermontov (1956)
High Requiem (1956)
Johnny Goes East (1958)
Johnny Goes North (1956)
Johnny Goes South (1959)
Johnny Goes West (1959)
Johnny on the Belgrade Express
  (1960)
Mountainhead
Swastika Hunt
Timelock (1967)
Trieste

36 JONAS WILDE (Andrew York)
The Co-Ordinator (1967)
The Deviator (1968)
The Eliminator (1966)
The Expurgator (1973)
The Infiltrator (1971)
The Predator (1968)

37 LADY FROM L. U. S. T.
  Series (Rod Gray)
Lady from L. U. S. T. (1967)

(alt. title: Lust, Be a Lady
  Tonight)
Skin Game Dame (1968)

38 LANNY BUDD (Upton Sin-
  clair)
  1: World's End (1940)
  2: Between Two Worlds (1941)
  3: Dragon's Teeth (1942)
  4: Wide Is the Gate (1943)
  5: Presidential Agent (1944)
  6: Dragon Harvest (1945)
  7: World to Win (1946)
  8: Presidential Mission (1947)
  9: One Clear Call (1948)
10: O Shepherd, Speak! (1949)
11: Return of Lanny Budd (1953)

39 LUNATIC Series [Adventures
  of Mr. Francis Mandell-Es-
  sington] (Joseph Storer Clous-
  ton)
Best Story Ever (1932)
Count Banker (1907)
Lunatic At Large (1899)
Lunatic At Large Again (1923)
Lunatic in Charge (1926)
Lunatic in Love (1927)
Lunatic Still At Large (1924)
Mr. Essington In Love (1931)

40 MAN FROM CHARISMA
  Series (Ted Mark)
Man from Charisma (1970)
Right On, Relevant (1970)
Rip It Off, Relevant (1971)

41 MAN FROM O. R. G. Y. Series
  (Ted Mark)
Back Home at the O. R. G. Y.
  (1968)
Come Be My O. R. G. Y.
Hard Day's Knight (1966)
Here's Your O. R. G. Y. (1969)
Man from O. R. G. Y. (1965)
My Son, the Double Agent (1966)
Nine-Month Caper (1965)
Real Gone Girls (1966)
Square Root of Sex (1967)
Unhatched Egghead (1966)

42 MAN FROM PANSY Series
  (Don Rico)

1: The Man from Pansy (1967)
2: The Daisy Dilemma (1967)

43 MAN FROM T. O. M. C. A. T.
   Series (Mallory T. Knight)
   1: Dozen Deadly Dragons of
      Joy (1967)
   2: Million Missing Maidens (1967)
   3: Terrible Ten (1967)
   4: Dirty Rotten Depriving Ray ('67)
   5: Tsimmis in Tangier (1968)
   6: Malignant Metaphysical
      Menace (1968)
   7: Ominous Orgy (1969)
   8: Peking Pornographer (1969)
   9: Doom Dollies (1970)
  10: Bra-Burners' Brigade (1971)

44 MAN FROM U. N. C. L. E.
   Series (various authors)
   1: The Thousand Coffins Affair,
      by Michael Avallone (1965)
   2: The Doomsday Affair, by
      Harry Whittington (1965)
   3: The Copenhagen Affair, by
      John Oram (1965)
   4: The Dagger Affair, by
      David McDaniel (1966)
   5: The Mad Scientist Affair,
      by John T. Phillifent (1966)
   6: The Vampire Affair, by
      David McDaniel (1966)
   7: The Radioactive Camel
      Affair, by Peter Leslie
      (1966)
   8: The Monster Wheel Affair,
      by David McDaniel (1967)
   9: The Diving Dames Affair,
      by Peter Leslie (1967)
  10: The Assassination Affair, by
      J. Hunter Holly (1967)
  11: The Invisibility Affair, by
      Thomas Stratton (1967)
  12: The Mind Twister's Affair,
      by Thomas Stratton (1967)
  13: The Rainbow Affair, by
      David McDaniel (1967)
  14: The Finger in the Sky Af-
      fair, by Peter Leslie (1967)
  15: The Utopia Affair, by David
      McDaniel (1968)
  16: The Splintered Sunglasses
      Affair, by J. Hunter Holly

(1967)
  17: The Hollow Crown Affair,
      by David McDaniel (1969)
  18: The Unfare Fare Affair,
      by Peter Leslie (1969)

45 MARK HOOD (James Dark)
Assignment--Hong Kong (1966)
   (alt. title: Hong Kong Inci-
   dent)
Assignment--Tokyo (1966) (alt.
   title: Operation Miss Sat)
Bamboo Bomb (1965)
Come Die With Me (1965)
The Invisibles
Operation Ice Cap
Operation Scuba (1967)
Sea Scrape (1971)
Sword of Genghis Khan (1967)
Throne of Satan (1967)

46 MATT HELM (Donald B.
   Hamilton)
   1: Death of a Citizen (1960)
   2: The Wrecking Crew (1960)
   3: The Removers (1961)
   4: The Silencers (1962)
   5: Murderer's Row (1962)
   6: The Ambushers (1963)
   7: The Shadowers (1964)
   8: The Ravagers (1964)
   9: The Devastators (1965)
  10: The Betrayers (1966)
  11: The Menacers (1968)
  12: The Interlopers (1969)
  13: The Poisoners (1971)
  14: The Intriguers (1971)

47 MAX SMART (William Johnston)
1: Get Smart! (1965)
2: Sorry Chief.... (1966)
3: Get Smart Once Again! (1966)
4: Max Smart and the Perilous
   Pellets (1966)
5: Missed It By That Much!
   (1967)
6: And Loving It (1967)

48 MISS SEETON (Heron Carvic)
Miss Seeton Draws the Line
   (1970)
Miss Seeton Sings (1973)

Witch Miss Seeton (1971)

49 MR. MOTO (John Marquand)
Last Laugh, Mr. Moto (1942)
Mr. Moto Is So Sorry (1938)
Mr. Moto Takes a Hand (1940)
Mr. Moto's Three Aces (1956)
No Hero (1935) (alt. title: Your
    Turn, Mr. Moto) (1935)
Stopover Tokyo (1957) (alt. title:
    Last of Mr. Moto)
Thank You, Mr. Moto (1936)
Think Fast, Mr. Moto (1937)

50 MRS. POLLIFAX (Dorothy
    Gilman)
Amazing Mrs. Pollifax (1970)
Elusive Mrs. Pollifax (1971)
Palm for Mrs. Pollifax (1973)
Unexpected Mrs. Pollifax (1966)

51 MODESTY BLAISE (Peter
    O'Donnell)
I, Lucifer (1967)
Modesty Blaise (1965)
Sabre Tooth (1966)
Taste for Death (1969)

52 NICK CARTER "KILL-
    MASTER" (various authors)
The Amazon (1969)
Amsterdam
Arab Plague
Assignment: Israel (1967)
Assault on England (1972)
Berlin
Black Death (1970)
Bright Blue Death
Bullet for Fidel (1965)
Cairo Mafia (1972)
Cambodia
Carnaval for Killing (1969)
Casbah Killers
Checkmate in Rio (1964)
Chile (1972)
China Doll (1964)
Chinese Paymaster (1967)
Cobra Kill (1969)
Code Name: Werewolf (1973)
Danger Key (1966)
Death Strain
The Defector (1969)
Devil's Cockpit

Doomsday Formula (1969)
Double Identity (1967)
Dragon Flame
The Executioners (1970)
Eyes of the Tiger (1965)
Filthy Fine
14 Seconds to Hell (1968)
Fraulein Spy (1964)
Golden Serpent (1968)
Hanoi (1966)
Hood of Death
Human Time Bomb
Ice Bomb Zero
Inca Death Squad (1972)
Istanbul (1965)
Jewel of Doom (1970)
Judas Spy
Korean Tiger
The Liquidator (1973)
Living Death (1969)
Macoa (1968)
Mark of Cosa Nostra (1971)
Mind Killers
Mind Poisoners (1966)
Mission to Venice
Moscow
Night of the Avenger (1973)
Omega Terror (1972)
Operation Che Guevara
Operation Moon Rocket
Operation Skyjack (1970)
Operation Snake
Operation Starvation (1966)
Peking/The Tulip Affair
Red Guard (1969)
Red Rays
Red Rebellion
Red-Winged Death (1972)
Rhodesia
Run, Spy, Run (1964)
Safari for Spies (1964)
Saigon (1964)
Sea Trap (1969)
Seven Against Greece (1967)
Spy Castle (1968)
Strike Force Terror (1973)
Target: Doomsday Island (1973)
Temple of Fear
Terrible Ones
13th Spy (1965)
Time Clock of Death
The Vatican (1971)
Weapon of Night (1968)

Web of Spies

53 NOTEBOOKS Series (Sam
  Picard)
1: Mission No. 1 (1969)
2: Man Who Never Was (1971)
3: Dead Man Running (1971)

54 OPERATION HANG TEN
  Series (Patrick Morgan)
Beach Queen Blowout (1971)
Cute and Deadly Surf Twins
  (1970)
Deadly Group Down Under
  (1970)
Death Car Surfside (1972)
Girl in the Telltale Bikini
Hang Dead Hawaiian Style (1969)
Scarlet Surf at Makaha
Too Mini Murders (1969)
Topless Dancer Hangup

55 OTLEY Series (Martin
  Waddell)
Otley (1966)
Otley Forever (1968)
Otley Pursued (1966)
Otley Victorious (1969)

56 PRIVATE ARMY of Colonel
  Tobin Series (Alan Caillou)
1: Dead Sea Submarine (1971)
2: Terror in Rio (1971)
3: Congo War Cry (1972)
4: Afghan Assault (1972)

57 SAM DURRELL "Assignment"
  Series (Edward S. Aarons)
Assignment--Angelina (1958)
Assignment--Ankara (1961)
Assignment--Black Viking (1967)
Assignment--Budapest (1971)
Assignment--Burma Girl (1961)
Assignment--Carlotta Cortez
  (1966)
Assignment--Cong Hai Kill
  (1959)
Assignment--Helene (1959)
Assignment--Karachi (1962)
Assignment--Lili Lamaris (1961)
Assignment--Lowlands (1961)
Assignment--Madeleine (1971)
Assignment--Maltese Maiden

(1972)
Assignment--Manchurian Doll
  (1968)
Assignment--Mara Tirana (1966)
Assignment--Moon Girl (1967)
Assignment--Nuclear Nude
Assignment--Palermo (1966)
Assignment--Peking (1969)
Assignment--School for Spies
  (1970)
Assignment: Silver Scorpion
  (1973)
Assignment--Sorrento Siren (1963)
Assignment--Stella Marni (1965)
Assignment--Suicide (1966)
Assignment--Sulu Sea (1964)
Assignment--The Cairo Dancers
Assignment--The Girl in the
  Gondola (1964)
Assignment--The Golden Girl
  (1971)
Assignment--The Star Stealers
  (1970)
Assignment--The White Rajah
  (1970)
Assignment to Disaster (1955)
Assignment--Tokyo (1971)
Assignment--Treason (1967)
Assignment--Zoroya (1960)

58 SAM DURRELL "Assignment"
  Series (cont. by Robert C.
  Galway)
Assignment--Andalusia (1965)
Assignment--Argentina
Assignment--London (1963)
Assignment--Malta (1966)
Assignment--New York (1963)
Assignment--Sea-Bird (1969)
Assignment--Tahiti

59 SCARLET PIMPERNAL
  (Baroness Emmuska Orczy)
Adventures of the Scarlet Pim-
  pernel (1929)
Eldorado (1913)
Elusive Pimpernel (1908)
First Sir Percy (1921)
I Will Repay (1906)
League of the Scarlet Pimpernel
  (1919)
Lord Tony's Wife (1917)
Pimpernel and Rosemary (1925)

Scarlet Pimpernel (1905)
Sir Percy Hits Back (1927)
Sir Percy Leads the Band (1936)
Triumph of the Scarlet Pimper-
    nel (1922)
Way of the Scarlet Pimpernel
    (1934)

60 SECRET MISSION Series
    (Don Smith)
 1: Secret Mission: Peking (1968)
 2: Secret Mission: Prague (1968)
 3: Secret Mission: Corsica (1968)
 4: Secret Mission: Morocco (1969)
 5: Secret Mission: Istanbul (1969)
 6: Secret Mission: Tibet (1969)
 7: Secret Mission: Cairo (1970)
 8: Secret Mission: North Korea
    (1970)
 9: Secret Mission: Angola (1970)
10: Secret Mission: Munich
    (1970)
11: Secret Mission: Athens
    (1971)
12: Secret Mission: The Krem-
    lin Plot (1971)
13: Secret Mission: Marseilles
    Enforcer (1972)
14: Secret Mission: Death Stalks
    in Spain (1971)
15: Secret Mission: Haiti (1972)

61 STEVE AUSTIN-Cyborg-Super
    Agent (Martin Caiden)
Bionics Man (1972)
Operation Nuke (1973)

62 WITHERED MAN series
    (Norman Deane)
Dangerous Journey (1939)
I Am the Withered Man (1941)
Seven Times Seven (1932)
Withered Man (1940)

About the Authors

JAMES ROBERT PARISH, New York-based freelance writer, was born near Boston on April 21, 1944. He attended the University of Pennsylvania and graduated Phi Beta Kappa with a degree in English. A graduate of the University of Pennsylvania Law School, he is a member of the New York Bar. As president of Entertainment Copyright Research Co., Inc., he headed a major researching facility for the film and television industries. Later he was a film reviewer-interviewer for Motion Picture Daily and Variety. He has been responsible for such reference volumes as The American Movies Reference Book: The Sound Era, and The Emmy Awards: A Pictorial History. He is the co-author of The Cinema of Edward G. Robinson and The MGM Stock Company: The Golden Era, and the author of such volumes as The Great Movie Series, The Fox Girls, and The Paramount Pretties. He recently compiled Actors' Television Credits (1950-1972).

MICHAEL R. PITTS, a journalist and freelance writer, is currently the entertainment editor of the Anderson Daily Bulletin in Indiana where he resides. A graduate of Ball State University (Muncie, Indiana), with a B.S. in history and a master's degree in journalism, he has been a frequent contributor to such cinema journals as Films in Review, Filmography, Film Fan Monthly, Classic Film Collector, Castle of Frankenstein, Cinefantastique, and Focus on Films. Presently he is working on A Guide to American Directors with Mr. Parish, and is also preparing Celluloid Sleuths: The Great Movie Detectives. Formerly in public education, Mr. Pitts was born July 31, 1947 in New Castle, Indiana.